The author of Hebrews is insistent: without holiness, no one will see the Lord. Holiness, therefore, understood as Jesus-likeness that every Christian ought to display consequent to conversion, is absolutely essential. And radical holiness, as depicted here in these pages, demonstrates the seriousness with which we ought to pursue it. Where humility, a watchfulness against sin, a love for righteousness, putting others first and loving Christ with joyful passion, and so much more are missing, something less than biblical holiness and Christ-like holiness are on display. Drs Beeke and Barrett will not settle for anything less than total commitment to pursue holiness, whatever the cost. If you can settle for less, then don't read this book. But settling for less may cost you dearly.

DEREK W. H. THOMAS
Senior Minister, First Presbyterian Church, Columbia, South Carolina

The angels in the presence of God sigh to one another, 'Holy! Holy! Holy! Isn't Jehovah holy?' They themselves are also holy like the Lord of Hosts, but they can't get over God's eternal and infinite holiness. Then the command comes to the weakest lambs in the flock of Christ and to the newest converts, 'Be ye holy!' And the standard for us is exactly this, 'As I am holy.' What a gulf, but also what certainty that this is to be the predestined destination of all, even the very greatest of all sinners who has put his trust for salvation exclusively in the Lord Christ. So, do you see your holy calling, brothers and sisters? We who have this hope in us must make ourselves holy. This book has come to you at this moment to help you magnificently to address your life, and increasingly so, to this incredible end of attaining more and more of the holiness of God. What a goal! What a heavenly purpose for daily living. Pursue it by His sufficient grace!

GEOFFREY THOMAS
Pastor of Alfred Place Baptist Church, Aberystwyth, Wales

I warmly recommend this fine book on holiness written by authors valued and respected for their theological excellence and their service to Christ in our modern world. Holiness is the hardest part of the Christian's life and demands that we make it our life-long study and practice. The biblical emphasis of this book, strongly reinforced by excellent Puritan teachings, makes this volume a golden treasury for the modern reader. All who are travelers on the road of true holiness have heaven itself as their sure destination.

MAURICE ROBERTS
Emeritus pastor, Free Church of Scotland (Continuing), Scotland

This is the perfect book for those who still think the message of *sola gratia* is a threat to living a holy life. This is also the perfect book for those who still think that calling for sanctification is a threat to preaching justification. But most of all this is the perfect book for anyone—young as well as more mature believers—longing to live a God-pleasing life. In brief, Drs Beeke and Barrett have provided us a great tool to assist us in practicing biblical holiness.

HERMAN SELDERHUIS
President, Theological University Apeldoorn, The Netherlands

Although there is no shortage of books on sanctification, few if any deal with this subject as thoroughly and exhaustively as Joel Beeke and Michael Barrett have done in *A Radical, Comprehensive Call to Holiness*. The title says it all: it is a radical call in that it points to the fundamental change that takes place when a sinner is born from above. It is a comprehensive call because just as sin permeates every part of the natural man, grace also manifests itself in every faculty of the new creature in Christ. Furthermore, it is also a convicting call because the holiness that God requires is so all-embracing that even though the new convert desires to live according to all the commandments of God, he finds it impossible to meet the divine standards perfectly. His old nature, while being put to death, is dying so slowly that it often leaves the believer discouraged and longing to be delivered from 'this body of death' (Rom. 7:24). The authors offer much needed instruction on all issues that arise in connection with sanctification. They explain the difference between positional and progressive sanctification, warn against half-hearted and selective holiness, point out the errors of perfectionism but also, and above all, they speak glowingly of the rewards of holiness: the sweet communion with God in Christ. Their main sources besides the Scriptures, are the profound insights of the Puritans on this vital doctrine of godly living. I heartily recommend this valuable resource of solid spiritual food at a time when many are tempted to get by on fast-food substitutes.

CORNELIS PRONK
Emeritus Minister, Free Reformed Church, Brantford, Ontario

It is genuinely refreshing to find a current book on holiness so vigorous and earnest, concerned to unite faith and life so closely and warmly. Christ-centered at its core, it is sweetly clear in its doctrine and strongly compelling in its demands, while always pastorally sensitive and practically helpful. Its sweep carries us through all aspects of holiness, from the new birth to the glory to come, encouraging us in the way and warning us from error with lessons from across the history of the Christian church. It is a book full of truth which needs to be not merely approved and applauded, but laid hold upon and lived. It is one thing to endorse such teaching, and another to embrace it: I gladly do the former because I trust that, by God's grace, I and many others will do the latter.

JEREMY WALKER
Pastor at Maidenbower Baptist Church, Crawley, England

In recent days, we have witnessed a renewed interest in Reformed theology, and in this we rejoice. But there is one area that has been sadly overlooked and needs to be addressed, namely, the doctrine of sanctification. This book, *A Radical, Comprehensive Call to Holiness*, provides the necessary antidote to this omission. Well-designed and thoroughly studied, this volume by Drs Joel Beeke and Michael Barrett is certain to be a valuable and trusted aid in your Christian walk.

STEVEN J. LAWSON
President, OnePassion Ministries; Professor,
The Master's Seminary, Sun Valley, California
Teaching Fellow, Ligonier Ministries

With exegetical precision, theological clarity, and pastoral experience, the authors walk the reader through Scripture to see and to embrace the beauty of holiness in all of life. By locating holiness in the person and Work of Jesus Christ, the joy of holy living becomes attractive. Holiness is Christlikeness, and this book will aid the Christian in this glorious pursuit!

CHARLES M. BARRETT
Pastor, Wayside Presbyterian Church (PCA), Walden, Tennessee

A Radical, Comprehensive Call to Holiness is the mature articulation of this vital subject by two seasoned shepherds of the flock of the Lord Jesus Christ. From a variety of vantage points, they expound the premise that holiness is Christlikeness— that union to Christ manifests itself in likeness to Christ. Very ably they argue that genuine holiness is the experiential affirmation of true saving faith—that all who truly believe the gospel will also live the gospel. This book, saturated with Scripture, will be a valuable and trustworthy resource for all who love the Lord Jesus Christ in sincerity, and whose heart's desire is to honor the Living Word by honoring His written Word.

BARTEL ELSHOUT
Pastor, Heritage Reformed Church, Hull, Iowa

Drs Beeke and Barrett have provided a resource that resonates with the Church's greatest need in these strange and unsettling times. If 'without holiness no one will see the Lord,' it is vital that Christians understand what the Bible means by holiness. The twenty-nine chapters can be read sequentially or occasionally as a particular topic is experientially relevant. The Church is indebted to these authors for promoting true godliness.

IAN HAMILTON
Professor of Historical Theology,
Westminster Presbyterian Theological Seminary, Newcastle, United Kingdom

Anyone who ever teaches you evangelical obedience and holiness has done you the greatest favour on this side of eternity. That is what Joel Beeke and Michael Barrett have done for all of us. In this book, as they have opened up the subject of holiness, they have plumbed the depths of doctrinal and exegetical clarity, spied out the land of practical Christian living, and then soared to the heights of devotional ecstasy. Read this book for your good, for the good of your family, and for the good of your church. You will be glad that you did so!

CONRAD MBEWE
Pastor, Kabwata Baptist Church, Lusaka, Zambia

A RADICAL, COMPREHENSIVE

CALL

to

HOLINESS

Joel R. Beeke &
Michael P. V. Barrett

Copyright © Joel R. Beeke and Michael P. V. Barrett 2021

hardback ISBN 978-1-5271-0611-6
epub ISBN 978-1-5271-0683-3
mobi ISBN 978-1-5271-0684-0

10 9 8 7 6 5 4 3 2 1

Published in 2021
in the
Mentor Imprint
by
Christian Focus Publications Ltd,
Geanies House, Fearn, Ross-shire,
IV20 1TW, Great Britain.

www.christianfocus.com

Cover design
by
Rubner Durais

Printed
by
Bell & Bain, Glasgow

CONTENTS

For

Paul Washer

a lover of holiness in Christ,
a winner of souls by Christ,
a treasured brother in Christ.

"I thank my God upon every remembrance of you"
(Philippians 1:3).

— JRB —

❄ ❄ ❄

And for

Chadwick Charles Barrett
Charles Michael Barrett

My two sons:
Testimonies to God's covenant faithfulness

"I have no greater joy than to hear that my children walk in truth"
(3 John 4)

— MPVB —

Introduction:
Holiness Explained

GRACE never leaves a man where it finds him. Grace always transforms the sinner into a saint – a holy man. 'For we are his workmanship, created in Christ Jesus unto good works, which God hath before ordained that we should walk in them' (Eph. 2:10). God's will is for His people to be holy. The objective of His electing grace is to bring us into conformity to the image of Jesus Christ (Rom. 8:29), and every true Christian has a desire for that Christ-like holiness.

Notwithstanding God's will and the Christian's desire, the experience of holiness does not come easily. We seem to be in constant struggle against the external enticements to sin that so effectively appeal to the internal impulses of our own carnal desires. Every victory that we win over sin seems only to increase the intensity of the next battle. Every defeat weighs heavily on our conscience as we wonder if God will forgive us again. The question presses us: How can we achieve victory over sin and live the Christian life successfully? Is such victory even possible?

Sadly and wrongly, many Christians give up, resigning themselves to what appears to be the fact of the matter – they can't quit sinning. Consequently, Christianity has become for some people nothing more than a theoretical set of beliefs that have little bearing on life; for others it is a rigid set of standards that relentlessly rule life. Neither of these alternatives produces much joy in the Lord, and neither leads to a victorious life. Whatever initial enthusiasm existed at conversion dwindles, and disillusionment sets in; faith loses its attraction. Further testifying to the problem are the plethora of how-to books offering supposedly new formulas for successful Christian living, and the proliferation of parachurch seminars offering practical, character-building principles or psychological tricks for increasing personal resolve. Many well-meaning but ultimately deleterious efforts have capitalized on the dissatisfaction of Christians who have somehow failed to understand what the Bible teaches about the Christian life. The tendency has been to substitute virtuous character traits for genuine holiness. Too much stress has been placed on being like some person mentioned in the Bible. It is little wonder that Christianity degenerates to the drudgery of doing this or not doing that when Christians ignore the God-given key to holy and happy Christian

9

living. Successful Christian living and victory over sin are possible if we stick to the path God has laid down for us in His Word. The key to happy holiness is the gospel of Jesus Christ.

The doctrine that concerns our daily duty of holiness is *sanctification*. Sanctification is God's will for every believer. First Thessalonians 4:3 is explicitly clear: 'For this is the will of God, even your sanctification.' Doing the will of God is our duty, but, as always, duty must flow from doctrine. The more we understand the doctrines of the gospel, the more we can do our duty. The gospel is like a chain with many inseparable links: election, regeneration, conversion, union, justification, adoption, reconciliation, sanctification, glorification, etc.[1] Successful sanctification is going to depend on how we see sanctification coupled with the other links. Too often Christians are frustrated in their efforts at holiness because they have uncoupled and isolated sanctification from all the other gospel components. Attempting to live a Christian life apart from the bedrock of Christian theology is presumptuous folly, but it is not a new mistake. Paul saw this same proclivity for will power rather than gospel power among the Galatians: 'Are ye so foolish? having begun in the Spirit, are ye now made perfect by the flesh?' (Gal. 3:3). His right answer to their mistake was to direct their eyes again to Christ who had been 'evidently set forth' before them (Gal. 3:1). Seeing Christ and our place in Him is going to be the solution for us as well. We are complete in Him.

In this book, we want to expound the doctrine of sanctification and show its connection to our complete salvation by discussing specific aspects of Scripture's radical and comprehensive call to holiness. Very simply, we are going to see that sanctification is the application of the gospel in our daily lives. Perhaps the axiom 'right thinking about the gospel produces right living in the gospel' applies more directly to this element of salvation than to any other. Whereas the other links in the gospel chain focus on our position, privileges, and prospects in Christ, sanctification concerns where and how we live right now. Sanctification is the believer's becoming in experience what grace has purposed him to be. Sanctification is living in the reality of gospel grace. Since in our justification God regards us as holy and righteous, we should live as though we are. Although holiness is not the prerequisite for salvation, it is the evidence of it. Sanctification is the essential and certain effect of the gospel.

God's call to holiness is radical, and it is comprehensive. Holiness is a topic that demands and deserves constant visitation, both from the pulpit and from the pew – indeed, both in the pulpit and in the pew. The divine call to holiness is a daily task involving the core of religious faith and practice. Calvin said, 'The whole life of Christians ought to be a sort of practice of godliness, for we have been called to

---

1. John Murray *Redemption Accomplished and Applied* (Grand Rapids: Eerdmans, 1989). Michael Barrett, *Complete in Him: A Guide to Understanding and Enjoying the Gospel* (Grand Rapids: Reformation Heritage Books, 2017). Both of these books provide helpful summaries of these links in the gospel chain.

sanctification.'[2] Holiness is the commitment of the whole life to live Godward – to be set apart to the Lordship of Jesus Christ.

In stark contrast to the postmodern ethic that conveniently compartmentalizes beliefs and practices into separate drawers of life, biblical holiness of heart must be cultivated in every sphere of life – in secret with God, in the privacy of homes, in the places of business, in the pleasures of our social friendships, in all of public life and in worship. The call to holiness extends to every part of life. It encompasses the whole being in every movement of body, spirit, and soul.

In both Testaments, holy means separated and set apart for God. Negatively, holiness is separation from sin. Positively, holiness is consecration to God and, specifically, conformity to Christ. The mandate for holiness is based in the very character and person of God: We are to be holy because God is holy. God's holiness is His unique essence. God is infinitely different from everything else that is. The answer to the Bible's question, 'Who is like unto thee, O LORD?' (Exod. 15:11), is unequivocally clear: No one nor anything is even comparable to God (see Isa. 40:18).

Significantly, the antonym of holiness in the Old Testament refers to that which is common, ordinary, or mundane. God is infinitely extraordinary; God's holiness is the sum of His glory and beauty. Edwards said, 'The holiness of God has always appeared to me the most lovely of all his attributes.'[3] This is echoed by a contemporary definition of the Lord's holiness: 'It is the sum of all His attributes, the outshining of all that God is.'[4] Since God calls His people to holiness and holiness is the sum and outshining of who and what He is, it ought to be the sum and outshining of His people as well.

The concept of holiness is positional (justification), practical (sanctification), and perfected (glorification). Understanding the connection between these aspects is crucial and requires attention because subjective experience must flow from objective truths. Consequently, this study will address some of those objective truths, but the focus will be on the experience of heeding and obeying God's radical and comprehensive call to live holy before Him in the present evil world.

To live holy is to live godly. The New Testament designates this kind of living with a word most often translated 'godliness' in the KJV (*eusebeia*, ευσέβεια). This godliness is the sum of piety, practical holiness, or true religion. It includes the idea of awe or fear in the presence of the majestic God, but it goes beyond mental awareness to stress the worship and obedience generated by that reverence. It is the right attitude about God that elevates God to the place He ought to occupy in the

---

2. John Calvin, *The Institutes of the Christian Religion*, ed. John T. McNeill, trans. Ford Lewis Battles (Louisville, Ky.: Westminster John Knox Press, 2006), 1:835. This quote comes from Book 3, Chapter 19, section 2.

3. Jonathan Edwards, 'Personal Narratives,' (c. 1740, Yale: Jonathan Edwards Center, 2005), p. 11.

4. *The New Bible Dictionary*, s. v. 'Holiness' (Grand Rapids: Eerdmans, 1962), p. 530. Though these words have been attributed to Edwards by some, this precise quote comes from Roderick A. Finlayson in his article on holiness. Nevertheless, the truth and emphasis of these words certainly appears in Edwards.

lives, the thoughts, and devotion of His people. The word reminds us that saving faith commands all of life. This word of true religion reminds us of what must be the governing principle of life.

Interestingly, surveying the occurrences of this word in the New Testament touches on most of the specific issues that we will address in this study. Six propositions sum up the evidence.

First, godliness is focused on Jesus Christ. Christ reveals the very essence of godliness. According to Paul in 1 Timothy 3:16, the mystery of godliness is that in Jesus 'God was manifest in the flesh.' The mystery in the New Testament, of course, does not refer to an enigma but to that which is known only by means of revelation. It was part of the work of the Incarnation that Jesus was the perfect example of true piety, true fear of God, and true holiness and righteousness. Since the purpose of our predestination is to be conformed to the image of Christ, it only makes sense to look to Christ to see what we are supposed to be. Godliness is not following rules or principles; it is being like Christ. Peter assures us that this godliness comes through the knowledge of Christ and that God in Christ supplies the power to perform (2 Pet. 1:3). This union with Christ is the starting place for every experience of piety.

Second, godliness is linked to doctrine. Paul refers to 'the words of our Lord Jesus Christ, and the doctrine which is according to godliness' (1 Tim. 6:3) and again to 'the acknowledging of the truth which is after godliness' (Titus 1:1). Throughout the Bible, doctrine and duty go hand in hand. Right thinking determines right behavior. Practical piety is the product of sound theology. The folly of so much of modern Christianity is that it demands certain traditions of life-practice while ignoring the eternal truths that define those practices. Sadly, even doing the 'right thing' apart from the conscious application of biblical truth is not godliness. It may be conservative and contrary to popular practices, but it is not godliness. True religion is not thoughtless or heartless mimicking of some list of do's and don'ts; it is a conscious living with reference to God and truth. Since the Word of God is the revelation of truth, it is imperative to read, study, and meditate on the Scripture. We are to live 'by every word that proceedeth out of the mouth of God' (Matt. 4:4).

Third, godliness is motivated by the light of eternity. After Peter describes the passing away of the world that now is, he draws this conclusion: 'Seeing then that all these things shall be dissolved, what manner of persons ought ye to be in all holy conversation and godliness' (2 Pet. 3:11). He then sketches what this with-a-view-to-eternity godliness is going to look like. It is marked by anticipation (3:12), diligence to be like Christ (3:14), meditation ('account') with thanksgiving that God has delayed the day of judgment long enough for our salvation (3:15), cautious perseverance in truth (3:17), and sanctification, or progressing in holiness, by knowing Christ (3:18). A life of holiness never gets away from Christ.

Fourth, godliness matures through effort. There is no such thing as passivity in the Christian life of sanctification. Godliness is not the result of some divine 'zap' but rather matures through struggle. In 1 Timothy, Paul uses two images to describe this effort. On the one hand, it requires exercise (4:7-8). Interestingly, our word 'gymnasium' comes from the Greek word here translated 'exercise.' Athletic skills or physical fitness do not just happen; they do not even happen by reading 'how-to' books on achieving this or that skill or goal. They result from strenuous practice and single-minded determination. An athlete will habitually drill on the various fundamentals of his sport. Gymnasiums are full of equipment labeled to address certain muscle groups or cardio health and stamina. But just learning what the equipment is for does not produce a physical benefit. The only way to develop skills or to strengthen weakness is to 'work on it.' So it is that the only way to strengthen areas of spiritual weakness or to progress in holiness is to implement what the Scripture informs. On the other hand, godliness involves pursuit. Paul instructs the man of God to 'follow after righteousness, godliness, faith, love, patience, meekness' (6:11). The word 'follow' is both a military and a hunting term. As a soldier fights the good fight of faith (6:12) as though his life depended on it, or as a hunter strategizes and tracks his quarry, so the Christian must resolve to pursue and 'catch' Christlikeness.

Fifth, godliness is marked by attendant circumstances. Or rather, it does not exist in isolation; it always has effects. Living godly in Christ Jesus can bring trouble (2 Tim. 3:12). Being different from the world and living by a different set of standards can be perilous. Christians can be an aggravating presence in the world just like salt in a wound. But that is what Christ has instructed us to be (Matt. 5:13). Being godly means, though, that the believer is more concerned about what God thinks than what the world thinks. To be like Christ will mean that the world will treat us as it treated Christ. Hence Christ told us that we should not be surprised by the world's hatred: 'If the world hate you, ye know that it hated me before it hated you' (John 15:18). Being hated by the world is part of Christlikeness. Living godly has the positive effect of breeding brotherly love (2 Pet. 1:6, 7). Godliness will dispel strife, disunity, envy, or bitterness among or between believers. Godliness causes a selflessness that enables believers to esteem others more highly than self and to submit to one another in the fear of God. Happily, godliness is marked by God's special attention: 'if any man be a worshipper of God, and doeth his will, him he heareth' (John 9:31). The word 'worshipper' comes from the same root word as 'godliness' though with a different prefix, but the sense is essentially the same. The happy thought is that the throne of grace is open to the true worshipper, the one who is living godly in Christ. True religion brings the great blessing of God's presence and communion.

Sixth, godliness begins at home. In giving instructions regarding the care of widows, Paul says, 'let them learn first to shew piety at home' (1 Tim. 5:4). That principle extends beyond the context of widow-care for sure. Godliness is not confined to the church or just displayed in public; it must be the character of home life. In many ways, religion is no more real than it is in the home. Religion that is displayed in public but disguised at home is nothing more than hypocrisy; it is irreligion. This is why family worship is such a vital part of God's call to comprehensive holiness. The most important works of religion are done at home, and there is a solemn connection between good churches and good homes.

In so many ways, this one word 'godliness' has encapsulated the biblical concept of holiness that we want to examine in this book. The topics and particularly the Scripture passages which are exegeted in no way are exhaustive of the subject, but it is our prayer as we now consider specifics of God's demand for holiness that He will use these meditations as a means of increasing desire for godliness and holiness and of pointing the way to achieving and practicing that holiness in life with a view to the life to come. Personal holiness doesn't just happen; it must be cultivated. But it is possible. Obeying God's radical call to holiness is possible because of grace. Obeying the call is possible because He has given us a pattern to follow. That pattern is the triune God Himself and especially Jesus Christ. Stephen Charnock rightly said that the way to honor the Lord is 'to live to Him in living like Him.'[5] Obeying the call to holiness is possible because God has supplied the means to achieve it through His Word, the sacraments, the care of the church and fellowship with other believers, since association promotes inculcation.

Last but not least, obeying the call is possible because He has not left us alone. We have a Companion with us who never leaves us alone – the blessed Holy Spirit. The indwelling Holy Spirit is the irrefutable evidence that we belong to Christ: 'Now if any man have not the Spirit of Christ, he is none of his' (Rom. 8:9). The Spirit who raised up the Lord Jesus from the dead and made us spiritually alive (Rom. 8:11) is the same Spirit who constantly abides with us. Every believer has dwelling within him that death-defying infinite Power as a constant resource in the daily battles for holiness. Although the presence of the indwelling Spirit provides the believer with many blessings and benefits (assurance, fellowship, guidance, conviction, etc.), the primary ministry of the Spirit in our sanctification is to incite and enable us to holiness. It is 'through the Spirit' that we are able to 'mortify the deeds of the body' (Rom. 8:13). God's promise to Zerubbabel applies to sanctification as much as to any other work for the glory of God: 'Not by might, nor by power, but by my spirit, saith the Lord of hosts' (Zech. 4:6).

The Spirit operates in our sanctification as He directs us to the application of the gospel. We have received 'the spirit which is of God; that we might know the things that are freely given to us of God' (1 Cor. 2:12). It is by the Spirit of the Lord that we are changed into the image of Christ from glory to glory (2 Cor. 3:18). In the light of this provision, it should be our daily prayer 'to be strengthened with might by his Spirit in the inner man' (Eph. 3:16). God has given us the infallible Guide to lead us to walk contrary to the flesh (Rom. 8:4). Indeed, the promise is that if we walk in the Spirit, we 'shall not fulfill the lust of the flesh' (Gal. 5:16). Paul's

---

5. Stephen Charnock, *The Complete Works of Stephen Charnock* (Edinburgh: James Nichol, 1864), 2:268.

argument is that since 'we live in the Spirit,' we should 'also walk in the Spirit' (Gal. 5:25). The particular word for 'walk' in this verse brings the issue down to the basics. We are literally to walk in a straight line or row, step by step following the path set by the Holy Spirit. The way of holiness is certainly not a game, but it does involve 'following the Leader.' We must submit ourselves to that holy influence and follow God's provision, our faithful Companion, relying on His might to lead us to victory. Following the Holy Spirit will lead us not only away from sin but also toward the positive marks of godliness: 'love, joy, peace, longsuffering, gentleness, goodness, faith, meekness, temperance' (Gal. 5:22-23).

For the Christian, religion should be the governing principle of existence. No part of the redeemed life has been untouched by grace, and no part of redeemed living is exempt from evidencing that grace. Consequently, in writing this book, we wish to express heartfelt gratitude to our holy triune God who – despite our ongoing battles with sin and shortcomings – sanctifies us in Christ Jesus (1 Cor. 1:30) by His Holy Spirit (1 Cor. 2:14), as well as to our wives, Sandra (Barrett) and Mary (Beeke), who model holiness for us in real and tangible ways, and in so doing, serve as treasured gifts of God to us. Hearty thanks also to Andrew Farr and Ian Turner who assisted us so helpfully and faithfully in a variety of ways in completing this book. It was a joy to write this book together (Michael: chapters 1–10, 12, 13, 15, 25; Joel: chapters 11, 14, 16–24, 26–29 – and then we edited each other's chapters), as strong friends in Christ and colleagues at Puritan Reformed Theological Seminary. It is our prayer that this book will assist you (and us!) in pursuing God's radical and comprehensive call to holiness.

— MPVB/JRB

HOLINESS DEFINED

CHAPTER 1

GRAPPLING WITH POSITIONAL AND PROGRESSIVE HOLINESS

THE issue of this chapter is crucial both theologically and experientially: the relationship between positional and progressive holiness. In more doctrinal terms, the question is the relationship between justification and sanctification. To reverse the order of these two components of salvation destroys the gospel; to blur the distinctions between them is deleterious to the enjoyment of the gospel. The two doctrines cannot be separated, and neither can they be confused. Justification addresses the legality of the gospel; sanctification concerns the effect of the gospel. The subject of this book is sanctification, but it is impossible to understand sanctification apart from justification.

KEY DEFINITIONS

The Westminster Shorter Catechism offers a concise definition of justification: 'Justification is an act of God's free grace, wherein he pardoneth all our sins, and accepteth us as righteous in his sight, only for the righteousness of Christ imputed to us, and received by faith alone' (Q. 33). In justification, the believer receives by faith and rests in what God alone does. Justification is a forensic or legal act, a one-time event, by which God declares or pronounces the guilty sinner to be righteous. Being righteous in this theological context means that all the requirements of God's inflexible law have been met. To justify is a legal expression referring to the adjudication of the Judge that proclaims the defendant to be innocent of the charges against him and not liable to the punishment that guilt would have incurred.[1] The man whom the court declares innocent is free to go because the decision of the court is binding and irreversible. This is exactly what God does when He justifies sinners: He declares them to be righteous (completely conformed to His unyielding law), thereby freeing them from any penalty.

---

1. 'Justification is a legal, or forensic, term, and is used in Scripture to denote the acceptance of any one as righteous in the sight of God' (James Buchanan, *The Doctrine of Justification* [Edinburgh: Banner of Truth, 1984], p. 226). In the Reformed tradition, Buchanan's work is considered one of the classic works on justification.

It is absolutely imperative to restrict the act of justification to the legal sphere. In other words, justification does not impart or infuse any righteousness into the believer.[2] It does not create any moral change; it is something God does outside the believer, not inside. Justification concerns how God regards the believer and deals with him in terms of His law. It is His decision. This is possible because God imputes Christ's righteousness. Imputation underscores the objective nature of justification. To impute does not mean to impart, but rather the concept means to consider, think about, or reckon. In the theology of justification, imputation has a twofold focus. On the one hand, God imputed the sinner's guilt to Christ, and on the other hand, He imputed Christ's righteousness to the sinner. In other words, God regarded Christ as guilty and dealt with Him accordingly, and He regards the believer as righteous and deals with him accordingly. On the cross God dealt with Christ in terms of His guilty people; in justification God deals with His people in terms of Christ. The believer's acceptance before God is in Christ the beloved (Eph. 1:6); therefore, that standing before God can never change. It is neither diminished nor enhanced by the believer's behavior.

These are crucial thoughts when we consider justification as it relates to sanctification.[3] We cannot understand justification apart from the righteousness of God; we cannot understand God's righteousness apart from His perfect law. The gospel does not replace the law; it fulfills it for every believer. 'Christ is the end of law for righteousness to every one that believeth' (Rom. 10:4). This is why justification addresses the legality of the gospel.

The Westminster Shorter Catechism also provides a succinct definition of biblical sanctification: 'Sanctification is the work of God's free grace, whereby we are renewed in the whole man after the image of God, and are enabled more and more to die unto sin, and live unto righteousness' (Q. 35). This definition suggests two key truths: (1) sanctification is something God graciously does in us; (2) sanctification is something we obediently do in response to and in evidence of what God does. In other words, as believers we cooperate with God. If we remain passively inactive in the face of sin, waiting for God to do it all, we will be overrun. If we are active in the face of sin without conscious reference to what God has done,

---

2. 'The Roman Catholic idea is that grace is infused into the soul of a person at baptism, making the person inherently righteous, so that God therefore judges him to be righteous. But the Reformers insisted that we are justified when God imputes someone else's righteousness to our account, namely, the righteousness of Christ' (R. C. Sproul, *Are We Together? A Protestant Analyzes Roman Catholicism* [Orlando, Fla.: Reformation Trust, 2012], p. 43). Sproul's whole work is a careful analysis of the difference between Roman Catholicism and Protestantism. His chapter on justification is helpful in distinguishing between the infusion of righteousness and the imputation of righteousness.

3. See also J. V. Fesko, *Justification: Understanding the Classic Reformed Doctrine* (Phillipsburg, N.J.: P&R, 2008); John Piper, *The Future of Justification: A Response to N. T. Wright* (Wheaton, Ill.: Crossway, 2007). Fesko's work is a contemporary analysis of justification and deals with some of the modern threats to the biblical and Reformed understanding of justification. Piper's book, as noted in its title, is directed at one modern threat to justification. Since a proper understanding of justification is so crucial to sanctification, both of these books are helpful as further reading for understanding what the Bible says concerning justification.

we will be overrun. Leviticus 20:7-8 effectively unites these two essential elements. The Lord first commanded His people, 'Sanctify yourselves therefore, and be ye holy.' Then He affirmed, 'I am the LORD which sanctify you.'

That the catechism refers to sanctification as the work of God's free grace and the dying to sin and living to righteousness as taking place 'more and more' underscores a vital truth: sanctification is a progressive and not a once-for-all operation. That is in contrast to justification's being an act. In sanctification, something happens on the inside as God renews the whole man in His image. There is a subjective inward change, in contrast to the complete external objectivity of justification. Notwithstanding the clarity of the confessional definitions, confusion exists both in practice and in understanding.

KEY WORD

Part of the confusion stems from the use of the vocabulary of sanctification. Accurate definitions of the key theological vocabulary are always the first step in understanding any theological proposition. Therefore, we must understand the significance of the biblical terms translated 'to sanctify' or 'sanctification.' The words for sanctification in both the Old and the New Testaments have the same essential idea: holiness. In both Hebrew and Greek, the fundamental concept of holiness is separation. The concept of sanctification, therefore, refers to the act or process of setting something apart, thereby making it holy, separate and distinct from something else.[4]

In dealing with words, it is important to keep in mind the distinction between a word's information and its reference. The information of a word is its essential definition, the components of thought that combine to form the word's meaning. Reference is the actual reality that is in view. For instance, the word 'flower' can refer to a rose, but 'rose' is not a component of the definition of flower. So the word group for 'sanctification' conveys the meaning of setting something apart, but refers to various realities. There must be caution not to confuse a word's specific references with its basic information.

Be aware that, particularly in the Old Testament, the word 'sanctification' does not always occur in a salvation or gospel context. For instance, the fourth commandment says, 'Keep the sabbath day to sanctify it' (Deut. 5:12). This simply means that the Sabbath is to be set apart and treated differently from all the

---

4. 'What then is God's holiness? ... We mean the perfectly pure devotion of each of these three persons to the other two. We mean ... absolute, permanent, exclusive, pure, irreversible, and fully expressed *devotion.*' While not disagreeing with the idea of separation, Ferguson's stress in these opening pages of his book highlights the positive aspect of devotion rather than the more negative aspect of being separate. He takes this route to emphasize the fact that while 'there were personal *distinctions* within the fellowship of the Trinity (Father, Son, Holy Spirit), ... there was no *separation*, no *being placed at a distance from* each other' (Sinclair B. Ferguson, *Devoted to God: Blueprints for Sanctification* [Edinburgh: Banner of Truth, 2016], p. 2). With that in mind, he defines holiness more as devotion to God as opposed to separation unto God. While using a slightly different starting point, Ferguson winds up emphasizing the same truth as those who define holiness as being separate and distinct.

other days of the week. In another instance, the Lord identified the Medes as the particular people that He had sanctified or set apart for the specific purpose of defeating the Babylonians (Isa. 13:3). They certainly were not a godly people. However, when the word does occur in the context of salvation or the gospel, it refers to separation from sin unto God. A sanctified life is a distinct and separated life – consecrated to God and pure from sin.

This distinction between information and reference is even more crucial in the New Testament. The New Testament uses the word group (different forms of the same root) 'to sanctify' to refer to three inseparable, yet individually identifiable, aspects of salvation. The failure to recognize the multiple uses or referents of the word has led to some significant errors in the theology of sanctification; so we want to be careful in our interpretation.

First, it refers to *positional* sanctification. This is most likely the sense intended by Paul when he identified the believers in Corinth 'as sanctified in Christ Jesus, called to be saints' (1 Cor. 1:2; see also 6:11). The whole point of the epistle is that in practice, the Corinthians were not acting like saints (literally, holy or sanctified ones), although in reality and fact they were saints. This positional sanctification essentially equates with justification and designates the acceptance the believer has before God in Jesus Christ.[5] At regeneration, every believer is set apart unto God and guaranteed a full salvation. Positional sanctification is entirely the gracious act of God. Every believer, regardless of the degree of personal holiness, is equally justified. Every believer enjoys the same position before God in Christ.

Second, it refers to *perfected* sanctification – every believer's ultimate glorification. This meaning looks to that time when we will experience total separation from sin's power and sin's presence. This is the ultimate end of Christ's sanctifying His bride: 'That he might present it to himself a glorious church, not having spot, or wrinkle, or any such thing; but that it should be holy and without blemish' (Eph. 5:27). In death, to be absent from the body is to be present with the Lord and, therefore, to be removed from sin's presence (2 Cor. 5:8). At death, every saint takes his place in the heavenly Jerusalem with 'the spirits of just men made perfect' (Heb. 12:23). The word 'perfect' in Hebrews 12:23 is a different word, meaning 'to be brought to maturity.' But to be separated from sin by death is not the end. Perfected sanctification will at the end include our bodies as well as our souls. This final act and eternal condition of sanctification is again the sole agency of God. With a power that is uniquely divine, God will 'change our vile body, that it may be fashioned like unto his glorious body' (Phil. 3:21).

Third, it refers to *progressive* sanctification. This concerns the course of life between the moment of our positional sanctification that separates us from sin's

---

5. 'It is important for every Christian to keep in mind the great difference between his position and his practice, his standing and his state. God sees us as righteous, because He sees us through His righteous Son, who has taken our place.... Christians do not always act like Christians, but they are still Christians' (John MacArthur, *The MacArthur New Testament Commentary: 1 Corinthians* [Chicago: Moody Press, 1984], p. 6).

penalty and our perfected sanctification that separates us from sin's presence. Progressive sanctification is the experience of separation from sin's power in our daily lives. As the catechism says, we are 'enabled more and more to die unto sin, and live unto righteousness.' Remember the statement in Hebrews 12:23. The fact that it is in heaven that the just men have been brought to maturity indicates that none of them had achieved spiritual maturity or perfection before they died. According to Hebrews 12:14, this sanctification is something that we must pursue: 'Follow peace with all men, and holiness [sanctification], without which no man shall see the Lord.' The verb 'follow' suggests a couple of key thoughts: (1) Its literal meaning, 'to chase' or 'to pursue,' implies an expenditure of effort. (2) Its tense intimates that this fervent pursuit is constant and unceasing. (3) Its mood (imperative) directs the issue to our wills and demands obedience. Whereas positional and perfected sanctification require no effort on our part, progressive sanctification requires trust and obedience. We must trust what God has done in making us holy and obey what He commands to achieve that holiness. In short, we are to live distinct and separated lives, performing our duty in the light of God's provision.

So although the word 'sanctification' in the Bible encompasses salvation from start to finish, the *doctrine of sanctification* concerns the application of the gospel during the journey, from start to finish. It is the day-by-day effect of the gospel. Knowing that the primary significance of the word 'sanctification' is separation (from sin to God) will help us to identify key passages in Scripture pertinent to the doctrine of sanctification, even if the actual word does not occur. Any passage directing us to quit sin or to do right concerns progressive sanctification.

KEY DISTINCTIONS

Although the term 'sanctification' sometimes applies to justification and glorification as well as sanctification, it is vital for us to maintain the distinction between these gospel components while at the same time maintaining their inseparable connection. Remember that the doctrines are not to be confused, but neither are they to be disjoined. If there is justification, sanctification in this life and ultimate glorification in eternity necessarily and certainly follow. The main confusion concerns the relationship between justification and sanctification.

Position vs. Experience

First, we must maintain a distinction between our legal position and our daily experience. Without simply repeating what the key words have indicated, I do want to underscore this vital distinction. Justification concerns our legal position before the bar of divine justice, where God pardons our guilt and regards us as righteous by imputing Christ's righteousness to us. Sanctification, on the other hand, concerns our everyday experience in which we strive by faith in Christ to be righteous, yet never attain that perfect righteousness in this life.[6] Justification is a legal transaction outside of us, whereas sanctification is moral transformation within us. Legally, believers are as righteous as Jesus Christ; experientially, believers are not. Believers are accepted completely by God and, on the basis of that acceptance, they desire to please God. Position is irrevocably fixed; experience fluctuates.

The failure to grasp this difference stirs up many questions. Students, for instance, have often asked me, 'If God has pardoned all our guilt and will never condemn us, why must we continue to confess our sins, seeking forgiveness from God?' I am happy they recognize that sin requires confession and necessitates forgiveness, but I grieve that many labor under the impression that their failures to please God somehow jeopardize their standing before God. I have often used marriage to illustrate the issue. Pardon a personal illustration, but it addresses the point. My marriage to Sandra is a legally binding relationship. When we got married, we bought a license that had to be filed with the state. I have been married for over forty years, and I suppose that if I looked hard enough, I could find the papers to prove it. Notwithstanding that legal relationship and the unforced desire I have to please her, I have over the years done a few odd things that have hurt Sandra's feelings and created a bit of friction between us. She cries, and I feel bad. I don't like it. I have learned to admit that it is always my fault, to say I'm sorry, and to ask for her forgiveness so we can enjoy each other once again. So far, she has been most willing to forgive. Now here's my point. My fatuous behavior does not in the least alter the fact that I am married to Sandra; our marriage is established by law. However, my behavior sometimes mars the experience because I am not a perfect husband.

So it is with our relationship to God. Justification legally and irrevocably fixes the relationship. Sanctification pertains to the unforced desire of those justified to please God. Our failure to please God may rob us of the joy of fellowship, but it does not change our legal standing. The only way to restore the marred relationship is to admit our fault, confess our sorrow at grieving Him, and seek His forgiveness. Thankfully, 'If we confess our sins, he is faithful and just to forgive us our sins, and to cleanse us from all unrighteousness' (1 John 1:9). Don't confuse position with experience.

Monergistic vs. Synergistic

Monergism and synergism may be strange-sounding words, but they are easily definable. Monergism simply means 'working alone.' Synergism means 'working together.' It is imperative to keep these notions distinct when comparing justification with sanctification. Justification is monergistic; it is the work of God alone. In justification God graciously pardons a guilty sinner, exempts the pardoned from the penalty of his sin, and regards the sinner to be righteous – all on the basis of the righteousness of Jesus Christ. It is a single, judicial, completed act done outside

---

6. 'God's sanctifying work is "imperfect in this life." It is not defective, but it is incomplete' (Chad VanDixhoorn, *Confessing the Faith: A Reader's Guide to the Westminster Confession of Faith* [Edinburgh: Banner of Truth, 2014], p. 182).

of the individual without causing any change in character but resulting in an equal standing for all so justified. The sinner makes no contribution; by faith he simply receives and rests on what God has done in and through the Lord Jesus Christ.

Sanctification is synergistic; that is, it is the cooperation of God and the believer working to produce actual holiness. Failing to see the synergism of sanctification results in two potential errors: either passivity in waiting for God to do it all, or frustrating hyper-activity by trying to do it all alone. Sanctification is not a divine 'zap' that automatically makes the believer irreversibly holy. There is a common saying, 'Let go, let God.'[7] That is true enough for justification, but it does not apply to sanctification. Neither is sanctification simply the exercise of will power, although the Christian must exercise his will not to sin. In sanctification God makes the believer a new creature, renews him in the image of God, imparts righteousness, removes the pollution of sin, and defeats its power – all on the basis of the work of Jesus Christ. In sanctification the believer reacts to all that God has done inside of him, gradually changing more and more into the image of Jesus Christ by obeying God's word and by appropriating through faith all that Christ has done.

The next section, 'Holiness Exegeted,' includes an overview of the book of Joshua as a template of progressive sanctification. Israel's conquest of the Promised Land is perhaps one of the clearest illustrations of this necessary cooperation between God and the believer. Over and over again God told the nation to possess the land because He had driven out every enemy. God achieved and assured victory for His people by virtue of His promises to give them the land and to expel the Canaanites who stood in the way of their possessing the promise. The Israelites, nonetheless, had to cross the Jordan and drive out the enemy for themselves in deadly battle. Listen to what Moses told them on the border of the land: 'Understand therefore this day, that the LORD thy God is he which goeth over before thee; as a consuming fire he shall destroy them, and he shall bring them down before thy face' (Deut. 9:3; see also 7:2). That was God's part. He continues, 'So shalt thou drive them out, and destroy them quickly, as the LORD hath said unto thee.' That was their part. Both parts were essential for victory.

The Canaanites did not roll over and play dead or pack their bags and leave voluntarily; they fought back. The Canaanites were naturally stronger than the Israelites, and the Israelites stood little chance against them in their own strength (Deut. 7:1). But believing that God had given them the victory, they entered and fought in the light of that certain victory. Unconventional tactics, such as marching

---

7. 'Let this analogy teach you what it means to rest in the Lord. Let your soul lie down upon the couch of His sweet will, as your bodies lie down in their beds at night. Relax every strain, and lay off every burden. Let yourself go in a perfect abandonment of ease and comfort, sure that, since He holds you up, you are perfectly safe. Your part is simply to rest. His part is to sustain you; and He cannot fail' (Hannah Whitall Smith, *The Christian's Secret of A Happy Life* [New York: Fleming H. Revell, 1916], p. 42). Smith was extremely influential in propagating this theology of letting go and letting God. This quotation from her influential book clearly demonstrates the concept of passivity in sanctification.

around Jericho or praying for the sun and moon to stand still, testified to God's supernatural intervention, but the Israelites conquered Jericho only by obeying God's command and they defeated the coalition of nations only by using their swords in conjunction with God's hailstones. Note this lesson as well: one victory led directly to the next conflict – there was always an Ai to follow Jericho. The battles to possess the land were unrelenting, and the possession of new territory was gradual.

Similarly, Christ has achieved our victory over sin. But sin does not flee from us just because we have been saved; it does not give up its hold on us without a fight. If we attempt to battle against sin in our own strength, defeat is certain, because sin is stronger than we are. Conversely, if we do not strive to fight against sin, defeat is just as certain. But if we engage in the conflict claiming all that God has promised and Christ has won, fighting against sin with all our renewed resolve, we can enjoy the victory.[8] Even when we experience victory, though, we can never let our guard or our faith down because we live in a world filled with the Canaanites of sin and temptation. One victory only leads to the next conflict. Remember how the catechism's definition of sanctification suggested this necessary cooperation. 'Sanctification is the work of God's free grace, whereby we are renewed in the whole man after the image of God, and are enabled....' That's God's part. 'More and more to die unto sin, and live unto righteousness.' That's our part, and it takes a lifetime.

The Westminster Larger Catechism clearly identifies the key and essential distinctions between justification and sanctification:

> Although sanctification be inseparably joined with justification, yet they differ, in that God in justification imputeth the righteousness of Christ; in sanctification his Spirit infuseth grace, and enableth to the exercise thereof; in the former sin is pardoned; in the other, it is subdued: the one doth equally free all believers from the revenging wrath of God, and that perfectly in this life, that they never fall into condemnation; the other is neither equal in all, nor in this life perfect in any, but growing up to perfection (Q. 77).

The following chart and bullet points sum up the salient facts to keep in view in comparing justification and sanctification:

Distinctive Aspects

Justification	Sanctification
A judicial act outside the believer	A moral work inside the believer
Imputed righteousness	Imparted righteousness
Concerns legal position	Concerns daily experience
Restores rights as children of God	Renews in God's image

---

8. VanDixhoorn, *Confessing the Faith*, p. 184. 'Let us be earnest in our dependence on the Word and the Spirit, for it is through humble dependence on God's power that the strongholds of sin are brought down, and holiness is brought to completion.'

Justification	*Sanctification*
Removes guilt of sin	Removes pollution of sin
Cancels penalty of sin	Defeats power of sin
A single completed act	A continuing process
No change in character	A gradually changed life
Equal standing for all believers	Different stages of progression

Shared Aspects

- Although justification and sanctification are theologically distinct, they are practically inseparable. Sanctification is the *necessary* effect of justification. Sanctification is living in the reality of justification.

- Both require the grace of God.

- Both require faith in the blood and righteousness of Jesus Christ.

- Both require the operation of the Holy Spirit to apply God's grace and Christ's merit.

KEY PROBLEM

The key problem confronting every Christian in sanctification is further proof that sanctification is progressive. That every believer struggles against sin and temptation requires no argument. Experience proves it. It is not insignificant that Israel's conquest of Canaan stands as the great type (inspired analogy and picture prophecy) of the Christian's battle for sanctification. Because sanctification is not a single, perfect act making us holy once for all, simply living in this world means that we are surrounded by temptations. Throughout the Bible, we see examples of the godly men, the great heroes of the faith, failing and falling. Even Job, who was 'perfect and upright' (Job 1:1) and in his day the most holy man on earth (Job 1:8), struggled with bitterness and doubt in the fray of his great battle. He confessed his own awareness of his moral imperfection: 'If I justify myself, mine own mouth shall condemn me: if I say, I am perfect, it shall also prove me perverse' (Job 9:20). His perfection consisted in his wholehearted dedication and consecration to fear God and turn from evil, but he recognized it did not actualize in sinlessness. So we have to face it: every Christian is in a battle for holiness. The problem for sanctification is that we cannot avoid encountering the enemy. In any war, identifying the enemy is essential. The battle for sanctification rages on two fronts.

The External Enemy

The Bible is clear that there are two principal enemies that assault the believer from the outside: the world and Satan.

The World

James 4:4 draws the battle line: 'Know ye not that the friendship of the world is enmity with God? whosoever therefore will be a friend of the world is the enemy of God.' Therefore, as believers we are not to be 'conformed to this world' (Rom. 12:2). James and Paul use two different words to designate the world that opposes Christians in their pursuit of holiness. The word 'world' in James 4:4 refers not to the planet earth, but to the organizational orders, viewpoints, systems, and philosophies of the inhabitants of this planet that scheme and conspire against the order of God. Paul's word choice defines the world as a temporary, transient place that will soon pass away. This temporary world is a hostile environment for Christians. This world is no friend of grace; it never has been and never will be.[9]

To side with the world is to stand against God. How foolish it is for Christians who are destined for eternal glory to be consumed with and taken in by an anti-God and anti-Christ system that is doomed to destruction. Following this path leading along the broad way to hell may be easier than travelling the narrow way, but the eternally different destinations make the narrow way the only way to go. The problem is that for now, the broad way with all of its attractions is still in plain view as believers walk the narrow way; and therefore, the temptation is always present to go the way of the world. There are so many things in the world that can get us. We are surrounded, frequently ambushed, and too often subdued by sin. Therefore, we must be on constant guard. It is encouraging beyond words to know that our blessed Savior has prayed for us as we live in this hostile place: we are in the world, but we are not of the world (John 17:15-16).

I think that the Old Testament laws of cleanness and uncleanness (Leviticus 11–15; Deuteronomy 14) provide a great illustration of this conflict that every believer faces by living in the world. I am well aware that these sections of the Old Testament seem strange, and it is easy to get bogged down or sidetracked just trying to figure out what a 'pygarg' or a 'chamois' is. Notwithstanding the specific difficulties for us and for the Israelites in discerning what was clean or unclean, there was a very obvious lesson that God was teaching His people and one that we must learn as well: fellowship with God demands purity. Whatever else may have been the point in all the regulations, it was clear that to be unclean precluded participation in the rituals and ceremonies of worship. Therefore, Israel was to be vigilant in avoiding whatever would produce uncleanness.

Even though I may not be able immediately to identify every pollutant, I get the impression every time I read these laws that there were many, many things constantly surrounding the people that could potentially render them unclean and

---

9. Robert S. Candlish, *1 John* (Edinburgh: Banner of Truth, 1973), p. 169. 'For the world, – what is it? Fallen human nature acting itself out in the human family; moulding and fashioning the framework of human society in accordance with its own tendencies. It is fallen human nature making the ongoings of human thought, feeling, and action its own. It is the reign or kingdom of "the carnal mind," which is "enmity against God, and is not subject to the law of God, neither indeed can be." Wherever that mind prevails, there is the world.'

thus rob them of fellowship with God. That should be the primary point and warning for us. We can't walk in this world without being surrounded by unclean things that can potentially defile us and rob us of our enjoyment in the Lord. Therefore, as we walk, we must be vigilant in avoiding whatever would render us unclean. Fortunately, in the Old Testament there was always an appropriate sacrifice to restore to cleanness. And there still is: the blood of Jesus Christ keeps on cleansing us from all sin (1 John 1:7).

Satan

Behind all the worldly attractions and assaults against our progress in holiness is the 'god of this world' (2 Cor. 4:4) who hates God, Christ, and all that belong to Them. We therefore must not be ignorant of Satan's devices lest he 'should get an advantage of us' (2 Cor. 2:11). First Peter 5:8 says, 'Be sober, be vigilant; because your adversary the devil, as a roaring lion, walketh about, seeking whom he may devour.' Similarly, Paul warns about our dangerous spiritual enemies and admonishes us 'to put on the whole armour of God' so that we 'may be able to stand against the wiles of the devil' (Eph. 6:11-12). Satan's attack against Job, attempting to put a wedge between him and God by provoking him to sin against God, was not a unique or isolated occasion. A spiritual battle rages between God and Satan, and believers are very often the battlefield (see Revelation 12 for a synopsis of the spiritual warfare). Satan's efforts to thwart the sanctification of those Christ has delivered from his realm persist, even though he is a defeated enemy and his power over the believer has been subdued by the Lord Jesus Christ. In crushing the serpent's head, Christ both conquered Satan himself and destroyed his works (Gen. 3:15; 1 John 3:8; Heb. 2:14).[10] Although defeated and doomed, Satan now is running around like the proverbial chicken with its head cut off. He is frantic, but ultimately he will fall. In the meantime, we must be on guard.

The Internal Enemy

In this battle against sin, we are our own worst enemies. The temptations outside would not be such a threat were it not for the spiritual traitor inside. Every Christian has residing within him that which answers to sin and finds it appealing. The Scripture identifies this traitor as the flesh or the old man. 'For the flesh lusteth against the Spirit, and the Spirit against the flesh: and these are contrary the one to the other: so that ye cannot do the things that ye would' (Gal. 5:17). Even Paul confessed, 'For I know that in me (that is, in my flesh,) dwelleth no good thing: for to will is present with me; but how to perform that which is good I find not' (Rom. 7:18). Every Christian knows by experience the inner struggles with sin and

---

10. Candlish, *1 John*, p. 334. 'It was a great blow to the works of the devil; it cut up by the roots the very pith and staple of his power to work at all; when the Son of God was thus manifested.'

the constant frustrations caused by succumbing to sin. Inside is where the battle rages most fiercely.

It is important not to confuse what the Bible calls 'the flesh' or 'the old man' with what we theologically refer to as 'nature.' The term 'nature' refers to the intrinsic and essential characteristics of something. The most common analogy I have heard over the years to describe the inner struggle for sanctification has been a conflict between the black dog and the white dog. These two dogs presumably represent the two natures of the Christian. Both dogs are barking and battling for attention and dominance. Whichever dog we choose to feed wins: thus, all we have to do to be holy is feed the white dog and starve the black dog. This sounds simple enough, but it either exhibits or leads to some fundamental theological errors. It reflects a careless or incorrect understanding of the new nature that the believer has. The believer, just like the unbeliever, has only one nature. The new nature is different from the old, but it is not an additional nature. The black dog/white dog theory implies that alongside the original sin nature, which is totally corrupt and depraved without any desire or ability to please God, is placed another nature that is perfectly holy and pure.[11] This suggests that the Christian can be governed sometimes by the old nature that has no interest in God, and sometimes by the new nature that is perfectly in tune with God. Neither of these options is true or even possible. I have seen too many Christians beating themselves up and driving themselves spiritually crazy trying to control the dogs. If we don't identify the enemy properly, we will have little success in fighting him.

Although this inner struggle is unavoidable, it should not discourage us or paralyze us in the conflict. *Don't begrudge the struggle, for the struggle is itself an evidence of grace.* Sin finds a peaceful existence in the old nature, but it never exists peacefully in the new. David expressed the feeling of every genuine believer when he acknowledged that his sin was ever before him as a constant hostile presence (Ps. 51:3; cf. Ps. 32:3-4). When God renews in us the whole man after His image, He does not eradicate every element of the old man. In regeneration, God gives us a new nature. It is new, but it is not perfect. The Westminster Confession of Faith succinctly describes the situation: 'This sanctification is throughout, in the whole man; yet imperfect in this life, there abiding still some remnants of corruption in every part; whence ariseth a continual and irreconcilable war, the flesh lusting against the Spirit, and the Spirit against the flesh' (13.2).

---

11. John Eaton, *The Honey-Combe of Free Justifcation by Christ Alone: Collected out of the meree Authorities of Scripture, and common and unanimous consent of the faithull Interpreters and Dispensers of Gods mysteries upon the same, especially as they expresse the excellency of Free Justification* (London: R.B. at the Charge of Robert Lancaster, 1642), p. 305. 'The Apostle likens this righteousnesse of the Gospel to the soule; as if a Christian had two soules in him, first as he is man; and secondly, as he is a Christian: his soule as he is a man, is his natural soule, by which he lives truly only to this world: but his soule as he is a Christian, is Christs righteousnesse, that also sanctifies him.' Eaton seems to be an early proponent of this erroneous view of the Christian having two natures. For further analysis of Eaton, see Jonathan Beeke, 'Hogs, Dogs, and a Wedding Garment,' *Puritan Reformed Journal* 4, no. 2 (2012), pp. 50-71.

No analogy is perfect, but I prefer the following one. In renewing the whole man after His image, God plants within the believer the seed of holiness that sprouts, takes root, grows, and bears fruit. The corruption within us tends to choke and slow the progress of growth, but there will be growth. We must be on guard and vigilant in pulling the weeds. The Confession puts it this way: 'In which war, although the remaining corruption, for a time, may much prevail; yet, through the continual supply of strength from the sanctifying Spirit of Christ, the regenerate part doth overcome; and so, the saints grow in grace, perfecting holiness in the fear of God' (WCF, 13:3).

There is hope after all. Having identified the enemies, we are ready to get the victory. The fact of the conflict is the occasion for conquest, not retreat. The only way to conquer sin and win the victory is by living in the reality of what God has provided in and through the Lord Jesus Christ. The Christian's daily battle against sin really should not be a fair fight because God has given us everything necessary to live godly lives. Consider this amazing promise: 'According as his divine power hath given unto us all things that pertain unto life and godliness, through the knowledge of him that hath called us to glory and virtue: Whereby are given unto us exceeding great and precious promises: that by these ye might be partakers of the divine nature, having escaped the corruption that is in the world through lust' (2 Pet. 1:3-4). Remember the adage: right thinking about the gospel produces right living in the gospel. Practical piety (our duty) is the product of sound theology (our doctrine).

CHAPTER 2

UNDERSTANDING UNION WITH CHRIST

UNION with Christ is an essential and most wonderful component of the gospel. The believer's security and acceptance with God depend on his association—indeed, his union—with Jesus Christ. Because believers and Christ are mutually united—believers in Christ (Col. 3:3) and Christ in believers (Col. 1:27; see also 1 John 3:24 and 4:13)—all the merit and infinite worth of Jesus Christ become the shared experience and possession of every believer. This is mind-boggling when we realize that in Christ dwells 'all the fulness of the Godhead bodily' and that believers are complete in Him (Col. 2:9-10).[1]

Tragically, too many Christians, who are in fact united to Christ, do not consciously and deliberately take advantage of what that union means and all it guarantees for a happy Christian life. As a result, these Christians struggle with doubt, intimidation, and fear, facing the issues of life and death as though they were alone. Many genuine and sincere believers, desiring with all of their hearts to serve the Lord and do what pleases Him, live under the constant burden of guilt. They realize correctly that all of their best efforts are tainted with sin and imperfection, but under that load of guilt, they constantly search for more and more issues in their lives that they can surrender to salve their consciences for a while.[2]

If only Christians would realize that regardless of personal failures, imperfections, and sins, the merit of Jesus Christ encompasses and subsumes all of their service to Him. What we do personally cannot increase or decrease God's acceptance of us. What we do as believers is pleasing and acceptable to God because He always sees us together with His Son, His dearly Beloved. Sadly, the reality of the believer's union with Christ, which is so much a part of gospel theology, is so

---

1. 'The reality [of our union with Christ] far surpasses the ability of human language to describe it' (Robert Letham, *Union With Christ: In Scripture, History, and Theology* [Phillipsburg, N.J.: P&R, 2011], p. 1).

2. Andrew Naselli, *No Quick Fix: Where Higher Life Theology Came From, What It Is, and Why It's Harmful* (Bellingham, Wash.: Lexham, 2017). Naselli provides a concise overview and critique of a movement that teaches this sort of sanctification theology.

little a part of modern Christianity.[3] I don't know how many times in my teaching career I have addressed this particular theme only to find students supposing it to be some new doctrine. They have often asked me, 'Why haven't we ever heard this before?' I could never answer that question.

Let me, however, add this caution. Do not take this truth in the wrong direction, and beware of those who do. The fact that our personal behavior neither adds to nor distracts from our acceptance before God in Christ is not license to sin or reason to abandon the pursuit of personal purity. Rather, it is faith in the reality of our union with Christ that leads to the proper obedience of God's laws for holiness. Right thinking about the gospel produces right living in the gospel, not wrong or careless living. Fixing our minds on the amazing truth that we are united to Christ will profoundly impact the way we live. It will give us boldness and motivation for life and confidence for death. It is as we learn to take advantage of everything that we are and have in Christ that we will experience all the benefits of our completeness in Him.

Union with Christ—this nexus in the gospel—itself is multifaceted.[4] On the one hand, one of the greatest advantages that union with Christ provides is the profound sense of assurance and security flowing from the knowledge that God deals with us only and always in terms of Christ. On the other hand, this union puts progressing in holiness in proper perspective. This aspect addresses directly the issue of this book concerning God's radical and comprehensive call to holiness. The knowledge of union with Christ generates the appropriate motivation for obeying that call. Progressing in holiness is not in order to somehow gain favor or acceptance with God; it is in view of and because of the acceptance fixed in Christ. The Scripture reveals this essential doctrine from different perspectives, each of which has its own application and all of which coalesce to form one glorious and indissoluble union with the Savior.

UNITED TO CHRIST REPRESENTATIVELY

That Christ is the federal, covenantal, or representative head of His people is the beginning point for any consideration of the believer's union with Christ. In this context these terms (federal, covenant, and representative) can be used interchangeably. This aspect of our union primarily concerns our legal standing before God. One essential reason I can say God only and always deals with us as

---

3. 'The task of understanding what this means is made a lot harder by the limits of our human finitude.... Being united to Christ involves union with the Son of God, who himself transcends our finitude. Being indwelt by the Holy Spirit entails union with the whole Trinity. This goes beyond what we can even imagine' (Letham, *Union With Christ*, p. 1). The magnitude of union with Christ may be one reason why it is so little a part of modern Christianity. We do not stretch our minds to think about the incomprehensible, and so we set aside this doctrine to the detriment of our own souls. Letham's work is an attempt to reintroduce the theology of union with Christ into modern Christianity.

4. William Evans, *Imputation and Impartation. Union with Christ in American Reformed Theology* (Colorado Springs, Colo.: Paternoster, 2008). Evans provides an in-depth, technical analysis of union with Christ throughout the teachings of several theologians in the Reformed tradition.

He deals with Christ is that Christ stands as our legal representative before God. When God sees Christ, He sees us.

Our guilt before God is linked directly to our relationship with Adam and his sin. Because God had ordained Adam to be a public or representative man, his obedience or disobedience to the terms of the probation (Gen. 2:16-17) would affect the entire human race that was in him as the first man. When he sinned, he earned death both for himself personally and for the entire human race corporately united to him. The Scripture is emphatically clear: 'In Adam all die' (1 Cor. 15:22). In addition to placing humanity under the death penalty, Adam plunged the human race into such inherent and individually deserved guilt and corruption that successfully earning salvation became absolutely and totally impossible. Adam's first sin justly counted as ours, and union with him resulted in every man's personal inability not to sin as well. Man's just condemnation is why the gospel is necessary.

God's matchless, infinite grace is why there is a gospel. Man needed a new representative who could and would fulfill the requirements for life. God appointed His Son to that position. The Lord Jesus Christ is the only One divinely chosen and qualified to be the Savior of sinners. As the Scripture declares: 'In Christ shall all be made alive' (1 Cor. 15:22). Whereas by nature, all men in Adam are under the sentence of death, by grace, all believers in Christ are alive and have received a new nature capable of pursuing holiness. The representative to whom we are united determines our eternal destiny. Christ, like Adam, was ordained to be a public or representative man. In order for the Son of God to be our representative, He had to become the Son of Man. In His Incarnation, the eternal Son of God partook of the same flesh and blood as those He came to represent – His brethren, the children given to Him (Heb. 2:11-14). The Incarnation was Christ's identifying Himself with us.[5]

Three key texts that contrast Christ's success as the second man with the first man's failure stand out – Psalm 8, Romans 5, and 1 Corinthians 15. Indeed, I believe that the Old Testament text was the foundation for the New Testament's development. Psalm 8 is a messianic song highlighting the greatness and grace of God and pointing to the Lord Jesus as the only means by which fallen man can come to the enjoyment and experience of the privileged rank God assigned to man in creation. For now, I want to focus attention on Psalm 8:4-6, the principal

---

5. Mark Jones, *Knowing Christ* (Edinburgh: Banner of Truth, 2015). His chapter on the Incarnation explores this theme of Christ identifying Himself with His people. See especially pp. 31-34.

'For the Son of God, the incarnation meant a whole new set of relationships: with his father and mother; with his brothers and sisters; with his disciples; with the scribes, the Pharisees and the Sadducees; with Roman soldiers and with lepers and prostitutes. It was within these relationships that he lived his incarnate life, experiencing pain, poverty and temptation; witnessing squalor and brutality; hearing obscenities and profanities and the hopeless cry of the oppressed. He lived not in sublime detachment or in ascetic isolation, but "with us", as "the fellow-man of all men", crowded, busy, harassed, stressed and molested. No large estate gave him space, no financial capital guaranteed his daily bread, no personal staff protected him from interruptions and no power or influence protected him from injustice. He saved us from alongside us' (Donald Macleod, *The Person of Christ: Contours of Christian Theology* [Downers Grove, Ill.: InterVarsity, 1998], p. 180).

messianic statements. Having considered the vastness of creation, David raised the question as to why God would give such special attention to man, particularly since man had so tragically fallen from his original glory. He used two terms for man that contrast the diminutiveness of man with the vastness of creation: 'What is *man*, that thou art mindful of him? And the son of *man*, that thou visitest him?' The first word for 'man' emphasizes man's frailty and mortality. The second expression, 'son of man (*adam*),' also underscores man's inherent weakness and insignificance as earthy. This is why, I think, in one of the key New Testament commentaries on this 'man theology' Paul said, 'The first man is of the earth, earthy' (1 Cor. 15:47).

According to Paul, whereas the first man was of the earth, the second man is 'the Lord from heaven' (1 Cor. 15:45-47). David's description of the ideal man in Psalm 8:5-6, though not as explicit, matches Paul's. The apostle speaks of a man ('the last Adam,' 'the second man') who, unlike the first man, honorably and unfailingly fulfilled the high station God intended for mankind. In His condescending and humiliating Incarnation, the Second Person of the eternal Trinity was temporarily diminished to a position lower than that of the angels in order to perform the necessary obedience to merit and restore life to the race of which He was the Head. He was the ideal Man. Having fulfilled the necessary requirements to satisfy God's demands, He was then crowned with glory and honor. Christ's commissioned humiliation led to His earned exaltation, whereas Adam's created exaltation crashed into deserved humiliation. Everything the first Adam lost the second Adam regained.

Paul effectively demonstrates that what Christ did in fulfilling the requirements of life and regaining Paradise, He did as a public figure. There is a remarkable connection between our representative and us. Just as in Adam 'we have borne the image of the earthy,' in Christ 'we shall also bear the image of the heavenly' (1 Cor. 15:49). Romans 5:12-19 is unquestionably the most explicit biblical exposition contrasting the corporate effect of Adam's disobedience with the corporate effect of Christ's obedience. In our place and as our representative, Christ fulfilled every demand of God's righteous law. He worked so that we might receive grace. There is an important connection between our justification and our representative union with Christ. God's just imputation of our guilt to Christ and His equally just imputation of Christ's righteousness to us (the essence of justification) are righteously legal acts because Christ is our covenant Head, our representative. Accordingly, the prophet Isaiah in one of his famous Servant Songs records God's word to His Servant that identifies Him in terms of the covenant: 'I will preserve thee, and give thee for a covenant of the people' (Isa. 49:8; see also Isa. 42:6).

All of this deals with the issues of legality. As our representative, Christ accepted our liabilities, and His merit accrues to us. This understanding of federal theology answers two crucial questions, 'If Adam did it, how come I'm guilty?' and

'If Christ did it, how come I'm innocent?'[6] If it was a just thing for God to condemn us in Adam because he was the head of the whole human race, it is a just thing for God to justify us in Christ because He is the Head of the redeemed race. Christ's righteousness counts for us. Therefore, there is no condemnation to those who are 'in' Christ Jesus (Rom. 8:1). We are graciously accepted by God in Christ, the Beloved (Eph. 1:6). To be thus united to Christ is to be in the safest place possible. Here is the real security of the gospel.

UNITED TO CHRIST MYSTICALLY

The believer's union with Christ is mystical. Don't be afraid of this word. Theologically, 'mystical' refers to spiritual truth that surpasses human comprehension because of the transcendence of its nature and significance, and thus, it is a most appropriate word to designate our union with Jesus Christ.[7] This mystical union is a truth that, notwithstanding its reality, defies explanation. If I may, let me put it in these terms: union with Christ is so profound, it is almost too good to be true. Yet it *is* true, and we must believe it on the authority of God's certain revelation and learn to live in its reality.

Being in union with Christ goes beyond enjoying His legal representation or even His constant company. The Lord Jesus promised that He would be with us, even to the end of the world (Matt. 28:20). The inspired apostle assures us that the Lord will never leave us or forsake us, giving us the boldness to affirm, 'The Lord is my helper, and I will not fear what man shall do unto me' (Heb. 13:5-6). If that uninterrupted companionship were the only level of our association with Christ, it would be wonderful and far beyond what we deserve. The witness of Scripture, however, is not just that Christ is with us but that we are in Him. Read particularly the books of Ephesians and Colossians and just count the number of times we are actually said to be in Christ. It is astounding. We are not just experiencing His presence nor are we somehow appended or attached to Him; we are actually in Him.

---

6. John L. Girardeau, *The Federal Theology. Its Import and Its Regulative Influence* (Greenville, S.C.: Reformed Academic Press, 1994). This republished work of Girardeau provides a concise introduction to the basic tenants of Federal Theology. In dealing with these tenants of Federal Theology, Girardeau unpacks the important answers to these two crucial questions.

7. 'This union the orthodox divines have called mystical, borrow the expression, most likely, from Eph. 5:32…. Orthodox divines have rather meant thereby, what is the proper, scriptural idea of the word μυστηριον, from μυω, something hidden and secret: not something incomprehensible and incapable of being intelligibly stated. The spiritual union is indeed mysterious in that sense…. But the tie is called mystical, because it is invisible to human eyes; it is not identical with that outward or professed union…. It is a secret kept between the soul and its Redeemer, save as it is manifested by its fruits' (Robert Lewis Dabney, *Systematic Theology* [Edinburgh: Banner of Truth, 1985], p. 614). Dabney seems to acknowledge that 'mystical' has two meanings and that both meanings can be applied to the mystical union. But he prefers 'hidden' to 'incomprehensible.'

K. Scott Oliphint, *The Majesty of Mystery: Celebrating the Glory of an Incomprehensible God* (Bellingham, Wash.: Lexham Press, 2016). Oliphint's book, especially his opening chapter, wrestles with the theological understanding of 'mystery.' It provides a helpful understanding for someone who is interested in studying how spiritual truth surpasses human comprehension because of the transcendence of its nature and significance.

How can I explain that? I can't. It is a mystical union. Yet there are two things about this union that I do want us to think about.

A Spiritual Union

Although believers consciously enter into union with Christ through faith (Eph. 3:17; Col. 2:12), the execution of the union and the attestation to its reality are the operations of the Holy Spirit. In Ephesians 2:20-22, Paul used the analogy of a building to explain the believer's union with Christ: 'And are built upon the foundation of the apostles and prophets, Jesus Christ himself being the chief corner stone; in whom all the building fitly framed together groweth unto an holy temple in the Lord: in whom ye also are builded together for an habitation of God through the Spirit.'

Not only does he make it clear that Christ, as the foundation and cornerstone, is essential to the building's existence, but he also explains that the components of the superstructure (i.e., believers) are put into place through the agency of the Holy Spirit. In 1 Corinthians 12, the apostle uses another analogy, describing the church as the body of Christ. Although his focus of application is on the unity that all the individual members have in the body, he does make a significant statement revealing how believers become part of this body of Christ: 'For by one Spirit are we all baptized into one body' (12:13). Obviously, Paul is not referring to water baptism, which is a visible sign administered by an ordained minister that publicly identifies an individual as a member of the church. Water baptism, regardless of its great importance, does not and cannot save. Rather, Paul is speaking of that spiritual baptism whereby the Holy Spirit of God actually accomplishes and effects a real and spiritual union with the Savior. By some divine and inexplicable means, the Holy Spirit places us in Christ.

The beauty of this action, being a spiritual work, is that the Holy Spirit, just like the Father and the Son, never fails in what He does. Thankfully, we are not left to ourselves to figure out how to achieve or attain this necessary element of our salvation. It is a divine work, requiring no contribution from us. Although we cannot comprehend how this spiritual union occurs, the Holy Spirit has given to us an internal witness that assures us that He has done His job. As evidence that we are in Christ, we have the Spirit of Christ in us: 'If any man have not the Spirit of Christ, he is none of his' (Rom. 8:9). As evidence that we have the Spirit of Christ, the Holy Spirit bears witness with our spirit not only that we are the children of God, but also that we share with Christ everything from His sufferings to His glorification (Rom. 8:16-17).

A Spiritual Communion

Being in union with Christ means that every believer jointly participates and shares in the work of the Lord Jesus. This particular truth really staggers the mind. In a way that we cannot fathom, in Christ—and therefore together *with* Christ—

believers partake in all Christ did to accomplish redemption, and they share jointly in the success of His work.[8] Once again, I'm glad that truth is not limited within the bounds of my comprehension. Nevertheless, to encourage our contemplation of this aspect of our union, I want to discuss some of the things that the Bible reveals we experience with Christ.

Union with Christ's Death

In union with Christ, believers died with their Savior. Consider these astounding statements that declare the believer's communion with the death of Christ: 'I am crucified with Christ' (Gal. 2:20); 'We are buried with him by baptism into death' (Rom. 6:3; also Col. 2:12); 'Our old man is crucified with him' (Rom. 6:6); 'If one died for all, then were all dead [i.e. all died]' (2 Cor. 5:14). Obviously, we did not hang on the cross along with Christ to suffer all of the physical agony and torment that He endured in both body and soul. In the physical sense, Christ suffered and died alone as the substitute for His people. He bore our penalty and exempted us from ever having to pay the price of our sin. Yet mystically we were united to Him. When Christ died, all of His people died with Him. God counted believers as being in His Son.

This union guarantees that everything our Lord purchased on the cross is the certain possession of all those united to Him. When Christ was crucified, He satisfied God's righteousness, secured the forgiveness of sin, and severed the connection to sin's doom and dominion. So if we died with Him, God's law has no more claim against us – justice has been served. If we died with Him, we have received pardon from guilt and forgiveness for all our sins. We have every right to face our sins and claim the blood of Christ to keep on cleansing us every time we need forgiving (1 John 1:7). If we died with Him, we have been freed from sin's dominating power over us (Rom. 6:14). In Christ, we possess definitively the power to be free from the whole oppressive burden of sin. In Christ, we have the freedom to pursue holiness.

Union with His death not only provides certain security in our knowing that we are the partakers of all He purchased, but it also generates both the motive and the power for holy living. A united life leads to a transformed life. This is clearly Paul's logic in Colossians 3. Paul first declares the united life: 'For ye are dead, and your life is hid with Christ in God' (3:3). Note carefully the verb tenses. The expression 'ye are dead' does not refer to being in a condition or state of death; rather, it refers to a past act—that time when the believer died with Christ—and could be translated 'you died.' The next statement could be translated 'your life has

---

8. 'It must have sounded particularly shocking for Paul to suggest that he had any part in Christ's crucifixion. It still does! Paul is not suggesting that anything he has done has *added* to what Christ accomplished in his death. Rather, he is drawing on the doctrine of our union with Christ as believers. When Christ died to the law's curse, we also died to it. In union with Christ we share in the great redemptive moments associated with Christ: we are thereby crucified, raised, and ascended in him' (Derek Thomas, *Let's Study Galatians* [Edinburgh: Banner of Truth, 2004], p. 61).

been hidden with Christ.' This particular tense expresses a completed past act that has continuing consequences. Here is the idea: when we died with Christ, we were at that very time placed in Christ, and there we constantly remain.

Paul next defines the transformed life. The apostolic application of this gospel is simply that we are to quit sinning: 'Mortify therefore your members which are upon the earth.... Put on the new man' (3:5, 10). This dying to sin and living to righteousness becomes normal behavior in the light of Christ's being 'all, and in all' (3:11). Paul reasons the same way in Romans: 'Knowing this, that our old man is crucified with him, that the body of sin might be destroyed, that henceforth we should not serve sin' (6:6). Here is part of the secret to victorious living. We must learn to look down on sin from the vantage point of the cross, for we indeed were crucified with Christ. The sin that is so alluring when in our face will lose its appeal from the perspective of the old rugged cross.

Union with Christ's Resurrection

In union with Christ, believers have been raised from spiritual death to spiritual life and have the certain prospect of the bodily resurrection as well. By His death, our Savior 'abolished death, and hath brought life and immortality to light through the gospel' (2 Tim. 1:10). When Christ rose from the dead, we rose from the dead with Him. The Scripture is explicit in what it teaches. 'Even when we were dead in sins, hath [God] quickened us together with Christ ... and hath raised us up together' (Eph. 2:5-6). 'For if [since] we have been planted together in the likeness of his death, we shall be also in the likeness of his resurrection' (Rom. 6:5). 'Now if [since] we be dead [died] with Christ, we believe that we shall also live with him' (Rom. 6:8). 'Ye are risen with him through the faith of the operation of God, who hath raised him from the dead. And you, being dead in your sins and the uncircumcision of your flesh, hath he quickened together with him' (Col. 2:12-13). 'If [since] ye then be risen with Christ, seek those things which are above' (Col. 3:1). Christ Himself assures us that because He lives, we will live also (John 14:19). In the immediate context of that promise, the Lord Jesus defined that mutual life as evidence of union with Him: 'At that day ye shall know that I am in my Father, and ye in me, and I in you' (John 14:20).

Communion with the death of Christ necessarily means communion with His resurrection and life. It is impossible to be united to His death without being united to His life. 'It is a faithful saying: For if we be dead with him, we shall also live with him' (2 Tim. 2:11). Just as certainly as believers partake of what Christ achieved by His atoning death, so they partake of all the victory of His glorious resurrection. This shared life includes the spiritual life generated by the new birth (requiring resurrection power, Eph. 1:19-20) as well as the future resurrection when 'this corruptible must put on incorruption, and this mortal must put on immortality' (1 Cor. 15:53). 'God hath given to us eternal life, and this life is in his Son. He that hath the Son hath life' (1 John 5:11-12).

This union with Christ that has secured our newness of life and immortality demands modification in our lives. Since we are new creatures in Christ, our view of life must radically differ from the one we held when we were dead in sin: 'Old things are passed away; behold, all things are become new' (2 Cor. 5:17). In Colossians 3, Paul issues two sweeping imperatives that flow from the fact that we are risen with Christ. First, we are to seek the things that are above where Christ sits at the right hand of God (3:1). Seeking includes more than casual or curious investigation; it requires the concentration of effort necessary to obtain the object of the search.[9] As we live in this world, we must diligently and continually bring heaven to bear on the issues of life. That we are united to Christ is for us a fact of life that we must factor into life. Second, we are to set our affections on things above (3:2). What the Authorized Version translates as 'set your affections' is actually one word and could be translated more literally as 'think.' We are to be thinking about the things above. Right thinking always focuses on Christ and our place in Him.[10] That is the essence of Paul's application. Since we have been raised with Christ, think about it. The only question is 'Why don't we?'

Union with Christ's Session

By the law of this spiritual and mystical union, believers sit with Christ on His throne. Since we are united to Christ, it is impossible for Christ to be where we are not or for us not to be where He is. As part of His earned exaltation, after His resurrection He ascended into heaven and took His seat of honor at the right hand of His Father. And inexplicably yet absolutely, so did we. I confess that the fact that we are enthroned with Christ as He sits exalted in His session at the right hand of God totally confounds me. It is amazing beyond words. It occurs to me that sometimes we read the Scripture so casually that we do not take the time to let the truths really sink into our minds and hearts. Listen to what the Scripture says, and just think about it: 'Blessed be the God and Father of our Lord Jesus Christ, who hath blessed us *with all spiritual blessings in heavenly places in Christ*' (Eph. 1:3 emphasis mine); 'But God, who is rich in mercy ... hath raised us up together, and *made us sit together in heavenly places in Christ Jesus*' (Eph. 2:4, 6 emphasis mine). If these were predictions of what God would do for us someday, we would have something wonderful to look forward to. But these are not prophecies; they are declarations of what God has already done.[11] So as I sit here struggling over words,

---

9. 'The word translated "seek" carried overtones of longing or yearning for something – having a deep desire that controls the whole direction of life' (Mark Johnston, *Let's Study Colossians and Philemon* [Edinburgh: Banner of Truth, 2013], p. 86).

10. 'That is, the need to consciously nurture those longings of the heart by literally seeking the object of its desire, namely Christ.... It is strange that Christians and churches all too often preoccupy themselves with the earthly trappings of the Christian life rather than with Christ himself' (Mark Johnston, *Let's Study Colossians*, p. 86).

11. Carson poetically expresses the truth of Ephesians 1 this way: 'We were blessed in the heavenly realms long before being included in Christ. Since we heard the good news, overwhelmed, we reach forward to seize Paradise. We shall see Him ourselves face to face to the praise of His glorious grace'

I am even now in heaven in throne-union with Jesus Christ. What is more real: where I am here or where I am there?

As confounding as all this may be to reason, what wonder it imports for our faith. The implications of this throne-union to the issues of life are extensive. We ought not to live any part of our life *here* without the consciousness that we are in reality *there*.[12] We need to live in the light of spiritual reality. This throne-union with Christ ought to assure us of our absolute security in the gospel. If we are spiritually present in heaven in Christ now, then there is no possibility that we can ever perish in hell. Union with Christ is an excellent argument for our eternal security. This union ought also to strengthen us through all the struggles and sufferings of this life. Just as certain as is suffering is the fact that 'we shall also reign with him' (2 Tim. 2:12; see also Rom. 8:17 where joint suffering leads to joint glorification). Even when all of life seems to be against us, we have reason for confidence and joy, knowing by faith that appearance and reality are not the same. 'Who is he that condemneth? It is Christ that died, yea rather, that is risen again, who is even at the right hand of God, who also maketh intercession for us' (Rom. 8:34).

Can you see it? Christ died; we died with Him. Christ is risen; we rose with Him. Christ is at the right hand of God; we are sitting with Him. Therefore, no one or nothing can condemn us or separate us 'from the love of God, which is in Christ Jesus' (Rom. 8:39). May God help us to think more and more about this mystical union and communion that we have with Christ. It will do us good.[13]

UNITED TO CHRIST VITALLY

Believers are also united to Christ vitally. By vital, I simply mean that which is necessary for the existence and continuation of life. Apart from Christ, spiritual life does not exist, but in Christ there is abundant life. Everything necessary to generate and sustain life flows freely from the Savior. Spiritual life and survival, therefore, depend on union with Christ. Paul recognized the vital union between himself and Christ when he testified, 'I am crucified with Christ: nevertheless I live; yet not I, but Christ liveth in me' (Gal. 2:20). What was true for Paul is true for every individual believer. The more we are conscious of the animating power within us, the more we can draw from Christ's infinite energy to enable us to live in the flesh

---

(D. A. Carson, 'To the Praise of His Glorious Grace' in *Hymns Modern and Ancient* [Roswell, Ga.: Heart Publications, 2011]).

12. 'In our generation, which reflects too little on the future and almost never on eternity, it is distressingly obvious that we need help, help from God, so as to be able to know the hope to which we have been called. Only then will we become more interested in living with eternity's values constantly before our eyes' (D. A. Carson, *A Call to Spiritual Reformation: Priorities from Paul and His Prayers* [Grand Rapids: Baker Books, 1992], p. 176).

13. 'We need to know who we are, as God sees us. Paul wants us to appreciate the value that God places on us, not because we are intrinsically worthy but because we have been identified with Christ…. If we maintain this vision before our eyes of who we are—nothing less than God's inheritance!—we will be concerned to live in line with this unimaginably high calling' (Carson, *A Call to Spiritual Reformation,* pp. 176-77).

by faith in the Son of God who loved us and gave Himself for us (Gal. 2:20). At this point I want to explore three scriptural analogies of this vital union to increase our understanding of this oneness with Christ. Our success as Christians living in this present evil age will be in direct proportion to the degree to which we see Christ and recognize our place in Him.

The Food and Life Analogy

I suppose that some people live to eat; everyone, though, has to eat to live. I cannot explain how eating works. How the body reacts with food to extract all of the necessary vitamins, minerals, and whatever else is beyond my knowledge. I just enjoy the food and let my body do what it does naturally. Although it is not completely true that we are what we eat, what we eat does become a part of us. From food we get the energy that is essential to life. The Lord Jesus used this daily necessity to teach a fundamental lesson about a far more essential feeding: spiritual eating. After He had miraculously fed the huge crowds with natural food, He identified Himself as the Bread of Life (John 6:48). He then issued this 'dietary' ultimatum: 'Except ye eat the flesh of the Son of man, and drink his blood, ye have no life in you. Whoso eateth my flesh, and drinketh my blood, hath eternal life; and I will raise him up at the last day. For my flesh is meat indeed, and my blood is drink indeed. He that eateth my flesh, and drinketh my blood, dwelleth in me, and I in him. As the living Father hath sent me, and I live by the Father: so he that eateth me, even he shall live by me' (John 6:53-57).

To interpret this instruction literally would be linguistically absurd and theologically aberrant. The Lord is obviously making a comparison between eating physically and eating spiritually. Eating Christ is a spiritual act of faith, not a physical act of chewing and swallowing. The point of correspondence is not in the mechanics of the eating process, but in the consequence. Eating is a fitting figure of appropriating to oneself what is necessary for life. As we believe Christ and His gospel we receive life and enter into a mutual bond with Christ: 'He that eateth my flesh, and drinketh my blood, dwelleth *in me*, and I *in him*' (emphasis mine).[14]

In the physical realm we understand the necessity of eating regularly and healthily to sustain life. Without food, our bodies will shrivel and waste away. Without food, we will become faint, having no energy to function. Unless we are physically sick or emotionally unstable, eating is natural, and mealtimes are enjoyable experiences. The same is true spiritually. Partaking of Christ by faith ought to be the normal and happy experience of every believer. We must have a regular, daily diet of eating the Bread of Life and drinking the Living Water if we

---

14. 'We need only understand that Jesus is using language that points to intimate communion. Just as the shared life of the persons of the Godhead is bound up with the intimate and eternal communion they enjoy, so the new life of the believer is bound up with the profound union and communion he or she has with Christ (6:57). The life of faith then is the life of conscious recognition of what Christ is as Son of God and as Savior of the world, and conscious dependence upon him for new life in fellowship with God' (Mark Johnston, *Let's Study John* [Edinburgh: Banner of Truth, 2003], p. 104).

are going to grow in grace and in the knowledge of God. What is great about eating and drinking Christ is that it is always the right thing to do and it is impossible to eat too much. As I have grown a bit older, I have been instructed to watch what I eat. I can't have this or that because I have to maintain a certain ratio in my cholesterol count. But Christ is always a feast. The more we feast on Him, the more spiritual strength we are going to gain. By faith we must procure to ourselves all that Christ is and all that Christ has for His people. He is our life.

The Head and Body Analogy

Christ is the Head of His people not only in a covenant sense, but in a vital sense as well. Paul expressed his desire for the spiritual growth of the Ephesian believers using this analogy: 'But speaking the truth in love, [we] may grow up into him in all things, which is the head, even Christ: From whom the whole body fitly joined together and compacted by that which every joint supplieth, according to the effectual working in the measure of every part, maketh increase of the body unto the edifying of itself in love' (Eph. 4:15-16).

Similarly, he identified Christ as 'the head over all things to the church, which is his body' (Eph. 1:22-23). In Colossians he also forthrightly declared that Christ 'is the head of the body, the church' (1:18).

The vital connection between head and body is obvious. The head is the command center for all the operations of life. From the head flow all the impulses and instructions for the body to function. A headless body is lifeless. It is only in union with its head that a body can live. What a vivid analogy to illustrate the inseparable connection between Christ and His people! As the body, His people do not and cannot exist without Him.[15] But united to Him, they have everything necessary for spiritual life and function. In addition, they enjoy the security based in the fact that God sees the body only through the head and deals with the body only in terms of the head.

But there is another side to this analogy that should increase our sense of security and our sense of duty. If it is true that a headless body is lifeless, it is equally true that a bodiless head cannot exist. Now follow carefully what I am going to say; I do not want to be misunderstood. Believers cannot exist apart from Christ, and *Christ* does not exist apart from His body, the church. I am not saying that the eternal Son of God, the Second Person of the holy Trinity, does not exist apart from the church. As God, He is absolutely independent, the eternal and immutable self-existent Deity. I am intentionally referring to the Savior as Christ, the title designating Him as the anointed One – eternally chosen to be the one and only Mediator between God and men, the ideal Prophet, Priest, and King. The gracious reason that God ordained His only begotten Son to be that Mediator was that He might become the Son of Man,

---

15. 'Separate the church as a body from Christ as its head and it becomes a lifeless institution and not the living organism it is meant to be. Too often the church looks to "other things" to inject life and vitality into it; when what it really needs is to appreciate its need for meaningful communion with Christ' (Mark Johnston, *Let's Study Colossians and Philemon*, p. 31).

that He might become Jesus who came to save His people from their sins (Matt. 1:21). Christ, the Messiah, came to save a people, and save a people is exactly what He did. As certainly as there is a Christ, there is a people who belong to Christ – His body, the church. Every believer, therefore, testifies to the existence of the Savior. This is why I say that union with Christ should stimulate our desire to reflect Him. Just as there is a sense in which God sees the body only through the head, there is a sense in which the world sees the head only through the body. It is vital, therefore, that we as members of His body become more and more conformed to His image, which is the purpose of our predestination to this glorious position (Rom. 8:29). Because we are in Christ, God always thinks well of us. Because we are in Christ, may sinners seeing us come to think well of Him. This is why union with Christ relates directly to obeying the call to holiness.

The Vine and Branches Analogy

Perhaps the most thorough analogy describing the believer's vital union with Christ comes from the teaching of Jesus Himself. In John 15, the Lord identifies Himself as the vine and true believers as the branches. The primary point of the analogy is the life connection between the vine and branches.[16] The vine is the stem and root, which supplies the life and fruitfulness of branches. The branches are the natural outgrowth of the vine and have no independent existence. Let me summarize Christ's teaching under three heads.

(1) Union with Christ Explained

Jesus emphasizes two principal aspects of this vital union. First, union involves communion. The verb 'to abide' occurs nine times in verses 4-9. This word means to remain, to continue, or to take up residence, and it expresses an intimacy of relationship. This union entails mutual abiding as Christ remains in us and we in Him (15:4-5). The vine shares its life juices with the branches that draw what they need for life from that constant circulation. So the believer shares in and draws, from the life of Christ, what is necessary for spiritual, eternal, and abundant life.

Second, union implies dependence.[17] The branch cannot function or survive apart from the vine (15:4, 6). Jesus said, 'Without me ye can do nothing' (15:5). Note particularly how personal Christ makes this: 'without me.' Christ is everything to and for His people. Observe, as well, the absoluteness of Christ's statement: 'ye can do nothing.' He does not say that we can do things better with Him; He forthrightly says we can't do anything. Why then do we so often attempt things without Him? Although we know our flesh is weak, in our spiritual stupidity we

---

16. 'Whatever is involved in this intimacy between Christ and Christians, it stands at the heart of spiritual vitality' (D. A. Carson, *The Farewell Discourse and Final Prayer of Jesus: An Exposition of John 14–17* [Grand Rapids: Baker, 1980], p. 91).

17. 'Continuous dependence on the vine, constant reliance upon him, persistent spiritual imbibing of his life – this is the *sine qua non* of spiritual fruitfulness' (D. A. Carson, *The Pillar New Testament Commentary: The Gospel According to John* [Grand Rapids: Eerdmans, 1991], p. 516).

often feel obligated to give ourselves a chance before resting upon Christ. Trying to approach sanctification or service without consciously relying on faith in Christ is folly and doomed effort. We can do all things through Christ who strengthens us (Phil. 4:13), and we can do nothing without Him. That's an important lesson to learn.

(2) Union with Christ Evidenced

To be united to Christ shows itself in life: spiritual life does not look like or act like spiritual death. Jesus highlights two essential proofs of abiding in Him.

First, union with Christ is evidenced by *the production of fruit*. In verses 6-11, the Lord refers to fruit six times. This fruit is not the result of human effort or achievement; it is the result of abiding in Christ. Note carefully that fruit does not procure union; instead, it reveals the fact of union (15:2, 6, 8). Bearing fruit is not optional; it is an essential mark of union with Christ. Even though Christ does not here specify the identity or properties of the fruit, we do know that the law of fruit necessitates that kind produces like kind. If the life of Christ flows through us, it must be likeness to Christ that emanates from us. As fruit brings glory to the vine, so must we radiate glory to Christ.

It is the fruit that attracts attention to the vine. Some interpreters mistakenly limit the fruit-bearing to efforts in evangelism. Although they are contextually wrong in identifying the fruit as new converts, there is an important sense in which the fruit that we bear—the evidences of spiritual life in Christ—ought to attract men to Christ. It is best to see the fruit as the evidence of a transformed life produced by the Spirit of God. According to Scripture, the kind of fruit required is defined in terms of love, joy, peace, longsuffering, gentleness, goodness, faith, meekness, and temperance (Gal. 5:22-23). The amount of fruit may vary between branches, but the existence of fruit on them does not. As the branch draws from the life juices of the vine, it will yield more fruit. In like manner, as by faith we draw from the resources that Christ supplies, the evidences of grace will increase in our lives.

Second, union with Christ is evidenced by *the Father's care*. In Christ's analogy, God the Father is the husbandman, i.e., the proprietor and gardener (15:1). The branches are not wild growth; rather, they are the objects of special cultivation, care, and concern. The owner of the vineyard does everything that is necessary for the production of fruit (see Isa. 5:1-2). Good gardening requires great skill, particularly in the pruning of vines and fruit trees. Cutting too much will kill; pruning too little does not further proper growth. Christ reveals that God knows precisely what is necessary for each individual branch to produce fruit. At the beginning of this passage He says, 'Every branch in me that beareth not fruit he taketh away' (15:2). On the surface this sounds like a contradictory statement. If the branch is in Christ, how can the branch be taken away? Let me here interject one of the key principles of interpretation: a verse cannot mean what it cannot mean.

Christ is unmistakably referring to a branch in Him – a genuine believer. The crux of meaning lies in the verb translated 'taketh away,' the primary meaning of which is 'to raise' or 'to lift up.' This explains the image: some branches the Father lifts up. He carefully raises the branch that has fallen to expose it more advantageously to the light of grace that it might grow.[18] What a beautiful statement this is!

In the second part of this verse, the Savior continues, 'Every branch that beareth fruit, he purgeth it, that it may bring forth more fruit' (15:2). God will prune by cutting away what chokes out or competes for the production of fruit. More fruit is His objective. Again, it is clear that fruit in the life of the Christian is not the result of natural energies; it is the result of divine operation. The branches can never take credit for fruit, and Christians can never take credit for godliness. Fruitfulness is thriving in grace.

(3) Union with Christ Enjoyed

The benefits that flow from union with Christ are indescribably wonderful. Four blessings stand out in Christ's analogy. Each of these could potentially lead to long

---

18. D. A. Carson, *The Pillar New Testament Commentary Series: The Gospel According to John* (Grand Rapids: Eerdmans, 1991), pp. 514-15. Carson has a different take on this verse. He translates the Greek verb as 'cuts off.' One reason that he goes with this translation is that he sees no major significance to the words 'every branch *in me*.' In his view, there are only two possible groups in mind: apostate Christians or ethnic Jews. 'It is more satisfactory to recognize that asking the *in me* language to settle such disputes [as to whether the dead branches are apostate Christians or Jews who were once in God's vine] is to push the vine imagery too far. The transparent purpose of the verse is to insist that there are no true Christians without some measure of fruit.' He makes no provision that this phrase 'in me' is union with Christ language. For him, the whole metaphor of the vine is about fruitfulness. Unfruitfulness is a sign of a false profession. He is joined in this view of the words 'in me' by Andreas J. Kostenberger, *Baker Exegetical Commentary on the New Testament: John* (Grand Rapids: Baker Academic, 2004), pp. 451-52. See especially p. 451, n. 16.

Many commentators view the branches not bearing fruit as false professors. William Hendriksen takes this view in *New Testament Commentary: John* (Grand Rapids: Baker Book, 1979), Leon Morris in *The New International Commentary on the New Testament: The Gospel According to John* (Grand Rapids: Eerdmans, 1971), and J. C. Ryle in *Expository Thoughts on the Gospels: John: Volume 3* (Edinburgh: Banner of Truth, 1987). John MacArthur takes this view as well: 'The phrase *in Me* in this case cannot have the Pauline connotation of believers' union with Christ; it merely describes those who outwardly attach themselves to Him' (*The MacArthur New Testament Commentary: John 12–21* [Chicago: Moody, 2008], p. 152). What is interesting is that MacArthur does not treat these verses in order. He deals with the groups and what the passage has to say as a whole about his view of the two groups – those who bear fruit and those who do not bear fruit. MacArthur's problem is that he is pitting Pauline and Johannine theology against each other. Paul and John proclaim a united message given to them by the supreme Author of Scripture: the Holy Spirit. This phrase 'in me' carries many overtones throughout Scripture that speak to the fact of union with Christ. Therefore, the interpretation of this one phrase dictates how one takes the whole passage. If a person is in Jesus Christ, he cannot be cut off from Jesus and cast into a punishing fire. If a person is in Jesus Christ, he can be lifted up out of the mire of worldliness and have the unnecessary dross pruned away so that he will be more fruitful. That dross is burned up in God's refining fires of sanctification (cf. 1 Pet. 1:6-7).

R. C. Sproul takes a mediating position where he does not come down either way but presents both views as options (*St. Andrew's Expositional Commentary: John* [Orlando, Fla.: Reformation Trust], 2009). R. Kent Hughes only addresses believers and does not really answer the question of whether or not apostate Christians are in view in these verses (*Preaching the Word: John* [Wheaton, Ill.: Crossway], 1999). A. W. Pink does agree with the emphasis of 'in me' being union with Christ and the necessary translation of the verb being 'lift up' instead of 'cut off.' See his discussion in his *Exposition of the Gospel of John: Three Volumes Complete and Unabridged in One* (Grand Rapids: Zondervan, 1975), pp. 805-10.

discussions, but I am merely going to identify them for your further consideration. First, union with Christ means escape from destruction (15:6). Eternal destiny is linked to where we are in relationship to Christ. The man out of Christ is like a branch that is withered (void of life and vitality) and burned. To be outside of Christ is death, now and forever, but to be in Christ is life, both now and forever.

Second, union with Christ guarantees answers to prayer (15:7). The language of this verse is significant. The text marks as a privilege both praying and being answered in our prayers. If we abide in Him, we *will ask* and it *will become* reality for us. Prayer is the exercise of our union and communion with Christ. The more conscious we are of that union and our consequent dependence on Him, the more we will pray.

Third, union with Christ assures us that we are the objects of God's love (15:9-10). It is the only way that we can ever personally know and experience the love of God. Christ is the supreme object of the Father's love and those in Christ share in that never-ending, never-changing love.

Fourth, union with Christ produces joy. Christ concludes His analogy with the statement, 'These things have I spoken unto you, that my joy might remain in you, and that your joy might be full' (15:11). This is the ultimate issue. The consolation, peace, and satisfaction resulting from our meditation on union with Christ will overwhelm us with spiritual joy and contentment. And in union with Christ, even this joy is mutual. It is easy enough to understand why we should rejoice in Christ, but that He acknowledges His own joy in us is astounding (similarly, see Isaiah 62:4-5: 'the Lord delighteth in thee…. So shall thy God rejoice over thee'). God, Christ, and we have every reason to be satisfied. Why has the remarkable thrill of this union become so ignored by so many who have every right to enjoy it?

UNITED TO CHRIST INTIMATELY

There is no relationship on earth more intimate than that between husband and wife. Adam, in his yet sinless state, expressed his understanding of the inseparable connection between himself and the partner God had made especially for him: 'This is now bone of my bones, and flesh of my flesh' (Gen. 2:23). In his inspired commentary on and application of Adam's statement, Moses made it clear that the marriage bond superseded every other human connection. 'Therefore shall a man leave his father and his mother, and shall cleave unto his wife: and they shall be one flesh' (Gen. 2:24). In arguing for the sexual purity of believers, Paul used the theology of Moses to explain the relationship of the believer to Christ: 'But he that is joined unto the Lord is one spirit' (1 Cor. 6:17). He later said to the same group of believers that they had been espoused to one husband, Christ (2 Cor. 11:2). In Ephesians 5—perhaps the most explicit passage expounding the gospel according to the symbol of marriage—the apostle goes right back to Adam's confession when he describes the believer's union with Christ: 'For we are members of his body, of his flesh, and of his bones' (5:30).

It is not surprising that Scripture so frequently uses marriage as the choice symbol of the intimate and eternal relationship that exists between Christ and His bride, the church. The parallels are many and the theology illustrated is magnificent. In marriage, God ordained that two become one flesh; in the spiritual union, the believer becomes one with Christ. In marriage, two people traditionally share a name; in the spiritual union, Christians are called by His name. In marriage, two people share one life: in the spiritual union, Christians, being one with Christ, are beneficiaries of the grace of His life. In marriage, two people have in this life a common destiny: what God has joined together, man cannot put asunder. Likewise, nothing can separate the Christian from the love of Christ. In marriage, two people live in constant company and fellowship; so in the spiritual union believers abide in Christ and He abides in them. In marriage, two people share a mutual attraction and affection. Each sees something in the other that generates and feeds love. The Song of Solomon portrays a marriage that was a mutual admiration society consisting of two members. Such love points to a love that is even nobler. For Christ loved us first with a love that was not mutual. He loved us, but we saw no beauty in Him that we should desire Him, even though He is the altogether lovely One. But His gracious Spirit wooed us and drew us irresistibly to Him, and now we love Him because He first loved us. And here is the real mystery. He loved us not because we were lovely, but in spite of our ugliness and sin. His love for us is single, exclusive, and undivided. It is amazing that Jesus would love even *me*. But it is an overwhelming thought that in union with Him, Jesus loves *especially* me.[19] As any bride is special to her husband, so are we believers special to Christ.

Let me suggest one final thought about the wonder of our marriage union with Christ. As a husband, I cherish the union with my wife and have often reflected on what our marriage means as a picture of the marriage between Christ and His church. I pray that in some way our marriage has been a living gospel sermon. Yet as the father of two married sons, I have come to a new understanding and appreciation of the marriage bond. When my first son married, I experienced emotions that I did not know I was capable of. It is difficult to put into words the joy and satisfaction I felt toward my son's bride. Perhaps the strangest and newest thing for me was the total absolute acceptance and family-love I have for his wife. Because of her oneness with my son, she is one with my family. So it is for my younger son and his bride. This whole business of having married sons has helped me understand a little of how our Heavenly Father views us as the bride of Christ. The Father is pleased with us because we are united to His Son. United to Christ, the Father loves us as He loves His Son and accepts us completely and unreservedly. In His great intercessory prayer for His people, the Lord Jesus said to His Father, '[Thou] hast loved them, as thou hast loved me' (John 17:23). Amazing!

---

19. 'The Bridegroom will greatly desire His bride for her beauty. A gorgeous bridal gown will adorn her' (R. B. Kuiper, *The Glorious Body of Christ* [Edinburgh: Banner of Truth, 1966], p. 366). Kuiper is echoing the words of Psalm 45:11: 'So shall the king greatly desire thy beauty.'

What a sense of security to know we are loved, to know we are special to God. When we are conscious of the love that binds us inseparably to the Savior, our response should be to reciprocate with mutual love to Him. Christ should be our life – our reason for living. Pleasing Him should be our chief desire.

UNITED TO CHRIST ETERNALLY

There is one final aspect of our union with Christ that I want us to see. It is an indissoluble union, meaning that union with Christ is eternal. The old hymn puts it well:

> *His forever, only His –*
> *Who the Lord and me shall part?*
> *Ah, with what a rest of bliss*
> *Christ can fill the loving heart!*
> *Heav'n and earth may fade and flee,*
> *Firstborn light in gloom decline;*
> *But while God and I shall be,*
> *I am His, and He is mine.*[20]

The Scripture reveals that the believer's mystical union is not just everlasting (no temporal ending), but it is in fact eternal (no temporal beginning, either). There is obviously a temporal beginning to our union when by faith we consciously enter into a saving relationship with Jesus Christ and are baptized by the Holy Spirit into His body. Yet in the mind of God, what transpires in time manifests His eternal purpose. The eternal nature of the believer's spiritual union with Christ puts in boldface the believer's security in the gospel.

United Before Time

Ephesians 1 is one of those high watermarks in the Scripture. In this chapter the imprisoned Paul set forth a breathtaking view of God's eternal strategy and purpose in Christ. Paul himself was obviously overwhelmed with the view, because once he started describing it, he had a hard time stopping. Verses 3-14 form one complex sentence heaping one glorious truth on top of another. At the end of verse 7 and the beginning of verse 8, he defines it all in terms of 'the riches of his grace which he has lavished upon us' (my translation). All of this divinely lavished grace is known in Christ. At least ten times in this run-on sentence Paul uses the construction 'in Christ.' God the Father is the source of grace, and Christ is the mediator of it. Paul makes it explicitly clear that it is only in union with Christ that men can experience saving grace. Among the many benefits and spiritual blessings that God reveals in Christ is the fact of the believer's eternal election in Him. God has 'chosen us *in* him before the foundation of the world' (1:4).

---

20. George W. Robinson, 'Loved with Everlasting Love' in *Trinity Hymnal: Revised Edition* (Suwanee, Ga.: Great Commission Publications, 1990), p. 703.

It is sad that the doctrine of election has become such a subject of controversy among Christians, when the Scripture treats it exclusively as a source of blessing. The Bible never makes election a matter of speculation or introspection, but it does present it as a chief reason for praise and confidence in grace. Sinners are never told to ascertain their election before being converted; they are told to come to Christ. But saints, having been converted, are to consider the fact of their election as grounds for their security and peace. I love the way the Savior links these two noncompetitive truths: 'All that the Father giveth me shall come to me; and him that cometh to me I will in no wise cast out' (John 6:37). The Father's giving the sinner to Christ guarantees the sinner's coming to Christ. The sinner's coming to Christ is the evidence of the Father's giving the sinner to Christ. God's purpose never fails. As mysterious as the doctrine of election may be, it is clear enough that election does not exist apart from Jesus Christ. All we have to do is get to Christ. And getting to Christ ought to engender confidence when we realize that our getting to Christ is not just a momentary crisis decision on our part: it is time witnessing to eternity. That the divinely stated purpose of election is holiness (Eph. 1:4) and conformity to Christ (Rom. 8:29) brings this right back to how union with Christ relates to sanctification.

United After Time

The union that God conceived before time and that we experience now by faith will continue forever. A 'time' is coming when time as we know it will cease to exist. The end of time, however, will not mark the end of the believer's union with Christ. Rather, it will magnify it by finally making it not a matter of faith but a matter of sight. In that everlasting day, believers will see His face (Rev. 22:4). 'What a day that will be, when my Jesus I shall see!'[21]

Paul draws attention to that moment when our faith will become sight in his great exposition of the second coming of Christ. In 1 Thessalonians 4 and 5, the apostle sets down five indisputable facts about the return of the Lord Jesus. (1) Christ's coming will be on schedule (5:1). Although it is not for us to know the day and the hour of His coming (Matt. 24:36), His coming 'the second time without sin unto salvation' (Heb. 9:28) will be in the fullness of time. (2) Christ's coming will be in person (4:16). It was the incarnate Christ who ascended into glory; it will be the same incarnate Christ who in glory returns from glory. (3) Christ's coming will be brilliantly obvious (4:16). His first coming in humiliation was without fanfare – only a few scattered shepherds heard the announcement of His birth. His second coming in exaltation will take place with much fanfare – a shout, the voice of the archangel, and the trump of God. (4) Christ's coming will be magnetic (4:14-17). Those in Christ, physically dead or alive, will irresistibly rise and join the Savior. (5) Christ's coming will be a happy event (4:17). This is the primary point of application for us in this discussion. There will be immediate

---

21. Jim Hill, 'What a Day That Will Be' in *Praise* (Grand Rapids: Zondervan, 1979), p. 470.

happiness as we meet Christ for the first time, face to face in the air. It is hard to imagine what that experience will be like. And Scripture guarantees us unceasing happiness as we shall 'ever be with the Lord' (4:17). From that moment on, we will forever know by our glorified sight what we now know only through our so-often weak faith. I cannot possibly add to Paul's inspired application: 'Wherefore comfort one another with these words' (4:18).

The truth of union with Christ offers much food for thought; it is an essential component of right thinking about the gospel. It secures for us every blessing of the gospel of grace. Let it be our prayer that God will increasingly enable us to understand and to utilize all that we have in Christ. May God help us to see ourselves as He sees us. May God help us to see Christ.

CHAPTER 3

THE FEAR OF THE LORD

EVERYONE fears something. Some fears are healthy, and some are not. But all fears share this component: what we fear controls us. On one occasion when I was doing a conference in Singapore, my wife's fear of heights kept her from exploring the wonders of a mountain cave in Borneo and saved me several dollars because of her adamant refusal to ride the Singapore Flier, a huge, slow moving Ferris wheel designed to give a bird's eye view of the city. Whether rational or irrational, fear is a powerful and persuasive motivating emotion.

It is not surprising that the Bible is so concerned about what we fear – because what motivates us is so important. So often and in so varied of circumstances, the Lord commands us to stop fearing certain things. That is not always an easy command to obey since it usually concerns scary situations, whether the presence of enemies, storms, trials, or just the face of man. The grip of fear has the power to paralyze. Fear results from the overwhelming awareness of something that we perceive to be threatening. Sight is the mechanism that triggers fear. Not to fear what we would naturally be afraid of requires a conscious ignoring of what we perceive to be the threat. Not fearing what is seen requires a reassessment of what is real. In this biblical context, not fearing is walking by faith rather than sight.

Although the Bible identifies many things not to fear, it isolates one object of legitimate and necessary fear: God. This does not imply that God is 'scary,' but it does demand that the conscious awareness of God should govern life.[1] It is the fear of God that dispels the fear of other things. Thus, David could say that even though he walked through deep darkness (where scary things would lurk), he would not be afraid of the potentially harmful things because of his awareness of God's presence (Ps. 23:4). Being more aware of God, who he could not see with physical

---

1. 'What then is the fear of the Lord? It is not a cringing dread before the Lord. It is not a guilty "Oh no, here comes God. I'm in for it now." The fear of the Lord is openness to him, eagerness to please him, humility to be instructed by him.... It takes us to that place of maturity where no one has to follow us around with a tedious list of do's and don't's, constantly telling us what to do. We are motivated from deep within. We know what is right, and it is what we love, because it is of God' (Raymond C. Ortlund, Jr., *Proverbs: Wisdom that Works* [Wheaton, Ill.: Crossway, 2012], p. 30).

53

sight, kept him from fearing whatever dangers were lying in wait in the darkness. That is walking by faith and not sight.

The Bible's demand for the fear of God is so all encompassing and all pervasive that it is the very essence of true piety and ultimately defines true religion.[2] The fear of God is the principle for worship, the directive against sin, the dynamic of spiritual life, and the main spring of Christian service. Simply said, the fear of God governs both worship and ethics, affecting both attitudes and actions. It is not surprising that the fear of God along with obeying God is the sum of man's duty to the Lord (Eccles. 12:13; see also Deut. 10:12). Not only is it the mandated duty, it is the mark of those who live in such a way as to delight the Lord. The Psalmist affirmed, 'The LORD taketh pleasure in them that fear him' (147:11).

Because the fear of God is such an all-pervasive component of true religion, it relates directly to obeying God's call to holiness. In essence, to fear God is to live in the conscious awareness of God as He has revealed Himself in holiness, factoring Him into every situation and circumstance of life. Living in the fear of God is living in the reality of God. Recognizing and acknowledging God for who He is demands the response of fearing Him. Moses clearly made that connection in Deuteronomy 10 where he sets out the requirements of true religion. Deuteronomy 10:17 sums up who God is: 'For the LORD your God is God of gods, and Lord of lords, a great God, a mighty, and a terrible ....' The expressions God of gods and Lord of lords are Hebrew idioms designating a superlative idea: the Lord is the supreme God and supreme Sovereign. The word 'terrible' is a bit misleading according to modern usage, but literally means 'One who is to be feared, reverenced or honored.'[3] After identifying who God is, Moses issued the imperative: 'Thou shalt fear the LORD thy God; him shalt thou serve, and to him shalt thou cleave, and swear by his name. He is thy praise, and he is thy God ...' (Deut. 10:20, 21). So fearing God with all its attendant circumstances affecting the practice of life begins with the knowledge of God. I can sum it up this way: Fearing God starts in the head with the knowledge of God; it is expressed with the heart through worship; it is evidenced through the hands in holy behavior. The purpose of this chapter is to consider how the fear of God relates to God's call to holiness, but the 'doing' or 'hand' part of fear cannot be understood in isolation. Holy living does not happen with an empty head or an unfeeling heart.

HEAD TO HEART

There is an inseparable link between knowing God and fearing God. Not to fear God equates to ignorance of who He is. Proverbs 1:7 says, 'The fear of the LORD is the beginning of knowledge,' and Proverbs 9:10 says, 'The fear of the LORD is the

---

2. 'Any sphere of knowledge you're engaged in—every aspect of your workaday world—should be to you as a believer a source of wonder and worship and should be used as a means of glorifying God. And it will be if you enjoy the fear of God' (Jerry Bridges, *The Joy of Fearing God* [Colorado Springs, Colo.: Waterbrook Press, 1997], p. 5).

3. 'A profound sense of awe toward God is undoubtedly the dominant element in the attitude or set of emotions that the Bible calls "the fear of God"' (Bridges, p. 18).

beginning of wisdom.' Although two different Hebrew words for 'beginning' occur in the two statements, they convey essentially the same ideas, denoting fear as both the starting point and chief principle of knowledge and wisdom. Fearing God is the consequence of knowing God and is the core of wisdom. That is significant since Proverbs, as a blueprint for the practice of true religion, sums up that pious practice in terms of wisdom. In Hebrew, the word 'wisdom' means 'skill' or 'ability.' In Proverbs, wisdom designates the skill or ability to live in a way that pleases God. In other words, wisdom is a life of sanctification, a life pursuing holiness. Knowing God leads to the fear of God which in turn generates genuine awe. The fear of God starts in the head and governs the heart. So it is vital to know God.

God is not the figment of imagination. What we know of God, indeed what is knowable about God, is what He has chosen to reveal of Himself, whether through the means of natural or special revelation. It is obviously beyond the scope and purpose of this study to develop an extensive theology proper, that is the doctrine of God. That would require volumes. But the Scripture does give guidance concerning the foci of the revelation of God that should inform our fear-generating knowledge. The Psalmist enjoined in the final inspired model for worship, 'Praise ye the LORD .... Praise him for his mighty acts: praise him according to his excellent greatness' (Ps. 150:1-2). The point very simply is that God deserves to be feared because of who He is, what He is like, and what He does. Fearing God results from attention to God's august Person, His attractive perfections, and His awesome works.[4] The more we know about Him, the more we will fear Him.

That fear will manifest itself in genuine spiritual worship. A key component of fearing the Lord is the attitude about Him, an attitude of awe and reverence in the heart. Stephen Charnock comments on the necessary connection between knowing God's person, perfections, and works and worshipping Him rightly:

> When we see, therefore, the frame of the world to be the work of his power, the order of the world to be the fruit of his wisdom, and the usefulness of the world to be the product of His goodness, we find the motives and reasons of worship; and weighing that his power, wisdom, goodness, infinitely transcend any corporeal nature, we find a rule of worship, that it ought to be offered by us in a manner suitable to such a nature as infinitely above any bodily being. His being a Spirit declares what he is; his other perfections declare what kind of Spirit he is .... How cold and frozen will our devotions be, if we consider not his omniscience, whereby he discerns our heart! How carnal will our services be, if we consider him not as pure Spirit![5]

Or we can sum it up in terms of Scripture: 'For thou are great, and doest wondrous things: thou are God alone. Teach me thy way, O LORD; I will walk in thy truth: unite my heart to fear thy name' (Ps. 86:10-11; see also Pss. 33:8; 89:7).

---

4. 'To fear God is to cherish an awesome sense of His greatness, grandeur, and excellence as these perfections are revealed to us both in His Word and His works' (Bridges, p. 59).

5. Stephen Charnock, *The Existence and Attributes of God* (Grand Rapids: Baker Books, 1979), 1:207.

To know God in His Infinite Being and perfections and to consider His works of creation, providence, and redemption stagger the mind. It is always the case that such recognition of the Lord's immensity, majesty, and might heightens the sense of personal smallness. Seeing God always magnifies Him and reduces every sense of self. Consider how both Ezekiel and John could only fall on their faces when overtaken by the glory of God (Ezek. 1:28; Rev. 1:17). A genuine fear of God will express itself in true and reverential worship.[6] So close is the connection between fearing God and worshipping Him that the terms are interchangeable. Jesus Himself makes the correlation. In response to one of Satan's temptations, Christ said, 'Thou shalt worship the Lord thy God, and him only shalt thou serve' (Matt. 4:10). As in each of His answers of resistance Christ quoted a text from Deuteronomy, here from 10:20 that says 'Thou shalt fear....' Interestingly, the Septuagint of Deuteronomy 10:20 uses the Greek word for fear; so Christ is giving the divine interpretation of what it means to fear the Lord.

The level of genuine, heartfelt, and heart active worship will always be in proportion to how much we are impressed with the object of worship. True worship, therefore, arises from the knowledge of God. The greater the knowledge of God, the greater will be the exercise of true worship. Worship conducted in the fear of God will always seek to elevate God to His proper place and prevent elevating self. This was the counsel of the Preacher when he instructed, 'Keep thy foot when thou goest to the house of God ... for God is in heaven, and thou upon earth' (Eccles. 5:1-2). Keeping the foot simply means to guard the steps, to be careful about conduct, to exercise personal restraint. As we become increasingly conscious that worship brings us into the holy presence of God, we must become increasingly cautious that we do nothing to offend that holy presence. We are to worship in the fear of the Lord.

HEAD TO HANDS

Worship with sincere awe and reverence is an essential element of the fear of the Lord, but how fear affects the hands or behavior is the principal concern of this study. The fear of God that starts in the head and governs the heart also dictates the hands. Attitude affects actions. Knowing God and living in the reality of God (fearing Him) leads to practical holiness by putting temptations to sin in proper perspective. It is almost inconceivable that one could submit to temptation if and when, at the moment of temptation, he is factoring the reality of God into the situation.[7] How can sin be attractive when the reality of God grips and fills the mind? The bottom line is that the fear of the Lord is a motivation for sanctification,

---

6. 'The fear of God ... is the fear which constrains adoration and love. It is the fear which consists in awe, reverence, honor, and worship.... It is the reflex in our consciousness of the transcendent majesty and holiness of God' (John Murray, *The Fear of God: The Soul of Godliness* [Birmingham, Ala.: Solid Ground Christian Books, 2008], p. 12).

7. 'The first thought of the godly man in every circumstance is God's relation to him and it, and his relation to God. That is God-consciousness and that is what the fear of God entails' (Murray, *The Fear of God*, p. 14).

for dying to sin and living to righteousness. Proverbs clearly draws the line between fearing God and avoiding sin. For instance, Proverbs 16:6 says, 'by the fear of the LORD men depart from evil.' Similarly, 3:7 says, 'Be not wise in thine own eyes: fear the LORD, and depart from evil' and 8:13 says, 'The fear of LORD is to hate evil.' Job illustrates the connection as he was described as a man 'that feared God, and eschewed evil' (Job 1:1, 8; 2:3).

Just like worship, this element of fear flows from the knowledge of God, particularly in terms of what is known about His hatred of sin. Knowing the consequences of sin and how sin displeases the Lord should be powerful motivators to resist sin's temptations. In terms of worship, fearing God is reverential awe. In terms of ethics, fearing God is the dread to disobey and displease Him.[8] This dread follows two tracks of motivation. One may reflect more maturity than the other, but both are motivations to avoid sin and pursue holiness.

Dread of Chastisement

Disobedience has consequences. This is a lesson that parents are obliged to teach their children. Discipline is necessary but never pleasant, either to the parent who grieves over the misconduct or to the child who suffers pain. Proverbs, on multiple occasions, gives instructions to parents: 'He that spareth his rod hateth his son: but he that loveth him chasteneth him betimes' (Prov. 13:24); 'Chasten thy son while there is hope, and let not thy soul spare for his crying' (Prov. 19:18); 'Foolishness is bound in the heart of a child; but the rod of correction shall drive it far from him' (Prov. 22:15); 'Withhold not correction from the child: for if thou beatest him with the rod, he shall not die. Thou shalt beat him with the rod, and deliver his soul from hell' (Prov. 23:13-14); 'The rod and reproof give wisdom: but a child left to himself bringeth his mother to shame. Correct thy son, and he shall give rest; yea, he shall give delight unto thy soul' (Prov. 29:15, 17). A common notion in all these references is that this chastisement is remedial rather than simply punitive. But it would hurt, nonetheless.

Significantly, the Psalmist compares the Lord's dealing with His people in parental terms. Psalm 103:13 avers, 'Like as a father pitieth his children, so the LORD pitieth them that fear him.' Part of the exercise of that fatherly compassion is the necessary discipline. Thus, Hebrews declares, 'For whom the Lord loveth he chasteneth, and scourgeth every son whom he receiveth' (12:6). This divinely administered discipline is an evidence of sonship and is remedial but unpleasant, nonetheless.

Notwithstanding parental discipline's link to love, no child wants to experience it. The fear of discipline can be an effective motivator for obedience. Confessedly,

---

8. '"Reverence" carries a positive connotation. It describes a sense of awe as we perceive the majesty of God. "Godly fear," on the other hand, is a sense of profound awe and intimidation as we see the power and holiness of God, who "is a consuming fire." That refers to His power to destroy, His holy reaction against sin' (John MacArthur, *Worship: The Ultimate Priority* [Chicago: Moody, 2012], p. 115).

as a boy there were times when I behaved myself properly in the face of temptations because I knew the consequences if my dad found out about my misbehaving. Maybe I should say *when* he found out, because it seemed he always found out. Although I still remember times years ago when I did not resist the temptations and suffered from the weeping willow switch, I can also say that I cannot remember any occasion when I was punished for doing something that pleased my parents. They administered punishment only when my behavior displeased them because I had broken a family rule, and they did not want me to do it again. The weeping willow tree in the front yard stood as a deterrent to misbehavior. I loved my parents and held them in the highest respect, but I did fear them and what they could do with a switch. Fear of the switch may well have been an immature motive for obedience, but it worked – most of the time.

This fear of chastisement is a legitimate motive for avoiding sin and pursuing holiness.[9] When the Lord warned His people about disobeying the rules of the covenant, He described the various forms of fear-producing chastisement that He would inflict upon them (Deut. 28:66). Fear is part of sin's punishment. When the Lord, in time, executed that chastisement, He explained His remedial purpose in disciplining: 'I will go and return to my place, till they acknowledge their offence, and seek my face: in their affliction they will seek me early' (Hosea 5:15). In one of his protestations of innocence, Job expressed his fear of divine chastisement as a reason for his integrity: 'For destruction from God was a terror to me' (Job 31:23).

It may be argued that fearing God because of potential chastisement is an immature motive for holiness. After all, John says that 'There is no fear in love; but perfect love casteth out fear: because fear hath torment. He that feareth is not made perfect in love' (1 John. 4:18). John's word for 'perfect' actually means 'mature.' Maturity is the process of growth and presupposes a period of immaturity. The word 'torment' means 'punishment,' so the idea is that fear has something to do with punishment. Fear entails a bit of anxiety for sure. Such a fear may very well be immature, but an immature motive for holiness is far better than none. As maturity progresses, anxiety over punishment gives way to the focus on love for the person. The line of the familiar hymn describes this maturing transition: ''Twas grace that taught my heart to fear, and grace my fears relieved.'

Dread of Marring the Relationship

Remember that sanctification is progressive; it involves a growth in holiness. As the believer matures in his relationship with the Lord, the desire to do what pleases the Lord in no way diminishes. The more we grow in the knowledge of God (the head factor), the more we will behave in a way that pleases Him (the hands factor). Because the Christian grows in the experience of love for God, he grows in the fear

---

9. 'Worship is life lived in the presence of an infinitely righteous and omnipresent God by one utterly aware of His holiness and consequently overwhelmed with a sense of his or her own unholiness.... A true worshipper comes into the presence of God with a healthy but soul-shattering fear' (MacArthur, *Worship*, pp. 114-15).

of doing anything to offend Him. Loving God and fearing God are not mutually exclusive; rather, they are inseparable expressions of relationship.[10]

Pardon another personal illustration. I love my wife, but I can also honestly say that I fear her. I'm not afraid of what she can do to me, not even if we had a weeping willow tree. Because I love her, I fear doing anything that will displease her and interrupt or mar the relationship we have with one another. Because I know her, I pretty much know what pleases her and displeases her. Consequently, I try my best to do the one and avoid the other. Sometimes, not often I hope, I have failed and hurt her feelings. When that happens, she momentarily stops speaking to me and may even retreat to another room. The relationship has been marred, and I don't like it. So out of love and fear of marring the relationship, I try to be the best husband I can.

So should it be in our relationship with God. Mature believers don't ask, 'What will happen or what will God do to me if I do this?' On the contrary, they ask like Joseph, 'how then can I do this great wickedness, and sin against God?' (Gen. 39:9). Out of love for God, we should fear doing anything displeasing to Him.

This is the kind of fear that Job expressed. After the several calamities Job experienced including his own personal suffering, he confessed, 'For the thing which I greatly feared is come upon me, and that which I was afraid of is come unto me' (Job 3:25). This goes far beyond Job's saying he was afraid of calamity, loss or suffering. The narrator has already made it explicitly clear what Job feared; He feared the Lord (Job 1:1, 8; 2:3). His lamentation, therefore, must be understood in that light. From Job's perspective, it seemed as though God had withdrawn from him. His conscience was clear that he had done nothing to offend God, but yet he interpreted his trial as chastisement. A component of Job's fear of God was the dread of losing favor and fellowship with God. It appeared to him that his relationship with God had been marred, and he did not know why. We know he was wrong in his perceived assessment, but the statement nonetheless illustrates this aspect of fearing God.

The fear of God is manifold, involving the head, the heart and the hands. The fear of the Lord would be an appropriate topic in any discussion of true, biblical worship. The fear of God, produced by the knowledge of God, is a key factor in worshiping the Lord in the beauty of holiness that He deserves and requires. But it is an equally important topic in the discussion of sanctification. Fear governs behavior. The fear of God, produced by the knowledge of God, motivates purity. [11] The following diagram shows the manifold operation of the fear of God.

---

10. 'To disobey, then, is spiritual adultery, giving the affection that belongs to God to something or someone else. Transgressing God's boundaries or breaking his law is first about breaking relationship with him.... When a deep, reverential fear of God has captivated your heart, you will willingly and joyfully live inside the fences he has set for you' (Paul David Tripp, *Awe: Why It Matters in All We Think, Say and Do* [Wheaton, Ill.: Crossway, 2015], p. 81).

11. 'Obedience is not the impersonal following of a set of arbitrary and abstract laws. Obedience is being in such awe of God that you are blown away by his wisdom, power, love, and grace, which makes you willing to do whatever he says is right and best. Obedience ... is a response of joyful willingness ignited by, stimulated by, and continued by a heart that has been captured by God's glory, goodness, and grace' (Tripp, *Awe*, pp. 81-82).

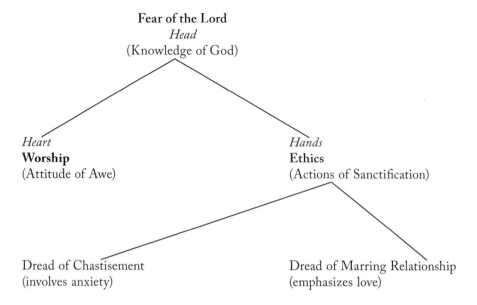

Fear of the Lord
Head
(Knowledge of God)

Heart
Worship
(Attitude of Awe)

Hands
Ethics
(Actions of Sanctification)

Dread of Chastisement
(involves anxiety)

Dread of Marring Relationship
(emphasizes love)

Every Christian should live in such a way so as to not offend the Lord, either in order to avoid discipline, or more maturely, to avoid the loss of communion. For whatever reason, there should be the fear to disobey. Fearing God is an integral part of holy living and can, in a sense, be understood as the motivating principle for every other exercise of holiness. Its association with walking in God's ways, serving the Lord, keeping the commandments, and indeed loving the Lord indicates how vital it is in the whole process and exercise of sanctification. Fearing God is living in the conscious awareness of God, and that has life-altering effects. Fearing God fosters obedience to God's radical and comprehensive call to holiness. Since what we fear governs both attitude and actions, there is no better way to end this meditation than with Peter's admonition: 'Fear God' (1 Pet. 2:17).

HOLINESS EXEGETED

CHAPTER 4

POSSESSING OUR POSSESSION: LESSONS FROM JOSHUA

BECAUSE God rules history and all of history serves His redemptive purpose, the Bible often records history to teach spiritual lessons. Thus the Psalmist said that he was going to open his mouth in a parable as he proceeded to give an overview of Hebrew history (Ps. 78:3). Similarly, after his historical review of God's past dealings with the nation, the people charged Ezekiel with speaking parables (Ezek. 20:49). There is more to history than just facts; history pointed to something beyond itself. Paul understood this when he observed that Israel's history served as examples and admonitions for the church (1 Cor. 10:6, 11).[1]

Israel's conquest of the Promised Land serves such a purpose. The conquest of Canaan is an illustration of progressive sanctification, particularly of the necessary cooperation between God and the believer.[2] Over and over again God told the nation to possess the land because He had driven out every enemy. God achieved and assured victory for His people by virtue of His promises to give them the land and to expel the Canaanites who stood in the way of their possessing the promise. The Israelites, nonetheless, had to cross the Jordan and drive out the enemy for themselves in deadly battle. Listen to what Moses told them on the border of the land: 'Understand therefore this day, that the LORD thy God is he which goeth over before thee; as a consuming fire he shall destroy them, and he shall bring them

---

1. 'Both the historical events and the inscripturated narrative are not simply history or isolated texts in Scripture; rather, behind all these things lies the eternal purposes of the living God, who knows the end from the beginning, and who therefore has himself woven the prefigurement into these earlier texts for the sake of his final eschatological people' (Gordon D. Fee, *The First Epistle to the Corinthians*, The New International Commentary on the New Testament [Grand Rapids: Eerdmans, 1987], pp. 458-59).

2. 'The book of Joshua not only exhibits the sovereign grace of God, His covenant-faithfulness, His mighty power put forth on behalf of His people, but it also reveals what was *required from them* in the discharge of their responsibility: formidable obstacles had to be surmounted, a protracted warfare had to be engaged in, fierce foes overcome, before they entered into the actual enjoyment of the land' (A. W. Pink, *Gleanings in Joshua* [Chicago: Moody Press, 1964], p. 12). Pink seems to take a mediating view between seeing Canaan as a type of heaven and the conquest of the land as a type of sanctification. But his strongest statements are in favor of the conquering nature of the Christian life between conversion and glorification.

down before thy face' (Deut. 9:3; see also 7:2). That was God's part. 'So shalt thou drive them out, and destroy them quickly, as the LORD hath said unto thee.' That was their part. Both parts were essential for victory.

The Canaanites did not roll over and play dead or pack their bags and leave voluntarily; they fought back. The Canaanites were naturally stronger than the Israelites, and the Israelites stood little chance against them in their own strength (Deut. 7:1). But believing that God had given them the victory, they entered and fought in the light of that certain victory. Unconventional tactics, such as marching around Jericho or praying for the sun and moon to stand still, testified to God's supernatural intervention, but the Israelites conquered Jericho only by obeying God's command and they defeated the coalition of nations only by using their swords in conjunction with God's hailstones. Note this lesson as well: one victory led directly to the next conflict – there was always an 'Ai' to follow a 'Jericho.' The battles to possess the land were unrelenting, and the possession of new territory was gradual.

Similarly, Christ has achieved our victory over sin. But sin does not flee from us just because we have been saved; it does not give up its hold on us without a fight. If we attempt to battle against sin in our own strength, defeat is certain, because sin is stronger than we are. Conversely, if we do not strive to fight against sin, defeat is just as certain. But if we enjoin the conflict claiming all that God has promised and Christ has won, and fighting against sin with all our renewed resolve, we can enjoy the victory.[3] Even when we experience victory, though, we can never let our guard or our faith down because we live in a world filled with the 'Canaanites' of sin and temptation. One victory only leads to the next conflict. Remember how the catechism definition of sanctification suggested this necessary cooperation: 'Sanctification is the work of God's free grace, whereby we are renewed in the whole man after the image of God, and are enabled'—that's God's part—'more and more to die unto sin, and live unto righteousness' – that's our part.

The Book of Joshua highlights two essential truths with multi-leveled applications about advancing God's kingdom, about possessing the possession. I want to focus on how these two truths relate to the pursuit of holiness, on what they teach about advancing or progressing in sanctification. On the surface, the two propositions appear to be mutually exclusive, but in reality, they underscore the essential principles of the doctrine: (1) Every advance depends on God, and (2) Every advance depends on us.

EVERY ADVANCE DEPENDS ON GOD

Israel's conquest of Canaan is a significant type of the believer's battle with sin. The battle plan that God revealed to Joshua was instructive not only for Israel as they prepared to take possession of their land inheritance, but for all believers as they

---

3. 'The contents of this book and the lessons which they are designed to teach us are greatly needed by our own generation … in setting before us, by clear exemplifications and striking illustrations, the rules and requirements upon which success is conditioned. Here, as nowhere else in Scripture, are we shown *how* we may be "overcomers"' (A. W. Pink, *Gleanings in Joshua*, p. 22).

take possession of the spiritual possession that rightfully belongs to them. Three components of God's part in the process stand out for consideration.

God's Promise

The Book of Joshua begins with the sweeping pledge to Joshua that 'every place that the sole of your foot shall tread upon, that I have given unto you, as I said unto Moses' (Josh. 1:3). Israel's possession of Canaan was linked inseparably to God's promise. That divine promise was the guarantee of victory. The Lord had first given the promise hundreds of years earlier to the patriarchs (Gen. 15:18), had repeated it to Moses and the people who were brought out of Egyptian bondage (Exod. 3:8), and now He renewed it to Joshua and the generation that would begin to enjoy the fulfillment. After God led the nation safely across the Jordan to the threshold of the promise, they stood before Jericho. What had been a theoretical enemy was now visibly real. The Lord encouraged the people by making the general promise of possessing the land very specific: 'See, I have given into thine hand Jericho, and the king thereof, and the mighty men of valour' (Josh. 6:2). Jericho stood as an obstacle to advancing into the full experience of the promise. If they could not get past Jericho, there was no going forward. God's using the past tense of the verb 'I have given' highlighted the certainty of the promise and generated confidence in the definite application. Before the army took the first step to Jericho, they had the assurance of victory.[4]

The parallels to sanctification are significant. Just as God promised Israel victory over Jericho and all the other Canaanites, He has promised believers victory over sin. For instance, in discussing the implications of union with Christ, the apostle Paul made some sweeping statements: those in Christ have been freed from sin, and sin no longer has dominion over those in Christ (Rom. 6:7, 14). These are wonderfully great promises. The first step in sanctification is to know that God has both purposed and promised victory for every believer.[5] Christians should learn specifically from Jericho that the promise of victory is not abstract theory. God's promise that Jericho would fall was just a specific component and application of the general promise that they would take possession of the land. Likewise, there is no specific sin that stands outside God's general promise that sin no longer has dominion. It sounds too good to be true, but 'all the promises of God in him [Christ] are yea, and in him [Christ]

---

4. 'It was God who gave the victories and the Israelites who reaped the benefits.... This land had been promised for centuries to Abraham and his descendants, and the book tells of the joyful fulfillment of God's long-standing promises' (David M. Howard, Jr., *The New American Commentary: Joshua* [Nashville, Tenn.: Broadman & Holman, 1998], p. 26).

5. 'As we shall see, God's people had a large part to play in the conquest and destruction of the city of Jericho. It was not delivered to them on a plate, as it were, by overwhelming supernatural intervention that required them to do nothing. But the way in which the victory came was chosen by the Lord, so that it would be ingrained in their memory that this first victory was the gift of their gracious, sovereign commander. What happened at the beginning was to be the pattern for all their future advance into this land of promise and rest' (David Jackman, *Joshua: People of God's Purpose*, Preaching the Word [Wheaton, Ill.: Crossway, 2014], p. 67).

Amen' (2 Cor. 1:20). The presence of sin is a challenge to faith, but God's promise is the solid ground for confidence, assurance, and encouragement. Victory in Jesus is more than a song; it is the promise of God.

God's Acts

God works in various ways to accomplish His purpose and to keep His word. Moses had predicted that God would drive out the enemy (Deut. 7:1), but he did not specify how. God did not always work the same way in defeating the enemy and not always as expected. But one thing was for certain: God's promises are always sure because of God's power.

Sometimes His work was obvious. Jericho, the first obstacle to possessing the land, is a case in point. Defiant Jericho became a token that God had the ability to make every promise good. The detailed plan for Jericho's fall and execution of that plan certainly included human involvement, but the nature of that involvement served to accent God's working (6:3-16). All the people had to do was to march around the city, blow some trumpets, and take possession of what God provided for them. What happened to Jericho was a miracle. Although Jericho was an impenetrable and immovable obstacle to Israel, it was nothing to God. His might was greater than Jericho's. It is significant that God's plan for defeating Jericho focused on the Ark of the Covenant (6:4, 6-9, 11-13). The ark with the mercy seat was the important symbol of the Lord's presence with His people and the visible reminder of the necessity of atonement.[6] It was only as Israel's army remained in union with the ark that they saw Jericho fall. This was the first and most important lesson for Israel to learn as they began their journey into the Promised Land.

So, it is in sanctification that the power for victory resides in the Lord. Sin is far stronger than any Christian, but it is not stronger than Christ. The New Testament declares that the cross work of Jesus Christ marked the end of sin's power (Col. 2:14-15; Heb. 2:14-15). The power over sin resides in the blood of the Savior. Victory is possible only as believers look to that blood and their union with Christ in each battle with sin. This truth makes little sense to natural reasoning, but neither did marching around Jericho. Israel experienced other obvious occasions of God's acting – such as His manipulating the sun and moon and sending hailstones at the battle of Gibeon (Josh. 10); but the first display at Jericho taught the lesson that is so vital for the experience of sanctification: don't lose sight of the ark, or in New Testament terms, don't lose sight of Christ.[7]

---

6. Michael P. V. Barrett, *Beginning at Moses: A Guide for Finding Christ in the Old Testament* (Grand Rapids: Reformation Heritage Books, 2018). See the discussion of the ark of the covenant on pp. 282-84.

7. 'What occupied the central place in the army's procession? The ark of the covenant. This symbol of God's presence went in the midst of the people, and as if its presence were not enough, the priests with the trumpets drew attention to it. The unmistakable lesson that comes from this order is that God stands at the center of all his people's victories. The Christ-centered life is the life lived in the power of the gospel.... At the end of the day success in our efforts and strivings for holiness results from living with the Lord Jesus at the heart of all that we do' (Rhett P. Dodson, *Every Promise of Your Word: The Gospel According to Joshua* [Edinburgh: Banner of Truth, 2016], p. 121).

Sometimes God's work was not obvious. Throughout the conquest, He often did things behind the scenes to ensure victory. The Lord told the people that He had sent 'the hornet' before them to deliver into their hand the Amorites, Perizzites, Canaanites, Hittites, Girgashites, Hivites, and Jebusites (Josh. 24:11-13). Interpreters differ as to the identity of the hornet, but whether it refers to a literal swarm of insects or to His preemptive strategy through whatever means is ultimately irrelevant to the point.[8] The point is that God so controlled circumstances to pave the way for victory over the Canaanites, every last one of them (Josh. 12:9-24). It was the Lord who put the fear of Israel into the hearts of Jericho's citizens before Joshua led them across the Jordan (Josh. 2:9-11; 5:1). It was the Lord who maneuvered the hearts of the heathen kings, contrary to typical practice, to ally themselves against Israel and to fight in the open, abandoning their walled cities (Josh. 11:20; see also 10:10, 14, 42).[9] After all, Jericho proved that those walls, the chief defensive structures for those cities, meant nothing. At first sight, these Canaanite coalitions would have appeared as evidence that God had left them to face insurmountable odds. Undoubtedly, Israel feared when all those different enemies gathered against them at once; yet, the coalition was God's way of working to give Israel a remarkable victory. Bringing the Canaanites out of their strongholds was the divine means of defeating multiple enemies all at once rather than one city at a time. The Lord always knows what's best for His people.

This too suggests a couple of things that parallel the battle for holiness and sanctification. Often times, the believer becomes overwhelmed with all the temptations and obstacles that threaten his progression in holiness. The struggle is great. But just as God did not abandon Israel to the enemy, neither does He abandon the Christian to sin's temptations. Indeed, with every temptation there is 'a way to escape' (1 Cor. 10:13). That escape route from sin's temptation is always the way of the cross. Resisting the devil and all his devices with the power of the cross is the certain way to make him flee (James 4:7). Similarly, as God worked behind the scenes to prepare the way for Israel's advance, so we may never know how much His preemptive providence has protected us and prevented the insurmountable temptations from confronting us at all. Christ instructed us to pray, 'lead us not into temptation, but deliver us from evil' (Matt. 6:13). We must believe that God has answered that prayer over and again.

---

8. 'There is no unanimity about the identity of the *hornets* which the Lord is to have sent ahead of Israel to drive out the Canaanites before them. Some think the Hebrew word does not refer to insects but to a condition of irrational fear or panic.... In spite of some uncertainty as to detail, the main thrust of the verse is clear. It means to stress ... the gratuitous nature of the gift God gave to his people in granting them the land' (Marten H. Woudstra, *The Book of Joshua*, The New International Commentary on the Old Testament [Grand Rapids: Eerdmans, 1981], p. 349).

9. 'It was God who was waging war—and even leading the Canaanites out to war, so that in many respects Israel was waging a defensive campaign—so that he might judge them for their sin. Canaanite disobedience is thus contrasted with Israelite obedience, showing that it was their rebellion which led to their armed resistance and ultimately their destruction, since their hardening of heart was really God giving them reason to follow their own foolish inclinations, just as Pharaoh had done' (David G. Firth, *The Message of Joshua*, The Bible Speaks Today [Downers Grove, Ill.: InterVarsity Press, 2015], p. 137).

God's Method

God is active, and He often works in ways that unmistakably and undeniably reveal His hand. The fall of Jericho (Josh. 6) and the abnormal movement of the sun and moon (Josh. 10) demonstrate that direct divine intervention. Those supernatural displays were extraordinary. Likewise, He often works through secondary agents to accomplish His purpose. This method of God's working is ordinary but is nonetheless His working.

The normal pattern throughout the conquest of Canaan was for God to instruct Joshua, who in turn passed the instructions and commands to the people who were then responsible for carrying out those orders. You can see that pattern, for instance, in Joshua 1:1-9 (the Lord's word to Joshua) and 1:10-11 (Joshua's word to the people); in 3:7,8 (the Lord's word to Joshua) and 3:9-13 (Joshua's word to the people); in 4:1-3, 15-16 (the Lord's word to Joshua) and 4:4-7, 17 (Joshua's word to the people); and in 6:2-5 (the Lord's word to Joshua) and 6:6-7 (Joshua's word to the people). That's the same pattern that the Lord used with Moses, but he was now dead (1:1-2). No one leader is indispensable, but every chosen leader is God's gift to the people to direct them in their efforts to do what God has commanded and purposed for them.[10]

This divinely defined pattern continues and relates directly to the believer's progression in sanctification. Among the gifts the ascended Christ has given the church are the pastor/teachers 'for the perfecting of the saints, for the work of the ministry, for the edifying of the body of Christ: Till we all come in the unity of the faith, and of the knowledge of the Son of God, unto a perfect man, unto the measure of the stature of the fulness of Christ' (Eph. 4:11-13). It is imperative that ministers faithfully proclaim God's Word and that believers consistently sit under the preaching of that Word. God has ordained preaching as a means of disseminating the gospel (i.e. evangelism) and of exhorting and admonishing His people to holiness (i.e. edification). In the battle against sin, every Christian needs all the help he can get. In His good providence, the Lord has not left the believer to struggle alone; He continues to supply the church with the essential leadership to feed, strengthen and protect the church against all the enemies that are set on drawing believers away from truth and piety (see Acts 20:28-30). A key component in that leadership is the preaching of the Word, which presupposes that the minister has first himself heard from the Lord. Joshua's authority was only valid as he declared what God had commanded. When the people followed those mediated instructions, they were able to claim more territory in their promised possession.

---

10. 'No man is indispensable, but every man is unique. Men are dispensable; but this does not mean that one man fills another man's place in the same way as a person would remove one concrete block and put another concrete block in its place. In the final analysis, nobody takes the place of anybody else. This is the wonder of personality and the wonder of God using personality in leadership' (Francis A. Schaeffer, *Joshua and the Flow of Biblical History* [Downers Grove, Ill.: InterVarsity Press, 1975], p. 25).

The Westminster Larger Catechism sums up the importance of preaching as one of the 'outward and ordinary means whereby Christ communicates to his church the benefits of his mediation' (Q. 154). The answer to Question 155, 'How is the Word made effectual to salvation,' provides a fitting conclusion to this point about God's ordinary method of working: 'The Spirit of God maketh the reading, but especially the preaching of the Word, an effectual means of enlightening, convincing, and humbling sinners; of driving them out of themselves, and drawing them unto Christ; of conforming them to his image, and subduing them to his will; of strengthening them against temptations and corruptions; of building them up in grace, and establishing their hearts in holiness and comfort through faith unto salvation.'

EVERY ADVANCE DEPENDS ON US

God's sovereignty and providential government are never advanced in contradiction of man's responsibility and willful actions. Notwithstanding God's promise, purpose, and program to drive out the Canaanites from the land destined to be Israel's possession, the Canaanites did not passively retreat from it nor did Israel passively receive it. There were battles on both fronts. The Canaanites did everything they could do to retain possession; the Israelites had to fight their way in, claiming every acre of their promised possession. Possessing their possession was contingent upon how they responded to what God had done and had promised to do. Such is the pattern for sanctification. God, having defeated sin and Satan by the blood of Christ's cross, renews the believer in his whole man after the divine image, thus enabling the believer to die to sin and live to righteousness. The Christian's enjoyment and experience of the divinely accomplished victory depend on his active dying to sin and living to righteousness. From Israel's side, the successful conquest of Canaan depended on faith in what God said and obedience to His commands. That simple pattern applies to the Christian's conquest of sin. Notwithstanding the verity of God's Word concerning the promised victory over sin, without believing it and doing it, the Christian will never enjoy or experience what should be his possession. Sanctification is conditioned by faith and obedience. As the old hymn admonishes, we are to trust and obey.[11]

Hebrews 11:30 says, 'by faith the walls of Jericho fell down, after they were compassed about seven days.' God said Jericho would fall; Israel believed God; they acted in the reality of what they believed. Faith often contradicts sight. When Israel was confronted with hostile coalitions determined to stop their progress into the land, it had to be a daunting and intimidating sight (Josh. 10-11). These Canaanite kingdoms were far more experienced in warfare than Israel was and had

---

11. 'The victor was always Yahweh, and never Israel alone. However, that is not the whole of the emphasis, for it was also an action that involved faithful human response – and all that was done was in accordance with what Yahweh had commanded Moses. The advance came through obedience' (Firth, *The Message of Joshua*, p. 137).

a more sophisticated arsenal. But in the face of that danger, the Lord commanded Joshua and the people not to fear: 'Fear not, nor be dismayed, be strong and of good courage; for thus shall the LORD do to all your enemies against whom ye fight' (Josh. 10:25; 11:6). Not fearing is part of the vocabulary of faith. We tend to be afraid of what we see. Seeing the enemy was reason to be afraid and had the potential to cause the people to retreat or, at best, to stall. Not being afraid in that fearful situation required awareness and confidence in what could not be seen, namely, the reality of God and His Word. Allowing the Canaanites to make them afraid was tantamount to walking by sight. Not being afraid was walking by faith.

The cooperation between God and Israel in Jericho's destruction and the defeat of the coalitions parallels nicely the process of sanctification. Significantly, Paul compares our efforts toward sanctification to military action: 'Follow after ... godliness' (1 Tim. 6:11). The word 'follow' involves more than just a casual game of 'follow the leader.' It means to pursue or chase after something. The word can designate either military or hunting activity, both of which require strategy and strenuous effort. The word suggests the intense resolve to catch and to conquer. Since the next verse says, 'Fight the good fight of faith,' the military idea is most likely in view. Soldiers struggle passionately and vigorously, because their lives frequently depend on their efforts. So must we fight with might and faith in order to win the victory, which is godliness. The chase after godliness will take us through hostile territory and threats of ambush (just like Israel in Canaan), but we must keep on pursuing, using all the armor and weaponry in our arsenal, all of which is supplied in Christ and God's Word.

So although the power for victory over sin is in Christ and His blood, the believer cannot be inactive in experiencing that victory. God's Spirit applies the benefits of Christ. By faith the Christian must look to Christ and his part with Christ and then live in the reality of that victorious union. Faith is never passive. It lays hold of the truth of God's Word and acts accordingly. Faith is the means of appropriating the promise and living as though it is really true. [12] It is not wishful thinking; it flows from confidence in God's Word. It is always the case that the object of faith determines the value of faith. Saving faith saves because Christ is its object. Sanctifying faith sanctifies because Christ is its object. To try to stop sinning without reference to Christ and His cross is as much folly as Israel's storming Jericho or any other Canaanite fortress without reference to the Lord's provision and promise.

Faith translates theory, or better yet, theology, to experience. The appropriate activity flowing from faith is obedience. Joshua kept God's Word before the

---

12. 'Real faith shows itself in obedience.... That incentive to keep on keeping on seems also to be the purpose of chapter 12 of Joshua, which to our eyes and ears may at first seem a somewhat tedious list. But in the context of what we have already seen in Joshua, it is in fact a glorious celebration.... As each one is delineated, with the repeated "one"tolling like a bell, they represent the removal of those impossibly strong opposition forces at the hand of the living God and his limitless sovereign power.... Whatever spiritual blessings we enjoy, whatever victories are won, whatever experience of God's rest is currently ours, it is not due to us but to our great God and Savior Jesus Christ' (Jackman, *Joshua*, p. 134).

people and admonished them to obey it. After the tragic defeat at Ai and the subsequent victory, Joshua made a copy of all the law of Moses and then read it before all the people, highlighting the blessings for obedience and curses for disobedience (Josh. 8:32-35). He admonished the people to 'take diligent heed to do the commandment and the law, which Moses the servant of the LORD charged' (Josh. 22:5) and not to 'turn aside therefrom to the right hand or to the left' (23:6). There would be no chance for the nation to advance in Canaan if they were disobedient to God's Word.

The personal battle for holiness requires the same commitment to the Word of God. Significantly, in Paul's description of the Christian's armor for his warfare in the world, he identifies the Word of God, the sword of the Spirit, as the only assault weapon to be used against the enemy (Eph. 6:17). It is not the sword in the sheath that cuts; it is the sword unsheathed and brandished that puts the enemy to flight. Only the *open* Bible that is known and applied has the power. The Lord Jesus showed this in His temptation. Although He is the Son of God, He answered every temptation with a specific word of Scripture. With every thrust of the sword, the devil was silenced and finally compelled to flee. It is imperative to know what God has commanded and to follow His orders implicitly. Without God's Word we would not know what holiness was supposed to look like. The way of holiness, the course of sanctification, is not haphazard; God does not leave His people to wander their way to a closer walk with Him. The condition or formula for holiness is simple: know it, believe it, and do it by the Spirit's grace.

Israel's conquest of Canaan illustrates that the way to possess the promised possession may have been simple enough, but it was not easy. It was warfare with battle following battle. One victory only led to the next confrontation. First was Jericho, then Ai, then twenty-nine more (see Josh. 12:9-24). The enemy changed and tactics varied, but victory was possible every time they followed God's orders.

Notwithstanding a common notion that crossing the Jordan into Canaan is a picture of the Christian's passing through death into glory, the biblical account of entering Canaan is a picture of struggle and conflict. Rather than pointing to the rest of glorification, it points to the lifelong struggle that every believer will have as he battles to progress in his sanctification. It is a struggle that every believer knows all too well (see Rom. 7). But God has recorded Israel's history for our learning, admonition, and encouragement. Seeing how God enabled Israel, in spite of weakness and inexperience, to gain more and more territory of their promised possession should motivate and embolden us to press on in a relentless pursuit of the holiness God has intended for all who are in Christ. The struggle is tough, but let us not begrudge the struggle. The struggle exists because sin is our enemy with whom we cannot peacefully coexist. Christ has defeated every enemy. In union with Christ we participate in His victory. By the Spirit's grace, let us by faith and by fighting possess our possession.

CHAPTER 5

AVOIDING THE GREATEST SIN

(DEUTERONOMY 6 AND MARK 12)

THE Westminster Shorter Catechism teaches, and our own sensitivity recognizes, that 'some sins in themselves, and by reason of several aggravations, are more heinous in the sight of God than others' (Q. 83). Today's environment is crowded with sights, sounds, and situations that ought to cause any decent person to blush. We can hardly escape exposure to sins that we could otherwise hardly imagine. Yet, it is sobering and fearful to acknowledge that there is no sin—regardless of how heinous—that is beyond any man's ability to commit. Although it is contrary to expectation for a Christian so to sin, there are Christians who have murdered, committed adultery, stolen, lied, and the list could tragically go on. Although we are all capable of any sin, we are not all susceptible to specific sins to the same degree. The level and intensity of the temptations necessary to induce us to those particular sins to which we are not attracted would have to be great. But there are sins for which our temptation threshold is low, and we must be extremely cautious when confronted with such besetting sins.

The tragedy is that we are highly susceptible to the greatest sin of all. The greatest sin may not make the list of most heinous sins as identified by society or self. Even that we don't recognize its gravity is part of the tragedy. Since 'sin is the transgression of the law,' the logical deduction is that the greatest sin would be the transgression of the greatest law.[1] When the religious leaders asked Jesus to identify the first or chief commandment, He said without hesitation, 'thou shalt love the Lord thy God with all thy heart, and with all thy soul, and with all thy mind, and with all thy strength: this is the first commandment' (Mark 12:30; see also Matt. 22:37-38). Before finishing His answer, Jesus inseparably linked the second greatest commandment ('Thou shalt love thy neighbor as thyself') to the first concluding, 'There is none other commandment greater

---

1. 'It seems to me that if the Great Commandment is to love the Lord our God with all our heart, soul, mind, and strength, the great transgression is the failure to keep this commandment' (R. C. Sproul, *Mark*, St Andrew's Expositional Commentary [Orlando, Fla.: Reformation Trust, 2011], p. 319).

than these' (Mark 12:31). The account in Matthew further explains, 'On these two commandments hang all the law and the prophets' (Matt. 22:40). As this second principal commandment flows from the first, so every other specific commandment flows from these two.

Significantly, the Lord is not telling His antagonists anything new. He repeats what is known as the *Shema* ('Hear, O Israel: The LORD our God is one LORD'), the summary expression of true religion, which issues forth in the greatest command to love the Lord (Deut. 6:4-5). Then, in identifying the second greatest command, the Lord quotes Leviticus 19:18, from a chapter that begins with God's command 'Ye shall be holy: for I the LORD your God am holy' (Lev. 19:2). These two umbrella statements sum up the whole moral law and stand as heads over the two divisions of the Decalogue, the first four words or commandments specifying love for God, and the last six love for neighbor. There is warrant for saying that transgressing this first and greatest commandment opens the way to committing every other sin, and that a heart to keep this commandment is the safeguard against every other sin. To love God is to keep His commandments (1 John 5:3).

On the one hand, this sounds so simple; on the other hand, it seems so impossible. The pressing question is, what does this kind of total love or devotion to God look like in actual experience? The pressing desire of every genuine believer is to keep the greatest commandment in order to avoid the greatest sin and thus to set a course to pursue that radical and comprehensive holiness to which God has called every regenerated believer. This kind of devotion is not natural, but neither is it impossible for those who are the objects of God's love. It is vital to remember that 'We love him, because he first loved us' (1 John 4:19). Loving God is where is starts; it is the response to grace. Since this is so fundamental to the experience of progressive sanctification, understanding the principle and the practice of this greatest commandment is essential.

THE PRINCIPLE OF THE GREATEST COMMANDMENT

Its Logic

Understanding the *logic* of the greatest commandment is the foundational concern. It is a consistently biblical principle that duty flows from doctrine. Apprehending truth must affect experience. Spiritually speaking, the head must connect with the heart which in turn directs the hands. Putting Mark 12 in the context of Deuteronomy 6 suggests two reasons that wholehearted devotion to the Lord is our reasonable or logical service (see Paul's language in Romans 12:1).

(1) Who God is

Keeping the greatest commandment and thus avoiding the greatest sin makes sense, first of all, because of who the Lord is. When the scribe asked Jesus to identify the first commandment, He answered, 'The first of all the commandments is, Hear,

O Israel: The Lord our God is one Lord' (Mark 12:29). Meaningfully, He did not begin with an imperative but rather with a proposition, the *Shema*, which is one of those benchmark statements in the Bible full of significance and implication. Loving God is based on this fundamental fact of true religion: The Lord is the unique, exclusive, and sovereign Savior.[2]

Looking at the original statement in Deuteronomy provides some insight not directly on the surface in Mark, since the Greek word translated 'Lord' is not as specific as the Hebrew word it glosses. One of the helpful features of the KJV is how it distinguishes between two different words for 'Lord,' both of which refer to the one true God, but both of which the Septuagint renders with the same Greek word, the word that occurs in Mark 12:29. One word is *Jehovah* or *Yahweh*, the personal name of God, that the KJV translates as 'LORD'; the other is *Adonai*, always a divine title, that the KJV translates as 'Lord.' The translation of Deuteronomy 6:4 reflects the difference: 'Hear, O Israel: the LORD our God is one LORD.' In other words, 'Yahweh our God is one Yahweh.' Or it could be translated, 'Yahweh is our God; Yahweh is One.'

What this declaration reveals about God is manifold. Yahweh is the personal and covenantal name of the one true and living God. He is the absolute Being, eternal, and independent, completely unaffected by anything outside of Himself. Yet it reveals Him as a Person who enters into a saving and covenantal relationship with His people. That Yahweh is 'our God'—the general term for supreme and majestic deity—declares His grace: He who is transcendent is graciously immanent with His people. That Yahweh is one reveals both His uniqueness and unity.[3] This statement goes beyond an assertion of God's singular uniqueness; it includes God's Trinitarian unity as well, which is an essential component of divine uniqueness.[4] That God is one and that He is three are not mutually exclusive truths; indeed, it is the very essence

---

2. 'When the *Shema* was uttered and the Jews were directed to focus their affection on God, the object of their affection was not an impersonal cosmic force, an unnamed, unknown higher power. It clearly stated God's identity: "The LORD our God." This was the God of Abraham, Isaac, and Jacob, the God of Moses, the God who had delivered Israel from their slavery in Egypt' (Sproul, *Mark*, p. 317).

3. '"The LORD our God, the LORD is one." This could mean one or more of several ideas. It could mean that Yahweh is incomparable. Or it could mean that Yahweh is united in his will and purpose – what Wright describes as the integrity of God. More probably it means that Yahweh is the only God, not only for Israel but for the whole universe. Therefore Israel must have no other God. This phrase could also mean that God is a unity – one and not many. I think that the idea of God being the one and only is what is being communicated here' (Ajith Fernando, *Deuteronomy: Loving Obedience to a Loving God*, Preaching the Word [Wheaton, Ill.: Crossway, 2012], p. 258).

4. 'It is possible to understand verse 4 in several ways, but the two most common renderings of the last clause are (1): "The LORD our God, the LORD is one" (so NIV) or (2) "The LORD our God is one LORD." The former stresses the uniqueness or exclusivity of Yahweh as Israel's God and so may be paraphrased "Yahweh our God is the one and only Yahweh" or the like.... The latter translation focuses on the unity or wholeness of the Lord. This is not in opposition to the later Christian doctrine of the Trinity but rather functions here as a witness to the self-consistency of the Lord, who is not ambivalent and who has a single purpose or objective for creation and history. The ideas clearly overlap to provide an unmistakable basis for monotheistic faith. The Lord is indeed a unity, but beyond that he is the only God' (Eugene H. Merrill, *The New American Commentary: Deuteronomy* [Nashville, Tenn.: Broadman & Holman, 1994], p. 163).

of who God really is. Christianity is the only religion that recognizes and affirms this essential dogma. Although the *Shema* does not specifically identify God the Father, Son, and Holy Spirit, it does speak to the unity of the Godhead. Although no analogy can explain the mystery of the Trinity, the use of the number 'one' in the Old Testament at least illustrates the possibility of a single entity consisting of multiple parts. For instance, Ezekiel took two sticks, and he put them together to become one stick (Ezek. 37:17-22). It is not surprising that the Old Testament so often affirms something similar to Solomon's acknowledgement: 'LORD God of Israel, there is no God like thee, in heaven above, or on earth beneath' (1 Kings 8:23; similarly, Exod. 15:11; 2 Sam. 7:22; Jer. 10:6).

This absolute, Trinitarian monotheism is the very foundation of true religion and the logical ground of the greatest commandment. Because He is who He is, He is worthy of all worship, devotion, and love.

(2) What He Has Done

The logic of the greatest command is based not only on who God is but also on what He has done, particularly in His work of redemption. The preamble of the Decalogue explicitly links the two propositions as the starting point for issuing the specific commands: 'I am the LORD thy God, which brought thee out of the land of Egypt, from the house of bondage' (Deut. 5:6; Exod. 20:2). Although Moses sums up the greatest commandment immediately after the declaration of God's identity (Deut. 6:4, 5), his argument for obeying it focuses on the fact of redemption.

In Deuteronomy 6:12, he warns against forgetting the Lord, 'which brought thee forth out of the land of Egypt, from the house of bondage.' Similarly, in Deuteronomy 6:20-23 he links keeping God's commandments with the fact that 'the Lord brought us out of Egypt with a mighty hand.' Although the exodus from Egypt was a real, historic event that occurred in the mid-fifteenth century B.C., effecting the national deliverance of Israel from despotic domination, throughout Scripture it became a paradigm of spiritual deliverance from sin's dominion. The Exodus pictures the gospel.

In Egypt, Israel was held in a bondage from which they could not free themselves. From Egypt, Israel was delivered by sovereign grace they did not deserve. With immense power evidenced by the supernatural intervention of God's strong arm and the blood of the Passover lamb, God delivered them in fulfillment of covenant promises made to Abraham years earlier. In the light of covenant grace and redemption, total devotion to the gracious Redeemer is logical. The more we think about what God has done in saving, the more we will respond in love, obedience, and the pursuit of holiness. This was Paul's reasoning when he reminded the Corinthians that they had been bought with a price and that, therefore, they were to glorify God with the totality of their lives (1 Cor. 6:20). Similarly, he reasoned that thinking about Christ's redeeming death should preclude living by self-interest but should rather motivate the believer to live unto Him (2 Cor. 5:15). That kind of total devotion was living in the reality of Christ's constraining love (2 Cor. 5:14). Remembering redemption creates an attitude toward the Lord that makes worshipping Him, obeying Him, and loving Him both necessary and pleasurable.

Its Demand

Flowing directly from the *Shema*, the declaration of the Lord's uniqueness, is the imperative of total devotion: 'And thou shalt love the LORD thy God with all thine heart, and with all thy soul, and with all thy might' (Deut. 6:5; also Mark 12:30). The language is forceful; both the Hebrew of Moses and the Greek of Mark use verbal expressions that designate the strongest form of command and could be translated 'you must love the LORD.' There is no other legitimate option; this is the obligatory response in the light of who God is and what He has done.[5]

The command to love is itself significant. Love usually just happens; it is something that we have little control over. We tend to fall into it before we know what is happening. I still remember when I first fell in love with my wife; I just couldn't help myself. Nobody had to tell me to do it. But here, we are told that we must love God. We do not fall in love with God. Loving God is a matter of obedience; it is something over which we have control. Although both the Hebrew and Greek words for love include emotion and affection, they are principally volitional words requiring a conscious exercise of the will expressed in desire, inclination, preference, and choice of the loved object. This love requires a conscious rejection of every competitor.[6]

When I fell in love with my wife, I may have been temporarily out of control emotionally, but the time came when I made a conscious decision to choose her and reject every other woman on the face of the earth. That was love. So it is that loving God is a conscious choice of Him and a conscious rejection of anything and everybody else that compete for His rightful place. Loving God and loving anything else as God are mutually exclusive. This is the significance of Christ's caveat that discipleship hinges on hating father, mother, wife, children, brothers, sisters, and self (Luke 14:26; Matt. 10:37). Similarly, Joshua made it clear that serving God in sincerity and truth required putting away all other gods (Josh. 24:14). Therefore, he insisted, 'choose you this day whom ye will serve' (Josh. 24:15).

This kind of love for God is not an emotional fever that can be fanned into flame by manipulative worship tactics. It is a willful determination that governs

---

5. 'Jesus' answer emphasized the fact that God is never satisfied with anything less than the devotion of our whole life for the whole duration of our lives' (Sinclair Ferguson, *Let's Study Mark* [Edinburgh: Banner of Truth, 2002], p. 200).

   'In covenant terms, then, love is not so much emotive or sensual in its connotation (though it is not excluded in those respects), but it is of the nature of obligation, of legal demand. Thus because of who and what he is in regard to his people whom he elected and redeemed the Lord rightly demands of them unqualified obedience' (Merrill, *Deuteronomy*, p. 164).

6. 'Jesus demands a decision and readiness for God and for God alone, in an unconditional manner' (William L. Lane, *The New International Commentary on the New Testament: The Gospel of Mark* [Grand Rapids: Eerdmans, 1974], p. 432).

the totality of life. Emotion is variable, but the setting of will is a constant that should not vary regardless of outside stimuli. It is when people gauge love for God in terms of feeling that they conclude that keeping this greatest commandment is impossible. Loving God should not be void of feeling, but superseding emotion is the determination that God is supremely unique and nothing or no one can take His rightful place. In a sense, the words of the old hymn express the sentiment: 'Take the world, but give me Jesus.' This injunction to love the Lord is based on the precedent of His love: 'We love him, because he first loved us' (1 John 4:19). Because in eternity He chose His people, His people in time choose Him as their God and Savior. True believers may fluctuate in the degree of their devotion, but true believers do not renege on that choice. There are no options: true believers must love the Lord.

This exclusive love for God is all encompassing: 'And thou shalt love the LORD thy God with all thine heart, and with all thy soul, and with all thy might.' The linking of heart, soul, and strength is a way of stressing the totality of the commitment we owe the Lord.[7] There is no part of our being untouched by grace, and there should be no part of our being exempt from worshipping and loving the God whose grace and initializing love enable us to love Him at all. 'Heart' in the Bible refers to the entirety of the inner man: intellect, emotion, and will. 'Soul' is the word in the Old Testament that designates the whole man, the totality of the person, everything that there is about him – outwardly and inwardly. Loving with the heart means that we think about God, desire God, and embrace God. Loving with the soul means that all our inner faculties and outer deportment witness to our exclusive allegiance to God. Just in case we fail to grasp what it means to love God with everything in us and with everything we are, we are told to love with all our strength and energy. For further clarification, Jesus adds 'with all thy mind' (Mark 12:30). Loving God involves understanding. Right thinking leads to right behavior. The point is that loving God is neither casual nor occasional; it is consuming.[8]

---

7. 'Heart, soul, mind, and strength were not intended as a breakdown or a psychological analysis of human personality – they simply meant that everything was to be devoted to loving God. It does not take much of a man to be a believer, but it takes all there is of him!' (R. Kent Hughes, *Mark Volume 2: Jesus, Servant and Savior*, Preaching the Word [Westchester, Ill.: Crossway, 1989], p. 115).

8. The story behind the following quotation is somewhat vague. The words are most often attributed to a Zimbabwe pastor who was martyred for his faith. Regardless of its origin, these words encapsulate a consuming devotion to God: 'I'm part of the fellowship of the unashamed. I have the Holy Spirit's power. The die has been cast. I have stepped over the line. The decision has been made – I'm a disciple of his. I won't look back, let up, slow down, back away, or be still. My past is redeemed, my present makes sense, my future is secure. I'm finished and done with low living, sight walking, smooth knees, colorless dreams, tamed visions, worldly talking, cheap giving, and dwarfed goals. I no longer need preeminence, prosperity, position, promotions, plaudits, or popularity. I don't have to be right, first, tops, recognized, praised, regarded, or rewarded. I now live by faith, lean in his presence, walk by patience, am uplifted by prayer, and I labor with power. My face is set, my gait is fast, my goal is heaven, my road is narrow, my way is rough, my companions few, my Guide reliable, my mission clear. I cannot be bought, compromised, detoured, lured away, turned back, deluded, or delayed. I will not flinch in the face of sacrifices, hesitate in the presence of the enemy, pander at the pool of popularity, or meander in the maze of mediocrity. I won't give up, shut up, let up, until I have stayed up, stored up, prayed up, paid up, preached up for the cause of Christ. I am a disciple of

THE PRACTICE OF THE GREATEST COMMANDMENT

For sure, obeying the greatest commandment to love the Lord totally begins in the head and is felt in the heart, but it is not just a mystical knowledge that generates esoteric contemplations. Thinking must direct behavior, and the Lord teaches what a life of total devotion is going to look like in practice. Significantly, Christ designates this greatest commandment as the summary statement of all of God's revealed law, which is so intimately connected to the gospel of grace. Using the law and the gospel in obeying God's radical and comprehensive call to holiness is so essential for the practice of holiness that we will consider it specifically in the section 'Holiness Practiced.' For now, highlighting the essential components of total devotion that Moses delineated in his exposition of the *Shema* in Deuteronomy 6 will identify essential factors for the practical exercise of godliness. Obeying the greatest commandment with a view to avoiding the greatest sin is going to express itself in experience, and Moses explains how it should happen.

There are five components to this formula for total devotion, and Deuteronomy 6:13 is a key verse that links three of them: 'Thou shalt fear the LORD thy God, and serve him, and shalt swear by his name.' Christ demonstrated the power of the formula outlined in this verse to resist temptation and to avoid the greatest sin when He was tempted in the wilderness by Satan (Matt. 4:10). None other than Christ kept the greatest commandment perfectly; He is our perfect example.

First, loving God happens as we *fear God*. Two other times in Deuteronomy 6 Moses refers to the necessity of fearing God (vv. 2, 24). Fearing God is the distinctive expression of true religion and of a right relationship with God. The essence of fearing God is awareness of God, a God-consciousness defined by knowledge of Him. Knowing God as He reveals Himself will affect both what we think of Him and what we do before Him. Simply said, the fear of God defines both our attitude and actions, or in other words, our worship and ethics. On the one hand, being aware of God will cause us to hold Him in utmost reverence and respect, to bow in absolute awe of His being. On the other hand, being aware of God will move us to personal purity and piety. Fearing God is nothing more or less than living with the overwhelming awareness of the reality of God. The more we know Him the more we will fear Him, and the more we fear Him the more we will perform our duty to Him. Fearing God involves a dread of doing anything that would displease Him, anything that would mar our relationship with Him. That brings us to a key expression of love: we will always desire to please the one we love.

Second, loving God happens as we *serve God*. Serving God requires humble submission to His lordship, ownership, and authority. By virtue of His creating us and especially in light of His redeeming us, He owns us and all our rights.

Jesus. I must go till he comes, give till I drop, preach till all know, and work till he stops me. And, when he comes for his own, he will have no problem recognizing me. My banner will be clear' ('The Fellowship Of The Unashamed,' *McAlvany Intelligence Advisor*, accessed August 15, 2018, https://mcalvanyintelligenceadvisor.com/fellowship-unashamed).

Interestingly, Moses issues this command to serve the Lord right after reminding the people that God had brought them 'out of the land of Egypt, from the house of bondage' (Deut. 6:12). Significantly, the word 'bondage' comes from the same root as the verb 'serve.' Service to the hard taskmasters of Egypt was exchanged for service to the kind master of grace. Whether we like it or not, every man is slave to someone. All outside of Christ are subject to bondage (Heb. 2:15), being servants to sin (Rom. 6:16, 20). But those in Christ, being delivered, have become 'servants to righteousness unto holiness' (Rom. 6:17-19). Serving God is the consequence of grace and should be the grateful expression of love to God for who He is and what He has done. Submitting to Him is another way to avoid the greatest sin.

Third, loving God happens as we *commit ourselves to God*. This is the significance of swearing by His name. Swearing by His name is the oath or pledge of allegiance that we vow to the Lord. Committing to Him requires rejecting all other gods (Deut. 6:14), and loyally affirming Him as the one true God worthy of total devotion. Avoiding the greatest sin demands exclusive fidelity to God.[9]

Fourth, loving God happens as we *obey God* (Deut. 6:6, 17, 25). Verse 17, particularly, sums it up: 'Ye shall diligently keep the commandments of the LORD your God, and his testimonies, and his statutes, which he hath commanded thee.' Loving the Lord, who is the lawgiver, produces love for the law itself. It is impossible to love God and then be lukewarm or indifferent to His Word. God's Word is the projection of His thought—the mirror of His mind and will—and is, therefore, linked inseparably to His person. How we view the law of God is a certain index to how we love the Lord: 'For this is the love of God, that we keep his commandments: and his commandments are not grievous' (1 John 5:3). Christ also made the connection explicitly clear: 'If ye love me, keep my commandments' (John 14:15). Truly loving God and blatantly disobeying God cannot coexist. To put it simply, according to Deuteronomy 6:25, observing God's commandments is the right thing to do. To confess love for God is to confess with the Psalmist, 'O how love I thy law' (Ps. 119:97). Loving God manifests a swiftness to hear as well as the determination to do whatever God says (see James 1:19, 22).

Fifth, loving God happens as we *remember God* (Deut. 6:12, 6-9). Verse 12 states this component negatively by warning against forgetting the Lord. In the Old Testament, remembering and forgetting are always acts of will, not involuntary impulses of the mind. To remember is to think about something on purpose; to forget is purposefully to refuse to think about something. A true believer cannot live without reference to God. The more the Christian fixes his mind on the Lord and all His perfections and works, the more he will be moved to live in a way pleasing to the Lord. The old saying that someone can be so heavenly minded to

---

9. 'Anything short of total loyalty would bring in things that eat into our love relationship with God and spoil it.... In some ways the call to love God with our whole being is a call to total dedication. But for us total dedication is much more than obedience to some rules. It has to do with a relationship with God that oozes with love. To be totally dedicated to God is to be madly in love with him' (Fernando, *Deuteronomy*, p. 260).

be no earthly good is without biblical warrant. Indeed, the more heavenly minded one is, the better he will live on earth.

Remembering God is factoring Him into all the issues of life. A relationship with God cannot be compartmentalized; it must affect every sphere of life. This is the directive of Deuteronomy 6:6-9. Consciously and intentionally bringing devotion to God and His Word into every arena of life is a means of keeping the mind set on Him. All of life is religious: the home, the community, the heart. The polar expressions in verse 7 (sit/walk; lie down/rise up) are a literary device (merismus) that expresses totality. The physical displays in verses 8-9 are to be the means of jogging the memory to think about God. That is good, but be on guard, lest the external displays become a substitute for the inner reality. Many Jews of Christ's day displayed their phylacteries whereby they touted their spirituality when in reality they had no heart for God. Similarly, having plaques with Bible verses on our wall or refrigerator is good, but it is imperative to make sure that the Word is first and foremost in the heart.

The bottom line is that avoiding the greatest sin of not loving the Lord with the heart, soul, and strength requires consciously and actively factoring God into all of life. Deuteronomy 10:12-13 is a fitting conclusion: 'And now, Israel, what doth the Lord thy God require of thee, but to fear the Lord thy God, to walk in all his ways, and to love him, and to serve the Lord thy God with all thy heart and with all thy soul, to keep the commandments of the Lord … ?' Five infinitives outline the Lord's expectations for His people in chiastic order, which is typical of Hebrew structure. In chiasm, the first and last items are paired, then the second and fourth, leaving the middle statement as the principal focus. Significantly, fearing God is linked with keeping the commandments. According to the Preacher in Ecclesiastes, this sums up the whole duty of man (Eccles. 12:13). Walking and serving are paired together, referring to one's habitual manner of life that should be defined by humble submission to the Lord's authority. And then, loving God is right in the middle, the focal point of it all. That, for sure, ought to be the focal point of our lives. Attention to this greatest of all the commandments will be the safeguard against the greatest sin and all the others that flow from it.

CHAPTER 6

THE CRISIS OF UNBELIEF: LESSONS FROM THE BORDER

(NUMBERS 13–14)

THE Holy Spirit has recorded the history of Israel for us that we might learn from it. Many circumstances and experiences of the church corporately and of believers individually find almost exact parallels to those of ancient Israel. According to the apostle Paul in 1 Corinthians 10, the period of Israel's wilderness wanderings, specifically, provides obvious and necessary lessons for the church. It is the beginning of that wilderness experience that I want to focus on in this meditation, since it addresses some issues that relate directly to the believer's pursuit of holiness and his frequent reluctance to enter into the full experience and enjoyment of God's promises of victory over sin.

The newly formed nation was at the southern frontier of Canaan, the Promised Land. Egypt was not far behind, and God had confirmed to the nation over and again the sensibility of walking by faith. When they needed water or food or rest, God had provided it for them. Daily they enjoyed the manna as evidence of the fidelity of God's word of promise. The drama of the Exodus and the pedagogic journey from Egypt had reached what seemed to be a triumphant conclusion. But now at the border of the land that God had promised, they faced yet another crisis and test of faith. The tribal representatives sent into Canaan to spy out the land returned with vivid proof that the land was everything God had promised it would be. The evidence of blessing was unmistakable, but the spies also reported that taking possession of the land involved a visible and serious risk. There is a risk to walking by faith, or so it seems when all self-reliance must give way to simple trust in God. As Israel faced the border crisis of whether to possess their possession or not, so the same crisis confronts God's people today. So often it seems that Christians stand at the border of blessing without acting upon the promises that God has given about victory over self, sin, the world, and the devil.

This narrative about grapes, giants, grasshoppers, and God teaches some vital lessons about entering into the enjoyment of the kind of sanctified life that should be the experience of every believer. It teaches the necessity of walking by faith even when appearances argue against it. Three propositions about possessing the blessing of victory are on the surface of the narrative, which have direct application to our theme of pursuing holiness. The question to ponder as we reflect on Israel's border crisis is whether or not we have stalled in the progress of our sanctification – our lived experience of what God has promised in the gospel.

THE BLESSING IS REAL

The blessing ahead for Israel was both promised and proven. From Kadesh (Num. 13:26), at the southern border of Canaan, Moses instructed the spies to go 'southward' to 'see the land' (Num. 13:17-18). This obviously cannot refer to the direction they were to travel since they actually had to head north to enter the land. The word translated in the KJV as 'southward,' rather than referring to their route, refers to the southern district of Canaan called the *Negev*. Perhaps with a touch of narrative irony but certainly with theological import, their trek into the Negev took them to Hebron (Num. 13:22).

Hebron traces right back to Abraham and the covenantal promise he received from the Lord concerning this very land.[1] The Lord had told Abraham right after he left Ur and entered the land of Canaan, 'Unto thy seed will I give this land' (Gen. 12:7). Then, after his separation from Lot, he dwelled 'in the land of Canaan' (Gen. 13:12) and specifically, he pitched his tent 'in the plain of Mamre, which is in Hebron' (Gen. 13:18). It was there the Lord gave him an overview of the land that would be his and his seed's (Gen. 13:15), and the instructions to 'Arise, walk through the land in the length of it and in the breadth of it; for I will give it unto thee' (Gen. 13:17). So it was from Hebron that Abraham, at least symbolically, took possession of the land, claiming it with his footprints. It was from Hebron that Abraham set out in a bold demonstration of faith to defeat the coalition of kings who had invaded the territory of promise (Gen. 14). It was in Hebron, that Abraham was buried along with Sarah, the dust of their bodies becoming part of the land itself (Gen. 23:19; 25:9-10). You can see why I say there is significance in the spies' coming to Hebron.[2] What a history there was at Hebron! What a claim to

---

1. 'Those very words, *"the land of Canaan, which I am giving to the Israelites"* (2), recalled the twofold promise of both people and land made centuries earlier to Abraham.... The first part of the divine promise had been gloriously fulfilled. As this vast company of travelers stood on the threshold of the promised land, they were indeed "like the dust of the earth." God had assured the patriarch that his descendants would "take possession of the cities of their enemies." They had witnessed the first part of God's promise in the massive increase in their numbers; surely they could trust the second part about the guaranteed conquest' (Raymond Brown, *The Message of Numbers*, The Bible Speaks Today [Downers Grove, Ill.: InterVarsity, 2002], p. 115).

2. 'It may well be significant that the narrative devotes so much attention to Hebron. It was near Hebron that God first promised Abraham that he would inherit the land (Gen. 13:14-18). It was from that area that he set out to defeat the coalition of kings (Gen. 14:13ff). It was in Hebron that he acquired his only piece of real estate for the burial of his wife, and where he and the other patriarchs were buried (Gen. 23; 25:9; 35:27-29; 50:13). The narrator knew these traditions, and he assumes the spies did and that the reader does. It is essential that they be borne in mind as the rest of the story unfolds' (Gordon J. Wenham, *Numbers*, Tyndale Old Testament Commentaries [Downers Grove, Ill.: InterVarsity, 1981], pp. 118-19.

the land Hebron represented! At Hebron, the spies were standing on the promises.[3] Possessing the land was a real promise to be fulfilled and to be enjoyed.

And yet, the significance of the land goes far beyond the dirt of Canaan. It is beyond my scope here to develop all the theological truths associated with the land except to say this: the land was an important symbol (object lesson) and type (picture-prophecy) of the spiritual blessings that God promised and vouchsafed in Christ. Indeed, 'all the promises of God in him are yea, and in him Amen' (2 Cor. 1:20). The blessings of the gospel are real.

The truth of the matter is that if believers would progress in holiness in the light of and on the ground of all those gospel blessings touching spiritual life and living that God has promised, their conquest and possession of their spiritual land—their inheritance—would be steady and bold. Consider Peter's remarkable word that seems too good to be true but is one of those promised blessings that is absolutely real in Christ: 'According as his divine power hath given unto us all things that pertain unto life and godliness, through the knowledge of him that hath called us to glory and virtue: Whereby are given unto us exceeding great and precious promises that by these ye might be partakers of the divine nature, having escaped the corruption that is in the world through lust' (2 Pet. 1:3-4). Just as the spies in Hebron were standing on the place of promise, so every believer must take his stand on the promises that cannot fail.

Not only did God promise the land, He gave proof that the land was as good as He promised. God's promised blessing is not just theological theory, it is real. Providentially, the spies entered the land at 'the time of the first ripe grapes' (13:20). At the brook Eshcol, along with some pomegranates and figs, they harvested a cluster of grapes so large that they had to put it on a pole to distribute its weight between two of the spies for transport. That the name of the brook was Eshcol (the Hebrew word for 'cluster') suggests that this region was famous for the bounty of its vintage (Num. 13:23-24). When the spies returned to Kadesh, they showed the whole assembly of Israel the cluster of grapes and testified concerning the land that 'surely it floweth with milk and honey; and this is fruit of it' (Num. 13:26-27). Interestingly, the word translated 'told' in verse 27 has the idea of recounting in detail all that they had seen firsthand in the land. It is as though the spies just started listing one by one all the blessings of the land that they had seen for themselves. The souvenir grapes proved that everything God had said about the land was true. The grapes were a token sign of God's incomparable and immeasurable blessing.[4]

---

3. 'Those twelve spies were on ground hallowed by memories of God's faithfulness.... This very countryside offered its own rich testimony to the Lord's unchanging faithfulness. Surely, in such honoured territory, the spies would be encouraged that the Lord who had helped their forebearers would not fail them' (Brown, *The Message of Numbers*, p. 116).

4. 'What God had said to Moses as he had stood by the blazing bush in the desert of Midian was absolutely true.... The spies repeated God's words and produced visible evidence that it was exactly as the Lord has said.... That cluster of grapes, the present logo of the Israeli Tourist Board, symbolizes the prosperity of the land and the generosity of the God who gives abundantly to all his people' (Brown, *The Message of Numbers*, pp. 117-18).

When the Lord called Moses from the burning bush to commission him to lead Israel out of Egypt, He told Moses that from that place of bondage He would bring the people 'unto a good land and a large, unto a land flowing with milk and honey' (Exod. 3:8). The very fact that Israel was at Kadesh was irrefutable proof that God delivered them from bondage. The very fact of the grapes was irrefutable proof of the blessings of the promised inheritance. Although the text does not specify, it is not too much to assume that those grapes were on display for all to examine. Most likely, they looked at the cluster with aspirations to enjoy the bounty for themselves. Certainly, none could dispute the glory of the grapes. Seeing the grapes should have caused them to cross the border into the full enjoyment of the blessing.

The connection this draws to the Christian's experience is direct and suggestive. Believers, in union with Christ, possess all the promises and blessings of the gospel, including the assurance that 'sin shall not have dominion over you' (Rom. 6:14). What a 'grape' that is! What Christian can examine or contemplate that promise without aspirations to enjoy and experience its reality personally? But too often in experience the believer becomes content to only consider the truth without crossing over the border into full enjoyment. Truth is examined from every theological angle and admired, but there is hesitation to appropriate it because it seems too good to be true, at least too good to be personally true. So, notwithstanding the glorious realities of the 'grapes' of the gospel, not every believer picks those grapes for himself. This sad fact leads to the next proposition suggested by the narrative.

THE OBSTACLES TO BLESSING ARE JUST AS REAL

When God told Moses at the burning bush that He would deliver His people from Egypt to that milk and honey land, He also disclosed that they would be entering 'the place of the Canaanites, and the Hittites, and the Amorites, and the Perizzites, and the Hivites, and the Jebusites' (Exod. 3:5). They were leaving the presence of one enemy to face the presence of many. God made it clear from the start that there would be some resistance and blockades to their possessing the blessing. However, the divine deliverance from the one (i.e. the Egyptians) should have been sufficient proof that deliverance from the many (i.e. the multiple inhabitants of Canaan) was certain as well. With Egypt in the dust behind them (or rather in depths of the sea behind them), they should have crossed the border without hesitation.[5] But at the border, they are confronted with the reality of the obstacles, and face the crisis of unbelief.

Outside Opposition

The sight of giants obscured the sight of the grapes: 'Nevertheless the people be strong that dwell in the land, and cities are walled, and very great: and moreover we saw the children of Anak there' (Num. 13:28). That 'nevertheless' took over the

---

5. 'Egypt's superior strength, military resources and impressive chariots were nothing to God. He put them all under the water of the Red Sea.... The God who had vanquished the tyrants of the old land would overcome their enemies in the new one' (Brown, *The Message of Numbers*, p. 119).

rest of the spies' report. The milk and honey that God said would be in the land was there for sure, but so were all those people that He said would be there too. The blessing of the land was undeniably great, but the inhabitants of the land were big and strong (Num. 13:31-32); in fact, they were giants (Num. 13:33). This was no exaggeration. At this time, Canaan consisted of a number of independent city-states, governed by distinct nations of people who were accustomed to warfare as they encountered border conflicts with other states within the region. Their cities were strongly fortified, and they were experienced in battle, whereas Israel only knew how to make bricks. Israel was militarily outmatched for sure. What the spies saw was real, and what they saw became a challenge to faith in the promise.

Sometimes what is not said communicates more than what is said. When the spies returned to Kadesh, they reported concerning the land, 'surely it floweth with milk and honey' (Num. 13:27). Almost every other time this description of the land occurs, it is accompanied directly with some statement about God's promise to give it to the people (e.g. Exod. 3:8, 17; 13:5; 33:2-3; Lev. 20:24; Num. 14:8; Deut. 6:3; 11:9; 26:9, 15). Interestingly and suspiciously, the spies intentionally omitted any mention of God's assuring statements.[6] They were absolutely sure that the land measured up to all that they had heard it would, but they were not so sure that God would really give it to them.[7]

Intimidated by the sight of the giants, the spies gave a calumnious report ('evil report'), intimating that if they attempted to cross the border either the land would devour them or the giants would destroy them (Num. 13:32). Therefore, they became paralyzed at the border: 'We be not able to go up against the people; for they are stronger than we' (Num. 13:31). Sight prevailed over faith. The presence of the opposition was no surprise to the Lord and in no way altered His promise or frustrated His purpose. In fact, the opposition was integral to God's plan to teach the necessity of faith over sight. But the opposition was so visible!

That kind of faith crisis is all too common in the believer's battle for holiness. Too often spiritual paralysis results when the giants of the world or the Devil and his minions confront the Christian. Without question, this world is hostile to God and grace. There are many giants of temptation bombarding the believer from every direction, threatening to thwart any spiritual progress. Outside opposition to holiness is real. To minimize the opposition is foolish, for sin and Satan are inherently more powerful than self-generated courage. Sanctification is not the consequence of psyching oneself up to engage in spiritual battles.

---

6. 'A hint of the spies' attitude is given in their very first words. They call Canaan *the land to which you sent us;* usually when the land is qualified by a relative clause, it is described as the land "which the Lord swore to give them", or something similar (*cf.* 13:2; 14:16, 23, 30, 40; 15:2, *etc.*). Whenever the spies describe the land, they pointedly avoid this phraseology' (Wenham, *Numbers*, p. 119).

7. 'These first-hand details about the residents of the land gave the spies' report a touch of authority, and no doubt helped to convince the people of the impossibility of the conquest. But at the same time they obliquely, but totally, challenged the divine promises.... [The spies] look on the presence of these other nations as an insurmountable obstacle to entry, not as a confirmation of God's purpose' (Wenham, pp. 119-20).

Being blind to the giants standing in the way of holiness is just as dangerous as being blinded by them. The giants must not paralyze us to inactivity as they did to Israel; rather, they should be reasons to remember the promises. This is the essence of the crisis of faith: Do we act on the promises or stall at the border of blessing for fear of what lies ahead?

Inside Opposition

According to the spy report, entering the land would lead to a conflict between giants and grasshoppers: 'all the people that we saw in it are men of a great stature. And there we saw the giants ... and we were in our own sight as grasshoppers, and so we were in their sight' (Num. 13:32-33). The giant/grasshopper analogy symbolized the realization of self-insignificance and inadequacy that only magnified the immensity of the opposition. The fact of the matter is that their assessment was right on point, but their response was wrong.

The self-assessment caused the majority of the spies adamantly to warn Israel against crossing the border. By focusing on the bigness of the enemy and the smallness of self, they talked themselves out of the blessing. Sometimes self is the biggest obstacle of all to the experience and enjoyment of God's blessing. Their fear of risk in taking on the giants to possess what God had promised not only stalled them at the border; it led them to irrational thinking and conclusions. With fickle emotions getting the best of them, they concluded that dying in Egypt or in the wilderness would have been better than dying at the hand of Canaanites, and so they expressed their desire to go back to Egypt (Num. 14:1-3). They hardly were better off in Egypt, and ironically their failure to take the risk of faith granted them their wish of dying in the wilderness (Num. 14:23, 29-30). There are always consequences for not trusting the Lord.

Realizing the grasshopper-like nature of self must be kept in proper perspective and balance. Introspection is an important function in the Christian experience. Recognizing self-insufficiency and self-inability is a means to direct us to the all-sufficiency of Christ upon whom we must rest and in whom we must live. Victory over the giants of the world and the devil is achieved in Jesus, not in self. I'll have more to say about that below.

Introspection that terminates in self is always deleterious to successful and joyous Christian living; it must not become an excuse for inactivity. Far too often, Christians convince themselves that no matter how much they desire and admire the 'grapes,' they are undeserving and incapable of experiencing the blessings of gospel, including their sanctification. They conclude it is for others—the *Joshuas* and *Calebs*—but somehow not for them. So being overwhelmed by thoughts of self, they talk themselves out of blessing and avoid the risk of taking God at His word. They remain content to stay at the border, peering into the place of blessing, stalled by the crisis of unbelief. If it is fear of the obstacles on the outside and lack of confidence on the inside that prevents the enjoyment of God's blessing, the solution is to look away from both of those realities to that which is even more certain.[8] This leads to the final thought from the narrative.

THE BESTOWER OF BLESSING IS SUPREMELY REAL

The grapes of incomparable blessing, the giants of immense opposition and the grasshoppers of self-inadequacy were all real, but God is the ultimate reality – greater than them all. With God in view, there are no obstacles too great. This was the minority opinion expressed by Caleb and Joshua. Significantly, Caleb and Joshua saw what all the other spies saw (Num. 14:6). They saw the grapes, and they saw the giants. Nor did they dispute or deny that they were grasshoppers, but with the eye of faith they 'saw' something else. They were more conscious of God than they were of the giants, the grasshoppers, and even the grapes. Caleb's initial charge to the people was unequivocal: 'Let us go up at once, and possess it; for we are well able to overcome it' (Num. 13:30). This was not presumption, but an expression of faith in God. Significantly, when these two described the land as flowing with milk and honey, they included what the majority report omitted, that God would bring them into the land and give it to them (Num. 14:8). The plea of Caleb and Joshua (Num. 14:6-10) highlights three facts about God that should have caused Israel to march immediately into Canaan. The same facts ought to convince every believer to march on to Zion experiencing the victories over the world and sin that God has promised in Christ.

Invincible Power

From every human perspective, the defensive strongholds of the Canaanites appeared to be impenetrable. Israel, certainly, did not have the skill or arsenal to break through the fortifications. Nonetheless, Joshua and Caleb were so convinced that God would give them the land that they forthrightly declared, 'their defence is departed from them' (Num. 14:9). They knew that the Lord would take vengeance on the adversaries, and their defensive mechanisms would fail because He was great in power (see Nahum 1:2-3). The word 'defence' literally means 'shadow' and conveys the thought of protection. The power of the Canaanites was great, but as great as it was, it was nothing in comparison to the power of the Lord.[9] Remembering how God's power destroyed the Egyptians, at that time the greatest power on earth, should have been evidence enough that these Canaanite nations, superior in power

---

8. 'Instead of the land devouring the people, as the unfaithful scouts had threatened, Israel and God would consume those giants and occupy their land, for the time of the Amorites was at hand. But instead of reaching out for this opportunity for victory, they reacted ominously. Fear of the world was the foundation of their rebellion. Confidence in a faithful covenant God was their only hopeful recourse' (R. Dennis Cole, *Numbers*, The New American Commentary [Nashville, Tenn.: B&H, 2000], pp. 227-28).

9. '[The Canaanites] may look like demi-gods, but *their protection* (literally "shadow", an apt picture of divine protection in the hot lands of the Middle East, Pss. 91, 121:5) *is removed from them, and the LORD is with us*. The whole balance of power is altered' (Wenham, *Numbers*, p. 122).

to Israel but inferior to Egypt, had no chance of standing before God. We have only to fast forward forty years, to see how feeble that stone protection was before the Lord, who brought down the walls of Jericho with the sound of trumpets (see Josh. 6).

Whereas the majority saw the opposition as an excuse for retreat, Joshua and Caleb saw the opposition as occasion for God to show His power and as a reason to depend on Him alone for victory. Every opponent to their possessing what God had promised was doomed to defeat. Their ability to go forward was inseparably linked to the Lord's power. In Pauline terms, Joshua and Caleb were confident that if God was for them, then none could be against them (Rom. 8:31). There was no reason to stall at the border.

So it must be in the Christian's contest against sin that believers must rely on what Christ has powerfully accomplished in the gospel. By His powerful death, He destroyed 'him that had the power of death, that is the devil' in order to deliver His people who were held in the bondage of that death (Heb. 2:14-15). Consequently, sin no longer holds dominion over the believer (Rom. 6:14). Faith enables the Christian to live in the reality of that deliverance and freedom. Just as Caleb said, 'we are well able to overcome it,' so the Christian should confidently testify, 'I can do all things through Christ which strengthen me' (Phil. 4:13). Convinced of His invincible power, we can experience the blessing and pursue godliness with boldness in face of any opposition.

Immutable Purpose

Joshua and Caleb also pled with the people to cross the border in the light of God's unchanging purpose for them: 'If the Lord delight in us, then he will bring us unto this land' (Num. 14:8). This is not a statement of doubt or hypothetical speculation; rather, the grammatical construction indicates that the condition, technically the protasis ('if the Lord delights'), was regarded as already fulfilled. It is a statement of absolute fact with a significant implication. The absolute fact is God takes pleasure in His people. The significant implication is that what God delights in always translates to reality. His pleasure is not based on the performance or worth of the object, but is the expression of His sovereign will directed toward the object. The Psalmist penned, 'But our God is in the heavens: he hath done whatsoever he hath pleased' (Ps. 115:3; note 'pleased' and 'delight' are the same word in Hebrew). That the nation was camped at Kadesh on the border of the Promised Land was evidence of sovereign grace that had revealed the Lord's sovereign delight or pleasure for them. All this was based on His covenant promise, by which they had experienced deliverance from the bondage of Egypt and protection and provision on their journey to this point. That God was consistently and constantly orchestrating all their circumstances from Egypt to Kadesh confirmed His immutability that guaranteed their preservation (Mal. 3:6). There should be no doubt, then, that His good pleasure was to bring them into the land. What He begins He finishes.

Linking this truth to gospel blessings should be an overwhelming reason to live in the reality of all God has purposed for His people in Christ. Paul makes it clear that all the spiritual blessings belonging to believers in union with Christ are 'according to the good pleasure of his will' (Eph. 1:5, 9, 11). He further explains that the divine purpose covers everything in the believer's life from eternity to eternity (Rom. 8:28-30). Between those two eternities, we must live now according to His will. Since God has purposed that we be conformed to the image of His Son, it is imperative that we live pursuing the holiness that so perfectly marked His life. His purpose is to encourage us to enjoy the fullness of the blessings.

Immediate Presence

It follows that if God has an unchanging purpose and will for His people, He is not going to abandon them and leave them on their own. On the contrary, He will neither leave nor forsake them (Heb. 13:5). This is the last fact about God that Joshua and Caleb underscore in their exhortation to the nation to cross the border: 'The LORD is with us: fear them not' (Num. 14:9). This is the Immanuel concept ('God with us') that throughout redemptive history has been a source of comfort and courage for God's people. Resting in the reality of God's invisible presence dispels the fear of what is visible. This was the testimony of the Psalmist who even though he was walking in darkness he would not fear the legitimately scary things around him because he was confident that God was with him (Ps. 23:4). Trusting and resting in the reality of God's presence is the essence of walking by faith and not by sight.

Significantly, Joshua and Caleb did not try to dissuade the people regarding the presence and power of the Canaanites, who undoubtedly would resist their entering into the land. The potential threat was real. But they did try to persuade them of something more real than what they could see. If by faith they could rest in the certainty of God's presence with them, the Canaanite giants would be reduced to grasshopper status, for that's what they were in *God's* sight (Isa. 40:22).[10] Living in the awareness of God puts everything else in perspective. There is an old and admittedly trite statement that God and you make a majority. Notwithstanding the triteness, the truth of it ought to generate a boldness to advance and to lay hold of the blessings God has purposed. Not long after leaving Egypt, God assured Moses, 'My presence shall go with me, and I will give thee rest' (Exod. 33:14). Moses responded, 'If thy presence go not with me, carry us not up hence' (Exod. 33:15) and then acknowledged that the divine presence was evidence of grace (Exod. 33:16). The knowledge of God's presence was all that was needed.

---

10. 'That specific faith in the Lord's presence and favor with his people was what drove Joshua and Caleb's interpretation of the facts in front of them. They saw the same warriors as the majority did, protected by the same city walls, and yet concluded that those pagan nations not only *could* be defeated but *must* be defeated.... Giants may seem enormous from the perspective of shrimps, but comparing them with the power of the Almighty tends to cut them down to size' (Iain M. Duguid, *Preaching the Word: Numbers: God's Presence in the Wilderness* [Wheaton, Ill.: Crossway, 2006], p. 170).

The reality of God's immediate presence with His people remains the reason why Christians ought confidently to resist the temptations to sin and to make progress in the way of holiness. God has given to every believer the Holy Spirit as a constant, unceasing companion that leads in the way of Christ Jesus who has freed the believer from the law of sin and death (see Rom. 8:1-11). The conscious sense of that divine presence is a source of comfort and courage.

Israel's crisis of faith at the border led to one of the most tragic periods in the checkered history of the nation. Apart from Joshua and Caleb, that whole generation died in the wilderness, experiencing continuing evidences of God's covenant mercies but never experiencing the fullness of the blessing that should have been theirs to enjoy. Even in the wilderness God did not forsake them, but He gave them many gospel lessons because He had an unchangeable purpose that not even their unbelief could frustrate. For forty years they walked in circles, still as the covenant people, but making no progress and forever remembered for their bad example of lack of faith (see Ps. 95:8-11; 1 Cor. 10:5-10; Heb. 3:15-19). What a sad way to be remembered – so contrary to what should have been!

All of that is history, but the same issue confronts every Christian today. Will we take possession of our inheritance or not? Will we be content to stay at the border of all the blessings that Christ has purchased for us or will we by faith enter into the experience of victory over sin, the world, Satan, and self? Let us learn the lesson from the border. Let us move on from Kadesh, the place of crisis, to Hebron, the ground of promise.

CHAPTER 7

THE DIVINE ORDER FOR HOLINESS
(ROMANS 6:1-14)

NATURAL reasoning always perverts truth. Romans 5 is a theological high-water mark in the Scripture where Paul declares and expounds the glorious and liberating doctrine of justification, that component of salvation that is so foundational to the believer's acceptance before God and his life before the world. But tragically, Paul's exposition of a free justification by faith on the merits of Jesus Christ alone raised the absurd question 'shall we continue in sin, that grace may abound?' (Rom. 6:1). With forceful language, the apostle expressed his denial of that perverted reasoning.[1] Being justified freely by grace demands purity and holiness in life.[2] Receiving Christ's gracious deliverance from sin's penalty and guilt in order to remain in sin's power and domination is as illogical as it is perverse. Throughout his epistles, Paul exhorts converts to be holy because the gospel applied to the heart not only rescues the soul from condemnation, but also it inclines the soul in the direction of righteousness. Paul's argument for Christian holiness based on the application of the gospel is nowhere more compelling than in Romans 6.

Just as the atoning work of Christ is the ground of the sinner's justification, so is it the ground for the saint's sanctification. Justification has fixed the Christian's legal position and standing before God. In Christ, the believer stands before God as holy as Jesus Christ Himself. This is imputed righteousness. Sanctification is the believer's becoming in experience what the grace of the gospel has purposed him to be. Sanctifying grace enables the Christian to live piously – to live in the reality of what he is in Christ. This is imparted righteousness. Whereas justification is a single legal act or declaration of God, sanctification is a continuing work of God that progressively

---

1. 'Paul is not simply expressing a denial of that premise; the force of his language signals apostolic abhorrence. Paul would be appalled if he heard any true Christian say, "If I keep getting grace when I sin, I am just going to keep on sinning that grace may abound." God forbid' (R. C. Sproul, *Romans*, St. Andrew's Expositional Commentary [Wheaton, Ill.: Crossway, 2009], p. 182).

2. 'We cannot have saving faith unless the Holy Spirit has changed the disposition of our souls. Therefore, only the regenerate have faith. All the regenerate are changed. We cannot have the Holy Spirit changing the disposition of our hearts and bringing us to faith but then leaving us hanging there with no change in our lives' (Sproul, *Romans*, pp. 183-84).

matures during the lifetime of every justified saint. Theologically, it is imperative to maintain the distinction between justification and sanctification. Practically, it is imperative to demonstrate the inseparable connection between the two truths. Sanctification flows necessarily from justification.[3] Paul links these two aspects of salvation by demonstrating how the sacrifice of Christ is the ground for each.

While most Christians agree that holiness should mark the life, there are differing views concerning how to achieve that holiness. Unfortunately, many of the suggestions for obtaining victory over sin are based on psychological tricks to increase personal resolve and determination to win over temptation. Efforts in sanctification that are founded on personal resolve and will-power are doomed to failure and frustration.[4] It is imperative to return to the biblical theology of sanctification. Romans 6 reveals this important theology. Paul essentially argues that right thinking about the gospel produces right living.[5] His order of reasoning is clear. First, there must be a knowing of certain truths by experience (Rom. 6:3, 6). Second, there must be a reckoning of those truths by faith (Rom. 6:11). Third, there must be a doing of the truths by obedience (Rom. 6:12-13). This order cannot be successfully altered. To skip the first two points and jump into the third will result either in the frustration of failure or the bondage of a legalism that drains the joy out of holiness. It is always dangerous to do without thinking, and that is certainly true in the believer's battle against sin. The key truth that gives motion to sanctification is the believer's union with Jesus Christ. Three thoughts sum up Paul's exposition of this holiness producing union: its fact, design, and experience.

THE FACT OF UNION WITH CHRIST (ROM. 6:3-5)

There is no chance for holiness apart from spiritual union with Jesus Christ. This truth marks an essential difference between biblical Christianity and every other religion. Whereas in natural religion men try to live holy lives in order to get to God, in true Christianity men live holy lives after God has gotten to them.

Union with Christ's Death

Paul first expresses the believer's union with Christ's death in terms of baptism. He asks the Roman Christians whether they were ignorant of the nature and design of

---

3. 'The God who declares the sinner just at the same time, and in close connection with it, pours the sanctifying Spirit into his heart, producing holiness' (William Hendriksen, *Romans: Chapters 1–8* [Grand Rapids: Baker, 1980], p. 193).

4. 'Some people try to find the key in an intense emotional experience, thinking that if only they can make themselves feel close to God they will become holy. Others try to find sanctification through a special methodology. They think that if they do certain things or follow a prescribed ritual they will be sanctified. Godliness does not come in that fashion; in fact, approaches like these are deceiving. A holy life comes from *knowing*' (James Montgomery Boice, *Romans: The Reign of Grace (Romans 5–8)*, Volume 2 [Grand Rapids: Baker, 1992], p. 656).

5. 'It is an exercise in subjectively believing something to be true because it is objectively true. It is lining up our thinking with truth…. We are simply told to bring our thinking into line with God-given reality' (Christopher Ash, *Teaching Romans: Unlocking Romans 1–8 for the Bible Teacher*, Volume 1 [London: Proclamation Trust, 2009], p. 230).

baptism: 'Know ye not, that so many of us as were baptized into Jesus Christ were baptized into his death?' (6:3). As wonderful and as important as the sacrament of Christian baptism is, there is not a drop of water in Romans 6. Paul's reference must be to spiritual baptism, for no amount of water can effect the spiritual union that this passage describes.[6] To see this as water baptism is to see baptismal regeneration, and no orthodox view of baptism tolerates the notion of saving grace in association with the act of the church sacrament. Rather, the apostle refers to that gracious act of the Holy Spirit where we are 'all baptized into one body,' the body of Christ (see 1 Cor. 12:13). 1 Corinthians 10:2 illustrates this 'dry' sense of the word 'baptize.' Paul speaks of all those who were 'baptized unto Moses in the cloud and in the sea.' This refers to that generation of Israelites who identified with Moses and were united to him in his trek through the wilderness and across the dry bed of the Red Sea. To be baptized with Moses kept one dry in the Red Sea crossing. The point of the word is *union*.

So the basic significance of this spiritual act of baptism in Romans 6:3 is that it creates a vital, intimate union with the Savior Himself. In Galatians 3:27, Paul equates being baptized into Christ with putting on Christ. Although the mechanics of this union remain an inexplicable mystery to the finite mind, it is nonetheless a real

---

6. The following quotations demonstrate the difference among Reformed commentators on what is meant by the word 'baptism' in Romans 6. Some see no reference to water baptism. Others see a reference to the sacrament of baptism, but stress that baptismal regeneration is not and cannot be in view. They all agree on the fact that Paul is stressing the believer's identification with Jesus. They recognize that Paul's point concerns the doctrine of union with Christ. 'For the vast majority of today's people, the mere mention of baptism immediately sets them thinking about the sacrament of water baptism and blinds them to what any text that mentions baptism may actually be saying. It has blinded commentators, too, of course. They also think of the sacrament, and because they do they have produced many wrong interpretations of these verses based on their assumption. Some have taught that sacrament joins us to Christ and is therefore necessary for salvation. This view is called "baptismal regeneration."... But Paul is not thinking along these lines at all in these verses, and therefore any approach to them with the idea of the sacrament of water baptism uppermost in our minds will be misleading' (Boice, *Romans 5–8,* pp. 658-59).

'In essence, then, Paul is saying: "Look at what your baptism pictures; listen to what your baptism says; and as faith takes hold of its message remember what it tells you about who you are in Christ."... This, then, is the rhythm of the baptized life of faith: knowing that we are united to Christ; believing that this is so and acting on that conviction; and then discovering the power of the gospel to transform and sanctify' (Sinclair Ferguson, *Devoted to God: Blueprints for Sanctification* [Edinburgh: Banner of Truth, 2016], pp. 76, 88).

'This undoubtedly refers to the baptism of the Holy Spirit, rather than water baptism' (Francis A. Schaeffer, *The Finished Work of Christ: The Truth of Romans 1–8* [Wheaton, Ill.: Crossway, 1998], p. 153).

'The reason some have been hesitant to understand Romans 6 as referring to water baptism is usually plain. They fear that Paul will then be held to teach "baptismal regeneration", namely that the mere administration of water in the name of the Trinity automatically bestows salvation. But the apostle neither believed nor taught this.... The essential point Paul is making is that being a Christian involves a personal, vital identification with Jesus Christ.' Stott says this in the context of arguing that Paul is referring to water baptism in Romans 6 (John Stott, *Romans: God's Good News for the World* [Downers Grove, Ill.: InterVarsity, 1994], pp. 173-74).

'We have lost touch with the riches of the sacraments that God has given to his people.... Baptism is not what saves us, but in our baptism God gives us a tangible sign of his promise of redemption.... Baptism is a sign of our being regenerated by the Holy Spirit. It does not effect regeneration, but it is a sign of it. It is the sign of God's promise that all who believe will, in fact, be justified. It is a sign of our sanctification. It is a sign of our being indwelt by the Holy Spirit. It is a sign of our glorification. It is a sign of our identification with Christ. We are in Christ and he is our champion' (Sproul, *Romans,* p. 185).

union. The implications of this union boggle the mind and would be unbelievable if they were not the authoritative assertions of God Himself. God's Word declares that the believer's acceptance by God is 'in the beloved' (Eph. 1:6). The believer is positioned in Christ by an inseparable union. This position with Christ is so certain that the believer is blessed 'with all spiritual blessings in heavenly places in Christ' (Eph. 1:3). United with Christ, the believer is—inexplicably yet undeniably—where Christ is.

In this text Paul emphasizes that the believer is united to the death of Christ.[7] When Christ died, the believer died in Him. This obviously does not mean that believers physically hung on the cross with Jesus. On that cruel and rugged cross, He suffered all the indescribable agonies alone. But He did so as the Covenant Head of His people, as their Covenant Representative, suffering and dying as the perfect Substitute. In a most wonderful and mysterious sense, every Christian can say with Paul, 'I am crucified with Christ' (Gal. 2:20). There is an old hymn that asks the question, 'Were you there when they crucified my Lord?' The biblical answer is that every believer was there, for sure, in spiritual union with Christ.[8]

Because He is the Head and His church is His body, every believer, therefore, partakes of all the benefits that Christ accomplished by His atoning death. Christ purchased the believer's justification, adoption, assurance of divine forgiveness, peace, joy, and eternal life; and the list of benefits for both this life and the life to come goes on. The focus of this passage is that the Christian's holiness or sanctification was one of the benefits accomplished by Christ's death. Indeed, Christ gave Himself for the church 'that he might present it to himself a glorious church ... holy and without blemish' (Eph. 5:27).

Having stated the reality of union with Christ (Rom. 6:3), Paul reflects on the consequences of that union (Rom. 6:4). This spiritual baptism effected a burial with Christ. In the physical realm, burial is a means to dispose of the old corpse, to remove it from the presence of the living. It effects a separation. Thus in the spiritual realm, burial with Christ involves a separation from the world, the kingdom of Satan.[9] Although living in the world, the Christian is not of the world. Life in

---

7. 'We like to think of identifying with Jesus in terms of being with Him in the heavenlies (Eph. 2:6), or of His being the bridegroom and our being the bride, or of His being the vine and our being the branches. But let us never forget, as Christians, that if we are going to understand the Christian life we must also understand and then practice our identification, in this present life, with Christ's death' (Schaeffer, *The Finished Work of Christ*, pp. 153-54).

8. 'In a spiritual sense we died with him on Calvary. When he went to the cross, he went not for himself but for his sheep. He did a work there that we could not possibly do for ourselves. It was our sin that he was carrying in his death, so when he died, he did not simply die for us; we, by virtue of this spiritual union, died with him' (Sproul, *Romans*, p. 188).

9. 'The reason burial is an important step even beyond death is that burial puts the deceased person out of this world permanently. A corpse is dead to life. But there is a sense in which it can still be said to be in life, as long as it is around. When it is buried, when it is placed in the ground and covered with earth, it is removed from the sphere of this life permanently. It is gone. That is why Paul, who wanted to emphasize the finality of our being removed from the rule of sin and death to the rule of Christ, emphasizes it' (Boice, *Romans*, p. 662).

Christ demands and enables separation from the world (see 1 John 2:15-17). One aspect of sanctification is dying more and more to sin, living separate from evil. Once the Christian was dead in sin; now he must be dead to sin by virtue of his association with Christ.

Union with Christ's Life

The consequence of death and burial with Christ is life. Union with His death guarantees union with His life. Christ, having died, rose again. His resurrection was the certain and necessary consequence of His atoning death. His resurrection was heaven's affirmation and confirmation that Christ successfully accomplished all He intended in His sacrifice: God's wrath was appeased and His people were redeemed. Similarly, a new and holy life is the certain and necessary consequence of the believer's dying with Him. Newness of life is a reality in Christ. That is a fact. Sanctification is nothing more than living in the reality of what we have in Christ.

Sharing in Christ's death means sharing in Christ's victory and life. In verse 5 Paul confirms and expands his preceding thoughts suggested by baptism. Verse 5 defines the condition of the Christian: 'If we have been planted together in the likeness of his death.' The apostle's language in stating the believer's condition is significant. By using the simple condition formula, Paul assumes the reality of the protasis, the technical term for the 'if clause.' By substituting the word 'since' for 'if,' the force of this construction is more evident: 'Since we have been planted ... .' It is an established fact, an assumed reality, that the believer has been planted with Christ in His death. Planting is a new image that Paul uses to describe the nature of union with Christ. The word has the idea of a common origin, things that are born or produced at the same time, things that grow together. The perfect tense of the verb used in the protasis suggests that this planting was instantaneous and final with results that continue. Being well rooted in Christ produces an inevitable experience. The apodosis, the technical term for the 'then clause,' defines what that continuing, inevitable experience is. Since the believer is planted with Christ in His death, *then* he will be 'of the resurrection.' The future tense that occurs in the apodosis is a future of obligation; it refers not simply to what will happen, but what must happen. There is a certainty of sequence between the protasis and the apodosis. Because the one is true, the other is absolutely certain. Christ's death and resurrection secured for every believer a necessary and certain life. That life involves not only escape from sin's penalty and guilt (justification) but also cleansing from sin's power and pollution (sanctification).[10] So Augustus Toplady petitioned in his well-known hymn *Rock of Ages* concerning the shed blood of Christ: 'Be of sin the double cure, Cleanse me from its guilt and power.'

---

10. 'Many people seem to view the Christian life as some sort of gloomy struggle. It's as though the deaths of 6:2-4a were the end of the matter. Certainly there are the deaths, but the deaths are for a purpose. We don't just die in order to die. We die in order to live – and not just in the future life, mind you, but in this present life as well' (Schaeffer, *The Finished Work of Christ*, p. 154).

THE DESIGN OF UNION WITH CHRIST (ROM. 6:6-7)

The design of this union with Christ's resurrection relates to sanctification and is specifically stated in verse 6, where Paul remarks on the knowledge of the Christian: 'Knowing this, that our old man is crucified with him, that the body of sin might be destroyed, that henceforth we should not serve sin.' The word for 'knowing' involves more than merely head knowledge or creedal affirmation; it refers to a personal experience of gospel truths. There must be a vital experience of the old man's crucifixion with Christ. The old man designates the old depraved nature that is thoroughly corrupted with sin. Indeed, to pay the penalty of this sin was the reason Christ died. The experiential knowledge of this union is foundational to enjoying the evidences of the new life flowing from that death-union.

Having established the experiential association between 'our old man' and Christ's crucifixion, Paul uses two different purpose formulas to show the design of the union. First, the union was in order to destroy the body of sin. This sinful body most likely is synonymous with the old man. The old man was crucified in order to destroy its corruption. The corruption of the old nature did not immediately disappear (to which every believer, including Paul, can testify, see Romans 7), but the antidote to sin's corruption was injected, making it possible for the believer to die more and more to sin.

Second, the union with Christ and consequent destruction of the old man was in order that the believer might not be a servant to sin. To live free from sin is to fulfill the purpose of salvation.[11] This second stated purpose is the practical evidence of the first stated purpose. Because of Christ's death, the Christian is no longer in bondage to sin. Outside of Christ, the sinner is in slavery to sin, a state of misery and bondage from which he cannot free himself. Sin is a terrible master that has sufficient power to coerce and control in spite of the sinner's best intentions or efforts. But in Christ are the basis, reason for and only hope of victory over sin's dominion. Because Christ destroyed sin's dominion by His death and because the believer was united to that death, it is illogical that the believer should continue under sin's control. On the contrary, it is logical for the believer to offer himself to God as living, holy, and acceptable sacrifice (Rom. 12:2).

In Romans 6:7 Paul summarizes the result of this union for the Christian: 'For he that is dead is freed from sin.' More literally this says, 'For the one who died has been justified from sin.' This freedom or justification is far-reaching. Judicially, union with Christ's death frees the believer from sin's penalty. Subjectively, union with Christ's death frees the believer from sin's power. Eternally, union with Christ's death will free the believer from sin's presence. This mystical union effects a radical change. To be in Christ is to be free, to 'be free indeed' (John 8:36). Freedom in Christ is freedom to be and do what was impossible outside of Christ. To live

---

11. 'Since sin's power over us has been broken, we should reflect that new freedom in the way we live' (Douglas J. Moo, *Romans*, The NIV Application Commentary [Grand Rapids: Zondervan, 2000], p. 198).

under sin's control is to fail to use the freedom that Christ has purchased by His atoning death. [12] Freedom from sin is not just a possibility; it is a reality in Christ. To understand this is to understand the basis of sanctification.

THE EXPERIENCE OF UNION WITH CHRIST (6:8-14)

All theology has application. God never reveals truth just to satisfy man's curiosity or answer his reason. Theology must make its way from the head to the heart and then to practice, or it has been abused. Conversely, there can be no proper Christian practice unless there is a theological basis. Realizing the vital connection between doctrine and duty, Paul applies the theology of union with Christ to the experience of the everyday conflicts with sin. In theory and theology, the Christian has victory over sin. In practice, how is that victory to be experienced? That is the question, and that is the battle confronting every Christian.

The link between theology and practice is faith.[13] Twice in verses 8-14 the apostle uses the vocabulary of faith to give further impetus to his practical instructions. First, he uses the word 'believe' (Rom. 6:8). Once again Paul uses a simple condition to assume the reality of the protasis (the 'if' clause) in this conditional sentence. Since it is a fact that we died with Christ, we are constantly believing (present tense) that we will live with Him. This faith rests firmly on Christ. The value of faith is always determined by the object of faith. Just as Christ is the object of justifying faith, so must He be the object of sanctifying faith. Sanctification does not progress because of self-determination or willpower; it progresses as Christ and the benefits of His sacrifice are appropriated by faith. In verses 9 and 10 Paul demonstrates the sensibility of such faith in Christ by directing our attention to facts about the Savior's death and resurrection. He describes the permanent life of the risen Christ to show that the Christian's new life must be permanently free from sin's domination. Believing that there is victorious life in Christ is not just wishful thinking; it is reality.

Second, he uses the word 'reckon' (Rom. 6:11). This word means to consider or regard something as being true. This word emphasizes the vital appropriation of what is believed. It is one thing to believe something to be generally true; it is another thing to regard it as personally true. What the Christian is to reckon is the same thing he is to believe: deadness to sin through union with Christ. This is the doctrine that Paul had set forth in the opening verses of the chapter. It is true;

---

12. 'The God who raised us from spiritual death has given us the grace to resist. No longer do we sin under compulsion as slaves. We have been set free, but our liberty is extremely weak. We are not accustomed to the power of the resurrection. Our comfort zone is still back in the graveyard of spiritual death even though we really have been set free by the power of the Holy Spirit' (Sproul, *Romans*, p. 193).

13. 'So how do I lay hold of all this? The answer is in verse 11: "Likewise reckon ye also yourselves ...." We lay hold of it through the "reckoning" of faith. Let me repeat again what a calling this is. Jesus died in history. Jesus rose physically from the dead in history. We died when we accepted Jesus as our Savior, once for all. We will be raised in history in the future. Through faith we are now to live on the basis of all these great truths' (Schaeffer, *The Finished Work of Christ*, p. 160).

therefore, the believer must acknowledge the personal relevance of the truth. The Christian must consider himself to be in experience what he is positionally and legally in Christ. The believer must never lose sight or thought of what he is and what he has in the Lord Jesus Christ. It is noteworthy that this word 'reckon' occurs also in connection with the doctrine of justification (see Rom. 4:3-4). However, in justification God is the subject of the verb. He looks at the merits of Christ's atonement and considers the sinner who believes in Christ to be legally free from sin. In sanctification, the saint looks at the same merits of Christ's atonement and considers himself to be experientially free from sin. Faith is the victory because faith lays hold of Christ.

Knowing the truth and believing the truth lead to doing the truth. In Romans 6:12-14 Paul issues the imperatives not to let sin rule and not to yield to sin's domination. Unfortunately, many interpreters and preachers begin their explanation and exposition of sanctification with the imperatives of Romans 6:12-13. To tell anyone not to sin without explaining where the ability not to sin comes from can only breed failure and discouragement in the efforts toward holiness.[14] It must be emphasized that successful obedience to these commands is possible only because of what Christ has done and because of the inseparable union that Christ has with His people.

Although victory over sin is possible because the atonement defeated sin and Satan, the Christian nonetheless has to do his part in realizing victory. The believer is not passive in sanctification; indeed, he cooperates with God as he continually dies to sin and lives to righteousness. The Christian's responsibility in sanctification is essentially twofold. On the one hand, he is to refuse submission to sin.[15] In Romans 6:12 Paul gives the admonition that sin should not so reign that we would obey its lusts. The word 'lust' refers to those cravings and desires generated by sin. To allow these sinful inclinations to dominate and direct the life is contrary to God's desire for our conformity to Christ. Believers must resist sin's rule. In Romans 6:13 Paul continues this aspect by commanding Christians not to yield themselves to become agents for unrighteousness. This word 'yield' simply means to put at someone's disposal. To put oneself at sin's disposal is nothing more than surrendering to sin's domination. To surrender to sin's persistent domination is to become a traitor. 'No surrender to sin' must be the Christian's battle cry. The tense

---

14. 'The presupposition of the exhortation is not that sin reigns but the opposite, that it does not reign, and it is for that reason that the exhortation can have validity and appeal. To say to the slave who has not been emancipated, "Do not behave as a slave" is to mock his enslavement. But to say the same to the slave who has been set free is the necessary appeal to put into effect the privileges and rights of his liberation.... Deliverance from the dominion of sin is both the basis of and the incentive to the fulfillment of the exhortation, "Let not sin reign"' (John Murray, *The Epistle to the Romans*, The New International Commentary on the New Testament [Grand Rapids: Eerdmans, 1980], Vol. 1, p. 227).

15. 'Sin is conceived of as a master at whose disposal we place these members in order that they may be instruments to promote unrighteousness. The exhortation is to the effect that we are not to go on placing our physical organs at the disposal of sin for the furtherance of such an end' (Murray, *The Epistle to the Romans*, Vol. 1, pp. 227-28).

of this prohibition is significant; it is the present imperative, which in prohibition requires the ceasing of an act assumed to be in progress. 'Stop surrendering to sin!' The very grammar of the text conforms to daily experience. Every Christian knows well that the conflict against sin rages constantly. One victory over sin's temptations leads only to the next temptation. In daily experience, the one united to Christ's triumphant death can never let his or her guard down.

On the other hand, the Christian is to submit to God.[16] This is the positive element in sanctification: living unto righteousness. Paul uses the same word 'yield' to refer to this positive aspect. Every Christian is to place himself at God's disposal, to surrender to God and the cause of righteousness. Whereas Paul used the present tense to express the prohibition against yielding to sin, he uses the aorist imperative to command allegiance to God. The use of the aorist does not preclude the idea of a continual yielding, but it emphasizes the urgency and necessity of the action. This is the proper course of action for those who are alive from the dead. Regeneration has given the Christian a new nature, a new inclination, a new power. It is by virtue of this resurrection power that willing submission to God and willing rejection of sin are possible.

Paul concludes this section with the explicit declaration that sin will 'not have dominion' (Rom. 6:14). The Greek word for 'have dominion' is the verb form of the root meaning 'lord' or 'master.' Christ's people are free from sin's lordship because they are under grace and not law. Paul is not inserting here a dispensational observation about the church age; he is making an observation that is vitally necessary for victory over sin. The word 'law' does not refer here to the Mosaic era or the Old Testament at all; it designates, rather, the principle of doing.[17] This statement of being under grace and not law parallels Paul's question to the foolish Galatians: 'Having begun in the Spirit, are ye now made perfect by the flesh?' (Gal. 3:3). It is impossible to achieve victory over sin merely by striving to do things. All of salvation is by grace. Sanctification is God's gracious working just as justification is God's gracious act. Too often Christians today behave like the Galatians of Paul's day. They realize that they come into salvation by grace through faith in Christ. But for whatever reason, they attempt to live the Christian life by self-power without reference to the grace of the gospel. Paul thus reminds us of the grace of God, which in this entire context finds expression in the atoning sacrifice of Christ. Paul's instructions concerning sanctification can be reduced to this: 'Do not go beyond the cross.' When temptations come, we should consciously direct our thinking to the cross of Christ and what He accomplished for us. It is impossible to yield to sin while at the same moment placing ourselves at the disposal of God.

16. 'Since we are alive to God, it is only appropriate that we should offer ourselves and our faculties to him.... As those who are alive from death, we must offer ourselves to his service' (Stott, *Romans*, p. 181).

17. 'To be *under law* is to accept the obligation to keep it and so to come under its curse or condemnation' (Stott, *Romans*, p. 181).

Right thinking about the gospel will result in right behavior. To forget about the gospel in the daily battle against sin is to enter the conflict unarmed. We stand little chance against sin by ourselves. Lewis Jones, the hymn writer, reflected well Paul's theology of sanctification: 'Would you o'er evil a victory win? There's wonderful pow'r in the blood.'

Sanctification is not a divine 'zap' that automatically makes the believer irreversibly holy. It is a lifelong battle that requires the saint to lay hold by faith of the victory that Christ has accomplished on the cross and actively to enjoy that victory by living in its reality.[18] Remember that the Christian's daily battle with sin is much like ancient Israel's conquest of the Promised Land. Over and again God told the people to possess the land because He had driven out the Canaanites from before them. As we considered in our meditations from Joshua, although God had won the victory, the Israelites had to cross the Jordan and fight the Canaanites in deadly battle. The Canaanites did not roll over and play dead or pack their bags and leave voluntarily just because Israel entered the land; they fought for their land. The Canaanites were naturally stronger than the Israelites, and the Israelites stood little chance against them in their own strength. But, believing God had given them victory, they entered and fought in the light of that certain victory. Similarly, Christ has already achieved our victory over sin. But sin does not disappear from us just because we are saved. It does not give up its territory without a fight. If we attempt to fight by ourselves, defeat is certain because sin is much stronger than we are. But if we enter the conflict claiming Christ's victory and our part in it, sin and Satan must flee from us.

Read on into Romans 7 and you will see something of the struggle with the presence and practice of sin that is a part of spiritual life. Christians are at war with sin, and all too often we lose skirmishes and battles. It is imperative to remember that deliverance is 'through Jesus Christ our Lord' (Rom. 7:25). That gives us cause to say with Paul, 'I thank God.'

---

18. 'The victory over sin that God has won for us in Christ is a victory that must be appropriated. Putting away those sins that plague us will be no automatic process, something that will happen without our cooperation' (Moo, *Romans*, p. 200).

CHAPTER 8

LIVING FOR JESUS

(ROMANS 12:1-2)

TRUTH and duty are two sides of the same coin. This coupling is nowhere more evident than in the letters of Paul. The book of Romans—the greatest of his theological treatises—is a paradigm for the truth/duty union. The apostle traces the gospel from man's condemnation to glorification. He has shown God's way for the condemned sinner to be freed from both the guilt and the liability of punishment of his sin, and for the saint to live righteously in this life and to know the assurance of future glory. The foundation of his argument is that favor and acceptance with God cannot be earned but must be received, experienced, and enjoyed by faith in the gospel, which is summed up in Christ. This gospel of salvation is based on the free and sovereign grace of the infinitely merciful God. Paul expounds these essential gospel truths in the first eleven chapters of the book. The exposition is deep and high all at once. But once he has laid the foundation with truth, he transitions to the necessary duty. Life in Jesus demands living for Jesus.[1]

Romans 12 introduces what is typically identified as the practical section of Romans. This designation does not suggest that practice is isolated from truth, but on the contrary, practice flows from it. Truth in the head must affect the heart and direct the hands. Christ Himself said, 'If ye know these things, happy are ye if ye do them' (John 13:17). Romans 12:1-2 particularly chart the course for the kind of holy living required by the gospel. They are familiar verses that have been expounded in many sermons and have been committed to memory by many believers. That is good, but sometimes familiarity distracts from thoughtful consideration and application. Too often, we can hear words pass easily from lips without really listening to what they say. What we are and what we will be for Christ depends in great measure on the application of these verses that direct us to

---

1. 'The good news of Jesus Christ is intended to transform a person's life. Until individual Christians own and live out theology, the gospel has not accomplished its purpose' (Douglas J. Moo, *Romans*, The NIV Application Commentary [Grand Rapids: Zondervan, 2000], p. 393).

dedication to Christ. Dedication has become a trite word even in Christian talk, but its significance is vital. In this text, Paul details what it means to be a dedicated Christian – what it means to live for Jesus. He makes it clear that living for Jesus is logical, progressive, and worth the effort.

LIVING FOR JESUS IS LOGICAL

Paul sums up his apostolic directive to dedication and duty by calling it the believer's 'reasonable service.' The English word 'logic' derives straightly from the Greek word translated 'reasonable.' That's why I say the kind of living that Paul is going to detail is the only logical course of action for the Christian.[2] For a redeemed person not to pursue this lifestyle is illogical and absurd, even apart from the more serious assessment that it is sin. Interestingly, Paul designates this logical behavior as 'service.' He uses a Greek word that in the Septuagint (the Greek version of the Old Testament) uniquely refers to divine service, and that sense carries over into the New Testament usage (see Heb. 9:1, 6). The word describes the liturgical service and operations of the priesthood. This suggests that there is a logical link between worship and life. There is more to worship than just sitting through a church service. To be deficient in a living, personal holiness taints every other expression of worship.[3] Any disconnect between worship and holy living is illogical. It follows to reason that if we are saved, we should serve Him. This kind of logical Christian living is motivated by mercy and expressed in consecration.

Motivated by Mercy

Paul begins his appeal for Christian living with a note of urgency: 'I beseech you.' The form of the verb (present tense) suggests that he is persistent and insistent in his urging, begging, and imploring them concerning an essential matter. All believers, not just those in first century Rome, must listen well and take this apostolic exhortation seriously. The basis for his admonition is what God has done.[4] In fact, it is through the agency or instrumentality of God's mercies that they are to live for Jesus. Living for Jesus makes no sense apart from the overwhelming knowledge of the richness of God's grace. This kind of distinctively Christian living does not occur in a theological vacuum. That 'mercies' is plural suggests the

---

2. '"Spiritual" translates *logikos*, which could mean either "reasonable" (AV) or "rational." If the former is correct, then the offering of ourselves to God is seen as the only sensible, logical and appropriate response to him in view of his self-giving mercy' (John Stott, *Romans: God's Good News for the World* [Downers Grove, Ill.: InterVarsity, 1994], p. 321).

3. 'Worship is the way we live, not what we do on Sunday morning .... We worship God, says Paul, by giving ourselves in sacrificial service to our Lord. We are to serve him every day, every hour, every minute' (Moo, *Romans*, p. 397).

4. 'Whenever we teach any part of 12:1–15:13 we must remember it builds on eleven chapters of exposition of the sovereign, free, undeserved kindness of God toward us in Jesus' (Christopher Ash, *Teaching Romans: Unlocking Romans 9–16 for the Bible Teacher*, Volume 2 [London: Proclamation Trust, 2009], p. 152).

multiple manifestations of divine compassion and pity that Paul has expounded in his theological treatise leading up to this exhortation.[5]

Reflecting on the exposition of the gospel leading up to this charge should fill the heart with gratitude for the sovereign and undeserved displays of God's free grace and mercy. Mercy is best understood in the light of the misery of sin and its just condemnation. Thus Paul begins his treatise by proving that all have sinned and are guilty before God, whether Jew or Gentile. Misery gives way to the revelations of God's mercies in justification, reconciliation, life in union with Christ, adoption, the gift of the indwelling Spirit, and election to grace. It is these amazing saving mercies that Paul alludes to as the motive for Christian living. God's mercies are what make living for Jesus the logical service that every Christian should render in thanksgiving for grace. Paul sums up this logic succinctly in his own personal testimony: 'For the love of Christ constraineth us; because we thus judge, that if one died for all, then were all dead: and that he died for all, that they which live should not henceforth live unto themselves, but unto him which died for them, and rose again' (2 Cor. 5:14-15). It just doesn't make any sense, spiritually, to live by self-interest when we look at life through the spectacles of Christ's love.[6]

The tragedy is that so many Christians never give a second thought to what the apostle identifies as the principal motivating influence in the pursuit of holiness. Too many strive for virtue without any reference to grace. Consequently, the Christian lifestyle is often reduced to legalistic list-keeping or frustrating failures. Let us all learn to think about God's gospel mercies, all of which flow through the mediation of Christ, as the reason for and as the means by which we can live for Jesus. The proper 'why' leads to the proper 'what': right thinking causes right behavior.

Expressed in Consecration

Paul explains what a consecrated life looks like in terms of an Old Testament sacrifice: 'that ye present your bodies a living sacrifice.' His choice of the aorist infinitive 'to present' conveys a sense of urgency and necessity. There were two broad categories of ceremonial sacrifices: those that pictured propitiation and expiation and those that pictured consecration. There has only been one sacrifice that effectively and successfully appeased God's wrath against offending sinners and cleansed them from guilt. That was the once-for-all sacrifice of Jesus Christ to whom all of the Old Testament sacrifices pointed. Any self-hatched attempt to

---

5. 'Paul makes his plea in light of God's tender mercies, which he has just finished expounding in chapter 11, and those mercies are these: (1) we are justified by faith; (2) our sins are forgiven through the atonement of Christ; (3) God works all things together for our good; and (4) God calls people to himself. Everything Paul has expounded throughout the doctrinal section of the epistle, chapters 1–11, points back to God's mercy' (R. C. Sproul, *Romans*, St. Andrew's Expositional Commentary [Wheaton, Ill.: Crossway, 2009], p. 406).

6. 'It is right and proper—hence logical, reasonable—that those who have been highly favored should offer themselves to God wholeheartedly, as sacrifices, living, holy, and well-pleasing to him' (William Hendriksen, *Romans Chapters 9–16* [Grand Rapids: Baker Book House, 1981], p. 402).

quench God's anger or work off the guilt of sin is offensive to God, only incurring more wrath and guilt. Believers know that and have thus placed their trust in the atoning work of Christ as their only hope of salvation. Yet even genuine believers sometimes fall into the delusion that pursuing holiness is a way to keep God happy with them or to work off the guilt of spiritual failures. That is folly because it cannot work, and it is frustrating because it never leads to any sense of confidence that enough has been done. It should go without saying that Paul is not telling Christians to offer themselves as a sin or guilt offering.[7]

The sacrifice in view is most likely the whole burnt offering, one of the sweet savor offerings. The distinctive feature of the whole burnt offering was that after the propitiatory components were completed, the whole sacrificial victim was left to be consumed completely on the altar as a picture of dedicating everything to the Lord. This complete consecration was not made with a view to appeasing wrath but because the wrath had already been appeased by the shedding of the blood. The burning of the carcass, though likely offensive to human nostrils, smelled good to the Lord. In the ultimate sense, the burnt offering in all of its components was a picture sermon about Christ, who gave 'himself for us an offering and a sacrifice to God for a sweetsmelling savour' (Eph. 5:2). No one ever lived, or could ever live, a more perfectly consecrated life before God than Jesus Himself. But here Paul applies the language of the whole burnt offering to describe the kind of consecrated life every believer owes to the Lord because of bestowed mercies. It is the logical consequence of grace.

The *extent* of the consecration is total: Christians are to present their bodies. There is something quite ordinary yet intimate about the body. The body is the external instrument of activity; yet it has no existence apart from spirit. Therefore, it represents the totality of life.[8] Significantly, Paul links body and spirit when admonishing the Corinthian believers to flee fornication as a key expression of holy living: 'What? know ye not that your body is the temple of the Holy Ghost which is in you, which ye have of God, and ye are not your own? For ye are bought with

---

7. 'The apostle is not telling us here that we can save ourselves by offering ourselves to God .... Because of the mercies of God, because Christ is the one and only offering, because everything has been done, now you must present yourselves in this way to God' (Martyn Lloyd-Jones, *Romans 12: An Exposition of Christian Conduct* [Edinburgh: Banner of Truth, 2000], p. 38).

8. 'We tend to think of worship as spiritual rather than physical, so we might wonder why Paul asks us to present our bodies rather than our souls. Actually, Paul is writing about the entire person. God wants us to give ourselves' (Sproul, *Romans*, 407).
    'It has been maintained that he uses the term "body" to represent the whole person so that the meaning would be "present your persons." Undoubtedly there is no intent to restrict to the physical body the consecration here enjoined. But there is not good warrant for taking the word "body" as a synonym for the whole person .... Paul was realistic and he was aware that if sanctification did not embrace the physical in our personality it would be annulled from the outset' (John Murray, *The New International Commentary on the New Testament: The Epistle to the Romans* [Grand Rapids: Eerdmans, 1980], Vol. 2, p. 110). Murray's interpretation does not differ in its final outcome, since he acknowledges that there is no restriction of consecration to merely the physical body. He chooses to emphasize the necessity of the consecration of the physical body in this passage and therefore does not apply it further to the whole person. His conclusion is sound in that if sanctification does not embrace the physical body it cannot embrace the whole person.

a price: therefore glorify God in your body, and in your spirit, which are God's' (1 Cor. 6:19-20). To present the body as a sacrifice is to lay everything on the altar, keeping nothing back. Since the body is the 'container' of life, our reasonable service to the Lord requires it. Service is impossible without the body. There is no part of the redeemed life untouched by grace; there should be no part of the redeemed life exempt from living for Jesus.[9]

Three qualifiers mark the *character* of consecration. First, it is a *living* sacrifice. In the Old Testament sacrifices, the life of the victim was consumed in the offering. Living this sacrificial life for Jesus may not involve the forfeiture of physical life, but it does require putting to death the flesh (see Colossians 3:5: 'mortify therefore your members which are upon the earth'). It also requires putting to death the self-interests that conflict with the cross work of Jesus (2 Cor. 5:14-15). Simply said, being a living sacrifice means death to sin and self, and life to God. The burnt offering was a daily sacrifice, so presenting our bodies as a living sacrifice must be a daily operation.[10] This daily renewal is crucial, since a living sacrifice is prone to crawl off the altar.

Second, it is a *holy* sacrifice. God is holy, and those who approach Him must have clean hands and a pure heart (Ps. 24:3-4). In the Old Testament dispensation, the Lord set rigid regulations and strict qualifications for legitimate sacrifices. The potential sacrificial victims had to be without any blemish or defect. Any offering that was defective was offensive to God (see Mal. 1:7-8). This requirement for physical perfection was a salient component in the visible sermon pointing to the moral perfection of Jesus Christ who shed His precious blood 'as of a lamb without blemish and without spot' (1 Pet. 1:19). Significantly, Peter later says that believers are to 'be found of him in peace, without spot, and blameless' (2 Pet. 3:14). Accordingly, Paul says that Christ died 'to present you holy and unblameable and unreproveable in his sight' (Col. 1:22). Since the believer's predestination is with a view to being conformed to the image of Christ (Rom. 8:29), it follows that believers must be holy. Obviously, the practical, experiential holiness of the believer will never in this life match the perfection of the Savior, but progressing in holiness does mark the kind of consecrated offering expected of every believer. We must offer the best that we can unto the Lord for all the benefits of grace He has bestowed on us.[11]

Third, it is a sacrifice *acceptable unto God*. This is incredibly amazing. The idea is that God delights in and is well pleased with this kind of offering. This

---

9. 'This is an appeal to those who have been set free by grace to live under grace by presenting all that they are to God.... To offer our bodies (or in 6:13, 19, our "members") is to offer everything that we are, all that we think or feel, all the influence we can exert over others, all the difference we can make in the world' (Ash, *Teaching Romans*, p. 153).

10. 'It is possible that the word "living" also reflects on the permanence of this offering, that it must be a constant dedication' (Murray, *The Epistle to the Romans*, Vol. 2, p. 111).

11. 'When we give ourselves as living sacrifices to God, he wants that sacrifice sanctified or consecrated. In the words of the old hymn, "Give of your best to the Master." We are to give the most sanctified portion of our lives as an act of praise to God' (Sproul, *Romans*, p. 408).

statement parallels the description of Old Testament's whole burnt offering as a sweet-smelling savor, referring to that step in the procedure after the propitiatory rites were completed. In gratitude for the atonement, all was placed on the altar in complete consecration to the Lord. As the smoke of the burning flesh ascended from the altar, the Lord was pleased. It follows that no life can begin to be pleasing to God until the saving benefits of the blood of Christ's atoning sacrifice have been applied. Consecration of life is not in order to acceptance but because of it. The believer's union with Christ guarantees acceptance before God and generates a gratitude that motivates consecration of life. It is astounding that God takes pleasure in the consecrated lives of His people. To God, the destruction of our flesh smells good.[12]

LIVING FOR JESUS IS PROGRESSIVE

Paul's exhortation 'to present' our bodies as a living sacrifice in Romans 12:1 was direct and urgent; the tense of the infinitive (aorist) underscores the fact that consecrated living for Jesus is not optional for the believer in view of all of God's saving mercies. The shift to the present tense imperatives in verse 2 is significant as well. In Greek, the present tense often designates progressive action, that which is constant, continual, and habitual. Living for Jesus is not a one-off operation; it is a way of life.[13] If verse 1 defines the logic of holy living, the imperatives of verse 2 focus on the mechanics of the process. Paul, in very practical terms, shows how to live for Jesus.

Requires Repentance

Repentance involves a change. Paul's language makes it clear that repentance is not a single, past decision, but rather one that involves a new way of life. It entails turning from what we were and becoming what we should be. Thus, Paul develops this requirement from two perspectives, negatively and positively.

Negatively, he issues the imperative 'be not conformed to this world.' That translation is clear enough, but there are couple of noteworthy observations from the Greek text. The verb translated 'be ... conformed' is best understood as a middle voice, which in Greek highlights the personal involvement and interest in the verbal action. In addition, the grammatical construction suggests that they were conforming themselves to the world, and it was time to stop. The word for 'world' specifically refers not to planet earth but to the present age which is transient and

---

12. 'You must present your body, he says, that it will come up with a most beautiful aroma to God. Because you are a Christian, and because you want to show your gratitude to God, you should keep your body in such a condition that as you present it day by day there will be "a sweet-smelling savour" that will go up, as it were, to God, and He will be very happy to accept your offering' (Lloyd-Jones, *Romans 12*, p. 54).

13. 'It is a *process*. The fact that Paul calls on believers to engage in this renewing of the mind shows that it does not automatically happen to us when we believe …. The ruts of the old life are not always easy to get out of. Some of our ways of thinking are deeply ingrained, and they will not disappear overnight' (Moo, *Romans*, p. 398).

evil.[14] If we put all that together, Paul's injunction is this: 'Stop modelling yourself after this momentary, evil time.' This age opposes spiritual and godly pursuits and represents everything contrary to the way of righteousness. Living for Jesus requires resisting the temptation to live for the present, realizing that Jesus 'gave himself for our sins, that he might deliver us from this present evil world [age]' (Gal. 1:4). To wrap oneself up in the things of this temporary world defies the objective of Christ's atonement. Therefore, it is illogical, in view of all the mercies of God received through Christ, to live like the sinful world, which is marked by corruption (Matt. 6:19) and doomed to destruction (1 John 2:17, which uses a different word for world but intends the same destiny). So if you are patterning your life like the world around you, stop it.[15]

Positively, he commands, 'be ye transformed.' Just as in the previous prohibition, this positive command is in the middle voice, suggesting our personal interest and involvement in the ongoing transformation process. Our English word 'metamorphosis' is simply a transliteration of this Greek word and reflects the sense of Greek word quite well. This transformation is a revolutionary change from the inside out; it is an outward expression of an inward reality. Like the butterfly who exits the cocoon coffin constructed in a 'former life,' so must the Christian exit the corpse of the old man to live in the newness of life. Grace has made the believer a new creation; living for Jesus in consecration and in the pursuit of holiness is simply living in the reality of what grace has intended. The believer has no business masquerading like the world or remaining in the cocoon of the old life. There is no sphere of life unaffected by grace, and there should be no sphere of life exempt from the evidences of grace. Social life, leisure, business and most certainly family life should show the wonder of our spiritual metamorphosis.

Achieved by Right Thinking

The evidence of repentance is outward, but its impetus is inward. It involves a change of mind that results in a change of life. Not surprisingly then, Paul identifies the means of the required transformation as the renewal of the mind. In this 'X of Y' construction, word Y (mind) functions as the object of word X (renewal). Although the agent of the renewing is not expressly stated, it is theologically implied. Unquestionably, the agent of the renewal is the Holy Spirit.[16] The full thought would be 'the Holy Spirit renews the mind' and with that renewed mind

---

14. 'The word "age" (NIV "world") refers to a change of epoch rather than a change of place, as in Ephesians 1:21' (Ash, *Teaching Romans*, p. 155).

15. 'As for the change which takes place in the people of God, … it is a fundamental transformation of character and conduct, away from the standards of the world and into the image of Christ himself. These two value systems (*this world* and *God's will*) are incompatible, even in direct collision with one another…. The two sets of standards diverge so completely that there is no possibility of compromise' (Stott, *Romans*, pp. 323-24).

16. 'By grace this mind is changed so that right at the core of our humanity we love God's law (7:22, 25). This renewal of the mind is the work of the Holy Spirit (cf Titus 3:5, where the same word is used in the expression "renewal (transformation) by the Holy Spirit")' (Ash, *Teaching Romans*, pp. 155-56).

the transformed life of living for Jesus takes place. This mind-renewal is one of the affected parts of the Spirit's work of regeneration. In regeneration or the new birth, the Holy Spirit implants the principle of spiritual life into the dead heart, resulting in a new way of thinking, a new way of feeling, and a new way of doing (the mind, the affections, and the will). There is a real sense in which holy living starts in the head. Right thinking leads to right behavior.[17] What we think about determines what we do. So in the pursuit of holiness we must use the minds that the Holy Spirit has given us and think according to His leading. Second Corinthians 3:18 is a key text that explains what the Holy Spirit leads us to think about: 'But we all, with open face beholding as in a glass the glory of the Lord, are changed into the same image from glory to glory, even as by the Spirit of the Lord.' The Spirit opens our understanding to the mirror of God's Word and so we see the Lord and thus are changed.[18] Interestingly, the word 'changed' in 2 Corinthians 3 is the same word as 'transformed' in Romans 12. The spiritual holiness-pursuing metamorphosis occurs as we think about Christ. Thinking about Jesus is the secret to living for Him. There is something about seeing Jesus that transforms the beholder into His image. It sounds simple enough. It should be.

LIVING FOR JESUS IS WORTH THE EFFORT

Living for Jesus is worth all our struggles with temptations and sin because the goal of godly living is so worthwhile. Paul concludes his exhortation and instructions in holy living with a statement of purpose: 'that ye may prove what is that good, and acceptable, and perfect, will of God.' Some lexical and grammatical observations point to Paul's particular emphasis. Lexically, the word 'prove' has the idea of examining, discovering, and finding by experience. Grammatically, that Paul uses the present tense for the word 'prove' shows the need for this experience to be a constant habit of life. There is ultimately nothing more vital than knowing and doing the will of God. Too often Christians project the notion of God's will into the distant future, wondering what God's will might be rather than searching for what God's will is right now. The apostle makes it clear that the attention given to discovering God's will should be a daily exercise.

The sentence structure of this purpose clause heaps up descriptions of God's will that show how important and attractive to the believer knowing God's will should be. With a single definite article Paul coordinates three qualifiers to explain God's will: God's will is good, acceptable, and perfect.[19] The word

---

17. 'A new orientation in our thinking leads to a new orientation in our behavior. Here Paul touches on the heart of New Testament ethics' (Moo, *Romans*, p. 395).

18. 'Here then are the stages of Christian moral transformation: first our mind is renewed by the Word and Spirit of God; then we are able to discern and desire the will of God; and then we are increasingly transformed by it' (Stott, *Romans*, p. 324).

19. 'The thought is rather that the will of God is "the good, the acceptable, the perfect".... We may never fear that the standard God has prescribed for us is only relatively good or acceptable or perfect, that it is an accommodated norm adapted to our present condition and not measuring

'good' designates that which is morally good and beneficial. The word 'acceptable' refers to that which is well-pleasing – both to God who wills and the believer who acts. The word 'perfect' implies that which is complete, requiring no improvement or amendment. So discovering God's will is beneficial, pleasurable, and full.[20] Living for Jesus with this objective in view is certainly worth the effort.

Although these two verses are familiar and often quoted, the familiarity must not minimize the importance or cloud the clarity of this divinely inspired, apostolic formula for Christian dedication. The apostle provides a distinct directive that is motivated by divine mercy, defined as total sacrifice, and demanded by logic. Paul makes it clear that this dedication is to be a way of life characterized by ongoing repentance and gospel thinking. It is, indeed, to be a daily discovery of what is pleasing to God and good for us. In many ways, Paul's simple definition of God's will in 1 Thessalonians 4:3 sums it all up: 'For this is the will of God, even your sanctification.' Since God has called us 'unto holiness' (1 Thess. 4:7), it is His will that we should live holy lives.[21] The bottom line, therefore, is this: living for Jesus is living like Jesus.

---

up to the standard of God's perfection. The will of God is the transcript of God's perfection and is the perfect reflection of his holiness, justice, and goodness' (Murray, *The Epistle to the Romans*, Vol. 2, pp. 115-16).

20. 'The verb translated "test and approve" means here to recognize that God's way is the best and really to want to go that way' (Ash, *Teaching Romans*, p. 156).
  'If life is aimless, stagnant, fruitless, lacking in content, it is because we are not entering by experience into the richness of God's will .... There is not a moment of life that the will of God does not command, no circumstance that it does not fill with meaning if we are responsive to the fulness of his revealed counsel for us' (Murray, *The Epistle to the Romans*, Vol. 2, p. 115).

21. 'God's will for each of us is that we grow into spiritual maturity, that our lives become more fully set apart and consecrated by the Holy Spirit, and that our minds are changed. After that we will be able to tell what is pleasing to God. Then we will be able to know what he wants us to do – that good and acceptable and perfect will of God' (Sproul, *Romans*, p. 411).

CHAPTER 9

THE 'DOS' AND 'WHYS' OF THE TRANSFORMED LIFE

(1 PETER 1:13-21)

CONVERSION is the start of something, not the end. Too often the assumption is that the initial act of faith—that crisis and momentary decision—satisfies every duty to God and makes every other aspect of Christianity automatic. For certain, regeneration—the mysterious and supernatural life-imparting act of the Holy Spirit in the heart of a dead and spiritually insensitive sinner—is instantaneous. That new birth, evidenced by conscious faith and repentance, begins a new life, evidenced by a consequent transformation of living. Indeed, there is no regeneration without the resulting reformation of life.[1] Grace finds sinners where they are, but grace never leaves sinners where they were.

The demand for a transformed life confronts every believer in Christ. Holiness is not just the mark of the 'super-saint'; it is the mandated course for every new creature in Christ Jesus. Everything old has passed away; everything has become new. In this text before us, Peter makes a compelling appeal based on the profound truths of the gospel to convince and challenge us to live like grace has made a difference in our lives. The initial 'wherefore' of 1 Peter 1:13 flows from the apostle's summary exposition of the Trinitarian gospel certainties expressed in verse 2: salvation is founded on the authority of the Father, administered by the application of the Holy Spirit, and all with respect to or in view of the accomplishments of the Son.[2] Peter reasons with typical apostolic logic that Christian living should testify to the power and greatness of saving grace. Ethical demands flow from revealed and experienced truth. There are 'dos' in Christianity; there are also 'whys.' To try to 'do' without

---

1. 'The new birth given by God the Father (1:3) necessarily implies a decisively altered way of life that is characterized by the new knowledge of God and Christ' (Karen H. Jobes, *Baker Exegetical Commentary on the New Testament: 1 Peter* [Grand Rapids: Baker Academic, 2005], p. 112).

2. 'The imperatives of Christian living always begin with "therefore." Peter does not begin to exhort Christian pilgrims until he has celebrated the wonders of God's salvation in Jesus Christ .... Because we have been given hope, we are called to live in it' (Edmund P. Clowney, *The Message of 1 Peter*, The Bible Speaks Today [Downers Grove, Ill.: InterVarsity, 1988], p. 61).

thinking about 'why' is hopeless, resulting in either heartless legalism or frustration. But in the light of the 'whys,' the 'dos' are both possible and pleasurable.

According to 1 Peter 2:9, believers enjoy a special position and privilege: 'But ye are a chosen generation, a royal priesthood, and holy nation, a peculiar people.' That special privilege serves a special purpose: 'that ye should shew forth the praises of him who hath called you out of darkness into his marvellous light.' The position of the believer is glorious; the experience or practice of the believer should correspond to the reality of his position before God in Christ. With that in mind, I want to think through Peter's imperatives and logic for Christian living delineated in 1 Peter 1:13-21: the 'dos' and 'whys' of the transformed life.

THE DOS

In the Greek text of 1 Peter 1:13-17, Peter issues three imperatives or commands to direct the believer in his Christian walk. The commands are broad in their scope but clearly mark the manner and course for the transformed life. Imperatives are always directed to the will, calling for urgent and conscious obedience. The 'dos' of Christian living are deliberate.

Persevere

First Peter 1:13 begins this section: 'Wherefore gird up the loins of your mind, be sober, and hope to the end for the grace that is to be brought unto you at the revelation of Jesus Christ.' Three thoughts flow from the statement. First, there is the *command to hope*. Although the translation links three imperatives (gird, be sober, hope), only the verb 'hope' is actually an imperative in the Greek text. The expression 'to the end' is an adverb meaning fully, perfectly, or completely. The command, therefore, is to hope fully, a reference to maintaining a steadfast or persevering hope. Hope is part of the vocabulary of faith; it is faith's future focus.[3] Biblical hope is anything but a cross-your-fingers wish for something beyond realistic expectation. Hope is the personal expectant reliance on God's Word with the certainty that it cannot be anything else but true.[4] Hoping, with its future focus, makes it clear that saving faith is not just a past crisis decision, but a constant exercise that must persist until what is believed is confirmed by sight.

Second, Peter identifies the *object of hope*: 'for the grace that is to be brought unto you at the revelation of Jesus Christ.' The value of faith, including hope as faith's future focus, always depends on its object – what is believed or hoped for. This is why I stress that hope is not just wishful thinking regardless of how sincere or intense that wishing may be. Hope is not empty or futile, since it rests on the person

---

3. 'Those redeemed by Christ and regenerated by God's Holy Spirit have an ultimate hope which, when rightly grasped by faith, sustains them in time just as much as it compensates them inconceivably in eternity' (William W. Harrell, *Let's Study 1 Peter* [Edinburgh: Banner of Truth, 2012], p. 23).

4. 'Since our hope is sure, we can bank on it. It is not so much an attitude to be cultivated as a reality to be recognized. To set our hope is to believe the gospel' (Clowney, *The Message of 1 Peter*, pp. 61-62).

of Jesus Christ. In this context, 'hope' is specifically the revelation or full disclosure of Christ that will occur at His return and the eschatological consummation of God's gracious redemptive purpose for His people.[5] The transformed life now keeps an eye on the glorious future.[6] This hope keeps the believer from being entangled with the affairs of this life. Hoping in that certain culmination of grace is a key component in the transformed life. John put it this way when speaking of the future appearance and revelation of Jesus: 'And every man that hath his hope in him purifieth himself, even as he is pure' (1 John 3:3). That's Peter's logic as well.

Third, the apostle instructs concerning our *manner of hope*. Although translated as imperatives, the verbs 'gird up' and 'be sober' are participles that are circumstantially subordinate to the principal verb 'hope.' They describe how to hope: hope by girding up and being sober. Girding up the loins is a common biblical image to describe preparation for vigorous activity.[7] The typical attire of the day consisted of a flowing garment that was suited for normal movement but would be a hindrance to quick maneuvering. So the flowing robe would be hitched up around the waist to remove the impediment and to allow freedom of movement. The image is similar to our expression of rolling up the sleeves as a preparation for strenuous activity. Significantly, the participle is in the middle voice, a grammatical form to underscore the personal involvement or interest in the verbal idea. To gird up the loins is intentional and intense; there can be no slackness. Even more significant is that this process of preparation takes place in the mind, the place of thinking: 'gird up the loins of your mind.' The 'dos' of holiness cannot take place in a mental vacuum. It is a spiritual principle that right thinking determines right behavior. It must be the discipline of the Christian mind to think about things that are true, honest, just, pure, lovely, of good report, virtuous and praiseworthy (Phil. 4:8). That whole list can be summed up in terms of thinking about Christ, who is the epitome of every holy perfection.[8]

Not only are we to hope by girding up the loins but also by being sober. Being sober refers to a calm, steady, well-balanced state of self-control that is not under the influence of the intoxicating delusions of the world. There are so many things in this old world that have the power to attract and the potential to control and subdue.

---

5. 'We look to God, hear his word of promise, see his salvation in Christ, and fix our hope on him. Peter makes this clear by defining again the object of our hope. It is the grace that is being brought to us at the revelation of Jesus Christ. To fix our hope is to fix our gaze on the coming glory of Christ's appearing' (Clowney, *The Message of 1 Peter*, p. 62).

6. 'Grace is what the Puritans rightly called *young glory*. It is that grace culminating in glory which is to be the focus of our hope' (Harrell, *Let's Study 1 Peter*, p. 24).

7. 'The image Peter employs is vivid and instructive. It alludes to the instruction God gave his people on the eve of their exodus from Egypt. They were to eat the Passover lamb with girded loins, sandals on their feet, and staff in hand (*Exod.* 12:11). In other words, when the people of God partake of the saving provision of God, they are to be prepared for empowerment to walk in freedom and holiness' (Harrell, *Let's Study 1 Peter*, p. 22).

8. 'We gird our minds when we direct our thoughts consistently to the mercies of God in Christ.... Peter calls his readers to gather up their distracted thoughts, focusing them on the truth of God in Christ' (Harrell, *Let's Study 1 Peter*, p. 22).

The only way to avoid the worldly distractions, delusions and spiritual disasters is to control the mind, 'bringing into captivity every thought to the obedience of Christ' (2 Cor. 10:5). Spiritual self-control is the consequence of having a mind that is under the control of Christ. Christian living requires a mind that is fixed on things above.[9]

Be Holy

Biblical hope breeds biblical holiness (1 John 3:3).[10] First Peter 1:14-16 transition from the imperative to hope to the command to be holy. The command actually occurs twice, first in verse 15 as the direct command flowing from the apostle's argument and then in verse 16 as part of the quotation from Leviticus 11:44 that states the reason for the present injunction. So for analysis purposes, I am counting the imperative in verse 15 as Peter's prescription for what to do in living the transformed life and am regarding the quoted imperative in verse 16 as explaining the logic for Peter's admonition. This is why I've said this section (1 Pet. 1:13-17) issues three imperatives mapping the course of transformed living.

The construction in verse 15 is intensive: 'you yourself be holy.' This goes beyond recommendation to emphatic obligation. Holiness is not optional for the Christian; it is a requirement. This holiness involves a life that is set apart and distinct from the kind of living that characterizes the world apart from God. A holy life is different from its worldly surroundings; it is a transformed life. First Peter 1:14-16 highlight three thoughts about this life of personal holiness: its recipients, its requirements, and its reason.

First, Peter identifies the *recipients* of the charge to be holy as 'obedient children' (v. 14). The phrase is literally, 'children of obedience,' and 'children,' of course, is not a designation of age but rather refers to those belonging to the class of people characterized by the genitive 'obedience.'[11] Simply, these are people who obey. That is an amazing description that highlights the essence of a transformed life, particularly in light of Paul's identification of the unconverted as 'sons of disobedience' and 'children of wrath' (Eph. 2:2-3). Significantly, Paul concludes

---

9. 'Drunken stupor is the refuge of those who have no hope. But Christians who look for the coming of the Lord live in hope. They will not seek escape in the bottle, for they have tasted of the Spirit of glory. Alive and alert, they look for the Lord' (Clowney, *The Message of 1 Peter,* pp. 62-63).

   'Peter instructs his readers to set their hope on the grace that will be theirs when Jesus returns by being fully able to think and act on the basis of their true nature in Christ, despite whatever hostility such a lifestyle might provoke from their society. Peter's readers cannot resolve to make the hard ethical choices he will enjoin on them if they do not have their minds fixed on the final outcome of that resolve' (Jobes, *1 Peter,* p. 111-12).

10. 'True hope, fixed on Christ, begets in us a desire and determination to be like Christ, and, more specifically, to become closer now to what we shall be forever in the final day when we shall see the face of our Saviour and reign with him in glory' (Harrell, *Let's Study 1 Peter,* p. 24).

11. '*As obedient children* views Peter's readers as children in God's family whose lives are characterized by obedience to their heavenly Father.' Grudem goes on to say in footnote 19, 'The Gk. Phrase is literally "as children of obedience", a construction echoing the Heb. Construct state by use of a genitive of definition' (Wayne A. Grudem, *Tyndale New Testament Commentaries: 1 Peter* [Downers Grove, Ill.: InterVarsity, 1988], p. 82).

that these disobedient and doomed-to-wrath children who by grace have been made alive in Christ (Eph. 2:5) are God's 'workmanship, created in Christ Jesus unto good works, which God hath before ordained that we should walk in them' (Eph. 2:10). So when Peter directs the command to be holy to obedient children, he is not demanding the impossible. Rather, he is commanding what regenerating grace has made possible and what God's design for believers requires. The call to holiness is within the ability of the converted because the ability to obey is a consequence of regeneration. Holiness, therefore, is not optional for believers; the pursuit of holiness marks the distinction between life and death. It bears repeating because it is a crucial point. For sure, the pace and progress of the pursuit will differ among believers, but to some degree every true believer is a child of obedience.

Second, Peter describes the *requirements* of holiness, both negatively and positively. Negatively, believers are not to fashion themselves according to the desires or lusts done formerly in their state of spiritual ignorance (1 Pet. 1:14). Peter uses the same word Paul used when he told believers not to be conformed to the world (Rom. 12:2).[12] Believers are to break the mold of their old conduct, separating themselves from their old desires and habits.[13] What was done formerly in spiritual ignorance as a way of life becomes repulsive to the new way of thinking. Second Corinthians 5:17 sums it up well: 'Therefore if any man be in Christ, he is a new creature: old things are passed away; behold, all things are become new.'

Positively, believers are to fashion or model themselves after a new model. Although the participle 'fashioning' is not repeated, the strong contrastive particle 'but' in 1 Peter 1:15 implies its positive use. The thought would be this: don't model yourselves after your former ways but model yourselves according to the pattern of the One who called you to be holy. This divine call includes salvation's beginning by divine initiative and salvation's experience by divine enabling. That He has called believers to be holy is salvation's requirement. Too often the pursuit of holiness is defined in terms of 'not doing' without the positive perspective of 'doing.' Turning away from sin involves turning to the Lord. God is the ultimate and absolute standard of what holiness is. In a very real sense, pursuing holiness is imitating God.[14] This mandated imitation extends to 'all manner of conversation.' This conversation refers not just to verbal communication but to all of life's movements, actions, and habits. There is no part of life that can be exempt from

---

12. '*Do not be conformed* uses a word which occurs elsewhere in the New Testament only at Romans 12:2. It means "to pattern one's actions or life after", and reminds these Christians that obedience to God and holiness of life (see v. 15) are radically different from a life that follows "natural" (that is non-Christian) desires wherever they lead' (Grudem, *1 Peter*, p. 83).

13. 'Holiness means loving the things God loves, and turning away from the things that are an affront to God's character' (Brandon D. Crowe, *The Message of the General Epistles in the History of Redemption: Wisdom from James, Peter, John, and Jude* [Phillipsburg, N.J.: P&R, 2015], p. 34).

14. 'To be holy means that Christians must conform their thinking and behavior to God's character .... The Christian's morality would be defined by, and derived from, the character of God their Father as first revealed in Scripture and then ultimately in the life of Jesus Christ' (Jobes, *1 Peter*, pp. 112-13.)

holiness. This is a key thought particularly in this post-modern world where life tends to be compartmentalized into seemingly unrelated categories. The typical notion is that one's social life, work life, family life, political life, moral life or religious life operate independently one from another. Transgressions in one sphere supposedly have no bearing on other. On the contrary, the biblical ethic is pervasive. As 'obedient children,' Christians must consciously factor in their 'religion' to every sphere of life.[15]

Third, Peter declares the authoritative *reason* for the believer's personal holiness: 'Because it is written, Be ye holy; for I am holy' (1:16). The apostolic command to be holy is not a new command or demand; it is based on the authority of the Word of God. He appeals to what had been written in Leviticus 20:26: 'And ye shall be holy unto me: for I the LORD am holy.' The Lord then expounds on that command by telling the covenant people that He had severed or separated them from other people that they may be His (see also Leviticus 20:24). Because of grace, they were to be different from people around them. Because the Lord is holy, His people must be holy too. What was true for the Old Testament covenant people applies as well to God's covenant people of any age or place.[16] Significantly, Peter employs Old Testament covenant language to underscore the continuity of God's people throughout the ages: 'But ye are a chosen generation, a royal priesthood, an holy nation, a peculiar people; that ye should shew forth the praise of him who hath called you out of darkness unto his marvelous light' (1 Pet. 2:9; see Exod. 19:5-6; Deut. 26:16-19). Remember that being holy is not optional; it is the revealed will and design of God for all who belong to Him by redemption. Being holy like the Lord will make God's people different from the world.

Fear

Living in fear is the final 'do' of the transformed life outlined by Peter: 'And if ye call on the Father, who without respect of persons judgeth according to every man's work, pass the time of your sojourning here in fear' (1 Pet. 1:17). The imperative 'pass' does not refer to inactive resignation but rather to how one behaves or conducts himself. A more literal translation can sharpen the focus: 'Since you are calling on the Father, the One who evaluates impartially according to the work of each one, behave yourself during the time of your exile

---

15. *'Be holy yourselves in all your conduct* speaks of a pattern of life that transforms every day, every moment, every thought, every action .... To be holy "as God is holy" includes a full and pervading holiness that reaches to every aspect of our personalities. It involves not only avoiding outward sin but also maintaining an instinctive delight in God and his holiness as an undercurrent of heart and mind throughout the day' (Grudem, *1 Peter*, p. 84).

16. 'Peter assumes that the OT writings are authoritative and normative for his Christian readers, regardless of their previous ethnic origin. He makes no distinction between the Jewish and Gentile Christian in his application, nor does the span of time between Leviticus and his letter mitigate the relevance of God's ancient revelation of himself .... In terms of moral transformation, the goal of both the old and new covenants is the same – to create a people who morally conform to God's character' (Jobes, *1 Peter*, p. 113).

in fear.' Peter packs a lot in this statement calling for a life of reverence that can be summed up in two thoughts.

First, he identifies the basis for fear by using a conditional statement. Greek has various grammatical constructions to express different kinds of conditions. The construction here is called a simple condition. Bear with me as I explain a couple of technical terms. Conditional statements have two parts: the protasis (the 'if' clause) and the apodosis (the 'then' clause) – 'If this, then this.' The significance of the simple condition is that the protasis is assumed to be true; it is regarded as fact. That is why in the literal translation, I used the word 'since' which conveys the idea more specifically in English than 'if.' Peter, then, is basing his argument on the fact of a Father/child relationship between God and the believer.[17] That believers call upon God as Father has far-reaching implications, not the least of which is that God deserves honor and respect. The Lord Himself made that link when addressing Malachi's congregation: 'A son honoureth his father ... if then I be a father, where is mine honour?' (Mal. 1:6). It is normal for a child who honors his father to desire to do those things that are pleasing to him and to know his father's approval. It is normal for a father to supervise and evaluate his child's behavior in order to ensure that the child conducts himself according to family rules. As a father of two sons, I was pretty good at finding things out about their behavior even when I could not directly observe it. I'm sure that my sons' knowledge of that skill kept them from doing certain things that would have displeased me. I have since learned from the grinning confessions in their manhood that I didn't know everything. But God does not need to discover anything about His children's behavior; He knows all and deals with all impartially and fairly. Since that is true, there is reason to fear and impetus to behave in a way that is pleasing to Him.

Second, he issues the imperative to behave in fear during the time of our sojourning. This is the way we are to live so long as we are aliens in this world. The word translated 'sojourning' is a compound word in Greek having the transparent idea of 'outside the house.' In a very real sense, believers are 'outsiders' in the world.[18] This world is transient and hostile to God and grace; it is not home for the Christian. Having this perspective of our temporary residence helps to pursue the kind of holiness and worldly difference that God has designed for His people. Putting the world in its proper place is the consequence of putting God in His proper place. This is why Peter says we are to conduct ourselves in fear.

Although the object of this fear is not explicitly expressed, it is unquestionably God since over and again the Scripture admonishes that we are not to fear men or circumstances. But fearing God, with its corollary of obeying God, is the essence of piety and, according to the inspired Preacher, sums up God's expectations: 'Let us

---

17. 'The first-class conditional (or condition of fact) in verse 17 ... indicates Peter's understanding that since they have become God's children by virtue of being born again (1:3), they consequently have a new life that is to be lived markedly different from the old one' (Jobes, *1 Peter*, p. 115-16).

18. 'In spite of their humanness, Christians are "extra-terrestrials" at heart. Or, better, they are "neo-terrestrials", representatives of the new humanity in Jesus Christ' (Clowney, *The Message of 1 Peter*, p. 68).

hear the conclusion of the whole matter: Fear God, and keep his commandments: for this is the whole duty of man' (Eccles. 12:13). Fearing God involves both an attitude of reverence for who God is and actions of obedience to what God requires. Fearing God affects worship and defines ethics. Fearing God is linked directly to the knowledge of God and can be defined simply as the awareness of God. If we live being overwhelmed with the reality of God, the pursuit of holiness will be our desire. Fearing God is factoring the reality of God into every situation of life.[19] Factoring the reality of God into every situation of life is a strong motivation for every 'do' of the transformed life.

THE WHYS

The biblical paradigm for holiness is that duty flows from doctrine. Right thinking about theology fosters transformed living. Doing the right things apart from the foundation and framework of right theology may produce a morally conservative lifestyle that is out of sync with worldly practices, but unless such living is the conscious application of Christian truth, it can degenerate into drudgery or thoughtless traditions. Peter links his apostolic admonitions regarding the 'dos' of holy living to the verities of the gospel (v. 18-21). Verse 18 begins with a causal participle that grammatically connects to the immediately preceding imperative 'pass' (behave yourselves), but logically governs the other 'dos' as well. The transformed life is the logical, reasonable way to live because of something you know. The verb 'to know' refers specifically to the intellectual apprehension of something; it is the knowledge of certain facts that demands duty. Peter brings together two things to know and think about that demand the transformed life.

The Cost of Redemption

The cost of redemption demands a transformed life. First Peter 1:18-19 put in bold terms the high cost of redemption that should cause those who have been redeemed to live selflessly before the Lord in grateful obedience. The word 'redeem' refers to an act of deliverance or rescue, often in reference to freeing slaves by paying a ransom price.[20] It is a fitting word to describe what Christ has done in rescuing His people from the bondage of sin and misery from which they could not free themselves. The knowledge of this incredibly expensive ransom is a motivating truth.[21]

---

19. 'Our highest regard must constantly be for God, and neither for men nor for the circumstances surrounding us, whether they be enticing or intimidating…. We should be fixed with reverent attention upon our God' (Harrell, *Let's Study 1 Peter*, p. 28).

20. 'The term "redeem" and the word group recalls Israel's liberation from Egypt. The term also is applied to the liberation of individuals, and in Isaiah the return from exile is portrayed as a second exodus. In the Greco-Roman world those captured in war could be redeemed, and slaves were often manumitted, meaning that their freedom was purchased' (Thomas R. Schreiner, *The New American Commentary: 1, 2 Peter, Jude* [Nashville, Tenn.: B&H, 2003], p. 84).

21. 'God has claimed us as his own, claimed us at a cost that sears our minds with the flame of his love. Peter appeals to the two most profound emotions our hearts can know. One is love, love that sees

Peter first explains this high price negatively; he identifies a currency that would have no value for this costly transaction: 'ye were not redeemed with corruptible things, as silver and gold, from your vain conversation received by tradition from your fathers.' If the weight of all the material assets and treasures of the world were placed on the scale against the value of a soul, each individual would tip the balance. Human resources and human efforts are of no value in this spiritual transaction. The Psalmist, hundreds of years before Peter's assessment, comes to the same conclusion. Speaking of those who trust their riches, the Psalmist says in Psalm 49:7-8, 'None of them can by any means redeem his brother, nor give to God a ransom for him: (For the redemption of their soul is precious, and it ceaseth for ever).' When he says that 'it ceaseth for ever,' he means that any and every attempt of human effort or payment comes to nothing; it never works because the value of the soul is beyond the resources of any man. The point is clear from the Psalmist and from Peter that nothing associated with man or the world has enough worth to redeem or deliver the soul.

The beauty of the gospel is that God does for man what man cannot do for himself. Verse 19 begins with the beautiful 'but' that introduces the antithesis to the repudiated corruptible and worthless currency of verse 18. The only currency recognized as valid in heaven for the redemption of the sinner is 'the precious blood of Christ, as of a lamb without blemish and without spot.' That it is precious blood means that it has high value; indeed, it has infinite worth as it is the blood of the God/Man who gave Himself as the perfect sacrifice for the sins of His people to deliver them from the bondage and misery of their plight. To grasp the full significance of the statement would require an analysis of the whole Levitical system of sacrifice that was set in place as a picture prophecy of the true and ideal Lamb of God. As tempted as I am to draw all the lines from the Old Testament pictures to Christ, I must restrict my comment to the point at hand. The cost of Calvary was beyond human computation and comprehension as Christ paid this infinite price to redeem His people from the curse. It is the recognition of what redemption cost that puts the redeemed under obligation to live worthy of the cost incurred. When we think about the fact that Christ died for us, it should be unthinkable to live with a view to ourselves and self-interests.[22] Here's how Paul reasoned. 'For the love of Christ constraineth us; because we thus judge, that if one died for all, then were all dead: And that he died for all, that they which live should not henceforth live unto themselves, but unto him which died for them, and rose again' (2 Cor. 5:14-15).

If we can learn to keep the cross between us and every onslaught of temptation to transgress and wander from the way of holiness, those temptations, so attractive in themselves, will lose their allurement. Christ shed His precious and infinitely

---

the price God paid to redeem us. The other is fear, the fear of despising God's love' (Clowney, *The Message of 1 Peter*, p. 69).

22. 'The price of our redemption was infinite, and its cost was undertaken graciously by God. How could we, who have received this gift, live in any way other than the way of godly fear and gratitude?' (Harrell, *Let's Study 1 Peter*, p. 31).

valuable blood to deliver us not only from sin's penalty but from sin's power. Viewing temptations through the lens of the cross exposes sin for what it is. Because of the cross, believers are to be holy.

The Purpose of Redemption

The purpose of redemption demands a transformed life. Christ died to present the redeemed to the Father as holy, without blame and beyond reproach (see Colossians 1:22). Christians must live in the reality of this truth. In 1 Peter 1:20-21, Peter draws attention to God's eternal plan and purpose of redemption by referring to Christ as the slain Lamb (1:19) who was 'foreordained before the foundation of the world' (see also Revelation 13:8). Significantly, Peter began this epistle by assuring believers that they were part of God's saving foreknowledge (1 Pet. 1:2), and now he links them to Christ whose redeeming work was central to that eternal knowledge. The words 'foreknowledge' in 1:2, referring to believers, and 'foreordained' in 1:20, referring to Christ, come from the same root or stem word, the only difference being the part of speech. First Peter 1:2 has a noun whereas verse 20 has a participle, but the thought is the same. The word refers to God's eternal decree. The amazingly wonderful thought is that God's decrees cannot be frustrated. The Psalmist affirmed this: 'But our God is in the heavens: he hath done whatsoever he hath pleased' (Ps. 115:3). Christ was ordained to be the only Redeemer of God's elect before sinners existed in the framework of time. The atoning work of Christ was not a remedial afterthought on God's part to deal with man's miserable estate; it was the eternal plan.[23]

What was purposed in eternity was guaranteed for time. Thus, Peter says that the foreordained Redeemer 'was manifest in these last times for you' (1 Pet. 1:20). What the KJV translates as 'for you' is specifically 'because of you.' If redemption was the eternal plan, then the believer's life in Christ is the determined result. This is a truth that must sink deep into our souls. All who believe in God through the mediation of Christ ('by him' in 1 Pet. 1:21) constitute the reason Christ came to die and shed His precious blood. God's acceptance and vindication of Christ's sacrifice, evidenced by Christ's resurrection and earned glory (1 Pet. 1:21), is the guarantee of the believer's acceptance as well. Therefore, faith and hope in God (1 Pet. 1:21) is not wishful thinking; it is certain.

So if the purpose of redemption was to bring elect sinners to life through the sacrifice of Christ, then those elect sinners, whose election is evinced by faith in Christ, should be overwhelmed first with humble gratitude and then with happy compliance with the purpose of grace to be conformed to the image of Christ (Rom. 8:29). Since all those saved by Christ were bought at such a high cost, they should live so as not to frustrate or betray the purpose of saving grace. Transforming grace is going *to look like something* in life. The more we think about why, the more we will desire to do.

---

23. 'God's sovereign purpose centers on Jesus Christ; all history culminates in him…. God's purpose, even before creation, was that Christ would come to die and rise again for the salvation of all who are chosen in him' (Clowney, *The Message of 1 Peter*, p. 72).

HOLINESS PRACTICED

CHAPTER 10

EXPERIENCING THE NEW BIRTH

SANCTIFICATION is progressive. The very thought of progression suggests both a beginning and an end. Sanctification started someplace, and it is going to end some place. Sanctification is a journey, and every step is leading to the ultimate end when salvation will be complete – glorification. Thus, Paul could say that he was pressing 'toward the mark for the prize of the high calling of God in Christ Jesus' (Phil. 3:14). Every Christian should say the same. But just as it is certain that sanctification will be perfected in eternity, it is certain that sanctification begins in time. Something had to happen to initiate the process.

What had to happen is what makes God's call to holiness so radical. Without special divine intervention, man is incapable of obeying that call or even taking the first step in the journey of holiness. With divine intervention, man receives a new nature and disposition which are capable and desirous of the demanded holiness. This divine intervention is the new birth, or regeneration. Without the experience of the new birth, holiness is impossible.[1] Without holiness, seeing God is impossible. Without God, there is no hope. This is why Christ so adamantly declared, 'Ye must be born again' (John 3:7).

In order to understand why the experience of the new birth is such an essential element in obeying God's call to holiness, it is important to reflect on the inherent problem that makes pursuing holiness impossible for man and the graciously sovereign solution that starts the believer on the journey. The problem is death; the solution is life.

THE PROBLEM

Sinners are spiritually dead. In Ephesians 2:1, Paul identifies the state of believers prior to salvation as being 'dead in trespasses and sins.' In this context, being dead refers to the absence not of physical life but of spiritual life. Being spiritually dead renders one insensitive and unresponsive to the things of God (1 Cor. 2:14). The

---

1. 'It is that change of heart which is the distinguishing mark of a true Christian man, the invariable companion of a justifying faith in Christ, the inseparable consequence of vital union with Him, and the root and beginning of inward sanctification' (J. C. Ryle, *Regeneration: Being 'Born Again': What It Means and Why It's Necessary* [Fearn, Scotland: Christian Focus, 2003], p. 16).

most important part of man's person—his eternal soul—is dead to the most vital part of life – God. Because of trespasses and sins, man is spiritually dead. It is the fact of original sin that renders every man spiritually dead; it is the fact of spiritual death that impels every man to actual sin. Spiritual death buries a man in the dirt of sin. Spiritual death renders man thoroughly corrupt (a stinking corpse) and completely incapable of generating spiritual life.[2] Theologically, we refer to this condition as man's total depravity and total inability. The Scripture presents three important perspectives of this universal problem of spiritual death.

Dead in Adam

The Bible teaches, and experience verifies, that sin is universal. According to Scripture, the explanation for this universal presence of sin in the human heart lies in Adam's first sin, the fall of the human race. First Corinthians 15:22 declares explicitly, 'In Adam all die.' Romans 5 is a weighty text for many reasons, particularly for its explanation that links our guilt to Adam's sin. 'Wherefore, as by one man sin entered into the world, and death by sin; and so death passed upon all men, for that all have sinned' (v. 12). Consider also these statements: 'For if through the offense of one many be dead ...' (v. 15); 'For the judgment was by one to condemnation ...' (v. 16); 'For if by one man's offence death reigned by one ...' (v. 17); 'By the offence of one judgment came upon all men to condemnation ...' (v. 18); and 'For as by one man's disobedience many were made sinners ...' (v. 19).

All this raises an important and legitimate question: If Adam did it, how come I'm guilty? Theologians have long debated this question, often allowing the limitations of finite reason and a perverted, selfish sense of fairness to cloud the evidence of Scripture. There are many wrong answers to this question and what I believe to be one right answer.

Some Wrong Answers

One theory, called Pelagianism, denies that there is any constitutional connection between Adam's sin and the guilt of humanity. This view holds that all humanity, just like Adam, comes into the world balanced on the fence of morality, with an equal chance of sinning or not sinning. Accordingly, Adam, being morally indifferent, alone bore the responsibility for his sin, and neither his sin nor its consequences affect the human race. At worst, Adam set a bad example, and his descendants simply follow his bad example by sinning themselves. On the surface, the notion of individual responsibility sounds fair, but it ignores the explicit biblical data and wipes away the other side of Paul's argument in Romans 5 that links Christ's obedience to justification. If Adam's sin was just a bad example, then it follows that Christ's obedience was just a good example that ultimately contributes

---

2. 'This change is one which no man can give himself, nor yet to another. It would be as reasonable to expect the dead to raise themselves, or to require an artist to give a marble statue life' (Ryle, *Regeneration*, p. 15).

nothing to the salvation of sinners. Every man would be left to his own attempts to be perfect, attempts that are doomed to failure. That is hardly good news. This is an obvious and deleterious error.

An adaptation of Pelagianism called semi-Pelagianism teaches that man inherited from Adam a moral corruption that renders him spiritually sick but not dead.[3] Semi-Pelagians define sin as conscious, voluntary acts; sin is not a condition, but just a type of behavior. Since man was not a voluntary participant in Adam's transgression, he cannot be liable for Adam's guilt. Inherited corruption, though not sin, gives occasion to actual sins. Although man may theoretically be capable of not sinning, this sickness and corruption render man hard-pressed not to sin, without God's help. Sinful urges exist, but man can still initiate right behavior toward God, in spite of his innate moral sickness, without divine intervention; God then responds to man's feeble efforts with aiding grace.[4] Semi-Pelagianism led eventually to what we know as Arminianism. Arminianism, rather than saying God responds with aiding grace to man's initiating efforts, asserts that God gives grace equally to all men, enabling them to believe if they so choose. This is generally designated as prevenient grace, a term derived from Latin meaning 'to come before.' Arminianism argues that it is God's prevenient grace in the soul of every man that renders a spiritually sick man capable of responding to the gospel and thus, by his response, making the gospel personally effective. Again, the emphasis on individualism and personal responsibility makes this sound fair, but it hardly agrees with the biblical data that declares man spiritually dead, not just morally sick. Salvation is reduced to possibility rather than actuality.

There is one more wrong answer that I will mention. This system of doctrine is called New School or New Haven theology because it emerged from Yale in the early nineteenth century. Concerning the matter of Adam's sin, this theory teaches that man inherits from Adam an inherent tendency to sin. Although this tendency invariably leads to sin, the tendency itself is not sin because, according to this view also, sin consists exclusively in conscious, intentional violations of the law. In simple terms, men are not corrupt because they are guilty in Adam; they are guilty because they are corrupt. Men are guilty sinners only because they sin. This view essentially claims that behavior determines nature, whereas the Bible teaches that nature determines behavior. The bottom line, however, is this: 'Men are not sinners because they sin; men sin because they are sinners.'

---

3. 'The idea is not that man is still good enough to work his way into the kingdom of God through his own merits, he can't possibly get there without grace. The grace of God is as necessary, according to semi-Pelagianism, for salvation, as medicine is to heal this dying man. But a type of co-operation must take place between the patient and the physician for the healing medicine to have its effect. What happens is that God provides the medicine and he brings it to the dying man, but the dying man must co-operate by opening his mouth to receive it' (R. C. Sproul, *Ephesians: The Purpose of God* [Fearn, Scotland: Christian Focus Publications, 2006], p. 46).

4. 'Some tell us that a regenerate man has a certain power within him which enables him to repent and believe if he thinks fit, but that he still needs a further change in order to make him a true Christian' (Ryle, *Regeneration*, p. 17).

The Right Answer

Federal Theology best explains the connection between Adam's sin and man's consequent guilt. Federal Theology essentially affirms that God ordained Adam as the representative head of the human race. I believe this best explains the language of Scripture, particularly Romans 5 and 1 Corinthians 15.

As the first man, Adam stands naturally as the father of mankind. Every human being who has ever lived can trace his or her ancestry back to Adam by natural generation. In fact, as evidence of the real humanity of Jesus Christ, Luke traced the Savior's lineage right back to Adam (Luke 3:38). If we believe what the Bible teaches about creation, recognizing the natural headship of Adam is easy. Federal Theology also maintains that Adam was the covenant head of the human race. God established Adam as the representative head not only in a parental sense but also in a federal sense – the human race was in union with him. In the first covenant, which dictated the terms of life and death (Gen. 2:16-17), God would deal with the race as He dealt with Adam. After all, when God dealt with Adam in this covenant, Adam *was* the human race.

As the covenant head, Adam's behavior toward the terms of the covenant affected the whole race both because he represented the race and because the entire race was quite literally in him. Had Adam obeyed the conditions of the probation placed on him in Eden, he would have earned eternal life for himself and his descendants. Unlike the Pelagian notion, Federal Theology maintains that Adam was not created tottering precariously on the edge of right and wrong, but he was created with a positive bias toward God with spiritual knowledge, righteousness, and true holiness (see Col. 3:10; Eph. 4:24). Since God gave Adam every spiritual advantage, it was hard for him to sin. This increases the heinousness and seriousness of his sin. Adam did not uncontrollably slip and slide into sin. Solomon said that God made man upright, but that contrary to that original righteousness, he sought out many schemes (Eccles. 7:29). Remember how plainly Paul explained it: 'Adam was not deceived ... in the transgression' (1 Tim. 2:14). Let's be sure to base our theology of Adam's fall on Scripture and not on nursery rhymes. I certainly agree that Humpty Dumpty had a great fall and that, despite the efforts of all the king's horses and all the king's men, Humpty could not be put back together again. But Humpty—i.e., Adam—was not an egg balanced on a wall. He was put in the middle of Paradise, so he had to take a long, running jump to get over the wall God had erected. Not easy for an egg.

When Adam deliberately and willfully disobeyed God, he corrupted himself, incurred guilt, and became subject to death. But Adam's disobedience was not confined to himself. Because he was our federal representative, we shared equally in his disobedience and consequent guilt. God justly imputed Adam's sin in breaking the terms of the covenant to the human race, which was in Adam and which consequently was involved in his sin. Through the disobedience of Adam, the entire race is justly considered guilty and is condemned before God (Rom. 5:17-19).

Therefore, all men are conceived in iniquity, born in sin, and naturally guilty.[5] The immediate results of Adam's first sin have persisted throughout his race: shame (Gen. 3:7), alienation from God (Gen. 3:8), guilt (Gen. 3:10), and the sentence of death (Gen. 3:19, 22).[6] Note that we are not responsible for any of Adam's subsequent sins, only the first sin that plunged humanity into guilt and spiritual death. Listen again to Paul: 'By one man sin entered into the world, and death by sin; and so death passed upon all men, for that all have sinned' (Rom. 5:12). That's pretty clear. From the very beginning of our existence, therefore, we needed a gospel.

Although our guilt in Adam may seem logically complicated and the implications of it unflattering, the biblical declarations of it are forthright. Consider the statements of the Westminster Larger Catechism, which remarkably abstracts the key points of Scripture:

> The covenant being made with Adam as a publick person, not for himself only, but for his posterity, all mankind descending from him by ordinary generation, sinned in him, and fell with him in that first transgression (Q. 22).

> The sinfulness of that estate whereinto man fell, consisteth in the guilt of Adam's first sin, the want of that righteousness wherein he was created, and the corruption of his nature, whereby he is utterly indisposed, disabled, and made opposite unto all that is spiritually good, and wholly inclined to all evil, and that continually; which is commonly called Original Sin, and from which do proceed all actual transgressions (Q. 25).

Dead in Person

Although we are guilty in Adam, we cannot blame Adam for our own spiritual lifelessness. Other than Jesus Christ, no man is personally exempt from guilt and corruption. There is not a just man on the earth (Eccles. 7:20). We have to face it: every man from the beginning of his physical life bears the defilement and guilt of sin. David confessed, 'Behold, I was shapen in iniquity; and in sin did my mother conceive me' (Ps. 51:5). When excoriating the people of Israel because of sin, the Lord declared, 'Thou ... wast called a transgressor from the womb' (Isa. 48:8). We are by nature children of wrath and children of disobedience (Eph. 2:2-3).

What the Scripture expressly asserts it also vividly illustrates. Two significant object lessons in the Old Testament dispensation depicted the natural corruption that coexisted with the beginning of life. Though the object lessons are no longer operative, the truth portrayed is still the truth. The first was the ceremony of

---

5. 'Original sin means that we are born with natures inclined to evil .... This truth can be proved by the sinfulness of our children from the most tender age .... Transgression and sin come naturally to our race without instruction' (Richard Phillips, *Ephesians*, A Mentor's Expository Commentary [Fearn, Scotland: Christian Focus Publications, 2016], p. 134).

6. 'We inherit the fallen nature of Adam by which we are spiritually separate from God and subject to the desires of the world and its way of thinking. In this natural condition we, "like the rest," are also subject to the wrath of God' (Bryan Chapell, *Ephesians*, Reformed Expository Commentary [Phillipsburg, N.J.: P&R, 2009], p. 80).

circumcision. Circumcision required the excision of the foreskin of the flesh, itself a symbol of sin and corruption. Significantly, the New Testament equates being dead in sins to the uncircumcision of the flesh (Col. 2:13). Although the significance of circumcision as a sign of the covenant has many important implications (see Gen. 17:10-14), at the very least the fact that it was performed on the infant suggests that the problem of sin is a problem from birth.

The second object lesson was one of the laws defining ceremonial cleanness and uncleanness. The overall purpose of these laws—dealing with everything from diet to household scum—was to teach the people that fellowship with God demanded purity and that sin precluded such fellowship. Interestingly, one of the natural circumstances of life that rendered a woman ceremonially unclean was childbirth (see Lev. 12). Children are without question a wonderful gift from the Lord, and having children is an occasion for happiness (Ps. 127). But regardless of how cute and cuddly a newborn child is, God wanted everyone to know that a child is born a sinner. Job's question and his own answer sum up the perpetual problem of 'man that is born of a woman .... Who can bring a clean thing out of an unclean? not one' (Job 14:1, 4).

Not only does the Bible make clear that man is a sinner from the start of life, but it also teaches that guilt and corruption infest man's innermost being. Not only are all men sinners, but all of man is sinful. Man is totally depraved. He is devoid of any good that can please God; he is without any spark that could possibly flame into spiritual life.[7] Sin is a matter of the heart: 'The heart is deceitful above all things, and desperately wicked' (Jer. 17:9). Jeremiah describes the heart as being a 'Jacob' (same basic word as deceitful) and completely malignant and pernicious. Throughout the Scripture, the heart designates the inner man – the mind, the emotions, and the will. The natural mind is incapable of understanding anything spiritual (1 Cor. 2:14) because the understanding is darkened (Eph. 4:18). The whole 'mind and conscience is defiled' (Titus 1:15). The natural affections are devoid of any love for God (John 5:42), being spiritually callous – past feeling (Eph. 4:19). The natural will deliberately chooses the way of death, rejecting the way of life (Prov. 8:36 – note that the words 'hate' and 'love' are primarily volitional rather than emotional terms).

Romans 3:11-18 is perhaps the most extensive catalog of man's sin nature in the New Testament. Note the following statements that particularly focus on the condition of the naturally depraved heart. First, that 'there is no fear of God before their eyes' (Rom. 3:18) suggests the depraved disposition of natural man. The sinner lives without an awareness of God that checks and restricts the evil passions. If Job's fear of God caused him to turn from evil (Job 1:1), it follows that without the fear of God, men turn to evil following a mindset that is hostile to God (Rom. 8:7). The

---

7. 'To say it is God's work is to say that the soul is passive, in a state of spiritual death, until the gift of regenerating grace is imparted by God' (Paul Helm, *The Beginnings: The Word and Spirit in Conversion* [Edinburgh: Banner of Truth, 1986], p. 15).

sinner lives without any holy motive or impulse. Second, that 'there is none that understandeth' (Rom. 3:11) suggests the imbecility of the depraved mind. In this total spiritual ignorance, even the beauty of Christ and the claims and offer of His gospel make no sense. Third, that 'there is none that seeketh after God' plots the course of the depraved will. Nowhere is the depravity of man more painfully vivid than in the exercise of the fallen will. The first act of Adam's fallen will was not to seek God but to hide from Him. That is always the direction taken by the sinner when following his natural inclinations. Those who are in the flesh can mind only the things of the flesh (Rom. 8:5). Similarly, Jeremiah described the cursed man as one 'whose heart departeth from the LORD' (Jer. 17:5). To have such a heart is death (Rom. 8:6).

Left alone, man is in serious trouble because he cannot resurrect himself from this spiritual death or cure himself from this spiritual depravity. As the Ethiopian (or anyone else for that matter) is incapable of changing his skin, and a leopard (or any other animal) is incapable of changing its appearance, so sinners, who are 'accustomed to do evil,' are unable to do anything that is good (Jer. 13:23).[8] 'They that are in the flesh cannot please God' (Rom. 8:8). Our total inability to change our nature is the inevitable corollary to our total depravity. Admitting and remembering our helpless estate puts the grace of the gospel in the right perspective.

Dead to Godliness

Man may be dead in trespasses and sins, but paradoxically, he is living in sin quite actively. Like spiritual zombies, sinners live unconscious of their death. The apostle Paul describes this zombie-like condition in Ephesians 2:1-3 when he details how the spiritually dead walk: 'You ... who were dead in trespasses and sins; wherein in time past ye walked according to the course of this world, according to the prince of the power of the air, the spirit that now worketh in the children of disobedience: among whom also we all had our conversation in times past in the lusts of our flesh, fulfilling the desires of the flesh and of the mind; and were by nature the children of wrath, even as others.'

The ideas of 'walking' and 'conversation' both imply the course, habits, and tendencies of life. The text identifies the three morbid guides that the spiritually dead follow. (1) They follow the world. This refers to that transient system that is inherently opposed to truth, righteousness and God. To follow this world and the spirit of this age is to be at enmity with God.[9] (2) They follow the devil. This

---

8. 'Even when we do the right thing morally, we do it for the wrong reasons – to justify ourselves and bring ourselves glory. This is one reason the Bible describes us as dead and not just sick (Eph. 2:1-3). Like a dead person, we are incapable of loving God for God's sake' (Michael Lawrence, *Conversion: How God Creates A People* [Wheaton, Ill.: Crossway, 2017], pp. 24-25).

9. 'Those without Christ are captive to the social and value system of the present evil age, which is hostile to Christ. They are willing slaves to the pop culture of the media, the "group think" of the talk shows, post-Christian mores, and man-centered religious fads. The spiritually dead are dominated by the world' (R. Kent Hughes, *Ephesians: The Mystery of the Body of Christ*, Preaching the Word [Wheaton, Ill.: Crossway, 1990], pp. 66-67).

accuser, tempter, corrupter, and arch-liar is at the head of the parade leading to eternal death. Elsewhere, the Bible calls him 'the god of this world' who blinds the eyes of unbelievers (2 Cor. 4:4) and holds them captive at his will (2 Tim. 2:26). (3) They follow the lusts of the flesh. Nature again rules. The bent of natural inclinations yields to the passions of sin, and the desires of the mind are inherently predisposed to evil. It would be impossible to list all the conceivable sins that man is capable of committing against God and His law that render him culpable before God and subject to the just penalty of the broken law. Some sins are outward acts; others are inward thoughts. Some sins are against fellow men; other sins are against self. Some sins are more heinous than others, but all sins are against God (Ps. 51:4).

This is the problem with having a rotten heart: out of the heart come all the issues of life (Prov. 4:23). Consequently, from the evil heart proceed all kinds of defilement (Matt. 15:19; Luke 6:45). The original sin that corrupts the heart always issues forth into actual sins. We do what we do because we are what we are. We don't necessarily do everything we are capable of doing in the sphere of sin, but the great pity is that we are capable of doing the worst.[10] In that catalog of sin in Romans 3, Paul's attention to man's depraved nature leads to his focus on man's depraved behavior. Since there is none righteous (Rom. 3:10), it follows that 'there is none that doeth good, no, not one' (Rom. 3:12). Read Romans 3:13-14 and see how the mouth mirrors the heart. From the abundance of the spiritually dead heart emanates untruthfulness, slander, and profanity. Romans 3:15-17 describe a lifestyle characterized by violence, ruin, distress, affliction, and wretchedness. Sin defiles everything. If we are left alone, it doesn't look good for us.[11]

THE SOLUTION

Man's sinful nature renders him incapable of holiness: he is spiritually dead. The only solution to spiritual death is spiritual life: a radical change is necessary. There is a striking parallel between the beginning of physical life and the beginning of spiritual life. Genesis 2:7 is a key text: 'And the Lord God formed man of the dust of the ground, and breathed into his nostrils the breath of life; and man became a living soul.' In the first creation, Adam had no physical life until he received the special breath of God. The molded dirt may have resembled Adam's eventual appearance, but it was just a lifeless sculpture until God breathed into it. As a lifeless shape, the first man could contribute nothing to his becoming alive. But when God breathed into the lifeless form, man came alive, and he lived as proof

---

10. R. Kent Hughes, *Ephesians*, p. 67: 'The Biblical doctrine of depravity means that every part of the human person is tainted by sin. It does not mean that all humans are equally depraved, for most do not go near the depths they could go. As John Gerstner says, there is always room for "deprovement."' See also Sinclair Ferguson, *Let's Study Ephesians* (Edinburgh: Banner of Truth, 2005), p. 41.

11. 'This is what Paul means when he says that we are *by nature children of wrath*. This phrase, like "sons of disobedience" (2:2), is a Hebrew way of saying "marked by", "characterized by", or "destined for" – in this instance "destined to experience the wrath of God". Wrath is the settled hostility of God's holy will towards everything that rebels against him' (Ferguson, *Let's Study Ephesians*, p. 42).

of his having received the principle of life. Apart from that special divine breath, Adam was insensitive to paradise.

Significantly, the Scripture refers to the beginning of spiritual life in terms of creation. 'Therefore if any man be in Christ, he is a new creature [creation]' (2 Cor. 5:17). 'For in Christ Jesus neither circumcision availeth any thing, nor uncircumcision, but a new creature' (Gal. 6:15). 'For we are his workmanship, created in Christ Jesus' (Eph. 2:10). In the initial process of natural creation, man was insensible to the physical world without the life-imparting breath of God; so in spiritual creation, man remains dead to anything spiritual without the life-imparting Spirit of God (see 1 Cor. 2:14). In a most tragic sense, every sinner is dead to paradise. Just as Adam required God's breath for physical life, every sinner requires a gracious and special intervention of God to bring him to spiritual life.[12] Consequently, the Scripture speaks of God's making dead sinners alive. 'But God, who is rich in mercy, for his great love wherewith he loved us, Even when we were dead in sins, hath quickened us [made us alive] together with Christ' (Eph. 2:4-5). 'And you, being dead in your sins and the uncircumcision of your flesh, hath he quickened [made alive] together with him' (Col. 2:13). That is radical.

The Definition of New Life

This component of the gospel that concerns the inception of spiritual life is *regeneration*. Regeneration refers to the implantation of the principle of spiritual life into the heart of the sinner that results in an instantaneous, radical, and obvious change of nature affecting the whole governing disposition of life.[13] The prophet Ezekiel explained regeneration in terms of God giving the sinner a new heart and a new spirit: 'A new heart also will I give you, and a new spirit will I put within you: and I will take away the stony heart out of your flesh, and I will give you a heart of flesh' (Ezek. 36:26). The heart, of course, refers to man's mind, emotions, and will. The spirit refers to the impulses that direct and regulate the desires, thoughts, and conduct of life. The prophet's description of the old heart as stony portrays an inward nature that is cold, unfeeling, and hard. A petrified heart is utterly dead, incapable of functioning. It is a graphic image of the helpless condition of the sinner, devoid of any spiritual life or responsiveness. In regeneration, God graciously turns the heart of stone into viable flesh that responds to spiritual stimuli. This regeneration creates a revolutionary change in the way the sinner thinks, what he desires, and how he chooses to live. He has a new nature that is capable of spiritual activity.

---

12. 'Here is the amazing truth of our spiritual re-creation. Just as God breathed into lifeless dust to give life to Adam, the Lord gives spiritual life to those who were spiritually dead. This God alone can do' (Chapell, *Ephesians*, p. 83).

13. 'Doubtless it is no outward, bodily alteration, but undoubtedly it is an entire alteration of the inner man. It adds no new faculties to a man's mind, but it certainly gives an entirely new bent and bias to all his old ones. His will is so new, his tastes so new, his opinions so new, his views of sin, the world, the Bible, and Christ so new, that he is to all intents and purposes a new man. The change seems to bring a new being into existence' (Ryle, *Regeneration*, p. 14).

One moment the sinner was dead; the next he is alive. Consequently, 'old things are passed away; behold, all things are become new' (2 Cor. 5:17).

Regeneration is the application of spiritual life that awakens the sinner from the stupor of spiritual death, enabling him to see, to understand, and to grasp Christ as He is offered freely in the gospel. The Westminster Standards define this regeneration in terms of effectual calling:

> Effectual calling is the work of God's almighty power and grace, whereby (out of his free and special love to his elect, and from nothing in them moving him thereunto) he doth, in his accepted time, invite and draw them to Jesus Christ, by his word and Spirit; savingly enlightening their minds, renewing and powerfully determining their wills, so as they (although in themselves dead in sin) are hereby made willing and able freely to answer his call, and to accept and embrace the grace offered and conveyed therein (Westminster Larger Catechism, Q. 67).

> Effectual calling is the work of God's Spirit, whereby, convincing us of our sin and misery, enlightening our minds in the knowledge of Christ, and renewing our wills, he doth persuade and enable us to embrace Jesus Christ, freely offered to us in the gospel (Westminster Shorter Catechism, Q. 31).

What God does so graciously and powerfully in this life-giving call to spiritual life is illustrated in Christ's raising from physical death Jairus's daughter and His friend Lazarus. As Christ stood over the dead girl, He simply said, 'Talitha cumi: which is being interpreted, Damsel, I say unto thee, arise' (Mark 5:41). At Christ's command, the girl immediately arose and walked (Mark 5:42). Having received life, she lived; she did not choose rather to stay dead. Standing outside the tomb of Lazarus, Jesus cried out, 'Lazarus, come forth' (John 11:43). At Christ's command, Lazarus immediately emerged from the tomb (John 11:44). Lazarus likewise did not reject Christ's command, choosing to stay dead; he exhibited all the vital signs of life. Something in Christ's call both instilled life and made living irresistible.

My point is that anyone else could have said 'Talitha cumi' all day long without any effect on the dead girl. Anyone else could have commanded the remains of Lazarus to come out of the grave without any effect whatsoever on the corpse. But in the command of Christ was the power to live. His call was effectual and irresistible.[14]

So it is every time God by His Spirit through His Word brings dead sinners to spiritual life. Whereas it was the power of the Living Word that gave life to the little girl and Lazarus, it is the written Word, the Spirit-used means of grace, that speaks the life-giving command to sinners (see 1 Pet. 1:23). Without that special and irresistibly effective application by the Spirit, we can command sinners all day long to live with the same ineffectiveness that we would have experienced standing outside the tomb of Lazarus. But when the Spirit of God implants the

---

14. 'Lazarus responded, but this was because Jesus gave him ears to hear, strength to move, breath to live, and the will to obey. Lazarus responded but Jesus was responsible for the new life, because Lazarus was dead .... Since we are spiritually dead prior to God giving us new life, the spiritual life we have must be his doing and is to his glory alone' (Chapell, *Ephesians*, p. 81).

principle of life within the soul, the regenerated soul will evidence all the vital signs of spiritual life.

Regeneration is good news for dead sinners. Without it, sinners remain spiritually lifeless and forever doomed. Man is in such a desperate condition that without a radical change of heart, he has no hope. His best efforts in reformation of character are folly and amount to nothing in the attainment of spiritual life.

The Exposition of New Life

The doctrine of regeneration directs us to our most fundamental and basic need. Being dead in our trespasses and sins means that more than anything else we need life, and God graciously according to 'his divine power hath given unto us all things that pertain unto life and godliness' (2 Pet. 1:3). Although the Scripture uses various images to describe the essence of regeneration – (e.g., circumcision (Deut. 30:6); resurrection (Eph. 2:5-6); creation (Eph. 2:10); spiritual baptism (1 Cor. 12:13); new covenant (Jer. 31:33) – perhaps the most expressive is that of the new birth (see John 1:12-13; Titus 3:5; 1 Pet. 1:3, 23; 1 John 5:4). Nowhere is the new birth defined in more detail and with more precision than in John 3 where the Lord Jesus explained to Nicodemus what it means to be born again.

Five important lessons summarize Christ's teaching about the new birth; these flow from two great statements of necessity: (1) you *must* be born again (John 3:7) and (2) the Son of man *must* be lifted up (John 3:14). These two necessities are inseparably linked – the possibility of the first depends on the performance of the second. Every other statement in this most famous of texts hinges on these two 'musts.' I want us to take our place in the night class along with Nicodemus and listen and learn from the Master Teacher as He explains these five principles of the new life that is provided in the gospel and required for entrance into the kingdom of heaven.

The Necessity of New Life

Christ makes it unmistakably clear that new life requires a new birth. As in the first birth a physical life issues from previous nonexistence, so in the second birth a formerly nonexistent spiritual life comes into being. Without a physical birth there is no physical life. Similarly, if there is no new birth, there is no salvation. The new birth, therefore, is not optional for spiritual life; it is necessary. Twice in this passage Jesus tells Nicodemus that being 'born again' is indispensable to salvation (John 3:3, 7). That Christ demands another birth to follow natural birth makes the Authorized Version's translation 'again' appropriate. However, the word translated 'again' also means 'from above.' This sense of the word is perhaps more pertinent to man's need because it calls special attention to the divine source of spiritual life which guarantees the necessary qualifications for entrance into the kingdom of God.[15]

---

15. 'This regeneration is *another*, a word that can mean "from above" or "again".... But what stands behind this expression? And to what kind of experience does it refer?... The focus here is not on the

The significance is that a new birth is necessary for salvation because the first birth does not produce the kind of life that is fit for God's kingdom. Christ's statement in John 3:6 is most telling: 'That which is born of the flesh is flesh.' This reveals the folly of Nicodemus's comment about entering as a grown man into his mother's womb to be born again (John 3:4). Even if that were possible, it would neither solve man's fundamental problem nor provide the necessary qualification for citizenship in God's kingdom. A second birth from his mother's womb would produce the same sinful and corrupt flesh as the first birth. The flesh can give birth only to more flesh: Kind propagates according to its kind.[16] Every man owns David's confession: 'Behold, I was shapen in iniquity; and in sin did my mother conceive me' (Ps. 51:5). Fallen sinful flesh is unfit for glory: 'So then they that are in the flesh cannot please God' (Rom. 8:8). Indeed, to live after the flesh leads inevitably to death (Rom. 8:13). Therefore, by Christ's definition, being born again is not just a fresh start or a second chance at life. It must be a birth of a completely different sort from the first birth. It must be a birth that changes the fleshly nature that is so naturally corrupt and bent against God. It is more than simply being born again; it must be being born from above. As we will see, 'That which is born of the Spirit is spirit' (John 3:6).

What Christ requires is a change of nature that affects the whole man. Although the new birth will reveal itself in moral reforms and character improvements, the transformation of life flows from a new nature that innately has new desires, impulses, and inclinations. The new birth is a change from the inside out that comes from above and enables holy living.

The Agent of New Life

The apostle John, in his opening discourse, explicitly identified God as the source of the birth of the sons of God, those who believe on His name: 'Which were born, not of blood, nor of the will of the flesh, nor of the will of man, but of God' (John 1:13). Likewise, Peter recognized the heavenly source of the new birth when he blessed 'the God and Father of our Lord Jesus Christ' who had 'begotten us again' (1 Pet. 1:3). Though not using the language of birth, Paul named the Holy Spirit as the agent of regeneration (Titus 3:5). All this accords with Christ's demand for a birth from above. That God the Father through the action of the Holy Spirit issues life to sinners, bringing them forth to spiritual life, highlights the absolute grace demonstrated in this component of the gospel. No man authored his own existence in the first birth, and no man can give life to his soul in the second birth. But what man cannot do for himself, God graciously

---

potential convert's humility, brokenness or faith, but on the need for *transformation*, for new life from another realm, for the intervention by the Spirit of God' (D. A. Carson, *The Gospel According to John* [Grand Rapids: Eerdmans, 1991], p. 190).

16. 'Like generates like. *Flesh gives birth to flesh* .... The point is that natural, human birth produces people who belong to the earthly family of humankind, but not to the children of God. Only *the Spirit gives birth to spirit*' (Carson, *The Gospel According to John*, p. 196).

does. In this text, the Lord Jesus isolated two essential truths about the new birth that feature the special operation of the Spirit.

First, Christ defined the spiritual character of the work. In John 3:5 He declared emphatically, 'Except a man be born of water and of the Spirit, he cannot enter into the kingdom of God.' The focus here is on the primary notion of being born 'from above.' The grammatical construction of verse 5 provides the best interpretation. The translation in the Authorized Version is quite literal, except that no definite article governs the word 'spirit.' The problem is not so much with the translation as with the common failure to recognize the figure of speech that Christ employed. The linking of 'water and spirit' is a literary device called *hendiadys*. This is itself a Greek word that means 'one through two.' It refers to the linking of two nouns by the conjunction 'and' to express one complex idea that would normally be expressed by an adjective modifying a noun. Being born 'of water and of spirit' refers, consequently, to *spiritual water*, which pertains ultimately to *spiritual cleansing*.[17]

By defining the new birth in terms of a necessary spiritual cleansing, Jesus links His exposition of regeneration to other Scripture. Ezekiel, immediately before citing the Lord's promise to give a new heart and new spirit (regeneration), communicated the Lord's promise that He would 'sprinkle clean water upon you' (Ezek. 36:25-26). Recognizing this obvious link to Ezekiel explains for us Christ's query to Nicodemus, 'Art thou a master [teacher] of Israel, and knowest not these things?' (John 3:10). I believe that Christ was simply asking Nicodemus if he had ever read Ezekiel 36. He should have known the theology of regeneration: it was Old Testament theology as well as New. Similarly, Paul spoke of the 'the washing of regeneration, and renewing of the Holy Ghost' (Titus 3:5). Thus, Christ is teaching that the new birth involves an inward cleansing from the filthiness and pollution that preclude entrance into heaven. Such a cleansing is spiritual work because man is absolutely incapable of cleansing himself (see Jer. 2:22).

Christ affirms the success of this spiritual cleansing: 'That which is born of the Spirit is spirit' (John 3:6). As certainly as flesh begets flesh, so the Spirit begets spirit. This certain offspring parallels Ezekiel's declaration that when God promises to sprinkle clean water on you, the certain consequence is that you will be clean (Ezek. 36:25). Because the source of the new birth is from above and because the agent of the new birth is the Holy Spirit, there is never a miscarriage. The new birth always works; it always fits the sinner for the kingdom.

Second, the new birth is a sovereign work. Life is mysterious. Its origin and perpetuation are beyond human comprehension. As inexplicable as natural life is, the mystery of spiritual life is infinitely more unfathomable. The application

---

17. 'In short, *born of water and spirit* ... signals a new begetting, a new birth that cleanses and renews, the eschatological cleansing and renewal promised by the Old Testament prophets' (Carson, *The Gospel According to John*, p. 195).

of the new birth by the Holy Spirit is the sovereign work of God.[18] Its execution is according to God's gracious good pleasure, and it defies human explanation. But we should not stumble over what we cannot explain. Although the mechanics and the administration of this gracious work may be mysterious, sovereign, and incomprehensible, its effects are always evident.

The Lord Jesus compared the efficacious operation of the Holy Spirit in the new birth to the blowing of the wind. 'The wind bloweth where it listeth, and thou hearest the sound thereof, but canst not tell whence it cometh, and whither it goeth: so is every one that is born of the Spirit' (John 3:8). This is a most vivid analogy because the Greek terms for 'wind' and 'spirit' are exactly the same word. We may not be able to control the wind's direction or force, but it always makes its presence known. To one degree or another, we can hear it and feel it.

So it is with the life-giving operation of the Holy Spirit. Why He moves as He does and where He moves is beyond our knowledge and beyond our control, but His movements are always discernible. The new birth is the consequence of the Spirit's breathing that cannot be hidden.[19] The hymn writer expressed well the theology of Christ's wind/spirit analogy: 'I know not how the Spirit moves, convincing men of sin, revealing Jesus through the Word, creating faith in Him.' But the evidence of that working is obvious: 'But I know whom I have believed, and am persuaded that He is able to keep that which I've committed unto Him against that day.'[20] The sovereign act of the new birth always issues forth in spiritual life that lays hold of Christ in faith. When we are born of the Spirit, we will know it.

The Provision for New Life

New life via new birth is necessary for all aspects of salvation, including sanctification. That is fact, but it is hardly good news. Commanding a dead man to live is futile: death cannot generate life. Spiritual life must come from above, not from within. The gospel, the good news, is that God has provided the means whereby dead, spiritually oblivious sinners can receive the life necessary for salvation. Grace provides what the requirement for life demands. Grace makes possible what is humanly impossible. In His discourse to Nicodemus, the Lord Jesus made two astounding statements concerning the provision of new life.

First, this provision is based in the love of God. The provision for new life, spiritual and eternal, flows from God's wondrous, incomprehensible, and mysterious love. Christ declared this amazing love in what is without doubt the most famous and most frequently quoted verse in the Bible: 'For God so loved the world, that

---

18. 'The wind does as it pleases. So does the Spirit. Its operation is sovereign, incomprehensible, and mysterious' (William Hendriksen, *The Gospel of John* [Edinburgh: Banner of Truth, 1959], p. 135).

19. 'We can neither control him nor understand him. But that does not mean we cannot witness his effects. Where the Spirit works, the effects are undeniable and unmistakable' (Carson, *The Gospel According to John*, p. 197).

20. *Trinity Hymnal: Revised Edition* (Philadelphia: Great Commission Publications, 1990), p. 705.

he gave his only begotten Son, that whosoever believeth in him should not perish, but have everlasting life' (John 3:16). Who in the world cannot find hope in this astounding declaration?

Although this wondrous statement can stand by itself in its unparalleled clarity, let me make some observations to put in boldface the full significance of the divine love that expressed itself in the giving of Christ and applies itself in the giving of new life. The word 'love,' of course, is that great New Testament word that finds its most expressive definition in God Himself, who is love (1 John 4:8). Love's stimulus is within God, who loves, and not in the world, which is loved. Humanly speaking, God's love for the world makes no sense, since the world consists of sinners who are repulsive and unworthy of love. Why God loves a world of sinners is answered only within the sovereign will and good pleasure of God.

The word 'so' in 'God so loved …' designates not the degree to which God loves but the way in which God demonstrated His love for the world. The two 'that' statements (different words in the Greek text) define the consequence and purpose of God's love. The *consequence* of the divine love is that He gave His own eternal Son. Because He loved, He gave. Although the world is filled with sinners who are unlovely, unresponsive, and ungrateful, yet for His own sake He loved them. Given that the supreme and eternal object of the Father's love is His only begotten Son (John 17:23-24), the sacrificial giving of the Son heightens the magnitude of God's love for the world. What an unspeakable gift to a lost and dying world (2 Cor. 9:15)! The *purpose* of His having given the Son is to rescue the perishing by providing the necessary new, spiritual, and everlasting life. Notice how the apostle Paul similarly and pointedly links God's love with the work of regeneration: 'But God, who is rich in mercy, for his great love wherewith he loved us, even when we were dead in sins, hath quickened us together with Christ' (Eph. 2:4-5).

God did not give His Son in vain; God's purpose always translates to reality. In His love God gave His Son to provide life for dead sinners, and Christ fulfilled that purpose. New life is in Christ, and being in Christ is the only way to know and experience God's love. The apostle John makes this point in what seems to be his inspired commentary on John 3:16: 'God hath given to us eternal life, and this life is in his Son. He that hath the Son hath life' (1 John 5:11-12). 'In this was manifested the love of God toward us, because that God sent his only begotten Son into the world, that we might live through him' (1 John 4:9). God's love is the sinner's only hope.

Second, this provision is purchased by Christ's atoning death. Although God's love is the basis of the sinner's hope, the sinner's salvation is that God's love moved Him to give Christ to die and thereby to purchase every element of salvation, including the new birth. 'Herein is love, not that we loved God, but that he loved us, and sent his Son to be the propitiation for our sins' (1 John 4:10). Again we see that no part of the gospel message is ever very far from the cross of Jesus Christ. Significantly, the Lord Jesus coupled 'ye must be born again' (John 3:7) with 'even so must the Son of man be lifted up' (John 3:14). The unfailing purpose of His being lifted up was that believers 'should not perish, but have eternal life' (John 3:15).

Christ compared His being lifted up on the cross with Moses' lifting up the serpent in the wilderness (see Num. 21:9). The parallels between that ancient action and Christ's eternally efficacious act are obvious and instructive. The only cure for those suffering the curse from the deadly venom of the fiery serpents was for them to look in faith to the emblem of the curse itself. The emblem of destruction was at the same time the emblem of healing. So the only remedy for those under the curse of sin is to look in faith to the cross work of Jesus. Christ purchased the remedy from the curse by becoming the curse: He who knew no sin became sin. Christ's being lifted up reveals and declares both the wrath of God in the condemnation of sinners and the love of God in the pardon of all those who believe. His death is the believer's life. His cross is the believer's title to God's kingdom. His being lifted up is the believer's ladder to heaven.

The 'must' of the new birth is possible because of the 'must' of the cross.[21] It is because God loved us and Christ died for us that the Holy Spirit imparts to us new life through the new birth. From plan to execution to application, salvation is of the Lord.

The Appropriation of New Life

Sinners appropriate new life by way of the new birth by means of faith. Throughout this discourse Christ limited the benefits of the new birth to those who believe. In the historic context of the Old Testament picture prophecy of Moses' lifting up the serpent, every Israelite who looked to the poled serpent was healed. So it is that whoever in the world looks to Christ is saved: 'Look unto me, and be ye saved, all the ends of the earth: for I am God, and there is none else' (Isa. 45:22). The Son of man had to be lifted up 'that whosoever believeth in him should not perish, but have everlasting life' (John 3:15). God so loved the world and gave His Son 'that whosoever believeth in him should not perish, but have everlasting life' (John 3:16). The infallible promise is that 'he that believeth on him is not condemned' (John 3:18).

Nothing apart from faith can secure interest in Christ and His atoning death. But this raises a serious question: How can a sinner who is dead in trespasses and sin—blind and insensitive to spiritual matters—exercise faith, which is obviously a spiritual act? Every orthodox theologian agrees that both faith and regeneration are necessary for the experience of new, spiritual life. Without the new birth there is no salvation; without faith there is no salvation. Some theologians argue that faith is the necessary prerequisite to the new birth – that faith precedes regeneration. Others argue that the new birth is the prerequisite to faith – that regeneration precedes faith.

---

21. 'The lifting up of the Son of man is presented as a "must." It is not *a* remedy; it is *the only possible* remedy for sin, for in this way only can the demands of God's holiness and righteousness—and love!—be met' (Hendriksen, *The Gospel of John*, pp. 138-39).

It is not my purpose in this practical exposition to defend or refute all the issues in this debate. However, it is impossible for me to say anything without revealing my interpretation. So let me quickly lay it on the table. I believe that biblically, theologically, logically, and temporally, regeneration precedes the exercise of faith. The new birth is the work of the Holy Spirit; saving faith is the evidence of the new life.[22] In regeneration, the Holy Spirit changes our nature and secures for us and in us the holy exercise of a new disposition, thereby enabling us and inciting within us the desire to repent from our sins and believe the gospel. Although the fact of the new birth precedes faith, the consciousness of the new birth follows faith. Awareness of life exists only after life. I know I was born naturally because I am now alive and do the stuff that living people do. I know I was born spiritually because I am now alive spiritually and do what spiritual people do – not the least of which is believing the gospel. Just as my breathing is the indication and not the cause of life, so my believing is the evidence of spiritual life, not the cause of it.

However, I must issue a word of caution and encourage us to stick to the language and logic of Scripture. In His conversation with Nicodemus, Christ did not make the new birth a matter of introspective speculation. While addressing the necessity of being born again, Christ focused on the evidence of new life and the necessity of belief. The commands of Scripture are always addressed to man's consciousness, to where he is. It is not for us to wonder whether God loved us and Christ died for us; it is for us to believe the gospel with the heart and confess with the mouth that Jesus is Lord (Rom. 10:9-10). Christ, the Living Word and the whole of the written Word, offers the gospel of new life to anyone in the world of sinners. The guarantee of the whole Scripture is that those who so believe are indeed born again. To be part of the 'whosoever' that believes and calls on the Lord for salvation is to be guaranteed the promised everlasting life. This ought to give us the assurance that saving faith is not self-generated, but it is rather the irrefutable evidence of the regenerating work of the Holy Spirit of God.

The Forfeiture of the New Life

Christ, having just announced God's gracious love in sending Him to die, declares just as emphatically that apart from Him, sinners will experience nothing of that divine love. Jesus concluded His lesson to Nicodemus about the new birth with a solemn warning to those who refuse to believe. Sinners forfeit life when they refuse to believe in Jesus Christ. Eternal destiny is defined and determined ultimately by one's relationship to the Lord Jesus Christ. He that is condemned is condemned 'because he hath not believed in the name of the only begotten Son of God'

---

22. 'It is important, however, to take note of the fact that Jesus mentions the necessity of regeneration before he speaks about faith. The work of God *within* the soul ever precedes the work of God in which the soul cooperates. And because faith is, accordingly, the gift of God, its fruit, everlasting life, is also God's gift. God gave his Son; he gives us the faith to embrace the Son; he gives us everlasting life as a reward for the exercise of this faith. To him be the glory forever and ever!' (Hendriksen, *The Gospel of John*, p. 142).

(John 3:18). It is that simple. What Christ said to Nicodemus in this text parallels closely what He said as the Wisdom of God: 'For whoso findeth me findeth life, and shall obtain favour of the LORD. But he that sinneth against me wrongeth his own soul: all they that hate [reject] me love [choose] death' (Prov. 8:35-36).

The Savior's condemnation of unbelievers emphasizes why the new birth is so essential.[23] The Lord's warning underscores the depth of spiritual death and blindness that keeps sinners willfully in darkness even in the presence of the light: 'And this is the condemnation, that light is come into the world, and men loved darkness rather than light, because their deeds were evil. For every one that doeth evil hateth the light, neither cometh to the light, lest his deeds should be reproved' (John 3:19-20). Man left to himself relentlessly follows his own natural inclinations and always chooses the way of darkness and death. Choosing the way of light and life, on the other hand, is the evidence of doing those things that are wrought by God (John 3:21).

The new birth cannot be experienced without faith in Jesus Christ. As we seek to understand and enjoy regeneration, we have to direct our thinking to Christ. As believers we ought to rejoice in the life that we have in, through, and because of Christ. We don't have to understand the mysterious mechanics of how the new birth operates or even be right in our understanding of the order of salvation, but we must understand that 'he that hath the Son hath life' (1 John 5:12). It doesn't matter what else we have or do not have; we must have Christ to have life. Heaven may be gained without money, education, fame, and many other things, but heaven cannot be gained without the new birth made possible by the atoning death of God's only begotten Son. Regeneration, like every other component of the gospel, exists only in terms of Christ.

Thanks to God's sovereignly gracious work of regeneration, those who have experienced the new birth are on the path to glorification. The new beginning leads to the perfect ending. The new nature is not in this life perfect, but it dies more and more to sin and lives more and more to righteousness with a new way of thinking, new affections and desires, and a new will that is bent toward God and holiness. The new birth is a prerequisite to obeying God's call to holiness.

---

23. 'The perishing of which this verse speaks indicates divine condemnation, complete and everlasting, so that one is banished from the presence of the God of love and dwells forever in the presence of the God of wrath' (Hendriksen, *The Gospel of John*, p. 141).

CHAPTER 11

CULTIVATING HOLINESS

THE godly farmer who plows his field, sows seed, fertilizes and cultivates, is acutely aware that, in the final analysis, he is utterly dependent on forces outside of himself for an assured crop. He knows he cannot cause the seed to germinate, the rain to fall, or the sun to shine. But he pursues his task with diligence, nonetheless, looking to God for blessing and knowing that if he does not fertilize and cultivate the sown seed, his crop will be meager at best.[1]

Similarly, the Christian life is like a garden that must be cultivated in order to produce the fruits of holy living unto God. 'Theology is the doctrine or teaching of living to God,' wrote William Ames in the opening words of his classic, *The Marrow of Theology*.[2] God Himself exhorts His children, 'Be ye holy; for I am holy' (1 Pet. 1:16). Paul instructs the Thessalonians, 'God hath not called us unto uncleanness, but unto holiness' (1 Thess. 4:7). And the author of Hebrews writes, 'Follow peace with all men, and holiness, without which no man shall see the Lord' (Heb. 12:14). The believer who does not diligently cultivate holiness will not have much genuine assurance of his own salvation (2 Pet. 1:10).[3] In this chapter I will focus on the Christian's scriptural call to cultivate Spirit-worked holiness by diligently using the means God has provided to assist him.

THE CALL TO CULTIVATE HOLINESS

Holiness is a noun that relates to the adjective *holy* and the verb *sanctify*, which means to 'make holy.'[4] In both biblical languages *holy* means separated and set apart for God. For the Christian, to be set apart means, negatively, to be separate from sin, and, positively, to be consecrated (i.e., dedicated) to God and conformed to Christ. There is no disparity between Old Testament and New Testament concepts of holiness, though the Old Testament stresses ritual and moral holiness; the

---

1. This chapter is a modified and updated version of chapter 18 in Joel R. Beeke's *Puritan Reformed Spirituality* (Darlington, England: Evangelical Press, 2006).

2. *The Marrow of Theology*, trans. and ed. John D. Eusden (1629; Boston: Pilgrim Press, 1968), p. 77.

3. Jerry Bridges, *The Pursuit of Holiness* (Colorado Springs: Navpress, 1978), pp. 13-14.

4. This is apparent from the Dutch word for sanctification, *heiligmaking* (literally: 'holy-making').

New Testament stresses inward and transforming holiness (Lev. 10:10-11; 19:2; Heb. 10:10; 1 Thess. 5:23).[5]

Scripture presents the essence of holiness primarily in relation to God. The focus of the sacred realm in Scripture is God Himself. God's holiness is the very essence of His being (Isa. 57:15);[6] it is the backdrop of all else the Bible declares about God. His justice is holy justice; His wisdom is holy wisdom; His power is holy power; His grace is holy grace. No other attribute of God is celebrated before the throne of heaven as is His holiness: 'Holy, holy, holy, is the LORD of hosts' (Isa. 6:3). 'Holy' is prefixed to God's name more than any other attribute.[7] Isaiah alone calls God the 'Holy One' twenty-six times. God's holiness, John Howe wrote, 'may be said to be a transcendental attribute that, as it were, runs through the rest, and casts lustre upon them. It is an attribute of attributes, ... and so it is the very lustre and glory of His other perfections.'[8] God manifests His majestic holiness in His works (Ps. 145:17), in His law (Ps. 19:8-9), and especially at the cross of Christ (Matt. 27:46). Holiness is His permanent crown, His glory, His beauty. It is 'more than a mere attribute of God,' says Jonathan Edwards, 'It is the sum of all His attributes, the outshining of all that God is.'[9]

God's holiness denotes two critical truths about Him: first, it conveys the 'separateness' of God from all His creation and His 'apartness' from all that is unclean or evil. God's holiness testifies of His purity, His absolute moral perfection or excellence, His separateness from all outside of Him, His complete absence of sin (Job 34:10; Isa. 5:16; 40:18; Hab. 1:13).[10]

Second, since God is holy and set apart from all sin, He is unapproachable by sinners apart from holy sacrifice (Lev. 17:11; Heb. 9:22). He cannot be the Holy One and remain indifferent to sin (Jer. 44:4); He must punish sin (Exod. 34:6-7). Since all mankind are sinners through both our tragic fall in Adam and our daily transgressions, God can never be appeased by our self-efforts. We creatures, once made after the image of our holy Creator, voluntarily chose in our covenant-head Adam to become unholy and unacceptable in the sight of our Creator. Atoning blood must be shed if remission of sin is to be granted (Heb. 9:22). Only the perfect, atoning obedience of a sufficient Mediator, the God-man Christ Jesus, can fulfill the demands of God's holiness on behalf of sinners (1 Tim. 2:5). And blessed be

---

5. Cf. Lawrence O. Richards, *Expository Dictionary of Bible Words* (Grand Rapids: Zondervan, 1985), pp. 339-40.

6. See especially Rudolf Otto, *The Idea of the Holy*, trans. J. W. Harvey (London: Oxford University Press, 1946).

7. Stephen Charnock, *The Existence and Attributes of God* (repr. Evansville, Ind.: Sovereign Grace, 1958), p. 449.

8. *The Works of the Rev. John Howe* (1848; repr. Ligonier, Penn.: Soli Deo Gloria, 1990), 2:59.

9. *The Works of Jonathan Edwards* (1834; repr. Edinburgh: Banner of Truth Trust, 1974), 1:101; cf. R. C. Sproul, *The Holiness of God* (Wheaton, Ill.: Tyndale House, 1985).

10. R. A. Finlayson, *The Holiness of God* (Glasgow: Pickering and Inglis, 1955), p. 4.

God, Christ agreed to accomplish that atonement by the initiation of His Father, and did accomplish it with His full approbation (Ps. 40:7-8; Mark 15:37-39). 'For he hath made him to be sin for us, who knew no sin; that we might be made the righteousness of God in him' (2 Cor. 5:21). As the Dutch Reformed Lord's Supper Form states, 'The wrath of God against sin is so great, that (rather than it should go unpunished) He hath punished the same in His beloved Son Jesus Christ with the bitter and shameful death of the cross.'[11]

By free grace, God regenerates sinners and causes them to believe in Christ alone as their righteousness and salvation. As Christ's disciples, we are made partakers of Christ's holiness by means of divine discipline (Heb. 12:10) and called by God to be more holy than we shall ever become by ourselves during this life (1 John 1:10).[12] He calls us to separate from sin and to consecrate and assimilate ourselves to Himself out of gratitude for His great salvation. These concepts— separation from sin, consecration to God, and conformity to Christ—make holiness comprehensive. Everything, Paul tells us in 1 Timothy 4:4-5, is to be sanctified, that is, to be made holy.

In the first place, personal holiness demands personal wholeness. God never calls us to give Him only a piece of our hearts. The call to holiness is a call for our entire heart: 'My son, give me thine heart' (Prov. 23:26).

Second, holiness of heart must be cultivated in every sphere of life: in privacy with God, in the confidentiality of our homes, in the competitiveness of our occupation, in the pleasures of social friendship, in relation with our unevangelized neighbors and the world's hungry and unemployed, as well as in Sunday worship. Horatius Bonar writes:

> Holiness ... extends to every part of our persons, fills up our being, spreads over our life, influences everything we are, or do, or think, or speak, or plan, small or great, outward or inward, negative or positive, our loving, our hating, our sorrowing, our rejoicing, our recreations, our business, our friendships, our relationships, our silence, our speech, our reading, our writing, our going out and our coming in – our whole man in every movement of spirit, soul, and body.[13]

The call to holiness is a daily task and encompasses a whole-life commitment to live 'God-ward' (2 Cor. 3:4), to be set apart to the lordship of Jesus Christ. As John Calvin put it, 'The entire life of all Christians must be an exercise in piety.'[14]

Thus, holiness must be inward, filling our entire heart, and outward, covering all of life. 'And the very God of peace sanctify you wholly; and I pray God your whole spirit and soul and body be preserved blameless unto the coming of our Lord Jesus

---

11. *The Psalter* (Grand Rapids: Eerdmans, 1991), p. 136.

12. Stephen C. Neill, *Christian Holiness* (Guildford, England: Lutterworth, 1960), p. 35.

13. Horatius Bonar, *God's Way of Holiness* (repr. Pensacola, Fla.: Mt. Zion Publications, 1994), p. 16.

14. Quoted in Donald G. Bloesch, *Essentials of Evangelical Theology* (New York: Harper & Row, 1979), 2:31.

Christ' (1 Thess. 5:23). 'Holiness,' Thomas Boston maintained, 'is a constellation of graces.'[15] In gratitude to God, a believer cultivates the fruits of holiness, such as meekness, gentleness, love, joy, peace, patience, kindness, goodness, mercy, contentment, gratitude, purity of heart, faithfulness, the fear of God, humility, spiritual-mindedness, self-control, and self-denial (Gal. 5:22-23).[16]

This call to holiness is not a call to merit acceptance with God. The New Testament declares that every believer is sanctified 'through the offering of the body of Jesus Christ once for all' (Heb. 10:10). Christ is our sanctification (1 Cor. 1:30); therefore, the church, as the bride of Christ, is sanctified (Eph. 5:25-26). The believer has a sanctified *status* before God, on account of Christ's perfect obedience which has fully satisfied the justice of God for all sin.

The believer's status, however, does not imply that he has arrived at a wholly sanctified *condition* (1 Cor. 1:2). The relationship between the believer's status and his condition before God was famously summed up by Luther's phrase, *simul justus et peccator* ('at once righteous and a sinner'). That is to say, the believer is both righteous in God's sight because of Christ and remains a sinner as measured by his own merits.[17] Though the believer's status from his regeneration onward makes an impact on his condition, he is never in a perfectly sanctified condition in this life. Paul prays that the Thessalonians may be sanctified wholly, something that still had to be accomplished (1 Thess. 5:23). Sanctification *received* is sanctification well and truly *begun*, though it is not yet sanctification *perfected*.

Holiness must be cultivated and pursued. Growth in holiness must and will follow regeneration (Eph. 1:4; Phil. 3:12). New Testament language stresses a vital, progressive sanctification in which the believer must strive for holiness (Heb. 12:14).

Thus, true believer, holiness is both something you have before God in Christ and something you must cultivate in the strength of Christ. Your status in holiness is conferred; your condition in holiness is to be pursued. Through Christ you are made holy in your standing before God, and through Christ you are called to reflect that standing by being holy in daily life. Your context of holiness is justification through Christ; and your route of holiness is to be crucified and resurrected with Him, which involves the continual 'mortification of the old, and the quickening of the new man' (Heidelberg Catechism, Q. 88). You are called to be *in life* what you already are *in principle* by grace.

---

15. Quoted in John Blanchard, *Gathered Gold* (Welwyn, England: Evangelical Press, 1984), p. 144.

16. Cf. George Bethune, *The Fruit of the Spirit* (1839; repr. Swengel, Penn.: Reiner, 1972); W. E. Sangster, *The Pure in Heart: A Study of Christian Sanctity* (London: Epworth Press, 1954); John W. Sanderson, *The Fruit of the Spirit* (Grand Rapids: Zondervan, 1972); Jerry Bridges, *The Practice of Holiness* (Colorado Springs: NavPress, 1983); Roger Roberts, *Holiness: Every Christian's Calling* (Nashville: Broadman Press, 1985).

17. Cf. Heidelberg Catechism, Question 1 (the believer's status) and Question 114 (the believer's condition).

What Must be Cultivated

Concretely, then, what must you cultivate? Three things:

1. Imitation of the Character of the Father

God says, 'Be ye holy; for I am holy' (1 Pet. 1:16). The holiness of God Himself ought to be our foremost stimulus to cultivate holy living. Seek to be like your heavenly Father in righteousness, holiness, and integrity. In the Spirit, strive to think God's thoughts after Him via His Word, to be of one mind with Him, to live and act as God Himself would have you do.[18] As Stephen Charnock concludes: 'This is the prime way of honouring God. We do not so glorify God by elevated admirations, or eloquent expressions, or pompous services for him, as when we aspire to a conversing with him with unstained spirits, and live *to* him in living *like* him.'[19]

2. Conformity to the Image of Christ

This is a favorite Pauline theme, of which one example must suffice: 'Let this mind be in you, which was also in Christ Jesus: who ... made himself of no reputation, and took upon him the form of a servant ... and ... humbled himself, and became obedient unto death, even the death of the cross' (Phil. 2:5-8). Christ was humble, willing to give up His rights in order to obey God and serve sinners. If you would be holy, Paul is saying, be like-minded.

Do not aim for conformity to Christ as a condition of salvation, but as a fruit of salvation received by faith. We must look to Christ for holiness, for He is both the fount and path of holiness. Seek no other path. Follow the advice of Augustine, that it is better to limp on the path than to run outside of it.[20] Do as Calvin taught: Set Christ before you as the mirror of sanctification, and seek grace to mirror Him in His image.[21] Ask in each situation encountered: 'What would Christ think, say, and do?' Then trust Him for holiness. He will not disappoint you (James 1:2-7).

There is unending room for growth in holiness because Jesus is the bottomless well of salvation. You cannot go to Him too much for holiness, for He is holiness *par excellence*. In fact, 'the pursuit of holiness is the pursuit of Christ.'[22] He lived holiness; He merited holiness; He sends His Spirit to apply holiness. 'Christ is all, and in all' (Col. 3:11) – including holiness. Christ in us (*Christus in nobis*)

---

18. A. W. Pink, *The Doctrine of Sanctification* (Swengel, Penn.: Bible Truth Depot, 1955), p. 25.

19. Charnock, *The Existence and Attributes of God*, p. 453.

20. Aurelius Augustine, *Against Two Letters of the Pelagians*, 3.5.14, in *A Select Library of the Nicene and Post-Nicene Fathers*, first series, ed. P. Schaff (repr. Grand Rapids: Eerdmans, 1982), 5:404.

21. John Calvin, *Institutes of the Christian Religion*, ed. John T. McNeill, trans. Ford Lewis Battles (Philadelphia: Westminster Press, 1960), 3.14.4ff.; cf. Thomas Goodwin, *The Works of Thomas Goodwin*, ed. John C. Miller (Edinburgh: James Nichol, 1864), 6:220.

22. Kevin DeYoung, *The Hole in our Holiness* (Wheaton, Ill.: Crossway, 2012), p. 98.

is an essential complement to Christ for us (*Christus pro nobis*).[23] As Luther profoundly set forth, 'We in Christ=justification; Christ in us=sanctification.'[24]

3. Submission to the Mind of the Holy Spirit

In Romans 8:6, Paul divides people into two categories – those who let themselves be controlled by their sinful natures (i.e., the carnally minded who follow fleshly desires) and those who follow after the Spirit (i.e., those who *mind* 'the things of the Spirit,' Rom. 8:5).

The Holy Spirit was sent to bring the believer's mind into submission to His mind (1 Cor. 2). He was given to make sinners holy. Let us beg for grace to increasingly bow as willing servants under His control more fully and more consistently.

How does the Spirit make us holy and work this holy grace of submission to His mind?

- He shows us our need for holiness through conviction of sin, righteousness, and judgment (John 16:8).

- He implants the desire for holiness. His saving work never leads to despair but always to sanctification in Christ.

- He grants Christlikeness in holiness. He works upon our whole nature, molding us after Christ's image.

- He provides strength to live a holy life by indwelling and influencing our soul. If we live by the Spirit, we will not gratify the desires of our sinful nature (Gal. 5:16); rather, we will live in obedience to and dependence on that Spirit.

- Through humble feeding on Scripture and the exercise of prayer, the Spirit teaches us His mind and establishes an ongoing realization that holiness remains essential to being worthy of God and His kingdom (1 Thess. 2:12; Eph. 4:1) and for fitness in His service (1 Cor. 9:24-25; Phil. 3:13).

Ephesians 5:18 says, 'Be not drunk with wine, wherein is excess; but be filled with the Spirit.' Thomas Watson writes: 'The Spirit stamps the impression of his own sanctity upon the heart, as the seal prints its likeness upon the wax. The Spirit of God in a man perfumes him with holiness, and makes his heart a map of heaven.'[25]

HOW TO CULTIVATE HOLINESS

It is clear that believers are called to holiness, but the cardinal question remains: How does the believer cultivate holiness? Here are seven directions to assist us.

---

23. Cf. Bonar, *God's Way of Holiness*, chapter 2.

24. Quoted in John Blanchard, *More Gathered Gold* (Welwyn, England: Evangelical Press, 1986), p. 147.

25. Thomas Watson, *A Body of Divinity* (1856; repr. Grand Rapids: Sovereign Grace Publishers, 1970), p. 173.

1. Know and love Scripture so as to grow in holiness

Scripture is God's primary road to holiness and to spiritual growth – the Spirit as Master Teacher, blessing the reading and searching of God's Word. Jesus prayed, 'Sanctify them through thy truth: thy word is truth' (John 17:17). And Peter advised, 'Desire the sincere milk of the word, that ye may grow thereby' (1 Pet. 2:2).

If you would not remain spiritually ignorant and impoverished, read through the Bible at least annually. More importantly, memorize the Scriptures (Ps. 119:11), search (John 5:39) and meditate upon them (Ps. 1:2), live and love them (Ps. 119; 19:10). Compare Scripture with Scripture; take time to study the Word. Let Proverbs 2:1-5 set your agenda for serious personal Bible study: receiving God's words (teachability), storing God's commandments (obedience), applying the heart (discipline), crying for knowledge (dependence), and searching for hidden treasure (perseverance).[26] Do not expect growth in holiness if you spend little time alone with God and do not take His Word seriously. Rather, 'Let the word of Christ dwell in you richly' (Col. 3:16), for 'we take hold of Christ as his words take hold of us.'[27] When plagued with a heart prone to be tempted away from holiness, let Scripture teach you how to live a holy life in an unholy world. Let Scripture be your compass to guide you in cultivating holiness, in making life's decisions, and in encountering the high waves of personal affliction.

2. Use the sacraments of baptism and the Lord's Supper diligently as means of grace to strengthen your faith in Christ

God's sacraments complement His Word. They point us away from ourselves. Each sign—the water, the bread, the wine—directs us to believe in Christ and His sacrifice on the cross. The sacraments are visible means through which He invisibly communes with us and we with Him. They are spurs to Christlikeness and therefore to holiness.

Grace received through the sacraments is not different from that received through the Word. Both convey the same Christ. But as Robert Bruce put it, 'While we do not get a better Christ in the sacraments than we do in the Word, there are times when we get Christ better.'[28]

Flee often to Christ by Word and sacrament. Faith in Christ is a powerful motivator for holiness, since faith and the love of sin cannot mix. Be careful, however, not to seek your holiness in your experiences of Christ, but in Christ Himself. As William Gurnall admonishes:

> When thou trustest in Christ *within* thee, instead of Christ *without* thee, thou settest Christ against Christ. The bride does well to esteem her husband's picture, but it were

---

26. Bridges, *Practice of Holiness*, p. 52.

27. DeYoung, *The Hole in our Holiness*, p. 131.

28. Robert Bruce, *The Mystery of the Lord's Supper*, trans. and ed. Thomas F. Torrance (Richmond: John Knox Press, 1958), p. 82.

ridiculous if she should love it better than himself, much more if she should go to it *rather than to him to supply her wants.* Yet thou actest thus when thou art more fond of Christ's image in thy soul than of him who painted it there.[29]

3. Regard yourself as dead to the dominion of sin and as alive to God in Christ (Rom. 6:11)

Dr Martyn Lloyd-Jones writes, 'I can say to myself that not only am I no longer under the dominion of sin, but I am under the dominion of another power that nothing can frustrate.'[30] Although sin no longer reigns over us as believers, we still have a duty actively to fight against sin. Bridges rightly admonishes us that it is disastrous 'to confuse the *potential* for resisting sin (which God provided) with the *responsibility* for resisting (which is ours).'[31]

Seek to cultivate a growing hatred of sin *as sin*, for God hates sin (Prov. 6:16-19; Ps. 5:5). When tempted, say with Joseph, 'How then can I do this great wickedness, and sin against God?' (Gen. 39:9). Look for heart-idols. Pray for strength to uproot them and cast them out. Attack all sin, all unrighteousness, and all devices of Satan.

Strive for daily repentance before God. Never rise above the publican's petition, 'God be merciful to me a sinner' (Luke 18:13). Remember Luther's advice to exercise 'lifelong repentance' before God.

Believe that Christ is mighty to preserve you alive by His Spirit. You live through union with Christ, therefore live unto His righteousness. His righteousness is greater than your unrighteousness. His Saviorhood is greater than your sinfulness. His Spirit is within you: 'Ye are of God, little children, and have overcome them: because greater is he that is in you, than he that is in the world' (1 John 4:4). Do not despair: you are strong in Him, alive in Him, and victorious in Him. Satan may win many skirmishes, but the war is yours, the victory is yours (1 Cor. 15:57; Rom. 8:37). In Christ, the optimism of divine grace reigns over the pessimism of human nature.

4. Pray and work in dependence upon God for holiness

No one but God is sufficient to bring a clean thing out of an unclean (Job 14:4). Hence, pray with David, 'Create in me a clean heart, O God' (Ps. 51:10). And as you pray, work.

The Heidelberg Catechism (Q. 116) teaches that prayer and work belong together. They are like two oars, which when both utilized, will keep a rowboat moving forward. If you use only one oar—if you pray without working or you work without praying—you will row in circles.

---

29. Quoted in Joel R. Beeke, *Holiness: God's Call to Sanctification* (Edinburgh: Banner of Truth Trust, 1994), pp. 18-19.

30. D. Martyn Lloyd-Jones, *Romans: An Exposition of Chapter 6 – The New Man* (Edinburgh: Banner of Truth Trust, 1972), p. 144.

31. Bridges, *Pursuit of Holiness*, p. 60.

Holiness and prayer are inseparable. Both are central to the Christian life and faith; they are obligatory, not optional. Both originate with God and focus upon Him. Both are activated, often simultaneously, by the Spirit of God. Neither can survive without the other. Both are learned by experience and through spiritual battles.[32] Neither is perfected in this life, but must be cultivated lifelong. Both are easier to talk and write about than to exercise. The most prayerful often feel themselves to be prayerless; the most holy often regard themselves as unholy.

Holiness and work are also inseparable, especially the work of nurturing and persevering in *personal discipline*. Discipline takes time and effort. Paul exhorted Timothy, 'Exercise thyself rather unto godliness' (1 Tim. 4:7). Holiness is not achieved sloppily or instantaneously.[33] Holiness is a call to a disciplined life; it cannot live out of what Dietrich Bonhoeffer called cheap grace – that is, grace which forgives without demanding repentance and obedience. Holiness lives out of costly grace – grace that cost God the blood of His Son, cost the Son His own life, and costs the believer daily mortification so that, with Paul, he dies daily (1 Cor. 15:31).[34] Gracious holiness calls for continual commitment, continual diligence, continual practice, and continual repentance.[35] 'If we sometimes through weakness fall into sin, we must not therefore despair of God's mercy, nor continue in sin, since ... we have an eternal covenant of grace with God' (*Baptism Form*).[36] Rather, resolve with Jonathan Edwards: 'Never to give over, nor in the least to slacken, my fight with my corruptions, however unsuccessful I may be.'[37]

These two things, *fighting against sin* and *lack of success*, appear contradictory but are not. Failing is not the same as becoming a failure. The believer recognizes he will often fail. Luther said that the righteous man feels himself more often to be 'a loser than a victor' in the struggle against sin, 'for the Lord lets him be tested and assailed to his utmost limits as gold is tested in a furnace.'[38] Nevertheless, the godly man will persevere even through his failures. Failure does not make him quit; it makes him repent the more earnestly and press on in the Spirit's strength. 'For a just man falleth seven times, and riseth up again: but the wicked shall fall into mischief' (Prov. 24:16). As John Owen wrote, 'God works in us and with us, not against us or without us; so that his assistance is an encouragement as to the facilitating of the work, and no occasion of neglect as to the work itself.'[39]

---

32. James I. Packer, *Rediscovering Holiness* (Ann Arbor: Servant, 1992), p. 15.

33. Cf. Jay Adams, *Godliness Through Discipline* (Grand Rapids: Baker, 1973), p. 3.

34. Dietrich Bonhoeffer, *The Cost of Discipleship*, trans. R. H. Fuller (London: SCM Press, 1959).

35. Bridges, *Practice of Holiness*, pp. 41-56.

36. *The Psalter*, p. 126.

37. For Edwards' seventy resolutions to promote holiness made at nineteen years of age, see *The Works of Jonathan Edwards*, 1:xx-xxii.

38. *Luther: Lectures on Romans*, trans. and ed. William Pauck (Philadelphia: Westminster Press, 1961), p. 189.

39. Owen, *Works*, 6:20.

Let us never forget that the God we love, loves holiness – hence the intensity of His fatherly, chastising discipline (Heb. 12:5-6, 10)! Perhaps William Gurnall says it best: 'God would not rub so hard if it were not to fetch out the dirt that is ingrained in our natures. God loves purity so well He had rather see a hole than a spot in his child's garments.'[40]

5. Flee worldliness

We must strike out against the first appearance of the pride of life, the lusts of the flesh and eye, and all forms of sinful worldliness as they knock on the door of our hearts and minds. If we open the door and allow them to roam about in our minds and take foothold in our lives, we are already their prey. 'Daniel purposed *in his heart* that he would not defile himself with the portion of the king's meat, nor with the wine which he drank: *therefore* he requested of the prince of the eunuchs that he might not defile himself' (Dan. 1:8; emphasis added).

The material we read, the recreation and entertainment we engage in, the music we listen to, the friendships we form, and the conversations we have all affect our minds and ought to be judged in the context of Philippians 4:8: Whatsoever things are true, honest, just, pure, lovely, and of good report, 'think on these things.' We must live *above* the world and not be *of* the world while yet *in* the world (Rom. 12:1-2). If you stand *on* the Word, you will not stand *with* the world.

6. Seek fellowship in the church; associate with mentors in holiness (Eph. 4:12-13; 1 Cor. 11:1)

The church ought to be a fellowship of mutual care and a community of prayer (1 Cor. 12:7; Acts 2:42). Converse and pray with fellow believers whose godly walk you admire (Col. 3:16). 'He that walketh with the wise shall be wise' (Prov. 13:20). Association promotes assimilation. A Christian life lived in isolation from other believers will be defective; usually such a believer will remain spiritually immature. We cannot have a *heavenly* fellowship if we promote a *hindering* fellowship.

Such conversation, however, ought not exclude the reading of godly treatises of former ages which promote holiness. Luther said that some of his best friends were dead ones. For example, he questioned if anyone could possess spiritual life who did not feel kinship with David pouring out his heart in the psalms. Read classics that speak out vehemently against sin. Let Thomas Watson be your mentor in *The Mischief of Sin*; John Owen, in *Temptation and Sin*; Jeremiah Burroughs, in *The Evil of Evils*; Ralph Venning, in *The Plague of Plagues*.[41] But also read J. C.

---

40. Quoted in I. D. E. Thomas, *The Golden Treasury of Puritan Quotations* (Chicago: Moody Press, 1975), p. 140.

41. Thomas Watson, *The Mischief of Sin* (1671; Pittsburgh: Soli Deo Gloria, 1994); John Owen, 'Temptation and Sin,' in *The Works of John Owen*, vol. 6 (1851; repr. London: Banner of Truth Trust, 1967); Jeremiah Burroughs, *The Evil of Evils; or The Exceeding Sinfulness of Sin* (1654; Pittsburgh: Soli Deo Gloria, 1992); Ralph Venning, *The Plague of Plagues* (1669; repr. London: Banner of Truth Trust, 1965).

Ryle's *Holiness*, Octavius Winslow's *Personal Declension and Revival of Religion in the Soul*, and John Flavel's *Keeping the Heart*.[42] Let these divines of former ages become your spiritual mentors and friends.

7. Live in a present-tense, total commitment to God

Form habits of holiness. Pursue harmony and symmetry in holy living. Root out all inconsistencies, by the grace of the Spirit, and enjoy godly activities. Be committed to not get dirty with this world's temptations and to remain clean by forgiveness from and consecration to your perfect Savior. Total commitment to God teaches us daily 'to educate, sensitize, and heed [our] consciences on all matters of divinely specified duty ... sanctify all relationships, handling them responsibly, benevolently, and creatively so as to please the God who calls for neighbor-love ... [and] delight in God and praise him joyfully at all times.'[43]

Don't fall prey to the 'just one-more-time' syndrome: postponed obedience is disobedience. Tomorrow's holiness is *today's* impurity. Tomorrow's faith is *today's* unbelief. Aim not to sin at all (1 John 2:1); ask for divine strength to bring every thought into captivity to Christ (2 Cor. 10:5), for Scripture indicates that our 'thought-lives' ultimately determine our character: 'For as he thinketh in his heart, so is he' (Prov. 23:7a). An old proverb says it this way:

> Sow a thought, reap an act;
> Sow an act, reap a habit;
> Sow a habit, reap a character;
> Sow a character, reap a destiny.

ENCOURAGEMENTS FOR CULTIVATING HOLINESS

The cultivation of holiness is demanding. Thomas Watson called it 'sweating work.' Happily, God provides us with several motives to holiness in His Word. To encourage us in the pursuit of holiness, we need to keep our eyes focused on the following biblical truths.

1. God has called you to holiness for your good and His glory

'For God hath not called us unto uncleanness, but unto holiness' (1 Thess. 4:7). Whatever God calls us to is necessary. His call itself, as well as the benefits which we experience from holy living as described below, should induce us to seek and practice holiness.

Holiness augments our spiritual well-being. God assures us that 'no good thing will he withhold from them that walk uprightly' (Ps. 84:11). 'What health is to the

---

42. John Charles Ryle, *Holiness: Its Nature, Hindrances, Difficulties, and Roots* (repr. Greensboro, N.C.: Homiletic Press, 1956); Octavius Winslow, *Personal Declension and Revival of Religion in the Soul* (1841; repr. London: Banner of Truth Trust, 1960); John Flavel, 'Keeping the Heart,' in *The Works of John Flavel*, 5:417-507 (1820; repr. London: Banner of Truth Trust, 1968).

43. J. I. Packer, *A Quest for Godliness: The Puritan Vision of the Christian Life* (Wheaton, Ill.: Crossway, 1990), p. 332.

heart,' John Flavel noted, 'that holiness is to the soul.'[44] In Richard Baxter's work on holiness, the very chapter titles are enlightening: 'Holiness is the only way of safety. Holiness is the only honest way. Holiness is the most gainful way. Holiness is the most honourable way. Holiness is the most pleasant way.'[45]

But most importantly, holiness glorifies the God you love (Isa. 43:21). As Thomas Brooks affirmed, 'Holiness makes most for God's honour.'[46]

2. Holiness makes you resemble God and preserves your integrity

Watson wrote: 'We must endeavour to be like God in sanctity. It is a clear glass in which we can see a face; it is a holy heart in which something of God can be seen.'[47] Christ serves here as a pattern of holiness for us – a pattern of holy humility (Phil. 2:5-13), holy compassion (Mark 1:41), holy forgiveness (Col. 3:13), holy unselfishness (Rom. 15:3), holy indignation against sin (Matt. 23), and holy prayer (Heb. 5:7). Cultivated holiness which resembles God and is patterned after Christ saves us from much hypocrisy and from resorting to a 'Sunday only' Christianity. It gives vitality, purpose, meaning, and direction to daily living.

3. Holiness gives evidence of your justification and election, and fosters assurance

Sanctification is the inevitable fruit of justification (1 Cor. 6:11). The two may be distinguished, but never separated; God Himself has married them. Justification is organically linked to sanctification; new birth infallibly issues in new life. The justified will walk in 'the King's highway of holiness.'[48] In and through Christ, justification gives God's child the *title* for heaven and the boldness to enter; sanctification gives him the *fitness* for heaven and the preparation necessary to enjoy it. Sanctification is the personal appropriation of the fruits of justification. B. B. Warfield notes, 'Sanctification is but the execution of the justifying decree. For it to fail would be for the acquitted person not to be released in accordance with his acquittal.'[49] Consequently, the justifying decree of Christ in John 8, 'Neither do I condemn thee,' is immediately followed by the call to holiness, 'Go, and sin no more' (v. 11).

Election is also inseparable from holiness: 'God hath from the beginning chosen you to salvation through sanctification of the Spirit' (2 Thess. 2:13). Sanctification

---

44. Blanchard, *Gathered Gold*, p. 144.

45. 'The Spiritual and Carnal Man Compared and Contrasted; or, The Absolute Necessity and Excellency of Holiness,' *The Select Practical Works of Richard Baxter* (Glasgow: Blackie & Son, 1840), pp. 115-291.

46. Blanchard, *More Gathered Gold*, p. 149.

47. Watson, *A Body of Divinity*, p. 172.

48. Owen, *Works*, 11:254ff.; Joel R. Beeke, *Jehovah Shepherding His Sheep* (Grand Rapids: Reformation Heritage Books, 1997), pp. 186-88.

49. B. B. Warfield, *Perfectionism* (Phillipsburg, N.J.: Presbyterian and Reformed, 1958), p. 100.

is the earmark of Christ's elect sheep. Election is always a comforting doctrine for the believer, for it explains the sure foundation of the grace of God working within him: sanctification visualizes election.[50]

While the believer receives comfort from election, Calvin insisted that the unbeliever is not called to consider it – rather, he is called to repentance. If we are discouraged by the doctrine of election, or we rely upon election without living a holy life, we fall prey to a satanic misuse of this precious, encouraging doctrine (cf. Deut. 29:29). As Ryle asserts, 'It is not given to us in this world to study the pages of the book of life, and see if our names are there. But if there is one thing clearly and plainly laid down about election, it is this – that elect men and women may be known and distinguished by holy lives.'[51] Holiness is the visible side of their salvation. 'Ye shall know them by their fruits' (Matt. 7:16).

Consequently, holiness fosters assurance (1 John 2:3; 3:19). 'Everyone may be assured in himself of his faith by the fruits thereof' (Heidelberg Catechism, Q. 86). Reformed divines agree that most of the forms and degrees of assurance that true believers experience—especially daily assurance—are reached gradually in the path of sanctification, through careful cultivation of God's word, the means of grace, and corresponding obedience.[52] An increasing hatred of sin, by means of mortification, and a growing love to obey God, by means of vivification, accompany the progress of our faith as it grows into assurance. Christ-centered, Spirit-worked holiness is the best and most sound evidence of divine sonship (Rom. 8:1-16).

The way to lose a daily sense of assurance is to forego the daily pursuit of holiness. Many believers live too carelessly, treating sin lightly or neglecting daily devotions and study of the Word. Others do not actively cultivate holiness, but assume the posture that nothing can be done to foster sanctification, as if holiness only 'happens' inside us on special occasions. To live carelessly or inactively is to ask for daily spiritual darkness, deadness, and fruitlessness.

4. As a believer, holiness purifies you for effective service to God

Conversely, 'unto them that are defiled is nothing pure' (Titus 1:15). We cannot exercise holiness if our hearts have not been fundamentally transformed through divine regeneration. Through the new birth, Satan is deposed, the law of God is written upon our hearts, Christ is crowned Lord and King, and we are made 'willing and ready, henceforth, to live unto Him' (Heidelberg Catechism, Q. 1). Through Christ, God sanctifies us and makes our prayers and thanksgivings

---

50. Cf. Walter Marshall, *The Gospel Mystery of Sanctification* (repr. Grand Rapids: Reformation Heritage Books, 2000), p. 220-21.

51. Ryle, *Holiness*, p. 27.

52. Joel R. Beeke, *Assurance of Faith: Calvin, English Puritanism, and the Dutch Second Reformation* (New York: Peter Lang, 1991), 160ff.; cf. Westminster Confession, Chapter 18, and the Canons of Dort, Head 5, for an appreciation of the intertwining of holiness and assurance.

acceptable. As Thomas Watson said: 'A holy heart is the altar which sanctifies the offering.'[53]

Paul joins sanctification and usefulness together: 'If a man therefore purge himself, he shall be a vessel unto honour, sanctified and meet for the master's use, and prepared unto every good work' (2 Tim. 2:21). God uses holiness to assist the preaching of the gospel and build up the credit of the Christian faith, which is dishonored by the carelessness of Christians and hypocrites who often serve as Satan's best allies.[54] Our lives are always doing good or harm; they are an open epistle for all to read (2 Cor. 3:2). Holy living preaches reality. It influences and impresses like nothing else can; no argument can match it. It displays the beauty of religion; it gives credibility to witness and to evangelism (Phil. 2:15).[55] 'Holiness,' writes Hugh Morgan, 'is the most effective way of influencing unconverted people and creating within them a willingness to listen to the preaching of the gospel' (Matt. 5:16; 1 Pet. 3:1-2).[56]

Holiness manifests itself in humility and reverence for God. Such are those whom God looks to and uses (Isa. 66:2). As Andrew Murray notes,

> The great test of whether the holiness we profess to seek or to attain is truth and life will be *whether it be manifest in the increasing humility it produces*. In the creature, humility is the one thing needed to allow God's holiness to dwell in him and shine through him. In Jesus, the holy one of God who makes us holy, a divine humility was the secret of his life and his death and his exaltation; the one infallible test of our holiness will be the humility before God and men which marks us. Humility is the bloom and the beauty of holiness.[57]

5. Holiness fits you for heaven (Rev. 21:27)

Hebrews 12:14 says, 'Follow [literally: *pursue*] ... holiness, without which no man shall see the Lord.' As John Owen wrote, it is foolish to think

> that persons not purified, not sanctified, not made holy in their life, should afterwards be taken into that state of blessedness which consists in the enjoyment of God. Neither can such persons enjoy God, nor would God be a reward to them. Holiness indeed is perfected in heaven: but the beginning of it is invariably confined to this world. God leads none to heaven but whom He sanctifies on the earth. This living Head will not admit of dead members.[58]

Holiness and worldliness, therefore, are antithetical to each other. If we are caught up with this world, we are not ready for the next.

---

53. Watson, *A Body of Divinity*, p. 167.

54. Ryle, *Holiness*, p. 62.

55. Leonard J. Coppes, *Are Five Points Enough? Ten Points of Calvinism* (Manassas, Va.: Reformation Educational Foundation, 1980), pp. 94-96.

56. Hugh D. Morgan, *The Holiness of God and of His People* (Bridgend, Wales: Evangelical Press of Wales, 1979), p. 9.

57. Andrew Murray, *Humility: The Beauty of Holiness* (Old Tappan, N.J.: Revell, n.d), p. 40.

58. Thomas, *Puritan Quotations*, p. 141.

OBSTACLES TO CULTIVATING HOLINESS

The cultivation of holiness will inevitably meet with numerous obstacles. Many things impede holiness. Five common problems against which we need to be on guard are these:

1. Our attitude to sin and life itself is prone to be more self-centered than God-centered

We are often more concerned about the consequences of sin or our victory over sin than about how our sins grieve God.[59] The cultivation of holiness necessitates hating sin as God hates sin. Holiness is not merely loving God and our neighbor; it also involves hatred. The hatred of sin is part of the essence of holiness. Those who love God hate sin (Ps. 97:10). We must cultivate an attitude that views sin as always being preeminently against God (Ps. 51:4).[60]

Low and distorted views of sin reap low and distorted views of holiness. 'Wrong views about holiness are generally traceable to wrong views about human corruption,' J. C. Ryle asserted. 'If a man does not realize the dangerous nature of his soul's diseases ... he is content with false or imperfect remedies.'[61] Cultivating holiness demands a rejection of the pride of life and the lusts of the flesh; it prays 'Give me the single eye, Thy Name to glorify' (Psalter 236, stanza 2). With eyes fixed on self rather than God's glory, we are more susceptible when 'the old nature presents something as being beneficial but conceals its sinfulness. It presents it as a necessity, as being delightful, as being advantageous, or as being honest .... and the old nature breaks through, one sin begetting another.'[62]

We fail when we do not consciously live with our priorities centered on God's word, will, and glory. In the words of the Scottish theologian, John Brown, 'Holiness does not consist in mystic speculations, enthusiastic fervours, or uncommanded austerities; it consists in thinking as God thinks, and willing as God wills.'[63]

2. Misunderstanding 'living by faith' (Gal. 2:20) to imply that no effort towards holiness is commanded of us hinders our progress

Bishop Ryle corrects the false idea that human effort sinful or 'fleshly':

> Is it wise to proclaim in so bald, naked, and unqualified a way as many do, that the holiness of converted people is by faith only, and not at all by personal exertion? ... I doubt it. That faith in Christ is the root of all holiness no well-instructed Christian will ever

---

59. Jerry Bridges, *Pursuit of Holiness*, p. 20.

60. William S. Plumer, *Psalms* (1867; repr. Edinburgh: Banner of Truth Trust, 1975), p. 557.

61. Ryle, *Holiness*, pp. 1-2.

62. Wilhelmus à Brakel, *The Christian's Reasonable Service*, ed. Joel R. Beeke, trans. Bartel Elshout (Grand Rapids: Reformation Heritage Books, 1994), 3:10.

63. John Brown, *Expository Discourses on 1 Peter* (1848; repr. Edinburgh: Banner of Truth Trust, 1978), 1:106.

think of denying. But surely the Scriptures teach us that in following holiness the true Christian needs personal exertion and work as well as faith.[64]

We are responsible for holiness. Whose fault is it but our own if we are not holy? As Ralph Erskine counsels, we need to implement the *fight-or-flight* attitude with regard to sinful temptations. Sometimes we simply need to heed Peter's plain injunction, 'Dearly beloved, I beseech you as strangers and pilgrims, abstain from fleshly lusts, which war against the soul' (1 Pet. 2:11). Often it is as simple as this – *Abstain!*

If you have put off the old man and put on the new (Eph. 4:22-32), live accordingly (Col. 3:9-10) – not as a form of legalism, but as a repercussion of divine blessing (Col. 2:9-23).[65] Make a covenant with your eyes and feet and hands to turn from iniquity (Job 31:1). Look the other way; walk the other way. Put away uncontrolled anger, gossip, and bitterness. Put sin to death (Rom. 8:13) by the blood of Christ. 'Set faith at work on Christ for the killing of thy sin,' wrote Owen, 'and thou wilt ... live to see thy lust dead at thy feet.'[66]

3. On the other hand, taking pride in our holiness and thinking we can somehow produce holiness apart from faith hinders our progress

From beginning to end holiness is the work of God and His free grace (Westminster Confession of Faith, Chapter 13). As Richard Sibbes maintained, 'By grace we are what we are in justification, and work what we work in sanctification.'[67] Holiness is not partially God's work and partially our work. Holiness manufactured *by our heart* is not holiness *after God's heart*. All working out of the Christian life on our part is the fruit of God working in us and through us: 'Work out your own salvation with fear and trembling, for it is God which worketh in you both to will and to do of his good pleasure' (Phil. 2:12-13). 'The regenerate have a spiritual nature within that fits them for holy action, otherwise there would be no difference between them and the unregenerate,' wrote A. W. Pink.[68] Nevertheless, self-sanctification, strictly speaking, is non-existent.[69] 'We do good works, but not to merit by them (for what can we merit?), nay, we are beholden to God for the good works we do, and not He to us' (Belgic Confession of Faith, Article 24). As Calvin explained, 'Holiness is not a merit by which we can attain communion with God, but a gift of Christ which enables us to cling to him and to follow him.'[70] John Murray put it this way: 'God's working in us is not suspended because we work, nor our working

---

64. Ryle, *Holiness*, p. viii.

65. Sinclair Ferguson, 'The Reformed View,' in *Christian Spirituality: Five Views of Sanctification*, ed. Donald L. Alexander (Downers Grove, Ill.: InterVarsity Press, 1988), p. 64.

66. Owen, *Works*, 6:79.

67. Blanchard, *More Gathered Gold*, p. 152.

68. Blanchard, *More Gathered Gold*, p. 149.

69. Peter Toon, *Justification and Sanctification* (Westchester, Ill.: Crossway, 1983), p. 40.

70. Blanchard, *More Gathered Gold*, p. 148.

suspended because God works. Neither is the relation strictly one of cooperation as if God did his part and we did ours ....God works in us and we also work. But the relation is that *because* God works we work.'[71]

> *And every virtue we possess,*
> *And every conquest won,*
> *And every thought of holiness,*
> *Are His alone.*

Kenneth Prior warns: 'There is a subtle danger of speaking of sanctification as essentially coming from our own effort or initiative. We can unconsciously do this even while acknowledging our need for the power of the Holy Spirit, by making the operation of that power dependent upon our surrender and consecration.'[72]

Our dependence on God for holiness ought to humble us. Holiness and humility are inseparable,[73] and neither one recognizes itself. The most holy complain of their impurity; the most humble, of their pride. Those of us who are called to be teachers and examples of holiness must beware of the subtle and insidious pride working its way into our supposed holiness.

Wrong views of how holiness relates to humility greatly hinders our holiness:

- As soon as we think, speak, or act as if our own holiness is somehow sufficient without being clothed with Christ's humility, we are already enveloped by spiritual pride.

- When we begin to feel complacent about our holiness, we are far from both holiness and humility.

- When self-abasement is lacking, holiness is lacking.

- When self-abasement does not make us to flee to Christ and His holiness for refuge, holiness is lacking.

- Without a life dependent on Christ, we shall possess no holiness.

4. Embracing unscriptural, erroneous views about holiness can greatly impede our holiness

Many erroneous interpretations of Scripture can skew a proper understanding of biblical holiness in our personal lives. Allow me briefly to address a few of these errors. The first error held by many is the need to experience 'the second blessing,' an earnest search for our own special gift of the Spirit. However, it is not just *the* second blessing that the believer needs, but he needs *a* second blessing, as well as a

---

71. John Murray, *Redemption Accomplished and Applied* (Grand Rapids: Eerdmans, 1955), pp. 184-85.

72. Kenneth Prior, *The Way of Holiness: A Study in Christian Growth* (Downers Grove, Ill.: InterVarsity Press, 1982), p. 42.

73. Cf. G. C. Berkouwer, *Faith and Sanctification*, trans. John Vriend (Grand Rapids: Eerdmans, 1952), chapter 6.

third and fourth and fifth – yes, he needs the continual blessing of the Holy Spirit in order to progress in holiness so that Christ may increase and that the believer may decrease (John 3:30).

A second error is making the exercise of charismatic gifts prerequisites for holiness, such as speaking in tongues or faith healing. Contrary to this, John Stott wisely comments that 'when Paul wrote to the Corinthians that they were not lacking in spiritual gifts (1 Cor. 1:7), he makes it clear that the evidence of the Spirit's fullness is not the exercise of His gifts (of which they had plenty), but the ripening of His fruit (of which they had little).'[74]

Finally, there is the error of accepting Jesus as Savior and not as Lord. The Heidelberg Catechism provides a summary corrective to the practice of separating the Savior from His lordship: 'One of these two things must be true, that either Jesus is not a complete Savior or that they, who by a true faith receive this Savior, must find all things in Him necessary to their salvation' (Q. 30).

5. We are prone to shirk the battle of daily spiritual warfare

No one likes war. The believer is often blind to his own real enemies – to a subtle Satan, to a tempting world, and especially to the reality of his own ongoing pollution which Paul so poignantly expresses in Romans 7:14-25. To be holy among the holy takes grace; to be holy among the unholy takes great grace. Maintaining personal holiness in an unholy world with a heart prone to backsliding necessitates a perpetual fight. It will involve conflict, holy warfare, struggle against Satan, and a battle between the flesh and the spirit (Gal. 5:17). A believer not only has peace of conscience, but also war within (Rom. 7:24–8:1). As Samuel Rutherford asserts, 'The devil's war is better than the devil's peace.'[75] Hence the remedies of Christ's holiness (Heb. 7:25-28) and of His Spirit-supplied Christian armor (Eph. 6:10-20) are ignored at our peril. True holiness must be pursued with an acute awareness of indwelling sin which continues to live in our hearts and to deceive our understanding. The holy man, unlike others, is never at peace with indwelling sin. Though he may backslide far, he will again be humbled and ashamed because of his sin.

THE JOY OF HOLINESS CULTIVATED

A holy life ought to be one of joy in the Lord, not negative drudgery (Neh. 8:10). We distort scripture by assuming that holiness requires a gloomy disposition. Jesus said, 'If ye keep my commandments, ye shall abide in my love; … These things have I spoken unto you, that my joy might remain in you, and that your joy might be full' (John 15:10-11). Those who are obedient—who are pursuing holiness as a way of life—will know that the joy which flows from communion with God is a supreme joy, an ongoing joy, and an anticipated joy.

---

74. John Stott, *The Baptism and Fullness of the Holy Spirit*, 2nd ed. (Downers Grove, Ill.: InterVarsity Press, 1975), p. 50.

75. Samuel Rutherford, *The Trial and Triumph of Faith* (Edinburgh: William Collins, 1845), p. 403.

1. The supreme joy: fellowship with God

No greater joy can be had than that of communion with God. 'In thy presence is fulness of joy' (Ps. 16:11). True joy springs from God enabling us to walk in fellowship with Him. When we break our fellowship with God by sin, we need to return, like David, with penitential prayer to Him: 'Restore unto me the joy of thy salvation' (Ps. 51:12). The words Jesus spoke to the thief on the cross represent the chief delight of every child of God: 'To day shalt thou be with me in paradise' (Luke 23:43).

2. The ongoing joy: abiding trust

True holiness obeys God, and obedience always trusts God. It believes, 'that all things work together for good to them that love God' (Rom. 8:28) – even when it cannot be seen. Like faithful workers on a Persian carpet, who blindly hand up all colors of strand to the overseer working out the pattern above them, God's intimate saints are those who hand Him even the black strands He calls for, knowing that His pattern will be perfect from above, notwithstanding the gnarled mess underneath. Do you too know this profound, childlike trust in believing the words of Jesus: 'What I do thou knowest not now: but thou shalt know hereafter' (John 13:7)? Such ongoing, stabilizing joy surpasses understanding. Holiness reaps joyous contentment; and 'godliness with contentment is great gain' (1 Tim. 6:6).

3. The anticipated joy: eternal, gracious reward

Jesus was motivated to endure His sufferings by anticipating the joy of His reward (Heb. 12:1-2). Believers too may look forward to entering into the joy of their Lord as they pursue lifelong holiness in the strength of Christ. By grace, they may joyously anticipate their eternal reward: 'Well done, thou good and faithful servant .... Enter thou into the joy of thy Lord' (Matt. 25:21, 23). As John Whitlock noted: 'Here is the Christian's way and his end – his way is holiness, his end, happiness.'[76]

Holiness is its own reward, for everlasting glory is holiness perfected. 'The souls of believers are at their death made perfect in holiness' (Westminster Shorter Catechism, Question 37). Also their bodies shall be raised immortal and incorruptible, perfect in holiness, complete in glorification (1 Cor. 15:49, 53). Finally the believer shall become what he has desired to be ever since his regeneration – perfectly holy in a triune God. He shall enter into the eternal glory of Jesus Christ as a son of God and fellow-heir with Him (Phil. 3:20-21; Rom. 8:17). He shall finally be like Christ, holy and without blemish (Eph. 5:25-27), eternally magnifying and exalting the unfathomable bounties of God's sovereign grace. Truly, as Calvin stated, 'the thought of the great nobility God has conferred upon us ought to whet our desire for holiness.'[77]

---

76. Thomas, *Puritan Quotations*, p. 140.

77. Blanchard, *More Gathered Gold*, p. 153.

Concluding Application

I once read of a missionary who had in his garden a shrub that bore poisonous leaves. At that time, he had a child who was prone to put anything within reach into his mouth. Naturally, he dug the shrub out and threw it away. The shrub's roots, however, went very deep. Soon the shrub sprouted again. Repeatedly, the missionary had to dig it out. There was no solution but to inspect the ground every day and to dig up the shrub every time it surfaced. Indwelling sin is like that shrub. It needs constant uprooting. Our hearts need continual mortification. As John Owen warns us:

> We must be exercising [mortification] every day, and in every duty. Sin will not die, unless it be constantly weakened. Spare it, and it will heal its wounds, and recover its strength. We must continually watch against the operations of this principle of sin: in our duties, in our calling, in conversation, in retirement, in our straits, in our enjoyments, and in all that we do. If we are negligent on any occasion, we shall suffer by it; every mistake, every neglect is perilous.[78]

Press on in the uprooting of sin and the cultivation of holiness. Continue to fight the good fight of faith under the best of generals, *Jesus Christ*; with the best of internal advocates, *the Holy Spirit*; by the best of assurances, *the promises of God*; for the best of results, *everlasting glory*.

Have you been persuaded that cultivating holiness is worth the price of saying 'no' to sin and 'yes' to God? Do you know the joy of walking in God's ways? The joy of experiencing Jesus' easy yoke and light burden? The joy of not belonging to yourself, but belonging to your 'faithful Savior Jesus Christ,' who makes you 'sincerely willing and ready, henceforth, to live unto Him' (Heidelberg Catechism, Question 1)? Are you holy? Thomas Brooks gives us sixteen marks of 'how we shall know whether we have real holiness'; here are several of them: The holy believer 'admires the holiness of God, ... possesses diffusive holiness that spreads itself over head and heart, lip and life, inside and outside, ... stretches himself after higher degrees of holiness, ... hates and detests all ungodliness and wickedness, ... grieves over his own vileness and unholiness.'[79] It is a daunting list, yet a biblical one. No doubt we all fall far short, but the question remains: Are we striving for these marks of holiness?

Perhaps you respond, 'Who is sufficient for these things' (2 Cor. 2:16)? Paul's ready answer is, 'Not that we are sufficient of ourselves to think any thing as of ourselves; but our sufficiency is of God' (2 Cor. 3:5). 'Would you be holy? ... Then you must *begin with Christ* .... Would you continue holy? Then *abide in Christ*.'[80]

---

78. Owen, *Works*, 3:310.

79. 'The Crown and Glory of Christianity: or Holiness, The Only Way to Happiness,' in *The Works of Thomas Brooks* (1864; repr. Edinburgh: Banner of Truth Trust, 1980), 4:103-50. I have summarized Brooks' marks. His entire treatise on holiness (446 pages) is an invaluable classic, but has been strangely neglected in contemporary studies on holiness.

80. Ryle, *Holiness*, pp. 71-72.

'Holiness is not the way to Christ; Christ is the way of holiness.'[81] Outside of Christ there is no holiness; without Him, every list of marks of holiness must condemn us. Ultimately, of course, holiness is not a list; it is much more – it is a life, a life in Jesus Christ.

Holiness in believers proves that they are joined to Christ, for sanctified obedience is impossible without Him. But in Christ, the call to holiness remains within the context of *sola gratia* (grace alone) and *sola fide* (faith alone).[82] 'If thou, LORD, shouldest mark iniquities, O Lord, who shall stand? But there is forgiveness with thee, that thou mayest be feared' (Ps. 130:3-4).

'Since Christ cannot be known apart from the sanctification of the Spirit,' Calvin writes, 'it follows that faith can in no wise be separated from a devout disposition.'[83] Christ, the Holy Spirit, the Word of God, holiness, grace, and faith are inseparable. Make it your prayer: 'Lord, grant that I might cultivate holiness today – not out of merit, but out of gratitude, by Thy grace through faith in Christ Jesus. Sanctify me by the blood of Christ, the Spirit of Christ, and the Word of God.' Pray with Robert Murray M'Cheyne, 'Lord, make me as holy as a pardoned sinner can be.'[84]

---

81. Blanchard, *Gathered Gold*, p. 146.

82. Cf. Berkouwer, *Faith and Sanctification*, chapter 2.

83. Calvin, *Institutes*, 3.2.8.

84. Blanchard, *Gathered Gold*, p. 146.

CHAPTER 12

DEAD AND ALIVE: KILLING THE OLD MAN AND ANIMATING THE NEW MAN

(COLOSSIANS 3:1-17)

'WANTED: Dead or Alive.' These words may well apply to the FBI's most wanted list and indicate that either of these mutually exclusive conditions will satisfy justice. Such a wanted poster would be appropriate in the Post Office or Law Enforcement stations, but not so in the church. On the contrary, the poster in the Church would more appropriately read, 'Wanted: Dead *and* Alive.' Conditions which are mutually exclusive physically must coexist spiritually. Remember from the exposition of Romans 6 that believers are 'dead indeed unto sin, but alive unto God through Jesus Christ our Lord' (Rom. 6:11). Sanctification is the process whereby these two conditions of death and life become experience. Significantly, the definition of sanctification in the Westminster Shorter Catechism (Q. 35) highlights these two components: dying to sin and living unto righteousness.

Dying and living are paradoxical. But in reality, that which seems to be self-contradictory is only apparently so. The combination of killing and animating is essential to an effective response to and practice of God's radical and comprehensive call to holiness. Perhaps one of the clearest and most comprehensive passages in the New Testament that develop this dual activity of sanctification is Colossians 3:1-17. It is a text that in typical biblical logic links position with experience, thinking with doing. Here Paul makes it clear again that the gospel contains a dynamic to energize and guide the Christian life along the proper paths.[1] The apostle looks at the Christian's life from the inside and outside, proving, as he so often does in his epistles, that deep theology must translate into the practices of life. Two broad concerns elaborate his argument: the principle of death/life and the practice of killing/animating.

---

1. 'What God has done for his people in Christ is the grand argument and incentive for Christian living .... It is because believers have died with Christ and been raised to new life with him that their conduct is henceforth to be different' (F. F. Bruce, *The Epistles to the Colossians, to Philemon, and to the Ephesians,* The New International Commentary on the New Testament [Grand Rapids: Eerdmans, 1988], p. 134).

THE PRINCIPLE OF DEATH AND LIFE

In the opening four verses, Paul expounds the theology that is essential and foundational to both spiritual life and godly living. He draws our attention to the objective realities of the believer's union with Christ with all of its representative, vital, intimate, and mystical significance. This union is equally true for every genuine believer in Jesus Christ, but is not equally enjoyed or consciously experienced by all. Hence, Paul directs us how to think in light of the facts. Three thoughts stand out about the believer's hidden life.

1. The Fact of the Hidden Life

Colossians 3:3 declares the proposition: 'For ye are dead, and your life is hid with Christ in God.' This is an indisputable fact. The text more literally reads, 'you died.' Since he is writing to those who were very much alive physically, this past death refers to something spiritual, or dare I say, mystical. Theologically, this refers to spiritual truth that surpasses human comprehension because of the transcendence of its nature and significance. It is a most appropriate word to designate the believer's union with Jesus Christ, a truth that notwithstanding its reality defies explanation.[2] The statement 'you died' takes us to that mysterious and mystical union of every believer with Jesus Christ in His death on the cross. There is a sense, though incomprehensible, in which every believer jointly participates and shares in the work of the Lord Jesus. This staggers the mind. Consider these astounding statements that declare the believer's communion with the death of Christ. 'I am crucified with Christ' (Gal. 2:20). 'We are buried with him by baptism into death' (Rom. 6:4; Col. 2:12). 'Our old man is crucified with him' (Rom. 6:6). 'If one died for all, then were all dead' (i.e. all for whom He died, died, 2 Cor. 5:14). Obviously, we did not hang on the cross along with Christ to suffer all the physical agony and torment that He endured in both body and soul. In the physical sense, Christ suffered and died alone as the substitute for His people. He bore our penalty and exempted us from ever having to pay the penalty of our sin. He is our Federal or Representative Head who stands in our place, and we were, thus, united to Him. When Christ died, all of His people died with Him. God regarded believers— His elect and Christ's inheritance—as being in His Son. We considered these remarkable truths in our earlier discussion regarding the experience of union with Christ. Pardon any repetition, but it is vital to learn that all these gospel truths are interrelated and inseparably linked.

It is on the cross where satisfaction against our sin was secured, where the connection to sin was severed. Being crucified with Christ means that we should

---

2. 'The new age of God's kingdom has begun, in the death and resurrection of Jesus. And you, who have come to trust him, have been so united to him that you *died with him* and you were *raised with him*' (John Woodhouse, *Colossians and Philemon*, Focus on the Bible [Fearn, Ross-shire: Christian Focus, 2011], p. 180).

look down on sin and the old life from that vantage point. Sin that seems so alluring when in our face loses its appeal when viewed from the old rugged cross.

Ironically, although we died, our life has been hidden with Christ in God. This mystical death did not produce a lifeless corpse. On the contrary, union with His death always includes union with His resurrection and life. Consider Colossians 3:1 that assumes the fact that believers were raised with Christ. Community with His death always includes community with His life. Significantly, Paul uses a different verb form to express the hidden life. Whereas we died once for all, the form of the verb 'hid' addresses both the past act of being hidden and its continuing consequences. When we died with Christ, we were at that very time hidden in Christ, and there we constantly remain. Given where Christ is, sitting at the right hand of God (Col. 3:1), this is all the more remarkable. He's in heaven; we're in heaven in Him. By faith we must know and reckon for ourselves that we are in Him.[3] The implications and applications of this throne-union are far-reaching, both regarding our security with God and our duty in the world.[4] The world can't see us there (after all, we're hidden), but God does, since all things are open before His eyes. The head-body analogy is one way that Paul describes union with Christ (Col. 1:18). It is our security that God sees the body through the Head; it is our duty that the world sees the Head through the body. It is sobering to realize that the world's estimation of the Head is so often determined by what they perceive about the body. Realizing this will make a huge difference in how we live out our faith.

2. The Imperatives of the Hidden Life

Paul issues two imperatives in Colossians 3:1-2 that are the logical corollaries to his proposition regarding the believer's union with Christ. The logic is clear from the opening statement that assumes the reality of fact: 'since you were raised with Christ.'[5] Given the fact of life-union with Jesus Christ, there are some key things to think about. Both imperatives, 'seek' and 'set your affections,' involve thinking. Imperatives are always addressed to our wills and identify what we are obliged to do.

First, *be seeking the things above* (Col. 3:1). The form of the verb demands a continuing and habitual process. This is not to be an occasional thought but one that becomes a regular routine. Furthermore, this seeking does not refer simply to

---

3. 'Spiritually—that is to say, "in Christ"—they belong already to the age to come and enjoy its life .... Judge everything by the standards of that new creation to which you now belong, not by those of the old order to which you have said a final farewell' (Bruce, *Colossians, Philemon, and Ephesians*, p. 134).

4. 'Because we are in Christ and Christ is in God, we are inseparable and secure. Our lives are part of the "above".... In him there is fullness. His fullness has passed into our emptiness, his righteousness into our sinfulness, his life into our death' (R. Kent Hughes, *Colossians and Philemon: The Supremacy of Christ*, Preaching the Word [Westchester, Ill.: Crossway, 1989], p. 92).

5. '*If* does not suggest uncertainty about the fact to be stated. As in 2:20, "if" in this context almost means "since"' (Woodhouse, *Colossians and Philemon*, p. 180. Emphasis mine).

an investigation but includes a thoroughgoing effort to obtain what is sought.[6] The direction of this ongoing effort is upward, where Christ sits exalted in His session at the Father's right hand. This apostolic advice parallels the words of Christ Himself in His discourse on the Mount admonishing us to lay up treasures in heaven and not on earth because 'where your treasure is, there will your heart be also' (Matt. 6:19-21). There is no treasure more valuable than Jesus, the pearl of great price. Nothing else approaches His infinite value and intrinsic worth. To regard Him so is to have our earthly heart fixed where He is and where we are in union with Him. Again this seeking is more than just an examination of the doctrine but a striving to experience and possess the fullness of the blessing. Remember our exposition of Numbers 13. Too often Christians are like the ten spies who admired and could describe the grapes of Canaan but failed to possess them; they remained on the border of blessing. Examining and expounding gospel truth is fundamental, but it is vital that we go beyond its exposition to its experience. We must live in the reality of what we believe. Let us not live on the border of spiritual blessing, but let us enter its fullness. Let us be like Caleb and Joshua who entered into the possession of what God had promised and provided.

Second, *set your affection on things above*: literally, 'be thinking about the above things' (Col. 3:2). The form of this verb also demands continuing and habitual activity. Thinking is the exercise of the mind and is spiritually crucial. Paul uses the noun form of the verb 'think' in Romans 8:6 when he says, 'For to be carnally minded is death; but to be spiritually minded is life and peace.' One's mindset is a litmus test revealing what one really is.[7] Thinking is the first step to doing. Right thinking produces right behavior. It is imperative that the believer, therefore, habitually and routinely engage the mind on the things that are above, where Christ is and where he is with Christ, in that throne-union. I don't know how thinking works, but I know it works. I know that when you think about something hard enough and long enough, you can't stop thinking about it. I suppose the issue is what we're thinking about when we're not thinking! Habitual thinking wears grooves in the brain. In Philippians 4:8 Paul lists some of the things that are above which we must think about. We need 'to groove our brains' with things that are true, honest, just, pure, lovely, of good report, virtue, praise – all of which are subsumed in Christ Himself.

This obviously does not mean that we never think about other things that are unavoidable parts of life. But it does mean that all we think about and all we do is governed by the fact that we are united to Christ.

---

6. 'Our minds, our thinking, our understanding is to be focused and informed by the things above, by Christ, the reigning Messiah …. It will involve the *deliberate* turning of our minds and our affections to Christ, in such a way that he becomes the shaping power of our lives' (Woodhouse, *Colossians and Philemon*, p. 183).

7. 'What we set our minds on determines our seeking and thus the direction of our Christian lives. What do you think about when you have nothing else to do? … What will the divine postmortem reveal to be our highest priority?' (Hughes, *Colossians and Philemon*, p. 91).

3. The Prospect of the Hidden Life

The prospect of the hidden life is that it will not remain hidden. A day is coming when faith transitions to sight, when the invisible becomes visible, and when our subjective experience becomes one with our objective position. The Greek verb translated 'appear' means to be manifest, completely revealed and open. Christ, 'who is our life,'—the essence of the life we possess and the object of our passions—will one day be openly revealed in all of His splendid glory.[8] Adding to the wonder is the fact that we will be manifested in the same glory with Him. There is no separating Christ and His people, not then and not now. The prospect of that certain glory shared with Christ puts all the stuff of time in its proper place. Preoccupation with Christ is the secret to everything in the Christian life. So living out our faith means that we live now with a view to then.[9]

THE PRACTICE OF KILLING AND ANIMATING

What is true on the inside will show itself on the outside. Although our union with Christ is hidden from view, the evidences of that union should be seen. Doctrine breeds duty. Ethical demands flow from theological truths. Union with Christ looks like something. In verses 5-17, the apostle details the implications of being in Christ both in negative and positive terms. His logic was adopted by the Westminster divines in their classic definition of sanctification in the Shorter Catechism as 'the work of God's free grace whereby we are renewed in the whole man after the image of God and are enabled more and more to die unto sin and to live unto righteousness' (Q. 35). We want to follow that logic as well as we consider what the hidden life is supposed to look like.

1. Killing the Old Man

In Colossians 3:5-11 the focus is on the negative component of this sanctification: death to sin. Believers are to put off the vices belonging to the old life outside of Christ.[10] It only makes sense that if we died judicially to sin in union with Christ in His death on the cross, we should also die practically to sin as we live in union with His life in the resurrection. Here's how Paul put it in Romans 6:4: 'Therefore we are buried with him in baptism into death: that like as Christ was raised up

---

8. 'Often Christians suffer for their faith, but they continue with a life source unknown to those who do not know Christ. Someday, however, Christ will be revealed. When he is, the source of Christians' lives will become apparent to all persons. The reason Christians have had values, outlook, and service to God and others will be clear. The hidden life will be manifested' (Richard R. Melick, Jr., *Philippians, Colossians, Philemon*, The New American Commentary [Nashville, Tenn.: Broadman, 1991], pp. 282-83).

9. 'Let us covenant to not fix our thoughts on the material and immaterial things of this world, but to pray for minds set on things above, to hold the Scriptures close to our hearts, to reflect on our past history, and to rejoice in anticipation of our future in him' (Hughes, *Colossians and Philemon*, p. 93).

10. 'You have said good-bye to your old life; therefore have done with all those things that were characteristic of it .... In short, be (in actual practice) what you now are (by a divine act)' (Bruce, *Colossians, Philemon, and Ephesians*, pp. 139-40).

from the dead by the glory of the Father, even so we also should walk in newness of life.' Paul's imagery here is suggestive. In physical burial, the corrupting corpse is separated from the land of the living. In remarkable irony, in this spiritual burial with Christ, the 'living' corpse of the believer is separated from the corruption of the world. Paul's argument in Colossians 3:5-11 suggests three thoughts.

First, he demands *the duty of death*. Paul issues commands; therefore, these are not simply apostolic or pastoral suggestions for optional behavior but imperatives that demand obedience. We are to *mortify* our earthly members along with their sinful practices (Col. 3:5). The word 'members' usually designates physical limbs or body parts, but by metonymical extension it includes whatever in us that is of this world that is bent to sin. It parallels what Paul calls the 'old man,' which we will consider in a moment. In many ways, the biggest threat to our sanctification is self. Therefore, we must die to self. But this death is not from natural causes, for dying to self is most unnatural. The word 'mortify,' perhaps, has lost some of its shock in modern usage. The word means to kill, with all of its violent connotations. This is suicide. We must kill self, metaphorically speaking: put it to death. The language is blunt, forceful and a bit shocking, but no more so than Christ's counsel to eliminate offending body parts for the spiritual welfare of the soul (Matt. 5:29-30). This member-killing signifies an urgent and immediate effort to eliminate by execution everything and anything that is at odds with God. If our life is truly in heaven, then we must kill off the sinful stuff of our earthly existence. The consequence of Christ's dying for us and our dying in Him is that we should not live anymore with a view to ourselves – our interests, ambitions, or desires that would be contrary to grace (see 2 Cor. 5:15).

We are also *to put off* sinful practices (Col. 3:8), those things that stain and thus ruin the appearance of a garment. The imagery changes, but the topic is the same. By using an illustration about changing clothes, Paul makes the point clear that life in Christ cannot look the same as before. It is only logical that after a bath, you would not put on the filthy clothes that made the bath necessary to begin with. So also spiritually, after the washing of regeneration, we must put off the garments that have been mucked up from the dirt of this world. Life in union with Christ requires a visible transformation. The Bible knows nothing about a gospel that makes no demands on life or requires no change. Grace finds sinners in the most indescribable filth, but grace never leaves a sinner where it finds him.

Second, he identifies *the sins subject to death*. Paul gives two extensive but not exhaustive lists of sins to illustrate the kind of behavior that is incongruous to the hidden life in Christ (Col. 3:5, 8). It is not my intent to define or elaborate on each of the specific vices, but I do want us to get the principal point the apostle is making. Each group lists five sins, all of which relate to specific violations of the second division of God's moral law dealing with man's relationship to man. Transgression of the second division is evidence of transgression against the first. Man's relationship with his fellows is a mirror of his relationship with God. In

Colossians 3:5, the sins progress from outward acts to inward attitudes (fornication, uncleanness, inordinate affection, evil concupiscence, and covetousness) whereas in verse 8, the sins move from inward attitudes to outward acts (anger, wrath, malice, blasphemy, filthy communication). Putting the two groups together creates a logical *chiasmus* in which the center focus is on the inward attitudes and thoughts. *Chiasmus* is a common literary structure throughout the Bible. It's a different logic than modern westerners are accustomed to using, but recognizing it often helps us follow the progression of a biblical argument. It is like a big 'X' that draws attention to the center point where the lines intersect. So here at the point of intersection are the sins of the mind (covetousness, anger). This focus affirms our proposition that thinking determines behavior. Sins in the head are no less serious than sins of the hands.[11]

Another literary technique appears when all ten sins are combined. It would be a mistake to assume that these specifically designated sins are the only ones with which we must be concerned. Here Paul employs a device called *brachylogy*, which is a partial list of items to indicate the totality of something. Paul's point, therefore, is not just that we should deal with these sins specifically, but with sin generally. This is a representative list to include all vices that are contrary to holiness. The list of sins to which you may be particularly susceptible may differ from mine, but the text makes it clear that we must deal directly with the sins in our lives no matter what they are.

Verse 7 gives the hope that we can indeed mortify and put off our sins. There is power in the gospel to enable the transformation required by grace. The Colossian believers used to walk and live within the sphere of those sins, but now they don't. What used to characterize their lives no longer does. That reversal of lifestyle marks every genuine believer. No Christian is experientially as holy as he should be nor as holy as he will be when he appears with Christ in glory, but neither is he as unholy as he used to be. Every saint can say with John Newton: 'I am not what I ought to be, I am not what I want to be, I am not what I hope to be in another world; but still I am not what I once used to be, and by the grace of God I am what I am.'

Third, Paul explains *the reasons for death* to sin. He gives two reasons, one negative and one positive. Negatively, death to sin is necessary because sin angers God (3:6). Every sin is a violation of His righteous justice, and His wrath is poised against it. Whereas the sinful world stands already condemned, all those in Christ have been delivered from condemnation (Rom. 5:1). Insomuch as Christians, then, are no longer under God's wrath, sinfulness should no longer be their practice. We are no longer subject to God's wrath because of Christ's atoning work. The cross stands as the greatest evidence of God's justice and wrath against sin. God put the

---

11. 'I cannot help but noticing the wisdom of these words. If I don't deal with my covetousness, I am likely to be in trouble with my desires. If I don't deal with my desires, I will be in trouble with my thoughts. If I don't deal with my thoughts, then I am asking for trouble in my actions. "Put to death what is earthly in you." Decisive, firm, radical action is called for' (Woodhouse, *Colossians and Philemon*, p. 191).

cross of Christ in the place of our sins, and so must we. It was because of our sin that Christ died. To think of why He died and to remember that we died in union with Him is reason enough to die to sin.

Positively, death to sin is necessary because we have been restored in the image of God (Col. 3:9-10). Paul transitions to this argument by linking two causal participles (*put off* and *put on*) to the imperative 'lie not one to another,' suggested by the imagery of clothing. I don't think it is really true that clothes make the man, but they do reveal something about the man. I love to wear camouflage. So when I wear it, you would be safe to assume that I hunt and that I wish I were in the woods where neither you nor the deer could see me. On the other hand, if I were to wear the scrubs of a surgeon, that would be misleading and potentially dangerous if you believed what you saw. The point is simply this: dress according to what you are. To be hidden in union with Christ demands death to sin because we have put off the old man and put on the new. The simple fact of the matter is that those who trust Christ have changed clothes.

In his comments on Colossians 3:9, Calvin defines the 'old man' as 'whatever we bring from our mother's womb, and whatever we are by nature.' In this context, it designates the unregenerate state in which there is no spiritual life or sensitivity and no impulse toward God or spiritual things. It is that nature that gives rise and expression to every evil deed. No longer are they spiritually dead, insensitive, or motionless toward God. They look different because they have put on the new man.[12]

2. Animating the New Man

The 'new man' refers to that regenerate nature in which the Holy Spirit has implanted the principle of spiritual life. It is the new garment worn by everyone hidden in Christ. Paul describes the new man as being continually, habitually, progressively renewed in the knowledge of the Creator's image. This is the component of sanctification that the Westminster Shorter Catechism (Q. 35) refers to when it says we are renewed in the whole man after the image of God. It is not a sinlessness, but it wants to be and is headed in that direction. It is beyond the scope of our meditation here to think about the full meaning and many implications of the image of God. Suffice it to say that it was the unique mark of man's original creation that was tragically marred by the fall of man into sin and wonderfully restored by God's grace through the gospel. Jesus Christ is the ideal image, even the perfect manifestation of God (Col. 1:15), and it is only through Him and in Him that we are being renewed. Christ, the Second Adam, reversed the curse and restored all lost by the first Adam.

So regardless of race or nationality (Col. 3:11), every believer will look the same in this regard: they have all put on the new man. To wear the new man is

---

12. 'In these verses the Colossians were commanded to put on virtues which stood in brilliant contrast to the vices which the Colossians were previously commanded to put off. Here we have the wardrobe of the saints, and what beautiful garments they are!' (Hughes, *Colossians and Philemon*, p. 101).

to be adorned with Christ, who is all and in all: He is our uniform.[13] Christ is everything in the realm of grace; there certainly is no experience or enjoyment of grace without Him. We die to sin by looking to Christ. As we look, we are changed progressively from glory to glory (2 Cor. 3:18) until He appears when we will be like Him because we will see Him as He is (1 John 3:2). If seeing Christ with our eyes is how glorification works, it follows that seeing Christ with the eyes of faith is how sanctification works. There is something about seeing Jesus that makes us like Him.

Living out our faith is more than not doing bad things; it involves doing good things as well. A life of faith is not just negative; it is most positive. Again the Westminster Shorter Catechism says it well that in our sanctification we are enabled to live unto righteousness. Paul concludes his argument about the 'seen life' by expounding what it is to live spiritually (Col. 3:12-17). There are three points to his exposition.

First, he delineates the *marks of spiritual life*. He continues the clothes analogy with the imperative 'put on' and then lists the virtues that are to be seen in the new man, the style of clothing to wear. He addresses the imperative to those chosen by God, set apart as distinct, and the objects of fixed and continuing love – other ways of identifying those whose lives have been hidden with Christ in God.[14] Again it is not my intent to define each of the virtues, all of which follow the same pattern as the list of vices by relating to the second division of the Law. I want simply to draw some conclusions. Significantly, all of the virtues or marks are characteristics of Christ Himself.[15] That should not be surprising since Christlikeness is the ultimate objective of our salvation: God has predestinated us to be conformed to the image of His Son (Rom. 8:29). So to put on bowels of mercies is to be like Christ, and so it would be right down the list (kindness, humbleness of mind, meekness, longsuffering, Col. 3:12). Paul explicitly makes the connection to Christ when he sets Christ as the pattern for forgiveness: 'as Christ forgave you, so also do ye' (Col. 3:13). It is noteworthy that Paul isolates love as the bond or belt that keeps everything complete and together (Col. 3:14). The essence of this love is selflessness, and who more perfectly than Christ who demonstrated this selfless love to the climax of giving Himself for His church (Eph. 5:25). There is nothing that will spoil, spot, or stain the Christian's wardrobe more than self. So be like Christ.

---

13. 'We have Heaven's wardrobe from the hand of the Ultimate Tailor. It is revealing to note, as many have before, that all of these garments were perfectly worn by Christ. Therefore, when we put on these five graces, we are putting on a family resemblance to Christ' (Hughes, *Colossians and Philemon*, p. 104).

14. 'Before we can respond to the imperatives in verses 12-17 we must understand that this new identity has been given to us, not achieved by us. In Christ, it is who we are. This identity is utterly extraordinary. The words used to describe it in verse 12 are heavy with connotations. They describe the most privileged status conceivable' (Woodhouse, *Colossians and Philemon*, p. 202).

15. 'Paul's description of the character of God's chosen ones is surprising, and not what we are used to seeing in "important" people. The reason for this surprising description of attire to be put on by the most privileged people in the world is that each of the following words is a term that typically describes God or Christ' (Woodhouse, *Colossians and Philemon*, pp. 203-4).

I would suggest also that Paul in this list of virtues is employing the same literary device of brachylogy that he used to list all the vices. These are random representative virtues that imply every conceivable virtue that conforms to and expresses obedience to God's standard of righteousness, His Law and His Son. Remember, what the world sees in us determines what it will think of Christ. Ironically, as God sees us, the body, in Christ, the Head, so the world sees Christ, the Head, through us, the body. That is a sobering thought that should dictate our actions.

Second, Paul details the *method of spiritual life* (Col. 3:15-16). He issues three imperatives to explain how to live out our faith; all are in a form that express constant and habitual activity, underscoring the fact that living the Christian life is a fulltime occupation.

The first and third imperatives express tolerative ideas: 'let the peace of God rule' and 'let the word of Christ dwell' (Col. 3:15-16). This is what should happen, and we should do what is necessary to allow it to happen. The peace that comes only from God must rule in our hearts, our inner being, where we think, feel, and determine to act. Although this peace could refer to the subjective peace of soul that comes from God evidenced by assurance of faith, confidence in forgiveness, and contentment, I'm more inclined to take it to be the objective peace of reconciliation that Christ accomplished through His blood (Col. 1:20).[16] In a very real sense the peace of God is summed up in Christ. That may account for the textual variant adopted in some versions that reads 'the peace of Christ.' So much in the text has focused on Christ's death and what we are to think about it, that it makes sense that the reconciliation between God and us that He has enabled through His blood should factor into our relationship to the body. The word 'rule' is an athletic term meaning to act as an umpire, to arbitrate disputes, to make the calls. Peace with God will translate to peace within the body of Christ. That will happen when we allow Christ to settle every matter.

We should let the word about Christ (a topical genitive) dwell in us abundantly (Col. 3:16). To put it simply, the gospel should be at home in our hearts, where it will then impact every decision, plan, and activity of life.[17] We are to live within the sphere of God's Word. For this to happen, we must know what the Scripture says. *Sola Scriptura* is part of our Reformed tradition, but it must be more than just a component of our creed. Dwelling together implies intimacy,

---

16. 'He gives us his own *personal* peace. It is not just the peace we experience when there is no conflict. It is a sense of wholeness and well-being, completeness and totality. But it is even more – it is the *presence* of Christ. His peace and his presence are marvelously associated in both the Old and New Testament Scriptures ....It is this experience of peace—the cessation of hostility with God, the sense of well-being, and the sense of his presence—that has marked my life' (Hughes, *Colossians and Philemon*, p. 110).

17. 'This word is to be at home in the body of believers. It is to be dominant in their life together, shaping and directing their minds and hearts. The word of Christ is to be extravagantly spoken and heard among them' (Woodhouse, *Colossians and Philemon*, p. 208).

and if we confess love for the Word, it must be more than talk.[18] Paul uses a series of circumstantial participles to express what the indwelling Word is going to look like. First, it will affect our conversation with fellow believers (teaching and admonishing one another). Second, it will direct praise to God by singing the new song in our hearts, which He has put there by grace, by using psalms, hymns, and spiritual songs. As translated in the Authorized Version, psalms, hymns, and spiritual songs are the means of mutual teaching and admonition. I would prefer translating the verse with a slightly different punctuation (placing a comma after 'another'), which would more naturally link 'in psalms and hymns and spiritual songs' to singing rather than teaching: 'Let the word of Christ dwell in you richly, in all wisdom teaching and admonishing one another, in psalms and hymns and spiritual songs, singing with grace in your heart to the Lord.' But wherever the comma is placed, it is clear that the indwelling Word of Christ is going to be seen outwardly. That's our salient point for now. What is inside shows itself on the outside. This is the process of animating or stimulating the new man.

Sandwiched between the two tolerative imperatives is the command 'be ye thankful' (Col. 3:15). Constant and habitual gratitude is a key component of living out our faith.[19] It is a common theme throughout Paul's letters and in his personal testimony. No exposition is required at this point. How can we not be thankful when we think of Christ, His work, and what that means for us personally. That indeed underscores the Heidelberg Catechism's rubric of misery, deliverance, and gratitude.

Finally, Paul declares the *motive for spiritual life* (Col. 3:17). The reason why we do what we do is important: motives matter. For the Christian, Christ's name and glory should be the principal concern in everything we think, say and do. The Scripture disallows the modern—or perhaps I should say postmodern—notion of compartmentalizing life so that religious life is somehow unrelated to everything else. On the contrary, nothing about life is outside the scope of the relationship we have with Jesus Christ. Who Christ is, His authority over us, our identification with Him, our knowledge of His will, and our thankfulness to God for Him, all factor into every sphere of life. To speak and act consciously and intentionally in the name of Jesus will unquestionably affect what we say and do. Right thinking produces right behavior. We can't get away from this axiom.

Living out our faith equates simply to living in the reality of the religion we profess. There can be no disconnect between belief and practice, between doctrine and duty. Objective truth must transfer to subjective experience. The more we know

---

18. 'It is not just a question of disciplined study. It is a matter of the heart. It is Spirit-filled participation in Christ and his Word' (Hughes, *Colossians and Philemon*, p. 111).

19. 'Believers who are full of gratitude to God for his gracious calling will find it easier to extend to fellow believers the grace of love and forgiveness and to put aside petty issues that might inhibit the expression of peace in the community' (Douglas J. Moo, *The Letters to the Colossians and to Philemon*, The Pillar New Testament Commentary Series [Grand Rapids: Eerdmans, 2008], p. 285).

the gospel and our completeness in Christ the more we can enjoy and experience the gospel in life. Theology is the most practical of disciplines and sciences. In the head we must know the truth. In the heart we must believe the truth. With the hands we must implement and evidence the truth. Living our faith starts on the inside and shows itself on the outside. It shows itself by progressively putting to death the remains of the old self and animating the new man by looking alive.

CHAPTER 13

MAKING USE OF LAW AND GOSPEL

SANCTIFICATION concerns the believer's behavior or ethics. By definition ethics are the rules or standards that govern conduct. It is ironic that society, as a whole, laments the tragic absence of ethical behavior while at the same time rejects any fixed standards that would give definition to ethics. We live in a day when everyone does what is right in his own eyes, yet there is no concept of what is really right or wrong. The result is turmoil and moral anarchy. If there is such a thing as ethical behavior, there must be such a thing as absolute standards. The absolute standard is God and His revealed law. However, the ungodly one's attitude about God's law seems never to change. The Lord said to wicked and wayward Israel through the prophet Hosea, 'I have written to him the great things of my law, but they were counted as a strange thing' (Hosea 8:12). Sinners still regard God's law as strange and outmoded. Sadly, even Christians, who ought to know better, have ignored God's law for various reasons and as a result even they drift along in a sea of self-conceived liberty. Although all men are under obligation to live according to God's law and set standards, Christians above all others should live and move and choose their daily course within the parameters set by God's absolutes.[1]

This is so because there is an inseparable link between the directives of God's law and the grace of the gospel. The tension between law and gospel may exist in the mind of man, but the Scripture never puts them in opposition. It is only when the works of the law are elevated above the gospel of grace, or when the works of the law become a prerequisite to the gospel of grace, that problems ensue.

The Scripture provides two clear pictures illustrating the importance of keeping the gospel and law in a proper relationship with each other. Although the principles of the Decalogue were operative from the beginning, they were not inscripturated

---

1. 'He cites still further the grace which he bestowed upon the people, saying, *when he took them out of the land of Egypt, out of the house of bondage.* By this he means that he has truly bound them to himself so that the people cannot revolt against him without meriting further punishment. For seeing that they shall have forgotten the redemption by which they were redeemed, their ingratitude will be double. For since they were purchased by the hand of God, it was imperative that they give themselves in service to him who was their Redeemer' (John Calvin, *John Calvin's Sermons on the Ten Commandments* [Grand Rapids: Baker, 1980], p. 58).

until the middle of the fifteenth century B.C. by Moses. Happily, God did not issue the commandments to Moses at the burning bush as the conditions or prerequisites for His delivering the people from bondage. On the contrary, God graciously redeemed them with the strong arm of His power and by the blood of the sacrifice. It was not until the newly birthed nation arrived at Sinai that God inscribed the tablets. The law was given to show a redeemed people how they were to live in response to and in evidence of the redemption. The sanctifying use of the law followed the experience of the gospel.

Similarly, Paul's use of the Sarah/Hagar duel (Gal. 3; Gen. 21) illustrates the danger of elevating the works of the law above the grace of the gospel. Notwithstanding the hermeneutical questions raised by Paul's analysis of identifying Hagar with the works of law and Sarah with the promise of gospel, the bottom line is clear.[2] Significantly, Sarah and Hagar got along fine so long as Hagar occupied her place as servant to Sarah. It was only after she was elevated to a position of wife alongside Sarah that there was conflict. So it is that when the law is elevated to a position or function for which it is not designed that there is going to be tension. The sanctifying use of the law serves the gospel of grace.

So in this chapter, I want to consider how the law works with the gospel to lead God's redeemed people on the course of holiness. It is beyond the scope of our meditation to offer an extensive commentary of the law or to relate gospel truths to sanctification since that has been addressed in previous chapters. The focus here will be to reflect on the general principles for using the law in the process of sanctification.

THE PURPOSE OF THE LAW

Christianity is not just a religion; it is a vital personal relationship with Jesus Christ that determines and demands a certain way of life. Nothing in the life of a Christian can be separated from that relationship. Right thinking about the gospel, its grace, and its implications will produce the right, ethical conduct. The Christian's purpose in life is essentially threefold and the fulfillment of this purpose will always result in ethical behavior. First, he is to glorify God. 'Whether therefore ye eat, or drink, or whatsoever ye do, do all to the glory of God' (1 Cor. 10:31). Second, he is to enjoy God forever, as the Psalmist declared: 'God is the strength of my heart, and my portion for ever' (Ps. 73:26). Third, he is to be conformed to Christ. 'For whom he did foreknow, he also did predestinate to be conformed to the image of his Son, that he might be the firstborn among many brethren' (Rom. 8:29). Without Christlikeness, there is no way a Christian will either glorify God or experientially enjoy Him. Indeed, the glory of God is seen perfectly in the face of Jesus Christ (2 Cor. 4:6) and it is by looking in God's Word to see the Lord's glory that believers are changed into that glory (2 Cor. 3:18).

---

2. See my detailed exposition and explanation of Paul's hermeneutic regarding the Abraham/Sarah/ Hagar triangle in Michael Barrett, *Beginning at Moses: A Guide to Finding Christ in the Old Testament* (Grand Rapids: Reformation Heritage Books, 2018), pp. 261-68.

If the believer's purpose is to be conformed to Christ, there are a couple of basic questions. First, what was Christ like? Second, how can the believer know if he is conforming to Christ? Paul directs to the answers when he said that Christ in His humanity 'was made under the law' (Gal. 4:4). The same law that overshadows every man overshadowed Jesus. Whereas every man disobeys the law, Jesus obeyed the law absolutely and completely (see Rom. 5). Consequently, it is true of Jesus that He was 'holy, harmless, undefiled' (Heb. 7:26); that He 'did no sin' (1 Pet. 2:22) which is 'the transgression of the law' (1 John 3:4); that He pleased the Father (Matt. 3:17) and fulfilled all righteousness (Matt. 3:15). Christ's active obedience earned a perfect righteousness before God as He lived under the law. Theologically, righteousness is conformity to the standard of God's law. During His earthly life Christ conformed to that absolute standard and thus was holy, without sin. So the logic should be clear. If the believer is to be like Christ, he must live according to the precepts of the same law. In a very real sense, conformity to Christ is measurable by obedience to the law.[3]

Being like Christ, glorifying and enjoying God are not vague directions that God sets before His people. On the contrary He has made the means to the end very clear. He has given His Word, the only rule for faith and practice. God's law serves to help the believer fulfill his goal. He has also given His Holy Spirit to guide in the implementation and application of that Word.

At the risk of some repetition, I'm going to sum up the law's purpose particularly as it relates to the gospel. God's law is the capsule statement of His absolute requirements. Indeed, the Lord Himself is at the very heart and center of the law because it reflects and declares His very nature.[4] Consequently, Paul declared that this law is 'holy, and just, and good' (Rom. 7:12). The law serves many functions. Its demand for perfect obedience not only condemns sinners before the righteous God but is the schoolmaster that leads men to Christ whose perfect active and passive obedience is the only ground for a sinner's acceptance before God. This evangelical function, however, does not exhaust the law's purpose. Once delivered from the penalty of the broken law and the requirements of the law for spiritual life, the believer whose obligation is to holiness must live within the sphere of the law. The grace of the gospel does not give the Christian the right to do whatever he desires. To come to Christ is to be under a yoke. It is an easy yoke, but it is a yoke nonetheless (Matt. 11:28-29). The gospel has loving boundaries (2 Cor. 5:14), and for the genuine believer, living within those boundaries is pleasurable (1 John 5:3).[5] The liberty of the gospel involves freedom from the law as the means of gaining

---

3. 'Jesus is teaching that if we want to know what the law really means, we must look at him and what he does with it' (Sinclair Ferguson, *The Sermon on the Mount* [Edinburgh: Banner of Truth, 2009], p. 71).

4. '[The Law] expresses the character of God and his will for man's life' (Ferguson, *The Sermon on the Mount*, p. 70).

5. 'These commandments are the sacred way in which we are to walk. Rather than restrict us, these tracks give us freedom to move in a Godward direction' (Ferguson, *The Sermon on the Mount*, p. 75).

divine favor, freedom from the law's penalty and guilt, and the freedom to be holy. Holiness is not some abstract, indefinable virtue. Holiness is living according to the precepts of God's law. Nothing should be more desirable for a Christian than to do those things that are pleasing unto the Lord. God's law defines the sphere of pleasing behavior. Christians must endeavor to keep the law, not in order to gain divine favor or salvation (that would be legalism), but because they have received divine grace (that would be sanctification). Those in Christ are free from the law as a means of life, but they are not free from the law as a way of life. Pursuing God's call to holiness requires using the 'map' that He has given to lead in the way.

THE CATEGORIES OF THE LAW

The Westminster Confession of Faith clearly and correctly distinguishes three categories of law: moral, ceremonial, and civil or political (WCF, 19.2–3). The moral law, summed up in the two great commandments to love God totally and to love neighbor as self, is delineated in the Decalogue and remains inflexibly unchangeable.[6] The confession further says that the 'moral law doth forever bind all ... to the obedience thereof' and that the gospel does not in 'any way dissolve, but much strengthen this obligation' (WCF, 19.5). The ceremonial laws were picture prophecies of Christ and the gospel that have been fulfilled in the new dispensation and whose repetition, therefore, is strictly prohibited (see WCF, 19.3). Although the practice of the ceremonies is now obsolete, the pictures of the truth to which they pointed are still in focus. The civil laws were specific applications of the moral law that were given to Israel as a visible and political entity. As the confession says, these laws have 'expired together with the State of that people; not obliging any other now, further than the general equity thereof may require' (WCF, 19.4).

The special focus of this chapter is the use of the law as it relates to pursuing holiness as a way of life. Consequently, attention will be on the moral and civil laws. However, it is important to note that in the Old Testament dispensation, all three categories of law were operating together, and this is instructive for an understanding of the connection between gospel and law.[7] The ceremonial laws concerning the Tabernacle/Temple, the sacrificial system, and the clean/unclean classifications declared timeless gospel truths and implications in pictures. The law

---

6. 'While shaped for *later* human life in a *specific* place and time, it simultaneously gave expression to principles intended to be applicable to *any* place or time – simply because it reflected [God's] own character which he wanted his people to reflect. The Ten Commandments therefore expressed, largely in negative terms (because addressed now to sinners), what God originally willed in a positive way for Adam and Eve in the Garden of Eden' (Sinclair Ferguson, *Devoted to God: Blueprints for Sanctification* [Edinburgh: Banner of Truth, 2016], p. 167).

7. 'The Decalogue was accompanied by subsidiary laws about sacrifices for its breach (a liturgy governing the approach to God), and applications of its principles to society (a civil code). Thus the whole of life was governed by God's law. From one perspective then, the law was a seamless robe. Even if some commandments were more fundamental than others, the people could not pick and choose which commandments they would obey and which they could safely ignore. Yet at the same time a thoughtful old covenant believer would be able to see an inner substructure and dynamic built into the law. It was given in a three-dimensional form' (Ferguson, *Devoted to God*, p. 175).

and gospel were partners in defining and enabling the pursuit of holiness. That is the key lesson for now. Although the administration of the gospel message differs in the New Testament from the Old, the marriage between gospel and law remains.

Thoughts on Using the Moral Law

The Ten Commandments, the summary delineation of the moral law, are at the heart of the Mosaic covenant inaugurated at Mt. Sinai. They were central to the Israelite theocracy of the Old Testament, and the Lord Jesus made it clear in His teaching that the ancient code is equally valid for the Christian faith (Matt. 5:17-37; 19:16-20). In addition to recognizing their timeless validity, Christ also demonstrated the proper method of interpreting the commandments: the individual statements include within them all degrees and forms of the represented prohibition or command. The surface requirements of the law are clear. What God forbids should never be done, and what God commands should be done. But the spirit of the law goes beyond the surface. Included in a prohibition is the demand for the converse duty. Included in a duty is the prohibition of the converse sins. Included in a duty or prohibition are not only all the 'same kind' issues, but also the causes, means, and provocations associated with it. This hermeneutic that recognizes the spirit as well as the letter of the law is essential and makes the application of the commandments to the Christian profoundly simple.[8]

If the Ten Commandments (literally ten 'words') are the summary of the moral standards and requirements of God, then Christ beautifully summarized the commandments when He demanded total love for God and 'self-like' love for neighbors (Matt. 22:36-40). Not only does this encapsulate man's duty, but it suggests the principal divisions in the law: man's duty to God and man's duty to man. Through these laws God clearly reveals to man, and particularly to His people, the conduct that is pleasing to Him. These laws define the sphere of ethical behavior.

The Decalogue begins with a preamble, which, though not one of the ten words, constitutes a vital part of the whole. God identifies Himself as Jehovah, who redeemed the people from the bondage of Egypt (Exod. 20:2). Thus, the Lord highlights the covenant relationship that He had with His people and 'justified' His right to issue the following demands. It was the Exodus that demonstrated to

---

8. 'The genius lies in Calvin's two principles of interpretation: (1) The commandment addresses "inward and spiritual righteousness;" (2) the "commandments and prohibitions always contain more than is expressed in words"' (Stanley N. Gundry, ed., *Five Views on Law and Gospel* [Grand Rapids: Zondervan, 1999], p. 55).

'Often commentators provide specific rules for interpreting the Ten Commandments. Here are the most important ones. 1. The Decalogue must be interpreted spiritually .... Spiritual interpretation recognizes as well that we cannot suffice with an external obedience, but that the law demands of us our *heart* (Matt. 22:37-40; 1 Tim. 1:5). 2. The negative commandments ("You shall not ...") include positive commands, and vice versa. 3. Each commandment must be interpreted *per synecdoche*, which means that where one sin is mentioned, the commandment intends to cover the entire range of related sins. 4. Those commandments concerned specifically with love toward God weigh more heavily than those commandments concerned specifically with love toward neighbor .... 5. The starting point and goal of all the commandments is love' (J. Douma, *The Ten Commandments: Manual for the Christian Life* [Phillipsburg, N.J.: P&R, 1996], p. 12).

Israel that Jehovah was their God and they owed their existence to Him. Because of what God had done, His people were obligated to live a special way before Him.[9] It is significant that God gave these stipulations, not as the condition for their deliverance from bondage, but as the means for their living as a redeemed people. Even then, the law was not to be a means of life, but a way of life for God's people. Remembering their redemption would create within them an attitude toward the Lord that would make obedience both necessary and pleasurable. It is no less true for the Christian that a sincere acknowledgment of God's saving and faithful acts must inspire obedience and total, humble devotion. A saving, vital, personal relationship to God through the Lord Jesus Christ is the foundation for proper living. Right thinking about this sets the heart toward right living before God and man. Before God issued a command to obey, He declared the grace of the gospel to trust. Sinai sets the course for living out of Egypt; it marks the borders of holiness.

The first four commandments concern man's duty to God and the last six concern man's duty to fellow man. Although this is not the place for a full exposition of the Decalogue, a general summary is in order since it is so foundational to obeying God's call to holiness. As you meditate on and seek to conform to the Law's instruction, I would recommend referring to the thorough exposition of the commandments in the Westminster Larger Catechism (Q. 100–148). It is sobering.

The First Commandment (Exod. 20:3)

The purpose of the first commandment is to obtain exclusive allegiance to Jehovah.[10] It obviously requires knowing and recognizing the Lord to be the one true and living God and to worship and glorify Him as He deserves. As the only true and living God and as the God of covenant grace and mercy, the Lord will not tolerate divided worship; He must be the sole object of devotion. This commandment addresses every manifestation of our worship, obedience, and submission to Him. Its inclusiveness should guard against any and all offensive behavior and motivate pleasing conduct outwardly and meditation inwardly. The last two words, 'before me,' are important in understanding the full force of the commandment. The expression refers to personal presence, but can also have overtones of hostility or defiance (cf. Gen. 16:12; Ps. 21:12). Literally 'to my face,' the phrase is not unlike the similar statement in colloquial English 'in

---

9. 'When God reclaims us for himself, are we not all the more strictly obligated fully to unite ourselves with him, to hold ourselves under the obedience of the doctrine which is proclaimed to us in his name? And thus let us learn to hold ourselves truly to our God, to renounce anything that we might be able to forge in our head. For we no longer have to falter this way or that, or be troubled by anything whatever, for there is one sole God who wishes to possess us, who does not want his honor sullied by having it transferred to creatures, and who watches over us in order that we might realize that it is he alone whom we must invoke and in whose succor and grace our refuge lies' (Calvin, *Sermons on the Ten Commandments*, p. 64).

10. 'This may well lead the van, and be set in the front of all the commandments, because it is the foundation of all true religion. The sum of this commandment is, that we should sanctify God in our hearts, and give him precedence above all created beings' (Thomas Watson, *The Ten Commandments* [Edinburgh: Banner of Truth, 1970], p. 49).

your face.' Anything that distracts from or competes with the absolute devotion to God is a defiant insult to the great God who made us and the gracious God who saved us.[11] This commandment demands that everything else and everyone else be subservient to the Lord. It is only as He occupies His rightful place in the heart of His people that they can hope to live right in other areas. If this is not right, nothing will be right.

The Second Commandment (Exod. 20:4-6)

Whereas the first commandment identifies the object of worship, commandments two through four specify the way to worship. This commandment, specifically, involves prohibitions that forbid worshipping images of Jehovah. God forbids the making of images of any sort and especially those in the form of created beings. The word translated 'graven image' refers to something manufactured from wood or stone; however, it frequently describes images in general regardless of the manner of their manufacture. The expression 'likeness' refers to any form capable of being seen. Together the words eliminate all possible physical representations of God. God is Spirit and true worship must be in spirit and in truth. It is impossible to represent the infinite God by the finite notions of man. There is always the danger that the form may receive the worship in lieu of what it symbolizes. The vehicle of worship becomes the object of worship. The application and extent of this commandment is far-reaching. It forbids devising and using any religious worship that is contrary to God's revealed order.[12] It demands observing and keeping pure all that God has ordered for true worship. This commandment makes it clear that it is possible to worship the right God in the wrong way.[13] Too often the church worships the grandeur of its formalism, the distinctives of its denominationalism, or the methods and techniques of its zealous service more than God Himself. The result is idolatry. The basis for this prohibition is the jealousy of God. In His fervent zeal for His name, His law, and His people, God will not tolerate wrong worship. That God inspects and punishes the successive generations of violators and esteems and blesses those that obey suggests the seriousness of this commandment.

The Third Commandment (Exod. 20:7)

The third commandment prohibits the misuse and abuse of the divine name. The significance of names in the Old Testament is well known, and the name of God is

---

11. 'People can make idols out of almost anything. The erotic, the desire for power, reason, nature, tradition, and conscience – each of these can be absolutized in ways both uncultured and very refined. Everyday common things can get a person in their grasp' (Douma, *The Ten Commandments*, p. 17).

12. 'After the first commandment rejects all other gods, so that only Yahweh remains, the second commandment rejects every wrong form whereby people desire to worship Yahweh' (Douma, *The Ten Commandments*, p. 35).

13. 'In the first commandment worshipping a false god is forbidden; in this, [the second], worshipping the true God in a false manner .... The commandment forbids setting up an image for religious use or worship' (Watson, *The Ten Commandments*, p. 59).

particularly important. Not only does the divine name reveal characteristics of God's nature, it also stands, by association, for the very person of the Lord. Consequently, this commandment creates something of a paradox. Although Jehovah revealed His name and Himself so that His people might know Him intimately, this special knowledge could be the source of danger if misused. God makes it clear that He will not tolerate the empty, purposeless use of His name for any reason.

This commandment has far-reaching implications.[14] It certainly includes the ignorant, vain, irreverent, wicked use of His name or perfections by blasphemy or sinful cursing. It demands that in speech, thought, and action His person be regarded with holy reverence and honor. The creature must not trifle with the holy Creator. The command also prevents using God for personal gain. Man must not manipulate God for private purposes. In the ancient world 'name magic' was common as men would invoke the name of their god to somehow sanction the action or seduce their deity to do what they wanted it to do. Although modern 'incantations' may take a different form, the selfish use of religion is as common today as ever. Too often the world mentions God in order to sanction and promote some activity or program. Even Christians, sadly, sometimes attempt to use God to their advantage. Often the divine gift of prayer becomes a vehicle for gratifying personal interests as God is coaxed into a particular course of action. Such violates this commandment that demands respect, fear, and subservience to the holy name. This commandment includes any use of the divine name for empty or worthless reasons.

The Fourth Commandment (Exod. 20:8-11)

The fourth commandment requires the keeping of the Sabbath. The verb 'to remember' denotes not only mental recall, but, more importantly, a willful acknowledgment. Consequently, the statement in Exodus that commands the 'keeping' or 'observing' of the Sabbath day is virtually the same as in Deuteronomy. Although the Sabbath principle existed from creation, this is the first injunction to keep it holy. Perhaps the biggest misconception involving this fourth word concerns the meaning of the term Sabbath. In spite of the association of the word in this context with the seventh day, the term does not inherently refer to the seventh day. The word comes from a root that means 'to cease.' Simply, the Sabbath is a day which stops or a day which marks or sets a limit. It is a day of cessation, regardless of the day of the week so designated.

This day was to be kept holy. The basic idea of this verb signifies separation or withdrawal. The Sabbath is a day that is set apart from all others.[15] Exodus 20:9-11

---

14. Watson, *The Ten Commandments*, pp. 84-92. Watson provides a helpful summary of the many ways in which men transgress this commandment.

15. 'Out of his great mercy, God has provided a remedy: one whole day out of seven to rest in his grace. He has given us a rhythm of work and rest, with six days for labor and one day for leisure. And he grants us our leisure specifically for the purpose of his praise. The Sabbath is a day for worship, a day for mercy, and a day for rest' (Philip Graham Ryken, *Written in Stone: The Ten Commandments and Today's Moral Crisis* [Wheaton, Ill.: Crossway, 2003], p. 102).

describes the manner and purpose of separation. If the Exodus and Deuteronomy passages are considered together, there are two significant and related reasons why the Sabbath is required. The commandment positively states that work is to be done for six days. According to Exodus, the Sabbath day is to be free from all labor because of the example God established at creation; He rested. According to Deuteronomy, the Sabbath is to be observed because God delivered His people from bondage – again a link to the gospel. The Sabbath is a day of rest and remembrance.[16] Relief from the mundane affairs of life allows the time for proper reflection and worship of the Lord for who He is and what He has done. It takes time and a proper frame of mind to worship, and the Sabbath provides both.

Although the day of the weekly Sabbath has changed, there is still a Sabbath for the Christian. Just as the Old Testament weekly Sabbath looked back to the Exodus, the day of redemption, so the Christian Sabbath looks to the resurrection of Christ, which guarantees redemption. The Christian also must set himself apart from the labors and happenings of everyday existence in order to worship the Lord effectively. By setting aside those things that are lawful and necessary on other days and making it the delight of the heart to spend time in public and private worship and in sincerely performing works of necessity and mercy, the Christian will enjoy His God and find the necessary impetus to serve His God with fervent zeal. Suffice it to say that God deserves constant worship and praise. However, in His providence He has given us other things to do that demand our time and attention. In His law, He has set aside a time when we can and must give our full attention to Him. Without such a day, that kind of worship is not possible. Unfortunately, there are many Christians today who have interpreted or reasoned the fourth commandment away. That is tragic and dangerous.[17]

The Fifth Commandment (Exod. 20:12)

The fifth commandment is the fitting link between the two divisions of the Decalogue. This word requiring the honoring of parents sets forth the family as the primary social unit and establishes the principle that submission to all divinely ordained authority is necessary. Obedience to God's authority figures on earth is tantamount to obedience to God Himself. The word 'honor' expresses the attitude and behavior required toward parents. The word's use in the Old Testament indicates that the concept involves both an internal attitude and an external expression (cf. Ps. 50:15; Num. 22:17). The honor for parents is an internal reverence and gratitude that expresses itself in obedience and other external acts.

---

16. 'We are prone to forget the great work of God in creation and redemption. And when we forget, we fail to praise him for making us and saving us. But the fourth commandment is a reminder. It is God's memorandum to his people, reminding us to give him glory for his grace' (Ryken, *Written in Stone*, p. 103).

17. In this fourth appendix of his book, Ferguson offers a spirited defense of the Sabbath Day. His arguments for why the Christian ought to keep the Sabbath Day are well worth the read (Ferguson, *Devoted to God*, pp. 261-70).

Because honoring is internal as well as external, it is not always humanly possible to determine whether it is genuine. Only God knows the heart that motivates any action. An important aspect of this commandment is the promise of long life to those who obey. A comparison of this promise with the punishment mentioned in Exodus 20:5 establishes an important principle: religion is a family affair.[18] Those successive generations being visited (literally, 'investigated') by God in regard to iniquity no doubt followed the idolatrous example of their fathers. Deuteronomy 4:40 extends the promise of life and prosperity to the children of those who obey. Consequently, those who receive this promise attached to the fifth commandment are those who follow the instruction and example of their parents.

The scope of this commandment extends beyond the family unit to the duty man owes to other relationships as well: to subordinates, superiors, and equals.[19] The rest of Scripture demonstrates this wide scope of application. Paul says that we are to submit ourselves to one another in the fear of God (Eph. 5:21). Peter says that we are to 'Honour all men. Love the brotherhood. Fear God. Honour the king' (1 Pet. 2:17). Again Paul says, 'be kindly affectioned one to another with brotherly love; in honour preferring one another' (Rom. 12:10). It is necessary to search the Scriptures to define all the specific duties we owe to our various relationships.

The Sixth Commandment (Exod. 20:13)

The sixth commandment prohibits the illegal taking of life. The proper understanding of this word depends on the meaning of the verb 'to kill.' There are four words in the Old Testament which mean 'to kill.' The two most common words are often interchangeable and occur in similar contexts. They occur (1) in connection with the killing of enemies (both personal and political), (2) in reference to killing in war, and (3) in the execution of criminals deserving of capital punishment. In contrast, the Decalogue verb occurs only in personal situations. It never refers to killing in war and, with one possible exception, never denotes capital punishment (Num. 35:30 where the 'eye for an eye' principle occurs). Therefore, to use this command as an injunction against capital punishment or military service is illegitimate. It is significant that human life, either expressed or understood, is always the object. The main difference between this verb and the others is that it refers to illegal killing, whether intentional or unintentional.[20] Although both types of murder are

---

18. 'An attack on the authority of parents is most grievous because it threatens the most precious heritage of Israel, its knowledge of God, and thereby also threatens possession of the blessing flowing from this knowledge' (Vern S. Poythress, *The Shadow of Christ in the Law of Moses* [Phillipsburg, N.J.: P&R, 1991], pp. 88-89).

19. 'According to "the rule of categories," every commandment stands for a whole category of sins and duties. By implication, when God tells us to respect our parents, he is telling us to respect anyone who has legitimate authority over us' (Ryken, *Written in Stone*, p. 123).

20. 'The Hebrew text indicates that this commandment is dealing with *unlawful* killing, that is to say, with killing that violates justice. The word here (*rasah*) never appears in contexts involving God putting someone to death or putting to death an enemy in wartime. Nor does this command prohibit a killing that has been ordered by the court. The sixth commandment is speaking about a

prohibited, it is significant that the Old Testament makes provision in the cities of refuge for those guilty of unintentional murder (Exod. 21:13). In contrast, not even clinging to the horns of the altar could protect those guilty of intentional murder (1 Kings 2:28, 34). This corresponds to Christ's statement in Matthew 5:21, which stresses the evil attitude of malice rather than the actual act. Sinful anger, hatred, and desires for revenge would all be precluded by the command. The positive side of this prohibition would include the thoughts and expressions of compassion and kindness, readiness for reconciliation and willingness to forgive. Needless to say, the full compliance to this command encompasses virtually every aspect of good behavior toward fellow men.

The Seventh Commandment (Exod. 20:14)

The seventh commandment prohibits all sexual impurity. Strictly speaking, committing adultery refers to the violation of the marriage bond. The serious nature of this sin is evident from its penalty: death (Lev. 20:10). Although the specific word is restrictive, it is here representative of all sexual sins. Perhaps the Lord singled out adultery as the chief expression of sexual impurity because it involves unfaithfulness to a relationship as well as fornication. Despite the fact that general acts of fornication outside marriage are not punishable by death in the Old Testament theocracy, the Scripture, nonetheless, views them as serious transgressions. Christ again shows the full intent of the law when He declares the thought apart from the act to be a violation (Matt. 5:28). Paul equates abstaining from fornication as an integral part of God's will for the Christian's sanctification (1 Thess. 4:3). Obedience to this commandment demands purity in body, mind, affections, communication, and behavior. It requires that attention be given to modesty and care be exercised to avoid whatever would generate temptations to moral uncleanness. Living in this modern, perverse society that has elevated immorality and promiscuity to normal behavior means that Christians, who are bound to God's absolute standard of right and decency, must be on constant vigil to guard the senses and flesh.[21]

The Eighth Commandment (Exod. 20:15)

The eighth commandment prohibits theft and thereby protects rights of others. As in all the commands, the extent of the prohibition goes beyond the obvious. Not only would this include the robbery of things, but also fraudulent business ventures, breaking of contracts, violations of trust between parties, or any sort of dishonest gain, whether financial, material, temporal, or in personal reputation.[22]

---

very specific kind of killing, one that does not *serve* society, but rather violates society' (Douma, *The Ten Commandments*, p. 214).

21. 'The preservation of orderly sexuality is a natural consequence of the call to holiness' (Poythress, *The Shadow of Christ in the Law of Moses*, p. 89).

22. 'Every law-code everywhere has always protected property, condemned stealing, and required damages—restitution—in the way that Scripture does .... But wait. How does the principle apply?

The Ninth Commandment (Exod. 20:16)

The ninth commandment prohibits whatever is prejudicial to the truth. It promotes truthfulness between men, particularly as it relates to the giving of testimony. The principal statement is forensic, but the application embraces all of life. The word translated 'false' has the general idea of deceit. When Moses expounded on the commandments in Deuteronomy 5, he changed the word to a term that signifies something empty or without foundation. In so doing, he expanded the commandment to include not only false testimony, but anything that is not conducive to the propagation of truth. Lying seems to be the first recourse of action from the home to the school to the workplace to the media to the halls of government. Trust has given way to justified suspicion. God hates lying wherever it occurs. Christians must learn to love and practice truth whatever the cost.[23]

The Tenth Commandment (Exod. 20:17)

The tenth commandment requires man to be content with his condition and prohibits the envying of another's possessions or lot in life. Interestingly, this commandment along with the first creates a thematic *inclusio*. Whereas commandments two through nine state the injunctions in terms of external behavior that encompass internal attitudes, the first and last focus immediately and directly on the attitude of heart. The word 'covet' has the general idea of desire and does not imply something inherently evil. Such desire becomes sinful when it is generated and nourished by discontent with what God has ordained for our personal estate and when with envy and inordinate affections toward what God has given to others we despise them for having what we desire for ourselves. Obedience results from the total satisfaction that one's position in life is sovereignly and providentially in the hands of God and from the assurance that God demonstrates His goodness and His presence regardless of the situation (Phil. 4:11; Heb. 13:5).

Thoughts on Using the Civil Laws

The sphere of holiness set by the moral law is all encompassing, touching every area and circumstance of life. But in many ways, the Decalogue paints holiness in broad strokes. Applying a specific commandment to a particular situation requires thought. That is good, but how to think from commandment to application is sometimes

---

It reaches further than perhaps we realize. There is, for instance, theft of *time*.... It is theft too when a tradesman fails to give *value for money*. ... It is theft when *debts* are left unpaid .... Finally, it is theft to steal a *reputation*, destroying someone's credit by malicious gossip behind his back' (J. I. Packer, *The Ten Commandments* [Wheaton, Ill.: Tyndale House, 1982], p. 61).

23. 'Veracity is the strict observance of truth in all our communications. The importance and necessity of this appears from the fact that almost all that mankind knows is derived from communications. The value of those statements which we accept from others depends entirely on their verity and accuracy. If they are false, they are worthless, misleading, and evil. Veracity is not only a virtue, but it is also the root of all other virtues and the foundation of all right character. In Scripture, therefore, "truth" is often synonymous with "righteousness"' (A. W. Pink, *The Ten Commandments* [Grand Rapids: Baker, 1976], p. 59).

difficult. So God in His grace to Israel taught them how to think by detailing specific applications of the moral law relevant to their time and circumstance. The specific applications are the civil laws, and they are part of growing in holiness.

As a child matures from infancy to adolescence to adulthood, the manner of parental instruction changes. A wise parent wants ultimately for his children to make their own decisions, but that aspiration is off limits to toddlers. In the early stages of a child's life, the parent must be extremely specific in teaching what is right and wrong, what is proper and improper behavior. Hopefully, the long list of dos and don'ts transitions to principles designed to guide into good decisions. It is a joy to parents to see their grown children making good decisions and doing the right thing even in situations that were not governed by some specific rule when the child was under their direct care. So it is with God's teaching infant Israel what obeying the moral law was to look like in actual life.

One of the difficulties for Christians using the Old Testament is the high level of specificity of its commands. Much of the Old Testament law comes not in moral absolutes but in specific instructions distinctively relevant to particular times, people, and places. These civil laws constituted a 'do and don't' list designed to show that keeping the moral law extended to every situation of life.

So rather than being put off by the specific laws that seem to be irrelevant to modern life, the Christian, first of all, should learn that holiness extends to all of life and, second, recognize how to discover relevance in what appears to be irrelevant.

In this venue, I can only give some guidelines to follow when considering those very specific laws. This is the overriding principle: truth is timeless and universal, but the application of truth varies and is conditioned by time, culture, and situation. Some of the civil laws of the Old Testament were so temporally, culturally, or situationally specific that obeying them would be impossible. Hence, the soundness of the confessional statement that these laws have 'expired together with the State of that people; not obliging any other now, further than the general equity thereof may require' (WCF, 19.4). Not even the Lord Jesus Christ, who kept the law of God perfectly, was able to keep all the specifics of the laws given to ancient Israel. For instance, since Christ owned no property, He was incapable of obeying Leviticus 19:9 that prohibited the harvesting of the corners of one's field. But although He did not nor could not obey that specific command, He certainly demonstrated over and again His selfless compassion for others – loving His neighbor. That love of neighbor looked different for Christ than for landowners in the temporary theocracy, but He nonetheless fulfilled the spirit of the law perfectly. The truth was the same, but application was different. It is a serious hermeneutical error to confuse application of truth with the principle of truth itself.

Because the civil laws delineate what holiness to God was to look like to ancient Israel, it is important to know how to extract from those laws the timeless principles that are to direct us to what holiness is to look like for us. A major hermeneutical error in dealing with the civil laws is inconsistency. Many tend to pick and choose which ones are relevant based on their own particular views of holiness. For instance, some who would appeal to Deuteronomy 22:5 as a law against women wearing trousers would not think twice about wearing a silk necktie with a wool suit, although that would violate Deuteronomy 22:11. For now the point is not whether women should wear trousers or men should wear silk ties; rather, the point is that there is a need for establishing guidelines for using the Old Testament civil laws.

Extracting the timeless truths from the temporal civil laws requires thinking, but the interpretation strategy is simple enough. All that is required is thinking backwards from the specific command to the general principle and then applying the general principle to the situation at hand. Remember that there is a four-tiered hierarchy of law: (1) the first great commandment to love God totally, (2) the second commandment to love neighbor, (3) the Decalogue which develops the first two in ten parts, and (4) the civil laws that relate to one or more of the Ten Commandments.[24] In fact, every specific commandment, whether in the Old Testament or the New Testament, will fit in this rubric. Every specific command is an application of one of the Ten Commandments, which in turn explain some aspect of loving God or loving neighbor.[25]

This process of thinking parallels closely modern practices of jurisprudence. The Ten Commandments are to the civil or case laws of the Old Testament what legal precedents are to trial lawyers. That is, they extract legal principles from specific cases and apply the principles to a new case. So the interpreter of the Bible looks at the specific cases in Scripture and extracts the principle (ultimately one of the two great commandments) and applies the principle to a new situation. Consider again Leviticus 19:9-10 that prohibits the harvesting of the corners of agricultural property so that there will be provision for the poor and aliens. This prohibition is a specific application of the sixth commandment which forbids killing and conversely demands the preservation of life. Doing what is necessary to preserve the life of another is an application of the second great command to love one's neighbor as

---

24. Walter Kaiser referred to this hierarchy as 'four levels of generality and particularity in the Bible' and the process of thinking through the hierarchy as a 'ladder of abstraction' (Walter Kaiser, *Toward Rediscovering the Old Testament* [Grand Rapids: Zondervan, 1987], pp. 159, 165).

25. 'A believer, therefore, would have understood not only that the civil and liturgical dimensions of the law were applications of the moral dimension, but also that these applications constituted a temporary divine arrangement.... In Jesus' life, death, resurrection, ascension, and giving of the Spirit—these three dimensions of the law would be clearly seen for what they always were—moral prescriptions for the fallen image of God applied to both civil and religious life until the Savior came and the final international community of the people of God was born. In this community there is no need for the old ceremonial law governing animal sacrifices. This community does not require old covenant civil law in order to function maximally – for it exists everywhere. But since this is the community of the new humanity (those who are being recreated "after the likeness of God"), the great foundational principles of the Decalogue, reflecting God's original purposes for his image, remain in place. All this becomes clear in the way Jesus fulfilled the law by bringing out its various dimensions in the full light of the new day' (Sinclair Ferguson, *Devoted to God*, p. 178).

self. So Leviticus 19:9 teaches us that holiness requires humanitarian and charitable acts of kindness to those less fortunate than ourselves. The applications of the same holiness principle will vary depending on circumstances, but the civil law teaches that there must be specific applications of the general truths.

This is just an illustration, but it outlines the thinking procedure necessary for dealing with civil laws and should be an encouragement to use the many specific commandments that God gave in the past as a guide to holy living now. The Reformed tradition holds that strict adherence to these laws is no longer required, other than applying the general principles to the varied circumstances of life. They teach us that holiness must pervade life.

So in the pursuit of holiness, the gospel and the law are partners. The gospel is the ground, the rationale, and the motive to holiness. The law is the prescription of what holiness is. Using the law as the guide to holiness takes the guesswork out of obeying God's radical and comprehensive call to holiness.

CHAPTER 14

LIVING CHRIST AND DYING IN CHRIST

'For to me to live is Christ, and to die is gain'

(PHILIPPIANS 1:21)

THE apostle Paul did not have an easy life. He endured many a trial for the sake of Jesus Christ. One of those trials was imprisonment. Twice he was imprisoned in Rome. We read of his second and last imprisonment in 2 Timothy, written when he was expecting to soon be executed.

But during his first imprisonment in Rome, about A.D. 60, Paul had a certain degree of liberty. He was allowed to live in his own rented house. And it is from that house that he wrote the Epistle to the Philippians. Paul, who had persecuted the church of Christ for many years, is now a prisoner of the very Savior whose followers he once cast into prison.

Of this Savior he now says in our text, 'He is my life.' Paul the prisoner has become a free man in Jesus Christ. Jesus Christ has freed him from the law of sin and death. So he writes to Philippi with joy. While he is in prison he writes this epistle, often called *the epistle of joy*. Paul says to them, 'Rejoice ... and again I say, Rejoice.'

The church at Philippi had a special place in Paul's heart. This church was founded by Paul on his second missionary journey. It began with the conversion of Lydia and the Philippian jailer and his family. So Paul writes this letter full of reminiscence, affection, and gratitude. He thanks the Philippians for ministering to his physical and temporal needs, which was quite remarkable because the Philippians, in terms of earthly treasure, were a rather poor congregation. But he knows that these gifts show their love for him.

In Philippians 1:18 he speaks of his joy in the Lord and in verse 19 he says, 'For I know that this shall turn to my salvation through your prayer.' He knows that even his imprisonment must be subservient to his salvation through the Philippians' prayers and the supply of the Spirit of Jesus Christ (cf. Heidelberg Catechism, Q. 1). He says in effect, my imprisonment is going to work together for good, for Christ will be magnified even in this, 'whether it be by [my] life or by [my] death' (v. 20).

193

And then he says with great confidence, boldness, and simplicity—and this surely is the apex of this opening chapter of Philippians—'For to me to live … Christ, and to die … gain' (Phil. 1:21). Notice the word 'is' is in italic print in the Authorized Version; it was added to make a complete sentence, since the Greek text has no helping verbs. Paul says, 'What is my life? When I look to the future, to the past, and to the present – why am I here? What is my life all about? For me to live …' and you can see him pausing here with his pen, and he writes, 'Christ.' That's it—that's my life in one word—*Christ!* And then he says, 'and to die … gain'—gain because Christ is our life, we will die in Him, and thus, our death will be gain—yes, eternal gain.

That is what we need today and everyday as we look to the future. May this be the model for your church and your family. May this be your goal. May this be something you not only post on your refrigerator, but something you know, something you live, something you experience. May this be what all your prosperity and all your adversity look toward: for me to live—Christ; for me to die—gain! And these two are connected. When for us to live is Christ, then for us to die will be gain, because to die is to be with Christ forever.

Let's look more closely, then, at Philippians 1:21, 'For me to live is Christ, and to die is gain.' Under the theme, 'Living Christ and Dying in Christ,' let us consider, first, how Christ can be our life, and second, how death can be our gain.

HOW CHRIST CAN BE OUR LIFE

What does it mean to be able to say, 'To live is Christ'? I would like to suggest four things to you, revolving around the words link, life, love, and likeness.

1. We Are Linked with Christ

When Christ is our life, we have a special linkage with Him. As theologians say, we are united to Him. This union with Christ is foundational. We must be in Christ by faith. In a word, we must have a relationship with Him.

Someone was speaking with me this week and he said about a friend, 'I'm connected with him.' That is a popular word today. People want to feel connected with other people. When you are in Christ, when your life is Christ, you are connected with Jesus Christ.

Of course, that had not always been the case with Paul. Originally, as a Pharisee, he persecuted those who were connected with Jesus Christ. For Paul, prior to his conversion, to live was Moses. He did everything right, according to the law, and he would have said, 'For me to live is the law,' for he gloried in legalism and manmade righteousness.

But on the way to Damascus all that changed (Acts 9). A light shone from heaven; Paul fell to the earth trembling, astonished, blinded, and conquered by God. And you know the story – his friends brought him into Damascus. For three days he could not see, nor did he eat or drink. He could only pray.

And there in 'the street which is called Straight' the Holy Spirit showed him who he really was in the mirror of the holy law of God (Acts 9:11). Paul saw that 'for me to live is sin.' That was something he never learned at the feet of Gamaliel. But now he learned that he was a stranger to God, a stranger to grace, a lost sinner before a holy God. His uncircumcised heart was humbled, and there Paul accepted the punishment of his iniquity.

But there too in the street called Straight the Holy Spirit led this persecuting Pharisee to Jesus Christ. The scales fell from Paul's eyes and he says, 'It pleased God … to reveal His Son in me that I might preach him among the heathen' (Gal. 1:15-16). His life was henceforth linked to the life of Jesus Christ. He entered into a real and vital relationship with Jesus Christ. He came to love Jesus Christ, and in Christ he was filled with the peace that passes all understanding. Christ became his life.

From that moment on Paul is determined to know nothing, save Jesus Christ and Him crucified (1 Cor. 2:2). Acts 9:20 says that after Paul was converted and came to know Christ, 'Straightway he preached Christ in the synagogues, that he is the Son of God.' He says to the Philippians, 'What things were gain to me, those I counted loss for Christ. Yea doubtless, and I count all things but loss for the excellency of the knowledge of Christ Jesus my Lord … and do count them but dung, that I might win Christ, and be found in him, not having my own righteousness, which is of the law, but that which is through the faith of Christ' (Phil. 3:7-9). That is the way to live, linked up with Jesus Christ. He is our life. He is our righteousness. He is our foundation.

What is your life? Just fill in the blanks for a moment, think autobiographically about yourself. Don't think of anyone else. For me to live is … what? Is it Christ? The way you are living right now – is Christ your life?

What if you have to say, 'For me to live is work'? Or, 'for me to live is friends and popularity'? Or money? Or reputation? You fill in the blank. What is the highest point in your life? What is the lowest point? What is the foundation? What is your life? Can you say with John 17:3 that this is life eternal, to know God and Jesus Christ whom He has sent? Could you live without Jesus for a week? A month? A year? Are you linked with Jesus Christ?

2. We Have Life in Christ

When Christ is our life, we are not only linked to Him but we have life in Him. We are linked to Him and united with Him for our justification, finding atonement and forgiveness in Jesus Christ, but Paul's concern here is the living of our daily life. He is saying, 'The aim of my daily life, the means and the content of my daily life, is Christ.' In other words, Paul is discussing our sanctification.

He wants to know Christ better in His person, better in His natures, better in His offices, and better in communion with Him. 'For me to live – Christ,' says Paul. 'Day by day He is my teaching Prophet, and my sacrificial, interceding High

Priest, and my ruling and guiding King. The aim of my life is to commune with Him daily. If I don't have contact with Christ in a day it is an empty day, a sad day. But if I have union with Him, and communion out of that union through His Word, the means of grace, and the pursuit of other spiritual disciplines, I rejoice! For me to live is truly a life in Christ.'

For Paul everything outside of Christ is death. Only Christ gives real life. Sin means death for Paul. So Christ and sin are antithetical to each other. That is why Paul is so grieved about his indwelling or remaining sin. It is a sorrow for him. He wages war against it and cries out, 'O wretched man that I am!' (Rom. 7:24). He grieves when he sins because he knows that to sin is not to live in Christ.

What about you? Do you see the emptiness of all of life outside of Christ? Do you see death in all that is not Christ? When you look back over the last year is this what you valued? Did you grow in Christ in this past year? Did you commune with Christ? What is all the rest of life if you haven't had communion with Christ? It is empty, isn't it? Empty at best, and it will condemn you at worst. Oh, to live truly is to live in Christ, by Christ, for Christ!

3. We Have Love for Christ

To live Christ means not only to have linkage with Christ and life in Christ, but to have love for Christ. Paul loved the Lord Jesus Christ. If you love your earthly life partner so much you say, 'I love you so much, I could just love you to pieces. I think you are so special!' That is the way true Christians feel about Jesus Christ, and they say, 'I love Him so much.'

To the Ephesians Paul says he yearned for them to know the love of Christ in all its depth, height, and breadth, asserting that it passes all understanding (Eph. 3:17-19). To the Corinthians he writes that the love of Christ constrained him to preach the gospel and to warn against sin (2 Cor. 5:8-15). The love of Jesus Christ was Paul's greatest motivator. It is what made him get out of bed in the morning, so to speak. It is what made him tick all day long; it is what filled his mouth, filled his heart, and filled his life. It was the engine that moved him to do whatever he did. That is why Christ is everywhere in his letters.

I love what Luther said: 'Paul could not keep Christ out of his pen because the Holy Spirit kept Christ in his heart.' An old saying is that all roads led to Rome. For Paul, all matters large and small lead to Christ because Christ is all. 'For I am determined not to know anything among you, save Jesus Christ, and him crucified' (1 Cor. 2:2). That is Paul's great theme. He said to the Colossians, 'Christ is all, and in all' (Col. 3:11). That's it; everything we believe, and have, and are as believers, we believe and have and are in relationship to Jesus Christ. He is our only theme.

What is amazing about Paul is that even in practical areas of daily life, mundane things, or everyday problems, he is always taking us back to Christ. Are there divisions in the church in Corinth? He points them to Christ. He writes, 'Is Christ divided; was Paul crucified for you?' (1 Cor. 1:13). If the problem was an immoral man in the assembly, he points to Christ again. 'Purge out therefore the old leaven, that ye may be a new lump ... for even Christ our Passover is sacrificed for us' (1 Cor. 5:7). If the problem is immoral temptations, Christ crucified is once more the answer: 'And such were some of you: but ye are washed, but ye are sanctified, but ye are justified in the name of the Lord Jesus, and by the Spirit of our God' (1 Cor. 6:11).

What about living in the home as Christian wives or husbands? Again, he points to Christ. 'Wives, submit yourselves unto your own husbands, as unto the Lord' (Eph. 5:22). 'Husbands, love your wives, even as Christ also loved the church, and gave himself for it' (Eph. 5:25). 'Children, obey your parents in the Lord: for this is right' (Eph. 6:1).

For every aspect of life, every relationship, everything practical, everything spiritual, Paul takes us to Christ. When he tells us to forgive each other he reminds us of Christ who forgave us (Col. 3:13). When he exhorts us to be generous in our giving, he reminds us of Christ who gave so much for us (2 Cor. 8:9). When he exhorts us to humility he says, 'Put on the mind of Christ' (Phil. 2:5). When he exhorts us to everyday holiness it is on the ground that we are crucified and risen with Christ (Rom. 6:3-5). Christ is the answer to every human problem. To the lost or to the saved, it is all Christ. He is all I preach. He is the sum and substance of my ministry. For me to live is Christ; I love Him with all my heart, says Paul.

Do you love the Lord Jesus Christ? I know when you compare yourself to Paul you feel that you come up short. But can you say with Peter, 'Lord, although I don't love Thee as I should, Thou knowest all things. Thou knowest that I love Thee'?

4. We Have Likeness to Christ

Finally, when our life is Christ, we don't only have linkage with Him, and life in Him, and love for Him, but we also have likeness to Him. If we really love someone we start to become more like that person, don't we? It is such an intriguing thing to see an elderly couple who are still ravished with each other, still on their first honeymoon, as it were, fifty years after they are married. They are so close to each other. They think together, they speak together, they walk together, they talk together, they pray together, and they read together. They just love each other. They become like each other, even in physical appearance. After a while they almost look like sister and brother.

And so it is in a believer; when his life is Christ he becomes more like Christ. There is a savor of Christ that oozes out of him, says Paul elsewhere (2 Cor. 2:15). The fruits of Christ are the fruit of the Spirit: love, joy, peace, humility, temperance. All those fruits listed in Galatians 5:22-23 are really nothing but a moral profile of the Lord Jesus Christ. The believer begins to exercise these graces more and more. We become more like Christ, so that in the great day we can be fully like Him when we enter into glory and see Him as He is. As John says in 1 John 3:2, 'We shall be like him,' perfectly like Him on that day.

To become like Christ involves chiefly three things. First, it involves developing, by God's grace, *a servant heart*, thinking not of myself and what *I* want, and what *I* like, and what *I* wish for, but to think in terms of God and His people, and to think corporately in terms of *we* as believers, and in terms of *we* as God's family, and living a life of service to others in Christ's name.

Second, it involves developing *a loving heart*. Christ had such a loving heart. He was a people person. He loved people. He took up little babies in His arms. He healed the lepers, and dared to touch them though they were unclean. There was nothing that held Christ back from loving people. To be like Christ is to love as Christ loved.

Third, to be like Christ is to have *a humble heart*. He was meek and lowly. The more we are like Christ, the more humble we are. You know the famous story about when someone approached Augustine and asked, 'What are the three most important Christian graces we need?' His answer was, 'Humility, humility, humility.'

This is what Paul means then when he says, 'For me to live is Christ.' It means linkage with Christ, life in Christ, love for Christ, and likeness to Christ, all flowing out of knowing and experiencing Christ's love to us.

But then he adds these amazing words: 'To die ... gain.' This brings us to the second part of Philippians 1:21.

HOW DEATH CAN BE OUR GAIN

Is death gain? Why does Paul tie death to life? It is because the two belong together. It reminds us of Question 1 of the Heidelberg Catechism: *What is thy only comfort in life and in death?* The world and our natural hearts try to separate the two. I will live the way I want to; I will live for myself. I'll worry about death later. Paul says no; because I live in Christ, to die in Christ – that shall be gain to me. The two belong together; the one truth implies the other. What an amazing confession – death equals gain.

Death by nature is a heavy loss. We have to leave our husband, wife, father, mother, and children behind. What a loss! We have to leave our work behind, our relationships behind, leave behind everything we have acquired and enjoyed. We say to each other, and rightly so, 'You have my sympathy in your loss.' Paul says, 'For me it is not a loss; it is a gain.' It is not a loss for the people of God. For me to live is Christ and therefore death is gain, for we both live and die in the Lord.

There are two things we need to look at here if we are to understand this text: what the apostle leaves behind, and what he receives when he dies.

1. What Paul Leaves Behind

So what will he leave behind? He will leave behind his beloved brethren in the Lord. He will leave communion with the people of God on earth. He must leave his beloved son Timothy. He leaves his brother and friend Silas. He leaves all that is on earth behind.

But he also leaves behind the body of sin and death. He leaves behind that earthly state or condition which he frankly acknowledged and lamented: 'I am carnal, sold under sin. For that which I do I allow not: for what I would, that I do not; but what I hate, that do I' (Rom. 7:14b-15). He leaves behind the body of sin when he dies.

He also leaves behind a life which at best is only labor and sorrow. He leaves behind a life of afflictions. Twice he was beaten with rods. Once he was stoned. Thrice he suffered shipwreck. He was in the deep for a night and a day and had been in perils of waters, perils of the city and the wilderness and the sea, perils of false brethren, weariness and painfulness, and hunger and thirst. He underwent fastings and suffered cold and nakedness. All this he leaves behind.

And he leaves behind a life of temptation, a buffeting Satan, an enticing world – no more problems with the lust of the eye, with the lust of the flesh, or with the pride of life. He leaves behind that troubling thorn in his flesh – no more unanswered prayers, no more vexing riddles.

Death, dear believer, shall be gain for you as well. You will leave behind your sinful heart, the hardships of your difficult life, your temptations, and the thorns in your flesh. Think of it. There will be no more sin, no more Satan, no more worldliness, and no more old nature. All evil is walled out and all good is walled in. No more tears, no more pain, no more night, no more death, no more curse, no more temptation. For me to die is gain because of what I leave behind! But even more, dying is gain because of what we will receive.

2. What Paul Receives at Death

David Murray has written a wonderful article on 'Why do believers have to die?'[1] Consider his list of the benefits that a believer receives in death:

(1) 'Dying brings us into communion with Christ's sufferings.' That is a great benefit. Though our death does not pay the penalty for our sin, dying reminds us of how Christ died for us and connects us more deeply and lovingly to Him (Phil. 3:10).

(2) 'Dying gives us a unique experience of Christ's all-sufficient grace.' Dying can be very difficult, painful, and fearful. Christ will help you through your death hours.

(3) 'Dying transforms us into Christ's image.' What a glorious thing that is! Death can intensify our sanctification so that as the outer man decays, the inner man is renewed in spiritual growth (2 Cor. 4:16).

(4) 'Dying is our last and perhaps greatest opportunity to witness for Christ's glory.' The deathbed is a pulpit. It may be our supreme test of faith, and the occasion

---

1. David Murray, 'Why Do Believers Have to Die?' *The Banner of Sovereign Grace Truth* 20, no. 1 (Jan. 2012), p. 17.

for us to bear witness that Christ is enough. The Lord has saved many through the testimony of a dying saint. This brings us to the most important point.

(5) 'Dying brings us into Christ's presence.' That is what you will receive, and that is everything, dear believer. To be in His presence is everything you desire, everything you could hope for. This is the apex. This is heaven's heaven – to be with Christ, to be His bride, to be in perfect communion with Him, to enjoy knowing Him and seeing Him and loving Him and praising Him and communing with Him uninterruptedly! What a life, what a future awaits the people of God! For me, to die is gain because I will be with Jesus forever!

Of course, that involves so much more; so much surrounds being with Jesus. Let me unpack some of the blessings of going to be with Christ.

(1) Dying brings us to perfect eternal life with Christ. Our death is no satisfaction for our sins, but it is the abolishing of sin and entrance into the fullness of life. The eternal life that begins here on earth at regeneration shall now be made perfect. Jesus said, 'Because I live, ye shall live also' (John 14:19).

(2) Dying grants us perfect knowledge of Christ. Believers know Christ here on earth. But in death that knowledge will be perfected. Now I see through a glass darkly, but then I will see face to face. Here I know in part, but there I will know as I am known (1 Cor. 13:12).

(3) Dying initiates us into perfect activities. As the Westminster Shorter Catechism (Q. 37) says, 'the souls of believers are at their death made perfect in holiness.' We will do all things well as 'the spirits of just men made perfect' (Heb. 12:23).

We will worship God perfectly. Believers will 'stand on the sea of glass, having the harps of God. And they sing the song of Moses the servant of God, and the song of the Lamb, saying, Great and marvelous are thy works, Lord God Almighty; just and true are thy ways, thou King of saints' (Rev. 15:2-3).

We will serve God perfectly. 'Therefore are they before the throne of God, and serve him day and night in his temple: and he that sitteth on the throne shall dwell among them' (Rev. 7:15). We will reign with Christ.

We will have perfect fellowship with the saints in glory. They 'shall sit down with Abraham, and Isaac, and Jacob, in the kingdom of heaven' (Matt. 8:11).

(4) Dying welcomes us into a perfect home. We will enter into perfect mansions shining with the perfect light of our perfect God. We will perpetually feast with Him at whose right hand are pleasures forevermore (Ps. 16:11).

(5) Dying ushers us into perfect communion with the triune God in Christ. We will have more intimate communion with Christ than we have known in our highest peaks of spiritual joy on earth. We will have a clearer vision of Christ's glory than our most lucid insights here. We will forever bask in His smile, bathe in His glory, and feast in His presence.

Death does more for us believers than anything this earthly life can do for us. Death is gain, for it brings me to Jesus. Death is gain because it brings more of

Christ to Paul and more of Paul to Christ. The whole Christ comes no more through a glass darkly. Every believer will be brought to Christ in heaven to be with Him forever. That is why Samuel Rutherford (1600–1661) said that God could make ten thousand heavens full of good and glorious joys, but all of them together could not compare to Christ.[2] To die is gain, when to live is Christ.

But if Christ is not your life, your death is not gain. Your death is tragedy. Your death means hell. Your death means to live forever apart from God. Your death means being shut out of the favor of God, even the common grace you may have experienced in this life. So what we need to ask is this: Is my life Christ? Because only then when I come to die, will death be gain.

Death can't harm you, dear child of God. Death will only do you good; it will take you higher and farther than the Bible, and prayer, and the sacraments, and worship, and all the means of grace will take you in this life. It will take you right into the presence of Jesus Christ.

So Paul has this dilemma. He wants to remain here for certain reasons, but he also wants to depart to be with Christ. Here, as William Hendrickson observes, we have a 'temporary residence,' a mere tent; there, 'a permanent abode.' Here, 'suffering mixed with joy'; there, 'joy unmixed with suffering.' Here, 'suffering for a little while'; there, 'joy forever.' Here, 'absent from the Lord'; there, 'being at home with the Lord.' Here, 'the fight'; there, 'the feast.' Here, 'the realm of sin'; there, 'the realm of complete deliverance.'[3] To die in the Lord is great gain.

Are you ready to die? May I ask you that? Are you really living? That is the question. If you are living in Christ, you are ready; your house is set in order. If you are not living in Christ, you are not ready. Dear friend, you must be ready. You must be born again. There is no other way. The Puritans used to say that the way to get ready to die is to practice dying while you are here – dying to yourself, dying to everything that would draw you away from Jesus Christ.

Charles Spurgeon put it this way:

> No man would find it difficult to die who died every day. He would have practiced it so often, that he would only have to die but once more; like the singer who has been through his rehearsals, and is perfect for his part, and has but to pour forth the notes once for all, and have done. Happy are they who every morning go down to Jordan's brink, and wade into the stream in fellowship with Christ, dying in the Lord's death, being crucified on his cross, and raised in his resurrection. They, when they shall climb their Pisgah, shall behold nothing but what has long been familiar to them, as they have studied the map of death.[4]

---

2. Samuel Rutherford, letter of July 6, 1637, in *Letters of Samuel Rutherford*, ed. Andrew A. Bonar (Edinburgh: Oliphant Anderson & Ferrier, n.d.), p. 413.

3. William Hendriksen, *Exposition of Philippians*, New Testament Commentary (Grand Rapids: Baker, 1962), p. 78.

4. C. H. Spurgeon, 'Dying Daily,' sermon 828, on 1 Corinthians 15:31, in *Metropolitan Tabernacle Pulpit, Volume 14* (Pasadena, Tex.: Pilgrim Publications, 1976), p. 491.

I'm afraid that some of you are not ready to die, that some of you are still clinging to empty toys and trinkets of this world. For some of you, to live is your possessions, your wealth, or your legalism, or maybe, God forbid, some of you even live for sin, or friendships, even things legitimate in themselves, but you are not living for Christ. You are not ready to die. You are not really living! You could die at any moment!

Rutherford wrote, 'Build your nest in no tree here, for God has sold the forest to death.'[5] Repent, believe the gospel, and bow before the living God. Don't rest until you too can say, 'For me to live is Christ, and to die is gain.'

There was an Italian man named Galeacius who was converted at the time of the Reformation. He had to give up his estates in Italy and flee to Geneva. His loss was so considerable to the Church of Rome that he was offered a free passage back and restoration of his estates if he gave up his new-found Reformed faith. This is the note he sent back to Rome: 'Let their money perish with them, who esteem all the gold in this world worthy to be compared with one hour's communion with Jesus Christ and His Holy Spirit.'[6] One hour with Christ is better than a lifetime with this world.

I would also remind you of John Paton (1824–1907) who went to the New Hebrides in the late 1850s on the Island of Tanna. He was beset by great difficulties. Cannibals there had never heard the gospel. His wife died after childbirth and his little boy died also. Paton buried his wife and his child, and then had to sit on the grave to prevent the cannibals from digging up their bodies and eating them. He was left alone. Then his house was burned down by one of the cannibals. He lost everything; he had absolutely nothing. He spent the night hiding in a tree, trying to sleep in that tree. He tells us that in the middle of the night as he sat in that tree the words were as clear to him as if they were written across the sky in large letters of gold, 'Lo, I am with you alway, even unto the end of the world.'[7] That is the way to live.

For me to live is *Christ*, a Christ who is with me always until the end of the world. And to die is *gain!*

---

5. Samuel Rutherford, letter of January 15, 1629, to Lady Kenmure, in *Letters*, p. 41.

6. Cited in Thomas Watson, *The Duty of Self-Denial* (Morgan, Pa.: Soli Deo Gloria, 1996), p. 25.

7. See *John G. Paton: Missionary to the New Hebrides* (London: Banner of Truth, 1965).

HOLINESS PROMOTED

CHAPTER 15

STUDYING THE WORD

IN an academic environment, auditors are often the envy of their classmates. They enjoy the experience of the classroom without writing any papers or taking any exams: they don't even have to study. But at the end of the term, the only thing they have is the memory of the experience. On the other hand, those students who took the course for credit had to satisfy all the requirements, write all the papers, and take all the exams. They had to study, but they earned a grade that counted toward their fulfilling all the requirements for their degree program and ultimate graduation.

There is a parallel from this analogy to religious life and what is required in pursuing the goal of holiness. No analogy is perfect: it is impossible to audit Christianity. Every true Christian is 'enrolled for credit' and must learn the lessons of faith that will certainly involve tests. But the Lord has provided all that is necessary to learn the lessons and advance in the faith. Central to the work for any academic course is a good textbook written by an expert in the field that provides the knowledge necessary for successful completion. So it is that God has given a 'textbook' that provides the Christian everything he needs to know for life: the Bible, the very Word of God. Needless to say, every Christian should study the Bible as the principal source of instruction for growing and maturing in holiness. Significantly, Paul identified this goal as God's objective in giving the Scripture by inspiration: 'That the man of God may be perfect, throughly furnished unto all good works' (2 Tim. 3:17). The word 'perfect' has the idea, specifically, of being capable or proficient. Studying the Scripture, therefore, is the means of increasing proficiency in advancing in the holiness to which God calls His people.[1]

The Bible warrants the utmost attention. I remember from high school and college a series of short booklets called CliffsNotes used by some students to provide

---

1. 'Significantly, the text before us, containing the Bible's most famous statement of the inspiration of Scripture, is set in the context of continuance – going on, remaining in the gospel. What Christians believe about the Scriptures has everything to do with their continuance and service in the faith' (R. Kent Hughes, *1 & 2 Timothy and Titus: To Guard the Deposit*, Preaching the Word [Wheaton, Ill.: Crossway, 2000], p. 236).

a synopsis of the primary texts that were assigned in literature courses, whether Chaucer or Shakespeare. Those students got the gist and had a far easier read than the rest of us that slogged our ways through all the archaic language of the actual sources. Too often, Christians rely on books about the Bible rather than studying the Scriptures themselves. There is nothing wrong with books about the Bible; they can be helpful and edifying, and I've contributed my share to the stockpile. But there is no substitute for personal study. It is the entrance of God's Word into the heart that gives light to the path (Ps. 119:130), and it is that 'engrafted word' that is able to save the soul and must be attended to for setting aside wickedness (James 1:21). In simple terms, the Bible is a means of grace; it is a means of spiritual growth (1 Pet. 2:2).

The Westminster Larger Catechism sums up succinctly why it is so important to study the Scriptures: 'The Scriptures principally teach, what man is to believe concerning God, and what duty God requires of man' (Q. 5). Knowing those two things is crucial. Hence, Paul admonished Timothy and us, 'Study to shew thyself approved unto God, a workman that needeth not to be ashamed, rightly dividing the word of truth' (2 Tim. 2:15). Although the word 'study' literally means 'to be diligent,' it is an appropriate word to refer to what we mean by 'study.' Correctly using (rightly dividing) the word of truth requires more than just a casual reading; it requires assiduous attention. It demands study.

It is in the Bible that we learn that God's required duty for us is to be holy; it is in the Bible that we learn how to pursue that holiness. It would be good if every Christian could echo sincerely the testimony of the Psalmist: 'And I will delight myself in thy commandments, which I have loved' (119:47). Studying the Bible should be the lifelong practice of every believer. There are some key thoughts to keep in mind when opening the Bible.

HOW TO VIEW THE BIBLE

The Bible is unique; there is nothing like it. Sixty-six separate books written by multiple authors over a span of 1,500 years, the Bible is ultimately one book with one Author, God Himself. The Scriptures, therefore, are not what ancient men thought about God or divine matters; they are the very words of God expressing and revealing His mind. By a supernatural operation referred to as inspiration, God breathed out His words (2 Tim. 3:16) to holy men who were carried along in the writing process by the Holy Spirit (2 Pet. 1:21). The Bible is God's Word because it claims to be God's Word, and faith believes it. That may seem to be circular reasoning, and perhaps it is, but it is reason that rests on God who is incapable of lying (Titus 1:2).

When we view the Scriptures through faith, we do so with a set of beliefs that we take for granted to be true. These presuppositions are essential and inevitable. It is absolutely impossible to come to the Bible with an open mind.[2] Liberal

---

2. 'In our discussion hitherto we have approached the Bible as the Word of God and consequently, as perfectly trustworthy in all that is says. Behind this approach lies the assumption that there is a

scholars often claim they approach Scripture with an open mind in order to evaluate the Word of God and judge its accuracy. In reality they come with the presupposition that human reason is superior to divine revelation. That is not an open mind; it is a closed heart that evidences a mindset predisposed against God and truth. Man cannot stand as the judge of Scripture; Scripture stands as the judge of man. As believers, we must come with an open and receptive heart to receive and believe what God says. The mindset of a believer every time he opens the Bible must be the conviction that *whatever the Bible says is true.* The believer may not completely comprehend all that he reads, but he does not doubt its truth. We cannot trust our reason to determine what is true or false, right or wrong. By faith we believe in the inspiration of the Bible, and therefore we affirm its authority, infallibility, sufficiency, and effectiveness from cover to cover. Each of these corollaries to inspiration are topics for thorough treatises, but for now simple definition will suffice.[3]

By *authority*, we mean that the Word of God is the absolute standard of truth (matters of faith) and the absolute rule for living (matters of practice).[4] The Westminster Larger Catechism summarizes well: 'The holy scriptures of the Old and New Testament are the word of God, the only rule of faith and obedience' (Q. 3).

By *infallibility*, we mean that the Bible is free from error.[5] Truth is absolute, and all truth has its ultimate source in God, who is Truth and the revealer of truth. Infallibility extends to every statement of Scripture, including matters of history and science as well as matters of theology.[6] For sure, the Bible is not intended to be a textbook for history or science, but that does not mean it is inaccurate when touching on those matters. The Bible is the standard by which all matters of

---

God, even the one living and true Creator of heaven and earth. It is He in whose very hand is our life and breath, and to whom we owe our existence. Undergirding the entire argument, therefore, is the presupposition of Christian theism: God is, and God has spoken' (E. J. Young, *Thy Word Is Truth* [Edinburgh: Banner of Truth, 1972], p. 185).

3. Peter A. Lillback and Richard B. Gaffin, Jr., eds., *Thy Word is Still Truth: Essential Writings on the Doctrine of Scripture from the Reformation to Today* (Phillipsburg, N.J.: P&R, 2013). This volume contains an exhaustive treatment on the many topics related to inspiration. Someone looking to understand the historic, Reformed understanding of Scripture should start with this volume and the writings found in it.

4. 'For Jesus, it was enough simply to say, "It is written ...." He understood Scripture to be nothing less than God's Word of self-revelation. Because it was breathed out by God, it is flawless, beyond all contradiction, and to be obeyed immediately, not hesitatingly; absolutely, not selectively' (John MacArthur, ed., *The Inerrant Word: Biblical, Historical, Theological, and Pastoral Perspectives* [Wheaton, Ill.: Crossway, 2016], p. 84).

5. 'When God speaks, what he says is expressive of his character and is by implication therefore inerrant .... This divine testimony bears its own divine character, namely, inerrancy. Men and women may lie to the Holy Spirit, and do so. But he does not lie to them' (MacArthur, ed., *The Inerrant Word*, p. 273).

6. 'An inerrant Scripture cannot contain falsehood, fraud, or deceit in its teachings or assertions. The denial explicitly rejects the tendency of some to limit infallibility and inerrancy to specific segments of the biblical message, such as spiritual, religious, or redemptive themes, excluding assertions from the fields of history or science' (R. C. Sproul, *Scripture Alone: The Evangelical Doctrine* [Phillipsburg, N.J.: P&R, 2005], p. 151).

theology, history, and science are to be judged. The simple fact is that whenever or wherever something disagrees with the Bible, that thing is wrong.

By *sufficiency*, we mean that the Bible is all we need to direct us in how to know God and please Him. It is all that we need to direct us safely and surely through this life and to the life to come.[7] The Psalmist declared that 'the law of the LORD is perfect' (Ps. 19:7). The word *law* refers here to the whole body of God's revealed instruction, the whole of special revelation. The word *perfect* refers especially to its completeness or wholeness. In simple terms, God's Word is complete. According to His infinite wisdom and good purpose, God has revealed all that we need for the welfare of our souls.[8] Therefore, the Psalmist concludes that this complete Word converts the soul; that is, it has a restoring and revitalizing impact on the whole man. There is no need for humanly defined philosophy, psychology, opinion, or experience to supplement the Bible. It may sound trite, but it is true: if God said it, that settles it.

By *effectiveness*, we mean that there is an inherent power in God's Word to accomplish what it says. The Lord Himself declared, 'So shall my word be that goeth forth out of my mouth: it shall not return unto me void, but it shall accomplish that which I please, and it shall prosper in the thing whereto I sent it' (Isa. 55:11). The Word of God is the hammer that in judgment breaks rocks into pieces (Jer. 23:29); it is the means of grace whereby God communicates the message of the gospel that saves all who believe (Rom. 10:17).

The bottom line is that every time we open the Scripture, we must do so with awe and reverence generated by the certain knowledge that the Bible is not an ordinary book but the very Word of the eternal God, whose veracity is beyond question or doubt. The Bible is not what men define it to be; it is what God declares it to be.[9] Men can believe that or deny that, but they cannot alter that. The premise that the Bible is the inspired, authoritative, infallible, sufficient, and effective Word of God should be the foundation for the study of Scripture. All truth has its source in God and, consequently, His truth is universal and timeless. Although times change, truth is changeless. Although applications of truth can vary, truth is constant. This is good reason to make the Bible a subject for study.

HOW TO APPROACH THE BIBLE

Once we have established the proper presuppositions and mindset about the Scriptures, we must develop proper procedures for studying and properly

---

7. 'In sum, the God-breathed Word is "useful" for all of life, all doctrine and all duty, all creed and all conduct – everything!' (Hughes, *1 & 2 Timothy and Titus*, p. 239).

8. 'The word "law" is the Hebrew word *torah*. Sometimes this refers specifically to the Law of Moses, but here it refers to all Scripture. God's Word is perfect, complete, blameless, and without blemish. There is nothing missing from God's Word – it is completely sufficient' (James Johnston, *Psalms 1–41: Rejoice, the Lord is King*, Preaching the Word, The Psalms, Volume 1 [Wheaton, Ill.: Crossway, 2015], p. 208).

9. 'The Scriptures themselves represent the Scriptures as not merely containing here and there the record of revelations—"words of God," *toroth*—given by God, but as themselves, in all their extent, a revelation, an authoritative body of gracious instructions from God' (Benjamin B. Warfield, *The Inspiration and Authority of the Bible* [Grand Rapids: Baker Book, 1948], p. 101).

interpreting the Bible. Interpretation is simply the process whereby we determine what something means, whether we read it or hear it. It is something that we do all the time; it is an indispensable part of communication. We all know how important it is when speaking to others to be understood. We all can tell stories, tragic or comical, about some misunderstanding of language. Husbands and wives sometimes even argue because one reads something into what the other said that was really not intended. This really is an essential key in the interpretative process: we must be careful to figure out what the speaker or writer meant. When we start reading in meanings not intended, misunderstanding, and possibly serious consequences, can ensue. Those consequences will be more or less severe depending on the nature of the communication. It certainly makes sense that, if we are seeking to interpret God's Word, we should exercise every caution to figure out what God meant.

Truth is not what we define it to be; it is what God has revealed and declared it to be. One of the issues in modern discussions about biblical hermeneutics (the science of interpretation) is whether attention should be given to authorial intent or reader response. Focusing on authorial intent recognizes that there is an objective and understandable message conveyed that ought to be discoverable by the normal process of interpretation. It leads to objective truth. Focusing on reader response implies that what the author meant is irrelevant and indiscernible, and that therefore what the reader sees becomes truth. It eliminates the possibility of absolute truth; truth becomes some floating abstraction that subjectively changes from reader to reader. The authority resides in the reader and not in the Word. What God means is infinitely more important than how I feel about what He said. Truth is whatever the Bible says, not whatever man thinks the Bible says. It may be trite, but it is true: God means what He says, and He says what He means. The purpose of His Word is not to mislead but to lead men to truth.[10]

Since it is so important when studying the Scriptures to discern what God is saying and then to implement it by being doers of the Word (James 1:22-25), I am going to suggest some ways that every Christian should approach the Scriptures with a view to understanding it and applying it.

1. Prayerfully

Begin every session of Bible study with prayer. As the Psalmist prayed for God to open his eyes to behold the wondrous things of the law, so must we pray (Ps. 119:18). Both the Scripture and prayer are means of grace, instruments through which God works in us. Through the Scriptures, God speaks to us, and in prayer we speak to God. Bible study should be an occasion of communication, and God's Word should

---

10. 'The Christian accepts the Bible as the Word of God. The Spirit of God has persuaded him of this fact, and he knows that the words of the Scriptures are words which have found their origin in God. Hence, the humble and devout Christian believer, whether he be scholarly or uneducated, no matter who the opponents of the Bible may be, will accept the words of the Bible as true' (Young, *Thy Word Is Truth*, p. 196).

define the topic of that conversation. Prayer expresses our desire for God's Word to find lodging in our hearts and transform us to what God desires for us.

Psalm 19:11-14 demonstrates the link between God's Word and prayer. In the light of God's Word, David acknowledged the benefits of obeying the Word and admitted the inherent pitfalls within himself that would hinder his desired compliance. Consequently, he prayed specifically for two things: personal purity and pleasing behavior before the Lord. That is the pattern for us to follow.

In praying for personal purity, he first asked for forgiveness: 'cleanse thou me from secret faults' (Ps. 19:12). The verb 'cleanse' has the idea of acquitting or being declared free from punishment. David recognized the gravity of his crimes against the Lord, even those unknown to any other but him and God. There could be no way forward until he had the assurance of pardoning grace. But there was a way forward because God's wonderful Word revealed that the Lord is good, ready to forgive, and plenteous in mercy unto all who call on Him (Ps. 86:5). He then expressed his desire to be protected and preserved from future sins. Presumptuous sins are those insolent sins that David acknowledged would be so disrespectful to the holy God. It is always the case that the nearer one is to God the more sensitive one is to sin, seeing it as an affront against God. 'The great transgression' in the Hebrew text of Psalm 19:13 is actually indefinite, not referring to any one particular sin but any and all violations of God's standards of righteousness. He prays that he might be kept from great sin. That is a big request, but the sadly unfulfilled desire of those sincerely trying to follow God's Word is to be sin-free (Rom. 7). Believers universally experience the tension between the desire to be holy and the nagging presence of indwelling sin, but the way to victory over sin is clearly marked. God's Word directs us in the way of purity. That is wonderful; we are not left to wander our way to a closer walk with God.

David was concerned not only with avoiding sin, but also with expressing a positive dedication to the Lord in his activity, communication, and thought. He wanted his life to be 'acceptable' before Jehovah (his covenant God), his Rock (his stable foundation), and his Redeemer (his near Kinsman). He trusted that God would always act surely, reliably and appropriately to meet his needs.[11] The acceptance he desires does not refer to a legal standing that he sought to earn or merit, but refers rather to that behavior which would be pleasing to the Lord. Every believer wants to please the Lord. The wonderful thing is that God has not left His people guessing as to what pleases Him. He has revealed it in His word. The Bible, God's Word, is absolutely essential for every aspect of life, spiritual, temporal and eternal. So as we open it to read and study, we should pray for its effect to take place in our lives. It issues the call for holiness and instructs us in the way of holiness.

---

11. 'The significance of the figure, [the Rock], is broader than that because it represents God as the solid foundation of his life, his place of security and safety, and his strength .... The combination of "my rock" and "my redeemer" provides a powerful summary of the nature and provision of God' (Ross, *A Commentary on the Psalms: Volume 1* [Grand Rapids: Kregel, 2011], pp. 485-86).

2. Dependently

Being a student presupposes the need for a teacher. Occasionally, those who are self-taught succeed in learning sufficiently, but the norm is for teachers to give directions and to be available to clarify things for the students. Happily, every Christian can sit under the tutelage of the Ideal Teacher, the Holy Spirit. Every Christian should consciously depend on the Holy Spirit every time he opens the Bible, praying that the Holy Spirit will teach us truth.[12] The Lord Jesus promised His disciples that the Spirit of truth would guide them into all truth (John 16:13). Not only do the specific implications of that promise relate to the inspiration of the New Testament, but it also has great significance for every believer who seeks to hear God in the inspired Word. In 1 Corinthians the apostle Paul refers to the great truths of the gospel as those things God has revealed to us by His Spirit (1 Cor. 2:10). He then says concerning these truths that they are what the Holy Spirit teaches by 'comparing spiritual things with spiritual' (1 Cor. 2:13). This could be rendered literally 'expounding spiritual [truths] to spiritual [men].' This statement highlights two essential points. First, it is the ministry of the Holy Spirit to illumine and instruct believers in the things of God. The Holy Spirit is the ultimate and consummate teacher of every believer. Second, we must have regenerated hearts before we can understand anything God says. 'The natural man receiveth not the things of the Spirit of God: for they are foolishness unto him: neither can he know them, because they are spiritually discerned. But he that is spiritual judgeth [discerns] all things' (1 Cor. 2:14-15a). Understanding God's Word depends in great measure on knowing Him.[13] It is the Spirit of God that regenerates sinners, turning them into spiritual men and thereby introducing them to the knowledge of God; it is the Spirit of God that leads saints into a more intimate knowledge of God through the Word.[14] That is His job. As believers—whether preachers, seminary professors, or laymen—we must learn more and more to depend on the Holy Spirit.

3. Diligently

Even a cursory reading of Scripture can be profitable; just scratching the surface uncovers truths that will benefit the soul. But many Christians limit their use of the Bible to surfing for familiar and devotional texts. Familiar and devotional texts

---

12. 'The Spirit in his internal testimony works to confirm the reliability of Scripture, giving us certainty that the Bible is the Word of God' (Sproul, *Scripture Alone: The Evangelical Doctrine*, p. 92).

13. 'Human persons cannot search out the hidden things of God unaided, through their own limited resources of wisdom, knowledge, or stance' (Anthony C. Thiselton, *The First Epistle to the Corinthians*, The New International Greek Testament Commentary [Grand Rapids: Eerdmans, 2000], p. 256).

14. 'Here the emphasis lies on their inability. Again it is "like is known by like" (see v. 11); without the Spirit they lack the one essential "quality" necessary for them to know God and his ways – "because they are spiritually discerned. ..." For Paul, "to be spiritual" and "to discern spiritually" simply means to have the Spirit, who so endows and enables' (Gordon Fee, *The First Epistle to the Corinthians*, The New International Commentary on the New Testament [Grand Rapids: Eerdmans, 1988], p. 117).

are good. But such a restricted regimen of Bible reading can miss the blessing of finding precious nuggets of truth that can be found only by a diligent searching and studying of the Scripture. Proverbs 2 says that if we will seek truth as silver and search for it as if for hidden treasure, we will not be disappointed, for the Lord promises to give wisdom, knowledge and understanding. This passage, in fact, suggests that industry or diligence rather than ability is a key factor in studying the Scripture.

Solomon outlines three features that should mark our approach to God's Word. (1) It should be *sincere*: 'So that thou incline thine ear ... and apply thine heart' (Prov. 2:2). To incline the ear is literally to sharpen the ear, an idiom for paying careful attention. To apply the heart is to stretch out the heart, which entails the operation of the entire inner self: mind, emotions, and will. (2) It should be *earnest*: 'Yea, if thou criest ... and liftest up thy voice' (Prov. 2:3). The verbs crying out and lifting up or giving the voice are expressions of fervent appeal. (3) It should be *persevering*: 'If thou seekest her as silver, and searchest for her as for hid treasures' (Prov. 2:4).

Both the image of miners digging for their treasure and the verbal forms for seeking and searching picture an unrelenting, unrelaxing diligence of pursuit. Mining is hard work. Indeed, that God's Word is compared to silver and hidden treasures suggests that the prize is not always lying on the surface. Part of the problem in most Bible study is that unless the message is on the surface, the average reader moves on in his reading, kicking up dust, until he finds an obvious surface lesson. Shuffling along does not typically result in discovered treasures; sometimes we have to dig, and discovering even a nugget increases the desire for more. The digging becomes profitable and enjoyable when we realize we are handling the very Word of God – the Word without which we cannot survive. From Genesis through Malachi to Revelation, the Word of God reveals changeless and eternal truth. Let us keep our Bibles open and not give up until we discover the truth, since we know that God is the rewarder of those who diligently seek Him. The Lord promises that when we seek Him we will find Him if we seek Him with all our heart (Jer. 29:13). That is the truth.

4. Contemplatively

The blessed man is he whose 'delight is in the law of the LORD; and in his law doth he meditate day and night' (Ps. 1:2). Similarly, the Psalmist said, 'O how I love thy law! it is my meditation all the day' (Ps. 119:97). This word *meditate* has the idea of being consumed or preoccupied with something. The blessed man just cannot get the law out of his mind. This clearly defines the difference between what the Bible means by meditating and what the typical notion of the world is. Whereas worldly meditation seeks to empty the mind of everything, biblical meditation seeks to fill the mind with the Word of God.[15] According to that biblical definition,

---

15. 'The spiritual discipline of meditation, according to the Psalter, begins with the memorization of divine instruction so that all along the way by day, or on the bed at night, one could recall it and think about it' (Ross, *A Commentary on the Psalms: Volume 1*, p. 189).

there is precious little meditation in the average Christian's life. Far too frequently Christians read the Bible without thinking. The eyes fall mechanically over the ink for a designated number of pages without the mind comprehending a thing. Devotions sadly consist of little more than a few verses before leaving home at the beginning of a busy day, or a few verses before going to bed after a busy day. There is just so much to do, and we feel at a loss if we are not busy doing. But the amount of blessing we receive from the Bible and the degree to which we understand the Bible will be in proportion to how much time we meditate on what we have read. Very simply, meditating is thinking, and here is the proverbial rub: thinking takes time; thinking is work. But thinking time is not wasted time. Many Christians get nothing from the Bible not because they are ignorant but because they are thoughtless. At the very least, this exhibits irreverence toward God's holy Word. Although our tendency when we read Scripture is to skip over the parts we don't understand immediately, it is important just to pause and think and ask the Teacher, the Holy Spirit, to explain. Don't give up too quickly. Remember that the purpose of Scripture is to reveal the truth, not to conceal it. Take the time to pray and think over the open Bible. Time is like money: we don't have much of either to spend. But one way or another we seem to have money to spend on the things we really want, and we seem to have time to spend on the things that are most important to us. If we truly agree with the Psalmist that God's Word is more precious than gold, we will want to devote as much thinking time to it as we possibly can.[16]

There is something about the process of thinking that grooves the brain. Granted that is not a medical or scientific explanation, but it is accurate, nonetheless. If you think about something long and hard enough, you can't help but think about it more. Those are the thoughts that naturally come to mind when not consciously thinking about something else. This is why Paul's counsel is so much on point: 'whatsoever things are true, whatsoever things are honest, whatsoever things are just, whatsoever things are lovely, whatsoever things are of good report; if there be any virtue, and if there be any praise, think on these things' (Phil. 4:8).

This is why studying the Bible is such a crucial component of obeying God's call to holiness. It is the way of filling the mind with proper thoughts. Since right thinking determines right behavior, there is nothing better to think about than God's Word.

5. Submissively

At Israel's national constitution at Sinai, Moses relayed God's word to them that they would enjoy a unique and special status with the Lord if they would obey His

---

16. 'God's Word is the greatest treasure for those who love him. We love the Bible more than we love money, more than fine gold. God's Word is our greatest pleasure. Sweet honey represents the pleasure of the senses – the finest tasting food, the best-smelling perfume, the most fashionable clothes, the fastest cars, the best new songs. The Bible is better. Do you feel that way? Do you love the Bible and treasure it? If you know God, his Word will be your treasure and your delight' (Johnston, *The Psalms, Volume 1*, pp. 209-10).

voice and keep His covenant (Exod. 19:3-6). Although they did not follow through on their verbal commitment, Israel's initial response was on target: 'All that the LORD hath spoken we will do' (Exod. 19:8). At the end of Moses' last sermon to his wilderness congregation after they had gone back on their word so often, he implored them to 'set your hearts unto all the words which I testify among you' (Deut. 32:46). To set the heart was to incline the whole of their inner being—the mind, the affections, and the will—to the word that they had heard. They were to submit to its authority, evidencing that submission by obedience. Doing what God says to do was the right thing to do for Israel (Deut. 6:25). It continues to be the right thing to do for all of God's people. Many years later, James echoed the same thought when he implored the scattered tribes (James 1:1) to be doers of the word and not hearers only (James 1:22). Humbly and actively submitting in obedience to God's Word sums up what God expects and demands. The Preacher put it this way: 'Fear God, and keep his commandments: for this is the whole duty of man' (Eccles. 12:13).

Approaching the Scriptures submissively touches on what should be the fundamental objective in studying the Bible.[17] The Bible records many facts about history, people, and religion, all of which are good to know. Yet, it is possible to know all the facts without experiencing an effect in the heart. Secular universities and liberal seminaries are filled with Bible scholars who know the facts yet deny the authority and absolute truth of what they know the Bible says. They tend to make the Bible subservient to their own reason and logic. On the contrary, as we approach the Bible to study it to learn what God wants us to know and to do, we do so with submission to the Bible's claims over us and with the resolve to conform to its teaching. In obeying God's call to holiness, we must acknowledge that God's Word stands over us as the final authority for our faith and practice. The more we understand the Scripture's claims, the more its claims will control our thinking and our doing. So we study the Bible bowing to its authority.

HOW TO STUDY THE BIBLE

Students who have done poorly on a test often protest that they spent hours studying but somehow still failed to give evidence of learning. Indeed, they may have looked at the textbook for hours, but the problem is that they read without plan or purpose. They did not know what they were looking for and didn't recognize what was important when they saw it. To teach good study habits as well as the subject facts, teachers will often supply students with study guides or study questions to aid them in reading the textbook. These guides and questions teach the students where to focus their attention and hopefully how to establish sound methods and good habits of study.

---

17. 'The fact of the matter is that there is only one way in which we can legitimately study the Bible, and that is to approach it as those who have submitted their entire being to God, who have acknowledged Him as their Lord, and who come to His Word ready to hearken to all that it has to say' (Young, *Thy Word Is Truth*, p. 190).

Similarly, there are many Christians who claim they don't 'get anything' from their Bible reading even though they read it regularly. Part of the problem is they read without plan or purpose. To be sure, just the reading of the Scripture is profitable because it will help foster a familiarity with the content that aids in the interpretive exercise. But there is a difference between just reading the Bible and intentionally studying it. It is impossible in this one chapter to develop a whole course for Bible study, but some general suggestions are in order.

First, look for Jesus. Jesus is the key that unlocks the meaning and message of the Bible. Keeping in mind the purpose of Scripture as a whole will help to identify the purpose of each of the parts of that whole. The overriding purpose of special revelation is to guide men to a proper relationship with God. God's gracious salvation is the only way guilty sinners can experience that relationship, and God's gracious salvation is in and through and by His Son, the Lord Jesus Christ. It follows that if the purpose of Scripture is to guide men to the Lord, and if the only way to the Lord is through the redemption of the Lord Jesus Christ, then the revelation of Christ should be the grand and predominant theme of Scripture. All revealed truth in one way or another relates to and is ultimately defined by that central truth. Obviously, the New Testament develops that saving theme. The Gospels, with the narratives concerning His earthly ministry, introduce the performance of His saving work, the historic foundation of the gospel. Acts records the initial proclamation and dissemination of the message of His saving work. The Epistles explain and expound the nature of His person and work and the implications for personal and church life. The book of Revelation assures us of the consummation of all the glorious truths of His person and work. It is equally true that Christ is the key that unlocks the mysteries of the Old Testament. The Pentateuch, the first five books with all their religious rituals, prepares the way for the perfect Priest to stand between God and men as the perfect sacrifice for sin. The Historical Books draw attention to the perfect King, who would come to rule His people and subdue His enemies. The Prophets anticipate the perfect Prophet, who represents and reveals the only true and living God to man. The Poetical Books put it all together with the Christ as the great theme for worship and praise.

According to Paul in 2 Corinthians 3, it is finding Christ that always opens the eyes to the true meaning of Scripture. To miss seeing Christ, either in the overall scheme of Scripture or in any individual book is to miss the central message and to jeopardize the proper understanding of the rest of the message. So as you begin to study the Bible, do so through the lens of Jesus.[18]

---

18. 'Here are three great openings – the opening of the Scriptures, the opening of the eyes, and the opening of the mind. All three need to be reproduced in the life of every growing Christian. To have the Scriptures opened in the right way is to open the eyes to Christ. And this in turn opens our eyes in a new way to the Scriptures…. If this happens for you, the Bible will cease to be a book to be handled only and instead will become a tool to be looked through. It will become a telescope which will bring you close to the Lord Jesus' (James Montgomery Boice, *Why and How to Study the Bible* [Philadelphia, Pa.: The Bible Study Hour, 1990], p. 10).

Second, pay attention to the context. Taking something out of context is one of the most common errors of interpretation. We all know what it's like to come into the middle of a conversation and jump to the wrong conclusion because we heard only part of what was said. It is unfair to any writer or speaker to extract statements from here and there and thereby totally misrepresent the intended meaning. If fairness demands caution and care in everyday communication, how much more vital it is to interpret Scripture in its context. Sometimes the quest for 'proof-texts' or the attraction to isolated favorite verses has resulted in interpretations and applications that are far distant from what the original author intended. Giving attention to the context is only being fair to Scripture. If our desire is to discover what God means and not just to prove our point with 'biblical' evidence, then we will make sure to keep verses in context. To ignore the context is to jeopardize the authority of the message or at least make it suspicious.[19]

By context, we simply mean the location or environment in which the text occurs. It certainly includes the immediately surrounding verses, but it extends also to the larger context of the entire book and then ultimately to the whole context of divine revelation. It is like looking at a target, with the bull's eye in the center and the various rings extending from the center. The bull's eye is contained within the entire ring structure and has no significance as a bull's eye independent from the other rings. Obviously, to hit the bull's eye you must stay within all the rings. The point is that there is a unity of meaning in all of Scripture because all of Scripture, whether Old or New Testament and regardless of human author, has a single Author, the Lord God Himself. God is invariably consistent and so never contradicts Himself. This consideration of the larger context is often called the analogy of Scripture, which simply means that Scripture must be interpreted in the light of Scripture.[20] First Corinthians 14:32 may hint at this principle: 'And the spirits of the prophets are subject to the prophets.' The Bible is its own best commentary. The Westminster Confession summarizes this principle well: 'The infallible rule of interpretation of Scripture is the Scripture itself: and therefore, when there is a question about the true and full sense of any Scripture, (which is not manifold, but one), it must be searched and known by other places that speak more clearly' (1.9). Paying attention to context involves reading and knowing the content of the Bible. Read your Bible.

Third, use the appropriate tools. Regardless of how prayerfully, consistently, and thoughtfully we read the Scripture, there will still be statements difficult to

---

19. 'Because the Bible is *God's Word,* it has *eternal relevance;* it speaks to all humankind, in every age and in every culture. Because it is God's Word, we must listen – and obey. But because God chose to speak His Word through *human words in history,* every book in the Bible also has *historical particularity;* each document is conditioned by the language, time, and culture in which it was originally written' (Gordon D. Fee and Douglas Stuart, *How to Read the Bible for All Its Worth* [Grand Rapids: Zondervan, 2003], p. 21).

20. 'That analogy of faith is the rule that Scripture is to interpret Scripture.... This means, quite simply, that no part of Scripture can be interpreted in such a way as to render it in conflict with what is clearly taught elsewhere in Scripture' (R. C. Sproul, *Knowing Scripture* [Downers Grove, Ill.: InterVarsity, 1977], p. 46).

understand. How much we understand about anything we read or hear depends on the extent of our experience and knowledge of that subject matter. Because of my total lack of mechanical skills and ignorance of engines, I could listen to a conversation about cars and not have a clue about what I was hearing. I don't know the jargon; I don't know the location or function of the parts that make a car run. My ignorance does not affect the reality of those things or diminish their importance. Thankfully, there are those who have the skill and the knowledge of mechanics, and I am most happy to depend on them for what is beyond my knowledge or experience. On rare occasions I have ventured outside my sphere of knowledge only to regret a mess I made. A hole in the wall under our bathroom sink testifies to my botching a simple job that a plumber could have done correctly in a matter of minutes. There are times when we must rely on experts.

The same principle applies to the study of Scripture. Matters of ancient culture, ancient history, and ancient languages are factors in the overall interpretation of Scripture. These issues help us to put the Bible in the real context in which it was originally given. But not every Christian who desires to read and understand the Bible has this helpful knowledge. There are experts, though, who have studied these areas and who can provide counsel and help. Rather than despair about your lack of knowledge, be thankful and consider that this is part of God's order and purpose. Among the gifts that God has given the church are pastors and teachers 'for the perfecting of the saints, for the work of the ministry, for the edifying of the body of Christ' (Eph. 4:11-12). The same principle was true in the Old Testament. The detailed regulations in Leviticus concerning what was clean or unclean illustrate the point. God gave the people instructions that He expected them to understand and obey. They themselves had to take the Word and discern what it meant and how it applied. But there were some matters beyond the experience or knowledge of the people. In those instances, God instructed them to go to the priests, whose experience and knowledge could answer their questions. God held the people responsible for both what they discovered on their own and what they learned from the priest.

It is not my purpose here to list all the tools available for Bible study. But certainly every serious student of the Word should have a good concordance, a good Bible dictionary or encyclopedia, an atlas, and a book of systematic theology. A study Bible like the *Reformation Heritage KJV Study Bible* addresses the key issues of the text that could generate further study. In addition, its application suggestions for worship themes will give direction to devotional thoughts as well. And don't hesitate to ask the minister that God has given you. My guess is that any minister would be thrilled to learn that his people are becoming curious and serious about learning as much of God's Word as possible. That would be evidence that the body is being edified and that saints are being perfected for the work of the ministry.

Fourth, read purposefully. Reading the Bible devotionally with a view to daily benefit and application should be the common exercise of every believer.

Meditating on a key thought for the day is food for the soul. But systematic and thorough study of Scripture ought to be a part of every Christian's routine as well. There are many ways to go about Bible study, but I'm just going to suggest a couple of ideas to guide your thoughts in developing a plan for studying individual books of the Bible, one by one. This is going to require some time and effort, but it is study after all. Studying the Bible should discover the answers to three key questions.

First, what does the Bible say? The only way to answer this question personally is to read the Bible. As much as possible read the book completely in a single sitting. Longer books may require multiple sits. For the longer books, use the outline that you can find in a Study Bible as a guide to major sections and read as many of the sections as you can. One of the disadvantages of the chapter/verse divisions in our Bibles is that it tends to foster a segmented and disjointed reading of the text. A chapter or a few verses are read, and then by the time of the next day's reading the whole flow of thought has gone. The purpose of reading as much as possible all at once is to overview the general message and direction of the book. Reading the whole or large sections multiple times will help you determine the purpose of the book – why it was written and what it is about.

Discovering what the Bible says should also involve reading the book analytically, looking for specific themes. One way to do this is simply to identify the major loci or topics of theology. Note what the book says about God, Christ, man, sin, salvation, and judgment. It would be helpful in this analysis to use a copy of Scripture that you can mark. Copies of the Bible are readily available on computers so that chapters can easily be printed out. Using colored pencils to mark the different doctrines will help to visualize what themes are most common and where they occur in the argument of the book. In addition to the major doctrines, identify and mark repeated words or phrases that may suggest the major emphasis. It would be good to mark the imperatives that direct behavior as well as all the promises and warnings that may occur. Answering this first question involves collecting the data. Reread the book, observing how the marked themes work together to convey the principal message of the book. By looking at the colors, you should be able to identify the central theme and discover how the subthemes relate to its development and help to put things in perspective.

Second, what does the Bible mean? This step in the process involves interpretation. The essential perspicuity (inherent clearness) of the Scripture makes answering this question possible. In the Bible, God is communicating to us, and He expects us to understand what He is saying. The Westminster Confession of Faith puts it this way: 'All things in Scripture are not alike plain in themselves, nor alike clear unto all: yet those things which are necessary to be known, believed, and observed for salvation, are so clearly propounded and opened in some place of Scripture or other, that not only the learned, but the unlearned in a due use of the ordinary means, may attain unto a sufficient understanding of them' (1.7).

Yet, some things are harder to understand than others. Admittedly, what Peter said of Paul's writing applies to other portions of Scripture too: 'some things [are] hard to be understood' (2 Pet. 3:16). Therefore, determining what the Bible means may require some research. Use the appropriate tools and resources that will help answer the hard questions. Using your Study Bible and reading a few commentaries should help to discover the meaning.

Third, what does the Bible require? Answering this question is the ultimate objective of studying the Bible. The steps of Bible study must lead from examination (what it says) to interpretation (what it means) to application (what it requires). Without application, Bible study is reduced to merely an academic exercise. The facts, meaning, and significance of what the Bible says must be brought into personal experience. Knowing about God and what pleases Him is learnable; knowing God and doing what pleases Him is holiness.

CHAPTER 16

PUTTING ON THE WHOLE ARMOR OF GOD[1]

(EPHESIANS 6:14-18)

I ONCE heard a story about a farmer who responded to watermelon thieves by putting a sign in his field that said, 'Warning: One of these melons has been poisoned.' For a few days, he thought his idea had worked – no more watermelons were stolen. Then, one day, he discovered that the sign had been altered to read, 'Warning: Two of these melons have been poisoned.' The farmer had to destroy his entire crop, as he didn't know which other melon was poisoned.

The devil works in similar ways to thwart our Spirit-driven efforts to maintain and increase the fruits of righteousness and holiness in our lives. No matter what sign you put up, he changes it and comes up with something else. He is a master manipulator and deceiver. How will we ever fight against him successfully? How can we stand in defiance against Satan's sinister schemes to overthrow the holiness that is being worked-in by God and worked-out in our lives?

The eighteenth-century Scottish divine Ralph Erskine said the only choice we have in responding to Satan is 'flight or fight.' In light of that, the Christian soldier uses three major strategies to fight against Satan. The first we might call *strategic retreat*, or running for shelter to Christ. As Christian soldiers, we lean on the power of Christ's might, for we have no shelter from Satan but in Christ (Ps. 57:1).

Having learned where to find refuge in the evil day, we then use the second strategy of our military training, an *unyielding defense*. Much of Paul's famous spiritual warfare passage in Ephesians 6:10-18 describes this strategy against Satan. We stand, fight, conquer, and drive out Satan in the strength of God's armor.

The third strategy is an *aggressive offense*. In Ephesians 6:14-18, Paul describes the five pieces of armor that we use defensively against Satan, then three ways to fight him offensively.

---

1. This chapter contains material updated and revised, from chapters 3–4 of Joel R. Beeke, *Fighting Satan: Knowing His Weaknesses, Strategies, and Defeat* (Grand Rapids: Reformation Heritage Books, 2015).

'Put on the whole armour of God' (Eph. 6:11), Paul tells us. Partial equipment will not suffice; twice we are told to put on the 'whole armour' (vv. 11, 13). We put on God by putting on His armor. Christ Himself made and wore the armor, and the Holy Spirit fits it to us and makes it ours. We must fight through to the end until we hold the field against Satan. Then we must go on the offense, attacking him. Let's look at each of the eight pieces of armor that Paul counsels us to use, gleaning practical lessons for fighting Satan today and thereby pursuing holiness.

BUILDING AN UNYIELDING DEFENSE

The Belt of Truth

Truth is a means to sanctification, to holiness of life (Eph 4:24; John 17:17). 'Stand therefore, having your loins girt about with truth,' Paul says in Ephesians 6:14. In Bible times, the soldier fastened or buckled the girdle, or belt, at his waist around the short tunic he wore. The belt supported the 'loins,' or muscles, of the lower back and served as a foundation for much of his remaining armor. Both the breastplate and sword were attached to it. Thus, 'girt loins' symbolized readiness to do battle.

Loins girt with truth are a symbol of the Christian binding to himself the faith revealed in the Bible. The Bible is our objective standard of truth and our final authority for doctrine and life. It speaks of the loins of your mind rather than loins of your heart (1 Pet. 1:13) because before truth can get to your heart, it must pass through your mind. So if you would fend off Satan, you must first fill your mind with truth. Apart from God, Satan may be the most powerful mind in the universe. Human wisdom and reason are not sufficient to withstand Satan. But God's truth, as recorded in His Word and personified in His Son, is what we need to battle Satan.

Truth in our minds is not sufficient, however. We must also possess knowledge of the truth in our hearts, our inmost being, causing us to grow in 'true holiness' (Eph. 4:24). If we are going to fight the devil successfully, not only must we master the truth, but the truth must master us. Many people today are ruled by their feelings. Despising the very theology they need, they are 'carried about with every wind of doctrine' (Eph. 4:14). Don't be tossed about with your emotions. Ground yourself in truth. Proverbs 23:23 teaches us to 'Buy the truth and sell it not,' if we would be holy. As Thomas Brooks says in *Precious Remedies*, 'A man may lawfully sell his house, land and jewels, but truth is a jewel that exceeds all price, and must not be sold.'[2]

Jesus said, 'If ye continue in my word, then are ye my disciples indeed; and ye shall know the truth, and the truth shall make you free' (John 8:31-32). We find freedom in Christ and in His truth. Demons can attack us, but they cannot overcome us if we are grounded in Christ and in His truth. The power of Christ's resurrection is greater than the power of Satan. Satan has no effective weapons against truth. He may rave against you and send numerous demons to hound you,

---

2. Thomas Brooks, *Precious Remedies* (Edinburgh: Banner of Truth, 1968), p. 21.

but if you trust in Christ as the Truth of God, you will stand firm because your feet are planted on the Rock that cannot be moved.

Satan's first great weakness is that he is planted in a lie, and, ultimately, a lie cannot stand against truth. Truth will triumph in the end. Cling to it. Know it, love it, and live it. 'Let us therefore pray unto God,' counsels John Downame, 'that we may be sanctified with his truth, that not only whatsoever we do may be grounded on God's truth, but that we may do it in uprightness of heart.'[3] Abide in Christ who is Truth, and you will gain the victory over Satan.

The Breastplate of Righteousness

The second piece of armor is the 'breastplate of righteousness' (Eph. 6:14). In Paul's day, soldiers wore a protective breastplate made of metal or very tough leather. The breastplate covered the chest and the abdomen, protecting vital organs from swords and other weapons. The breastplate was a critical defense against mortal and lesser wounds.

The Bible uses the heart and reins (kidneys) to refer to the seat of the thoughts and the deep motives and emotions of men. People in Paul's day believed that organs such as the heart and the kidneys were the center of the affections where emotions such as joy or anger originated. The apostle Paul used this understanding, unscientific though it was, to teach important spiritual lessons about protecting the vital parts of the inner man and its faculties against the attacks of Satan. In their conflict with the invisible powers, believers are most vulnerable in their thoughts, motives, and emotions. They need strong protection—a breastplate of righteousness—to keep from being wounded in their inmost being. By this piece of armor, Downame concludes, 'we are to understand a good conscience, true sanctification and a godly life, which ... we are to put on according to the example of our grand Captain Christ' as Isaiah 59:17 says, 'For he put on righteousness as a breastplate, and an helmet of salvation upon his head.'[4]

The righteousness of the breastplate is provided by God in Christ. Christ earned that righteousness through His passive and active obedience. In passive obedience, Christ satisfied God's penal justice by fully paying the penalty of sin through His sufferings and death. In active obedience, He satisfied God's perfect demand that His holy law be kept flawlessly in order to merit eternal life. Only this combination of passive and active obedience was sufficient to fully satisfy God's justice. All other forms of righteousness are worthless.

Since no mere man can perform either aspect of this righteousness (for who can pay the eternal price of death and hell, and who can keep the law perfectly?), every sinner must depend on Christ to perform it for him. Christ can do this as a

---

3. John Downame, *The Christian Warfare: Written Especially for Their Sakes who are Exercised in the Spirituall Conflict of Tentations, and are Afflicted in Conscience in the Sight Ande Sense of Their Sinnes* (London: William Stansby, 1634), 1:22.

4. Downame, *The Christian Warfare*, 1:23.

substitute for sinners since He is also God. Because Christ is God, infinite value is attached to His sufferings and His obedience to the law. That's why though a sinner can never pay for sin, Christ could pay for all the sins of all believers in a matter of hours. Each one of us urgently and desperately needs to receive Christ's righteousness by Spirit-worked faith, for if we have this righteousness, we have forgiveness of sins and eternal life. If we lack this righteousness, we will perish in our sins.

Paul said that his great goal in life was to win Christ 'and be found in him, not having mine own righteousness, which is of the law, but that which is through the faith of Christ, the righteousness which is of God by faith' (Phil. 3:9). Paul says, as it were, 'Everything else is dung, garbage. I used to be proud of my zeal and obedience. They were my breastplate; I relied on my own righteousness. But that is altogether different now.' Now, as the hymn says, 'My hope is built on nothing less / Than Jesus' blood and righteousness.'

Have you learned to see your own righteousness as the filthy rags that Isaiah speaks of (64:6)? Are you clothed instead with the white-robed righteousness of Jesus Christ?

Satan schemes to keep us from resting in Christ's righteousness. He tries to get us to base our hope for salvation on our own thoughts and feelings. Then, when our feelings dissipate and grow lukewarm, Satan whispers: 'You are not a child of God – otherwise you wouldn't feel this way; you would be much more holy than you are.'

It is easy to give way to Satan's suggestion to rely on our own thoughts and feelings, for feelings are an important part of true religion. True religion is more than notion; it also involves a person's will and emotions. We cannot be saved without feelings, for Christianity is not a stoical religion, but Satan exaggerates their importance. The righteousness of Christ is our protection against relying too much on feelings. As the hymn says:

> *I dare not trust the sweetest frame*
> *But wholly lean on Jesus' Name.*
> *On Christ, the solid rock I stand.*
> *All other ground is sinking sand.*[5]

Feelings are not the foundation of our salvation. Faith comes first. Feelings are the fruit of faith in Christ's righteousness. We must learn to cast ourselves on what Christ has done, how He brought about the astonishing reality of bringing unsanctified sinners like us into fellowship with a holy God; and if we cast our anxieties, feelings, and cares upon Christ by the grace of God, then we will experience feelings of joy and peace. We must not believe Satan's lie that faith is spun out of the web of our feelings. That is a dangerous, soul-damning, and hopeless task.

---

5. Edward Mote, 'My Hope Is Built on Nothing Less,' stanza 1 and refrain.

Shod Feet

In Ephesians 6:15 Paul tells us about the third piece of Christian armor: 'feet shod with the preparation of the gospel of peace.' The Roman soldiers, with whom Paul was well acquainted, wore sandals with strong straps that were thickly studded with sharp nails, which kept soldiers from slipping. Good footwear was a critical factor in the victories of Julius Caesar and Alexander the Great. Their soldiers won many battles partly because of military shoes that allowed them to cover long distances in a short time, catching their enemies off guard.

Paul says that Christians must have the right footwear for battling against Satan, and this footwear is 'the preparation of the gospel of peace.' Christians must always be ready and prepared to do battle with the forces of Satan. Without the right footwear, a Christian will slip and slide into defeat. If a Christian enters the battle halfheartedly, not quite sure if it's worth the effort, he is already defeated. A believer must always be ready to fight and be willing to endure hardship in the battle. A true soldier of Christ knows that the battle against Satan will be tough.

The gospel of peace is the pair of nail-studded sandals that enables the Christian to put his feet down and stand firm in battle. Like Luther, the Christian says, 'Here I stand,' or like Paul, he says, 'Stand fast in the faith' (1 Cor. 16:13).

The best way to stand up to the devil is to have the clearest possible understanding of the gospel and to experience gospel peace that passes all understanding through the blood of Christ. True knowledge of the gospel makes believers 'little to regard the foulness and unpleasantness of the way, and though Satan trouble them in their march, setting upon and assaulting them, yet they easily resist the fury of his temptations, and go on forward in the profession and practice of their Christianity, if they be armed with the knowledge of the gospel of peace.'[6] Our identity, comfort, and stability depend on knowing the gospel intellectually and experientially. Then you can look Satan in the eye, and say, 'If God be for us, who can be against us?' (Rom. 8:31). You can say with assurance that 'the God of peace shall bruise Satan under your feet shortly' (Rom. 16:20).

The Shield of Faith

The fourth piece of armor is the shield of faith. Paul says this shield enables the believer to 'quench all the fiery darts of the wicked' (Eph. 6:16). Roman shields in Paul's day were about four feet long by two feet wide, large enough to cover most of the body. They had fireproof metal coverings, with which a soldier could stop and extinguish fiery darts and flaming arrows.

Satan's devices are like fiery darts and flaming arrows. He has thousands of ways to attack believers with his darts, including blasphemous thoughts about God, sinful suggestions, and corrupt desires. He shoots darts outwardly at believers as well as inwardly at their hearts and minds. We need the shield of faith to withstand Satan's assaults for two reasons.

---

6. Downame, *The Christian Warfare*, 1:23.

First, faith helps us recognize satanic devices. William Gurnall says, 'Faith hath a piercing eye …. It looks behind the curtain of sense, and sees sin, before its finery was on and it be dressed up for the stage.'[7] Faith sees the ugliness and hellishness of sin without its camouflage.

Second, faith puts Christ between Satan and us, 'for he that putteth on faith, doth put on Jesus Christ also.'[8] Christ's blood is the fireproof covering in our shield of faith. Christ's blood and righteousness intervene between Satan and us, guarding us against Satan's fiery attacks.

Our biggest problem in battling Satan is that we forget to hold up the shield of faith. If you're a believer, raise high the shield of faith. Hide behind Christ. He will take the blows of Satan for you. He has already warded off every fiery dart to be your perfect Savior. Trust Him; He will never leave you nor forsake you.

Satan's tactic is to push aside your shield, then stab you under your armor. Do not let him do that. Take good care of your shield by living in faith. Rest in the person of Christ – come, hear, see, trust, take, know, embrace, rejoice, love, and triumph in Christ. By faith, lay hold of Christ, surrendering every part of yourself. Cling to Him the way the prongs of a ring cling to its diamond. Rely on His promises. Faith honors Christ, makes us strong, comforts us, makes us useful, and guarantees Satan's defeat. E. M. Bounds said, 'No battle was ever planned by hell's most gifted strategist which can conquer faith. All its inflamed and terrible darts fall harmless as they strike against the shield of faith.'[9]

Failing to use faith as a shield—that is, to walk in unbelief—is sure to be dangerous, if not fatal. Unbelief dishonors us, weakens us, destroys our comfort, and prevents our usefulness. Deny your doubts; quench your questionings. Refuse to surrender to your daily lusts. Battle Satan with the shield of faith. Trust in the Lord at all times. Remember, a faith that never withstands hell's temptations will not take you to heaven's rewards.

The Helmet of Salvation

'And take the helmet of salvation' (Eph. 6:17). The helmet of salvation is a critical piece of armor. No matter how well a soldier's body is protected, if his head is left uncovered, his chance of survival is minimal. A soldier must wear his helmet.

When an enemy is spotted in battle today, soldiers are ordered to take their battle stations. The first thing a soldier does after positioning himself behind a gun is to put his steel helmet on for protection from enemy shells or shrapnel. The Roman helmet of Paul's day was a leather cap covered with plates of metal. It was adorned with a kind of ornamental crest or plume. First Thessalonians 5:8 tells us that this helmet is 'the hope of salvation.'

---

7. William Gurnall, *The Christian in Complete Armour*, two vols. in one (1864; repr., Edinburgh: Banner of Truth, 1964), 2:79.

8. Downame, *The Christian Warfare*, 1:23.

9. E. M. Bounds, *Satan: His Personality, Power, and Overthrow* (Grand Rapids: Baker, 1972), p. 152.

Discouragement is a common ploy of Satan. Satan wants Christians to think that they have been battling him for a long time and that they have made little headway in the fight. They stumble into sin every day so that there seems to be little point in going on. 'My struggle against sin is useless,' they tell themselves. 'My attempt to live a holy life is hopeless. It is of no use to serve God.'

Satan digs in, tempting believers to become deserters from Christ's army. The only answer for this fiery dart is our hope of future salvation, or, as Romans 8 tells us, our hope of glory. Salvation in the past is justification, salvation in the present is sanctification, and salvation in the future is glorification. Glorification is what Paul has in mind here.

When Satan makes you feel like giving up in the battle against sin, put on your helmet of hope, Paul says. Believe that you have been saved, that you are being saved, and that you shall be saved. Cling to your only hope, Jesus Christ (1 Tim. 1:1), who is the same yesterday, today, and forever. By His resurrection, you are newly born to a living hope (1 Pet. 1:3-4) and will abundantly increase in hope through the Holy Spirit (Rom. 15:13).

One object of this abounding hope is the ultimate blessedness of God's kingdom (Acts 2:26; Titus 1:2). Hope produces joyful confidence in God (Rom. 8:28), patience in tribulation (Rom. 5:3), purity (1 John 3:3), and perseverance in prayer. It anticipates actual righteousness (Gal. 5:5) and is thus good, blessed, and glorious (2 Thess. 2:16; Titus 2:13; Col. 1:27, respectively). It anchors the soul by linking it to God's steadfastness in Christ (Heb. 3:6; 6:18-19).

If you are a Christian, you have a wonderful future. Your salvation cannot be taken from you. So look to the future. Look to glory, and do not lose heart.

In Romans 8:29-30, which describes the process of salvation from eternity past to eternity future, Paul speaks of glorification in the past tense: 'For whom he did foreknow ... them he also glorified.' Paul speaks of the future event of heavenly glorification as if it has already happened because his hope for the future is inseparably tied with what God has done for him in the past: predestination, calling, faith, justification, sanctification, and glorification are all linked together. The chain of salvation cannot be broken – each link is anchored in God's eternal, predestinating love.

Dear believer, be of good hope. No one can pluck you from the Father's hand, nor from Christ's hand (John 10:28-29). The Savior who persevered for you in the thick of battle will give you hope to stay the course in His strength. By wearing the helmet of hope, you will be prepared for every battle with Satan. Christ will sustain you in the fight and will bring you victory. When you see the enemy Satan coming, run to your battle station and put on the helmet of hope. Let hope be your ornament, your plume of eternal victory. Consider how the coming of the Son of Man draws near. Soon you will no longer need your helmet, for your battle will be over and Satan will be eternally crushed.

You will reign with the Captain of your salvation. You will come out of the great tribulation, wearing robes made white in Christ's blood. You will stand before the throne of God, praising the Lamb of God. The Lamb will lead you to living fountains of water; you will forever bask in His smile, bathe in His glory, and feast in His presence. You will find communing with Christ to be the essence of heaven. You will eternally rejoice in knowing, seeing, loving, praising, and glorifying Him. 'If we do not put on this helmet, we shall not dare to lift up our heads in the day of battle: for as those who are encouraged with hope of victory and the spoil ensuing, do fight valiantly.'[10] Lift up your head and put on your helmet: that is the only way to survive.

Do you hope in Jesus Christ? Everyone hopes in something – we cannot live without hope. But do you have the sure hope of the true Christian? Are you abounding in hope? Do you think often of the hope of heaven? You will fight Satan feebly if you view heaven dimly. But if hope is your helmet, you will be protected against blows to your head. You will withstand the crushing discouragement of the evil one.

BUILDING AN AGGRESSIVE OFFENSE

In January 2002, when I returned to my flat after lecturing on the doctrine of salvation in an Eastern European country, I was assaulted by two men who knocked me down, tied and gagged me, and ran a knife up and down my back, all the while shouting, 'Mafia, Mafia!' God graciously spared me and comforted me immeasurably with His Word throughout this forty-five-minute ordeal, but you can understand that I considered myself a dead man.

The Mafia is not always so blatantly or aggressively open, however. More often than not, they, like Satan, run a camouflaged organization and operation. We probably don't know the addresses of Mafia leaders, nor can we recognize them beneath their business suits. We know that the Mafia controls money-laundering businesses, various rings of prostitution, and all kinds of crime, but it is difficult to pin them down; and, because of their corrupting influences or intimidation tactics, it's difficult sometimes even to get juries to convict them.

Satan's spiritual Mafia controls people and nations – sometimes openly and blatantly, but more often in a camouflaged way. We need much wisdom and strength not only to defend ourselves against his attacks but also to offensively search him out and go on the attack in the strength of our God. Paul goes on in Ephesians 6:17-18 to tell us how to do that, presenting us with three powerful weapons in our battle against the archenemy of our Savior: 'Take ... the sword of the Spirit, which is the word of God: praying always with all prayer and supplication in the Spirit, and watching thereunto with all perseverance and application for all saints.'

The Sword of the Spirit

The sword of the Spirit, which is the Word of God (6:17), is a unique piece of armor in fighting Satan, for it attacks the enemy as well as repels him. God magnifies His Word by using it as a double-edged sword (Heb. 4:12). The Holy Spirit, the author

---

10. Downame, *The Christian Warfare*, 1:25.

of God's 'breathed-out' Word, enables us to interpret and use it. The sword of the Spirit can be used to combat Satan in two ways.

First, it is a *defense* against Satan. Jesus sets the example here. He responded each time to Satan's temptations in the desert with 'It is written' (Matt. 4:1-11). His words from Scripture plunged like steel into Satan's heart. That is how we, too, need to respond to Satan. When Satan says, 'You will one day fall at my hand,' faith says no and lifts up the Word of God as a sword, saying, 'I am persuaded that he that has begun a good work in me will perform it until the day of Jesus Christ' (see Phil. 1:6). When Satan hurls the doubt, 'Your sin is too great,' faith responds by saying, 'He is able also to save them to the uttermost that come unto God by him' (Heb. 7:25). For every dart of Satan, God has provided a sure defense in His Word. 'The only way to overcome him,' Calvin wrote, 'is by keeping to the Word of God in its entirety.'[11] Hand-to-hand combat with Satan and with temptation never works; we need hands gripping firmly the sword of the Spirit – clinging in faith to the promises of God (see 2 Sam. 23:10).

Second, the sword of the Spirit is an *offensive* weapon against Satan. Just as we fight Satan by finding shelter in Christ for an unyielding defense, we also fight Satan by taking the offense against him. The sword of the Spirit, which is the Word of God, gives us clear directions, powerful motives, rich encouragements, and instructive examples that equip us well for confronting Satan. Live not by bread alone, but by every word of God. Become intimately acquainted with your Bible: study it and memorize it daily. That will keep God's sword sharp. Live the Bible's truths each day; that will keep God's sword polished and bright. Keep the sword ready at all times through constant prayer. Speak out; bear witness to Scripture truth. Carry the light of God's word into a dark world, shining its light into every dark corner.

Pray and ask God for the wisdom of the Holy Spirit to wield the sword of Scripture against Satan. The Spirit is the ultimate author and interpreter of God's Word, so seek His wisdom. The Spirit delights to open our minds to His Word. He will teach us how to use it as a sword against Satan.

To the blind, the Bible is an ordinary book, full of mistakes. In the hand of the Spirit, the Bible 'is quick, and powerful, and sharper than any two-edged sword, piercing even to the dividing asunder of soul and spirit' (Heb. 4:12). When you use God's Word with skill against demonic attack, the sword of the Spirit cuts away the devil's strength and all his wisest plans. In dependence on the Spirit, use the sword of the Bible to stand your ground against Satan, to assail him, to run at him, to rout him, and to drive him from the field. Have confidence in the Word of God. It will never fail you, not even in the thick of battle with Satan, or Apollyon, which Bunyan so poignantly depicts when Christian is in the valley of humiliation:

---

11. John Calvin, *Sermons on Galatians*, trans. Kathy Childress (Edinburgh: Banner of Truth Trust, 1997), p. 51.

But as God would have it, while Apollyon was fetching his last blow, thereby to make a full end of this good man, Christian nimbly stretched forth his hand for his sword, and caught it, saying, 'Rejoice not against me, O mine enemy: when I fall I shall arise'; and with that gave him a deadly thrust, which made him give back, as one that had received his mortal wound. Christian, perceiving that, made at him again, saying, 'Nay, in all these things we are more than conquerors through him that loved us.' And with that Apollyon spread forth his dragon wings, and sped him away.[12]

Praying in the Spirit

'Praying always with all prayer and supplication in the Spirit' (Eph. 6:18). Prayer is the second offensive weapon against Satan. D. A. Carson observed that the enemy may 'unload massive doses of guilt and despair and shame on us. Sadly, because we are so insensitive to the possibility that these bouts of depression may be related to our calling as Christians, we may foolishly try to overcome them and cheer ourselves up .... How seldom do we think of Paul's first recourse – his immediate desire to seek the face of the Lord Jesus in prayer.'[13] Martin Luther said, 'Prayer is a strong wall and fortress of the church; it is a goodly Christian's weapon.'[14] The greatest weapon in God's armory is prayer.

Prayer is critical because every piece of Christian armor is useless without it. Prayer is like oil. Just as every part of an engine is useless without oil, so every part of Christian warfare is vain without prayer. It is Christ, not our armor in itself, that secures the victory: 'it behoveth us after we have armed ourselves at all points, not to trust altogether in our armour, but to have our recourse unto our grand Captain Christ Jesus, acknowledging our own weakness, and desiring his aide and assistance.'[15] Fighting Satan without prayer is like David fighting Goliath in Saul's armor. The armor doesn't fit, and it is ineffective against the blows of the enemy.

In withstanding Satan through prayer, Paul gives us four instructions. First, we should *pray always*. Some generations ago, several ministers gathered in the Scottish Highlands to discuss what it meant to 'pray without ceasing' (1 Thess. 5:17). After considerable discussion, one minister asked a young woman who waited on them if she knew what it meant. 'Yes, sir,' she said. 'As I arose this morning from bed, I prayed that the Sun of righteousness would arise with healing in His wings over me today. When I got dressed, I prayed that I might be clothed with Christ's righteousness. As I dusted the furniture in this room before you arrived, I prayed that the Lord would wipe my heart clean through the blood of Jesus. When I made your refreshments ready, I prayed that Jesus Christ would be my food and drink. Sir, I pray my way through each day, for prayer is my breath, my life.'

---

12. John Bunyan, *Pilgrim's Progress*, in *The Works of John Bunyan* (Edinburgh: Banner of Truth Trust, 1991), 3:113.

13. D. A. Carson, *A Call to Spiritual Reformation* (Grand Rapids: Baker Academic, 1992), pp. 211-12.

14. Luther, *Table Talk*, p. 156.

15. Downame, *The Christian Warfare*, 1:27.

Praying without ceasing means praying at set times and seasons as well as sending up short petitions to God throughout the day. It means praying at stated times of prayer and praying whenever you feel the least impulse to do so. Praying is more important than whatever else you are doing. Spurgeon said, 'Prayer must not be our chance work, but our daily business, our habit and vocation .... so must we addict ourselves to prayer.'[16]

Second, we are to *pray with prayer and supplication*. Though Paul appears to be repeating himself in Ephesians 6:18, he is not. Paul is saying, 'Pray with heartfelt, pleading prayer. Truly pray in your prayer.' Tragically, we often fail miserably in using the weapon of prayer. Satan can doze beside our prayerless prayers.

The marginal notes on James 5:17 in the King James Version of the Bible say that Elijah 'prayed in his prayer.' That means the prophet truly prayed with all his heart. Samuel Rutherford said that the condition of the heart in prayer is more important than the words that are said. He wrote that a mute beggar receives mercy at Christ's door when his tongue cannot say anything, yes, precisely because he cannot speak: 'Tears have a tongue, a grammar, and a language that our Father knoweth.'[17] Bunyan put it this way, 'When thou prayest, rather let thy heart be without words, than thy words without a heart.'[18]

Third, *pray with all prayer*. That means praying while acknowledging God in all your ways and trusting that He will direct all your paths (Prov. 3:5-6). Bring all your needs to God, great and small. Tell the Lord everything about yourself, as if He knew nothing about you, yet knowing that He knows all things. Entrust yourself and all of your needs into God's all-sufficient hands if you would defeat Satan on things small and large.

Finally, *pray in the Spirit*. Romans 8:26 says that the Holy Spirit helps us to pray in our infirmities and intercedes for us with groanings that cannot be uttered. The Holy Spirit shows us how miserable we are by nature and how great our debt is to God. The Spirit also enables us to think saving thoughts of God, of Christ, and of blessed things. He grants us faith and helps us express our needs and thoughts in prayer. He keeps us from hypocrisy, coldness, and all that is unseemly.

Let me illustrate how the Holy Spirit does this. A small boy was being taught by his father how to steer a ship. As the boy began to steer, his father stood directly behind him. The father knew that if he didn't help his son, the boat would crash on the rocks or be swept away in the swift current. The father did not push his son aside, though, telling him it would be better for him to take the helm. He leaned over his son, put his hands upon his son's hands, then guided his son's hands on the wheel. Through the father's guidance, the son steered the ship to safety.

---

16. Charles H. Spurgeon, *Morning and Evening: Daily Readings* (Grand Rapids: Zondervan, 1955), p. 31 [Jan. 15, Evening].

17. Samuel Rutherford, *The Trial and Triumph of Faith* (Edinburgh: The Assembly's Committee, 1845), p. 68.

18. Bunyan, 'Dying Sayings,' in *Works*, 1:65.

Likewise, we pray best when the Spirit grips our hearts and guides our thoughts, steering us in the course that He has charted for us. Just as this boy could not steer the ship on his own, so we cannot pray rightly without the Holy Spirit. Nor can we pray properly without Spirit-worked 'lowliness of mind' and 'holiness of life'; the more we pursue holiness, the more we will pray; the more we pray, the less holy we will esteem ourselves to be. William Gouge reminds us of Abraham's attitude in prayer – 'I am but dust and ashes' (Gen 18:27); and Job's – 'I am vile' (Job 40:4). Indeed, 'He that duly pondereth with himself, how his sins for number are innumerable, and for weight infinite, and how all his righteousness is as filthy rags, defiled with that sink of corruption which is in him, cannot but utterly deny himself, and so be of a lowly mind, not puffed up with any conceit of himself.'[19] Let us therefore have confidence in Him and seek to be filled with Him as we pray (Eph. 5:18).

Martyn Lloyd-Jones said, 'Everything we do in the Christian life is easier than prayer.'[20] If you desire to pray in the Spirit to fight Satan, do the following:

- Lean on Christ. In Him all prayer is made effective.

- Make prayer a priority. Bunyan said, 'You can do more than pray after you've prayed, but you can't do more than pray until you've prayed.'[21]

- Find sweetness in prayer. When I was nine years old, my dad told me, 'Always remember that a true believer has a place to go – the throne of grace. Prayer is God's gift to go to Himself. He is a prayer-giving, a prayer-hearing, and a prayer-answering God.' William Bridge said, 'It is a mercy to pray, though I [may] never have the mercy prayed for; thereby God doth come down to us, and we go up to God.'[22] Joseph Hall put it this way: 'Good prayers never come weeping home: I am sure I shall receive, either what I ask, or what I should ask.'[23]

- Repeat God's promises. God is tender to His own Word. Take Him at His word. He will make prayer effective for you.

If Satan rests content beside us because he knows that we lack the breath and vitality of genuine prayer, our prayer will be powerless against him. We must use what Bunyan called the 'weapon' of 'all-prayer.'[24] If we believe that man is man and God is God, we must be persistent in praying in our prayers.

---

19. William Gouge, *The whole-armor of God: or A Christians spiritual furniture* (London: John Beale, 1627), pp. 352-53.

20. D. Martyn Lloyd-Jones, *Studies in the Sermon on the Mount* (Grand Rapids: Eerdmans, 1976), p. 322.

21. I. D. E. Thomas, comp., *The Golden Treasury of Puritan Quotations* (Chicago: Moody, 1975), p. 210.

22. William Bridge, *A Lifting Up for the Downcast*, in *The Works of the Rev. William Bridge* (London: Thomas Tegg, 1845), 2:51.

23. Joseph Hall, *Meditations and Vows*, XLIX, in *The Works of The Right Reverend Father in God, Joseph Hall*, ed. Josiah Pratt (London: C. Wittingham, for Williams and Smith, et al., 1808), 6:13.

24. Bunyan, *Pilgrim's Progress*, in *Works*, 3:115.

Watch with Perseverance

'[Watch] thereunto with all perseverance and supplication for all saints' (Eph. 6:18). The true soldier must stand guard at his post; he must be vigilant, watchful, and alert. Likewise, the soldier of Christ must watch and pray to ward off the attacks of Satan.

Paul brings praying and watching together in one verse (Eph. 6:18) because they are truly inseparable. Our day often goes poorly because we have failed to begin in heartfelt prayer. We also pray poorly as we retire in the evening because we haven't been watchful through the day. 'Watch and pray,' Jesus said (Matt. 26:41).

The devil loves to work with drowsy Christians. The foolish virgins missed welcoming the bridegroom because their lamps ran out of oil. In *Pilgrim's Progress*, Bunyan's Christian lost his roll, symbolizing his assurance of faith, when he fell asleep.[25]

We can defeat Satan only if we watch and pray. We do this in the following ways:

By being constantly aware. We must be aware of what is going on in our hearts and in our family and our home. We must be aware of the needs of our church and the children of God. We must be aware of the needs of our city, state, and nation. We must be aware of what is happening in the government and world affairs. We must broaden our sense of awareness, for that will give us more material for intercession.

By interceding for others. We should pray for ministers and the progress of the gospel. Paul pleads for that in Ephesians 6:19-20. We should also make 'supplication for all saints' (v. 18). We are never more like Christ than when we are engaged in heartfelt intercession. T. J. Bach said, 'Many of us cannot reach the mission fields on our feet, but we can reach them on our knees.'[26] Intercession delivers us from selfishness, which Satan so delights to see; it lifts us above ourselves, gives us joy in service, and enables us to keep Satan at bay.

By persevering. Pray like a hunter; pursue until you get your prey. Press on as you watch, remembering that 'in due season we shall reap, if we faint not' (Gal. 6:9). Keep knocking on the door of God's grace. Don't leave after one knock, like a disheartened salesman. Be like Mercy in Bunyan's *Pilgrim's Progress*, who kept knocking to the point of fainting until God answered her.[27] Watch for God's answers. Do not turn your back on Him.

By watching in all things. That is what Paul commanded Timothy (2 Tim. 4:5). Obey the calling: 'Let every one that nameth the name of Christ depart from iniquity' (2 Tim. 2:19). As E. M. Bounds writes, '"Watch" is the keynote of

---

25. Bunyan, *Pilgrim's Progress*, in *Works*, 3:105.

26. Cited in Curtis C. Thomas, *Practical Wisdom for Pastors: Words of Encouragement and Counsel for a Lifetime of Ministry* (Wheaton, Ill.: Crossway 2001), p. 182.

27. Bunyan, *Pilgrim's Progress*, in *Works*, 3:179-80.

safety .... [We must be] wide awake not only when we see his form and fear his presence, but wide awake to see him when he is not to be seen, to repel him when he comes in any one of his ten thousand guises or disguises – this is our wise and safe course.'[28]

CONCLUDING APPLICATION: STAND UP FOR JESUS

Paul's well-outfitted soldier in Ephesians 6:14-18 gives us a comprehensive picture of how to fight against Satan. In dependency on the Spirit and in Christ's strength, use each piece of armor prayerfully every day, remembering what Samuel Rutherford said: 'The devil is but God's master fencer, to teach us to handle our weapons.'[29] Don't let any pieces of God's weaponry hang in the back of your closet unused. You need every one. Trust God to help you; don't lean upon your own understanding. As Calvin warned, 'If we contend with Satan, according to our own view of things, he will a hundred times overwhelm us and we can never be able to resist him.'[30]

Look to Christ, remembering that He wore the weapons of Ephesians 6 Himself, as Isaiah points out in the Old Testament. Powlison writes,

> The *Messiah* girds his loins with the truth, by fearing God and walking in the power and wisdom of the Spirit (Is. 11:5). The *LORD God* puts on the breastplate of righteousness to deliver his people from bondage to sins (59:17). The *LORD* himself comes—his feet shod—bearing good news of peace to those captivated in sin and judgment (52:7). The *LORD* himself is the shield behind which faith takes refuge from enemies. The *LORD* wears the helmet of salvation as he brings deliverance from the power of sin and gives his Spirit and Word (59:21). The sword of the Spirit is God's Word and proceeds from the mouth of the *Messiah*, the Servant who will deliver the nations from the power of darkness (49:2). Prayer is the way all this happens, for prayer relies on the Lord.[31]

As a believer in Christ, put your spiritual warfare into Christ's hands. Remember that ultimately the battle against Satan is not yours, but His (2 Chron. 20:15). Jesus Christ will not lose the battle against the prince of this world. You are part of His body, the church, and He will not relinquish His bride.

Take heart, soldier. Your comforts are many. You are in a strong position, being in Christ. You have all the equipment you need – the whole armor of God. You have the help of a master warrior, David's own teacher and guide, the Holy Spirit (Psalms 18; 144). He makes the devil to be your 'polisher, while he intends to be [your] destroyer,' wrote Stephen Charnock.[32] Brooks urges us to

---

28. Bounds, *Satan*, p. 144.

29. *Letters of Samuel Rutherford*, ed. Andrew A. Bonar (1891; repr., Edinburgh: Banner of Truth, 1984), p. 290,

30. John Calvin, *Commentaries on the Twelve Minor Prophets*, trans. John Owen (Grand Rapids: Baker, 2003), 4:58 [Hab. 2:1].

31. David Powlison, *Power Encounters* (Grand Rapids: Baker, 1995), p. 114.

32. Stephen Charnock, *Discourse on the Existence and Attributes of God*, in *The Complete Works of Stephen Charnock* (Edinburgh: James Nichol, 1864), 2:364.

consider this same truth when we are beset with myriad temptations, that '*all the temptations that befall the saints shall be sanctified to them by a hand of love.* Ah! the choice experiences that the saints get of the power of God supporting them, of the wisdom of God directing them (so to handle their spiritual weapons, their graces, as not only to resist, but to overcome), of the mercy and goodness of the Lord pardoning and succouring of them.'[33]

Not only do you have the enabling grace and responsibility to use your spiritual armor, but also you have the promise of help in the evil day and victory guaranteed at the last day. You are on the winning side; righteousness and holiness will by the Spirit's grace have the victory in your heart. Ultimately, as Gurnall wrote, 'God sets the devil to catch the devil.'[34] You may lose some skirmishes to Satan, but through Christ Jesus, you will win the war.

> *Stand up, stand up for Jesus,*
> *Stand in His strength alone;*
> *The arm of flesh will fail you,*
> *Ye dare not trust your own.*
> *Put on the gospel armor,*
> *Each piece put on with prayer;*
> *Where duty calls, or danger,*
> *Be never wanting there.*[35]

Let us pray with a Puritan:

> O thou whose very promise is balm,
> every touch life,
> draw near to thy weary warrior,
> refresh me, that I may rise again to wage the strife,
> and never tire until my enemy is trodden down.
> Give me such fellowship with thee that I may defy Satan,
> unbelief, the flesh, the world ....
> Give me a draught of the eternal fountain
> that lieth in thy immutable, everlasting love and decree.
> Then shall my hand never weaken, my feet never stumble,
> my sword never rest, my shield never rust,
> my helmet never shatter, my breastplate never fall,
> as my strength rests in the power of thy might.[36]

---

33. Thomas Brooks, *The Complete Works of Thomas Brooks*, ed. Alexander Balloch Grosart (Edinburgh; London; Dublin: James Nichol; James Nisbet and Co.; G. Herbert, 1866), 1:114.

34. Gurnall, *The Christian in Complete Armour*, 1:102.

35. George Duffield, 'Stand Up, Stand Up for Jesus,' stanza 3.

36. Arthur Bennett, ed., *The Valley of Vision: A Collection of Puritan Prayers and Devotions* (Edinburgh: Banner of Truth Trust, 1975), p. 181.

CHAPTER 17

CONDUCTING FAMILY WORSHIP[1]
(JOSHUA 24:15)

EVERY church desires growth. Surprisingly few churches, however, seek to promote internal church growth by stressing the need for fathers and mothers to raise their children in covenantal truth. Few seriously grapple with why many adolescents become nominal members with mere notional faith or why 75 per cent or more of our young people abandon evangelical truth and evangelical churches for unbiblical doctrine and modes of worship.

I believe one major reason for this failure is the lack of stress upon family worship. In many churches and homes family worship is an optional thing, or at most a superficial exercise such as a brief table grace before meals. Consequently, many children grow up with no experience or impression of Christian faith and worship as a daily reality. When my parents commemorated their fiftieth anniversary, all five of us children decided to express thanks to our father and mother for one thing without consulting each other. Remarkably, all five of us thanked our mother for her prayers and all five of us thanked our father for his leadership of our Sunday evening family worship. My brother said, 'Dad, the oldest memory I have is of tears streaming down your face as you taught us from *Pilgrim's Progress* on Sunday evenings how the Holy Spirit leads believers. At the age of three God used you in family worship to convict me that Christianity was real. No matter how far I went astray in later years, I could never seriously question the reality of Christianity, and I want to thank you for that.'

How critical is family worship to you? Is it the most important part of your day? You may remember how the Space Shuttle Columbia tragically disintegrated during its high-speed re-entry into the atmosphere in 2003. The commander of that mission was Colonel Rick Husband. Before he launched into space, he had prepared 18 devotions on video for each of his two children to watch during the 18 days he would be in orbit. Here was a man who was so committed to leading his children in family worship that he made thirty-six video devotions so that he

---

1. Much of this chapter is a revision of material condensed from Joel R. Beeke, *Family Worship* (Grand Rapids: Reformation Heritage Books, 2009) as well as an address given at a Desiring God Conference by Joel R. Beeke in 2011, https://www.desiringgod.org/messages/leading-family-worship.

could lead them even when he was gone. In a video-taped interview with his pastor which was played at a memorial service, Husband said,

> If I ended up at the end of my life having been an astronaut, but having sacrificed my family along the way, or living my life in a way that did not glorify God, then I would look back on it with great regret. Having become an astronaut would not have meant that much. I came to realize that what meant the most to me was to try to live my life as God wanted me to do, to be a good husband to Evelyn, and a good father to my children.[2]

How precious do you think those videos are to Rick Husband's family today? Isn't this the kind of legacy you and I want to leave our children and grandchildren?

Christians have long recognized that God often uses the restoration of family worship to bring reformation and revival to the church. For example, the 1677 church covenant of the Puritan congregation in Dorchester, Massachusetts, included the commitment 'to reform our families, engaging ourselves to a conscientious care to set before us and to maintain the worship of God in them; and to walk in our houses with perfect hearts in a faithful discharge of all domestic duties, educating, instructing, and charging our children and households to keep the ways of the Lord.'

As goes the home, so goes the church, and so goes the nation. Family worship is a most decisive factor in how the home goes. Matthew Henry wrote, 'Here the Reformation must begin.'[3]

Family worship is not the only factor, of course. Family worship is not a substitute for other parental duties, not to mention your personal walk with God. Family worship without parental example is futile. Spontaneous teaching that arises throughout a typical day is crucial, yet set times of family worship are also important. Family worship is the foundation of biblical child-rearing.

Family worship is also deeply rooted in our theology. Our God is a triune God, a God of familial relationships. His fatherly love overflows into the world He created because God created us in His image. God deals with the human race through covenant and headship, where fathers such as Abraham lead and represent families in God's promises. In the New Testament, we see families converted together and called to grow in holiness together in the life of the church.

As Douglas Kelly concludes, 'Family religion, which depends not a little on the household head daily leading the family before God in worship, is one of the most powerful structures that the covenant-keeping God has given for the expansion of redemption through the generations, so that countless multitudes may be brought into communion with and worship of the living God in the face of Jesus Christ.'[4]

---

2. 'Rick Husband, Mike Anderson "fervently lived for God"' (Baptist Press, February 3, 2003), http://www.bpnews.net/BPnews.asp?ID=15150, accessed January 24, 2011.

3. Matthew Henry, 'A Church in the House, a Sermon concerning Family Religion,' in *The Complete Works of the Rev. Matthew Henry* (repr., Grand Rapids: Baker, 1978), 1:259.

4. Douglas Kelly, 'Family Worship: Biblical, Reformed, and Viable for Today,' in *Worship in the Presence of God*, ed. Frank J. Smith and David C. Lachman (Greenville, S.C.: Greenville Seminary Press, 1992), p. 110.

Whether you are a minister or a head of household, this chapter aims to help you think through what family worship is, how to lead it, and why it is important. If you are a minister, examining your own practice of family worship is an important first step since, as Robert Murray M'Cheyne observed, people will seldom rise higher than their own pastor's level of holiness; I desire to move you to consider preaching on this important subject. Equip the fathers of your church to practice family worship; visit their homes, if necessary, and lead them in family worship so that the father can watch you do it and then do it himself.

Let us examine the subject of leading family worship under four headings: (1) duty; (2) implementation; (3) objections; and (4) motivation.

THE DUTY OF FAMILY WORSHIP

Given the importance of family worship as a potent force in winning untold millions to gospel truth throughout the ages, we ought not be surprised that God requires us as heads of households to do all we can to lead our families in worshiping the living God. Joshua 24:14-15 says, 'Now therefore fear the LORD, and serve him in sincerity and in truth: and put away the gods which your fathers served on the other side of the flood, and in Egypt; and serve ye the LORD. And if it seem evil unto you to serve the LORD, choose you this day whom ye will serve; whether the gods which your fathers served that were on the other side of the flood [i.e. back in Ur of Chaldees], or the gods of the Amorites, in whose land ye dwell [i.e. here in Canaan]: but as for me and my house, we will serve the LORD.'

Notice three things in this text: First, Joshua did not make worship or service to the living God optional: serving the Lord voluntarily and deliberately in our families (v. 15) is an important part of what it means to 'fear the LORD, and serve him in sincerity and in truth' (v. 14).

Second, not only is Joshua speaking for his own household ('as for me and my house,' v. 15), he is addressing the various leaders in Israel (v. 1) and charging them likewise to follow his example to 'serve the Lord.' Several factors reinforce this bold declaration:

- Joshua, remarkable in zeal as an aged man, makes this declaration when he is more than one hundred years old.

- Joshua is confident that although he will soon die, as God told him, his influence will continue in his family, and they will not abandon serving the Lord after he dies.

- Having just told the people to put away false gods (v.14), Joshua knows that his family will be swimming against the stream of Israel's remaining idolatry – yet he emphatically commands his family to serve the LORD anyway.

- The historical record shows that Joshua's influence was so pervasive that most of the nation followed his example for at least one generation. Joshua 24:31 says, 'And Israel served the LORD all the days of Joshua, and all the days of the elders that overlived Joshua [i.e. for the next generation], and which had known all the works of the LORD, that he had done for Israel.' What an encouragement to God-fearing parents to know that the worship they set up in the home may last generations after them!

Third, the word *serve* in verse 15 is translated as *worship* many times in Scripture; it not only conveys the sense of serving God in every sphere of our lives, but also in *special acts of worship*. Let us not miss the critical fact that Joshua had several things in mind, including obedience to all the ceremonial laws involving the sacrificing of animals, which point to the coming Messiah, whose blood sacrifice would be effectual for sinners, once and for all.

Surely every God-fearing husband, father, and pastor must say with Joshua, 'As for me and my household, we will serve the Lord. We will seek the Lord, worship Him, and pray to Him as a family. We will read His Word, replete with its instructions, and reinforce its teachings in our family.' Every father must realize, as Douglas Kelly says, 'that the head of each family is to represent his family before God in divine worship and that the spiritual atmosphere and long term personal welfare of that family will be affected in large measure by the fidelity—or failure—of the family head in this area.'[5]

According to Scripture, God should be served in special acts of worship in our families today in the following three ways:

1. Daily instruction in the Word of God

God should be worshiped by daily reading and instruction from His Word. Through questions, answers, and instructions, we and our children are to daily interact with each other about sacred truth. As Deuteronomy 6:6-7 says, 'And these words, which I command thee this day, shall be in thine heart: And thou shalt teach them diligently unto thy children, and shalt talk of them when thou sittest in thine house, and when thou walkest by the way, and when thou liest down, and when thou risest up' (cf. Deut. 11:18-19).

The activities this text commands are *daily* activities: lying down at night, rising up in the morning, sitting in the house, and walking by the way. In an orderly home, these activities are done at specific times of the day. They offer opportunities for regular, consistent, and daily times of instruction. Moses wasn't suggesting a little talk, but diligent conversation and diligent instruction that flow from our burning hearts as fathers. Moses says that words from God should be in our *heart*. We fathers must *diligently* teach these words to our children, he says.

2. Daily prayer to the throne of God

The command to 'pray without ceasing' includes when we are with our families. Our families must daily pray together unless providentially hindered. If you want

---

5. Kelly, 'Family Worship: Biblical, Reformed, and Viable for Today,' in *Worship in the Presence of God*, p. 112.

to eat and drink to the glory of God (1 Cor. 10:31), and the food you are about to eat is to be set apart for that purpose, you must sanctify it by prayer, Paul says (1 Tim. 4:4-5). And just as we pray that our food and drink may be sanctified and blessed to the nourishment of our bodies, so we should pray for God's blessing of His Word to the nourishment of our souls, for 'Man shall not live by bread alone but by every word that proceedeth from the mouth of God' (Deut. 8:3; Matt. 4:4).

Furthermore, don't our families commit daily sins? Shouldn't we daily seek forgiveness? Does not God bless us in many ways every day? Should we not acknowledge these blessings with daily thanksgiving? Should we not daily acknowledge God in all our ways, begging Him to direct our paths? It used to be commonly said in former centuries that a family without prayer is like a house without a roof, open and exposed to all the storms of heaven.

3. Daily singing the praise of God

Psalm 118:15 says, 'The voice of rejoicing and salvation is in the tabernacles [or tents] of the righteous: the right hand of the LORD doeth valiantly.' The psalmist says this singing *is* (not simply *ought to be*) in the tents of the righteous. Philip Henry, father of the famed Matthew Henry, believed this text provided a biblical basis for the daily singing of psalms in our families. He argued that joyful singing comes from the individual tents of the righteous. It involves family singing as well as temple singing.

The Lord is to be worshiped daily by the singing of psalms in our homes. God is glorified, and our families are edified. Because these songs are God's Word, singing them is a means of instruction, enlightening the understanding. Singing promotes devotion as it warms the heart. The graces of the Spirit are stirred up in us, and our growth in grace is stimulated. 'Let the word of Christ dwell in you richly in all wisdom; teaching and admonishing one another in psalms and hymns and spiritual songs, singing with grace in your hearts to the Lord' (Col. 3:16).

Dear brothers, we must implement family worship in our homes. God requires that you worship Him not only privately as an individual, but publicly as members of the covenant body and community, and socially, as families. The Lord Jesus is worthy of it, God's Word commands it, and conscience affirms it as your duty.

Your family owes allegiance to God. God has placed you in a position of authority to guide your children in the way of the Lord. You are more than friends and advisors to your children; as their teacher and ruler in the home, your example and leadership are crucial. Clothed with holy authority, you owe to your children prophetical teaching, priestly intercession, and royal guidance. You must direct family worship by way of Scripture, prayer, and song. Pastors too must lovingly inform the heads of families in our churches that they must command their household to worship God as Abraham did. 'For I know him,' God said, 'that he will *command* his children and his household after him, and they shall keep the way of the LORD, to do justice and judgment; that the LORD may bring upon Abraham that which he hath spoken of him' (Gen. 18:19).

IMPLEMENTING FAMILY WORSHIP

In offering the following suggestions for establishing God-honoring family worship in your homes, I'll avoid two extremes: an idealistic approach that is beyond the reach of even the most God-fearing home, and a minimalist approach that almost abandons daily family worship because the ideal seems so out of reach.

- Family worship will require some preparation. You should pray for God's blessing upon that worship. Have your Bibles ready and a Scripture passage selected. Catechisms and books of questions and answers for children are very helpful. A good daily devotional can also be used. Sometimes you might read through a book like John Bunyan's *Pilgrim's Progress* or *Holy War* and discuss it together. Choose some psalms and hymns that are easy to sing. Pick a place to gather, such as the supper table or living room. Set the times for family worship, ordinarily at breakfast and supper, but as it fits your family's needs. Whatever times you set, carefully guard those times like a precious jewel.

- During family worship, aim for brevity. Don't provoke your children. If you worship twice a day, try ten minutes in the morning and twenty in the evening. Be consistent. It is better to have twenty minutes of family worship every day than to try for extended periods on fewer days – say forty-five minutes on Monday, then skipping Tuesday.

- Don't indulge excuses to avoid family worship. Even if you have been sinning—perhaps you lost your temper in dealing with a particular child thirty minutes before family worship—still lead family worship; just begin it with heart-felt confession and repentance. If you are tired, deny yourself out of love for God and your family. After all, Christ was bone-weary when He went to the cross for you, yet He carried on. Shouldn't we carry on in response to His love as well?

- Lead family worship with a firm, fatherly hand and a soft, penitent heart. Speak with hopeful solemnity. Talk naturally yet reverently during this time, using the tone you would use when speaking to a deeply respected friend about a serious matter. Expect great things from a great covenant-keeping God.

Let's get more specific:

1. For the reading of Scripture

- *Have a plan.* Be sure to read the entire Bible over a period of time. As J. C. Ryle said, 'Fill their minds with Scripture. Let the Word dwell in them richly. Give them the Bible, the whole Bible, even while they are young.' One way this can be accomplished is by reading ten or twenty verses from the

Old Testament in the morning and ten to twenty from the New Testament in the evening.

- *Account for special occasions.* On Sunday mornings you might want to read Psalm 48 or John 20. On the Sabbath when the Lord's Supper is to be administered, read Psalm 22, Isaiah 53, or Matthew 26. Before you leave home for family vacations, read Psalm 91 or Psalm 121.

- *Involve the family.* Every family member who can read should have a Bible to follow along. Set the tone by reading Scripture with expression, as the living, 'breathing' book it is. Assign various portions to be read by your wife and your children. I simply divide the verses by the number of family members present. Teach your children how to read articulately, with reverence and with expression. Don't let them mumble or speed ahead. If you feel a need to do so, provide some brief words of explanation throughout the reading, according to the needs of the younger children.

2. For biblical instruction

- *Be plain in meaning.* Ask your children if they understand what you are reading. Be plain in applying scriptural texts. The 1647 Church of Scotland Directory provides counsel here:

  The holy scriptures should be read ordinarily to the family; and it is commendable, that thereafter they confer, and by way of conference, make some good use of what hath been read and heard. As, for example, if any sin be reproved in the word read, use may be made thereof to make all the family circumspect and watchful against the same; or if any judgment be threatened or mentioned to have been inflicted, in that portion of scripture which is read, use may be made to make all the family fear lest the same or a worse judgment befall them, unless they beware of the sin that procured it: and finally, if any duty be required, or comfort held forth in a promise, use may be made to stir up themselves to employ Christ for strength to enable them for doing the commanded duty, and to apply the offered comfort. In all which the master of the family is to have the chief hand; and any member of the family may propose a question or doubt for resolution (par. III).

- *Encourage family dialogue* around God's Word in line with the Hebraic practice of household question and answer (cf. Exodus 12; Deuteronomy 6; Psalm 78). Especially encourage teenagers to ask questions; draw them out. If you don't know the answers, tell them so, and encourage them to do a little research. Have one or more good commentaries on hand, such as those by John Calvin, Matthew Poole, and Matthew Henry. Remember, if you don't provide answers for your children, they will get them elsewhere – and often those will be wrong answers.

- *Be pure in doctrine.* Titus 2:7 says, 'In all things showing thyself a pattern of good works: in doctrine showing uncorruptness, gravity, sincerity.' Don't abandon doctrinal precision when teaching young children; aim for simplicity *and* soundness.

- *Be relevant in application.* Don't be afraid to share your experiences when appropriate, but do it simply. If we read a verse that has meant a great deal to me in my life, I sometimes tell my children why that verse is special to me. I want them to understand that though all of the Bible is special revelation, God often impresses certain verses and truths in the lives of His children in powerful ways to teach them lifelong lessons. You might also want to use concrete illustrations to explain a text from your past reading or from the life experience of other Bible saints or Christians throughout church history. Finally, ideally, try to tie together biblical instruction with what you and your family have recently heard in sermons.

- *Be affectionate in manner.* Proverbs continually uses the phrase *my son*, showing the warmth, love, and urgency in the teachings of a God-fearing father. When you must administer the wounds of a father-friend to your children, do that with heartfelt love. Tell them you must convey the whole counsel of God because you can't bear the thought of spending eternity apart from them. My father often said to us, with tears: 'Children, I cannot miss any of you in heaven.' Then, when we were all converted, he prayed, 'Lord, now, please save all the grandchildren!' Tell your children: 'We will allow you every privilege an open Bible will allow us to give you – but if we say no to you, you must know that flows out of our love.' As Ryle said: 'Love is one grand secret of successful training. Soul love is the soul of all love.'[6]

  When your children are young, take them on your lap in family worship. Let them identify Bible teaching and discussion with the warmth of Daddy's lap and the love of Daddy's heart.

- *Require attention.* Proverbs 4:1 says, 'Hear, ye children, the instruction of a father, and attend to know understanding.' You have important truths to convey. You must demand a hearing for God's truths in your home. That may involve repeated statements at the beginning like these: 'Sit up, son, and look at me when I'm talking. We're talking about God's Word, and God deserves to be heard.' Don't allow children to leave their seats during family worship, except for emergencies. Don't answer the phone; your audience with God is far more important.

3. For praying

- *Be short.* With few exceptions, don't pray for more than five minutes. Tedious prayers do more harm than good. Don't teach in your prayer; God doesn't need the instruction. Teach with your eyes open; pray with your eyes shut.

---

6. J. C. Ryle, *The Duties of Parents* (Conrad, Mont.: Triangle Press, 1993), p. 9.

- *Be simple without being shallow.* Pray for things that your children know something about, but don't allow your prayers to become trivial. Don't reduce your prayers to self-centered, shallow petitions.

- *Be direct.* Spread your needs before God, plead your case, and ask for mercy. Name your teenagers and children and their needs one by one on a daily basis. That holds tremendous weight with them. I am surely not alone when I confess that my parents' prayers often kept me from sin. On one occasion, when tempted to commit a sin, I saw in my mind's eye my mother on her knees, and simply could not go forward. Never forget that your earnest prayers as a parent can make lifelong impressions upon your children.

- *Be natural yet solemn.* Speak clearly and reverently. Don't use an unnatural, high-pitched voice or a monotone. Don't pray too loudly or softly, too fast or slow.

- *Be varied.* Don't pray the same thing every day; that becomes tedious. Develop more variety in prayer by remembering and stressing the various ingredients of true prayer. I find it helpful to use the simple ACTS acronym: adoration, confession, thanksgiving, supplication. Adore God for Himself, His titles and attributes; confess your sins and the family's sins; give thanks for God's blessings, and praise Him for His kingdom, glory, and power; declaring your humble dependence and need, asking for family mercies (both material and spiritual), interceding for friends, churches, and the nations. Mix these ingredients with different proportions to get variety in your prayers.

- *Be a trainer.* Train even your young children to pray. Depending on age and ability, one of your children could pray or offer thanks to God for one specific thing; another child might handle the entire prayer. When our oldest child was three years old, he asked while he was on my lap if he could say the 'Daddy's family prayer.' I was a bit surprised, but said yes, and then told him that I would whisper in his ear what to say one thought at a time, and he should repeat it aloud. When he was four years old, I told him that he should take his turn to pray the family prayer now without promptings from me until he would run stuck; at that point, I would revert to whispering in his ear several more thoughts which he would repeat aloud. By the time, he was seven, he was praying the full prayer himself. I followed the same pattern with our two daughters, and found that, though the Holy Spirit alone can teach children to truly pray, this way of teaching them to pray was very helpful. For example, when their friends would come over for dinner when they were seven or eight years old, they did not hesitate to pray reverently in front of them.

4. For singing
- *Sing doctrinally pure songs.* There is no excuse for singing doctrinal error no matter how attractive the tune might be.

- *Sing psalms* first and foremost without neglecting sound hymns. Remember that the Psalms, called by Calvin 'an anatomy of all parts of the soul,' are the richest gold mine of deep, living, experiential scriptural piety available to us still today.

- *Sing heartily and with feeling.* As Colossians 3:23 says, 'And whatsoever ye do, do it heartily, as to the Lord, and not unto men.' Meditate on the words you are singing. On occasion discuss a phrase that is sung.

After Family Worship

As you retire for the night, pray for God's blessing on family worship. 'Lord, use the instruction to save our children and to cause them to grow in grace that they might put their hope in Thee. Use our praise of Thy name in song to endear Thy name, Thy Son, and Thy Spirit to their never-dying souls. Use our stammering prayers to bring our children to repentance. Lord Jesus Christ, breathe upon our family during this time of worship with Thy Word and Spirit. Make these life-giving times.'

OBJECTIONS AGAINST FAMILY WORSHIP

Some people object to regular times of family worship, citing these reasons:

- *Our family doesn't have time for this.* If you have time for recreation and pleasures but no time for family worship, think about 2 Timothy 3:4-5, which warns about people who love pleasures more than God; they have a form of godliness, but deny the power of it. Time taken from family activity and business to seek God's blessing is never wasted. If we take God's Word seriously, we will say: 'I can't afford *not* to give God and His Word priority in my family.' Samuel Davies once said: 'Were you formed for this world only, there would be some force in this objection, but how strange does such an objection sound coming from an heir of eternity! Pray, what is your time given to you for? Is it not principally that you may prepare for eternity? And have you no time for what is the greatest business of your lives?'[7]

- *There is no regular time when all of us can be together.* If you have conflicting schedules—particularly when older children are in college—you should do the best you can. Don't cancel family worship if some children are not home. Have family worship when most family members are present. If conflicts in scheduling arise, change or cancel the activity that threatens worship, if possible. Family worship should be a non-negotiable item. Business, hobbies, sports, and school activities are secondary to family worship.

- *Our family is too small.* You only need two for family worship. As Jesus said, 'Where two or three are gathered together in my name, there am I in the midst of them' (Matt. 18:20).

---

7. Samuel Davies, 'The Necessity and Excellence of Family Religion,' in *Sermons on Important Subjects* (New York: Robert Carter and Brothers, 1853), p. 60.

- *Our family is too diverse for everyone to profit.* Have a plan that covers all ages. Read a few minutes from a Bible story book for the little ones, apply a proverb for the older ones, and read a page or two from a book for teens. A wise plan can overcome any diversity of age. Besides, all age groups can sing and pray together. Then, too, remember that when you are addressing one age group, the others are listening too. While you're teaching younger children, older teenagers are listening in. They're also learning by example how to teach younger children. When they marry and have children, they will remember how you led family worship and probably imitate you.

- If you're a minister, some of your parishioners may object: *I'm not good at leading our family in worship.* Here are a few suggestions for you to pass on to them: First, read James W. Alexander or Matthew Henry on family worship. Don Whitney, Jerry Marcellino, and I have smaller booklets on how to lead family worship. Second, tell them to ask for guidance from you or other God-fearing fathers. Ask if they can visit your home and either show them how to lead family worship, or observe how you do it. Third, encourage them to start simply. If they are not already reading Scripture and praying together, tell them to start. If they are reading and praying together, tell them to add one or two questions on the portion read and sing a few psalms or hymns; then, they can add a minute or two each week until they are up to fifteen minutes or even a bit more perhaps as the children grow older.

  Encourage them that their skill will increase with practice. As George Whitefield said: 'Where the heart is rightly disposed, it doth not demand any uncommon abilities to discharge family worship in a decent and edifying manner.'[8] Most importantly, encourage them to ask the Holy Spirit to show them how.

  Could it be that our real problem in family worship is not our inability to pray, read, and instruct so much as our lack of grasping the astounding promises and power God has given us to shape His covenant children for His glory?

- *Some of our family members won't participate.* There may be homes in which it is difficult to hold to family worship. Such cases are rare, however. If you have difficult children, follow a simple rule: no Scripture, no singing, no praying, no food. Say, 'In this house, we will serve the Lord. We all breathe, therefore every person in our home must praise the Lord.' Psalm 150:6 makes no such exception, even for unconverted children. It says, 'Let every thing that hath breath praise the Lord. Praise ye the Lord.'

- *We don't want to make hypocrites of our unconverted children.* One sin doesn't justify another. The mindset that offers this objection is dangerous. An unconverted person may never plead an unconverted state to neglect duty.

---

8. George Whitefield, 'The Great Duty of Family Religion,' *The Banner of Sovereign Grace Truth* 2 (Apr-May, 1994): pp. 88-89, 120-21.

Don't encourage your children to use this excuse for avoiding family worship. Stress their need to use every means of grace.

- *I can't carry a tune.* Encourage your children to learn to play the piano. Or obtain a CD or MP3 files with printed lyrics for edifying psalms and hymns to the Lord.

    The Reformers were strong on using music. Luther said, 'He who does not find the gift and perfect wisdom of God in His wonderful works of music, is truly a clod, and is not worthy to be considered a man.'

MOTIVATIONS FOR FAMILY WORSHIP

Every God-fearing father and mother should establish and maintain family worship in the home for the following reasons:

1. The eternal welfare of your loved ones

God uses means to save souls. Most commonly He uses the preaching of His Word. But He may also use family worship. Like the connection between preaching and the salvation of souls in the congregation, there is a connection between family worship and the salvation of souls. Proverbs 22:6 says, 'Train up a child in the way he should go: and when he is old, he will not depart from it.' That rule has been confirmed for centuries.

Spurgeon clearly remembered his mother tearfully praying over him like this: 'Lord, Thou knowest if these prayers are not answered in Charles's conversion, these very prayers will bear witness against him in the Judgment Day.' Spurgeon wrote: 'The thought that my mother's prayers would serve as witness against me in the day of judgment sent terror into my heart.'[9]

Fathers, use every means to have your children snatched as brands from the burning. Pray with them, teach them, sing with them, weep over them, admonish them, plead with them and upon their baptism. Remember that at every family worship you are ushering your children into the very presence of the Most High. Seek grace to bring down the benediction of Almighty God upon your household.

2. The satisfaction of a good conscience

J. C. Ryle said, 'I charge you, fathers, take every pain to train your children in the way they should go. I charge you not merely for the sake of your children's souls; I charge you for the sake of your own future comfort and peace. Truly your own happiness in great measure depends on it. Children have caused the saddest tears that man has ever had to shed.' Such sorrows are heavy enough when fathers have faithfully discharged their duty yet still live with a prodigal son or daughter. But who can bear the reproach of a stinging conscience that condemns us because we never brought them up in the fear of the Lord? What shame to have failed to take

---

9. *The Autobiography of Charles H. Spurgeon*, vol. 1 (Chicago: Revell, 1898), p. 68.

seriously the vow we uttered at our children's baptism or confirmation to raise our children in our confessional doctrines.

How much better if we can say: 'Son, we taught you God's Word; we wrestled for your soul; we lived a God-fearing example before you. You didn't see in us a sinless piety but an unfeigned faith. You know we sought first the kingdom of God and His righteousness. Your conscience will bear witness that Christ is the center of this home. We sang together, prayed together, and talked together. If you turn away from this light and these privileges, and insist on going your own way, we can only pray that all your Bible study, praying, and singing will not rise up against you in the Judgment Day – and that you will come to your senses before it is too late.'

3. Assistance in child-rearing

Family worship helps promote family harmony in times of affliction, sickness, and death. It offers greater knowledge of the Scriptures and growth in personal piety both for yourself and your children. It nurtures wisdom in how to face life, openness to speak about meaningful questions, and a closer relationship between father and children. Strong bonds established in family worship in early years may be a great help to teens in years to come. These teens may be spared from much sin when recalling family prayers and worship. In times of temptation, they may say: 'How can I offend a father who daily wrestles with God on my behalf?'

4. The shortness of time

'For what is your life? It is even a vapour, that appeareth for a little time, and then vanisheth away' (James 4:14). Daily training is only for a mere twenty years or less, and even those years are not guaranteed. We ought to conduct family worship in the awareness of how brief life is in terms of never-ending eternity. Children will sense this reality if family worship is done with earnestness, love, warmth, and consistency.

5. Love for God and His church

Godly parents want to glorify God and serve His church. They want to give the church spiritually stalwart sons and daughters. Pray that your sons and daughters may be pillars in the church. Blessed is the parent who can one day see among the crowd of worshipers their own sons and daughters. Family worship is the foundation of such a future.

CONCLUSION

We have been given biblical examples of family worship – will we not follow them? Has God placed in our homes the souls of creatures made in His image, and will we not use all of our abilities to see our children bow in worship before God and His Son, Jesus Christ? Will we not strive to promote the Christ-centered piety in our home that family worship is so well-suited to promote? Will we trifle with the spiritual nurture, yes, with the eternity, of our own family members?

If your children are grown and out of our home, it is still not too late to do the following:

- Pray for them. Pray that God may make crooked sticks straight and bring good out of evil.

- Confess your sin to God and to your children. Give them sound literature on family worship.

- Speak to and pray with your grandchildren. Do for them what you didn't do for your children.

- Begin family worship with your spouse. Follow the advice of James W. Alexander, 'Fly at once, with your household, to the throne of grace.'[10]

- Do not become discouraged and give up family worship, no matter what happens. Start over afresh. Press forward. Be realistic. Don't expect perfection from your performances or your children's responses. All your perfection is in your great High Priest, who intercedes for you and has promised to be gracious to believers and their seed.

- Beg the Lord to bless your feeble efforts and save your children and grandchildren. Plead with Him to take them in His arms for all eternity. May God graciously grant His Spirit to assist you, for the good of souls, and for His name's sake.

Let me close with this illustration taken from the autobiography of John Paton (1824–1907). Paton served as a missionary to a cannibalistic people in the islands of the south Pacific Ocean. He faced enormous difficulties and sorrows. But he persevered in the name of Christ. One earthly means by which God prepared him for his labors was his father in Scotland. In later years John Paton looked back upon his father with great gratitude. Paton's father worked out of a shop in their house. Their family had a small room in their home which was their prayer closet. John was deeply affected by his father's regular devotion to prayer in that room. He remembered, 'Thither daily, and oftentimes a day, generally after each meal, we saw our father retire, and "shut the door"; and we children got to understand ... that prayers were being poured out there for us, as of old by the High Priest within the veil in the Most High Place.' The Paton children could sometimes hear their father's voice full of emotion, pleading for them before the throne of grace.

When John Paton left his home to go to Glasgow to study theology and do urban evangelism, he had to walk forty miles before coming to a train station. His father walked the first six miles out with him. They spoke about the Lord, and his

---

10. J. W. Alexander, *Thoughts on Family Worship* (Morgan, Penn.: Soli Deo Gloria, 1995), p. 238.

father gave him counsel. Then for the last half-mile they walked in silence. His father's lips still moved, but now in silent prayer for his son while tears streamed down his face. When they came to the place of their parting, father grasped son by the hand, said, 'God bless you, my son! Your father's God prosper you, and keep you from all evil.' Overcome by emotion, he could say no more, but his lips continued to move in silent prayer. John Paton wrote that while walking the remainder of the distance, 'I vowed deeply and oft, by the help of God, to live and act so as never to grieve or dishonor such a father and mother as He had given me.'

And then Paton added, 'How much my father's prayers at this time impressed me I can never explain, nor can any stranger understand. When on his knees and all of us kneeling around him in family worship, he poured out his whole soul in tears for the conversion of the heathen world to the service of Jesus, and for every personal need. We all felt as if in the presence of the living Savior, and learned to love and know Him as our divine Friend. As we rose from our knees I used to look at the light on my father's face and wish I were like him in spirit, hoping that in answer to his prayers I might be privileged to carry the gospel to the heathen world in some way' – and he went to the cannibals in response![11]

May God grant that you and I become fathers like that!

---

11. *John G. Paton, Missionary to the New Hebrides: An Autobiography*, ed. John Gibson Paton (London: Banner of Truth, 1965), 26.

CHAPTER 18

RELISHING THE LOVE OF GOD
(1 JOHN 4:8)

GOD calls us to live lives of holiness. We have seen how we progress in holiness through studying the Word, putting on the whole armor of God, and diligently maintaining family worship.

Now we will examine the grand motivation for holiness, namely, the love of God. Many years ago, Napoleon said that he had conquered the world by force. By contrast, Jesus Christ conquers the world by love. We love God because He first loved us (1 John 4:19). God's love 'is a wide and fertile field ... in which to grow human piety and justice.'[1] The true motivation to live in holiness is neither a legalistic spirit of bondage to the law, nor the fear of going to hell, but a child-like relationship with God, trusting in His love for us as our Father in heaven for Christ Jesus' sake, and loving Him in response by the Spirit's grace. This love is rooted in unsurpassable, unchangeable, steady, and unconditional love of a triune God in Jesus Christ.

This remarkable, unworldly love, this love that comes to us from outside of us, makes us yearn to be holy, and inclines us to love God and our neighbor. In pursuing this motivation for holiness, we will look at 1 John 4:8: 'He that loveth not, knoweth not God; for God is love' – and onwards, examining three thoughts: first, the centrality of God's love, second, the quality of God's love, and third, the efficacy of God's love.

THE CENTRALITY OF GOD'S LOVE

'God is love' (1 John 4:8, 16). What an amazing declaration this is, and how desperately it needs to be heard by people today. What an amazing discovery the love of God is, when we, by the Spirit of God, learn to drink deeply of this love through Jesus Christ. The love of God is a revolutionary concept. It is staggering. 'God's love is of himself. God's love does not arise from something outside of him,

---

1. Joel R. Beeke and Paul M. Smalley, *Reformed Systematic Theology* (Wheaton, Ill.: Crossway, 2019), 1:799.

253

but [it] is God's very life: he *is* love.'[2] We know that God is more than love; He is also righteous, He is holy, He is just, and He is true. Yet John singles out this particular attribute of God. John sets it before us at a very great height and yet very near to us by saying, 'God is love,' offering these three simple words as his account of why someone bereft of love is a stranger to God.

1. God's Personality

John gives the love of God preeminence for several reasons. First, he singles out this attribute of God because it profoundly exhibits *the personality of God*. John wrote his epistle to warn Christians about the Gnostics, who viewed God as an impersonal power or force. This power was not the personal God of the Scriptures, whose very being is permeated with love. John teaches that God is love, not a force but a person with a heart, so to speak. He knows His own; He calls them by name. He has a purpose in mind for each of them. He cherishes them as individuals, and takes an interest in all that concerns them. God gives Himself to others; He is a God who cares.

John stresses the personal love of God with the sweet words, 'Father' and 'Son.' The Son is exceedingly precious to the Father, His 'only-begotten' (1 John 4:9). By His grace God draws us into the family circle of His love in the Trinity. He writes in 1 John 1:3, 'Truly our fellowship is with the Father, and with his Son Jesus Christ.' God's fatherly love embraces us in the grace of adoption. John exults in 1 John 3:1, 'Behold, what manner of love the Father hath bestowed upon us, that we should be called the sons of God.'

The sovereignty of God is central to Calvinism. But if you view that sovereignty as the Muslims do, as a kind of impersonal force or fate, you have missed what Christianity is all about. Calvinism, as well as biblical Christianity and the Reformed faith, teaches us that the sovereign God is first and foremost a truly personal God, ever existing in the mutual love relationship of three persons: the Father, the Son, and the Holy Spirit. So John can say categorically, 'God is love.'

In John 17:24 we hear Jesus praying, 'Father, I will that they also, whom thou hast given me, be with me where I am; that they may behold my glory, which thou hast given me: for thou lovedst me before the foundation of the world.' The love of the Father for the Son did not begin after the incarnation (Matt. 3:17). The Father loved the Son in the Trinity from eternity past. Proverbs 8:30 puts these words in the mouth of Jesus: 'I was daily his delight, rejoicing always before him.' God promised the Messiah, 'Behold my servant, whom I uphold; mine elect, in whom my soul delighteth' (Isa. 42:1). The Bible is replete with verses like these that express Father's eternal love for the Son within the bounds of the Trinity. God's love to God is never unrequited. Some of us may know what it's like to have had a broken heart with unrequited love: somebody you have loved doesn't return it, or perhaps the love they had for you faded. That is sad, an effect of sin in the world. It can never

---

2. Beeke and Smalley, *Reformed Systematic Theology*, 1:792.

be like that within God. The Father and Son always took eternal love and delight in each other – and always will. Jonathan Edwards put it this way:

> The infinite essential love of God is, as it were, an infinite and eternal mutual holy energy between the Father and the Son, a pure holy act whereby the Deity becomes nothing but an infinite and unchangeable act of love which proceeds from both the Father and Son. 'Tis all an holy energy consisting in that infinite flame of pure love and holy delight that there is, from all eternity, between the Father and the Son, immensely loving and delighting and rejoicing in each other.[3]

'Even prior to creation, God's love involved relationships and self-giving within the Trinity .... The greatest display of God's love for us is grounded upon his love for his Son.'[4] Someone once asked Cornelius VanTil, 'What is the deepest thing you meditate on?' and in a flash he said, 'Oh, it is the ontological eternal Trinity. You are on holy ground just to meditate on this love between the members of the Trinity.'

2. God's Essence

Second, God's love receives preeminence because love is *the essence and being of God*, revealed to us in the gospel in and through His Son. In the very depths of His being, 'God is love.' This is so important to John that he writes it in 1 John 4:8 and repeats it again in verse 16. The word 'love' appears dozens of times in this short epistle, twenty-nine times in chapter 4 alone. God's love comes from Himself: His love is self-generated. The moon only reflects light; the sun emanates light. God is light, like that sun, His love doesn't reflect from some other source, it comes from His very being, because God is love. To expand on John's formula, the Old Testament insists many times, that God is 'merciful and gracious, longsuffering, and abundant in goodness and truth' (Exod. 34:6).

God is love, but He also has many other attributes. We dare not make any one of God's attributes primary at the expense of making the others secondary. If we make love God's main attribute, we usually downplay the holiness of God, and the effect is often seen in lifestyles of license. If we move to the opposite extreme and say God's main attribute is holiness, legalism will normally be the result. Nearly all practical errors can be traced back to a faulty view of God. Jeremiah Burroughs reminds us that 'There is anger and hatred in God as well as love: but God is never said to be anger or hatred; no, not justice itself: but he loves that expression of himself to the children of men, *God is love*.'[5]

God is holy, God is love, and there is a beautiful harmony in all of God's attributes. And that tells us that His holiness is a loving holiness, His love is a holy love.[6] It is the

---

3. Jonathan Edwards, *Heaven: A World of Love* (Amityville, N.Y.: Calvary Press, 1992), p. 11.

4. Beeke and Smalley, *Reformed Systematic Theology*, 1:792.

5. Jeremiah Burroughs, *Causes, Evils, and Cures of Heart and Church Divisions* (New York: Carlton & Phillips, 1855), pp. 103-4.

6. Beeke and Smalley, *Reformed Systematic Theology*, 1:792.

same thing with God's infinity. The infinite God is love, therefore, God is infinite in His love. He lavishes love on us, knowing there is more in His infinity than we will ever be able to exhaust. Spurgeon once said, 'We can no more exhaust the infinite love of God than a little fish can drink up the oceans.' Dear friends, we need the love of God, and we need never fear that God will have us wait in line because there is only so much to go around. God is infinite; God is love. Therefore, He is infinite in His love. And since it is a holy love, it is a pure love.

God's love is central to His character and pervades all His actions. There is no darkness or negative past in God, no strings attached to His love, no contradictions in His loving nature (1 John 1:5). Love is what He has always been from eternity past and what He will be in eternity future. God is never cold; He is never distant. God is burning, undying, compassionate love in Christ Jesus.

3. God's Heart for Sinners

Third, John gives God's love preeminence because it is *what we most sorely need to hear*. The greatest possible thing we could hear about God with reference to ourselves is that He loves us. As sinful men and women, teenagers, and children, we need to hear about God's love. We stand before God insignificant in our creaturely frailty. We sense our alienation from God because of inherited sin and corruption. And how quickly the waters of death enclose us. The world goes on, and we are soon forgotten. We are but tiny specks on a small planet in a little galaxy in an immeasurable universe. Sometimes when we look at the stars and consider the immensity of our Creator and our own smallness before Him, we wonder, 'Who are we?' But the beauty of the love of God is that God brings our lives into focus before Him. For Christ's sake, we become in His loving presence His own children, whom He loves one by one.

God, in love, has a profound commitment to all who believe in His Son. So, if I am a believer, I am not insignificant to God. I do not exist in an impersonal cosmos, aching for some personal love that will offer me comfort and give me a reason to exist. No, I have a living, loving relationship with the very Creator of the universe and the Redeemer of my soul. My life is caught up in the loving purposes and the loving heart of the Almighty Father and His redeeming Son, for God is love.

4. God's Motive for Redemption

Fourth, John stresses God's love because love is *the very heart of Calvary*: 'In this was manifested the love of God toward us, because that God sent his only begotten Son into the world, that we might live through him. Herein is love, not that we loved God, but that he loved us, and sent his Son to be the propitiation for our sins' (1 John 4:9-10). He loved us even when He hated our lifestyle, our attitudes, and our choices. He loved us when our sins made Him angry enough to send us to hell. It was in the cross of Christ that God gave us the supreme demonstration of what love is: divine love, supernatural love, undeserved love, amazing love, eternal love, super-abounding love – 'Behold what manner of love the Father hath bestowed on us!' (1 John 3:1).

Love is the heart of the atonement. In the depths of His loving heart, God looks not upon His own things but upon the things of others. He loves by giving the best He has—His own Son—for the worst He can find: hell-worthy sinners. Love is what Christ spoke out of the appalling darkness and suffering and agony on the cross. As the poet Thomas Kelly wrote:

> *Inscribed upon the Cross we see,*
> *In shining letters, God is love.*
> *He bears our sins upon the tree:*
> *He brings us mercy from above.*[7]

Calvary is the tremendous triumph of God's love. It is the conquest of all the powers of evil by love, for God is love.

At Calvary we see the proof that 'God so loved the world, that He gave His only begotten Son that whosoever believeth in Him should not perish but have everlasting life' (John 3:16). At Calvary the open arms of Jesus make the most extravagant offer of love this world has ever known: unconditional love for profligates and prodigals, for atheists and Pharisees, love for all those who truly repent and believe in the Son and trust Him alone for their salvation. Since the Son incarnate is the revelation of the love of God for sinners, we can say that the Lord Jesus Christ is the love of God in human flesh. It is good theology to say, 'Jesus is love incarnate.'

If you are not a believer, I urge you to consider the unsurpassable love of God. The Almighty God, who so loved sinners that He gave up His only Son to suffer and die for them so that He might love them as He loves His Son (John 17:23), is calling you to Himself, even now. He is coming to you in the preaching of His Word, offering His love to you. He is willing to be your Savior, your Refuge, your Shepherd, your Keeper, your Father, and your Friend. No matter how great a sinner you are, if you will but bend your knee and cast your sins at His feet and believe in His Son, crying out for mercy, God will forgive you. He will save you and lift you up.

Do not spurn God's love. Do not cast away the greatest gift in the world. Perhaps you have been looking for love in all the wrong places. Do you want real love? Come to Jesus. He is love in the flesh, perfect beyond your wildest imaginations. He is better than you could ever dream. He is love in the flesh. God calls you to share in the inheritance of Christ. He wants to place you there in the righteousness of His Son, the standing of His Son, the blessed eternity of His Son. In the glorious presence of His Son, seated at God's right hand, are pleasures forevermore. Oh, do not spurn the love of God!

---

7. Thomas Kelly, 'We Sing the Praise of Him Who Died,' Stanza 2.

God is love. That love which did not shrink from Golgotha's suffering or death, that love which did not count the cost but loved to the uttermost, that love is available to *you* today. And there are no limits, no measurements to that love. Scripture says that God's love surpasses all 'breadth, and length, and depth, and height' (Eph. 3:18). This love is communicated most powerfully through the cross of Christ. In love for His own, Jesus paid the whole price of the Fall. He paid in full the wages of sin, namely condemnation, death, and hell itself, to the very last penny. Love has taken away every liability; it has purchased the church, Christ's bride, with a full dowry price. Because of this love, Jesus' manhood has been broken in our place. His lifeblood has been poured forth, His heart broken, His very spirit torn asunder from His body. He has given all He is for us, and now offers to give it all to us. 'Greater love hath no man' (John 15:13). God is love.

THE QUALITY OF GOD'S LOVE

Luke 7:36-50 is a beautiful case study of how God works out that love to win over the hearts of His people and make them willingly love Him in return. How beautifully the woman who was a sinner responds to the love of her Savior. Verses 37-38 tell us that she 'brought an alabaster box of ointment, and stood at his feet behind him weeping, and began to wash his feet with tears, and did wipe them with the hairs of her head, and kissed his feet, and anointed them with the ointment.' What motivated her to do that was the love of Christ. This woman admired the Lord Jesus; she appreciated the skillful way He handled His opponents. She was excited by His teaching. His great signs and healings took her breath away. She felt at home when she was in Jesus' presence. She felt safe and content. But most of all, she loved him for His compassionate love to her, a great sinner, a weeping sinner, a believing sinner, a loving sinner. She was moved to love Jesus much because Jesus loved her much. That is why she took the most precious object she owned: a jar of fragrant and expensive perfume, and poured it over Jesus' feet, then wiped His feet with her hair. The Pharisee despised her for wasting such precious perfume, but Jesus understood and rejoiced that His love had made this holy impact upon her, and declared, 'Her sins, which are many, are forgiven; for she loved much, but to whom little is forgiven, the same loveth little' (v. 47).

When God the Son loves, His love conquers us, motivates us, subdues us, restrains us from sin, and moves us to righteousness. His love conquers our hearts. Our parents love us, our spouses love us, and our children love us, but our Savior loves us with the purest, sweetest love of all. When we truly understand that, we have all the motivation we need to live holy lives for Him.

Jesus Christ loves us in specific ways. Let me just mention five of them.

1. God's Love is First

First, He loves us *before we love Him*. He takes the initiative with us. 'Herein is love, not that we loved God, but that he loved us' (1 John 4:10). The world hates

God and Christ (John 15:18, 23-24). Engrave this truth upon your soul: you hated God and will hate Him all your life until He changes you (Rom. 8:7). How then does anyone love God? John said it so poignantly in 1 John 4:19, 'We love him, because he first loved us.'

Mary did not come to Christ to win His love with her expensive gift. She had already been conquered by His love and now came to Jesus in response to His love. Mary was a sinner; from her birth she had a deceitful heart of stone. She failed to do good because she was a sinner. She should have loved God with all her heart, but she failed. She should have loved her neighbor as herself, but she failed. By nature she resented God. There was nothing in Mary to love. Jesus knew that.

Yet, Jesus loves the unlovable. He loved Mary in all her awkwardness, in all her deformity, in all her unlovable ways. Love is the fountainhead from which the gospel springs. And so God takes the initiative and loves us first. He loves us when we hate Him. There is no reason why He should love you or me. But He does. He loves with an unbought, unsought, initiatory, free love. Thomas Brooks teaches that 'Rachel was dearer to Jacob than Leah, because she cost him more; he obeyed, endured, and suffered more by day and night for her than for Leah: Ah! sinners, the greatness of your sins does but set off the freeness and riches of Christ's grace, and the freeness of his love. This maketh heaven and earth to ring of his praise, that he loves those that are most unlovely, that he shews most favour to them that have sinned most highly against him.'[8] There is nothing so great and pure as this love. God is love.

2. God's Love is Free

God's love is unconditional, one-sided, and sovereign; nothing other than goodness proceeds from Him, and yet He can sovereignly direct the manner of His love to each of His creatures.

There is a sense in which God's love is universally directed to all creatures: 'The earth, O LORD, is full of thy mercy' (Ps. 119:64). And yet, God distributes His love diversely. The birds of the air and the flowers of the field are under God's care, but He places a far greater value upon humanity. Even within humanity, God expresses a *general* love, on the one hand, whereby He 'maketh his sun to rise on the evil and on the good, and sendeth rain on the just and on the unjust' (Matt. 5:45); but on the other hand, God expresses a *special*, salvific love for His elect, the people of God, 'holy and beloved' (Col. 3:12). The saints of God receive the special love of God '*as an observable indication* of his love for his Son ... as if God said, "Do you want to see how much I love my Son? Look at how I will love my people."'[9]

---

8. Thomas Brooks, *The Complete Works of Thomas Brooks*, ed. Alexander Balloch Grosart (Edinburgh; London; Dublin: James Nichol; James Nisbet and Co.; G. Herbert, 1866), 1:143.

9. Beeke and Smalley, *Reformed Systematic Theology*, 1:797-98. The preceding remarks also summarize the subsection 'God's Free and Sovereign Love' of chapter 41, 'God's Moral Excellence, Part 1,' on pages 797-99.

God's love is a sovereignly directed, free love, unconditioned on anything God may find within the sinner to compel Him to love. He loved us *because* He loves us (Deut. 7:7-8). As God spoke through the prophet Hosea, 'I will love them freely.' Brooks expounds this:

> As God loves you with a first love, so he loves you with a free love ... I know they are backslidden, but I will heal their backslidings. I know they have broken their bones by their fall, but I will make those broken bones to rejoice. I know there is nothing at all in them that is excellent or eminent, that is honourable or acceptable, that is laudable or lovely, yet 'I will love them freely' ... of mine own, free, rich, absolute, sovereign, and independent grace.[10]

How blessed we are when we learn that God's love is a matter of His sovereignty, that 'God's love is a free love, having no motive or foundation but within itself.' Not only is His love sovereign, but so is every aspect of the process of salvation:

> The people of God are freely loved: Deut. 7:6-8; and freely chosen, John 15:16-19, Eph. 1:4; and freely accepted, Eph. 1:6; and freely adopted, Eph. 1:5, Gal. 4:5, 6; and freely reconciled, 2 Cor. 5:18-20; and freely justified, Rom. 3:24, 'Being justified freely by his grace;' and freely saved, Eph. 2:5; 'By grace ye are saved,' ver. 8, 'For by grace ye are saved;' Tit. 3:5, 'Not by works of righteousness which we have done, but according to his mercy he saved us.[11]

3. God's Love is True

Third, Jesus Christ loves His people *truly*. There is a lot of pretend love in this world. Many sing of love or make promises about never-dying love; they write stories and make films about love. Love is everywhere, it seems, but so little of it is *true* love. John warned against mere talk about love in 1 John 3:18: 'My little children, let us not love in word, neither in tongue; but in deed and in truth.' But now we see real love demonstrated once for all in Christ. First John 3:16 says, 'Hereby perceive we the love of God, because he laid down his life for us.'

When Job was the most prosperous man in town, everyone loved him. But when he suffered terrible losses and became sick, only four people came to see him, yet they wound up accusing him of heinous sin and urging him to repent. Job knew fair-weather love, which deserted him when troubles came. That is the best we can do, since by nature we do not truly love. We do not love each other and we do not love God. We love ourselves and our own ends. In particular, we love our sins. A young man meets a young woman and tries to determine whether he loves her. But really, what he is thinking is, 'Will she meet my needs?' Or worse, 'Will she yield to my charm?' He thinks selfishly. But Christ's love is 100 per cent genuine; there is nothing counterfeit about it. It is unconditional *true* love.

---

10. Brooks, *Works*, 5:592.

11. Brooks, *Works*, 3:484.

God's love is genuine in its personal affection, kindness, and delight in the ones to whom He directs His love. Theologians describe God's love as *benevolent* (showing good will and kindness toward the beloved) and *complacent* (having satisfaction and delight in the beloved).

God's *benevolent* love 'is his gracious and merciful love for people apart from what they deserve' leading to 'generous acts of good,' like sending His own Son to save the loveless and unlovable; 'he is able to love those whom he hates for their sins, for his love springs from the bottomless riches of his own goodness' and flows 'from his mercy to our misery.' It is astonishing to think that 'even as he hated sinners for their sins, he loved them as his pitiful creatures.'[12] This is God's *benevolent* love.

God's *complacent* love is 'his pleasure and delight in those whom he loves'; just as God rejoiced at creation (Gen. 1:1-31), so he rejoices 'in his Son and those united to him.' God's complacent love is not the reason He saved sinners, but is the 'Father rejoicing in those whom he has saved by faith in Christ ... and in the fruit they produce by union with Christ.'[13]

We must emphasize both God's benevolent *and* His complacent love, for 'complacent love not grounded in benevolence degenerates into justification by works. Benevolent love without complacency invites antinomianism, for it makes God indifferent to the sin or obedience of his saints.'[14] The *benevolent* and *complacent* love of God is the love in 1 Corinthians 13 that does not fluctuate, does not wait for a response, and loves for love's sake. It is the love of Jesus, whose love is kind, does not envy, does not boast, is not proud, is not rude, is not self-seeking, is not easily angered, keeps no record of wrongs, and does not delight in evil. Jesus' love rejoices with the truth, always protects, always trusts, always hopes, always perseveres, and never fails. It is perfect love.

4. God's Love is Strong

Fourth, Jesus Christ's love is *strong*. His love can never be conquered. Song of Solomon 8:7 tells us, 'Many waters cannot quench love; neither can the floods drown it. If a man were to give all the substance of his house for love, it would utterly be contemned.' God's love is as strong as death.

Death lays hold of all of us. But Scripture assures us that God's love is so strong that it carries us through death, so that death is transformed from a punishment for sin into an emancipation from sin and entrance into eternal life. God's love is also fervent; it burns with passion. Jesus, the great Bridegroom, passionately loves His bride, the church. He laid down His life for her and died for her. He determined to save her because He loved her so much. His love is unquenchable. You could pour thousands of gallons of water on it, and the love of God would burn as brightly as

---

12. Beeke and Smalley, *Reformed Systematic Theology*, 1:795-96.

13. Beeke and Smalley, *Reformed Systematic Theology*, 1:796.

14. Beeke and Smalley, *Reformed Systematic Theology*, 1:796.

ever. God's love is immovable; rivers of waters cannot wash it away. A river can cut through granite mountains, but the love of Jesus Christ cannot be eroded. His love is eternal. It is also beyond price. All the riches of the world cannot purchase this love; it is altogether priceless and yet free.

Many years ago, the wealthy billionaire Aristotle Onassis tried to buy the love of Jacqueline Kennedy. He even got her to marry him, but she never really loved him. He gave her jewels and houses and money, but she did not love him. The love of Jesus is far stronger than the love of the rich and powerful. When Jesus loves us, He woos us and wins us. We cannot buy His love; we can only receive it as a gift.

5. God's Love is Enduring

Finally, Jesus Christ loves us *abidingly*. God loved us in 'that God sent his only begotten Son into the world, that we might live' (1 John 4:9). God's love saves us forever (1 John 5:11). It does not flit around, rising and falling like a little bird. His love rests upon us, takes up residence in our hearts, and never departs from us.

John 3:16 tells us, 'God so loved the world that he gave.' Note the past tense. God gave His Son on Calvary two thousand years ago, but that act in the past is present for us today. Recently, a nurse entered the room of an elderly friend in hospital, announcing to him just a few hours before he would die, 'I need to do some more blood-work on you,' she said. His sister told me that he replied to the nurse, 'That will not be necessary; all the blood-work that I have ever needed has been done for me two thousand years ago on Calvary's cross.' And he died in peace.

The blood of Jesus, shed those many years ago, abides for us today. In that sacrifice on the cross, Jesus covers our sins, shows us His love, and intercedes for us moment by moment. Today, at this moment, Jesus takes my worthless name upon His lips and confesses it before His heavenly Father so that I know with assurance, 'Who is he that condemneth? It is Christ that died, yea rather, that is risen again, who is even at the right hand of God, who also maketh intercession for us' (Rom. 8:34).

Jesus does that, dear believers, because He loves you and me. He loved us yesterday and He loves us today and He will go on loving us in all of our tomorrows. His love is not a momentary infatuation or a tentative reaching out to us to see whether we are worthy of His love. He loves us from eternity past and is determined to marry us in everlasting glory. He betroths Himself to us and, even now, is preparing the eternal wedding feast. Soon He will invite us to come to the marriage supper of the Lamb (cf. Rev. 19:6-9). He loves us for all time and eternity.

Some people love us for a while, then their love cools. Some of you know what it is like to feel the withdrawal of someone's love. Perhaps a fellow Christian loved you greatly, but then you had a problem and your friend turned against you. Jesus' love is not like that. His love does not change, does not fluctuate, does not grow wintry and cold. His love is always warm, always kind, always faithful. His love restores my soul and leads me into green pastures. Jesus is my Shepherd, so I shall not want. When He needs to rebuke me, it is done in love. When He is angry with me, He is motivated by love. When He humbles me, He does so in love.

The believer responds to this kind of love by showing love, and by offering up his life to the Lord as a living, holy sacrifice. As George Matheson expressed it:

> *O Love that wilt not let me go,*
> *I rest my weary soul in Thee;*
> *I give thee back the life I owe,*
> *That in Thine ocean depths its flow*
> *May richer, fuller be.*[15]

So we grow in holiness because we are motivated to do so by the love of Christ. For no other love has the divine quality of the love of Christ.

THE EFFICACY OF GOD'S LOVE

God's love is not a static, abstract concept floating around in space. God's love is a wise and powerful divine energy that accomplishes God's purposes for His glory. God is particularly glorified in the effects that His redeeming love generates in us. John expressed this in various places in this epistle where he wrote of God's love being 'made perfect' (1 John 2:5; 4:12, 17-18).

This idea shows up repeatedly in 1 John 4:11-18. Listen for the words 'perfect' or 'made perfect' in this Scripture passage:

> Beloved, if God so loved us, we ought also to love one another. No man hath seen God at any time. If we love one another, God dwelleth in us, and his love is *perfected* in us. Hereby know we that we dwell in him, and he in us, because he hath given us of his Spirit. And we have seen and do testify that the Father sent the Son to be the Saviour of the world. Whosoever shall confess that Jesus is the Son of God, God dwelleth in him, and he in God. And we have known and believed the love that God hath to us. God is love; and he that dwelleth in love dwelleth in God, and God in him. Herein is our love *made perfect,* that we may have boldness in the day of judgment: because as he is, so are we in this world. There is no fear in love; but *perfect* love casteth out fear: because fear hath torment. He that feareth is not *made perfect* in love. We love him, because he first loved us. (emphasis added)

Of course, John does not mean that there is anything lacking or imperfect in God's love. He means that God's love reaches its goal in the effects that it produces in our lives. John Owen said, 'The love of Christ, being the love of God, is effective and fruitful in producing all the good things which He wills for His beloved. He loves life, grace and holiness into us; He loves us into covenant, loves us into heaven.'[16] In terms of Christ's redeeming love, we can say that His love reaches its goal or fulfills its mission or comes to fruition in creating a certain kind of people whose lives are a constant response to divine love.

---

15. George Matheson, 'O Love That Wilt Not Let Me Go,' Stanza 1.

16. John Owen, *Communion with God* (Ross-shire, Scotland: Christian Focus, 2007), p. 112.

I will use the acronym PEACE to describe how the believer is to respond to God's love. Peace, in fact, is a good way to summarize the great effect of God's love: peace with God, peace within ourselves, and peace with other people. Let me break it down one letter at a time.

Participation

The 'P' in PEACE is for *participation in His love*. God's love reaches its fruition in us when we are united to the God of love and have the love of God in us. 'If we love one another, God dwelleth in us, and his love is *perfected* in us' (v. 12). When we trust in Christ, God opens the door of our hearts and pours His love into us.

When we respond to Christ's love, we respond to that love by believing in His love, embracing Him as the One who first loved us, and by cherishing the gift of His love. We become partakers of that love. We surrender ourselves to it. We taste it. We enjoy it. We are nourished by it. We receive the free offer of the Lord Jesus Christ. We 'close with Christ,' as our Puritan ancestors of faith said. We hold fast to Christ as the prongs of a ring hold fast to the diamond. He becomes our all and in all.

Furthermore, God's love motivates believers to come back to God when they have fallen. They never again have the right to conclude that anything they have done, though ever so sinful, will turn God away from loving them. A believer knows that because God is love, God will never let His child go. God will reach out to the prodigal, no matter how far he or she has strayed, and bring that person back to Himself.

God motivates His backsliding child to come back to Him by showing and declaring that His love does not change. Consider what turned the prodigal son from his wandering ways. It was the generous love of his father, even in regard to his hired servants. The prodigal remembered his father as he was sitting among the pigs, envying them for the scraps they were eating. The son came to himself, saying, 'In my father's house there is bread enough, and to spare. There's nowhere else to go, but to my father's house. There's nowhere else in all the world where I will receive such love.'

Returning prodigals realize the greatest lesson of all: that God is love. They keep coming back to participate in God's love in a deeper, richer way. And so must we.

Emulation

The 'E' in PEACE is for *emulating the example* of God's love. God's love reaches its goal when we follow His example by loving others. John wrote in 1 John 2:5-6, 'But whoso keepeth his word, in him verily is the love of God perfected: hereby know we that we are in him. He that saith he abideth in him ought himself also so to walk, even as he walked.' Christ becomes our great model of love as we walk in His footsteps.

In fact, the commandment to love each other is very old. It was written on man's heart in the garden of Eden, and proclaimed to Moses at Mount Sinai (Lev. 19:18). But in another sense, the commandment to love each other is very new, now that

Christ has come (1 John 2:7-8). No one ever loved as Jesus loved. We now see deeper into the loving heart of God than the law of Moses could take us. And every time we deny ourselves to enrich others and take up our crosses so that someone else might know true joy, we are following the example of Jesus (Luke 9:23).

Consequently, you should 'not rest upon inward wishes of love; examine yourself for practical fruits of love. How has love cost you time, money, and energy?'[17] If God's love is replicated in you, it will show; others may see it in you better and easier than you!

Assurance

The 'A' in PEACE is for *assurance*. When we taste the love of God, we are persuaded in our inmost being of this unspeakable love. We see Jesus Christ the perfect Redeemer sent by God's love. We see His love planted in us and beginning to transform us into His beautiful image. Our fear of punishment for our sins is replaced by the certainty that we are loved with an everlasting love. 'Herein is our love made perfect, that we may have boldness in the day of judgment: because as he is, so are we in this world. There is no fear in love; but perfect love casteth out fear: because fear hath torment. He that feareth is not made perfect in love' (1 John 4:17-18).

What a sweet thing the reality of God's love is compared to the time we found it so hard to believe that God really loved us, given the repulsiveness of our sinful lives. How beautiful it is to know that His love is expressed in promises that cannot fail. We respond, 'We have known and believed the love that God hath to us. God is love, and he that dwelleth in love dwelleth in God, and God in him' (v. 16). So we say with confidence: 'God loves me. He will never stop loving me. His love is inside of me!' We trust God's love and are assured by it. In that assurance we honor Him and glorify Him, for, as Stephen Charnock observes, 'If God be not first believed to be good, he would not be believed at all in anything that he speaks.'[18]

Community

The 'C' in PEACE is for *community* of love. God's love is not given to us to rest passively inside us, but branches out to form a network of loving relationships with others. We are loved, therefore we are to love. Notice that John does not write in terms of 'I' and 'me' but 'we' and 'us.' Our response to divine love must take into account the 'one another' aspect of being members of Christ's body, the church. John says, 'If we love one another, God dwelleth in us, and his love is perfected in us. Hereby know we that we dwell in him, and he in us, because he hath given us of his Spirit' (vv. 12-13). We become brothers and sisters in one family sharing one life together.

We cannot limit this to the existing church. God's love overflowed to those who do not yet love. We were outside God's circle of love, but God's love went

---

17. Beeke and Smalley, *Reformed Systematic Theology*, 1:802.

18. Stephen Charnock, *The Existence and Attributes of God*, 2:335-36.

outside to reach us. In the same way our love must go outside the circle. When we respond to the love of God, we cannot help but communicate the love of God to the unsaved. 'Love all men, even your enemies (Matt. 5:44-45) .... Shall God's heart be large and open to you, but your heart be narrow and closed to others?'[19] We should care about their souls and tell them about Jesus Christ. When Christ becomes ours through faith, we are compelled to offer Christ to others as well. God draws us into the community of His love, and we become community builders by reaching out to others.

Echo

The final 'E' in PEACE is for the *echo* of God's love that is sounded forth by those He loves. Children delight to shout by caverns and cliffs so that they can hear their own voices echo back. God's voice speaks to us in the gospel; it shouts to us a proclamation of His love. We too become living echoes of the gospel. Jonathan Edwards said, 'If holiness in God consists chiefly in love to Himself, holiness in the creature must chiefly consist in love to Him.' When we seek for true holiness without love, that is not holiness. Genuine holiness is bathed in the effectual love of God. When coupled with worship, it becomes a loving worship, a worshipful love, what the old theologians called 'adoration.' We enjoy a holy, loving, intimacy with God. 'We love him, because he first loved us' (1 John 4:19). In loving Him we likewise echo His love for men, women, and children.

Isn't that a beautiful thought, that you can become an echo of the gospel of Jesus Christ? Every act of devotion to God is an echo of how He gave Himself for you. Every sacrifice you make of your time and finances is an echo of His sacrifice of His dear Son. Every act of patience and kindness towards the unconverted is an echo of the voice of Jesus saying, 'Come unto me, all ye that labour and are heavy laden' (Matt. 11:28).

This is the PEACE produced by the efficacy of God's love: participation, example, assurance, community, and echo. By sovereign grace, we participate in God's love as the love of Christ dwells in us, moving us to follow His example in the way of the cross, increasing our assurance that we are His and He is ours, building us into a community of faith and love that is a living echo of the gospel on earth.

Are you walking in the peace of God's love? Are you growing in divine love? Is God's love being perfected in you? It is the great aim of the cross of Jesus Christ.

Knowing and relishing the love of God, however, is not an easy matter of merely reading a book and remembering slogans. Relishing God's love is a matter of divine strengthening and enabling. We must not forget that Paul found it necessary to pray that God 'would grant you ... to be strengthened with might by his Spirit in the inner man ... that ye, being rooted and grounded in love, may be able to comprehend with all saints what is the breadth, and length, and depth, and

---

19. Beeke and Smalley, *Reformed Systematic Theology*, 1:802.

height; and to know the love of Christ, which passeth knowledge' (Eph. 3:16-19). God's love is not properly understood apart from His enabling; God must grant us 'strength' to comprehend something of His love. The love of Christ, which comes from beyond ourselves and takes us beyond ourselves, requires power from beyond ourselves to grasp it. It is no trifle to have our eyes opened to God's love, so that we know it and relish it. Let us pray to this end – that God would enable us by His 'strength' to comprehend this love, and that His love would become the cornerstone for all the various ways we pursue holiness.

May the Holy Spirit apply to us now what Jesus purchased so long ago, that the love of God may dwell in us. Then also our lives will be motivated by the love of the Triune God in Christ, 'which passeth knowledge' and fills us 'with all the fullness of God' (Eph. 3:19), so that we would pursue holiness with zealous love.

CHAPTER 19

Highlighting the Puritan Contribution[1]

WHEN we think about the impact of the Puritan legacy on the doctrine and practice of holiness in the Christian life, the oracle from God to Jeremiah appropriately illustrates the value many have found in the works of the Puritans: 'Thus saith the LORD, Stand ye in the ways, and see, and ask for the old paths, where *is* the good way, and walk therein, and ye shall find rest for your souls' (Jer. 6:16a). There is a certain wisdom in recognizing that many of the confusions that entangle the modern church's teaching and practice of holiness in the Christian life stem in large part from our departure from the ways of wiser Christians who have gone before us. A wise course of action would be to seek out and return to those paths. The Puritans, as continuing reformers of the Reformation, stand as exemplars in thinking through and applying *to all of life* the principle, 'Be ye holy; for I am holy' (1 Pet. 1:16).

The spirituality that was cloistered behind monastery walls for many centuries reduced piety to celibate, ascetic, and penitential devotion. Reformed theologians, however, helped Christians to understand that true spirituality flows from its principal source, Jesus Christ. The Christians' actions in the family, field, workshop, and marketplace—in short, the entire scope of life—are to be a grateful, pious reflection of the grace found in Jesus Christ.[2]

The Puritans thus stand out as models for all believers when it comes to sanctification. They did not minimize their depravity, or the intensity of the war involved in walking the King's highway of holiness. Rather, they thought long and hard on the process of sanctification in the Christian life, identifying many spiritual disciplines believers can follow, and then providing specific and practical directions on how to engage these disciplines. In Puritan thinking and living in this area, we see Calvinism in its most practical form.

---

1. Some of the material used in this chapter was drawn from chapters 14 and 15 of Joel R Beeke, *Living for God's Glory: An Introduction to Calvinism* (Lake Mary, Fla.: Reformation Trust, 2008).

2. Joel R. Beeke, and Mark Jones, *A Puritan Theology: Doctrine for Life* (Grand Rapids: Reformation Heritage Books, 2012), p. 843.

Let us first consider the Puritan contribution to the doctrine of sanctification, and second, some of the spiritual disciplines that the Puritans practiced as means of sanctification. With the Spirit's blessing, Christians who understand and implement this teaching can grow substantially in the faith.

THE PURITAN DOCTRINE OF SANCTIFICATION

The singular aspect of the Puritan doctrine of sanctification is its full development and balanced perspective. Owen Watkins says the Puritans took up the work of the Continental Reformers on justification (what God had done for sinners at Calvary) and completed it with detailed studies of sanctification (what God does within the soul and body of the believer).[3]

As we saw in chapter 11, *sanctify* means 'to make holy,'[4] and with reference to the Christian life it denotes the process of being separated from sin and consecrated to God. The classic Puritan definition of sanctification is stated in the Westminster Shorter Catechism. Question 35 asks, 'What is sanctification?' The answer runs thus: 'Sanctification is the work of God's free grace, whereby we are renewed in the whole man after the image of God, and are enabled more and more to die unto sin, and live unto righteousness.' This definition implies that the Puritans saw the word *sanctification* as describing the entire process of being conformed to Christ's image. This process begins with the new birth and continues throughout the life of the saint until his days on earth end.

Key Aspects of Sanctification

For the Puritans, there were several key ideas or aspects of sanctification that could not be neglected in a thorough discussion of this doctrine.

1. Sanctification is rooted in God's holiness

First Peter 1:16-17 says, 'But as he which hath called you is holy, so be ye holy in all manner of conversation; because it is written, Be ye holy; for I am holy.' God is holy. The holiness of God entails His moral purity and separateness from creation. With respect to our sinful condition, holiness evokes dread. But holiness, being 'God's crowning attribute,' as the Puritans said, also 'sheds light on all his other attributes,' so that His love is a holy love; His wisdom a holy wisdom, His majesty a holy majesty.[5] God's holiness therefore is a delight when sinners are brought into fellowship with God by His righteous Son who, having suffered for the unrighteous, brings us to God (1 Pet. 3:18). Our call to sanctification is rooted in the fact that God is holy.

---

3. Owen Watkins, *The Puritan Experience* (London: Routledge and Kegan Paul, 1972), pp. 5-16.

4. This relationship is apparent in the Dutch word for sanctification, *heiligmaking* (literally, 'holy-making').

5. Beeke and Jones, *A Puritan Theology*, p. 528.

2. Sanctification is both definitive and progressive

Scripture expresses our once-for-all sanctified *status* before God that can never be changed: 'We are sanctified through the offering of the body of Jesus Christ once for all' (Heb. 10:10). As the Puritan Walter Marshall explains, the believer's *status* before God is one of sanctity in Christ on account of His perfect obedience, which has fully satisfied the justice of God for all sin.[6] However, we still need to pursue a sanctified *condition* as we live before God: 'For this is the will of God, even your sanctification, that ye should abstain from fornication' (1 Thess. 4:3). The first type of sanctification we may call our *definitive* sanctification (status); the second is *progressive* sanctification (condition).

The Puritans usually mean *progressive* sanctification of our condition when they speak of holiness. It progresses toward that goal, but, as Romans 7 tells us, our moral and spiritual reach exceeds our moral and spiritual grasp. Many Christians today fail to understand this because their notion of what constitutes perfect righteousness is so dreadfully low, such as in the common idea that holiness means just avoiding sin, which completely misses the flip-side: that holiness entails a continual delight and desire for doing the will of God in community with other image-bearers, for God's glory.

The Westminster Larger Catechism conveyed a fuller picture of righteousness through its teaching on the Ten Commandments: sanctification involves motives as well as actions and each prohibition in God's law includes a corresponding directive (see Chapter 13).[7] The Puritans set sanctification within the framework of the Ten Commandments, summed up in the command to love the Lord our God with all our hearts and to love our neighbors as ourselves (Matt. 22:37-39). Once we grasp this concept, they said, we begin to see how high Scripture's standard of holiness is and how urgently we need to take refuge in Christ's perfect obedience every day.

Righteousness goes hand-in-hand with repentance; together they represent the twofold nature of turning from sin to obedience. Repentance is turning from sin, the Puritans said. It is a daily work of faith; it would not be a good work were it otherwise (Isa. 1:16-17). Righteousness means I am motivated to love God, which I express in worship, adoration, and devotion to Him. It means that I am motivated to love my neighbor, which I express in helpfulness, sympathy, edifying advice and speech, and acts of kindness toward others. Righteousness motivates me to surrender myself to help and encourage others, however little I may feel connected to them.

As the Christian pursues a righteous life, the law produces spiritual conflict because of the indwelling (though no longer dominant) sin still present in the

---

6. Walter Marshall, *The Gospel Mystery of Sanctification* (Grand Rapids: Reformation Heritage Books, 1999), 40ff., 228ff. In the twentieth century, John Murray developed this idea most robustly under the nomenclature of 'definitive sanctification' (John Murray, *Collected Writings of John Murray* [Edinburgh: Banner of Truth Trust, 1977], 2:277-84).

7. The best study on the Puritan view of the law is Ernest Kevan, *The Grace of Law: A Study in Puritan Theology* (repr., Grand Rapids: Reformation Heritage Books, 2013).

believer, combined with worldly pressures to succumb to various temptations, and the Devil who continually seeks to prevent our advance in holiness and to subvert our practice of righteousness. These enemies keep us from mortifying sin, and they work to undermine the reality of our repentance. In the Puritan vision, we must battle for holiness every step of the way, or we will not progress (Heb. 12:14).[8]

This is why, in order for sanctification to progress, we need 'the continued application of the blood of Christ to the believer by the Spirit,' as Thomas Boston said.[9] The believer 'does not stay at a standstill, but grows from one degree and measure of grace to another, "until he come to a perfect man, to the measure of the stature of the fullness of Christ" (Eph. 4:13),' adds Andrew Gray. 'He is like the morning sun, "that shineth more and more unto the perfect day."'[10] 'Sanctification is progressive,' says Thomas Watson. 'If it does not grow it is because it does not live.'[11]

In the mind of the Puritans, then, it was essential for the believer to recognize his conflict with sin and seek to maintain habits of righteousness. Others will see that a believer is changing from one degree of glory to another (2 Cor. 3:18), though he usually cannot see it himself. What he knows most vividly is not growth but the battle that he must continually fight against temptation. So he cries out: 'Lord, I am weak; help me to be strong and to do righteousness.'

Thomas Brooks encourages us to pursue this work, saying that 'he that hungers and thirsts not only after some grace, but all grace; not only after some holiness, but all holiness' will at last be filled: 'He that hungers and thirsts after the righteousness of Christ imparted, as well as after the righteousness of Christ imputed, after the righteousness of sanctification, as well as after the righteousness of justification, he is a blessed soul, and shall at last be filled.'[12]

Sanctification is definitive and yet progressive. We are called to be in life what we already are in principle by grace (Rom. 6:11-12). Our faithful Savior pledges that the work of God in us will continue until glory so that, though we are yet imperfect, the work of sanctification itself will prove to be invincible (Phil. 1:6, 11).

3. Sanctification is a divine work of renewal that is comprehensive and moral

Sanctification makes us increasingly conform to the image of Jesus (2 Cor. 5:17). It springs from a renewal of the heart (the core of the person), which is true

---

8. Thomas Boston, *The Complete Works of Thomas Boston* (Stoke-on-Trent, U.K.: Tentmaker Publications, 2002), 6:585-86.

9. Boston, *Works*, 6:591.

10. Andrew Gray, *A Door Opening into Everlasting Life* (Sioux Center, Iowa: Netherlands Reformed Book and Publishing, 1989), p. 88.

11. Quoted in John Blanchard, *The Complete Gathered Gold* (Darlington, England: Evangelical Press, 2006), p. 303; cf. John Owen, *The Works of John Owen* (Edinburgh: Banner of Truth Trust, 1965), 3:386-405.

12. Thomas Brooks, *The Complete Works of Thomas Brooks*, ed. Alexander Balloch Grosart (Edinburgh; London; Dublin: James Nichol; James Nisbet and Co.; G. Herbert, 1866), 3:270.

transformation. God changes the heart, and out of that change comes new character. Brooks explains, 'The righteousness of sanctification ... lies in the Spirit's infusing into the soul those holy principles, divine qualities, or supernatural graces, that the apostle mentions in Galatians 5:22, 23.'[13]

This change is comprehensive, meaning that it ought to affect all of one's life at all times. The word the Puritans used to describe this process was *universal*.[14] They often quoted 1 Timothy 4:4-5, which tells us that *everything* is to be sanctified.[15] No relationships, endeavors, or times are exempt from the call to holiness; it must be practiced every hour of every day.

Puritan sermons often focused on sanctification. Without a doubt, the Puritans were evangelistic – in fact, they were the first to create extended evangelistic tracts.[16] But when the Puritans wrote those tracts, they did so to lead people out of sin into the Christian life, in which they were to practice holiness to the glory of God. Thus, the theme of sanctification was never out of sight. When the Puritans dealt with assurance, they stressed what Question 36 of the Shorter Catechism also stresses: you cannot hope that God's Holy Spirit will give you strong, joyful assurance unless you are laboring on a daily basis to live a holy life. 'Holiness to the Lord' was the Puritan motto for everyone's life at every point, just as it was their motto for community life at every point. No group of divines focused on sanctification as much as the Puritans.

4. Sanctification is trinitarian and covenantal

The agent of sanctification is the triune, covenant God. The Puritans taught that the covenant faithfulness of the Father, Son, and Spirit motivates the believer to covenant faithfulness. So they presented the gospel as God's extension of His covenant to the sinner and they identified the church as God's covenant people. The Puritans explained sanctification as the Christian's proving and experiencing of God's covenant faithfulness. In short, they saw it as the Christian walking in covenant with His God.

The Puritans believed that God was a covenant God. They believed that the covenant was at the very heart of the Bible and that Scripture itself teaches us to integrate all of its teaching about God's mercy within this covenantal frame of reference. In undertaking to be the God of certain people, God required them to be His people in the world. The Puritans loved to preach on passages such as Galatians

---

13. Brooks, *Complete Works*, 3:270.

14. For example, see Thomas Manton, *The Complete Works of Thomas Manton*, ed. T. Smith. (1870; repr., Worthington, Pa.: Maranatha, 1980), 17:449, and Boston, *Complete Works*, 6:559.

15. Thomas Goodwin, *The Works of Thomas Goodwin* (Grand Rapids: Reformation Heritage Books, 2006), 3:389.

16. The first extended evangelistic tract was Richard Baxter's *A Call to the Unconverted* (repr., Grand Rapids: Zondervan, 1970). Later in Baxter's lifetime, Joseph Alleine lifted numerous points from Baxter and reproduced them as his own in his evangelistic work *Alarm to the Unconverted* (repr., Edinburgh: Banner of Truth Trust, 1995).

3 and Hebrews 11, in which all these truths are clearly set forth. Brooks said, 'sanctification is a precious benefit of the covenant of grace, as well as justification.'[17] Sanctification must be viewed as covenant blessing from a covenant God who has laid hold of us and brought us to new birth in order to bring us to glory, they said.

The Puritans also stressed sanctification as the special work of the Holy Spirit as sanctifier. The Spirit acts alone in initial sanctification, which coincides with regeneration, but He continues to work in progressive sanctification, which also involves the believer's activity. So the believer 'acts not but as he is acted [upon] by the Holy Spirit.'[18] And the Spirit perseveres in His work of sanctification and does a complete work in the end.[19] Reflecting on this truth, John Owen says that sanctification 'is the immediate work of God by his Spirit upon our whole nature, proceeding from the peace made for us by Jesus Christ, whereby, being changed into his likeness, we are kept entirely in peace with God, and are preserved unblameable or in a state of gracious acceptation with him, according to the terms of the covenant, unto the end.'[20] Through His sanctifying work, the Holy Spirit produces Christlikeness in His people, who are new creatures in Christ, risen with Him out of spiritual death. In them, the Christ-nature—that is, the sum total of all that His human life is—finds new expression.

In explaining the sanctifying change that the Spirit works in believers, the Puritans stressed the importance of *habit*. This concept had been basic in explaining spiritual life at least since Thomas Aquinas (1225–1274), whose understanding of habit was not much different from ours, though we probably would opt for the word *orientation* today. Likewise, the Puritans viewed habit as a behavioral pattern. So love, peace, and other fruits of the Spirit are holy habits of acting and reacting to circumstances. The believer aims to keep rejoicing, whatever may be going on; to keep loving, whatever may be happening; to remain at peace in himself before the Lord, whatever may be transpiring. He does not allow his conduct to be determined by what goes on around him; rather, he strives to live out the disposition of Jesus Christ in every circumstance, whatever that circumstance may be. He yearns for what Boston calls 'habitual holiness, that is, a habitual aversion of the soul to evil, and inclination to good.'[21]

The Object of Sanctification

The Puritans also spoke of the 'object of sanctification,' which is the believer. They viewed the believer from three perspectives.

First, the believer was considered to be *a human individual*. From the Puritan perspective, the human individual is best thought of in terms of three capacities:

---

17. Brooks, *Complete Works*, 3:250.

18. Boston, *Complete Works*, 1:655-56, p. 659.

19. See Robert Traill, *Works of Robert Traill* (Edinburgh: Banner of Truth Trust, 1975), 3:78-100.

20. Owen, *The Works of John Owen*, 3:369.

21. Boston, *Complete Works*, 1:659.

the capacity to think, the capacity to make decisions, and the capacity to feel. Thus, the Puritans talked about three faculties: the faculty of reason, the faculty of will, and the faculty of affection (or emotion). They said that in evangelizing or discipling others, it is wise to focus first on what the mind must grasp; second, on what the will must decide; and third, on the affections, or the fruits and marks of grace (such as Galatians 5:22-23 and the Beatitudes in Matthew 5). One would thus show how the qualities of love, joy, hope, and desire provide energy for the continued acts of the will that form the path of godly behavior. A wise preacher, the Puritans maintained, applies Scripture to instruct the mind, direct the will, and draw out the affections.

Second, the believer was considered *fallen and disordered*. Before grace comes, a person is fallen and disordered. He does not live rationally, for he does not live according to the truth that the mind is supposed to grasp. He does not live sensibly, because his will is led by irrational feelings rather than by known truth. His moral nature has been twisted; he is essentially egocentric.

Even after he is regenerated, the believer remains fallen and disordered due to ongoing battles with his old nature and with sin (Rom. 7:14-25). Boston summarizes this well, saying: 'Although the whole man is sanctified, yet no part of the man is perfectly sanctified in this life. It is neither midnight to them as with the unregenerate, nor mid-day as with the glorified, but twilight, which is a mixture of darkness and light. Hence arises the combat betwixt the flesh and Spirit (Gal. 5:17). Every grace has a weed of the contrary corruption by the side of it, which occasions this struggle, and imperfection in the best of their works.'[22]

The intent of gospel teaching is thus to restore us to God-centeredness and to help us in our battles with sin, the Puritans argued. That is the framework for teaching the gospel as it applies to the Christian life.

Third, the believer was considered to be *redeemed and justified*. Those who are being sanctified are those who have been redeemed by Christ's blood and justified through faith. Those whom the Spirit justifies, He sanctifies. As Robert Traill writes, 'Never a man is justified but he is also sanctified; and never a man is sanctified but he is also justified; all the elect of God, all the redeemed, have both these blessings passing upon them.'[23]

Because the believer is redeemed by Christ and justified in Him by grace, the Puritans could appeal to believers to resort to the same grace of God for sanctification. Since 'justification is an act of God as a gracious judge,' Traill wrote, believers may be comforted that 'sanctification is a work of God as a merciful physician.'[24] May all praise be given to God, who as gracious Judge is ever willing to be the merciful Physician and Sanctifier.

---

22. Boston, *Complete Works*, 1:658.

23. Cf. Traill, *Works of Robert Traill*, 3:72.

24. Traill, *Works of Robert Traill*, 3:73.

Motives to Sanctification

As we saw above, motive was an important factor when considering the pursuit of sanctification. Flavel says the standard of our conduct largely depends on the condition of our hearts. If we sanctify the inner life, and even our motives, we will grow in integrity and in all the graces of God, a condition that will provide more stability in times of temptation and trial.[25] Though pursuing holiness is hard work, the Puritans taught that God provides us with several motives to be holy.

1. Gratitude for gospel grace was often discussed as a primary motive for sanctification: Flavel observes that 'so in love is Christ with holiness that He will buy it with His blood for us.'[26] The Puritan Peter Vinke devoted a full sermon to the question, 'How is Gospel-Grace the Best Motive to Holiness?'[27] Richard Sibbes adds, 'By grace we are what we are in justification, and work what we work in sanctification.'[28]

2. Hatred for sin is another motive. Brooks says, 'A sanctified person detests sin, because of the hell that is in sin; but an unsanctified person detests sin, because of the hell that follows sin.'[29]

3. Our hope for heaven is yet another motive for pursuing holiness. Through Christ, justification gives God's child the *title* for heaven and the boldness to enter, while sanctification gives him the *fitness* for heaven and the preparation necessary to enjoy it. Life is a brief shadow. Ultimately, it is meant to prepare us to meet God in righteousness and peace. That kind of meeting is impossible for someone who does not bear fruits of holiness, for 'without [holiness] no man shall see the Lord' (Heb. 12:14). John Owen makes the same point:

> There is no imagination wherewith man is besotted, more foolish, none so pernicious, as this – that persons not purified, not sanctified, not made holy in their life, should afterwards be taken into that state of blessedness which consists in the enjoyment of God. Neither can such persons enjoy God, nor would God be a reward to them. Holiness indeed is perfected in heaven: but the beginning of it is invariably confined to this world.[30]

Edwards notes: 'The heaven I desired was a heaven of holiness.'[31] That is the desire of every true believer, for unholy people would not feel at home in a holy heaven. Watson puts it this way: 'If God should justify a people and not sanctify them, He

---

25. Flavel, *Keeping the Heart*, pp. 37-45; cf. Daniel Webber, 'Sanctifying the Inner Life,' in *Aspects of Sanctification*, pp. 54-56, and Boston, *Complete Works*, 6:602-604.

26. Flavel, *The Works of John Flavel*, 1:538-49.

27. Peter Vinke, in *Puritan Sermons, 1659–1689* (Wheaton, Ill.: Richard Owen Roberts, 1981), 4:264-84.

28. Quoted in Blanchard, *The Complete Gathered Gold*, p. 308.

29. Brooks, *Complete Works*, 3:317-18.

30. Quoted in I. D. E. Thomas, *The Golden Treasury of Puritan Quotations* (Chicago: Moody Press, 1975), p. 141.

31. Quoted in Blanchard, *The Complete Gathered Gold*, pp. 309, 311.

would justify a people whom He could not glorify.'[32] Accordingly, Thomas Brooks writes, 'The way of holiness that leads to happiness is a narrow way; there is but just room enough for a holy God and a holy soul to walk together.'[33]

4. Finally, to *confirm our election* is a legitimate motive for sanctification (2 Pet. 1:10), since holiness is one of the *purposes* of our election: 'he hath chosen us in him before the foundation of the world, that we should be holy and without blame before him' (Eph. 1:4).

Benefits of Sanctification

Pursuit of sanctification sustains joy in the Christian life. Earlier we saw in Question 35 of the Westminster Shorter Catechism how the Puritans defined sanctification. Moving to Question 36, we can also see why the Puritans considered the theme of sanctification so important. The question asks, 'What are the benefits which in this life do accompany or flow from justification, adoption, and sanctification?' The answer is: 'The benefits which in this life do accompany or flow from justification, adoption, and sanctification, are, assurance of God's love, peace of conscience, joy in the Holy Ghost, increase of grace, and perseverance therein to the end.'

Taken together, Questions 35 and 36 reveal the Puritan passion to see young believers grow in Christ into the assurance of God's love, peace of conscience, joy in the Holy Spirit, and increasing grace. The Puritans viewed the benefits of fellowship with God, assurance of faith, and an increase of grace and joy as fruits of sanctification. They also understood sanctification as the basic disposition of a true believer. From their perspective, believers who do not seek to advance in sanctification dishonor God and impoverish their spiritual lives. Let us seek sanctification for the glory of God and the good of our souls.

THE PURITAN PRACTICE OF SANCTIFICATION

The fact that the Puritans gave fuller shape to the *doctrine* of sanctification is only half the story of the Puritan contribution to the doctrine of sanctification. Just as importantly, they continually fleshed out the *practice* of sanctification in every sphere of life. The conviction that drove the Puritans never to be satisfied merely to articulate the doctrine of sanctification, but constantly to develop its practice, has been called a pilgrim mentality, seeing themselves as travelers through this world on a mission to manifest the gospel 'in every sphere of life, in every culture, and to every people group on our planet' as they made progress toward heaven.[34]

So, having delved into the Puritan doctrine of sanctification, let us consider how they put their comprehensive views on sanctification into practice. The

---

32. Quoted in Blanchard, *The Complete Gathered Gold*, p. 309.

33. Brooks, *Complete Works*, 4:81.

34. Joel R. Beeke, and Mark Jones, *A Puritan Theology: Doctrine for Life* (Grand Rapids: Reformation Heritage Books, 2012), p. 843.

Puritans practiced sanctification through diligent use of the means of grace and various spiritual disciplines. The best way to practice sanctification, according to John Flavel, is to pursue 'a diligent and constant use and improvement of all holy means and duties, to preserve the soul from sin, and maintain its sweet and free communion with God.'[35]

The Puritans suggested a variety of spiritual disciplines to help cultivate Christlikeness and holiness. We can classify these divisions into four groups – private, family, corporate, and neighborly disciplines. Since several of these disciplines are covered elsewhere in this book (e.g., see chapter 17 for family worship), I will discuss only a few of the major private and corporate disciplines here and briefly summarize the major neighborly disciplines.

A Word-based Sanctification: Scripture for Meditation and Life

The Puritans viewed the Bible a road-map for sanctification; that which it denied us we must deny to ourselves; that which it commanded we must obey.[36] We should desire the Word, for God uses the Word to sanctify us (1 Pet. 2:2; John 17:17).

There is more detail in chapter 11 on how using Scripture cultivates holiness. But a few brief remarks on the Puritan understanding of Scripture's role in our holiness will be helpful. Basic to the Puritan conviction was that the Word should be central to our Christian lives. In fact, we should begin each day with the Word; As Thomas Case said:

> It is no small advantage to the holy life to 'begin the day with God.' The saints are wont to leave their hearts with Him over night, that they may find them with Him in the morning. Before earthly things break in upon us, and we receive impressions from abroad, it is good to season the heart with thoughts of God, and to consecrate the early and virgin operations of the mind before they are prostituted to baser objects. When the world gets the start of religion in the morning, [we] can hardly overtake it all the day.[37]

Because the Puritans understood that the Spirit uses our Bibles to sanctify us, they were diligent in mining the Scripture. Richard Greenham asserts that we should read our Bibles with more diligence than men dig for treasure. He says diligence makes rough places plain, the difficult easy, and the unsavory tasty.[38]

Don't forget to sing the Scriptures, too. Psalm-singing has been a great boon for private devotions for believers who have engaged in it.[39]

---

35. John Flavel, *The Works of John Flavel* (Edinburgh: Banner of Truth Trust, 1968), 5:423.

36. Beeke and Jones, *A Puritan Theology*, p. 846.

37. Quoted in I. D. E. Thomas, *The Golden Treasury of Puritan Quotations* (Chicago: Moody Press, 1975), p. 141.

38. Richard Greenham, *The Works of the Reverend and Faithfull Servqnt of Iesvs Christ, M. Richard Greenham*, ed. H[enry] H[olland] (London: Felix Kingston for Robert Dexter, 1599), p. 390.

39. See Joel R. Beeke and Ray B. Lanning, 'The Transforming Power of Scripture,' in *Sola Scriptura! The Protestant Position on the Bible*, ed. Don Kistler (Morgan, Pa.: Soli Deo Gloria, 1995), pp. 257-60.

Do not expect to grow in holiness if you spend little time alone with God and do not take His Word seriously. When you are tempted to pursuits off the road of holiness, let Scripture teach you how to live a holy life in an unholy world. Follow the advice of Henry Smith: 'We should set the Word of God always before us like a rule, and believe nothing but that which it teacheth, love nothing but that which it prescribeth, hate nothing but that which it forbiddeth, do nothing but that which it commandeth.'[40] If we do these things, we will concur with Flavel, who attested that 'the Scriptures teach us the best way of living, the noblest way of suffering, and the most comfortable way of dying.'[41]

A frequently overlooked means to growth in holiness is *meditating on the Scriptures*. After reading Scripture, we must meditate on it (Ps. 1:2). Reading offers knowledge, but meditation and study add depth to that knowledge. The difference between reading and meditation is like the difference between drifting in a boat and rowing toward a destination.

The Puritans spoke often of meditating on God's Word and wrote forty books on the subject! Thomas Hooker defines the art of meditation as 'a serious intention of the mind, whereby we come to search out the truth and settle it effectually upon the heart.'[42] He and other Puritans suggest the following ways to meditate on Scripture:

1. Pray for the power to harness your mind – to focus by faith on the task of meditation.

2. Read the Scriptures, then select a verse or two or a doctrine upon which to meditate.[43]

3. Memorize the verse(s) to stimulate meditation, to strengthen faith, to help you witness to and counsel others, and to serve as a means of divine guidance. Brooks expresses it well: 'A sanctified memory is a rich cabinet full of the choicest thoughts of God ... that rich treasury' where we store up thoughts of God that are more and more holy, honorable, reverent, comforting, tender, and compassionate. 'Take a Christian in his ordinary course,' says Brooks, 'and you shall find that wherever he is ... his thoughts are still a-running out after God; and into what company soever he is cast, whether they are good or bad, yet still his thoughts are running out after God.'[44]

4. Meditate on what you know about your verse(s) or subject, probing the book of Scripture, the book of conscience, and the book of nature.[45] As you meditate,

40. Henry Smith, *The Works of Henry Smith* (Edinburgh: James Nichol, 1860), 1:494.

41. John Flavel, *Keeping the Heart* (Morgan, Pa.: Soli Deo Gloria, 1998), http://www.iclnet.org/pub/resources/text/ipb-e/epl-10/web/flavel-keeping.html

42. Thomas Hooker, *The Application of Redemption by the Effectual Work of the Word and Spirit of Christ, for the Bringing Home of Lost Sinners to God* (London: Peter Cole, 1659), 2:210.

43. For a list of profitable subjects for meditation, see *The Works of Stephen Charnock* (Edinburgh: James Nichol, 1865), 3:307.

44. Brooks, *Complete Works*, 2:83.

45. George Swinnock, *The Works of George Swinnock* (Edinburgh: Banner of Truth Trust, 1998), 2:417.

think of applications to your own life. 'Take every word as spoken to yourselves,' Thomas Watson writes.[46]

5. Meditate until you stir up good and holy affections within you, such as love, desire, hope, zeal, and joy, so as to glorify God.[47]

6. Arouse your mind to some duty and holy resolution.[48] The Puritans often wrote these resolutions down in their spiritual journals, and would refer to them later for purposes of self-examination and to remind themselves of the sanctifying nature of such 'holy habits.'

7. Conclude with prayer, thanksgiving, and psalm-singing.[49]

A Throne-Storming Sanctification: Vital Prayer

Holiness and prayer are closely related because prayer is the primary means of maintaining communion with God. We discussed the role of prayer and work in chapter 11, but it is worth noting here that the Puritans were prone to give five methods for fighting our natural tendency to lapse into half-hearted prayer:

1. Give priority to prayer. Prayer is the first and most important thing you are called to do. 'You can do more than pray after you have prayed, but you cannot do more than pray until you have prayed,' John Bunyan writes. 'Pray often, for prayer is a shield to the soul, a sacrifice to God, and a scourge to Satan.'[50]

2. Give yourself—not just your time—to prayer. Remember that prayer is not an appendix to your life and your work, it is your life—your real, spiritual life—and your work. Prayer is the thermometer of your soul.

3. Give room to prayer. The Puritans did this in three ways. First, they had real prayer closets – rooms or small spaces where they habitually met with God. When one of Thomas Shepard's parishioners showed him a floor plan of the new house he hoped to build, Shepard noticed that there was no prayer room and lamented that homes without prayer rooms would be the downfall of the church and society. Second, block out stated times for prayer in your daily life. The Puritans did this every morning and evening. Third, between those stated times of prayer, commit yourself to pray in response to the least impulse to do so. That will help you develop

46. Thomas Watson, 'How We May Read the Scriptures with Most Spiritual Profit,' in *Heaven Taken by Storm*, ed. Joel R. Beeke (Morgan, Pa.: Soli Deo Gloria, 1992), pp. 113-29.

47. Richard Baxter, *The Saints' Everlasting Rest* (Ross-shire, U.K.: Christian Focus, 1998), pp. 579-90, and Jonathan Edwards, *The Religious Affections* (London: Banner of Truth Trust, 1959), p. 24.

48. William Bates, *The Works of the Rev. W. Bates D.D.* (Harrisonburg, Va.: Sprinkle, 1990), 3:145, and Thomas White, *A Method and Instructions for the Art of Divine Meditation* (London: for Tho. Parkhurst, 1672), p. 53.

49. See Nathanael Ranew, *Solitude Improved by Divine Meditation, or A Treatise Proving the Duty, and Demonstrating the Necessity, Excellency, Usefulness, Natures, Kinds, and Requisites of Divine Meditation* (repr., Grand Rapids: Reformation Heritage Books, 2019). For a fuller treatment of Puritan meditation, see Simon Chan, 'The Puritan Meditative Tradition, 1599–1691: A Study in Asceticality' (PhD dissertation, Cambridge University, 1986); David Saxton, *God's Battle Plan for the Mind* (Grand Rapids: Reformation Heritage Books, 2015); Joel R. Beeke, *Puritan Reformed Spirituality* (Darlington, England: Evangelical Press, 2006), pp. 73-100.

50. John Bunyan, *Prayer* (Edinburgh: Banner of Truth Trust, 1999), 23ff.

the 'habit' of praying, so that you will pray your way through the day without ceasing. Remember that conversing with God through Christ is our most effective way of bringing glory to God and of having a ready antidote to ward off all kinds of spiritual diseases.

4. Give the Word to prayer. The way to pray, said the Puritans, is to bring God His own Word. That can be done in two ways. First, pray *with* Scripture. God is tender of His own handwriting. Take His promises and turn them inside out, and send them back up to God, by prayer, pleading with Him to do as He has said. Second, pray *through* Scripture. Pray over each thought in a specific Scripture verse. Matthew Henry's *Method of Prayer* is an exemplary guide for praying the Scriptures. In fact, all of the prayers in each of Henry's prayer categories and their subsections are comprised of paraphrased scripture (praise, confession, petition, thanksgiving, intercession). Indeed, 'if we consulted his book regularly for guidance ... Henry's method would give remarkable depth and variety to our prayers ... [and] deliver our prayers from bland repetition and thoughtless irreverence.'[51]

5. Give theocentricity to prayer. Pour out your heart to your heavenly Father. Plead on the basis of Christ's intercessions. Plead to God with the groanings of the Holy Spirit (Rom. 8:26). Recognize that true prayer is a gift of the Father, who gives it through the Son and works it within you by the Spirit, who, in turn, enables it to ascend back to the Son, who sanctifies it and presents it acceptable to the Father. Prayer is thus a theocentric chain, if you will – moving from the Father through the Son by the Spirit back to the Son and the Father.

Holiness and work are closely related because of the need to persevere in personal discipline, and discipline takes time and effort. As Paul advises Timothy, 'Exercise thyself rather unto godliness' (1 Tim. 4:7). Holiness is not achieved sloppily or instantaneously;[52] it calls for continual commitment, diligence, practice, and repentance.[53] 'If we sometimes through weakness fall into sin, we must not despair of God's mercy, or continue in sin, since ... we have an eternal covenant of grace with God.'[54] You and I must resolve, as did Jonathan Edwards, 'never to give over, nor in the least to slacken, my fight with my corruptions, however unsuccessful I may be.'[55]

A Spirit-minded Sanctification: Entertaining the Spirit

In the context of his pastoral work, Richard Sibbes contributed much insight on the role of the Holy Spirit in promoting a believer's sanctification. Through his books such

---

51. Beeke and Jones, *A Puritan Theology,* p. 886.

52. Cf. Jay Adams, *Godliness Through Discipline* (Grand Rapids: Baker, 1973), p. 3.

53. Bridges, *The Practice of Godliness*, pp. 41-56.

54. *The Psalter*, ed. Joel R. Beeke (Grand Rapids, Reformation Heritage Books, 2006), p. 126.

55. For Edwards' seventy resolutions to promote holiness made at nineteen years of age, see Jonathan Edwards, *The Works of Jonathan Edwards*, ed. Edward Hickman (Edinburgh: Banner of Truth Trust, 1974), 1:xx-xxii.

as *A Fountain Sealed* and *Exposition on 2 Corinthians Chapter 1*, he helped Christians see the Holy Spirit as an integral part of their lives:

> Sibbes advised that we should make a daily effort to appreciate the Holy Spirit, and to share our thoughts and plans with him as we gaze by faith in to the face of God. We should walk in daily communication with the Spirit through the Word, relying on every office that the Holy Spirit provides, as described in Scripture ... The Spirit must be entertained in every facet of Christian life and experience. We must relish His indwelling, His sealing, and His comforting work, while striving not to grieve Him.[56]

One way Sibbes described the grieving of the Holy Spirit is 'when the mind is troubled with a multitude of busyness; when the soul is like a mill where one cannot hear another,'[57] where we fill our lives with temporal concerns and push out spiritual matters – sometimes even under the guise of Christian activity. Living at such a frenetic pace of life disrupts our communication with the Spirit and renders our activity meaningless. Rather, we must seek to pace our lives around our daily communication with the Spirit through the Word, seeking to do all things in His strength and by His light.

A Community-Oriented Sanctification: Corporate Disciplines

The corporate disciplines revolve around the worship and life of the church.

First, the Puritans taught that we should make diligent use of the preached Word. Cultivate the habit of listening seriously and fervently to the sermons of your pastor on the Lord's Day. And listen throughout the week to sermons of other good preachers who encourage you to grow in sanctification.

The Puritans relished good sermons. They attended church faithfully, often took careful notes, and then talked and prayed their way through the sermon afterward with their children. These practices were the fruit of Puritan pastors teaching their people how to listen to sermons. Here is a digest of Watson's advice:

1. Prepare to hear the Word by bathing your soul in prayer.
2. Come to the Word with a holy appetite and a tender, teachable heart.
3. Be attentive to the preached Word.
4. Receive with meekness the engrafted Word (James 1:21).
5. Mingle the preached Word with faith.
6. Strive to retain what has been preached and pray about the Word proclaimed.
7. Put the Word into practice; be doers of it.
8. Beg the Spirit to accompany the Word with effectual blessing.
9. Familiarize yourself with the Word by sharing it with others.[58]

---

56. Beeke and Jones, *A Puritan Theology*, p. 584.

57. Sibbes, *A Fountain Sealed*, in Works, 5.422.

58. Watson, *Heaven Taken by Storm*, pp. 16-18, and *A Body of Divinity* (London: Banner of Truth Trust, 1971), pp. 377-79.

Point No. 7 is not merely a Christian cliché. Merely listening to the word without putting it into practice will contribute to our condemnation. Watson solemnly warns that 'the word will be effectual one way or the other; if it does not make your hearts better, it will make your chains heavier .... Dreadful is their case who go loaded with sermons to hell.'[59]

Puritan ministers frequently published their sermons in books. More than ninety percent of the seven hundred Puritan books reprinted since the beginning of the resurgence of Puritan literature in the late 1950s consist of revised sermons.[60] According to Alan F. Herr: 'The printing of sermons constituted a rather large business in Elizabethan England. It has been estimated that more than forty per cent of all publications issued at that time were religious or philosophical in nature and it is evident that sermons account for a large part of those religious publications.'[61] In the last three decades of the sixteenth century alone, more than three hundred volumes of Puritan sermons were published in England.[62]

As we mentioned in chapter 11, making diligent use of the sacraments is an indispensable practice of pursuing holiness, but to broaden this principle, we should, fourthly, sanctify the Lord's Day. Sabbath observance can greatly improve personal spirituality. We ought to view this day as a joyful privilege, not a tedious burden, in which our private worship of God, our use of spiritual disciplines, our visiting of the widows and the poor, and other godly practices can be sustained without interruption. In reflecting on the Puritan view of the Lord's Day, J. I. Packer concludes, 'We are to rest from the business of our earthly calling in order to prosecute the business of our heavenly calling.'[63]

A Mission-Minded Sanctification: Neighborly Disciplines

The neighborly disciplines govern our lives in relation to the world outside the church. These disciplines consist primarily of evangelization and service.

The Puritans taught that Christ expects us to witness to others and to serve them (Matt. 28:19-20; Heb. 9:14). We are motivated to do this by a sense of duty to obey (Deut. 13:4), gratitude (1 Sam. 12:24), gladness (Ps. 100:2), humility (John 13:15-16), and love (Gal. 5:13). Serving others is often hard work, but we are called to use every spiritual gift that God has granted us (cf. Rom. 12:4-8; 1 Cor. 12:6-11; Eph. 4:7-13).[64]

---

59. Watson, *A Body of Divinity*, p. 379.

60. For a listing and brief reviews of all of these titles, see Joel R. Beeke and Randall Pederson, *Meet the Puritans* (Grand Rapids: Reformation Heritage Books, 2006).

61. Alan F. Herr, *The Elizabethan Sermon* (New York: Octagon Books, 1969), p. 67.

62. Herr, *The Elizabethan Sermon*, p. 27.

63. J. I. Packer, *A Quest for Godliness: The Puritan Vision of the Christian Life* (Wheaton, Ill: Crossway, 1990), p. 239. Cf. Erroll Hulse, 'Sanctifying the Lord's Day: Reformed and Puritan Attitudes,' in *Aspects of Sanctification*, 1981 Westminster Conference Papers (Hertfordshire: Evangelical Press, 1982), pp. 78-102. For a helpful monograph on the Puritan Sabbath, see James Dennison, *The Market Day of the Soul* (Grand Rapids: Reformation Heritage Books, 2008).

64. Whitney, *Spiritual Disciplines for the Christian Life*, 93ff.

The Puritans taught that this kind of service is actually one of our greatest rewards in life. To see people drawn closer to Christ through the Spirit's blessing on God's Word and the use of our gifts is a profoundly humbling experience. It draws us closer to God. Thus, evangelism and service can be important means of grace and spiritual disciplines for our own profit.

THE CONCLUDING GOAL: MORTIFICATION AND SANCTIFICATION

The Puritans believed that the Christian who is undergoing sanctification by the means of grace and the spiritual disciplines must strive to be more like God by cleansing himself from all filthiness of the flesh and spirit so as to come to mature holiness in the fear of God (2 Cor. 7:1). That meant using the means of grace and the spiritual disciplines for a twofold purpose: mortification and vivification, both of which lie at the heart of our sanctification in our day-to-day lives.

A Sin-Killing Sanctification: Mortification

The Puritans also spoke of sanctification in terms of mortification, which involves putting to death every form of sin (see chapter 12). James Ussher (1581–1656) wrote that we are 'sure in Christ' and yet we engage in 'spiritual warfare' as 'a continual fighting against and struggling against the assaults of man's own flesh, against the motions of the Devil, and enticements of the world.'[65]

The Puritans understood Romans 7 as a depiction of the inner warfare every Christian wages. We are constantly plagued by an inclination to do evil, even though we want to carry out the good law (Rom. 7:21-23). This three-headed enemy of the world, flesh, and devil, as the Puritans would call it, can only be fought 'through Jesus Christ our Lord' (Rom. 7:25), since Christ has already triumphed over sin, death, hell, and the grave. Believers are therefore fighting a winning battle in the strength of Christ.

The Puritans used the word *mortification* to describe the discipline of watching and praying against sinful habits in such a way that, whenever a bad impulse arises, you immediately recognize what is happening and ask the Lord for strength to refuse it. You ask Him to drain the life of that impulse in you.

John Owen pictures this process of appealing to the Spirit as what the woman with the bleeding disorder did in touching the hem of Jesus' garment (Luke 8:43-48). She knew that if she could just touch Christ, she would be healed. Likewise, Owen says, we must stretch out the hand of faith and touch the Lord, from whom we gain strength to say no to sin and thereby take a step toward breaking a bad habit.[66]

---

65. James Ussher, *A Body of Divinity,* ed. Michael Nevarr (1648; repr., Birmingham, Ala.: Solid Ground Christian Books, 2007), p. 301 (32nd head).

66. John Owen, *Overcoming Sin and Temptation*, ed. Kelly M. Kapic and Justin Taylor (Wheaton, Ill.: Crossway, 2006), pp. 73-78.

Thomas Boston compares the believer to a man whose natural passions are being put to death. 'His lusts are upon the cross, nailed through and pierced to the heart, not to come down till they have breathed out their last (Gal. 5:24),' he says. 'Like a dying man taking leave of friends, he is parting with his old lusts.'[67]

A Heart-Transforming Sanctification: Vivification

Another element of sanctification, often called *vivification*, is being quickened from the heart to do the will of God. Ussher wrote that the two parts of sanctification are 'Mortification whereby our natural corruption is subdued; and Vivification or quickening, whereby inherent holiness is renewed in us.'[68] Vivification involves seeking God's strength to exercise good habits in obedience to the Decalogue, the Sermon on the Mount, and the ethical sections of the Epistles (e.g., Ephesians 5–6; Colossians 3; Gal. 5:22). Vivification makes us more responsive to God; it is as if we become more spiritually alive. Responsiveness to God is the essence of spiritual life, just as unresponsiveness to Him is the essence of spiritual death.

Boston pictures vivification as a man raised from the dead. He writes, 'So the sanctified sinner lives as one of another world, not conforming himself to the sinful courses of this world, but being transformed into the likeness to those of the better world.'[69]

That, after all, is what the Puritans meant by sanctification, so that through mortification and vivifications, marinated in the means of grace and the spiritual disciplines, the believer would increasingly become like his God – imitating the character of his Father, developing the mind of Christ (Phil. 2:5), and submitting to the will of the Spirit as recorded in the Bible. In other words, as Peter put it, 'Be ye holy, as I am holy' (1 Pet. 1:16).

---

67. Boston, *Complete Works*, 1:657.

68. James Ussher, *A Body of Divinity: Or, the Sum and Substance of Christian Religion*, Eighth Edition. (London: R. J.; Jonathan Robinson; A. and J. Churchill; J. Taylor; J. Wyatt, 1702), p. 491.

69. Boston, *Complete Works*, 1:657.

HOLINESS TESTED

CHAPTER 20

FIGHTING THE 'WRETCHED MAN'
(ROMANS 7:22-25)

TRUE believers are known for the peace they have with God through Jesus Christ. They are known for their hope of eternal bliss, their joy in God through Christ, and the love of God they show others by the Holy Spirit. If a believer's spiritual life is healthy, the unsaved person must confess: 'That believer possesses something I do not have. He or she has inward peace, strength, and comfort that rises above all the trials of life.'

In this chapter, we will consider how true believers are also known for their wrestling with spiritual warfare, dilemma, and strife. The joy and peace of believers often fluctuates, for spiritual strife and wrestling with sin endures to the end of life. As Paul teaches us in Romans 7:22-25, we fight the 'wretched man' within us until our last breath: 'For I delight in the law of God after the inward man: But I see another law in my members, warring against the law of my mind, and bringing me into captivity to the law of sin which is in my members. O wretched man that I am! who shall deliver me from the body of this death? I thank God through Jesus Christ our Lord.'

WRESTLING FOR INWARD HOLINESS

Romans 7 speaks of a holy war that rages in the hearts of born-again believers. As Luther famously said, 'In the Psalms, we look into the hearts of the saints,' so we may say that in Romans 7, we look into the heart of the apostle Paul. Paul's life involved continual conflict between the spirit and the flesh; he experienced ongoing strife between his new nature and the remains of his old one.

In Romans 7, Paul describes from personal experience the ceaseless conflict that rages within a believer. This conflict is different from the daily experience of many in our day. Some preachers say that Paul's struggle in Romans 7 must have taken place prior to his Damascus conversion. They cannot believe that a person who is converted will encounter such strife that he cries out, 'O wretched man that I am! Who shall deliver me from the body of this death?' (7:24). They believe that once a person is born again, he will have little spiritual strife, for believers delight in the

Lord without severe struggling against sin. Other Christian preachers take another view. Surprisingly, Dr. Martyn Lloyd-Jones taught that Romans 7 describes Paul's experience after being born again, but before he came to the consciousness of full assurance of faith.

Many preachers urge Christians to move past Romans 7 into Romans 8. But they forget that Romans 7 follows an earlier chapter in which Paul says, 'Therefore being justified by faith, we have peace with God through our Lord Jesus Christ' (Rom. 5:1). They do not understand that even after great spiritual experiences, such as those described in Romans 8, God's people may be brought back to the agony of Romans 7:24. It is best to see Romans 7 and 8 as complementing each other in describing the conflict that lies in the heart of every true Christian.

Paul summarizes that conflict in Romans 7:22-25. He begins in verse 22 by telling us the delight of his inner heart. He confesses, 'My heart delights in the law of God,' which echoes the words of David: 'O how love I thy law; it is my meditation all the day' (Ps. 119:97). Paul says he delights in doing what is consistent with God's law. He enjoys thinking consistently with God's law; he wants his thoughts to overflow into speech and actions consistent with God's law. He loves doing God's will, walking in His ways, and keeping His commandments.

The delight of born-again Christians is to serve God, cleave to Him, and obey Him. They are not satisfied merely with outward obedience and visible duties – like the Pharisees were; rather, they delight in the law of God from the heart, and desire that their heart would be sincerely engaged in all their duties. Their delight is to deny themselves, crucify the flesh, and flee from worldliness. They want to take up Jesus' cross, follow Him, and love Him with heart, soul, mind, and strength. They seek to tighten their grip on God and loosen their hold on sin. Likewise, as Brooks explains, 'a gracious soul grieves more that God by his sin is grieved and dishonoured, than that for it he is afflicted and chastened.'[1]

Do you delight in the law of God? Are you motivated to love God's law, or do you serve God to satisfy your conscience or avoid damnation? Can you truthfully say, 'Lord, Thou knowest all things; Thou knowest that I love Thee?' Can you say with Moses: 'I choose rather to suffer affliction with the people of God than to enjoy the pleasures of sin for a season, for I delight in the law of God after the inward man' (cf. Heb. 11:25)?

For believers, God's law does not function either as a means of salvation or as a dead letter. Rather, it should be the ruling principle by which we express our gratitude to God for salvation in Jesus Christ. Actually, the law has three purposes. Its first purpose is to convict us of sin, as Lord's Day 2 of the Heidelberg Catechism states clearly. Its second purpose is to restrain sin in society, and its third purpose is to serve as a rule of life and expression of gratitude for believers, as stated in Lord's Days 34–44 of the Heidelberg Catechism. Paul is obviously speaking of the third

---

1. Thomas Brooks, *The Complete Works of Thomas Brooks*, ed. Alexander Balloch Grosart (Edinburgh; London; Dublin: James Nichol; James Nisbet and Co.; G. Herbert, 1866), 2:424.

purpose of the law here, to urge us to sanctification and gratitude flowing out of the merits of Jesus Christ.

By nature, we do not delight in God's law. Paul makes that plain in Romans 8:6-7. By nature, we hate God's law – both its prohibitions of 'Thou shalt not' and its positive commands of 'Thou shalt.' By nature we love sin; therefore, we hate the law, since the law condemns sin. The law opposes everything that we by nature love.

Believers delight in what unbelievers hate. Notice here that Paul speaks of *delighting* in the law – not just *desiring* the law. Who can express the inward joy of serving God and obeying His law? Do you understand the sweetness of loving and serving God? Can you say: 'For a day in Thy courts is better than a thousand in the world; I had rather be a doorkeeper in the courts of God than to dwell in the tents of wickedness' (cf. Ps. 84:10)?

Can you say with Asaph, 'It is good for me to draw near to God' (Ps. 73:28)? Do you, like Mary Magdalene, delight to sit at Christ's feet? Do you find sweetness in being nothing in God's presence; sweetness in being drawn to God, sweetness in keeping His commandments and fleeing from sin? If heaven and hell did not exist, would you still find sweetness in walking in God's ways and keeping His commandments?

Does your heart resonate with David's when he says, 'O how love I thy law!' Does your heart yearn to obey God fully, to think God's thoughts after Him, to speak His Word, and to live out of Scripture and its promises?

THE INWARD DILEMMA

When we come to saving faith, we may think we said farewell to sin, the devil, and the world. We say with Joshua, 'As for me and my house, we will serve the living God of Israel' (Josh. 24:15), expecting to overcome sin and the world, to go from strength to strength, and to appear in Zion before God.

Early in our spiritual pilgrimage, however, we learn that encounters with sin are not resolved so easily. Overcoming sin involves great warfare. Formidable enemies stand in the way. Paul begins Romans 7:23 with the little word, *but*, saying, 'But I see another law in my members, warring against the law of my mind, and bringing me into captivity to the law of sin which is in my members.' We encounter another law, another principle, and another power that is contrary to the law of our renewed mind. The other law represents the remains of our fallen nature that is still within us. This law is the inclination to do evil.

John Owen suggests that believers experience sin as another kind of law. When we will to do good, sin is always near, Owen says. It is always at our elbow. Owen uses a Greek word, *parakeimai*, to show that sin is always at hand. It is like an unwelcome foreigner who walks uninvited into our home and then proceeds to nag us.

A feisty, eighty-five-year-old believer in Wales once told me that three thieves forced themselves into her home one day. They blindfolded her and tied her to a chair. When she heard them packing up her grandmother's heirloom china, she said sharply, 'You thieves, get out of here! You don't belong here. You are foreign intruders into my home. God will one day bring you to judgment for this. Now, be gone!'

One thief sat down beside her and began to repent. The others mocked him. They argued among themselves, then finally left, leaving all the china behind.

That woman responded to thieves the way we should respond to sin. When sin seeks to blindfold us and steal what we have in Christ, we should cry out, 'Sin, you are a foreign intruder. Get out of here. You don't belong here. I am a Christian – a new creation. I reckon myself dead unto sin and alive unto God through Jesus Christ (cf. Rom. 6:11). I will not sin against my precious Savior. Now, be gone, sin!'

The problem is that our old nature is inclined to commit evil. This inclination won't go away. It is active, present, and parallel with the good law. It argues against what is good. So when you proceed on a right course, the evil law begins to object. Paul says it 'wars against the law of my mind.'

This evil law knows no boundaries. There is no limit to the evil suggestions that it persuasively and energetically puts forward. This evil law will not be satisfied until it has made us its prisoner. It wants all of us, at any price. Today, we sometimes read about a black market that sells human body parts. Well, Satan owns the blackest market, and he works through this law, seeking to take possession of our eyes, our hands, our feet, our affections, our will, our heart – yes, every part of us.

Paul says these two laws within us are continually waging *jihad* (holy war) against each other. John Bunyan wrote a book on this theme titled *The Holy War*. In this book, Bunyan depicts the holy struggle that goes on within the soul of the 'city' of the true believer by means of the eye-gate, ear-gate, and other entryways into the city.

As true believers we find rest and peace with God in Jesus Christ; we find rest in the atonement. Paul says, 'Being justified by faith, we have peace with God through our Lord Jesus Christ' (Rom. 5:1). But we do not find peace with sin. As Thomas Brooks writes: 'the new creature can never, the new creature will never, be at peace with sin; sin and the new creature will fight it out to the death.'[2] Thus, we feel the clash of two great armies fighting within us. On one side, Satan seeks to bring our flesh and its lusts under his command; on the other, the Holy Spirit encourages the new principle of life planted in our heart. So flesh lusts against spirit, and spirit strives against flesh. They play tug-of-war against each other, trying to pull the rope in their direction, while toppling the other. Brooks explains this all-out internal war:

> The new man experiences a combat in every faculty. Here is the judgment against the judgment, and the will against the will, and the affections against the affections ... because there is flesh and spirit, sin and grace co-existent and cohabiting in every faculty of the

---

2. Brooks, *Works*, 5:279.

soul; renewing grace is in every faculty, and remaining corruption is also in every faculty, like Jacob and Esau struggling in the same womb .... The new man also combats with all sorts of known sins, whether they be great or small, inward or outward, whether they be the sins of the heart or the sins of the life ... a daily conflict, a constant conflict.[3]

Sadly, we do not always triumph in this strife. The expression *brings me under captivity* that Paul uses is translated more accurately from the original Greek as 'makes and takes me prisoner.' We believe that by the outpouring of God's grace in our souls, the Holy Spirit subdues our old natures. During our enjoyment of Christ's tender, saving presence, we even feel like we have overcome sin and worldliness. Yet, later we repeatedly experience the frustration of our spiritual enemies—the world, Satan, and our flesh—rearing ugly weapons against our new birth.

Happily, God assists us in that battle in remarkable ways. When we are confronted with temptation, He often removes the desire to sin; and when the desire to sin is present, He often removes the opportunity to sin. Thank God for such grace!

The remains of our old nature can resemble a volcano. Sometimes these remains lie dormant, sending up only a wisp of smoke. Fire may burn in the belly of the volcano and, if not restrained by grace, may build up to another eruption. Then we experience the power of the contrary law in our members, which brings us captive to the law of sin.

Do you, too, experience defeat in warring against our triple-headed enemy? Does this make you confess with Paul in Romans 7:19, 'For the good that I would I do not: but the evil which I would not, that I do'?

When we want to be holy, sin breaks out. When we would be heavenly-minded, earthly-mindedness drags us down. This dilemma makes us cry out with Paul, 'O wretched man that I am!' (v. 24).

Don't let these words drag you down. No one in this world is as happy as a true believer. God is his portion forever; he has found Christ and rests in His atonement. He has the Holy Spirit dwelling within him. His sins are forgiven; his guilt purged. He has the hope of eternal glory before him. Still, he often cries: 'O wretched man that I am!' (v. 24). It is a cry of grief! We cannot serve the Lord as sincerely as we desire. We cannot love the Lord as He is worthy of being loved.

No one grieves so much about sin as those who have been delivered from it by the blood of Christ. Those who have been forgiven much, love much. They often cry: 'O wretched man that I am!' (v. 24).

Paul was delivered by the blood of Christ. He was caught up into the third heaven, where he heard unspeakable words of glory. Yet with all those graces and blessings, Paul still cries out: 'O wretched man that I am!' (v. 24).

Paul's cry results from being taught in the school of Jesus. When we are taught by Christ, we know how far we have fallen short of God's standard and how much

---

3. Brooks, *Works*, 5:279.

less we are than what we ought to be. When we consider that we are bought with the blood of Christ and have promised to serve and glorify Him in spirit and body, then see how sinful we are, it is no wonder that we cry out, 'O wretched man that I am!' (v. 24).

Romans 7:24 does not come from the lips of a backslidden Christian, but from one who is in communion with God and Christ. This is not the cry of a man unschooled in communion with Christ, but a man to whom life was Christ and death was gain. In *The Unsearchable Riches of Christ*, Thomas Brooks reflects that it was Paul's *nearness* to God that made him cry out in Romans 7:24:

> He was a man that lived at as high a rate in God, as any we read of; a man that was filled with glorious discoveries and revelations, and yet under all discoveries and revelations, he remembers that body of sin and death that made him cry out, 'O wretched man that I am, who shall deliver me?, Who shall ease me of my burden, who shall knock off these chains that make my life a hell?'... Under his outward greatness he forgets not his former meanness. An humble soul is good at looking back upon his former low estate, upon his threadbare coat that was his best and only robe.[4]

The closer we draw to God, the more we discover the vileness of our nature. Not the weakest, but the strongest believer groans, 'O wretched man that I am!' (v. 24). Abraham, the father of believers and friend of God, confessed: 'Behold now, I have taken upon me to speak unto the Lord, which am but dust and ashes' (Gen. 18:27).

When the great patriarch Job encountered God, he cried out, 'I abhor myself and repent in dust and ashes' (Job 42:5-6). When Isaiah entered into the divine presence of God, he cried, 'Woe is me! for I am undone; because I am a man of unclean lips, and I dwell in the midst of a people of unclean lips: for mine eyes have seen the King, the LORD of hosts' (Isa. 6:5). When John met the exalted Savior on the isle of Patmos, he fell down as if dead. These were the confessions of some of the most eminent believers in the Bible.

Being at war with sin is a healthy sign. It is better than coming to a point where sin no longer troubles us, or we are no more burdened with our shortcomings in sanctification. When John Bradford, who was martyred during the reign of Queen Mary, wrote a letter to a fellow prisoner, he signed off as: 'the most miserable, sinful, hard-hearted, and unthankful sinner.' A few days later he joyfully died in Christ. Samuel Rutherford says of the war within, 'This body of sin and corruption embitters and poisons our enjoyment. Oh, that I were where I shall sin no more!' John Newton adds, 'I was ashamed of myself when I began to seek Christ, but I am more ashamed of myself now after I have found Him.' These words are strange to some people, who believe such confession is unhealthy. But Romans 7 makes it plain that verse 24 is the confession of a genuine believer who is growing in self-examination.

Such confessions are readily understood by conscience-stricken believers. I trust that you can identify more with Paul in Romans 7:24 than with people

---

4. Brooks, *Works*, 3:11.

who say they are beyond spiritual strife and can always be joyful and full of zeal for God and Christ.

On the other hand, we must not misunderstand Paul's complaint. Paul was not at peace with his imperfections; he was not content with the remains of his old nature. That is why he so earnestly asks: 'Who shall deliver me from the body of this death?' (v. 24b).

Paul does not mix Christianity and sin. He suffers agony because of sin. His wretchedness is brought on by the exertion of striving but without the satisfaction of living in complete harmony with God's will. He is weary from the battle.

Paul wants deliverance from this strife. He looks forward to the day when his internal dilemma will end. He wants to be delivered from the remains of his old nature. He is not resigned to his old nature. He does not shield himself behind the truth that even the best believers are imperfect, and therefore sin is not to be taken too seriously.

Rather, Paul yearns to be delivered from his body of death. This is a genuine mark of the saving work of the Holy Spirit. Unregenerate people are also under the power of sin, but sin does not drive them to their knees. They do not cry out for deliverance. Though the consequences of sin may trouble them, sin itself is not a heavy burden. By contrast, the believer suffers with the remnants of his old nature. The new man cries for deliverance, saying, 'Who shall deliver me from the body of the death?' (v. 24b).

Like Paul, have you tried to deliver yourself from sin? Do you know from experience that you cannot deliver yourself, despite your best intentions and most strenuous exertions? Do you know what it means to be grieved with yourself before God? Has Paul's cry, 'Who shall deliver me from the body of this death?' (v. 24b), ever been your cry?

O HAPPY DELIVERANCE

In time, Paul received the grace to find an answer to his agonizing question. His cry is of distress, but not of despair, for his question is answered by faith, which takes hold of a living Savior revealed in the Word. By the Spirit this faith is applied to the heart of wretched sinners. Paul then can say, 'I thank God through Jesus Christ our Lord' (v. 25).

By faith Paul sets his hope on Jesus Christ, who 'was delivered for our offences, and was raised again for our justification' (Rom. 4:25). He sets his hope on the Savior 'who of God is made unto us wisdom, and righteousness, and sanctification, and redemption' (1 Cor. 1:30). Paul sees by faith that in Christ God's people are more than conquerors. He sees that Christ has already won the battle for true believers. They may lose some skirmishes, particularly when they fight in their own strength, but they will ultimately win the war in the strength of Jesus Christ. As Joshua thanked the Lord for victory before his battle was finished, so Paul, looking to Christ, could say, 'I thank God through Jesus Christ our Lord' (Rom. 7:25).

Paul says, 'In Christ, I am already delivered. Christ has already defeated sin on the cross, where He has blotted out the law which was against us.' Paul speaks with full assurance. He knows that his death in Christ will be gain. To be with Christ is far better, for it means that sin will be left behind forever (Phil. 1:21-26). Conflict will not return. The body will be redeemed with all its parts at the resurrection.

Sin damages believers. It makes us suffer. It robs us of inward peace and disturbs communion with God; it can take heaven out of our souls. Yet sin can never keep the soul of a believer out of heaven. Sin will not win the final victory; Christ will.

Jesus Christ delivers true believers, not only in justification but also in sanctification. How blessed you are when the Spirit says you may find justification and sanctification in Christ. Oh, flee daily to the great heavenly High Priest who has overcome sin and is always making intercession for you!

No matter how intense spiritual warfare may become, and no matter how far the devil pursues Christians, they are more than conquerors under their leader, Christ. In Christ, there is sufficient grace for us until the end. In Christ, sin will one day be entirely rooted out! One day our groans will be turned into songs of praise.

With his eyes fixed by faith on this glorious future, Paul cries out in the midst of a holy war, saying that with his mind he serves the law of God, but with the flesh he still struggles against the law of sin.

So, lift up your head, dear believer. In Christ, you are more than a conqueror against sin. The flesh is an intruder that shall be overcome; it will lose the battle, not because of our goodness, but because of God's grace.

Dear child of God, we are fighting a winning battle! Christ has overcome all our enemies. He is now at the right hand of God, making intercession for His people.

Thus the message of Scripture for you is that sin will no longer have dominion over you because you are no longer under the law, but under grace. Under this reign of grace, God's people may say, 'I thank God through Jesus Christ our Lord.'

CONCLUDING APPLICATIONS

Let us conclude this message on a believer's struggle against sin with five applications:

1. Understanding our wretched state convinces us how much we need Christ

What would become of our humiliation, self-abhorrence, search for deliverance in Christ, and wonder of entering into heaven if with all the experiences and blessings received from the Lord, we remain miserable sinners who cry out, 'O wretched man that I am! Who shall deliver me from the body of this death' (v. 24)?

Paul later wrote to the Colossians that the Lord was pleased that all fullness should dwell in Christ Jesus. In us is nothing but sin and emptiness. We must learn these lessons all our life so that we do not become great in our own eyes and glory in our own conversions and experiences. Only in this way can the Lord make us realize that all salvation comes through Christ. A true Christian abhors his own righteousness and treasures the righteousness of Jesus Christ.

2. Understanding our wretched state shows us that struggle is part of sanctification

Sin is not eradicated from our lives all at once, but step by step. Just when we think we have conquered sin, it rises again. So we must continue to put God's spear through this enemy and kill it.

We must put sin to death. Sometimes sin is fleshly lusts; sometimes it is pride of the mind; sometimes it is covetousness. Sin is very deceitful; it comes in different forms. We need all Ten Commandments to tell us what sin is. And a continual struggle against sin is required for sanctification to progress. Owen explains, 'When sin lets us alone we may let sin alone; but as sin is never less quiet than when it seems to be most quiet, and its waters are for the most part deep when they are still, so ought our contrivances against it to be vigorous at all times and in all conditions, even where there is least suspicion.'[5] Romans 8 refers to this struggle as groaning, and the apostle Paul suggests that the whole world is groaning because it is affected by sin. We are part of this fallen world, which makes us groan, and in our groaning the Spirit comes to help.

The Holy Spirit groans as He assists us in our prayers to the Father. He helps us in the struggle against sin because we have not yet attained the new world. When we enter the new world of the resurrection, the struggle against sin will end because sin will then be banished, and we will be free of the flesh. We will have flesh, but it will not be sinful flesh. No residue of sin or its lusts will reside in us, for it will have been forever put to death.

3. Understanding our wretched state convinces us that we need the Holy Spirit

The Holy Spirit is determined that we will be sanctified. The Holy Spirit is jealous about us and watches over us, dear believers. He lives in us and gives us power over sin. He is our great sanctifying Friend. The dark spirit—the Devil—who lurks at your elbow is your great enemy, and only by the power of the Spirit will you defeat that enemy. We must fight sin and the enemy by the Holy Spirit, in His power and in His way. If we fight sin and temptation by using arguments about the shame we would feel if exposed, or the judgment of hell that could be suffered, this reveals that our hearts are caught up in the desire of the sin and that we would fully commit to the sin if such punishment or shame were not in the way. Owen says this is a dangerous frame of heart where our wills are under the seduction of sin. Rather, we must resist sin and lust from the 'gospel principles' of 'the death of Christ, the love of God, the detestable nature of sin, the preciousness

---

5. John Owen, *Of the Mortification of Sin in Believers*, in *Works of John Owen* (Edinburgh: Banner of Truth, 1968), 6: Chapter 2.

of communion with God, [and] a deep-grounded abhorrency of sin as sin.'[6] Joseph resisted temptation from gospel principles, that sin is evil, that sin offends God, and that sin would disrupt communion with God (Gen 39:9). How are we able to resist sin from gospel principles? 'The Spirit alone brings the cross of Christ into our hearts with its sin-killing power.'[7] If you are a Christian, the Holy Spirit will help you, for He is your Friend.

4. Understanding our wretched state helps us subject our conscience to the Word of God

Our guilt in Romans 7 must drive us to Romans 8, where our conscience finds peace in Christ, His Word, and His Spirit. The Puritans often said we must not let conscience overspeak the Word of God. That means a soul tormented by guilt must not consult his own feelings or attempt to read his condition in light of his present sense of misery. He must rather take hold of God's Word and its promises as the only exit from torment. Until the prevailing mood of self-condemnation has passed, the believer must direct the tiller of his mind in the way of God's Word. He must not trust either his feelings or his sickly conscience. This is hard work, but it is the true road back to comfort.

Let our advice to guilt-ridden Christians be as follows: 'All sin and blasphemy will be forgiven of the sons of men. For Christ will blot out as a cloud our sins, and as a thick cloud our transgressions. He will cast them into the sea and remember them no more. He is faithful and just to forgive us our sins and to cleanse us from all unrighteousness. If the Son makes us free, we are free indeed. Though our sins are as scarlet, He will make them like snow.' These and other promises must be held up to the believer in his hour of darkness, for these promises, not his own disordered self-accusations, offer the way back to the solid ground of faith and comfort.

The Holy Spirit offers believers the comfort of the gospel. That is a sacred moment, for deep floods of the soul now break up within the believer. Emotions gush forth. Feelings of delight overcome him till he weeps like a child into his heavenly Father's bosom. How precious, then, is the cross of Christ!

5. Understanding our wretched state teaches us to look for others to fight for holiness

As we fight the good fight of faith and wrestle for greater sanctification, we must remember that we have Jesus Christ, the best leader of all, to help us. We have the promises of our Father to comfort us. And we have the best guarantee for eternal results, for 'we know that all things work together for good to them that love God'

---

6. Owen, *Mortification*, Chapter 9.1.4. In this context Owen goes on to explain that if we fight against sin 'with hell and judgment, which are the proper arms of the law, it is most evident that sin hath possessed itself of his will and affections to a very great prevalency and conquest. Such a person hath cast off, as to the particular spoken of, the conduct of renewing grace, and is kept from ruin only by restraining grace; and so far is he fallen from grace, and returned under the power of the law.'

7. Owen, *Mortification*, Chapter 14.

(Rom. 8:28). So, however difficult it is to strive for holiness, let us not forget that holiness is ultimately God's blessing on the exercise of spiritual disciplines.

Let me close this chapter by asking: Are you a Christian? Is your delight the law of righteousness in Christ? Is sin your dilemma, your burden? Do you earnestly wish that all sin was dead in you? Who can deliver you from your sin? Can you find rest apart from Christ?

The three indispensable marks of the Christian is that he delights in God's law, considers sin as his dilemma, and looks to Christ for deliverance. If these marks are true of you, you will know the joy of crying out, 'I thank God through Jesus Christ our Lord.'

CHAPTER 21

HANDLING AFFLICTION
CHRIST-CENTEREDLY

AFFLICTION is a common experience for both Christians and non-Christians alike.[1] I sense that we all could with vivid words describe the bitter providences that we or people we know have experienced. Perhaps we also may be able to explain the theology behind affliction, for instance that all affliction is ultimately traceable to our tragic fall in Adam, and that all affliction is sent by a wise, fatherly God.

However, while the knowledge and experience of affliction may be common to us, the practice of handling affliction Christ-centeredly can be quite uncommon. As Christians, we do not have to look far to find affliction, but *experiencing* them *as a Christian* is something we must intentionally work at and grow in, by the Spirit's grace.

This chapter helps prepare us to handle affliction in a way that brings Christ into our pain—letting His person, word, and work speak to our affliction—so that we ourselves would grow closer to Christ and be able to handle our afflictions by the Spirit's help and for God's glory. To prepare ourselves to respond rightly to affliction *before* it comes is hard; to look back on it gratefully *after* it is over is harder; but to live Christianly *in* affliction is the hardest.

The question is not *when* affliction will come, or *how much* affliction we might endure, but *how* we will respond to and handle it. How can we combine our theological knowledge and daily experience into profitable practice? In other words, *How can we live through affliction more Christianly – in a way that is more like Christ? And how can we grow in grace while*—yes, while—*suffering affliction?*

Many of the insights I will share on how to live Christianly through affliction are gleaned from years of encountering affliction (including times of running from, wrestling with, resolving against, and—by grace—submitting to and bowing under it). We must always bear in mind, however, that even as I offer practical guidance on this aspect of Christian life, we are always dependent on the sanctification of the Holy

---

1. This chapter has been updated and revised from my booklet *How Should We Consider Christ in Affliction?* (Grand Rapids: Reformation Heritage Books, 2018).

Spirit at every juncture for real spiritual benefit. In other words, without the Spirit's gracious influences, affliction may readily lead us away from, rather than toward, God.

The focus of this chapter is that *the most effective means for living Christianly in affliction is to consider Christ, the fountainhead of all vital Christianity* (Heb. 3:1). To live Christianly in any sphere of life necessitates Spirit-worked faith to look to Him, to feast on Him, to depend on Him – yes, to find both our life in Him (on Calvary's cross), and our death in Him (as exalted Lord, to whom we belong). Consider Christ – that's the whole matter of coping with affliction well (Heb. 3:1; 12:3). How should we consider Christ in our afflictions? Let us unfold a variety of ways we must cope with affliction under three broad considerations of Christ: He has borne our pain; He gives more grace; He knows our way.

HE HAS BORNE OUR PAIN

As we trace the footsteps of Christ's life on earth, we find a pattern in which we too may walk as we cope with affliction. Several aspects of Christ's life stand out as relevant to the suffering saint—Christ's passion, power, prayers, and perseverance—which provide comfort and vigor in our times of affliction. We consider Christ and come away with comfort knowing He's 'plumbed the depths of my disgrace'; we also come away with vigor because, united to Him by the Spirit, Christ's perseverance has become ours.[2]

1. The Passion of Christ

First and foremost, consider the *passion of Christ*. Frequent meditation on the sufferings of our Lord Jesus is the greatest source of strength for living through and profiting from affliction. If Jesus suffered so much on behalf of His people, we should be able to endure, in His strength, the daily afflictions we must bear. What are our afflictions compared to His? Besides, was He not the Sufferer *par excellence* while wholly innocent, and are we not, at best, sufferers in His footsteps while wholly guilty?

When we consider Jesus' suffering compared with our own, our afflictions are scarcely worth mentioning. Herbert Carson explains:

> Whatever pains we face, whatever the loneliness or the misunderstanding, whatever the grief of spirit, nothing will ever begin to compare with the darkness of Golgotha. So, because He drank so deeply of bitter suffering, He is able to steady our hand as we drink what for us is a bitter draught but is, by comparison with His, a diluted cup.[3]

And then to consider that He died for us (rebellious, hell-worthy sinners) to make us true believers to live for Him – truly, we can scarcely take it in! It is almost too good to be true. If He *died* for us, shall we not at least *live* for Him?

---

2. Keith Getty and Stuart Townend, 'My Heart Is Filled With Thankfulness' (Brentwood, Tenn.: ThankYou Music, 2003).

3. Herbert Carson, *Facing Suffering* (Welwyn, Hertfordshire, U.K.: Evangelical Press, 1978), p. 45.

Moreover, there is not one affliction we must endure that He has not already endured in its essence. Is He not the 'breaker' to go before His flock (Micah 2:13), both in opening all our paths and in being tempted in all points as we are, yet without sin (Heb. 4:15)? All paths, all points – this is most encouraging. Jesus not only knows our affliction, but He has identified Himself with it. He has borne it, He will sanctify it, and He will grant you grace to bear it, so that He will deliver you even from the temptation to give up or run from the weight of affliction. 'There hath no temptation taken you but such as is common to man: but God is faithful, who will not suffer you to be tempted above that ye are able; but will with the temptation also make a way to escape, that ye may be able to bear it' (1 Cor. 10:13). Thomas Brooks said:

> Christ was much tempted, he was often in the school of temptation; and the more a Christian is tempted, the more into the likeness of Christ he will be transformed .... The image of Christ is most fairly stamped upon tempted souls. Tempted souls are much in looking up to Jesus, and every gracious look upon Christ changes the soul more and more into the image of Christ. Tempted souls experience much of the succourings of Christ, and the more they experience the sweet of the succourings of Christ, the more they grow up into the likeness of Christ.[4]

The more we look by faith to Christ crucified, the more strength we will discover within ourselves to sustain all the trials our heavenly Father is pleased to place upon us. Christ crucified is the best medicine for every affliction. 'His atoning death,' says Carson, 'is a pledge to us of His unending sympathy for us.'[5]

2. The Power of Christ

Second, consider the *power of Christ*. Being infinite God-man, Jesus received power on earth to bear infinite sufferings on our behalf. And through the merit of these sufferings, He now receives royal power in heaven from His Father to rule and strengthen us in our sufferings (Matt. 28:18). Translated practically regarding affliction, His heaven-earth power reads like this: if He desires to weigh us down with affliction—heavy, seemingly staggering affliction—we must not be alarmed, but must look to Him for strength.

Nor should we be ashamed of our lack of strength. When I worked for my father in my early youth, I was advised to carry only half bundles of shingles up the ladder to the roof, but I anticipated the day of greater maturity and strength when my shoulders could bear full, unsplit bundles as my older brothers' shoulders could. Similarly, afflicted believer, Jesus Christ tailors your afflictions to you. He has promised to fit your afflictions to your shoulders (1 Cor. 10:13). Neither be proud of slender shoulders nor ask for more affliction, but beg for broader shoulders that have been exercised in the weight room of Jesus' providential leading.

---

4. Thomas Brooks, *The Complete Works of Thomas Brooks*, ed. Alexander Balloch Grosart (Edinburgh; London; Dublin: James Nichol; James Nisbet and Co.; G. Herbert, 1866), 1:371.

5. Carson, *Facing Suffering*, p. 45.

As you and I realize, by grace, that the bearing of heavy burdens Christianly is a testimony of spiritual maturity and honors the Christ whom we love, we will be more submissive to being bruised as we groan under affliction's heaviness. Isn't this the encouragement that the Puritan George Downame intended to convey when he aptly penned, 'The Lord does not measure out our afflictions according to our faults, but according to our strength, and looks not [at] what we have deserved, but [at] what we are able to bear'?[6]

How great it is when we may look to the strength of Jesus Christ in all our weakness and apprehend our strength in Him (2 Cor. 12:9)! Then the power of the humiliated and exalted Jesus enables us to sing at times in the 'inner prison' depths with Paul and Silas (Acts 16:25) – yes, to rejoice that we are counted worthy to suffer for the name and sake of the Lord Jesus Christ (cf. 2 Corinthians 6 and 12).

3. The Patience and Perseverance of Christ

Third, consider the *patience and perseverance of Christ*. Chinese water torture, in which water is slowly dropped at regular intervals onto a person's forehead, gets all its power from the duration of the trial, not from the first one or two hundred drops. Insanity is often the end result.

And if it were not for Jesus, matters might end in the same way for us too: the severity of affliction is often in its duration. We wonder if there will ever be an end and, if so, how will we hang on until it is over?

But it is Christ who provides us the strength to bear one more drop, take one more step, and live one more day in the severest of tortures and persecutions. He has earned that provision of strength for us by enduring suffering all His life, and especially by enduring its intensity through to its completion. Gethsemane, Gabbatha, Golgotha – in each place, He confirmed that 'having loved his own ... he loved them unto the end' (John 13:1). Blood drop by blood drop, He poured out His life. And He never flinched. He never answered His mockers a word. He never yielded to their taunts: 'If thou be the Christ....'

If we think back to some of our heaviest afflictions, we must conclude that it was through Jesus' strength that we have endured the long nights, months, or years. When persecuted or taunted for being a Christian, we continued on and persevered only through the grace of God. Consider the depth of Paul's confession: 'By the grace of God I am what I am' (1 Cor. 15:10).

David experienced sixteen long years of persecution from Saul, but instead of perishing, he persevered by God's grace. Jesus has done too much, persevered too long (He is still persevering in intercession!) to let us slip through His fingers. 'I give unto them eternal life; and they shall never perish, neither shall any man pluck them out of my hand' (John 10:28). Thomas Brooks expounds the purpose of God in trials of long duration:

---

6. I. D. E. Thomas, comp., *The Golden Treasury of Puritan Quotations* (Chicago: Moody, 1975), p. 12.

God delays, that his people may set upon him with greater strength and importunity; he puts them off, that they may put on with more life and vigour; God seems to be cold, that he may make us the more hot; he seems to be slack that he may make us the more earnest; he seems to be backward, that he may make us the more forward in pressing upon him .... Anglers draw back the hook, that the fish may be the more forward to bite; and God sometimes seems to draw back, but it is only that we may press the more on .... so when a Christian prays, and prays, and yet catches nothing, God seems to be silent, and heaven seems to be shut against him; yet let him not cast off prayer, but mend his prayer; pray more believingly, pray more affectionately, and pray more fervently, and then the fish will bite, then mercy will come, and comfort will come, and deliverance will come.[7]

The key practice in our affliction must be to look more to Christ, trusting more in His promises, resting more in His perseverance, and seeking grace to imitate His patience under affliction. Trials that may alarm us will not finally destroy us. Our crosses are God's way to a royal crowning (Rev. 7:14).

Moreover, 'the longer any saint is afflicted,' says Brooks, 'the more into the image and likeness of Christ he will be transformed.' With passages in mind such as Romans 8:28 and Philippians 3:10, Brooks elaborates on this point:

It is one of God's great designs and ends in afflicting of his people, to make them more conformable to his Son; and God will not lose his end .... The longer they are afflicted, the more they are made conformable to Christ in meekness, lowliness, spiritualness, heavenliness, in faith, love, self-denial, pity, compassion, &c .... Nothing makes a man more conformable to Christ than afflictions.[8]

God orders even the duration of our afflictions to a purposeful end: conformity to Christ.

4. The Prayers of Christ

Fourth, consider the *prayers of Christ*. He often set time apart on earth to pray to His Father— especially in hours of need—and He continually prays in heaven for all His church. His prayers are effectual for all His people in whatever afflictions we find ourselves. Brooks explains:

Christ is a person of highest honour; he is the greatest favourite in the court of heaven; he always stands between us and danger. If there be any evil plotted or designed against us by Satan, the great accuser of the brethren, he foresees it, and by his intercession prevents it. When Satan puts in his pleas and commences suit upon suit against us, Christ still undertakes our cause ... and in despite of hell he keeps us up in divine favour.[9]

Prayer is one of those subjects that makes even seasoned Christians sigh in their hearts with a feeling that this is a neglected area. When it comes to spiritual

---

7. Brooks, *Works*, 1:388.

8. Brooks, *Works*, 1:358.

9. Brooks, *Works*, 1:367-68.

depression under affliction, however, we cannot afford to neglect prayer. We must learn to bring all our needs, concerns, anxieties, and thoughts steadily to our praying High Priest. We have every assurance from Scripture that Jesus Christ hears our every whisper, for His ear is ever tuned to hear the cries and sighs of His people.

A *prayerless* affliction is like an open sore, ripe for infection; but a *prayerful* affliction is like an open sore, ripe for the balm of Gilead – the healing ointment of Jesus' blood. 'Pray without ceasing' (1 Thess. 5:17).

If you feel like you are at your wits' end in the burning fiery furnace of affliction, even to the point that you can scarcely pray, don't give up. When you are brought to the end of your own prayers, cry out to your Savior, 'Lord Jesus, please pray for me when I can scarcely pray for myself, for Thy prayers are always answered by Thy Father, as Thou hast said, "Father, I thank thee that thou hast heard me. And I knew that thou hearest me always"' (John 11:41-42).

And when you grow drowsy or sloppy in prayer, pray standing, pray aloud, write down your prayers, or find a quiet place to walk in the fresh air to pray. Just don't stop praying. Conversation with God through Christ is the antidote that wards off spiritual depression in the thick of affliction.

HE GIVES MORE GRACE

Having considered the pattern Christ has given us by His footsteps on earth, let us now turn our gaze to His glorious rule on His heavenly throne for further resources for our afflictions. Thomas Goodwin asks whether Christ's tenderness toward us is at all diminished now that He is exalted in heavenly glory. Answering in the emphatic negative, Goodwin tells us that although 'now he is in heaven, his heart remains as graciously inclined to sinners that come to him, as ever on earth.'[10] Richard Sibbes concurs: 'God knows we have nothing of ourselves, therefore in the covenant of grace he requires no more than he gives, but gives what he requires, and accepts what he gives.' And what does Christ give to his afflicted saints? Sibbes continues:

> Why was he tempted, but that he might 'succor them that are tempted' (Heb. 2:18)? What mercy may we not expect from so gracious a Mediator (1 Tim. 2:5) who took our nature upon him that he might be gracious? He is a physician good at all diseases, especially at the binding up of a broken heart. He died that he might heal our souls with a plaster of his own blood, and by that death save us, which we were the procurers of ourselves, by our own sins. And has he not the same heart in heaven?[11]

And what does He give from His heavenly throne? He gives more grace (James 4:6). The astonishing thing the afflicted saint finds out, however, is that the grace Christ gives is Christ Himself.

---

10. Thomas Goodwin, *The Heart of Christ in Heaven Toward Sinners on Earth* (Edinburgh: Banner of Truth Trust, 2011).

11. Richard Sibbes, *The Bruised Reed* (Edinburgh: Banner of Truth Trust, 1998).

Christ Himself is the grace He gives to us. His own *preciousness* is what makes grace grace; He is *precious* grace in our afflictions, as He contains all of the varieties of grace necessary to fit the diverse needs of afflicted saints. What is more, the *preciousness* of Christ is *plentiful*, not limited by time, the vagaries of life, or the slowness of our spiritual growth; this *plentitude* is another grace in itself – a grace upon grace. Thirdly, piling on more grace is the grace of Christ's *presence* with us, an unspeakable privilege the Spirit brings to those united to Christ – an experiential fellowship with His presence that aids us in our afflictions.

1. The Preciousness of Christ

First, consider *the preciousness of Christ*. The Bible speaks of Jesus as precious. He is precious in His sympathy, precious to those who believe, and precious as the cornerstone of our salvation, but He is especially precious in shedding His blood for sinful, afflicted believers. First Peter 1:18-19 says, 'Forasmuch as ye know that ye were not redeemed with corruptible things, as silver and gold, from your vain conversation received by tradition from your fathers; but with the precious blood of Christ, as of a lamb without blemish and without spot.' Murdoch Campbell explains:

> As we grow more in grace our conscience becomes more tender, and our mind more sensitive to the sins which lodge within .... How often are we overcome with shame as we view our life in retrospect? ... To many choice saints the most wonderful and the most endearing word in the whole Bible is that which speaks of the infinite efficacy of Christ's blood .... 'The blood of Jesus Christ His Son cleanseth us from *all* sin' (1 John 1:7).[12]

Nothing is more precious than the blood of Jesus Christ. His blood is precious because of its centrality, its value, and its capability.

Consider the centrality of Christ's blood in the Bible. The Bible speaks of blood more than four hundred times. Blood is precious, for it is the most valuable thing in our bodies. Blood is essential to life. Even a perfectly healthy body, if drained of blood, will die. The life of the flesh is in the blood, the Bible says. Spiritually, the blood of Jesus Christ received by faith gives us spiritual life. In God's eyes, blood is sacred. Twice Hebrews 9 tells us that God cannot be approached without blood (vv. 7, 18). 'Without shedding of blood [there] is no remission' of sin (v. 22). That is the primary message of the entire Bible. When Adam and Eve fell, God shed blood to clothe them and cover their nakedness (Gen. 3:21). In Genesis 4, God showed He was pleased with Abel's sacrifice, which involved sacrificial blood. Hebrews 11:4 confirms that there can be no approach to God, no fellowship with Him by faith, no enjoyment of His favor, apart from blood.

From the beginning of Genesis to the end of Revelation, from the closing of the gates of Eden to the opening of the gates of the heavenly Zion, blood runs through Scripture, uniting all. Substitutionary blood gloriously restores what sin

---

12. Murdoch Campbell, *In All Their Affliction* (Northampton, U.K.: Flair Press, 1987), p. 34.

destroyed. Through His blood, the second Adam undid what the first Adam did, thereby reconciling sinners to God.

Let us take every affliction to Christ and rest in the saving efficacy of His blood, both to complete His sin-destroying work in us, to uphold us in every affliction, and ultimately to deliver us from every sorrow. Consider all peace and holiness and hope of heaven are bound up in the atoning blood of Immanuel.

Through our afflictions and the need they arouse in us, let us pray for grace to know and experience more fully the power of Christ's blood. Let us ask Christ to open our understanding to the efficacy of His blood, to grasp its necessity, to embrace its satisfaction, and to receive its beauty. Let us trust Christ to give us a deeper insight into His blood, that we may think of His blood as God thinks of it. Let us trust the eternal High Priest to work out in us the merits of His blood so that we may abide in the sanctuary of God's presence. We must ask for grace to draw nearer to God to meditate more on His blood-shedding, that His blood may become spirit, life, power, and truth to us. So let us bring our every affliction to this justifying and sanctifying blood, and you will find so much comfort that you will forever thank God for all your afflictions!

Consider the capability of Christ's blood. Christ's blood, dear believer, procures inexpressibly great and precious blessings for us even in the furnace of affliction. It not only accomplishes *full-orbed redemption* for us to justify us (Rom. 5:9) and to set us free from the slavery of sin (Rom. 8:12-16), from the curse of the law (Gal. 3:13), from the enslaving power of Satan (Heb. 2:14), and from the bondage of everlasting death (Rev. 21:1-9). It also *sanctifies* us. Through the process of sanctification, we are made holy to serve God. Blood separated the Israelites from the Egyptians. Likewise, Christ's blood calls us to separate ourselves from the world's sin, the world's religion, the world's sense of goodness, and the world's vileness. The more we rely on Christ's blood, the more we will be sanctified by the Holy Spirit. Even if it takes affliction to do this, we should pray with Charles Spurgeon, 'Oh, Lord Jesus Christ, burn up the love of the world! Let Thy death be the death of my sin. Let Thy life be the life of everything that is gracious, heavenly, eternal!'

Then too, Christ's blood *preserves and assures us* and *makes us victorious.* Christ's blood provides *confirming power.* Jesus' blood is the blood of the new covenant; it seals His last will and testament. His covenant blood confirms and assures us of our salvation. Christ's blood also provides *intercessory power.* Christ sprinkles His precious blood within the Holy of Holies in the heaven of heavens. He lives to make intercession for us (Heb. 7:25). And Christ's blood provides *victorious power.* As Revelation 12:11 says, 'They overcame him [Satan] by the blood of the Lamb.' Those who cling to the blood of Jesus in the midst of affliction have a weapon that makes hell tremble, heaven subservient, and earth obedient. Sin dies at the presence of Christ's blood; doubts and fears flee. Heaven opens its gates by that blood. Hell would lose its grip if that blood could operate there. Truly, we are more than conquerors through Him who loved us by giving His own blood. There is no victory without conflict and affliction, but there is true victory through faith in the blood of the Lamb. What glorious victory we have now and forevermore through the blood of the Lamb!

Finally, Christ's blood *opens heaven* for us. By Christ's blood, we *are made fit for heaven*. One of His most important ways to wean us from the world and ripen us for heaven is by sanctifying affliction to our soul so that we see clearly that there Christ's blood is our only passport into heaven. When Christ comes again, the trumpet will sound, the dead will rise, and everyone will surround the great white throne. There, wherever God sees Christ's blood, He will pass by in avenging justice. Sheltered under Christ's blood, believers will be washed from every stain of sin. Not a drop of divine wrath will fall upon them. They will be part of the heavenly choir that sings, 'Unto him that loved us, and washed us from our sins in his own blood, and hath made us kings and priests unto God and his Father; to him be glory and dominion for ever and ever' (Rev. 1:5-6). Oh, the joy of that moment when we find Christ to be all in all! Let us then, by the Spirit's grace, bring all our afflictions to Christ's blood and rely upon it alone.

2. The Plenitude of Christ

Second, consider the *plenitude of Christ*. In Him, there is 'bread enough and to spare' (Luke 15:17). Consider His names – each of the nearly three hundred titles and symbols given to Him in the Bible is a rich, divine gift of self-revelation. He is the Son of God and Son of Man, the express image of God; the Lamb of God, the Lion of the tribe of Judah, and the Lord Our Righteousness – all for us, His beloved afflicted people. Truly, He has a plenitude of names to strengthen you in every discouragement.

Let us consider His threefold office, through which He meets all our needs even in our deepest afflictions. As *prophet*, He teaches us in and through our afflictions, so that we later thank Him for those afflictions, recognizing in hindsight that we learned lessons through affliction that we never could have learned in any other way. As *priest*, He sacrifices, prays for us, and blesses us, saving us and keeping us saved by His amazing grace. As *king*, He guides us, rules over us, and defends us in countless ways that we will not even grasp until the day we enter into glory. All this makes us bow before Him as Savior and Lord, enabling us to receive the whole Christ to minister to the whole person—yes, to us—in all our need. Boston sees Christ's offices as particularly relevant in our times of affliction:

> Make use of Christ in all his offices for your humiliation under your humbling circumstances .... You have a conscience full of guilt, and that will make one uneasy in any circumstances, and far more in humbling circumstances; it will be like a thorn in the shoulder on which a burden is laid. But the blood of Christ [our Priest] will purge the conscience, draw out the thorn, give ease, and fit for service, doing or suffering .... We have need to be taught rightly to discern our humbling circumstances; for often we mistake them so far, that they prove an oppressive load; whereas, could we rightly see them, just

as God sets them to us [by Christ our Prophet], they would be humbling, but not so oppressive .... You have a stiff heart, loth to bow, even in humbling circumstances .... [Christ as King] is able to cause it to melt, and, like wax before the fire, turn to the seal.[13]

Moreover, consider the plenitude contained in His natures—divine and human—in one divine person! No other religion in the world offers such a Savior who is both almighty God and understanding man in one person, which is precisely what we need in times of discouragement and affliction, so that we can approach this wonderful God-man Savior by coming boldly and freely to His throne of grace in time of need (Heb. 4:14-16)!

Who can describe the value of Christ's states of humiliation and exaltation for discouraged believers! For afflicted believers, there is no end to the riches to be found in His humiliation through the steps of His humble birth (Luke 2:7), profound suffering (Isa. 53:3), substitutionary death (Phil. 2:8), remarkable burial (1 Cor. 15:4), and descent into hell (Matt. 27:46) – as well as in His exaltation through the steps of His miraculous resurrection (1 Cor. 15:4), essential ascension (Acts 1:9), intercession at the right hand of God (Rom. 8:34), and imminent return on the clouds to judge all people (Rev. 1:7).

Paul got it right when he wrote to the Colossians, 'Christ is all, and in all' (Col. 3:11). When our eyes are fixed on Him, and not on the waves we are encountering, we will not sink, for there is more plenitude in Him than in all the waves of all oceans combined!

3. The Presence of Christ

Third, consider the *presence of Christ*. He is at no time absent from us, even when our faith lacks active exercise to grasp Him. Even in our thickest hours of Egyptian darkness, He is close beside us. Only of Him can it be declared, 'The darkness and the light are both alike to thee' (Ps. 139:12).

Believers can draw much comfort from the fact that in all our dark afflictions, our High Priest retains us in His high-priestly eye, preserves us in His high-priestly heart, bears us on His high-priestly shoulders, removes us not from the engravings on His high-priestly hands, and never ceases to remember us in His high-priestly intercessions. 'He ever liveth to make intercession for them' (Heb. 7:25).

Christ's love toward us is so tender that, despite our negligence toward Him, He never forgets us. Our unbrotherliness to Christ never 'unbrothers' this precious Elder Brother from us. From His perspective, He ever remains a friend that sticks 'closer than a brother' (Prov. 18:24), even when you cannot see or feel Him. Even then He is whispering to you in midnight seasons, 'What I do thou knowest not now; but thou shalt know hereafter' (John 13:7).

We can take heart since Jesus, who never failed you in yesterday's afflictions (did He not rather give you extra tokens of His care?), is still present to give you today's

---

13. Thomas Boston, *The Crook in the Lot or The Sovereignty and Wisdom of God in the Afflictions of Men Displayed* (reprint, London: Simpkin, Marshall & Co., 1863), pp. 112-13.

strength (Matt. 6:34). Just as waves are cut down to melodious whimpers at the shore, so He will break down the waves of tomorrow's impossibilities as they break on the beachheads of our lives. Waiting on the ever-present Savior is never vain: He will not let you down. He is the same yesterday, today, and forever (Heb. 13:8). 'To quiet and silence your souls under the sorest afflictions and sharpest trials,' says Brooks, 'consider, *that your choicest, your chiefest treasure is safe*; your God is safe, your Christ is safe, your portion is safe, your crown is safe, your inheritance is safe, your royal palace is safe, and your jewels, your graces are safe; therefore hold your peace, 2 Tim. 1:12; 4:8.'[14]

HE KNOWS OUR WAY

We will meditate, finally, on the sovereignty of God in all our afflictions. Just as God knew His plans and purposes for Christ in His affliction, so Christ knows our path in our sufferings, and in our trials His ultimate goal and intent toward us is good – both for this life and the one to come.

1. The Purposes of Christ

Consider first the *purposes of Christ*. He lived to do His Father's will, to be sanctified through suffering, to merit salvation for His own, to present His church without spot or wrinkle to His Father. In a word, His life was God-centered.

His God-centered goals are numerous for us as well, in sanctified affliction: sanctified affliction humbles us (Deut. 8:2), teaches us what sin is (Zeph. 1:12), and causes us to seek God (Hosea 5:15). Affliction vacuums away the fuel that feeds your pride. Like a bell, the harder we are hit, the better we sound. We learn more under the rod that strikes us than through the staff that comforts us. Many Christians have discovered the truth of Robert Leighton's words: 'Affliction is the diamond dust that heaven polishes its jewels with.' Brooks explains the grace-refining quality that affliction has for believers:

> That scouring and rubbing, which frets others, shall make them shine the brighter; and that weight which crushes and keeps others under, shall but make them, like the palm tree, grow better and higher; and that hammer which knocks others all in pieces, shall but knock them the nearer to Christ, the corner stone. Stars shine brightest in the darkest night; torches give the best light when beaten; grapes yield most wine when most pressed; spices smell sweetest when pounded; vines are the better for bleeding; gold looks the brighter for scouring; juniper smells sweetest in the fire; chamomile, the more you tread it the more you spread it …. Afflictions are the saints' best benefactors to heavenly affections; where afflictions hang heaviest, corruptions hang loosest. And grace that is hid in nature, as sweet water in rose leaves, is then most fragrant when the fire of affliction is put under to distil it out. Grace shines the brighter for scouring, and is most glorious when it is most clouded.[15]

---

14. Brooks, *Works*, 1:393.

15. Brooks, *Works*, 1: 327-28.

Sanctified affliction also serves to keep us in Christ's communion, close by His side – to conform us to Him, making us partakers of His sufferings, image, righteousness, and holiness (Heb. 12:10-11). Like Stephen, the stones that hit us only knock us closer to our chief cornerstone, Jesus Christ, opening heaven wider for us. Affliction rubs the rust off our locked heart and opens our heart's gates afresh to our King's presence chamber. Yes, the rod of affliction is God's pencil for drawing Christ's image more fully upon us.

Sanctified affliction serves to wean us from the world and causes us to walk by faith. A dog will bite strangers, but not the owners of its home. Perhaps affliction bites us so deeply because we are too little at home with the Word and ways of God and too much at home with the world. Brooks helps us see the blessedness of the heart that is concerned more with getting rid of our sins than our sufferings:

> Paul does not cry out, O wretched man that I am! who shall deliver me from all my sorrows and sufferings? but 'O wretched man that I am! who shall deliver me from this body of death?' [Rom. 7:24]. A sincere heart, when he is himself, had much rather be rid of his sins than of his sufferings, yea, of the least sins than of the greatest sufferings. It was a sweet saying of Bernard: 'I had rather,' saith he, 'that God should better my heart than remove his hand; I had rather that God should continue my strokes than my sins.'[16]

'God,' says Thomas Watson, 'would have the world hang as a loose tooth which, being twitched away, does not much trouble us.'[17] In prosperity, we often talk of living by other-worldly faith, but in adversity, we are called upon to live our talk.

2. The Plan of Christ

Consider also the *plan of Christ*. Highly exalted, there is no name like His. At His name, every knee will bow (Phil. 2:10). Outside observers at Calvary may have concluded that the cross was the end of all Jesus' plans, but in reality, God's eternal plan was on track. The eternal plan lying behind all Jesus' affliction was eternal glory – not only for Himself but also for us. He returned to His Father differently than He came. He returned with His blood-bought bride, just as was planned in His eternal covenant with His Father. His church, positionally speaking, ascended into glory with Him, accepted by the Father in the Beloved (Eph. 1:6). Thinking more of God's eternal plan for us and our eternal destiny in glory will greatly help us be more submissive under affliction and teach us to praise God during trials and sufferings.

Our trials and sufferings in this life are but for 'ten days' (see Rev. 2:10), but our life-to-come glory is forever. The 'ten days' here are preparation for the glory to come. Affliction elevates the soul of the believer to heaven (Heb. 11:10) and paves his or her way to glory: 'For our light affliction, which is but for a moment, worketh for us a far more exceeding and eternal weight of glory' (2 Cor. 4:17).

---

16. Brooks, *Works*, 3:310.

17. Thomas Watson, *All Things for Good: An Exposition of Romans 8:28* (Shawnee, Kans.: Gideon House Books, 2015), p. 36.

We should not overestimate our rainy days on earth: they will soon give way to our coming crown and our eternal communion with God Triune, saints, and angels. 'He that rides to be crowned,' John Trapp wrote, 'will not think much of a rainy day.' As Frances Havergal (1836–1879) wrote in her well-known hymn 'Light after Darkness,'

> *Light after darkness,*
> *Gain after loss.*
> *Strength after weakness,*
> *Crown after cross.*
> *Sweet after bitter,*
> *Hope after fears.*
> *Home after wandering,*
> *Praise after tears.*
>
> *Sheaves after sowing,*
> *Sun after rain.*
> *Sight after mystery,*
> *Peace after pain.*
> *Joy after sorrow,*
> *Calm after blast.*
> *Rest after weariness,*
> *Sweet rest at last.*

We must remember that we are only renting *here* and that our personal home is reserved *there*. Let us not expect heaven on earth (apart from spiritual foretastes of glory by means of sanctified affliction). Rather, let us trust that one day we will be with Christ forever, overflowing with joy in a utopian marriage with Christ. We will be as holy as He is holy. We will see Him and love Him as He is, and be like Him (1 John 3:2). He will see no sin in us. No longer will we complain with Paul, 'Evil is present with me' (Rom. 7:21).

Not only will all evil be *expelled from* glory but all good will be *walled into* glory. We will enjoy perfect communion with God, with the redeemed made perfect, and with the holy angels. One will not have the least disagreement with another. Even Luther and Calvin will agree on everything. Our thoughts, our mind, and our souls – all will be made perfect.

Since the best is yet to come, we must not make too much of afflictions here in this world. God is using them to prepare His people for a better world – a world that focuses entirely upon Christ. If we hang on to this truth, we will never despair. What we often fear may be the worst thing that can happen to us – even death itself. But death, dear believer, will be gain for us, just as it was for Paul (Phil. 1:21), because of two things.

First, death will be gain because of what we will leave behind. We will leave behind a buffeting Satan and an enticing world. We will have no more problems with the lusts of the eye, the lusts of the flesh, and the pride of life. We will leave behind every troubling thorn in the flesh. There will be no more unanswered prayers, no more vexing riddles. Think of it – no more sin, no more Satan, no more world, no more old nature, no more tears, no more pain, no more night, no more death, no more curse, and no more temptation! Brooks, writing words of counsel to a friend, explains:

> (1.) Death will free you from the indwelling power of sin, Rom. 7:23. In heaven there is no complaints .... (2.) Death will free you from the power and prevalency of sin .... (3.) Death will free you from all provocations, temptations, and suggestions to sin. Now you shall be above all Satan's batteries. Now God will make good the promise of treading Satan under your feet, Rom. 16:20 .... (4.) Death will free you from all the effects and consequents of sin – viz., losses, crosses, sicknesses, diseases, disgraces, sufferings, &c. When the cause is taken away, the effect ceases; when the fountain of sin is dried up, the streams of afflictions, of sufferings, must be dried up; the fuel being taken away, the fire will go out of itself. Sin and sorrow were born together, do live together, and shall die together.[18]

For the believer death is gain because of what we leave behind!

Second, death will be gain because of what we will receive. Dying itself brings five great benefits: (1) Dying brings us into communion with Christ's sufferings; that is a great benefit. (2) Dying gives us a unique experience of Christ's all-sufficient grace; His grace will help us through our dying hours. (3) Dying will transform us into Christ's image; it is our last act of mortifying sin. What a glorious thing that will be! (4) Dying is our last and perhaps greatest opportunity to witness for Christ's glory; the deathbed can be the best pulpit ever! And finally, most importantly, (5) dying will bring you directly into the presence of Christ. To be in His presence is everything a believer could desire, everything we could hope for. This is the apex. This is heaven's heaven – to be with Christ, to be His bride, to be in perfect communion with Him, to enjoy knowing Him and seeing Him and loving Him and praising Him and communing with Him uninterrupted – forever basking in His smile and bathing in His glory and feasting in His presence with the whole redeemed person—soul and body—which will never grow weary! What a bright future it is that awaits the people of God. For us to die is gain because we will be with Jesus forever!

Being in heaven with Jesus in a perfect utopian marriage involves so much more. So much surrounds being with Jesus. There will be perfect eternal life and perfect knowledge. We will know Him face-to-face. There will be perfect activities to engage in – worshipping God, serving God, exercising authority with Christ in ways that we do not understand now, eternal fellowship and communion with the saints in heaven, a perfect home, perfect mansions, perfect light, perfect feasting, and so much more. But it all revolves around this – death is the wheelchair that

---

18. Brooks, *Works*, 5:452.

will roll us into the presence of the glorious King Immanuel, where no wheelchairs will ever be needed again. Death does more for us believers than anything in life has ever done or will ever do for us. Death is gain, for it brings us to Jesus. Death is gain because we will no longer see the whole Christ through a glass darkly.

Be assured that the Shepherd's rod does have honey at the end, so don't despair. All the believers' afflictions are imposed by a fatherly hand of love in the context of grace, not (as we are prone to think) by a punitive hand of judgment in the context of works. Our afflictions are all designed to bring us to heaven to be with Christ forever.

CONCLUSION: KEEP YOUR EYE ON CHRIST

As we experience affliction as believers we must consider Christ: (1) He's borne our pain in the experience of His passion, power, patience, perseverance, and prayers. (2) He gives more grace, consisting of His preciousness, plenitude, and presence. And (3) He knows our way, having fulfilled God's purpose in His life and sustaining His perfect purposes and plans for us. His life and afflictions were not only the means to our salvation but are also the means to perseverance through our trials and tribulations. Christ Himself—His Person, offices, life, afflictions, death, resurrection, ascension, and glory—must be the object of our attention as we suffer. Because there is conformity between our sufferings and the sufferings of Christ, says Isaac Ambrose,

1. We have Christ's strength to bear sufferings.

2. His victories to overcome sufferings.

3. His intercession to preserve us from falling away in sufferings.

4. His compassion to moderate and proportion our sufferings to the measure of strength which He hath given us.

5. His [S]pirit to draw in the same yoke with us, and to hold us under all sufferings, that we sink not.

6. His grace to be more glorious by our sufferings, as a torch when it is shaken shines the brighter.

7. His crown to reward our sufferings, when we shall have tasted our measure of them, 'For our light affliction which is but for a moment, worketh for us a far more exceeding and eternal weight of glory.'[19]

Let us seek grace to live Christianly today in and through our afflictions, and you will soon discover with the apostle, 'For to me to live is Christ, and to die is gain' (Phil. 1:21).

'Wait on the LORD: be of good courage, and He shall strengthen thine heart: wait, I say, on the LORD' (Ps. 27:14).

---

19. Isaac Ambrose, *Looking unto Jesus: A View of the Everlasting Gospel, or, The Soul's Eyeing of Jesus as Carrying on the Great Work of Man's Salvation from First to Last* (London, 1658), p. 406.

CHAPTER 22

OVERCOMING THE WORLD BY FAITH[1]
(1 JOHN 5:4-5)

There is a war waging for your heart – a very old war that began in the Garden of Eden (Gen. 3:1-6, 15) and will continue until the appearance of the new heaven and new earth. In this war, there are battles in our lives between sin and righteousness, holiness and wickedness; day-by-day we are living what Genesis 3:15 calls the enmity between the seed of the woman and the seed of the serpent, or between Christ and Satan. It is a war between the love of God and 'all that is in the world' (1 John 2:16). It is a conflict that spills over into all kinds of battlefields, such as in

- seats of government and centers of culture,
- the legislatures and courtrooms of the nation,
- the offices and workshops of business,
- the marketplaces and entertainment districts of cities,
- the dormitories and lecture halls of colleges and schools,
- the board rooms and sanctuaries of churches,
- our homes and families,
- and most importantly, in our hearts and minds.

Jesus does not intend for believers to retreat or escape from the world, but to overcome it (John 16:33; 17:15). We live in the world as it is, but we who are believers live here as the people of God, striving to live 'godly in Christ Jesus' (2 Tim. 3:12).

Obtaining and maintaining anything of value, however, takes work: a biblical and intimate marriage; close ties with family and friends; divine approval of our work; a personal, saving relationship with God; or a godly life in Christ Jesus that overcomes the world.

---

1. This chapter utilizes some material, updated and revised, from part 1 of Joel R. Beeke, *Overcoming the World: Grace to Win the Daily Battle* (Phillipsburg, N.J.: P&R Publishing, 2005).

None of these blessings can be taken for granted. In spiritual life, in inter-personal relations, in all of our work, the principle holds true: the way to gain is through pain.

The principle that growth requires struggle can be seen even in nature. For example, a man once found a cocoon of an emperor moth and took it home to watch it emerge. One day a small opening appeared. For several hours the moth struggled but couldn't seem to force its body past a certain point.

Deciding something was wrong, the man took scissors and snipped the remaining bit of cocoon. The moth emerged easily, its body large and swollen, but its wings small and shriveled. The man expected that in a few hours the wings of the moth would unfurl in their natural beauty, but they did not. The moth spent its life dragging around a swollen body and shriveled wings. The struggle and pain necessary to pass through the tiny opening of the cocoon are God's way of forcing fluid from the body of a moth into the wings. The merciful snip of the scissors was, in reality, most cruel.

Likewise, the Christian life demands entrance through a narrow gate and a daily walk along a narrow path. Living by faith through self-denying, holy warfare in the midst of a hostile world requires the Spirit's grace, the wisdom of Scripture, and our sustained, intentional effort.

To see how the believer overcomes the way of worldliness by faith, let's examine 1 John 5:4-5, which says, 'For whatsoever is born of God overcometh the world: and this is the victory that overcometh the world, even our faith. Who is he that overcometh the world, but he that believeth that Jesus is the Son of God?' We will consider overcoming worldliness by faith in four parts: (1) what it means, (2) when it begins, (3) how it is lived, and (4) why it lasts.

WHAT IT MEANS

Earlier in his epistle, John encourages us to flee worldliness. First John 2:15-17 says, 'Love not the world, neither the things that are in the world. If any man love the world, the love of the Father is not in him. For all that is in the world, the lust of the flesh, and the lust of the eyes, and the pride of life, is not of the Father, but is of the world. And the world passeth away, and the lust thereof: but he that doeth the will of God abideth for ever.'

In that passage, John contrasts love for the world with love for the Father. The two loves are incompatible. As Jesus said, 'No man can serve two masters: for either he will hate the one, and love the other; or else he will hold to the one, and despise the other' (Matt. 6:24).

One love must rule our life: the one holy passion for God and the things of God. The choice is clear and the directions simple, but the way is not easy. As Jesus said, 'Watch and pray, that ye enter not into temptation: the spirit indeed is willing, but the flesh is weak' (Matt. 26:41).

By 'the world' John does not refer to the physical world in which we live nor to the mass of people living on the planet. Rather, he uses the term to refer to Satan's kingdom of darkness in which its ruler and its inhabitants are lost in sin and wholly at odds with anything pleasing to God (1 John 5:4). In 1 John 2:15-17, 'the world' is a realm in opposition to Christ and His church. Though created to reflect the glory of God, it has become a fallen, disordered world in the grip of the evil one, and now stands in rebellion against the Lord and His Christ (Ps. 2:2). Despite its outward achievements, this world is lost. It is incapable of saving itself. It has lost its meaning. In this sense, the world is the mass of mankind that is estranged from God through sin and lives after the lusts of the flesh – the men, women, and children who focus on this world and neglect the world to come.

The goal of worldly people is to move forward rather than upward. They seek after outward prosperity rather than holiness. They burst with selfish desires rather than heartfelt supplications. They may not deny God, but they do ignore Him, forget Him, or use Him only for their selfish ends.

Worldliness, then, is the state of humanity without God. Someone who is of this world is controlled by worldly pursuits: the quest for pleasure, profit, and position. A worldly man yields to the spirit of fallen mankind—the spirit of self-seeking and self-indulgence—without regard for God. Each one of us, by nature, was born worldly. We belong to this evil world; it is our natural habitat.

By nature we have a worldly mind that is 'not subject to the law of God, neither indeed can be' (Rom. 8:7). As much as we were nourished by an umbilical cord in our mother's womb, so we were tied from birth to the world. Our understanding has been darkened (Eph. 4:18) by the guilt of Adam's sin, which was passed onto us.

Despite our natural worldliness, John speaks quite astonishingly of *overcoming* that liability. He says, 'For whatsoever is born of God overcometh the world.' John uses that phrase sixteen times in his writings – more than all the rest of the Bible writers put together. But what, exactly, does he mean by 'overcoming the world'?

John does not mean conquering the people of this world, winning power battles over our colleagues, or dominating others. He isn't referring to rulers such as Alexander the Great, who after conquering the world, regretted that he had no more worlds to conquer.

Nor does John mean withdrawing from the world, such as monks or Amish people tend to do in establishing their own communities. A Christian is called to fight *in* this world even though he is not *of* this world. To escape from the world is like a soldier avoiding injury by running from the battlefield. Escaping is not overcoming.

Overcoming also doesn't mean sanctifying everything in the world for Christ. Some parts of the world may be redeemed for Christ, but sinful activities cannot ever be sanctified. We don't need to Christianize drama or dance for public worship, for example, or try to Christianize what Hollywood has to offer.

For John, overcoming means fighting by faith against the flow of this present, evil world. Before we consider what that means, let us consider what overcoming the world involves.

Rising above This World's Thinking and Customs

Someone who wants to overcome the world realizes that he has something to overcome. He sees that he has been floating with this world's mentality – thinking and speaking the way this world does, and spending time and energy in the pursuit of worldly things. He now realizes that his thoughts, words, and actions have all been worldly – that he has done nothing to the glory of God or out of true faith in obedience to the spirit of God's law. 'I have wasted my life,' he cries out. 'Rather than overcoming this world, I have been overcome by this world. Its selfishness, pride, and materialism have swallowed me up.'

Someone who overcomes the world makes a clean break from worldly friends, worldly activities, and worldly customs. Like Joshua, he decides, 'As for me and my house, we will serve the Lord' (Josh. 24:15). He takes the cold plunge into potential rejection by the world, placing the fear of God above the fear of man, and esteeming God's desires of greater value than the desires of men.

Persevering in Freedom in Christ apart from Worldly Enslavement

Such perseverance takes great grace, for the battle against worldliness is intense (see Romans 7). Worldly people and temptations entice us. Internal worldliness afflicts us. Satan, ruler over many in this world, knows our weaknesses. At times, the attacks may be so powerful that we cry out with Paul, 'O wretched man that I am, who shall deliver me from the body of this death?' (Rom. 7:24).

By grace, one who would overcome the world strives for allegiance to God rather than the world. Finding freedom only in Christ and His service, he cries out, 'Lord, Thou hast loosed my bonds; I will fight against returning to the slavery of sin with all that is within me.' He sings with all his heart:

> *I am, O Lord, Thy servant, bound yet free,*
> *Thy handmaid's son, whose shackles Thou hast broken;*
> *Redeemed by grace, I'll render as a token*
> *Of gratitude my constant praise to Thee.*

(PSALTER 426, VERSE 9).

Being Raised above the Circumstances of This World

Paul learned to be content in whatever state he found himself. Neither poverty, wealth, sorrow, or joy could move Paul from Christ-centered living. That's what it means to overcome the world – to live above the threats, bribes, and jokes of the world for the sake of Christ. It means following the Lord fully like Caleb in the midst of complainers (Num. 14:24). It means remaining at peace in Christ when friends or people at work despise us for serving the Lord. It means patiently enduring all the persecutions the world throws at us.

A missionary in South Africa told me that every time he preaches in Sudan, he expects to be arrested and persecuted. When pressed for details on how he was persecuted, he said he had experienced only 'minor persecution,' such as having his head submerged in a pail of urine until he was forced to drink it, or having a bag tied around his head at the neck until he fainted from lack of oxygen. 'That's nothing compared to what our Lord experienced,' he quickly added. 'We Christians must count it all joy when we are persecuted for Christ's sake.'

Most of us will not suffer such persecution, but if we are to overcome the world, we must not expect to be friends of the world. As John tells us, worldly people who hated Christ will also hate His disciples. Luther said that suffering persecution is an inevitable mark of being a believer. If you are a true Christian, expect persecution. Second Timothy 3:12 says, 'All that will live godly in Christ Jesus shall suffer persecution.' Remember that a world that smiles upon you is a dangerous place.

Pray for grace to resist worldly temptation. Strive to follow Spurgeon's advice: 'Overcome the world by patiently enduring all the persecution that falls to your lot. Do not get angry; and do not become downhearted. Jests break no bones; and if you had any bone broken for Christ's sake, it would be the most honored bone in your whole body.'[2]

Living a Life of Self-Denial

When God called Abraham to leave his family and friends in Haran, Abraham obeyed, not knowing where he was going. When the well-watered plain of Jordan lay before him, he didn't ask to move there, as his nephew Lot did. When Lot was carried off into captivity, Abraham fought to free him, then refused to take anything from the defeated kings, though he had every right to the spoils of war according to the customs of his day.

Abraham also denied himself in the greatest possible test of his life. When God asked him to sacrifice his son Isaac, through whom all the promises of the covenant would come, Abraham unsheathed his knife and prepared to kill his son in obedience to God. May God grant us such self-denial, for that is what it takes to overcome the world.

WHEN IT BEGINS

By nature, we don't possess the faith of Abraham. We are dead in our sins (Eph. 2:1-2) until God graciously makes us His own (John 3:5). Only then are we called out of this sinful world to become living members of the kingdom of God. As John tells us, 'Whatsoever is born of God overcometh the world' (1 John 5:4).

To be born of God is to be regenerated. As we saw in chapter 10, regeneration is that secret act of God by which He gives new life to a sinner and makes holiness the governing disposition of his soul. Regeneration is not merely reformation, religion, or education, as Nicodemus discovered in his talk with Jesus (John 3). Rather, it is resurrection from the dead and a recreation that God miraculously works within us

---

2. C. H. Spurgeon, 'Victorious Faith,' in *Metropolitan Tabernacle Pulpit*, 47, no. 2757, p. 593.

(Eph. 2:1; 2 Cor. 4:6). As John Stott said, 'It is a supernatural event which takes us out of the sphere of the world where Satan rules, and into the family of God .... The spell of the old life has been broken; the fascination of the world has lost its appeal.'[3]

Those reborn of God have such a radical change of heart that they become new creatures with radically different views of sin, the world, Christ, and Scripture. They hate sin and long to flee from it. They hate what they used to love, and love what they used to hate. They long to know Christ and to live to please Him. Such people, John says, 'overcome the world.' This overcoming is a once-for-all, completed, and finished act. Everyone born of God *has* overcome the world.

Objectively, this act took place when the Son of God, lived, died, and rose from the dead, thus triumphing over sin and hell. Jesus Christ defeated Satan and the world on behalf of all those given to Him by the Father from eternity. Subjectively, this act takes place in the lives of sinners who are made partakers of Christ's great act of atonement through regeneration.

The Holy Spirit regenerates us, making us partakers of Christ by uniting us to Him. Paul tells us that believers share in Christ's death thereby dying to sin's power: 'our old man is crucified with him, that the body of sin might be destroyed, that henceforth we should not serve sin' (Rom. 6:6). If you have been united to Christ in His death, you are dead to your old Adamic nature which was enslaved to this world. Paul exclaims that 'in the cross of our Lord Jesus Christ ... the world is crucified unto me, and I unto the world' (Gal. 6:14). The saving virtue of Christ's death had been applied to Paul's soul, making the world totally undesirable to him.

Sharing in the death of Christ necessarily means sharing in His resurrection. It is impossible to be united to His death without being united to His life. 'It is a faithful saying: for if we be dead with him, we shall also live with him' (2 Tim. 2:11). The Christian has a new walk because of Christ's death-defying, sin-destroying power. The Christian, by virtue of Christ's resurrection, no longer walks in worldliness but in obedience to God. He is no longer given over to the powerful rule of the world, the flesh, and the devil. For 'if any man be in Christ, he is a new creature: old things are passed away; behold, all things are become new' (2 Cor. 5:17). If you are in Christ, you have received a new nature that is different from the world. You have been recreated unto obedience which you must walk in.

Because of their fellowship in Christ's death and resurrection, God's people have been plucked from the kingdom of this world and given to Christ and the kingdom of heaven. Through Jesus Christ, they have now overcome the world, the flesh, and the devil. As 1 John 2:13 says, 'I write unto you, young men, because ye have overcome the wicked one.'

We are victors, not because we are great warriors, but because we belong to the One who has triumphed. What a great thing to realize as we find ourselves at war with this world! We have overcome the world because we belong to the One who

---

3. John Stott, *The Letters of John* (Downers Grove, Ill.: InterVarsity Press, 2014), p. 173.

has overcome. But we must also strive to win daily battles against the world. By the grace of the Holy Spirit, here's how we are to do that.

HOW IT IS LIVED

Faith's Fight against Worldliness

When a person is born again, he begins to overcome the world. The Christian is still attracted to the world, however, because of the sin that remains in him. The Bible calls this remaining attraction 'the flesh.' Thus, while we must keep ourselves 'unspotted from the world,' as James says, we must remember that our 'flesh' is still inclined toward the world. That is why isolation from the world cannot keep us from sin. We who are believers carry a piece of the world within us.

No nature but the divine nature will strive to overcome the world. Believers, by grace, have that nature. They are, as Peter says, 'partakers of the divine nature' (2 Pet. 1:4). The Holy Spirit is in them. They are united to Christ Jesus. And they are adopted by the Father. By the grace of God, they can overcome the world. As 1 John 5:4 says, 'For whatsoever is born of God overcometh the world: and this is the victory that overcometh the world, even our faith.' In Christ, we have overcome the world, but we must also daily fight against the temptations of the world. That can only be done by faith.

In 1 John 2, John names three ways in which we are lured into the ways of the world: the lust of the flesh, the lust of the eyes, and the pride of life. In Christ's strength, faith battles against these paths of worldliness in order to overcome the world. Let's look at each path.

(1) Faith's Fight against the Lust of the Flesh

First, faith battles against *the lust of the flesh*. Faith refuses to love a world that delights in the lusts of the flesh. That means resisting temptations, such as drugs, smoking, overeating, or excessive drinking. The Bible repeatedly warns against such excesses. We must not be brought under bondage to anything physical but are to exercise self-control, for our body is the temple of the Holy Ghost (1 Cor. 6:19; 9:27; 3:17).

The prohibition against fleshly lusting forbids sexual immorality in all forms. It forbids any flirtation or physical intimacy outside of marriage. God has wisely placed sexual intimacy within the sanctity of marriage.

We must also be modest about the way we dress, so that it does not encourage lust. Clothing that calls attention to our nakedness arouses fleshly lusts that offend God. He blames those who provoke lust as much as those who lust after them.

Refusing to love the world means keeping ourselves and our children from worldly parties, worldly entertainment, and worldly music, all of which excite the lusts of the flesh. We must ask of all that we engage in: Can I pray over this? Does it glorify God or ignite fleshly lusts? Does it pass the test of Philippians 4:8, being honest, just, pure, lovely, and of good report? If it encourages lust, we should fight it and/or flee it.

Faith refuses to love this present evil world. Rather, it heeds Romans 13:14: 'Put ye on the Lord Jesus Christ, and make not provision for the flesh, to fulfill the lusts thereof.'

(2) Faith's Fight against the Lust of the Eyes

Second, faith battles against the *lust of the eyes*. Satan works hard to engage our eyes in worldly entertainment. Just as he tempted our first parents to believe that their Creator was hard and unbending, so he whispers to us, 'When did God say that you couldn't enjoy looking at whatever you desire to see? Doesn't he want you to know what's going on in the world? Only a hard, legalistic God would deny you such pleasures.'

Satan has been using such arguments since paradise. He knows his time is short, so he will do anything to persuade us to use our eyes to actively or passively participate in anything that breaks God's moral law. Perhaps the devil will even use a friend to entice you, as he used Eve to tempt Adam; Satan is a master at hiding himself under the cloak of friendship.

Today Satan makes such fruit even more tempting by allowing us to see worldly entertainment in the privacy of our homes – in videos or over the Internet or on our cell phones. We must say no to all forms of entertainment that glamorize sin through our sight. Such entertainment makes adultery look innocent, commonplace, or even exciting. Murder becomes thrilling. We cannot trust our own strength in watching whatever seeks to provoke lust through, as Bunyan would say, our 'eye-gate.' Even the apostle Paul admitted, 'For I know that in me (that is, in my flesh,) dwelleth no good thing: for to will is present with me; but how to perform that which is good I find not. For the good that I would I do not: but the evil which I would not, that I do' (Rom. 7:18-19).

Let us also rid our homes of unedifying magazines, trashy love novels, indeed, all printed material that contradicts the Ten Commandments. How can we ask not to be led into temptation while we continue to play with temptation? As James warns us, 'Every man is tempted, when he is drawn away of his own lust, and enticed. Then when lust hath conceived, it bringeth forth sin: and sin, when it is finished, bringeth forth death' (James 1:14-15).

Flee the lusts of the eyes. Practice self-denial. Follow Paul, who said, 'Herein do I exercise myself, to have always a conscience void of offense toward God, and toward men' (Acts 24:16).

(3) Faith's Fight against the Pride of Life

Finally, faith battles against *the pride of life*. How prevalent such pride is in our hearts. As George Swinnock said, 'Pride is the shirt of the soul, put on first and put off last.'[4] As a sin, pride is unique. Most sins turn us away from God, but pride

---

4. Thomas, *Puritan Quotations*, p. 224.

is a direct attack upon God. It lifts our hearts above God and against God. Pride seeks to dethrone God and enthrone itself.

Pride is complex. Twenty years after his conversion, Edwards groaned about the 'bottomless, infinite depths of pride' left in his heart. He said that pride takes many 'forms and shapes, one under another, and encompass the heart like the coats [layers] of an onion; if you pull off one, there is another underneath.[5] 'I know I am proud; and yet I do not know the half of that pride,' wrote Robert Murray M'Cheyne.[6] The pride of life includes:

Pride in ourselves and our accomplishments. By nature we are filled with self-gratification and self-fulfillment. We live for ourselves, applauding our own wisdom and accomplishments.

Pride in challenging the providential governing of God. Sects such as Mormonism and Jehovah's Witnesses, as well as Free Masonry and other secret lodges, challenge God's rule by asserting human efforts. So do the New Age Movement, transcendental meditation, and the occult, such as fortune-telling, horoscopes, ouija boards, and palm-reading. So do attempts to destroy life through artificial birth control, abortion, or euthanasia, all of which try to usurp the power of divine providence.

Pride of materialism. Materialism is dangerous because it is the practice of covetousness. Covetousness rules us from within. It is like a flood that bursts the banks of our hearts and spills over into our lives, wreaking destruction. Covetousness forgets that happiness does not consist in *things* but in *thoughts*. Loving possessions such as our homes or cars or clothing more than God is abominable idolatry in God's sight; it feeds our quest for pleasure. Dishonesty in business, tax evasion, and other unethical ways of increasing personal wealth feed the pride of life. So does envy or the wish to become rich at the expense of our spiritual welfare.

Faith strives against these and many more paths of worldliness. It gains victory over the subtle power of external and internal worldliness by focusing on Christ, pursuing God's will, living in hope, and especially, by cultivating holiness.

Faith's Cultivation of Holiness

Overcoming the world and pursuing holiness by faith begins with a Person: our Lord Jesus Christ. Only as faith grasps the Lord Jesus can we be led by Him to fight the world, fortify our hope, and pursue a life that is pleasing to God – one of holiness. Here are three ways John gives you to help you cultivate holiness:

(1) By Believing in Jesus the Son of God

When we become believers, we have a new nature that is different from the world. Our minds are enlightened, our consciences quickened, and our hearts stirred. In

---

5. Jonathan Edwards, *Thoughts on the New England Revival* (Edinburgh: Banner of Truth, 2005), p. 155.

6. *Memoir and Remains of the Rev. Robert Murray M'Cheyne*, ed. Andrew A. Bonar (Edinburgh: Banner of Truth, 2007), p. 17.

practice, this works through faith. By faith, we believe that Jesus is the Son of God. By faith we overcome conflict by looking away from ourselves and our weakness to Jesus as the strong Son of man and Son of God.

After writing about the conflict endured by biblical heroes of faith, the writer of Hebrews says the only way these people endured stonings, burnings, drownings, tortures, and other persecutions was by 'looking unto Jesus, the author and finisher of our faith; who for the joy that was set before him endured the cross, despising the shame, and is set down at the right hand of the throne of God' (Heb. 12:2).

If we would overcome the world, we must look by faith to Jesus, the Son of God, who endured the cross. The cross spelled victory for Christ, for it meant crushing the head of the serpent (Gen. 3:15) and finishing the work of suffering that His Father gave Him to do (John 19:30). Jesus chose to be nailed on the cross rather than be crowned king of the world. And in those dreadful hours on the cross, the world was vanquished at His feet.

Jesus' victory on the cross was for you, dear believer. The cross is also your way to glory. When you are faced with worldly temptation, ask yourself, 'How shall I do this great wickedness against my Savior and sin against His cross?' (cf. Gen. 39:9). Then confess with Paul, 'God forbid that I should glory, save in the cross of our Lord Jesus Christ, by whom the world is crucified unto me, and I unto the world' (Gal. 6:14). Sing with Isaac Watts:

> *Forbid it, Lord, that I should boast,*
> *Save in the death of Christ, my God;*
> *All the vain things that charm me most,*
> *I sacrifice them to His blood.*

You must also look to Jesus the Son of God as Almighty Intercessor and Advocate, very God of very God, if you would overcome the world. As Paul says, 'In Him dwelleth all the fulness of the Godhead bodily' (Col. 2:9). Everything you need in your battle against the principalities and powers of the world is to be found in Christ. You are more than conqueror through the One who loved you so much that He died for you.

Faith has victory over the powers of this world because faith connects our situation with Christ's resources. If you want your computer to work, you have to plug it into a power source. Likewise, faith takes our situation and plugs it into the mighty resources of the One who has overcome the world. Those resources include Christ's merits, His Spirit, and His graces.

Faith in Christ overcomes the world by reconciling us with God via the cross and delivering us from the kingdom of Satan. It makes us feel at home with God and His kingdom rather than with the devil and this world. It gives us new affections through the Holy Spirit. We can truly say with Paul, 'For me to live is Christ' (Phil. 1:21).

Trusting in Christ alone is so simple and yet so difficult. Such faith is utterly reliant upon the power of His might. Though it often misses the target due to the believer's inward pollution, faith never stops directing all to Christ. No wonder Matthew Henry said, 'Of all graces faith honours Christ most, therefore of all graces Christ honours faith most.'[7]

John says that if you have been born of God, then you will believe in His Son. You will love Him and His people, and you will overcome the world. No one but Christ can give you that power. You cannot give it to yourself. The church cannot give it to you. It is a divine gift, which enables you to say, 'Whom have I in heaven but thee? There is none upon earth that I desire beside thee' (Ps. 73:25).

(2) By Purifying Your Heart through Christ-centeredness

Faith is a heavenly plant that will not grow in impure soil. Faith is transforming. A homely person who looks at a beautiful object will remain homely. But a believer who fixes his faith on Christ is transformed into the image of Christ. Faith that looks at a bleeding Christ produces a bleeding heart; faith that looks at a holy Christ produces a holy heart; faith that looks at an afflicted Christ, produces sanctified affliction. And, according to Richard Cecil, 'One affliction sanctified, will do more in enabling the Christian to get a victory over the world, than twenty years of prosperity and peace.'[8]

As the chameleon takes on the hue of what it looks at, so faith that looks to Christ partakes of His moral excellence. By looking at and centering on Christ, the lusts of the world no longer have dominion over us. Worldliness is driven from the heart.

Christ overcame sin, Satan, death, and hell for us, but He also promises to be in us to purify us. That is the secret of overcoming the world, for, as 1 John 4:4 says, 'Greater is he that is in you, than he that is in the world.'

Faith helps us to see sin as it really is. Satan tries to make sin attractive. Sadly, we are prone to yield to that trick. We ask, 'What is the harm of listening to ungodly music or watching ungodly movies? Everyone else is doing it.' We then take sin as a sweet morsel on our tongue only to discover that it will turn bitter upon digestion.

That does not happen so easily when faith sees the sinfulness of sin behind the glamor that sin portrays itself to manifest. 'Faith looks behind the curtain of sense, and sees sin before its finery is on, and it be dressed on the stage,' wrote William Gurnall.[9] Faith sees the ugliness and heinousness of sin without its camouflage.

Of course, there will be times when the world appears to be overcoming us. There will be times when we forget that we have conquered our worldly flesh

---

7. *Matthew Henry's Commentary* (McLean, Va.: MacDonald, n.d.), 5:221 (on Matt. 15:28).

8. Richard Cecil, *The Works of the Rev. Richard Cecil* (New York: Robert Carter, 1847), 3:24.

9. William Gurnall, *The Christian in Compleat Armour*, 8th ed. (Glasgow: John Bryce, 1767), p. 381.

through Christ or fail to live in the freedom granted us through faith. Think of the American Civil War, when the edict of emancipation freed all slaves. Long after the war had been fought and won over that issue, some people went on living like slaves. They simply could not grasp the victory that was theirs.

So it is with us Christians. We have been freed from the slavery of the world through Christ, yet we can only live like free people if we resist the attractions of the world. And the only way we can do it is if we tell the world, by faith, 'All that you offer me is passing vanity. I belong to the King of kings, to the One who has triumphed. He gives me solid joys and lasting pleasure. He has bound me for His presence.'

When we fail to live according to that sense of victory, we need to be reminded of the Savior's words, 'In the world ye shall have tribulation; but be of good cheer; I have overcome the world' (John 16:33).

(3) By Living according to What Pleases God

By faith, we are pleased by what pleases God. We delight in God's delights. And, as our faith grows stronger, it increasingly tramples the world under its feet. It does this by obeying God's commandments. As John says, 'This is the love of God, that we keep his commandments ... *for* whatsoever is born of God overcometh the world' (1 John 5:3-4).

The aim of the world's commandments is to gain wealth, fame, social standing, secular power, and human pleasure. Jesus Christ aimed for none of that. He overcame the world by obeying God's commandments – loving God above all and His neighbor as Himself. That must be the goal of all those born of God. They must yearn to obey God's commandments. And if we keep God's commandments from the heart, we will overcome the world.

We need to avoid two extremes in obeying God's commandments, however. One is legalism, which adds to God's commandments. The other is antinomianism, which subtracts from the commandments. Today our greatest problem is antinomianism, which rejects the law of God as a rule of life. This kind of thinking finds the commandments of God too restrictive. It wonders how the God who gave them can be so strict. It obeys out of compulsion rather than delight. It tolerates little sins, reasoning that Christian living would be too much of a burden if it required complete obedience.

This kind of thinking can lead us into the swift current of worldliness. As soon as a believer rests his oars in his battle to keep God's commandments, he acts like the world and is swept downstream. He is then overcome by the world rather than overcoming the world in Christ.

Faith, like that of David and Daniel, finds obedience to Christ and His imperatives more important than life itself. That's why the apostles, prophets, and martyrs endured all kinds of hardships. They were stoned, sawn asunder, and slain by the sword, but none of those things took away their faith. Rather, they rejoiced that they were counted worthy to suffer for Christ.

When pleasing God becomes more important than pleasing people, the believer overcomes his love for this world's honor, riches, pleasures, entertainments, and friendships. Faith prepares him for submission in losses, self-denial, and enduring afflictions for Christ's sake.

(4) By Living for the Unseen World that Awaits Us

Faith refuses to call good evil and evil good. Faith dissolves the world's charms; it sees the world in its true colors, so that the world's control is broken.

Faith also sees the ultimate curse that awaits worldliness. God curses worldliness, John says, for 'the world passeth away, and the lust thereof' (1 John 2:17). The world's best pleasures are temporary. The world is our passage, not our portion. As Hebrews 9:27 says, 'It is appointed unto men once to die, but after this the judgment.'

This world will one day be burned up, together with all of those who lust after it. What is left when all the lusts for which people sell their souls, ruin their families, and stain their reputations have passed away? Nothing but dust, ashes, and the wrath of God. As Spurgeon said, 'If you had got all the world, you would have got nothing after your coffin lid was screwed down but grave dust in your mouth.'[10]

Faith sees that the world is unworthy of our attention. It sees that the world never gives what it promises. It is a gigantic mirage, a tragic fraud, a hollow bubble. As John Trapp wrote, 'Pleasure, profit, and preferment are the worldling's trinity.'[11] Long ago, Solomon discovered all three to be vanity. When you read Ecclesiastes, you will understand why John Bunyan called the world Vanity Fair. You also will realize why James asked: 'Know ye not that the friendship of the world is enmity with God? Whosoever will be a friend of the world is the enemy of God' (4:4).

Faith sees there are greater pleasures to be had by abstaining from sin than by indulging in it. Faith values the eternal rewards that Christ has laid up in heaven far more than all the treasures of the world. In abstaining from worldly pursuits, the believer experiences true happiness.

As we strive to overcome the world here, let us remember that we will be overcomers of the world perfectly in the age to come. Here on earth, heaven is in our hearts and in our deepest affections, yet the world and the devil are at our elbow. But in the new heavens and new earth to come, nothing but righteousness will dwell. By faith, we believe that Christ has gone to prepare that world for us and will return to put an end to the present evil one. Satan and all of his followers will one day be banished to eternal perdition. And the people of God will shine in the firmament of God's glory.

By faith, we believe that the best is yet to come. We look to a time when we will be forever saved from Satan, the world, and our old nature. Sin will be left behind;

---

10. Charles Spurgeon, https://www.frontline.org.za/index.php?option=com_content&view=article&id=1385:war-against-worldliness&catid=16:political-social-issues-cat&Itemid=201.

11. Thomas, *Puritan Quotations*, p. 67.

evil will be walled out. There will be no more tears, pain, sorrow, temptation, or death. We will worship and praise God, serve and reign with Christ, and fellowship with the saints and angels. We will find heaven a perfect place of perfect mansions, perfect gold, perfect light, and perfect pleasure. Above all, we will be in perfect communion with the Triune God, knowing, seeing, loving, and praising Him forever. Truly, 'our light affliction is but for a moment, working for us a far more exceeding and eternal weight of glory' (2 Cor. 4:17).

WHY IT LASTS

Overcoming the world by faith will last forever. That is because the object of faith is the Son of God, and the author of faith, the Spirit of Christ. The source of strength for the believer does not lie in himself or even in faith but in the object of faith, Jesus, the Son of God.

Christ died to cut the cord between sinners and the world. As Galatians 1:4 says, Christ 'gave himself for our sins, that he might deliver us from this present evil world, according to the will of God and our Father.' Christ didn't come just to deliver His people from eternal condemnation, great as that is, but to deliver them from this present evil world. He endured beatings and shame and pain and rejection to wrench those He called His own out of this present evil world and into the kingdom of God.

In Galatians 6:14, Paul says, 'God forbid that I should glory, save in the cross of our Lord Jesus Christ, by whom the world is crucified unto me, and I unto the world.' He is saying that the cross of Jesus Christ was so powerful that it made the world totally undesirable to him. The world lost its color for Paul and became remarkably bland.

All of this has much to say to us as believers in a world that seeks to trap us in its pleasures. Here are a few takeaways for us:

We must trust our great High Priest. When the power of the world threatens to invade our souls, we can take comfort in remembering that our great High Priest prayed, 'Father, I pray not that thou shouldest take them out of the world, but that thou shouldest keep them from the evil' (John 17:15). When our defenses are down, and we are most vulnerable to yielding to the enemy of our souls, we may hope for deliverance through the intercession of Jesus Christ and His Spirit. We may cry out, 'Dear Savior, were it not for Thy intercession, and blessed Spirit, for Thy preservation, in the hour of temptation we would have been swept into evil.'

We must use every means to strengthen ourselves against worldliness. We must listen to sermons, saturate ourselves with Scripture, read books that can make us wise to salvation, and pray without ceasing. We must fellowship with believers, observe the Lord's Day, evangelize unbelievers, and serve others. We must be good stewards of our time.

When Philip Henry, father of Matthew Henry, was thirty years old, he wrote in his diary, 'So old and older was Alexander when he conquered the great world;

but I have not subdued the little world of *myself*.[12] Is this your complaint? Do you also repent of your failures?

When we surrender to the devil's temptation, that failure is rooted in unbelief. Usually our guilt is neglecting to use the shield of faith and the means of grace to protect us from the enemy. Jesus often asked His disciples, 'Where is your faith?' He also asks us whenever we allow the fiery darts of Satan to enter our soul: 'Why don't you believe, watch, and pray?'

A faith that doesn't diligently use God's means of combat is no faith at all, for it does not change us from within. When God and others cannot see a difference in our lives as we move from unbelief to faith, our faith is not real.

Let us beware of anything that is rooted in worldly success, worldly theories, and worldly methods. For example, Christians who trust Christ and His Word should resist turning for help to therapists who approach their problems from the world's point of view. Too often, secular psychologists and counselors advocate self-reliance rather than reliance on God.

If J. C. Ryle could write, 'Worldliness is the peculiar plague of Christendom in our own era,'[13] how much more ought we to see it in our own generation. Myriads of nominal Christians today think like the world, look like the world, and act like the world. They appear morally decent, but Christ is not the focus of their lives. They are at home in this world and lack a passionate commitment to Christ and His Great Commission. They forget that when the worldly man thinks he has conquered the world, the world has conquered him. Then he is no longer salt and light in the world, and provides evidence that he is not born again after all.

If you have not been born of God, cry to Him immediately for a new heart. Without being born again, you will never overcome the world but will go to hell with the rest of the world. Turn from your sins, call upon Christ to save you, to give you faith and repentance, and to dwell within you by His Spirit. Pray for faith in Christ and His atoning death so that the world will lie as dead at your feet. 'Be not conformed to this world: but be ye transformed by the renewing of your mind, that ye may prove what is that good, and acceptable, and perfect, will of God' (Rom. 12:2).

Finally, we must remember that true faith has never failed to overcome the world. Like Christians of every generation, we grapple with besetting sins. Yet God has promised us the victory. Consider the heroes of faith in Hebrews 11. They believed in God in the worst battles of this world. They put on the 'whole armour of God,' especially 'the shield of faith' and 'the sword of the Spirit' (Eph. 6:10-18). So should we. 'Be faithful unto death, and I will give you a crown of life,' Jesus said.

Consider also Martin Luther, John Calvin, William Carey, David Brainerd, and hosts of less famous believers. By God's grace, millions of believers will say at the

---

12. Matthew Henry, *The Life and Death of the Rev. Philip Henry*, corrected and enlarged by J. B. Williams (London: B. J. Holdsworth, 1825), p. 1.

13. J. C. Ryle, *The Upper Room* (Edinburgh: Banner of Truth, 2004), p. 45.

throne of the Lamb on the Great Day of Judgment, 'I have fought a good fight, I have finished my course, I have kept the faith; henceforth there is laid up for me a crown of righteousness, which the Lord, the righteous Judge, shall give at that day: and not to me only, but unto all them also that love his appearing' (2 Tim. 4:7-8). And the Lamb shall say to them – as well as those of us who believe: 'To him that overcometh will I grant to sit with me in my throne, even as I also overcame, and am set down with my Father in his throne' (Rev. 3:21).

CHAPTER 23

ALLOWING ZERO TOLERANCE FOR LUST[1]
(EPHESIANS 5:3-4)

IN the last few years we have heard a lot of talk about possible radioactive contamination from the Fukushima Japanese nuclear reactor damaged in 2011 by the earthquake and tsunami. But the accident in Japan pales in comparison to the disaster that took place in 1986 in Chernobyl in the former Soviet Union. Even today, there is an exclusion zone in the Ukraine of a thousand square miles that prohibits public access. When the accident happened, many emergency responders rushed to the scene to put out the fire. They thought they were only battling fire and smoke. They did not understand that invisible to their eyes was the radioactive contamination in that smoke. Dozens of workers died within a few months, and hundreds suffered from acute radiation sickness. Downwind from the nuclear reactor, horses, cattle, and even trees died. No one knows how many people in Europe were affected.

Today I am warning you about a kind of contamination that is invisible to the eye, but just like the smoke of Chernobyl has the power to bring sickness and death. Many people today scoff at this warning, yet in their souls is a growing cancer that will ultimately destroy them if it is not removed by the great Physician. I am speaking not of a physical contamination such as radioactivity, but the spiritual contamination of sexual lust. 'What?' someone may say, 'Sexual lust is fun and natural. I enjoy it.' But like a poison that tastes sweet but destroys your life, so sexual lust is candy-coated death.

We must have zero tolerance for lust. Some places and schools have a policy of zero tolerance regarding harassment or drugs. Ephesians 5:3-4 calls upon Christians to have a personal policy of zero tolerance regarding sinful sexual lust: 'But fornication, and all uncleanness, or covetousness, let it not be once named among you, as becometh saints; neither filthiness, nor foolish talking, nor jesting, which are not convenient: but rather giving of thanks.'

---

1. This chapter is a revised version of sermon #15 from the Gospel Trumpet ministry, http://www. gospeltrumpet.net.

This Scripture speaks of 'fornication.' That means having a sexual relationship with someone with whom you are not married. It speaks of 'uncleanness.' That does not refer to getting dirt on your body but of contaminating yourself with things offensive to God and harmful to you, especially sexual sins of various kinds.[2] It also speaks of 'covetousness,' a super-sized desire for more and more, whether it is a desire for more money or more sexual pleasure.[3] Put these words together and you have worldly lust, especially sinful sexual lust.

When it comes to having zero tolerance for lust, this Scripture speaks to three questions. How do we have zero tolerance for lust? Why should we have zero tolerance for lust? What should we embrace or 'put on' instead of lust? So, with God's help, based on Ephesians 5:3-4, we want to consider the how, the why, and the what of *zero tolerance for lust*.

HOW DO WE HAVE ZERO TOLERANCE FOR LUST?

Ephesians 5:3 teaches us, 'Let it not be once named among you.' To 'name' something in this case means to mention it or talk about it.[4] That does not mean that we can't even say the words 'fornication,' or 'lust,' or 'immorality.' If it did, then we couldn't even read this verse of the Bible out loud. What it means is that sexual sin should be a matter of shame.[5] It is disgraceful. It should be such an unpleasant subject that we don't even want to talk about it if we don't have to. It is like a huge, disgusting sore that you just want to cover up so no one can see it. Ephesians 5:12 says, 'For it is a shame even to speak of those things which are done of them in secret.'

It is truly sad how our society has lost its sense of shame. While we should not seek to cause people inappropriate shame, there is a healthy and good kind of shame. Shame gives us a sense that some things are not normal; they are revolting, horrifying, and wrong. Shame is a voice inside of us that says we should avoid such things. It arises from a sense of the evil of sin. Sin damages us, for we were created in the image of God.

Sex is not a form of private recreation. Sex outside of marriage has huge personal consequences. A single sexual experience can affect you for the rest of your life. Fornicators sin against themselves, violating the natural principle of self-love. The Bible warns in 1 Corinthians 6:18, 'Flee fornication. Every sin that a man doeth is without the body; but he that committeth fornication sinneth against his own body.' Romans 1:24 warns that those given up to 'uncleanness through the lusts of their own bodies ... dishonour their own bodies.'

---

2. On the association of 'uncleanness' (*akatharsia*) with sexual sin, see Romans 1:24; 2 Corinthians 12:21; Galatians 5:19; Ephesians 4:19; 5:3; Colossians 3:5; and 1 Thessalonians 4:7 (in context).

3. Charles Hodge takes 'covetousness' (*pleonexia*) here to refer to materialistic greed. Andrew Lincoln takes it as sexual greed. See Charles Hodge, *Ephesians* (Edinburgh: Banner of Truth, 1991), p. 205; Andrew T. Lincoln, *Ephesians* (Dallas: Word Books, 1990), p. 322.

4. See Isaiah 19:17 and Jeremiah 23:36 (LXX), where the same Greek word for 'name' (*onomazō*) is used in the sense of to mention or speak of something.

5. The idea of shame is clear in the Greek text. The term 'filthiness' in Ephesians 5:4 is literally 'shamefulness' (*aischrotēs*), from the same root as 'shame' (*aischros*) in v. 12.

God created us to be men and women of honor and dignity. He did not make us to grovel in filth like animals but to walk with Him in holiness and ultimately to walk with Him in glory. Our noble calling on earth includes our sexuality. Sex itself, when properly enjoyed within the marital relationship, is beautiful and clean, not dirty or shameful. It is precisely because sex is good and honorable and promotes a good conscience that we should allow no tolerance for sins that twist and pervert God's good gift. Hebrews 13:4 says, 'Marriage is honourable in all, and the bed undefiled: but whoremongers and adulterers God will judge.' The 'bed' (the sexual union of a husband and wife) is inherently precious, honorable, and clean as God's plan and creation. The price of waiting for sexual relations until marriage is well worth the exercise of self-control to embrace the joy of beautiful marital relations.

Sexual sin and the evil desires that produce it therefore should be viewed as shameful, a kind of ugliness we want to avoid. There was a time in our society when getting pregnant without being married would have brought shame. Now many people think that living together outside of marriage is normal, desirable, and preferable. Pornography, homosexuality, or having multiple sexual partners,[6] are no longer done in secret, but celebrated, promoted, and forced upon us in the public square. One former U.S. president has persuaded his political party to inscribe into its political platform an unqualified support for homosexual marriage, while another U.S. president has had his reputation beleaguered by allegations of marital unfaithfulness and inappropriate sexual behavior. We are told that it is beautiful and normal and healthy and good for anyone to have sex with anyone so long as all the parties consent. But God, who made us and owns us, does not give His consent.

Having rejected God, our society is seeing the inevitable consequence described in Romans 1:32, 'Who knowing the judgment of God, that they which commit such things are worthy of death, not only do the same, but have pleasure in them that do them.' In many ways we are beginning to see North America slide into the same corruptions that wreaked havoc in the Roman Empire, the wicked society where Christianity had its beginnings. We see Ephesians 4:19 sadly fulfilled among us, as people are calloused to the evils they commit, 'who being past feeling have given themselves over unto lasciviousness, to work all uncleanness with greediness.'

It is time for Christians to rise up in holy rebellion against this evil, and to show the world what true love looks like. Romans 12:9 says, 'Let love be without dissimulation. Abhor that which is evil; cleave to that which is good.' Literally that could also be translated, 'Love without hypocrisy, hating the evil, clinging to the good.' Fake or hypocritical love may accept all kinds of evil with a mindless smile. Real love, however, must always include hatred against what is evil just as surely

---

6. We can expect to read of increasingly bizarre examples of this in the future, e.g., in Brazil a government official granted a 'civil union' to a trio (one man and two women). See Mariano Castillo, 'Unprecedented Civil Union Unites Brazilian Trio,' August 31, 2012, *CNN*, http://www.cnn.com/2012/08/31/world/americas/brazil-polyfaithful-union/index.html (accessed Sept. 13, 2012).

as it rejoices in what is good (1 Cor. 13:6). If we really care about people, then we will hate sin because sin destroys people.

How do we show zero tolerance for lust in practical ways? If fornication and uncleanness and covetousness are normal and acceptable in a wicked world, how can we be abnormal and radical in a good and holy way? Romans 13:14 says, 'But put ye on the Lord Jesus Christ, and make not provision for the flesh, to fulfil the lusts thereof.' Let me unpack that in five ways.

1. No tolerance for lustful talk

Ephesians 5:4 focuses the issue on how we talk: 'neither filthiness, nor foolish talking, nor jesting.' Does it surprise you that sexual sin often begins with how we talk? Immorality often begins with smooth, pleasant words (Prov. 6:24; 7:21). It might sound like a compliment about how good your body looks or how much someone likes you and wants to be with you – with sexual overtones that should be reserved for how a husband speaks privately to his wife. It might be a joke. This world is full of sexual innuendo. In fact, much of modern comedy consists of the clever use of words to make you think of sex when talking about other things. In other cases, people openly talk in a vulgar and filthy manner, such as in telling dirty jokes.

What should the Christian's response be to this kind of talk? We must have zero tolerance for it. We must never speak in a way that promotes fornication or uncleanness. If our friends ever talk that way, we should walk away, and if they insist on talking that way, then we should find better friends.

2. No tolerance for lustful looks

Christ taught us in Matthew 5:28, 'That whosoever looketh on a woman to lust after her hath committed adultery with her already in his heart.' You need to take severe action to avoid lustful looks. This is particularly a problem for many men, but women are increasingly falling prey to it. Like Job, you need to make a covenant with your eyes not to look upon someone's body with the intent of sexual desire and enjoyment, unless you are married to that person (Job 31:1).

Zero tolerance means you must cut out of your life everything that entices you to lust. If you have pornographic images in your possession, whether in print or stored electronically, destroy them. If you visit or are tempted to visit pornographic websites, establish an accountability partner and install a protection system on your computer that works. If a video game, movie, television program, or magazine entices your eyes, get rid of it. If a particular person allures you, find ways to avoid looking at that person in lustful ways.

3. No tolerance for lustful reading

Just as spoken words are powerful to excite our desires, so are written words. In fact, some women who have little interest in pornographic pictures may be caught up in reading books that excite romantic fantasies that are just as defiling. Furthermore, many science fiction and fantasy books popular among young people depict sexual immorality, sometimes subtly and sometimes scandalously, but always in a positive light without showing its tragic consequences.

Ask yourself, 'Does this reading material show the honor and dignity of sexual purity, or does it lift up sin?' Remember the command of Philippians 4:8, 'Finally, brethren, whatsoever things are true, whatsoever things are honest, whatsoever things are just, whatsoever things are pure, whatsoever things are lovely, whatsoever things are of good report; if there be any virtue, and if there be any praise, think on these things.'

4. No tolerance for lustful dress

Your actions express your character, and how you dress expresses your heart. Whether male or female, if you desire to draw attention to your body, then you will dress in a way that accentuates parts of your body to grab the attention and stir the desire of others. If you dress provocatively, the Bible says that your heart is wrong (Prov. 7:10). You will then attract to yourself the kind of man that would be attracted to a prostitute or to the kind of woman that would be attracted more to physique than a man's inner character. Perhaps you are beautiful or handsome, but Proverbs 11:22 says that a good-looking person without godly wisdom is like a piece of golden jewelry in the snout of a pig.

I am not suggesting that you should dress in a potato sack. There is nothing wrong with spending a moderate amount of time and money to wear attractive clothing. The Lord Himself showed a concern that people have adequate clothing after the fall of man (Gen. 3:21). But we should dress with modesty and put at least as much focus on the inward beauty of the heart as we do on our outward appearance, and certainly not flaunt our bodies (1 Tim. 2:9; 1 Pet. 3:3-4). Very soon these bodies grow old, die, and return to the earth.

5. No tolerance for lustful touch

As physical creatures, we were made to touch and be touched. In our culture, people use physical touch, such as a handshake or a hug, to greet and welcome each other (Rom. 16:16). There need not be anything sexual about such touching. However, there is such a thing as a sexual touch (1 Cor. 7:1). In order to bless us with a vibrant sexual life in marriage, God designed our bodies to respond to sexual touching and kissing. In marriage it is a beautiful and delightful thing to communicate our affection, friendship, and sexual desire through touch.

But kissing and touching can lead unmarried couples to lust and fornication (Prov. 7:13). Christians therefore need to exercise wisdom and self-control in how we touch people, especially someone to whom you are attracted but not married. There are some actions that the Bible clearly associates with making love, such as touching each other's private parts (Prov. 5:19-20). These are off limits for single people. And if someone touches you in that way against your will, you need to get away from him or her, end the relationship, and confide in a close friend or pastor, or, if you are young, tell your parents immediately.

With regard to holding hands and kissing in a courting or Christian dating relationship, it would go beyond the Scriptures to lay down laws for all Christians. Each Christian must know himself, be wise, and exercise self-control. Wise is the father who establishes guidelines and rules for his children in these areas for their protection and guidance. Wise is the couple that talks these matters over early on in their relationship, and with God's help, resolve to set firm biblical lines of self-denial for their premarital relationship.

Have zero tolerance for lustful touch, and ask yourself these questions: Does this activity stir sexual desires in me or the person I am with? If someone saw us doing this, would he think that we are likely headed for sexual intercourse? If my parents caught me doing this, would I feel ashamed? Dear friends, let there be not even a hint of sexual immorality among you!

WHY SHOULD WE HAVE ZERO TOLERANCE FOR LUST?

Why do love for God and love for people move us to firmly reject sexual sin? What motivates us to view fornication and uncleanness as shameful? Why should we have no tolerance for lustful talk, lustful looks, lustful reading, lustful dress, or lustful touch? Ephesians 5:3-4 and its context give us five reasons.

1. Lust is not love (v. 2)

It is no accident that just before warning us against lust, Paul wrote about true Christian love. Throughout history people have confused lust for love. Like Amnon towards Tamar, they can feel so much desire for someone it makes them feel sick. But their lustful desires have more in common with hatred than love (2 Sam. 13:1-2, 4, 15). No matter how much someone might say he loves you, if your companion tries to draw you into a sexual relationship before marriage, that is not love. It's probably mostly selfishness and using other people to get what he wants.

Ephesians 5:2 says, 'And walk in love, as Christ also hath loved us, and hath given himself for us an offering and a sacrifice to God for a sweetsmelling savour.' Notice here that the character of true love is self-sacrifice. Sacrifice is costly. It can be painful to wait until you are married. It's hard to say goodbye in the evening to someone for whom you have strong feelings. Nights can be long and lonely. But love is willing to sacrifice yourself for the good of the other; mutual self-restraint is well worth the price of preserving an unstained wedding day and of avoiding a bad conscience in marriage. Premarital relations have a way of wreaking havoc in the area of intimacy within marriage.

Seducing someone or allowing yourself to be seduced into fornication is the opposite of love; ultimately it is an act of hatred. The Bible says in 1 Thessalonians 4:6

that those who commit fornication 'defraud' others. The idea is that you greedily steal something precious from them.[7] For the sake of your own pleasure, you have led someone to sin against the living God. You have robbed that person of a good conscience and heavenly reward. You have used that person's body and jeopardized that person's eternal destiny. Furthermore, you have also defrauded that person's parents and family and your own family, bringing shame and dishonor upon them and robbing them of the joy of seeing their dear children walk in purity down the aisle at their wedding.[8]

Sexual sin has massive public consequences for a nation. Sexual sin is an act of hatred against society at large. Sex in marriage is the cement that holds together the foundation of our society: the family. Sexual immorality breaks up the foundation by weakening marriages. It spreads painful, embarrassing, and sometimes deadly diseases. Immorality also naturally produces children out of wedlock. Standard contraceptives still fail to prevent pregnancy in 9-15 per cent of cases per year.[9] Among teenagers the contraceptive failure rate is even higher. That means that tens of thousands of children are conceived every year by people using contraceptives. What will happen to these children if their parents are not joined in a loving marriage? How many are aborted? What is happening to our society right now as millions of people have grown up without a stable family? Is this love, to engage in an activity harmful to your friend, family, future children, and nation?

This is one great reason to have zero tolerance for lust: lust is not love.

2. Lust defiles desire (v. 3a)

Lust takes something good, useful, beautiful, and pleasing to God, and turns it into an evil monstrosity that is wasteful, ugly, and displeasing in the eyes of the Lord. In particular, it deforms our desires and makes them dirty. That is why sexual sin is called 'uncleanness' (v. 3). It is like throwing vomit and manure on an expensive painting by a gifted artist; sin casts spiritual dirt and filth upon God's amazing creation of our sexuality.

One way that lust does this is by wrapping itself in the lie that sex can be our god. Ephesians 4:22 speaks of 'deceitful lusts,' strong desires driven by lies. All sin is at root an attempt to treat God's creations as if they were the Creator instead of trusting Him who alone has never-ending happiness (Rom. 1:25). Sex is good,

---

7. The term 'defraud' (*pleonekteō*) means to take advantage of someone, often financially but also in other ways (2 Cor. 2:11; 7:2; 12:17-18). Interestingly, it is from the same root as the word 'covetousness' (*pleonexia*) in our text.

8. The text in 1 Thessalonians 4:6 says, 'defraud his brother,' not 'defraud the woman,' suggesting that the crime in view is particularly against the father of the woman. Under the Mosaic law (Exod. 22:17), a man who seduces a virgin must pay her father the bride-price even if they do not marry each other.

9. Haishan Fu, Jacqueline E. Darroch, Taylor Haas, and Nalini Ranjit, 'Contraceptive Failure Rates: New Estimates From the 1995 National Survey of Family Growth,' *Family Planning Perspectives* 31, no. 2 (March/April 1999): pp. 56-63, http://www.guttmacher.org/pubs/journals/3105699.html (accessed Sep. 13. 2012). Failure rate for the pill was 9% and for the male condom was 15%.

but it is not God. But when in lust we worship sex as our god, we hope for more than it can deliver.

This is a reason why fornication is connected to 'covetousness' or greediness (Eph. 5:3; Col. 3:5). Sinners think that if they will just feed their sin it will be quiet and satisfied. But the truth is the more they feed their lust, the more it consumes them and the greedier it gets. In the end lust will make you into an empty shell of hunger, always wanting more and never content with what you have. The only answer is not to feed lust but to kill it by the grace of Jesus Christ.

Have zero tolerance for lust, since it does not satisfy desire, but only defiles it.

3. Lust contradicts our holy calling (v. 3b)

In Ephesians 5:3 Paul reminds us that one reason we must give no place to lust is that this 'becometh saints.' In other words, sexual purity is fitting and proper for those called and consecrated to belong to God. The word 'saint' literally means 'holy ones' (Greek *hagioi*). It does not describe some elite class of super-spiritual people; all true Christians are saints by the blood of Christ (Eph. 1:1). Ephesians 5:8 tells us that we were once 'darkness' but now we are 'light in the Lord,' so we must walk as people who belong to the light. Lust is what we expect from people who do not know God (1 Thess. 4:5). It simply does not fit with who we are in Christ.

If you are a believer, God is building you, together with other believers, into His 'holy temple' where He lives (Eph. 2:21-22). The temple in the Old Testament was a beautiful building full of sparkling gold. Now people have become the temple, and we are beautiful in God's sight with the righteousness of Christ and the holiness of His Spirit. Do you want to spray-paint obscene graffiti on God's temple? That is what lust does. Don't you know that your body is the temple of the Holy Spirit? You are not your own. You were bought at the price of Christ's blood. Therefore glorify God with your body and spirit, which belong to God (1 Cor. 6:19-20). Submit to the Spirit's work, and grow into a beautiful and holy temple where God will live forever! We have a holy calling, and lust contradicts our holy calling.

4. Lust corrupts conversation (v. 4a)

Notice that the sins listed in Ephesians 5:4 revolve around how we talk: 'neither filthiness, nor foolish talking, nor jesting, which are not convenient: but rather giving of thanks.' Our ability to communicate in verbal language distinguishes us from the animals. Nothing like the complex and profound speech of human beings is found in the animal world. Lust takes the noble gift of human speech and turns your mouth into a sewer. There are some people whose speech is so filthy that even though you love them you hate being around them.

God gave us our mouths to speak the truth in love (Eph. 4:15). He especially gave us our ability to speak so that we could live to the praise of the glory of His grace (Eph. 1:6). Don't allow lust to pollute the streams of your words with the poison of sin. Keep them flowing clean and clear for the glory of God.

5. Lust damns sinners (vv. 5-6)

Paul's warning against lust and greed ends with these sobering words in Ephesians 5:5-6: 'For this ye know, that no whoremonger, nor unclean person, nor covetous man, who is an idolater, hath any inheritance in the kingdom of Christ and of God. Let no man deceive you with vain words: for because of these things cometh the wrath of God upon the children of disobedience.'

Dear young people, 'Let no man deceive you.' Lust is not healthy. Lust is not a joke. Lust, if it is not broken by the ruling power of Jesus Christ, will damn you and your friends to hell forever. If you continue in the path of sexual lust without repentance, then you are a fornicator at heart, and you have no place in heaven. Unless you declare war on your sexual sin, you remain at war with God. Will you trifle with a few passing pleasures and provoke the living God to anger? Will you for the sake of a few drops of gratification plunge yourself into a sea of fire? Hell is no party, but is a never-ending experience of the burning anger of God.

If, on the other hand, you truly repent of sexual sin committed in the past and forsake it, you will find forgiveness in Jesus Christ, even though the scars of sin may remain. As with the woman caught in the act of adultery, Jesus speaks to penitent sinners who are guilty of sexual sin, 'Neither do I condemn thee: go, and sin no more' (John 8:11).

Let us pray for God's grace to conquer this sin, so that we would have zero tolerance for lust. We must not pamper it. We must not permit it in our lives. We must turn from it in disgust and put on the Lord Jesus Christ.

CONCLUSION: TURN FROM LUST TO GRACE AND GRATITUDE

We must put off sexual lust and covetousness, throwing it away like an article of clothing stained by some putrid, repulsive, life-threatening contamination. And what shall we put on in its place? Every sin needs to be replaced by some fruit of righteousness and holiness (Eph. 4:22-24). Paul teaches us that we must replace lust with gratitude, writing in verse 4, 'but rather giving of thanks.'

Giving thanks for what? For the love of God in Christ. Ephesians 5:1-2 says, 'Be ye therefore followers of God, as dear children; and walk in love, as Christ also hath loved us, and hath given himself for us an offering and a sacrifice to God for a sweetsmelling savour.' Here is true love! Here is the God who loves sinners and makes them His 'dear children,' adopting them and embracing them with eternal affection. Here is Jesus Christ, giving His life as a sacrifice for our sins so that He can perfume us with the sweet smell of His obedience, instead of the revolting stench of our disobedience, and the Father will be pleased with us.

In some ways sexual lust is a twisted cry for love, but it seeks love in the wrong ways. But God's love is a love that can satisfy you and give you peace and contentment. If your heart is hard and cold, this love can give you a new heart that is soft and warm. If you have defiled your mind or body with uncleanness, here is love that can wash you as white as snow. If you have betrayed God with your sins, perhaps sins that no one else knows about, here is love that will accept the repentant sinner and He will be your shield, your glory, and the lifter of your head.

Revel in the grace of God and cultivate gratitude by trusting in Him. For gratitude will heal what lust has destroyed. Lust is not love, but thanksgiving to God ignites love. We love because we are amazed at how He first loved us. Lust defiles desire, but thanksgiving to God purifies desire. It sets us free to enjoy good things in their rightful place so as to let God alone be our God.

Lust contradicts our holy calling, but thanksgiving to God fulfills our holy calling. For God calls us to give thanks in all things to our God and Father in the name of Jesus Christ. Lust corrupts conversation, but thanksgiving to God gives honor and dignity to our conversation. Lust damns sinners, but thanksgiving to God springs from salvation by grace.

Ultimately the reason why Christians should have zero tolerance for lust is that Christians have no need for lust because we have a God who loves us as His dear children, a Savior who died for our sins – including lustful sins, and the Spirit who lives closer to our hearts than the most intimate companion. Repent of every known lustful sin, and entrust your soul and body to the triune God of grace, believing in His Son alone for salvation. Know this God, whom to know in Christ is life eternal (John 17:3), and be satisfied.

CHAPTER 24

RETURNING FROM BACKSLIDING[1]

EVERY Christian faces numerous discouragements in striving to follow Christ. Our knees go weak and our hands hang down when we face personal failure, when others let us down, or when providence denies our desires. Disappointment can lead to discouragement, and discouragement may end in doubt, fear, and even despair. We feel weak and tired, emotionally and spiritually, and may ask, 'Why should I persist in confessing a faith despised and hated in the world? It all seems pointless and hopeless.' We say with Asaph, 'Verily I have cleansed my heart in vain' (Ps. 73:13).

But we must press on. J. C. Ryle (1816–1900) said, 'We have a race to run.' He explained that every true Christian must endure great opposition:

> Without there will be fightings, within there will be fears; there will be snares to be avoided, and temptations to be resisted; there will be your own treacherous hearts, often cold and dead and dry and dull; there will be friends who will give you unscriptural advice, and relations who will even war against your soul ; in short, there will be stumbling-blocks on every side, there will be occasion for all your diligence and watchfulness and godly jealousy and prayer, you will soon find that to be a real Christian is no light matter.[2]

Florence Chadwick (1918–1995) was an American swimmer. In her prime, she swam the English Channel in record time. But when she attempted to swim the twenty-six miles from Catalina Island to the coast of California, a thick fog set in after fifteen hours in the water, and she could no longer see her goal. She grew discouraged and, an hour later, she asked to be pulled out by the people in boats accompanying her. Imagine her dismay when she discovered that she was only one mile away from the coastline! Two months later she tried again, and the same fog set in. But this time she fixed in her mind an image of the shore ahead of her, and pressed on to reach her goal.

---

1. This chapter is a condensed and revised version of Joel R. Beeke, *Getting Back in the Race: The Cure for Backsliding* (Adelphi, Md.: Cruciform Press), 2011.

2. J. C. Ryle, *The Christian Race and Other Sermons* (London: Hodder and Stoughton, 1900), p. 156.

Like a swimmer in the cold waters of the English Channel, our own sins constantly work to numb us and sap away our spiritual strength. To 'backslide' means to draw back from God, from our profession of faith, and from our commitment to follow Christ, and relapse into unbelief, sin, and spiritual numbness. Backsliding is an act of disloyalty and a form of rebellion. It can happen to an individual, a family, a church, even a whole denomination. Backsliding can leave people in a weakened spiritual condition for years before they recover. It can even lead to the final apostasy of giving up and walking away from the Lord forever.

Our perseverance is a fruit of God's preservation, but that perseverance is still ours, a fight we must fight, and a race we must run (see chapters 4, 11, 12, 16, and 20). All Christians are runners needing encouragement to keep running in the race, until they reach the goal, obtain the prize, and receive their crown from Christ in glory! In this chapter we will consider how to recognize backsliding believers and what the divine cure for backsliding involves.

RECOGNIZING INJURED RUNNERS

Picture in your mind a runner in a cross-country race. Off the mark things look great as he sets a strong pace, but as the race progresses, he gets a bit over-confident and careless. Soon, instead of paying attention to the terrain, he is dreaming about the shouts of admiration as he crosses the finish line in record time. So he fails to see a dip in the path, and suddenly falls to the ground, confused, discouraged, embarrassed, and unsure whether to give up now or try to keep going.

This is a moment of crisis and shame, *but the runner need not give up*. He can finish the race. And so can you, if you are a backslidden Christian and have fallen into sin, through your own weakness and carelessness.

Backsliding is a season of increasing sin and decreasing obedience in those who profess to be Christians. In backsliding, the cycle of repentance that characterizes the Christian life is broken and spiritual ground is lost.

All throughout the Bible, we are warned about backsliding.[3] The apostle James addressed the adulterous love of the world in the early church (James 4:1-10), and backsliding is still a perennial problem in the church today. 'My people,' the Lord Himself complains, 'are bent to backsliding from me' (Hosea 11:7). Yes, unbelievers and hypocrites in the church have a tendency to backslide, but it is easy even for true Christians 'to backslide from God ... without intending to do so, without putting forth any efforts to that effect ... [such as] prayer, self-denial, vigilance, violence, running, wrestling, fighting.'[4] Indeed, 'without great heed, you may fall into great decay of grace ... so that you shame the name of Christ, wound

---

3. See Quartus, 'Backsliding,' in *Fruitfulness in Christian Service* (Bristol: John Wright and Sons, 1916), p. 146. See also Jer. 2:19; 3:6, 8, 11, 12, 14, 22; 5:6; 8:5; 14:7; 31:22; 49:4; Hosea 4:16; 11:7; 14:4.

4. William S. Plumer, *Vital Godliness: A Treatise on Experimental and Practical Piety* (Harrisburg, Va.: Sprinkle, 1993), p. 152.

your conscience, grieve the Spirit, hurt the church, interrupt your fellowship with God, lose your assurance of salvation, and fall under God's discipline.'[5] What makes our backsliding all the more grievous and heinous is that we do it despite the immeasurable depth of God's love for us.

Perhaps there was a time when backsliding was foreign to your vocabulary; like Joseph you dreaded the thought of sinning against God (Gen. 39:9). But how is your spiritual life now? Do you see in yourself an inclination to go astray like a lost sheep, to return to a life you thought you'd left behind forever? Let us then explore how the sin of backsliding extends its deadly influence through our entire lives.

Signs of Sliding into a Spiritual Rut

As automobiles often get stuck in winter weather ruts, God's people let themselves drift and fall into backsliding, until they too are stuck. Here are six signs of backsliding.

1. Coldness in prayer

Formerly, backslidden believers anticipated prayer with delight, longing to pour out their hearts before God with all their needs, confessions, and vows, deeply aware that He knows their circumstances and needs better than they do.

Gradually, our zeal in prayer begins to fade away. Before we realize it, our prayers become more a matter of words than heart (Isa. 29:13).[6] Religious formality and deadness quench power and access. Heads are still bowed, words are still uttered, but where is the love, urgency, necessity, and sense of dependency? Ultimately, prayerlessness arises from unbelief. The visible beauty of the world seems more important, and the invisible, heavenly beauty of God seems less real. Prayer goes to the Lord as a thirsty man goes to a clear, cool river in order to drink (John 7:37-39); but unbelief has abandoned the fountain of living water for broken cisterns that hold no water (Jer. 2:13).

2. Indifference under the Word

As a Christian draws back from his Lord, he finds his affections towards God cooling, which especially shows itself in an indifference toward God's Word. The Bible is still read dutifully and regularly, but the spiritual relish with which it was read in former times has evaporated. This forecasts further decline due to spiritual malnourishment, for the Word is our life (Deut. 32:47; 1 Pet. 2:2). Dryness under the Word also implies backsliding from the Word made flesh, Jesus Christ, who

---

5. Thomas Vincent, *The Good Work Begun*, ed. Don Kistler (Morgan, Pa.: Soli Deo Gloria, 1998), pp. 84-86.

6. 'A man may pray with his lips and yet not pray with an intense desire of the soul.' Alexander Ross, *The Epistles of James and John*, The New International Commentary on the New Testament (Grand Rapids: Eerdmans, 1954), p. 102.

is the center and heart of all the means of grace. He who was the substance of our lives, the source of our sanctification, and the mark towards which we were always pressing, silently withdraws Himself.

3. Growing inner corruptions

During backsliding the secret sins of the heart begin to multiply as we neglect to put them to death. We no longer sincerely ask God to search us (Ps. 139:23-24). Instead we cover the evidence of our sin, hiding from God and blaming others – even the Lord (Gen. 3:12).

Blaming others for our sin encourages hypocrisy. So a *double life* begins to emerge of which God's children are only half-conscious. Instead of keeping the heart, they effortfully maintain outward appearance (Prov. 4:23; Matt. 23:26-27). Zeal for God's cause and honor burns low, while concern for our reputation takes the upper hand. We want others to think we are living *for* God when in reality we've stopped trying to live *with* God.

As *secret sins* multiply, vices we thought long gone in grace are resurrected with even more power than before. God's children may not run after sin as they did before regeneration, but now sin runs after them. And as their resistance against sin grows weaker, they welcome sin's approach. Offending God does not remain the overriding burden of sin; instead, the punishment of sin, or its offense to men, becomes our primary motive for resisting temptation. We may still confess sin as sin, and make vows to change, but both acts are done as an empty show of piety. We speak against sin, but in practice accommodate and fuel it, even in spite of the protests of our conscience (Rom. 13:14). Our confession is without repentance and our vows are not followed by change.

In spite of God's silence and their own failure to withstand trials, temptations, and weaknesses in their own strength, God's children continue to presume that all is well, perhaps even comforting themselves with their outward morality and form of religion (Luke 18:11).

4. The love of the world

When the Christian begins to backslide, one sign is an increase in worldliness, often the first mark which we notice. In everyday lives, in conversation, and even in dress and fashion, the spirit of the world begins to infest the church (see chapter 22). Backsliding can progress so far that increased worldliness of God's people will even be noticed by the world.

5. Declining love for believers

Backsliding can advance so far that *brotherly love*, one of the most basic marks of saving grace (1 John 3:14), seems to all but disappear among God's people. James 4:1 says, 'What causes quarrels and what causes fights among you? Is it not this, that your passions are at war within you?' Worldliness in the church foments wars in the church. Plumer said, 'As piety thus dies in the soul, charity diminishes, and censoriousness takes its place.'[7]

'Backsliders are commonly backbiters,'[8] so conflicts, troubles, disputes, and selfishness multiply. Instead of covering one another's faults, opportunities to talk against one another and to defend ourselves are gladly utilized.

6. Man-centered hopes

Into the vacuum created by God's departing glory rushes vainglory and man's love for strife (Phil. 2:3). If man is the center of the church, man becomes the subject of all talk. He is either idolized or criticized, and God and His Word are set aside.

Man-centeredness is an awful curse on the church, a dreadful blasphemy of God's name, the fruit of spiritual deadness, and a sure guarantee for no personal blessing unless the Lord breaks it down (Jer. 17:5-6). Backsliding produces false assurance and a feeble hope based on man's activities. Holy expectation is beyond self and man, and seeks the honor of God, the conversion of sinners, and the welfare of the church. The church's only hope is in God, for He alone can send forth His indispensable Spirit, increasingly conform us to His image, and revive both our churches and us (Col. 3:11; Rom. 8:29).

The Bitter Results of Backsliding

When we are 'bent to backsliding,' what are the tragic results of such sinfulness? Allow me to mention just four of many possible bitter fruits.

1. Injury to God's holy and worthy Name

When David sinned and tried covering it up, God rebuked him, saying, 'Thou hast despised me .... By this deed thou hast given great occasion to the enemies of the LORD to blaspheme' (2 Sam. 12:9-10, 14). How men will mock at Christ when they hear that those bearing His name acted shamefully! The worst thing about backsliding is that it will cast discredit on the name of the God who has given us so much grace. The life of a backslider is an insult to Christ's love, displayed for us at the cross.

2. Our own suffering

Backsliding causes a believer inwardly to experience more false peace than real peace. Yet there are times when conscience awakens and begins to roar (Pss. 32:3-4; 38:3-4). We should not underestimate God's power to discipline His children and afflict us for our own good (Heb. 12:4-11). Brakel wrote, 'Are you brazen toward the Lord? ... Consider that God will not put up with your sulking .... God may come and make life so bitter for you, that for the remainder of your life you will lament that you have been so rancorous toward the Lord. Therefore, take care that you regress no further.'[9]

---

7. William S. Plumer, *Vital Godliness*, p. 157.

8. Ebenezer Erskine, 'The Backslider Characterized,' in *Works*, 1:68.

9. Wilhelmus a Brakel, *The Christian's Reasonable Service*, 4:165.

If unchecked, backsliding leads to apostasy and damnation (Matt. 5:30). John Angell James wrote, 'Do not attempt while the sinful practice is continued, to gain any comfort of mind by the supposition that … you are a true Christian still, and shall one day be restored to God by penitence and faith.'[10] 'The Lord knoweth them that are his. And, Let every one that nameth the name of Christ depart from iniquity' (2 Tim. 2:19). You must repent and pursue holiness, and show yourself elect. As long as you rest in sin, you are on a trajectory towards hell.

3. The sin and apostasy of our children

It is not uncommon for children to follow their parents in sin 'unto the third and fourth generation' (Exod. 20:5). David repented of his sins, but his adultery and murder were followed by his son Amnon raping his half-sister Tamar, and another son Absalom becoming a deceiver, usurper, and traitor to David's own throne. Shall we pray for our children's salvation with our mouths but point them to damnation with our actions?

4. The decay of the church

Bad company corrupts good morals (1 Cor. 15:33). One person within the church whose heart is turning away from the Lord is like 'a root bearing poisonous and bitter fruit' (Deut. 29:18; Heb. 12:15). Do you want to be the cause of others stumbling? One accident on the highway can create a traffic jam stretching for miles. You are not an island, standing alone. Your progress towards Christ or backsliding from Him affects many others.

A Call for Godly Sorrow

The greatest evil of such backsliding is that *we do not feel any guilt for this.* We complain about spiritual dryness, the darkness of the times, the sad condition of the church and of God's people, but what does the Lord say of such complaints? They are nothing more than empty words in His ears if we do not repent of our role in causing the deadness and darkness (Jer. 8:6). Join with Jeremiah in saying, 'Oh that my head were waters and mine eyes a fountain of tears, that I might weep day and night for the slain of the daughter of my people!' (Jer. 9:1). Only when godly sorrow brings us to such a point can the first step be taken towards the healing of our backsliding.

RUNNERS RETURNING TO THE PHYSICIAN OF GRACE

When an athlete has injured himself, he quickly seeks the assistance of a physician, just as a backslidden Christian must return to the Lord.

Our Physician is full of wisdom, power, and grace for sinners, and He is willing to heal us even of the judgments which He Himself sent to chasten us (Exod. 15:26; Pss. 39:11; 99:8; Hosea 6:1). How can we return from our backsliding? Through

---

10. John Angell James, *The Christian Professor Addressed*, p. 307.

the prophet Hosea, God revealed a threefold way for obtaining healing from the Physician of grace.

True Repentance

The Lord says to His backslidden people in Hosea 14:1, 'O Israel, return unto the LORD thy God; for thou hast fallen by thine iniquity.' 'Return' or 'turn back' is a key word in Hosea for repentance.[11] Turning back to God often follows discipline from God, and is the proper way to respond to such discipline (Rev. 3:19; Luke 15:16-17) – 'to reenter the sphere of Yahweh's dominion … the sphere of Yahweh's love.'[12] What grace it is that the holy God invites, even commands, the backslider to return to Him! What follows are seven aspects of true repentance.

1. Recognize your sinful condition

Hosea gave a reason for repentance: 'for thou hast fallen by thine iniquity.' Without the illumination of the Spirit, sinners are blind to their spiritual need. J. G. Pike warned that 'secret backsliding is inexpressibly dangerous … [when believers] feel few or no suspicions respecting their real state.'[13] If you get a glimpse of how rotten your heart is, thank God for it, and pray for more.

2. Remembrance of your past obedience

By reminding God's people of their past, the Spirit plants deep convictions of spiritual blessings: '*Remember* therefore from whence thou art fallen' (Rev. 2:4-5a). Remember how sacred the throne of grace was, how frequently you resorted to it, how close your communion was with God.

3. Searching out sin

With repentance, the Spirit grants a holy zeal against sin, a burning desire to search out any and all sin that impedes your journey to everlasting life (2 Cor. 7:11; Ps. 139:23-24). Face the truth: you are not as you once were! The fruit of the Spirit has withered, the heart has lost its softness, and the throne of grace has lost its sweetness. Use the searchlight of God's Word to find the cause of your sad condition (Ps. 119:105, 130).

4. Grieving over sin

Discovering sin leads to true sorrow for sin, described by the Heidelberg Catechism (Q. 89) as 'a sincere sorrow of heart that we have provoked God by our sins.'[14] Hatred

---

11. The root idea of the Hebrew word for 'backsliding' is turning. The backslider has turned away, or turned back from following God. So in repentance, he turns once more, turning back in the right direction.

12. Thomas McComiskey, 'Hosea,' in *The Minor Prophets: An Exegetical & Expository Commentary*, ed. Thomas McComiskey (Grand Rapids: Baker, 1992), 1:229.

13. J. G. Pike, *A Guide for Young Disciples* (repr., Morgan, Pa.: Soli Deo Gloria, 1996), p. 309.

14. Joel R. Beeke, ed., *Doctrinal Standards, Liturgy, and Church Order* (Grand Rapids: Reformation Heritage Books, 2003), p. 68.

of sin goes beyond grieving over sin's *consequences;* true grief over sin is concerned with *sin itself,* as an offense to God. True sorrow that produces repentance is 'godly,' that is, God-centered, God-motivated, God-oriented, literally 'according to God' (2 Cor. 7:10). The sinner learns to grieve over sin more deeply because it dishonors or blasphemes (Rom. 2:21-24) the name of the God whom he earnestly desires to love and serve.

5. Confessing your Sin

True sorrow must pour out its heart before God, owning its own transgressions (Pss. 51; 32:5; 38:9). The Lord delights in such forthright acknowledgment of transgression from His backsliding child, 'Only acknowledge thine iniquity that thou hast transgressed against the LORD thy God ...' (Jer. 3:13-14).

6. Fleeing from sin

Counterfeit repentance goes no further than a measure of reformation, refusing to hate sin wholeheartedly and break from it completely. When sin comes and grasps hold of us, like Joseph we must flee and get away as fast as we can (Gen. 39:12). Whether it is love of money or youthful lusts (1 Tim. 6:11; 2 Tim. 2:22), we must not play with sin like a toy, but cast it away like a deadly rattlesnake.

True repentance cannot continue in sin, and it begs, 'Lord, keep me from falling (Prov. 28:13), grant me grace to flee from sin, to hate even the garment spotted by the flesh (Jude 23), and to abstain from even the appearance of evil' (1 Thess. 5:22).

7. Pursuing righteousness

Get back on track, fallen runner, and start running after holiness again (Heb. 12:12-14). At the end of the race stands the Lord Himself, ready to embrace you. Do not play games with the Lord.

F. B. Meyer counsels that if 'your life has been dry lately; no tear, no prayer, no fervor .... Get quiet and prostrate yourself before God [and pray] "May God forgive me! May God show me the sin, show me what it is that hinders me .... Whatever comes, may I not be a castaway, but still be used by Thee through the Holy Ghost for Christ."'[15]

Remember, there is no restoration without repentance. Don't listen to teachers who offer peace and pardon without brokenness over sin and turning from it (Jer. 6:13-14). How does a backslidden sinner repent? By using the means of grace.

True Use of the Means of Grace

Hosea 14:2 says, 'Take with you words, and turn to the LORD: say unto him, Take away all iniquity, and receive us graciously: so will we render the calves of our lips.' This verse teaches us *how* to 'turn to the LORD,' namely, by using God's

---

15. F. B. Meyer, *The Christ-Life for Your Life* (Chicago: Moody Press, n.d.), p. 19.

Word ('words'), which leads us to pray for grace ('say unto him'), so that we can offer a sacrifice of praise ('the calves of our lips').

But these means of grace can become another means of backsliding when we use them as if they were a magic formula to conjure up God's power like a genie out of a bottle. God is absolutely free to work when and how He pleases. Rather, the means are a beautiful path where God meets with us and walks with us, and they become the tools God uses to rebuild our broken lives, helping us 'to preserve the soul from sin, and maintain its sweet and free communion with God.'[16]

1. The means of the Word of God

'Take with you words,' Hosea said. Using the Word of God, the Holy Spirit not only works faith in the hearts of God's elect, but when that faith has been compromised by falling into sin, restores it when we return to the Lord. The Word is essential to the child of God (James 1:18; 1 Pet. 2:2; Jer. 15:16; John 6:68).

We must go back to the Bible, hearing it preached weekly, reading through the Bible daily, sharing regular devotions with your family, learning a good catechism, and memorizing particular verses and passages. One discipline that underlies all the others is *meditation* on the Word, which is the serious setting of your mind on a truth so as to search it and settle it powerfully in your heart.[17] Meditation cultivates *spiritual mindedness*, where grace engages the heart with truth producing holy joy and contentment in God.[18] You might meditate on a Scripture addressing the topic backsliders (Jer. 2; Pss. 25, 32, 51, 130; Hosea 14), or God's character, or Christ's person and work, or the sinfulness of sin. Don't just chew on the Word; digest it and incorporate it into your life.

2. The means of prayer

Hosea 14:2 says, 'Take with you words, and turn to the LORD: say unto him, Take away all iniquity, and receive us graciously.' If we ask why God needs words, Sibbes answers 'It is true; God needs no words, but we do, to stir up our hearts and affections.'[19] So pray the Scriptures back to God. Gurnall wrote that 'Prayer is nothing but the promise reversed, or God's Word formed into an argument, and retorted by faith upon God again.'[20]

Above all that you ask, pray for the fullness of the Spirit. Jesus taught in Luke 11:11-13: 'If ye then, being evil, know how to give good gifts unto your children:

---

16. *The Whole Works of the Rev. John Flavel* (London: W. Baynes and Son, 1820), 5:423.

17. Thomas Hooker, *The Application of Redemption By the Effectual Work of the Word, and Spirit of Christ, for the bringing home of lost Sinners to God. The Ninth and Tenth Books* (London: Peter Cole, 1657), p. 210.

18. John Owen, *Works*, 7:270. For a much fuller explanation of the art of meditation, see 'The Puritan Practice of Meditation,' in Joel R. Beeke, *Puritan Reformed Spirituality* (Darlington: Evangelical Press, 2006), pp. 73-100.

19. Richard Sibbes, *Works*, 2:260.

20. William Gurnall, *The Christian in Complete Armour*, 2:88.

how much more shall your heavenly Father give the Holy Spirit to them that ask him?' The Holy Spirit is the daily food we need more than bread and meat.[21]

3. The means of public worship

The fruition of the Word and prayer in our lives will be public worship, offering praise to God. So 'the calves of our lips,' a reference to the Old Testament's priestly worship, are 'the sacrifice of praise to God continually, that is, the fruit of our lips giving thanks to his name' (Hosea 14:2; Heb. 13:15).

A body of believers worshipping God in the Spirit, rejoicing in Christ Jesus, and putting no confidence in the flesh (Phil 3:3), can be the means of your rescue from the pit. Asaph's soul almost slipped through envy of the wicked, but in the sanctuary of God he saw the doom of the wicked and tasted afresh the sweetness of God (Ps. 73).

Find a church that faithfully preaches the Bible. Become a member and pour your life into it as a living sacrifice to God. Quit complaining, and start serving with your time, supporting with your giving, and showing gratitude to your leaders and fellow members. Much backsliding could be avoided or remedied simply by faithful participation in a healthy church.

4. The means of afflictions

Trials are used by the hand of God to heal the souls of His backsliding people, to humble us and show us our wicked hearts (Deut. 8:2), and to turn us away from our adulterous love affair with this world so that we seek Him again: 'and she shall seek them, but shall not find them: then shall she say, I will go and return to my first husband; for then was it better with me than now' (Hosea 2:6-7).

Even spiritual desertion serves God's loving purpose (Ps. 28:1; Ps. 13:1). Hosea 5:15 says, 'I will go and return to my place, till they acknowledge their offence, and seek my face,' so we must respond to trials with submission, not resentment and rebellion (Heb. 12:5-7). If you are suffering under God's hand, then humble yourself, meditate on His character and your sin, and thank Him that He did not merely cast you into hell, but pursues your heart with relentless love.

If afflictions come, do not let your hearts be unmoved, but cry out all the more for deliverance, beginning by asking for broken hearts.

5. The means of human accountability

In our individualistic age, we tend to view our spiritual lives as our own concern, and no one else's business. One of the best ways to prevent backsliding or arrest it early in its progress is voluntary accountability with a friend who is willing to ask

---

21. For additional material on prayer, see James W. Beeke and Joel R. Beeke, *Developing a Healthy Prayer Life: 31 Meditations on Communing with God* (Grand Rapids: Reformation Heritage Books, 2010); Joel R. Beeke and Brian G. Najapfour, eds., *Taking Hold of God: Reformed and Puritan Perspectives on Prayer* (Grand Rapids: Reformation Heritage Books, 2011).

hard questions on a regular basis and to lovingly administer warnings and rebukes when he sees you starting to slip in a particular area of temptation (Heb. 3:13; 10:24-25; Prov. 27:5-6).

Also, your church has a responsibility to correct you privately, to rebuke you publicly, and even to remove you from membership if you do not repent of your sin (Matt. 18:15-18; Heb. 13:17). The aim of such correction is to restore you from your fall and help you bear your spiritual burdens (Gal. 6:1-2). Love your elders for their efforts to help you. Forgive the imperfections of how they do it (Ps. 141:5). Christ Himself is present in church censures, sovereignly disciplining you, so let exhortations drive you to Christ (Matt. 18:20; 1 Cor. 5:4). It may very well save your spirit on Judgment Day (1 Cor. 5:5). This leads us to consider the third aspect of returning to the Physician.

True Reaffirmation of Faith

Reaffirmation of faith is the core of returning to the Lord, for the backslider's fundamental problem is one of misplaced trust (Hosea 2:5, 8, 12; 10:13). In our adulterous love for the world, the knowledge of God grows dim and weak – indeed we reject knowing Him (Hosea 4:1, 6; 5:4; 6:6-7). Perhaps you might object, 'But my sin has nothing to do with trusting in the Lord. My backsliding is about sexual lust, or the love of money, or laziness, or stealing at my job, or anger, or rebellion against authority ... I'm not even thinking about God when I sin.'

However, not thinking about God *is* the problem, for we treat God as irrelevant, not really believing that He is the only Lord and Savior. The root of all sin is a failure to embrace God as our only God.[22] So all sin is trusting in idols.[23] The issue in all backsliding is 'the all-sufficiency of Yahweh, with the question perhaps put this way: Where does life, in all its richness and fullness come from? ... if it comes from Yahweh plus others, then one will spread one's allegiance around, because Yahweh alone is not enough.'[24]

God's solution to backsliding is to reunite us to Himself in covenantal knowledge: 'thou shalt know no god but me: for there is no saviour beside me' (Hosea 13:4, cf. 2:20). Despite all we think we know, the Lord wants us to know Him in a deeper way than we have ever known Him before, in a way that engages all of our trust and hope.

Such knowledge involves realizing the horrible offense of your sins against God and the infinite riches of grace in Jesus Christ: 'In thee the fatherless findeth mercy' (Hosea 14:3). Go to your covenant God even now and say, 'LORD, be merciful unto me: heal my soul; for I have sinned against thee' (Ps. 41:4).

---

22. Sibbes, *Works*, 2:286.

23. See Matthew 6:24; Ephesians 5:5 on materialism; and Romans 1:21-26 and 1 Thessalonians 4:5 on sexual immorality.

24. Raymond C. Ortlund, Jr., *Whoredom: God's Unfaithful Wife in Biblical Theology* (Eerdmans: Grand Rapids, 1996), p. 49.

RUNNERS RECEIVING THE MEDICINES OF GRACE

With the rise of medical technology, competitive athletics, and exercise for personal fitness, sports medicine developed many different kinds of treatments and programs to heal, restore, and strengthen injured athletes. When the Christian runner receives a spiritual injury and begins to backslide, there is but one remedy: he or she must return to the Physician for healing. The medicine which He applies to our souls is God's grace.

In the deepest sense, God's grace is Christ Himself (John 1:14). When the Holy Spirit reveals a way of escape in Jesus Christ— the Savior whose blood is sufficient so that it 'cleanseth us from *all* sin'—there is true, spiritual healing (1 John 1:7; Mal. 4:2).

God has made Christ everything to the believer: He is the answer to all our burdens and wanderings. Are we nothing but sin? Christ became sin on behalf of His people to redeem them from it (2 Cor. 5:21). Are we separated from God? Christ was forsaken by His Father as Judge so that we will never be forsaken by Him (Matt. 27:46). Are we unrighteousness itself? Christ is the all-righteous one, having merited perfect righteousness through active and passive obedience (Isa. 61:10). Are we cursed? Christ died the accursed death as Curse-Bearer of His elect (Gal. 3:13). Are we under Divine wrath? Christ merits, keeps, and applies peace (Isa. 53:5).

Are we foolish? Christ is Wisdom (Prov. 8). Are we filthy? Christ is 'holy, harmless, undefiled, separate from sinners' (Heb. 7:26). Are we prone to temptation? Christ was 'tempted in all points like as we are, yet without sin' (Heb. 4:15). Are we in spiritual bondage? In Christ there is liberty, for 'if the Son shall make you free, ye shall be free indeed' (John 8:36). Are we prayerless and thankless? Christ is the praying and thanking High Priest, sitting at the right hand of the Father, who never ceases to make intercession for His people (Rom. 8:34). Are we restless? Christ went without rest for thirty-three years, and now has entered in His rest (Ps. 132:8, Heb. 1:3), causing His people to rest in Him as their Prophet, Priest, and King who has paid for everything on their behalf (Psalm 110).

Christ's offices and natures form a medicine cabinet out of which the Holy Spirit is able to remedy every disease that afflicts God's people. Here we will consider the three-fold promise of Hosea 14:4, 'I will heal their backsliding, I will love them freely: for mine anger is turned away from him.' Let us find the spiritual healing of Christ in this verse to bind our wounds with an unbreakable bandage of three strands: sanctification, adoption, and justification.[25]

Sanctifying Grace

The Lord says in Hosea 14:4a, 'I will heal their backsliding.' So far in Hosea 14, the prophet has addressed the people and given them words to speak in prayer to

---

25. Cf. Westminster Shorter Catechism (Q. 32).

God. But now God begins to speak to His people with the precious 'I will' of His promise. We struggle with our wicked hearts, trying to bend them to return to Him, but we discover that our hearts are desperately sick and deceitful. So we come to God saying, 'I cannot!' But God replies, 'I will.'

This promise belongs to the backslidden Christian, not to the hypocrite. So do not rest on this promise while resting comfortably in sin; rest on this promise of healing while you long for restoration and strive to repent (Jer. 3:22). It is a promise of victory to the fighter, not security to the sleeper.

Sometimes believers do not understand that they need Christ for everything in the Christian life, even true, healing sanctification. We repent and use the means *in dependence upon Christ*. He is not merely the provider of our strength, but *is* our strength. He not only heals but *is* our health.

Child of God, has this Physician ever applied the wrong medicine for your spiritual diseases? Indeed, sometimes His healing acts are painful, especially when He insists, as faithful Physician, on probing the depth of the wound. Yet for all the pain caused by the remedy of sanctification, you can trust Christ completely. After all, He is applying medicine to His own body (Eph. 5:29-30). We are a part of Him. He is as tender with us as we would be with our own flesh (Eph. 5:31-32). If it feels as though we were dying, it is only because He aims to raise us from the dead.

Because of the promise, 'I will heal their backsliding,' all God's people will learn the paradoxical way of sanctification, the way of gain through loss. United with Christ, they too take up their crosses, deny themselves, and begin to die unto sin: 'He himself bore our sins in his body on the tree, that we might die to sin and live to righteousness. By his wounds you have been healed. For you were straying like sheep, but have now returned to the Shepherd and Overseer of your souls' (1 Pet. 2:24-25).

Adopting Grace

Hosea 14:4b says, 'I will love them freely,' expressing the infinite affection and eternal loyalty which leaps forth from God's heart when all judicial wrath has been satisfied, and nothing is left but love.

Hosea was a living image of this love in his redemption of his unfaithful wife (Hosea 3:1); it displayed God's conjugal love by which the divine Husband embraces and kisses His bride, covering all the shame of her past with the shining white dress which He purchased for her by His blood. Hosea also displays God's love as a grace of *adoption*: 'When Israel was a child, then I loved him, and called my son out of Egypt' (Hosea 11:1). His great heart of compassion makes it impossible for Him to reject His children (Hosea 11:3-4; 8-9).

So, is God's love a conjugal love or an adoptive love? The revelation of the Trinity answers this question with beautiful clarity. We are the children of the Father and the bride of the Son. When God the Son takes His people as His wife, God the Father looks upon His Son's bride and says, 'Welcome, my child, to my family.'

The grace of adoption is a means by which God heals the backslidden runners in His race, like the father in Christ's parable, running to His prodigal child the moment that child returns home, interrupting even our confessions of sin (Ps. 32:5) with showers of hugs, kisses, and calls for a big celebration. It is He who heals your backsliding and carries you home on His shoulders. Sibbes wrote, 'Hath God planted an affection in us to love our children freely; and shall not God much more, who gives this love and plants it in us, be admitted to love freely?'[26]

God's love becomes real to us as the Spirit of adoption testifies with our spirits that we are children of God (Rom. 8:15-16; 5:5; 15:13). The grace of being called a child of God is a magnet that will draw and hold firm the most wayward heart (1 John 3:1).

Justifying Grace

God will heal Israel's apostasy and overflow with affectionate love, 'For mine anger is turned away from him' (Hosea 14:4c). The word 'for' tips us off to the fact that the previous blessings of sanctification and adoption rest upon this mercy – that God's righteous anger has been turned away because the demands of His righteousness have been satisfied.[27] With respect to Christ's work on the cross, this is called *propitiation*, the turning away of God's wrath and the satisfaction of His justice by the payment of redemption's great price (Rom. 3:25-26; 1 John 2:2). With respect to the application of Christ's work to our lives, this is called *justification*.

There are important ways in which justification and sanctification differ. Justification declares the sinner righteous and holy once and for all in Christ; sanctification makes the sinner righteous and holy progressively as a fruit flowing from Christ. Justification takes away the guilt of sin (having to do with the legal state of the elect sinner); sanctification takes away the pollution of sin (having to do with his daily condition).

God may be at peace with us, fully satisfied with His Son's work, but because of willful and persistent sin we might not perceive nor feel that peace. This is one reason why we must daily pray, 'Forgive us our debts,' knowing that 'if we confess our sins, he is faithful and just to forgive us our sins, and to cleanse us from all unrighteousness' (1 John 1:7–2:2). Christians need daily, sometimes hourly, to confess their sins to God and renew their dependence upon Christ's all-sufficient sacrifice and intercession. We should not sin, but we do sin, and so we must wash our consciences in the blood of Christ and count ourselves clean, trusting that 'the Lord fully, freely, and at once forgives the backsliding child who turns to Him, and says, with David, – "I have sinned."'[28]

---

26. Sibbes, *Works*, 2:317.

27. McComiskey, 'Hosea,' in *Minor Prophets*, 1:232.

28. Samuel Waldegrave, 'The Backslider Forgiven and Chastised,' in *Words of Eternal Life* (London: William Hunt and Co., 1864), p. 278.

Why do those who have backslidden feel such bitterness and deadness in their hearts? It is because they have forfeited their experience of peace with God by cherishing sin. We are not saved by works, but our assurance of justification is connected to our faithfulness (1 John 2:2-3).

Do you wish for a full consciousness of your acquittal so that you can boldly say, 'I am righteous in Christ, before God, and an heir of eternal life'?[29] Return to your God through repentance, the use of the means, and reaffirmation of your faith. God delights to comfort His people.

A Call to Return

Because of the grace of justification, adoption, and sanctification, Christ becomes everything to us – the Alpha and Omega (Rev. 1:8), the Author and Finisher of our faith (Heb. 12:2), the Horn of salvation (Luke 1:69), the Lord of lords (Rev. 17:14), and our Redeemer and Savior (Isa. 59:20; 1 Tim. 4:10). Should we not seek such great blessings from the Lord with longing, hunger, and expectant waiting? When we stumble and backslide, let us go to Him again for the medicines of grace.

RUNNERS RECOVERING BY THE HEALING OF GRACE

When Laura Wilkinson stood atop the diving platform in the final round of her Olympic competition in 2000, she was in eighth place, behind other divers who had performed impeccably, and she still bore the pain of an injured foot, broken six months prior to the Olympic Games. So as she looked down at the water ten meters below her, she had every reason to be discouraged.

Nevertheless, Wilkinson did her dive and, when the finals were done, she walked away with the gold medal, saying, 'I can do all things through Christ who strengthens me.'

Christian, it may be that your spiritual life has taken a fall: your sin may have broken your heart, dishonored your Lord, and damaged your ability to walk with God. But Christ can heal your soul, and by His grace, you can recover from your fall: you can do all things through Christ. God makes glorious promises to bring His people to full recovery.

Reviving Grace

Continuing in Hosea 14, we read the promise, 'I will be as the dew unto Israel ...' (v. 5). This promise in agricultural imagery assures us that God will give Himself to His people so that they will flourish spiritually under His grace. When God comes, He comes like 'the dew,' refreshing, renewing, invigorating, bringing life, growth, beauty, and fragrance. God's people will revive and become stably rooted and fragrantly beautiful (vv. 6-7). His gracious presence always changes us. His love makes us lovely. His life makes us lively.

---

29. Heidelberg Catechism, Q. 59.

Images of water (the "dew") in Scripture often refer to the third person of the Trinity, the Holy Spirit (Isa. 32:2, 15; 44:1-5; John 7:37-39). *To be filled afresh with the Holy Spirit's graces* is the great need and secret of all personal healing and spiritual revival. Through the graces poured out by the Spirit on backsliding believers, they are effectually renewed, and their backsliding souls are restored.

Dear backsliding believer, seek the Spirit's saving graces earnestly and believingly (Ps. 72:6). Reynolds wrote that 'God delights to have his people beg great things of him, to implore the performance of "exceeding great and precious promises" (2 Pet. 1:4); to pray for a share in "the unsearchable riches of Christ," to know things which pass knowledge, and to "be filled with all the fulness of God" (Eph. 3:8, 18, 19).'[30] We should have big dreams, big desires, and big prayer requests for our spiritual growth. God is able to do far more abundantly that we can ask or even imagine (Eph. 3:20). Imitate Paul by praying his grand prayers for spiritual growth (like those of Eph. 1:15-23; 3:14-21) for yourself, your family, your church, your seminary, and the churches of all nations.[31] Cultivate your hope in God's reviving grace. Don't settle for being a spiritual tumbleweed.

Sovereign Grace

Hosea 14:8 says, 'Ephraim shall say, What have I to do any more with idols? I have heard him, and observed him: I am like a green fir tree. From me is thy fruit found.' The essence of backsliding is a descent into the whirlpool of idolatry. Idolatry denies the sovereignty and sufficiency of God, imagining that a fruitful life requires something in addition to God.

Fruitfulness stands at the heart of our calling and identity as God's people. Israel was supposed to be God's vineyard bearing fruit for righteousness (Isa. 5:1-7). The very name 'Ephraim' means fruitful (Gen. 41:52). If the heart of backsliding is idolatry, then the heart of returning to the Lord is realizing that Christ is everything. The Lord is the sovereign dew that makes the vine to flourish, and He is the sovereign vine that fills the earth with fruit.

Christ is all. Christ is perfect God and perfect man. He is the Priest and the sacrifice. He became our curse and now is our blessing. He is the Prophet and the Word. He is the King and the Servant. He is the Mediator of the covenant and the essence of the covenant. He is the Way, the Truth, and the Life. He is the Bread we eat to live. He is the Shepherd and the One who laid down His life as the Lamb of God. He is our wisdom, righteousness, sanctification, and redemption. We trust in Him, love Him, and hope in His glorious appearance. He is our treasure, exceeding joy, and very great reward. We must embrace Him as our everything. He says to us still, 'From me is thy fruit found.'

---

30. Edward Reynolds, 'An Explication of the Fourteenth Chapter of Hosea,' in Burroughs, et al., *Hosea*, p. 658.

31. A helpful resource here is D. A. Carson, *A Call to Spiritual Reformation: Priorities from Paul and His Prayers* (Grand Rapids: Baker, 1992).

The Path of Restoration or the Pit of Destruction

Hosea 14:9 concludes the prophet's words with this appeal: 'Who is wise, and he shall understand these things? Prudent, and he shall know them? For the ways of the LORD are right, and the just shall walk in them: but the transgressors shall fall therein.'

Will we receive the wisdom God offers to backsliders? If we do, then we shall find a path of healing that leads us upward to glory. But if we despise God's advice, our backsliding will prove to be apostasy from the faith and we will die in our sins. Either way, God will be vindicated and glorified: 'for the ways of the LORD are right.'

In what condition is your soul? What is your trajectory – the path of restoration or the pit of destruction?

(1) *Are you a total stranger of the life of grace?* Then how poor you are! If God does not prevent it, you will appear one day before His judgment throne without an intercessor between you and an angry God, Christless and hopeless forever. Sinner, your need is urgent. Fly quickly to God's throne. No sinner, however vile, whose only plea is Jesus' blood, will ever be turned away from His presence.

(2) *Are you backsliding so far from God that you doubt that God ever began the good work of saving you?* Perhaps you groan, 'Oh, to return to the times when gospel sermons were the food of my soul, and secret prayer was kept up with delight. Now a guilty conscience, hard heart, and prayerless life have taken the place of everything I once thought I enjoyed.' Then you must pray, 'Lord, if this is Thy work within me, confirm it; if not, show me the truth, and begin thy saving work in me .... "turn thou me, and I shall be turned" (Jer. 31:18).'

(3) *Are you a backslider who cannot deny having been a subject of divine, sovereign grace, but yet you know that you are presently not in the right place before God?* Seek a full return. Avoid the sin of being only slightly affected with sin so as to be healed incompletely: 'give up your guilty sins, renounce all dependence upon finite help, and fall into the arms of your injured yet still tender and gracious Savior.'[32]

(4) *Are you a child of God who can honestly say you are not currently in a condition of 'perpetual backsliding' (Jer. 8:5), but rather, precious restoration (Psa. 23:3)?* Guard your revival of soul with a holy jealousy. Remember that you are still in a state of imperfection, snares, and dangers. You are not yet beyond the reach of temptation; fresh temptations may lead you to fall into the same sorrowful condition from which you recently emerged, except divine grace interpose to aid you.

This is sanctification: feeling more than ever the strength of sin and the weakness of the flesh, and knowing painfully what it is to be left to yourself. 'Hold up my goings in Thy paths, that my footsteps slip not' (Ps. 17:5).

---

32. Charles D. Mallary, *Soul Prosperity: Its Nature, Its Fruits, and Its Culture* (1860; repr., Harrisonburg, Va.: Sprinkle Publications, 1999), p. 348.

FINAL WORD TO CHRISTIAN RUNNERS

Christ faced nothing less than the cross and its shame. He let go of all dreams and desires of worldly success. He was stripped of all His earthly honor, all His human dignity, even the most basic human rights.

Darkness came upon Him, not just darkness in the skies but darkness in the soul, such that He cried out, 'My God, my God, why hast thou forsaken me?'

But Christ despised the pain and humiliation of the cross for the joy set before Him. He did not run the race for Himself but for us! He was bringing many sons to glory.

When we contemplate His agonies of body and soul, we see how very little it takes to make us stumble and turn away from obedience. How often have we sinned for the slightest pleasure, or to avoid the smallest disdain from men? But in the very contrast between our weakness and His strength we find hope.

Look to Him, and keep putting one foot in front of the other. And when your heart says, 'I can't do it; I'm too weak,' look at the great cloud of witnesses who have gone ahead of you (Heb. 12:1). They too were weak: Abraham, Moses, David, Peter, and others. They too stumbled. But by faith they ran the race. By faith they received strength. By faith they got back up when they fell down, and pressed on. By faith, you can do the same.

Christian runner, run the race to the end!

HOLINESS DISTORTED

CHAPTER 25

ERRONEOUS BELIEFS ON HOLINESS IN BIBLE HISTORY

ALMOST all good things have their imitations. Imitations can be attractive because they are usually cheaper than the original. To the untrained or unsuspecting eye, imitations appear to be genuine, and what is worthless can appear as having value. Sometimes imitations are harmless, but other times imitations can be most harmful. Occasionally when hunting, I will use a decoy that looks like the real thing to lure a deer into what seems to be, even to its keen senses, a safe place. But it is anything but a safe place for the deer; it is fatal.

Nowhere is imitation more dangerous than in religion. A bogus religion may be cheap and even give the appearance of being genuine, but it is a dangerously and eternally expensive alternative to genuine Christianity. Consider the time when Jesus was traveling from Bethany to Jerusalem, and He became hungry. He saw a fig tree in the distance that was full of leaves and the prospect of fruit. As the Lord approached the tree, it became clear that the tree that flaunted fruit was fruitless. He cursed the tree, and it withered away (Matt. 21:17-19). This episode has a spiritual parallel. There are those who bear some resemblance to having true faith, but like the fig tree they have no substance. Ultimately, trees are judged by their fruit, not their foliage (Matt. 7:16); and so it is that the heart rather than the appearance bears the evidence of true godliness. Tragically, it is possible to have a form of godliness without its power (2 Tim. 3:5), drawing near to the Lord with verbal pretense but with hearts distant from Him (Isa. 29:13).

The spiritually dangerous error of counterfeit religion is an all too common malady that takes many different forms. Three particular expressions of this error stand out in the Bible's history and have all too familiar manifestations in today's world.

ERROR 1: HOLINESS ATTEMPTED WITHOUT A MEDIATOR

Notwithstanding the many ways God revealed the truth of the gospel to ancient Israel, some were slow to learn it and some of the nation never got it. Displaying their spiritual ignorance, some in Israel had faulty notions about who God was, His holiness, His absolutely inflexible righteousness, and His amazingly sovereign grace. That ignorance displayed itself in various attempts to approach God apart from His revealed will. The narrative surrounding Korah's rebellion (Numbers 16–17) underscores the necessity of approaching God on His terms and the consequences of attempting to satisfy His holy demands by following one's own devices or relying on self-perceived merit. To be wrong on this point precludes any possibility of salvation. It is the fundamental truth of biblical religion that without holiness, seeing God is impossible, and without Christ, holiness—whether positional or progressive—is impossible.[1] There is but one Mediator between God and men, and that unique Mediator is Jesus Christ (1 Tim. 2:5). Moses reminded the people then that what happened to Korah was to be a sign for them (Num. 26:10), and Jude's reference to this event in his warnings against those who denied the Lord Jesus Christ indicates that this error did not end with Korah (Jude 4, 11). Lessons from the pit, the plague, and the bud vividly picture the error of attempting holiness without the Mediator of God's choosing. The story pictures the principle and points to the truth.

The Lesson from the Pit

The tragic scene that unfolds in Numbers 16:11-40 points to the necessity of the divinely chosen Mediator. The story begins with defiance and deliberate disobedience by two hundred and fifty eminent men led by Korah, Dathan, and Abiram, all of whom thought more highly of themselves than they ought and boldly rebelled against the God-ordained leadership of Moses and Aaron (16:1-3). Seemingly, they were not satisfied with their status and wanted more (16:9-10). Korah was a Levite responsible for the care of the tabernacle's sacred furniture, but he was not a priest. Dathan and Abiram were descendants of Reuben, Jacob's oldest son, but they did not enjoy the 'firstborn' preeminence among the tribes because of their ancestor's sin (Gen. 49:3-4).[2]

Rejecting the divine appointment of Moses and Aaron to their respective offices, the rebels charged Moses and Aaron with self-promotion (16:3). Undeniably, Moses and Aaron occupied weighty offices of great consequence, but the significance of their appointment went beyond their person to the function of foreshadowing the one and only Mediator between God and men, the Messiah Himself. Moses

---

1. 'Subsequent events demonstrate so frighteningly the dangers inherent in being called to be a holy nation that the survivors cry out for a priestly ministry that will act as mediator between them and God' (Gordon J. Wenham, *Numbers*, Tyndale Old Testament Commentaries [Downers Grove, Ill.: InterVarsity, 1981], p. 134).

2. 'As a southsider, part of the leading clan of the Levites, [Korah] didn't really want all social order eliminated .... While declaring all Israelites sacred before the Lord, what he really wanted was access for himself to the group that would be above the rest, the priesthood (16:10). Likewise, the Reubenites held a privileged place in the Israelite community; yet that was not enough for them. It still rankled them that their premier first place as firstborn of Jacob's sons had been stripped away because of Reuben's sins' (Iain Duguid, *Numbers: God's Presence in the Wilderness*, Preaching the Word [Wheaton, Ill.: Crossway, 2006], pp. 201-2).

anticipated the ideal Prophet who would come after him (Deut. 18:15). 'The office of Aaron the High Priest pointed especially to the unique office of Christ that God appointed and accredited: 'And no man taketh this honour unto himself, but he that is called of God, as was Aaron. So also Christ glorified not himself to be made an high priest, but he that said unto him, Thou art my Son ... saith also in another place, Thou art a priest for ever after the order of Melchisedec' (Heb. 5:4-6). So, for these rebels to reject Moses and Aaron was to circumvent God's order, assuming that they could approach the Holy God on their own without the appointed mediator.

The conflict led to a challenge with devastating consequences. Moses challenged Korah and his followers to put fire and incense in their censers (small pans) and to come before the Lord. Aaron was to do the same, and the Lord would make it clear whom He had chosen (16:5-18). The rebels presumed that they could get to the Lord on their own, so in their prideful ignorance they accepted the challenge; here was their 'chance.' Their using their own censers and incense was a picture of every gesture of self-righteous work and effort that finds all too many parallels even today. Many 'fill their censers' with tradition, heritage, church attendance, observation of the sacraments, or legalistic practices and trust in their own efforts to achieve the holiness essential to seeing God. Self-satisfaction tends to the supposition that God will be satisfied as well. In reality, self-satisfaction is self-deception.[3]

The consequences were severe. As Korah stood at the door of the tabernacle and the glory of the Lord appeared (16:19), it seemed at first sight that he may have been right. But it soon became evident that the divine glory would manifest itself in judgment, not salvation. Moses implored the congregation to take sides, either with Korah or Aaron (16:26). God's wrath was about to be let loose in a unique way, confirming that these rebels had provoked the Lord. Some were buried alive as the earth opened to swallow them (16:29-34), and others were consumed with fire (16:35). It had to have been a horrific scene. The dust of the disturbed earth and the smoke and stink of burning flesh proclaimed an unmistakable message.[4] It is no wonder that Moses said that 'they became a sign' (26:10). The people were to look and learn.

The point of this graphic picture highlights the necessity of the divinely chosen mediator. Two truths stand out. First, man cannot approach God on his own. Man's sin is too great, God's holiness is too restrictive, and God's righteousness is too demanding for man to come alone. Remember the rich young ruler who encountered Jesus. He was as good as he could be, but not good enough (Matthew 19). Second, the punishment for standing alone before God is eternally severe. The people's cry

---

3. 'Moses proposes that all who claim such a holy status should demonstrate it by undertaking a priestly task, the offering of incense. Since two of Aaron's sons had died for offering fire which the LORD had not commanded (Lv. 10:1-2), Korah's alacrity in submitting to this test is striking' (Wenham, *Numbers*, p. 135).

4. 'Those who believed Korah's words would inevitably find death instead of the freedom that he claimed it would bring. That is always the way it is with sin: it offers freedom to those who are "liberated" from God's Law, but in the end all it delivers is death' (Duguid, *Numbers*, p. 205).

timelessly rings true for all who attempt to do so: 'Behold we die, we perish, we all perish. Whosoever cometh anything near unto the tabernacle of the LORD shall die: shall we be consumed with dying?' (17:12-13). The death of the rebels was unusual and inescapable; but physical death is the least of concerns. Jesus said, 'Fear not them which kill the body, but are not able to kill the soul: but rather fear him which is able to destroy both soul and body in hell,' and 'Whosoever shall deny me before men, him will I also deny before my Father which is in heaven' (Matt. 10:28, 33). There is no hope without Jesus, the only Mediator able to reconcile unholy sinners to the holy God.[5]

The Lesson from the Plague

The people's reaction to the rebels' horrific punishment, the consequent plague, and Aaron's interference point to the efficacy of the chosen mediator (16:41-50). Notwithstanding the unmistakable visible sermon signified by the lingering dust from the massive grave and the putrid stench from the charred remains of those consumed, the people who witnessed it didn't all get the message. The next day after the drama of the burial and burning, the people complained to Moses that the 'the people of the Lord' had been unjustly executed (16:41). Their faulty view of Korah and his followers as good people betrayed a faulty view of the Lord. Their accusation reflected their notions that the way of the Lord was not fair, that His demands were too restrictive, and that His sentence was too harsh. They still did not comprehend how holy God is and how sinful men are.

Their sympathy for the rebels was tantamount to agreeing with them and thus earned them another display of God's glory and wrath (16:42, 45). The Lord told Moses to get away from the congregation because He was going to put an end to them quickly. This time His judgment was a plague. The Hebrew term refers generally to some kind of blow or affliction. But whatever it was, it was devastatingly swift as 14,700 people were slain immediately (16:46, 49). The lesson was clear again that God was and is inflexibly intolerant of any rejection of His chosen mediator.

Not only does the narrative repeat the truth regarding the necessity of a mediator, it reinforces that need by demonstrating the efficacy of the mediator's work. As soon as Moses saw that the judgment had begun, he rushed to appeal to grace, instructing Aaron, the priestly mediator, to take incense and make an atonement for the transgressors (16:46). Aaron did so, and with the smoke from his censer wafting heavenward 'he stood between the dead and the living' (16:48). What happened next was amazing: 'the plague was stayed,' literally, the pestilence was brought to a halt. The plague, the pouring out of God's wrath, could not get past Aaron. Aaron's interference worked!

---

5. 'Only the one whom God had chosen could draw near to him. There is no truth in the claim that all roads lead to God. Apart from the one he has chosen, all roads lead to a consuming fire' (Duguid, *Numbers*, p. 206).

It does not require much spiritual insight to get the point of this picture. Aaron's activity draws a direct line to the ministry of Christ, the ideal Priest and Mediator. By nature, all men are children of disobedience and are under the sentence of just condemnation. But God in grace sent His Son to make atonement, the only means by which His wrath could be appeased, His justice satisfied, sin cleansed, and man saved. Christ and the power of His cross stands between the believer and the curse, and God's wrath cannot get past the cross.[6] In making atonement, Christ took the full force of God's wrath for all those He represented. Christ's sacrifice was successful; here is the efficacy of Christ's mediation. Our only hope is to have Christ stand between us and God. Christ took to Himself the iniquity of His people; and His people experience the saving benefits of His holy righteousness. The successful cross, therefore, is where the pursuit of practical holiness must begin.

The Lesson from the Bud

The budding rod of Numbers 17 puts a halt to this exposé of the error of attempting holiness without a mediator by confirming the uniqueness of the divinely chosen mediator. Representatives from each tribe were to write their names on their rods and to bring them to the tabernacle and left overnight there. Aaron was to write his name on the rod of Levi. The rod that blossomed would be evidence verifying God's choice of priestly mediator. When Moses checked the rods on the next day, 'behold, the rod of Aaron for the house of Levi was budded, and brought forth buds, and bloomed blossoms, and yielded almonds' (17:8). Heaven's confirmation settled the matter once and for all as to whom God had chosen for this office. The budded rod was then to be kept as a token reminder of the uniqueness of God's choice of Aaron (Heb. 5:4). Remarkably, the rod was kept inside the ark (17:10; Heb. 9:4), a place where none could look but the Lord Himself. His covenant choice was always before Him.

The point of the picture underscores the uniqueness of the mediating priesthood of Christ. He is the eternal Priest by irrevocable decree (Ps. 110:4; Heb. 5) and the only Mediator between God and men (1 Tim. 2:5). God's choice of Aaron foreshadowed His choice of His Son over Aaron himself. The rod's seclusion in the ark, a climactic picture of God's immediate presence, declares that the central work of Christ is Godward, first as the sacrifice by which He entered the holy place (Heb. 9:12), and then by His continuing in God's presence for the sake of His people (Heb. 9:24). God sees His Son, and the glorified scars of His atonement, and remembers the covenant. All is well because of the necessary, successful, and unique Mediator.[7]

---

6. 'Israel's high priest *stood between the living and the dead* until *the plague stopped* (48), an arresting picture of an infinitely greater Mediator. God's Son entered a rebellious world where people were indifferent to the power and the consequences of sin, and its effects infinitely worse than the deadliest plague, but he *made atonement for them* (47). By his sacrificial death upon the cross, he stands between the living and the dead' (Raymond Brown, *The Message of Numbers*, The Bible Speaks Today [Downers Grove, Ill.: InterVarsity, 2002], p. 150).

7. 'There at the cross we see the true wideness of God's mercy. He does not admit all into his presence indiscriminately, ignoring their sin. Rather, he welcomes in all kinds of sinners as they trust in Christ and have their sins paid for at the cross. The way of salvation is as wide and as narrow as Christ. There

It is wise to learn from the mistakes of others. The dust from Korah's divinely dug grave has settled long ago and the stench of the rebels' charred flesh has dissipated, but the warning regarding their fatal error has been preserved for our admonition (see 1 Corinthians 10). The wandering Israelites were to look and learn, and so must we.

ERROR 2: HOLINESS MISTAKEN AS RELIGION

In one of His frequent exchanges with the Pharisees, the Lord Jesus said, 'In vain they do worship me' (Matt. 15:9; Mark 7:7). The sad danger is that vain worship is possible. Worshipping in vain is worshipping without purpose or result, in emptiness and deception. Two factors mark this worthless worship. First, it abandons God's directives in favor of man's traditions: 'Thus have ye made the commandment of God of none effect by your traditions ... teaching for doctrines the commandments of men' (Matt. 15:6, 9; see also Mark 7:7-8). Second, it is talk without heart: 'This people draweth nigh unto me with their mouth, and honoureth me with their lips; but their heart is far from me' (Matt. 15:8; Mark 7:6). That Christ quotes this indictment from Isaiah 29:13 indicates that it was not just a Pharisaical flaw. Heartless religion was possible in the Old Testament dispensation; it was rampant in the days of Christ's earthly incarnation; unhappily, it pervades even the best of churches today. God has never been and will never be satisfied with heartless worship.[8]

Tragically, the notion seems to be deeply ingrained in man that formal acts of worship—whatever form they take—constitute legitimate acts of holiness that will by their very performance be accepted by God. Men tend to form their opinions of God from their estimations of themselves. Because they satisfy themselves with outward acts of ritual, they assume that God must be satisfied as well. Many people today who are without Christ assume that going to church and keeping the golden rule will somehow work to their favor in the end. Even many who profess Christ allow their pious religious routines to substitute for personal holiness and a sincere heart. To conceive of God in this way is either to question His omniscience—that He is able to see the heart, or His moral perfection—that He cares about the heart. In contrast to all this human reasoning is the divine preference for heart obedience over manual religion: 'Behold, to obey is better than sacrifice' (1 Sam. 15:22).

Nonetheless, some are so convinced that their 'worship' works that they cannot fathom the notion that it does not. The Lord's incontestable indictment of Israel's heartless religion recorded in Micah 6 illustrates this unfounded confidence. The

---

at the cross, fearful rebels find peace with the Lord whom they spurned, in spite of their sin, and are safely drawn into intimate fellowship with him through Christ' (Duguid, *Numbers*, pp. 215-16).

8. 'This was the problem with Israel's attitude toward the Lord. They would offer burnt offerings, year-old calves, thousands of rams, and tens of thousands of rivers of oil. But they would not offer God what he asked for: themselves, their hearts, their undivided faith, their unfeigned devotion' (Richard Phillips, *Jonah and Micah*, Reformed Expository Commentary [Phillipsburg, NJ: P&R, 2010], p. 293).

nation defended itself against God's accusation by arguing that if God was not satisfied with what they were doing, it was His fault for not making His expectations clear. They claimed that they were willing to offer any sacrifice He wanted; all He had to do was ask: 'Wherewith shall I come before the LORD, and bow myself before the high God? shall I come before him with burnt offerings, with calves of a year old? Will the LORD be pleased with thousands of rivers of oil? shall I give my firstborn for my transgression, the fruit of my body for the sin of my soul?' (Micah 6:6-7). Their self-justifying questions concerning how to approach and satisfy God reveal both the false conception that external religion is enough to please Him and the frustration of not knowing how much is enough. This dilemma always plagues those who assume that outward displays of religion or personal deprivations please God. Since there can never be any certainty that enough has been done, the cyclical solution is to do more and more. Their quandary is evident in the intensification of their offers, ranging from the best of the animal sacrifices (calves of a year old) to exaggerated quantities of sacrifices (thousands of rams and ten thousand rivers of oil), to the desperate abomination of child sacrifice. Their willingness to stoop to heathen practice in order to reach the heights of God reveals their total ignorance not only of what God wants but of who God is. Ironically, rather than defending itself, Israel further incriminated itself by assuming God wanted things rather than hearts.

Condemning heartless religion as a substitute for personal and genuine piety was a common rebuke from the Old Testament prophets (see for instance, Isaiah 1; Hosea 6; Amos 4, 5; Jeremiah 7; Ezekiel 8). They preached against it so often because external religion can be so deceptive, breeding a sense of unfounded real security. The 'religious' tend to be the most difficult to reach with truth because they believe their religious rituals make all well. I want to reflect on this error from one of Jeremiah's great sermons. Often designated as the 'temple sermon,' this message in Jeremiah 7 cuts to the quick as it issues the warning against this serious danger.

Existence of the Error

Perhaps one of the most salient and sobering lessons from this temple sermon is that this problem can exist in the best places. The Lord instructed Jeremiah to 'stand in the gate of the LORD's house' (Jer. 7:2). As his pulpit platform, Jeremiah most likely used the steps on the south side of the temple leading up to one of the chief gates through which the people entered to worship. The point is sobering. This was not a message directed either to pagans or to the rabble in the back streets and alleys of Jerusalem or even to religious renegades. On the contrary, it was directed to the most outwardly religious segment of society. If I may put it in these terms, it was directed to respectable churchgoers who were members of the most conservative and orthodox church in town. Not only were these people going to the right place, but they were going for the right reason, too: 'to worship the LORD' (v. 2). They entered the temple gates with the pretense of bowing down before the Lord, giving

God His due. From the outside everything looked right: people in the right place doing the right things. That Jeremiah exhorted these worshippers to repent (v. 3) makes it all too clear that worship ritual does not guarantee that the worshipper is right with God. Mechanical worship is but a thin disguise for the hypocrite, and no church is exempt – no matter how right the rituals.[9]

Expression of the Error

With prophetic precision and inspired insight, Jeremiah identified two expressions of hypocrisy among his parishioners. First, the hypocritical worshippers affirmed a false creed. In other words, they believed the wrong thing – their theology was wrong. The threefold repetition of the phrase 'the temple of the LORD' expresses the unorthodox confession of faith of the seemingly orthodox worshippers (Jer. 7:4). The repetition of this 'temple theology' may have had some superstitious significance, as though by their saying it over and over, it would become true and ward off danger; or it may simply have signified the zeal and fervor with which they affirmed the creed. Regardless of why the statement was repeated, it evidences a misplaced confidence in the structure rather than the spiritual substance of the temple.[10] The temple was the sign of God's presence, and there was a long history of God's protecting His dwelling place against every enemy. Even the inspired songs of worship celebrated the Lord's special love of Zion and the certain hope that He would protect it (see, for instance, Pss. 69:35; 74:2; 76:2; 78:68; 129:5). Seemingly against all odds, God preserved His dwelling place against the Assyrians (2 Kings 18–19), so there was no reason to assume He would not spare it from the Babylonians, regardless of what Jeremiah threatened. The 'temple theology' attributed something magical to the place where the Lord had chosen to dwell. They apparently assumed that if they could keep God 'happy' by giving Him what they thought He wanted in the temple ceremonies, He would stay and all would be well. They expressed confidence in tradition, in location, and in practice, but not in the Lord Himself.

Second, the false creed gave expression to a false trust. Jeremiah declared that they were trusting 'lying words, that cannot profit' (Jer. 7:8; see also 7:4). The word 'trust' implies a feeling of strong confidence and safety in its object. But regardless

---

9. 'What boldness this action takes – a boldness surely perceived by most onlookers as arrogance, irreverence, or even outright delusion. How dare this lone prophet confront "all you people of Judah"! How dare he denounce and warn Yahweh's faithful worshipers! What effrontery! Yet these people who have so piously come to the temple to worship the Lord are also worshiping idols and are guilty of every kind of moral and social sin. As Malbim states, they suppose that the sacrifices and acts of worship are the very essence of what pleases the Lord' (Tremper Longman III and David E. Garland, eds., *Jeremiah and Ezekiel*, The Expositor's Bible Commentary, rev. ed., vol. 7 [Grand Rapids: Zondervan, 2010], p. 159).

10. 'Certainly the simple statement that these buildings are the Lord's temple is neither false nor misleading. What is false and deceptive is the wrong set of conclusions associated with that statement: first, that the very act of worshiping at the temple somehow vouchsafes God's favor; second, that the existence of the Lord's holy temple in their city and nation makes them special in God's sight; and third, the fact that the temple is standing and not destroyed guarantees their safety and reinforces their beliefs in the inviolability of Jerusalem' (Longman and Garland, *Jeremiah and Ezekiel*, p. 160).

of how safe they felt, they were not safe at all because they were trusting, literally, 'the words of the lie' (vv. 4, 8). Referring to something that is empty, worthless, and consequently futile, the word for 'lie' underscores a vital lesson about faith and trust: the *object* of faith determines the *value* of faith. It is not the fact of faith that saves; it is the object of faith that saves. That is, the object of faith saves when and only if the object is the Lord, His Word, and His Christ. These people trusted the temple with its external rituals without internalizing the divinely intended message of the rituals. That they trusted is without dispute; *what* they trusted was without power to save. There is always the danger of having a form of godliness without the experience of its power (see 2 Tim. 3:5). Religion, as I've said before, can be dangerously deceptive.

Exhibition of the Error

The disconnect between 'religious life' and 'real life' is a common mark of hypocrisy. Hypocrites tend to assume that religious activity earns them the freedom to live without restraint and with impunity. Jeremiah's temple congregation annunciated that assumption in these terms: 'We are delivered to do all these abominations' (Jer. 7:10). Notwithstanding their consistent worship in the temple, their lifestyle exhibited a disregard for God's law and a light regard for God's holiness. The list of crimes of which they were guilty violated both divisions of the Decalogue (v. 9 – theft, murder, adultery, false oaths, idolatry, and polytheism). True religion produces a desire in the heart to walk in holiness; life must correspond to profession. The apostle John concurs with the prophet Jeremiah in his assessment of those who live incongruously to their profession: 'If we say that we have fellowship with him, and walk in darkness, we lie, and do not the truth' (1 John 1:6). How one views the law of God is always an index to the genuineness of his religion. Obedience will never be perfect, but it is always the outgrowth of true trust.

How one regards the law of God is a reflection of how one regards the Lord Himself. Coming to stand before the Lord in His holy temple and claiming deliverance or sanction to sin (Jer. 7:10) exhibits a spiritual callousness and insensitivity to the holiness of God, a holiness which demands cleanness of hands and purity of heart for all who would approach the divine presence (Ps. 24:3-4). The very fact that they went through the motions of worship while at the same time blatantly transgressing God's law betrays a low estimation of who the Lord really is. Worshipping in the fear of God fosters daily living in the fear of God. True worship always connects with life.

Exposure of the Error

'The LORD is in his holy temple, the LORD's throne is in heaven: his eyelids try, the children of men' (Ps. 11:4). Indeed, 'all things are naked and opened unto the eyes of him with whom we have to do' (Heb. 4:13). Heartless, external, and hypocritical worship may satisfy the worshipper and impress the observer, but the Lord sees it for what it is and will deal with it according to His infallible knowledge and inflexible judgment.

Jeremiah 7:11 records some of the most sobering words of the passage: 'Is this house, which is called by my name, become a den of robbers in your eyes? Behold, even I have seen it, saith the LORD.' Although the temple should have been a most sacred place because it was hallowed by God's name, it had become a cave of thieves, a hideout for bandits. The imagery is telling. I must confess that every time I read this text I think of my youth when I would listen to the tales of the Lone Ranger. As I recall, the Butch Cavendesh gang caused constant havoc in the territory patrolled by the Lone Ranger and Tonto. Butch and his gang would rob a train or a bank or commit some other dastardly deed and then retreat to their secluded hideout for safety. So long as they could make it to the hideout, they were exempt from the arm of the law. Not even the Lone Ranger knew where the gang hid out. This is the analogy of the text. Israel would commit every conceivable crime on the outside (v. 9) and then retreat to the temple claiming to be delivered (v. 10). The temple was their place of refuge, their hideout, where they would be exempt from the demands and penalty of the law. But unlike the Lone Ranger, the Lord declared 'I have seen it' (v. 11). He knew right where they were, and the temple was no place of safety for them. Sadly, Israel's notion persists. Many today have turned church or the place of prayer into a hideout, assuming that no matter what they do everything will be okay if they can just get to church or say 'sorry' at bedtime prayer. But God is still incapable of being fooled; He still sees. Religion provides no refuge for hypocrites.

Not only does God know all about hypocritical worship, but He constantly warned against it and consistently judged it. The Lord reminded the people that He had been 'rising up early and speaking,' and that He had called to them without their hearing or answering (v. 13). 'Rising up early' is a Hebrew idiom that refers not to the time of action but rather to the zeal and fervency with which an action occurs. The divine warning against heartless religion was a high priority and a common component of inspired preaching from the days of Moses right through to the days of Jeremiah. The priority of the message has never diminished and therefore remains relevant. The hope is that those who hear the warning will heed it.

To illustrate His consistency in judging hypocrisy, the Lord gave a history lesson. Just as all of Israel's history serves as an example for us in this dispensation (see 1 Corinthians 10), so whatever amount of Israel's history existed at any given time served as an example for each succeeding generation in the old dispensation. The Lord told the temple worshippers in Jerusalem to remember what had happened to the tabernacle worshippers at Shiloh (Jer. 7:12, 14). The tabernacle, like the temple, was a place of worship, sacrifice, and revelation. But when the previous generation turned it into a hideout for all their wickedness, God did not spare it. Shiloh was not a safe place just because the tabernacle was there (1 Sam. 4). The demise of

Shiloh was concrete evidence of God's intolerance of talismanic religion.[11] God asked the temple hypocrites of Jeremiah's day, 'Where is the tabernacle?' God asks the church hypocrites of today, 'Where is the tabernacle? Where is the temple?' History makes it clear that God is not satisfied with religion. It is folly to think that what was inexcusable then will be overlooked now.

Excision of the Error

The only hope for the hypocrite is to quit his hypocrisy. The introduction to Jeremiah's temple sermon was the command to repent: 'Amend your ways and your doings' (Jer. 7:3). Amending one's ways required making good the whole course of life, including the inner inclinations, propensities, and desires of the heart, as well as the outward habits of living. Making good one's doings required changing the specific deeds that were generated by the inner character. This was not a call for reformation or for resolution to do better, but a call for the transformation of the heart, without which the hypocrisy would persist. Elsewhere Jeremiah made the appeal in terms of the circumcision of the heart (4:4), a most fitting analogy for those who took pride and confidence in the circumcision of the flesh (cf. Rom. 2:28-29). In Jeremiah 7:5-6, the prophet set down some specific guidelines for applying repentance to life. Interestingly, the specifics covered both divisions of the law, evidencing love for neighbor as well as love for God (kindness to orphans and widows, preservation of life, and ethical monotheism). It is always true that behavior toward men is an index of the extent of devotion to God. Regardless of the specific applications he made to the temple worshippers, Jeremiah's point is timeless: true religion always connects with behavior.

It is also invariably true that God accepts true repentance: 'The sacrifices of God are a broken spirit: a broken and a contrite heart, O God, thou wilt not despise' (Ps. 51:17). If Jeremiah's generation persisted in their hypocritical worship, they would find no salvation in the temple. But if they repented, God promised to keep them in the land of promise (Jer. 7:3, 7). There was a way to escape judgment. Although there are inherent dangers in religion, true religion in the heart is the sinner's only hope. The heart is the key.

Extent of the Error

Without genuine repentance, there is really no way of telling how far heartless, hypocritical worship can go in taking the worshipper away from God. Jeremiah's temple worshippers crossed the line of no return. So far gone were they that God forbade Jeremiah even to pray for them (Jer. 7:16) – a sobering and fearful

---

11. 'That Yahweh had once *established a dwelling place for* his *name* in what was some sort of a sanctuary (*my place*) did not in any way guarantee the inviolability of the town or the sanctuary when there was *wickedness* among his people. The people of Jeremiah's day thus had before them a powerful proof that God could dispense with the Jerusalem temple in the same way he dispensed with the Shiloh temple' (J. A. Thompson, *The Book of Jeremiah*, The New International Commentary on the Old Testament [Grand Rapids: Eerdmans, 1987], p. 282).

prohibition. Religious hypocrisy led to outright paganism. Even as the people were entering the temple under the pretense of worshipping the one true and living God (v. 2), they were all the while worshipping the queen of heaven (7:18; 44:17). This is a reference to the Assyro-Babylonian Astarte or Ishtar. In Mesopotamian myth, this goddess was designated either as queen or mistress and, as an astral deity, was commonly worshiped out in the open (Jer. 19:13; 32:29). The worship of this goddess along with all the host of heaven became popular in Judah during the wicked reign of Manasseh, who introduced all sorts of apostasy to the soon-to-be-doomed nation (2 Kings 21). It is as though in their religious ignorance and superstition they were trying to cover all the bases, giving to every deity what they heard would make that deity happy and earn them some relief.

But they were certainly not giving the true God what He wanted. There can be little wonder that this religious syncretism led to the dramatic indictment of the entire sacrificial system that was so integral to temple worship (Jer. 7:21-28). Critics often cite this condemnation of sacrifices to demonstrate a contradiction in Scripture. They argue that since God instituted the Mosaic sacrificial system, it is odd that He would now reject it.[12] Rather than seeing a contradiction between Moses and Jeremiah, we should recognize two significant facts about the Old Testament sacrifices, both of which are important and one of which has direct bearing on our topic. First, the Old Testament sacrifices had no inherent efficacy (see Hebrews 10). If God had intended the animal sacrifices to be a way of salvation, He would not have condemned them. This involves far-reaching theology that for now is beside our point. Second, the sacrifices had to be offered from a proper heart relationship to God. Ritual without obedience and a heart alive to God is absolutely meaningless. External religion is nothing unless the heart is right. This is very much to our point. Jeremiah, therefore, is not contradicting Mosaic law; he is stressing the spirit of the law that was intended from the beginning.

I hope that the point is clear for us. Whatever the form worship takes—whether suited to the old or the new dispensations—it must be in spirit and truth, or it is unacceptable to the God whom we profess to worship. Religious motion without heart devotion is an abomination to the Lord. Jeremiah is clear about that.

ERROR 3: HOLINESS EQUATED WITH TRADITION

Belief in the Bible must translate to behavior in life. True religion defines life action. Any disconnect between doctrine and duty reduces belief to theory. Conversely, any disconnect between duty and doctrine reduces behavior to lifestyle traditions. This error, perhaps, is the most common in evangelical and conservative settings.

---

12. 'At first sight God seems to be disowning the whole idea of sacrifice; and some early critics of Old Testament history seized on this to drive a wedge between the Prophets and the Law. But in fact this way of speaking is the Bible's strongest way of comparing one thing with another—here, the moral with the formal—putting it not in the mild form of "This is better than that," but with the starkness of "Not that, but this!"' (Derek Kidner, *The Message of Jeremiah*, The Bible Speaks Today [Downers Grove, Ill.: InterVarsity, 1987], p. 50).

Holiness is often perceived to consist of conformity to a list of dos and don'ts without consciousness of the theological whys (see Chapter 9). Somewhere in the process there has been a drifting away from truth – generating adherence to a set of practices isolated from truth.[13] Those traditions may very well be right-wing and conservative in comparison to worldly behavior, but merely being out of sync with the world does not equate to biblical holiness.

Adding to the error is the propensity of those following their adopted or inherited traditions to judge the spirituality of others in terms of conformity to their traditions. Holiness is not evidenced by how much one looks like Jesus, but by how much one looks like followers of the tradition. There is sometimes a drift, shifting authority from the Bible to what is believed about the Bible and then to how the Bible is applied. Truth is singular, universal, and timeless, and every true believer must affirm that whatever the Bible says is true. However, interpretations vary among believers for different reasons; not everyone sees things the same way. Applications of Scripture are multifaceted and are often colored by time and culture. This is true even regarding those who agree on an interpretation. Undeniably, holiness looks different today than it did when Moses defined the separatist lifestyle of the Nazarite (Numbers 6). To mark holiness today in terms of uncut hair and total abstinence misses the principal point. Caution is necessary to avoid elevating specific applications to the same authoritative level of the Bible. Living the Bible is holiness; ticking off a list of traditions may or may not be.[14]

In the Bible, none were more guilty of this error than the Pharisees. On more than one occasion, Jesus charged this religious sect 'with teaching for doctrine the commandments of men' and in so doing 'laying aside the commandment of God' (Mark 7:7-8; see also Matt. 15:6, 9). The Pharisees were so steeped in their traditions that they regarded Jesus Himself to be a sinner when Jesus, in order to keep God's law perfectly, challenged and violated their traditions. For instance, the Pharisees frequently condemned Jesus for what they regarded as violations of the Sabbath, even though Christ was the Lord of the Sabbath (Mark 2:27; 3:2, 6; John 5:10-18). The fact of the matter is that Jesus kept the Sabbath as divinely intended, but the Pharisees equated their tradition with holiness and elevated it above Christ Himself.

Part of the tragedy is that the Pharisees' traditions had a pious inception.[15] Many of the Jewish customs and institutions that were operating in New Testament

---

13. 'The Pharisees fulfilled the rites and rituals of worship. They prayed, read the law, sang songs, offered gifts, and fasted, but they slowly came to honor their own teachings more than they honored God's Word. For this reason, their worship was vain and worthless' (Daniel M. Doriani, *Matthew*, Reformed Expository Commentary, vol. 2 [Phillipsburg, N.J.: P&R, 2008], p. 41).

14. 'Unless the heart is right, holiness is impossible. Without love for God, the quest for holiness becomes legalistic. It substitutes human tradition for God's law and substitutes human effort for God's grace. The traditions of the Pharisees started with God's laws, then added mind-boggling details about rest, food, washing, and even spitting. The tradition regulated the wrong things, lesser things, and in the wrong way, leaving the heart untouched' (Doriani, *Matthew*, p. 41).

15. 'It is clear, both from Josephus and from the rabbinic sources, that fundamental in the Hakamic movement was a vision of holiness – a vision of implementing what God required of His people

times, including those of the Pharisees, originated in the crucial period between the Old and New Testament eras. A little digression into the historical beginnings will give some understanding as to why certain behaviors became temporally and culturally necessary. This brief survey will serve as a warning as to what can happen when traditions replace the conscious and Spirit-led application of truth.

Broadly speaking, three Jewish groups emerged in reaction to Antiochus IV, sometimes referred to as 'Epiphanes' because he regarded himself as a manifestation of Zeus. He was a Seleucid ruler who shrewdly and treacherously assumed power in Palestine when tensions were high between the Seleucids and Ptolemies, two divisions of the Greek Empire that struggled for supremacy after Alexander the Great. His fundamental policy was to unify the heterogeneous population under his rule by inculcating Greek culture into all of society. Hellenization was the missionary glue for cultural unity.

This policy was bound to collide with Jewish culture and religion. History records that Antiochus meddled in Jewish affairs and on multiple occasions perpetrated violence against both the people and their religion. Here are a few examples. During his reign, Onias III, the legitimate high priest, was assassinated, and Jason, a usurper of the post, was placed in the office with the understanding that he would help implement Antiochus' policies. A gymnasium was constructed for games. Given our understanding of sport and exercise, that might seem to us a benign gesture of good will. Sports were as fun then as they are now and clearly alluring to the young men. But since the Greek games were associated with the cult of Hercules and involved nudity and the consequent exposure of circumcision, participation resulted in religious compromise and, even worse, in apostasy, according to conservative Jews. Antiochus' encroachments into Jewish life intensified from temptation to forced compliance and outright violence. On one occasion during his return from Egypt, Antiochus attacked Jerusalem, plundered the temple and removed sacred vessels and furniture, slaughtered thousands of Jews, and enslaved others. Eventually, he took over the city and overturned Jewish customs and religious practices. He suspended the temple sacrifices and Sabbath observances. He destroyed copies of the Law and outlawed circumcision. He forced the eating of pork upon the penalty of death. He erected shrines to Greek gods throughout the land and, in an ultimate act of contempt, desecrated the temple by making it a shrine to Zeus and offering swine on the altar. This act most likely is that 'abomination that maketh desolate' (Dan. 11:31). Antiochus did what he could—whether out of rage, spite, or his own religious convictions—to eradicate God's chosen people and their distinctiveness in the world.

Opposition is almost too feeble a word to describe the blatant disregard for what was in that dispensation the scripturally proper way to worship the one true and living God. The three Jewish groups that arose in this period were the

if they were to be his people' (John Bowker, *Jesus and the Pharisees* [London: Cambridge UP, 1973], p. 15).

Maccabeans (military resisters), the Hellenists (political compromisers), and the Hasidim (religious separatists). The Hellenists and the offspring of the Hasidim remained into New Testament times. Of all the movements developing from this period, the Hasidim (pious ones) were primarily responsible for preserving the religious system necessary for the coming of Christ. Unhappily, the movement that was so faithful in preparing the way for Christ became one of the greatest instruments of opposition when He came. In all likelihood, the Hasidim were the predecessors of the Pharisees (meaning 'separated ones'), the religious order that was most vehemently aggressive in its opposition to Jesus Christ.

There is a terrible irony in this opposition that stands as a sobering warning. In their protest of the pagan encroachments of Antiochus, the Hasidim maintained strict adherence to the law of God and devised safeguards for its protection. In their effort to preserve the sanctity of the law, they specified applications of obedience designed to address the particular pressures of the day. Their motives were good and pure, and I believe that many of them were true believers, waiting and looking 'for redemption in Jerusalem' (Luke 2:38). They were the conservative evangelicals of the day. Tragically, it wasn't long before the traditions of their applications gained equal status and identification with the law itself. What they sought to protect became redefined and perverted in the process.[16] They erected a fence around the law that eventually became the law itself in their thinking. So convinced were they of their religious correctness that they accused the perfectly righteous Son of God of breaking the law. As we have already observed, it is true enough that Christ often violated the Pharisaical traditions and transgressed their fence, but the truth of the matter is that in order to keep perfectly the law of God, He had to break the laws of the Pharisees. In their legalistic pride and hypocrisy, it probably never crossed their minds that they could be wrong.

Herein lies the potential danger inherent in some segments of modern Christianity. Too often in the rush to scriptural relevancy and Christian practicality, applications of principles are made without due and necessary attention to what the Bible itself says. 'What to do' takes precedence over 'why' something should be done. Such dogmatism about particular applications of the Scripture can result in the same error of the Pharisees: when practice assumes parity with the Bible itself. Those who don't conform precisely and minutely to the outlined standards for conduct will then suffer the accusation of being compromisers or worse. I wonder sometimes if the Lord Himself would be excluded in some spheres of the church.

It bears repeating that the Bible is the only rule for faith and practice. Indeed, if what we believe doesn't translate into practice, it really doesn't constitute belief.

---

16. 'It is that by raising the human commentary to a level of importance equal to the divinely given law, they have actually negated the real purpose and spirit of the law itself. Thus they can go through the ritual of word and deed, dependent on the rules given in "the tradition", without being committed in their hearts to the spiritual intentions of the law. The final step, never originally intended, nor perhaps any part of the evolution of the tradition, is that God's law is actually set aside in favour of human teaching based on it' (Donald English, *The Message of Mark*, The Bible Speaks Today [Downers Grove, Ill.: InterVarsity, 1992], p. 143).

Christianity is more than just creedal theory; it is a way of life flowing from both a personal relationship with Christ and the propositional truths of God's Word. But we must be willing to see the difference between the authority of the Bible and our preferences concerning practices, regardless of how convinced we are of our own rightness. It may very well be that others who believe the Bible with the same degree of fervency can with the same intensity of conviction have different and equally legitimate preferences in application. I am speaking, of course, regarding those spheres of life where the Scripture allows the liberty of conscience, and not in the clearly black-and-white issues of obedience or disobedience. There are definitely clear-cut areas of right and wrong – whether some Christians acknowledge them or not. The drift of the genuine piety of the Hasidim to the hypocritical legalism Pharisees raises a red flag. Let us heed the warning lest our religion stand in opposition to Christ. The sad thing is that it can happen.

The danger of elevating tradition to be the measure of holiness is evident in Christ's frequent rebuke of the Pharisees for their self-righteousness throughout His ministry.[17] None have ever been better at keeping traditions and standards than the Pharisees and none more the object of Christ's scorn. The woes of Matthew 23 ought to be sufficient warning not to follow that path. But the persistent problem is that adhering to traditions makes holiness easy, or so it seems. Ticking off the list of things to do and avoiding the things not to do give a sense that all is well spiritually. But holiness is not just thoughtless habits of practice. It may very well be that 'traditions' are based on legitimate biblical principles, but blindly keeping them without the biblical 'why' in mind and heart downgrades them to custom rather than conviction. It may very well be that particular 'traditions' were generated by peculiar or temporal circumstances that had to be addressed in order to evidence biblical separation and holiness. When and where I grew up, roller skating was regarded as evil. No Christian would ever be found in a roller rink. So growing up, in compliance with that prohibition to safeguard holiness, I never roller skated even though I was never told why. It was a tradition that marked teenage holiness. You can imagine my shock when later in life I met some God-fearing Christians from a different region who grew up with roller staking as church-sponsored activity. We had the same Bible and the same desire for holiness, but different ways of living it out. To this day, I do not roller skate – but out of common sense rather than conviction!

Traditions in themselves may not be wrong; traditions by themselves are not spiritually threatening. The point is that we must guard against equating the external keeping of traditions as a substitute for the heart-desire to be like Jesus.

---

17. 'Quoting Isaiah, Jesus called attention to two parts of the human body – the lips and the heart. The lips are on the surface. The heart is the very core of a person's being. Jesus told the Pharisees and scribes: "Your lips move. You sing praises. You say prayers. You say that you love God, but it is no deeper than your lips. It doesn't come from the center of your being. My Father wants people to worship Him in spirit and in truth, not just with their lips, because lip service is the very essence of hypocrisy"' (R. C. Sproul, *Mark*, St. Andrew's Expositional Commentary [Orlando, Fla.: Reformation Trust, 2011], p. 158).

CHAPTER 26

MODERN CONTROVERSIES
ABOUT HOLINESS

THOUGH the doctrine of sanctification has not been the focal point of such intense controversy as the doctrine of justification, a number of erroneous ideas about it have challenged the church.[1] Doctrines of sanctification are not theories that have no bearing on how we live. False views of sanctification can lead to spiritual pride, hypocrisy, false assurance, discouragement for true saints, and even despair. A true view of sanctification provides both a vibrant hope and strong motivation for the daily battle to walk with God.

If we are Christians, then we approach sanctification as soldiers putting on their armor in the midst of a deadly war, a war not with other people but with invisible spiritual powers that aim to destroy us forever. Let us therefore take care to obtain our doctrine of sanctification from the mouth of God and embrace it in the depths of our souls.

CONTROVERSIES WITH ROMAN CATHOLICISM

There are important differences between the Reformed doctrine of sanctification and that of Roman Catholicism, given the manner in which extra-biblical traditions have formed in that religion a system of holy, priestly orders that administrate God's grace through the sacraments, and the peculiar honor it gives to virginity, celibacy, and monastic asceticism. Similar ideas and practices may be found in Eastern Orthodoxy and Anglo-Catholic theologians.

Sanctification by Sacramentalism

Roman Catholic theologians would agree that Christians need a continual supply of divine grace in order to walk in holiness, but they tie that grace to the sacraments of the church. They consider the Eucharist or Mass (Latin *Missa*) to be 'the source and

---

1. This chapter is adapted with permission from Joel R. Beeke and Paul M. Smalley, *Reformed Systematic Theology, Volume 3: Holy Spirit and Salvation* (Wheaton, Ill.: Crossway, forthcoming 2021), chapters 27–28.

summit of the Christian life,' containing 'the whole spiritual good of the Church, namely Christ himself.'[2] In the celebration of the Eucharist, Roman Catholicism asserts, the bread and wine become the very body and blood of Christ, who is then offered again to God for the redemption of sinners and worshiped by Catholics in the bread and wine.[3] When they receive the Eucharist with their mouths, their union with Christ increases and they participate more fully in spiritual life through Him.[4] This union with Christ is effective in 'cleansing us from past sins and preserving us from future sins,' for 'the Eucharist strengthens our charity.'[5]

In response, the Scriptures reveal Christ's institution of the Lord's Supper as an ordinance of worship, and Christians must obey His command, 'This do in remembrance of me' (1 Cor. 11:24-25). However, the relatively few references or allusions to the Lord's Supper in the New Testament hardly merit the elevation of it to the center of the Christian life. Aside from the Gospel parallels (Matt. 26:26-30; Mark 14:22-26; Luke 22:15-20), the Supper appears only in 1 Corinthians 10–11. The Romanists and some others would also allege John 6:51-58, but this is anachronistic because Christ had not yet instituted the Supper. His terminology of eating food is plainly a metaphor for faith (John 6:35).

Biblical texts that allegedly teach sacramental union with Christ emphasize faith in Jesus as the great means of receiving saving grace.[6] Thus, we commune with Christ by trusting in His Word, not relying upon the sacraments themselves. According to Christ, the primary means by which we commune with Him and grow in holiness is the Word of God. It is by abiding in Christ's Word that we know His truth and experience His power to liberate us from the slavery of sin (John 8:31-32, 36). When Christ spoke of Himself as the vine and His disciples as the branches, the means of abiding in Him that He highlighted was not the Supper, but the Word of God (John 15:3, 7). Christ identified eternal life not with the Eucharist, but with the knowledge of God revealed in the Word of Christ (John 17:3, 6). He prayed, 'Sanctify them through thy truth: thy word is truth' (John 17:17). Therefore, although the Lord's Supper assists believers in sanctification, it does so not by any inherent grace but only in conjunction with the word as believers exercise faith in the gospel of Christ.

Celibacy and Asceticism as Superior Forms of Holiness

The Roman Catholic Church further teaches that the high road to holiness is that of virginity and celibacy. Christ Himself is said to have presented us a model of celibacy, and 'from the very beginning of the Church there have been men

---

2. *Catechism of the Catholic Church* (New York: Doubleday, 1995), sec. 1324.

3. *Catechism of the Catholic Church*, sec. 1333, 1364, 1367, 1376, 1378, 1414.

4. *Catechism of the Catholic Church*, sec. 1391, citing John 6:56-57.

5. *Catechism of the Catholic Church*, sec. 1393-94.

6. John 6:29-35, 53-54; Romans 6:3-4, 17; Galatians 3:26-27; Colossians 2:12.

and women who have renounced the great good of marriage to follow the Lamb wherever he goes, to be intent on the things of the Lord, to seek to please him, and to go out to meet the Bridegroom who is coming.'[7] Virginity for the kingdom is thus a 'powerful sign' of God's grace and union with Christ.[8] Mary is the highest exemplar of this virtue, remaining a perpetual virgin and being 'full of grace' for the church of which she is the spiritual mother by her faith and obedience.[9] Furthermore, 'all the ordained ministers' (except permanent deacons) of the Roman Catholic Church are ordinarily celibate, for they are 'called to consecrate themselves with undivided heart to the Lord.'[10]

The Romanist denial of ordinary sexual intimacy in marriage to those seeking the highest consecration to Christ is part of a larger pattern of severe treatment of the body that is believed necessary to master oneself, perform satisfactory penance for sins, and progress in holiness.[11] Pope John Paul II regularly slept on a bare floor instead of his bed and whipped himself with a belt – and these practices, when discovered, were commended by Roman Catholics as acts of self-mortification.[12] Monks, nuns, and members of other special orders who take vows of 'chastity, poverty and obedience,' which require the practice of 'mortification' to the flesh are 'following Christ with greater freedom and imitating Him more closely.'[13] Theirs is 'a special consecration' that by 'renouncing the world they may live for God alone.'[14]

In response, we agree that Christ and Paul said that some people voluntarily embrace celibacy for the sake of serving the Lord without the distractions of domestic responsibilities (Matt. 19:12; 1 Cor. 7:32-35). However, Christ and His apostle said that celibacy is an extraordinary gift given only to some (Matt. 19:12; 1 Cor. 7:7). God's ordinary, creational pattern for sexual purity still holds: 'For this cause shall a man leave father and mother, and shall cleave to his wife: and they twain shall be one flesh' (Matt. 19:5), and, 'To avoid fornication, let every man have his own wife, and let every woman have her own husband .... For it is better to marry than to burn' (1 Cor. 7:2, 9). There is no biblical basis for thinking that celibacy is generally a higher pathway of holiness than married life, nor for restricting ministers

---

7. *Catechism of the Catholic Church*, sec. 1618. It uses the language of Revelation 14:4; 1 Corinthians 7:32; and Matthew 25:6.

8. *Catechism of the Catholic Church*, sec. 1619.

9. *Catechism of the Catholic Church*, sec. 496, 499, 508-11.

10. *Catechism of the Catholic Church*, sec. 1579.

11. *Catechism of the Catholic Church*, sec. 1460, 1734, 2015, 2339-40.

12. Colin Hansen, 'Why Pope John Paul II Whipped Himself,' *Christianity Today*, February 8, 2010, http://www.christianitytoday.com/ct/2010/februaryweb-only/16-11.0.html, accessed April 8, 2016.

13. Pope Paul VI, *Perfectae Caritatis* (Perfect Love), sec. 1, decree on October 28, 1965, of Vatican II, http://www.vatican.va/archive/hist_councils/ii_vatican_council/documents/vat-ii_decree_19651028_perfectae-caritatis_en.html. See *Catechism of the Catholic Church*, sec. 914-33.

14. Pope Paul VI, *Perfectae Caritatis*, sec. 5, 12.

of the Word from sexual activity in marriage. Peter and other apostles were married (Mark 1:30; 1 Cor. 9:5). The standard for a 'bishop' or overseer/elder in the church is not celibacy but faithfulness to God's law for marriage and family: 'the husband of one wife ... having his children in subjection' (1 Tim. 3:2, 4). To deny pastors the freedom to enjoy sexual intimacy with their wives is to open a door for Satan to tempt them to scandalous sin (1 Cor. 7:5). History testifies to the tragic results of this doctrine in the Roman church.

As to self-denial and controlling the body, we agree that Christ commended fasting as a spiritual discipline while we wait and long for His return (Matt. 6:1-18; 9:15). We must not let our physical desires master us but bring them into subjection to God's will (1 Cor. 6:12; 9:27). However, this does not justify the ascetic abuse of the body or severe abstinence from enjoyment of God's creation. When Paul wrote, 'I keep under my body' (1 Cor. 9:27) the verb (*hupōpiazō*) means to give a black eye, but in this context he was not speaking literally of bruising himself but using the athletic metaphors of a runner and a boxer (vv. 24-26). 'No boxer pummels himself with blows .... The expression is thus a figurative one.'[15]

The Spirit of God warned the apostolic church that false teachers would arise and forbid people to marry and require abstinence from food, but the truth is that God's creations are all good, and can be received in holiness if used with prayer, thanksgiving, and obedience to God's Word (1 Tim. 4:1-5). Paul warned us that the denial or severe treatment of the body may seem wise and godly, but in fact has no power to overcome inward sin; we conquer sin only by living in communion with Christ by faith in His death and resurrection (Col. 2:18, 23; 3:1). Therefore, we reject asceticism as a pathway to holiness.

SURVEY OF VIEWS ASSERTING
TWO-LEVEL CHRISTIANITY

The second major battlefront for the doctrine of sanctification pertains to refuting claims that the Holy Spirit brings some people to a level of Christian perfection in this life, where perfection may be variously defined. The problem of perfectionism is very old. Calvin complained in the sixteenth century of sects among the Anabaptists that taught God's children need not put their sins to death, but 'rather follow the Spirit as their guide, under whose impulsion they can never go astray'; thus believers need not fear, for 'the Spirit will command no evil of you if you but yield yourself, confidently and boldly, to his prompting.'[16] Other forms of perfectionism are less antinomian, and more nuanced in their assertion of a higher spiritual life. In this section, we will trace a line of perfectionism from eighteenth-century Wesleyanism

---

15. Gerhard Kittel, Geoffrey W. Bromiley, and Gerhard Friedrich, *eds, Theological Dictionary of the New Testament*, 10 vols. (Grand Rapids: Eerdmans, 1964), 8:591.

16. John Calvin, *Institutes of the Christian Religion*, ed. John T. McNeill, trans. Ford Lewis Battles (Philadelphia: Westminster Press, 1960), 3.3.14.

through its daughter movements in the subsequent centuries, including some that went far beyond anything John Wesley would have approved.[17]

Christian Perfectionism (Wesleyan Methodism)

John Wesley taught that a kind of Christian 'perfection' was attainable in this life. By 'perfection' he did not refer to freedom from ignorance, intellectual mistakes, or weakness of mind.[18] He spoke of a perfection consisting in a freedom from voluntary violations of God's laws, 'loving God with all the heart, so that every evil temper is destroyed and every thought and word and work springs from and is conducted to that end by the pure love of God and our neighbor.'[19] Wesley forcefully denied that 'all Christians do, and must commit sin, as long as they live.'[20]

Therefore, theologians in the Wesleyan Methodist tradition teach that some Christians walk on a different spiritual plane: the level of perfection. It should be noted that theologians from these traditions often attempt to qualify perfection as less than sinless fulfillment of the full extent of God's law while retaining the idea of 'entire sanctification' consisting in perfect love and an end of the inner battle against indwelling sin.[21] Oden calls it 'sustained radical responsiveness to grace,'[22] and marshals the following arguments: (1) God would not command holiness, perfection, and blamelessness in this life if it were impossible (Gen. 17:1; Matt. 5:48); (2) God would not promise full salvation and holiness without blemish if it were not possible (Ps. 119:1-3; 1 Thess. 5:23-24; 1 John 1:7, 9); and (3) Scripture provides examples of complete consecration in Enoch, Noah, Job, Barnabas, etc.[23]

In response, we argue: (1) It is a Pelagian argument to say that God's commands imply our spiritual ability, for it would lead to the conclusion that all mankind is capable of sinless obedience to God, a claim contradicted by Scripture (Rom. 3:9-18; 8:6-8). (2) God promises full salvation from the presence of sin in the life to come (Heb. 12:23; 1 John 3:2-3). In this life, God promises believers deliverance from the enslaving power of sin (Rom. 6:14), mingled however with the necessity of continuing to confess our sins (1 John 1:9), leaning upon Christ's death and intercession when we do sin (1 John 2:1-2), and pressing on in increasing holiness (Phil. 3:12-14). There is no person on earth who never sins,[24] and those

---

17. For a comprehensive study of nineteenth-century movements of this kind, see Benjamin B. Warfield, *Perfectionism*, 2 vols. (New York: Oxford University Press, 1931).

18. John Wesley, *Christian Perfection*, I.1-9, in *John Wesley's Sermons: An Anthology*, ed. Albert C. Outler and Richard P. Heitzenrater (Nashville: Abingdon, 1991), pp. 70-73.

19. Quoted in Thomas C. Oden, *John Wesley's Scriptural Christianity: A Plain Exposition of His Teaching on Christian Doctrine* (Grand Rapids: Zondervan, 1994), p. 323.

20. Wesley, *Christian Perfection*, II.7, in *Sermons*, p. 75.

21. See Anthony A. Hoekema, *Saved by Grace* (Grand Rapids: Eerdmans, 1989), pp. 215-16.

22. Thomas C. Oden, *Systematic Theology, Volume Three, Life in the Spirit* (Peabody, Mass.: Prince, 1992), p. 232.

23. Oden, *Systematic Theology*, 3:242-43.

24. 1 Kings 8:46; Ecclesiastes 7:20; Proverbs 20:9; James 3:2.

who claim otherwise are deceiving themselves and placing their souls in grave danger (1 John 1:8, 10). (3) When the Bible refers to saints on earth as 'perfect' (Hebrew *tamim*, Greek *teleios*), it refers to their spiritual maturity and a holistic life of godliness, not to perfection of life and freedom from all known sins (Gen. 6:9; 1 Cor. 14:20; Phil. 3:15).[25]

Therefore, we reject perfectionism, and warn our fellow believers against the spiritual elitism that generally arises from such teaching. Biblical realism demands that we face the ugliness of our remaining sin. However, we must also reject a lazy compromise with sin, and instead set our sights on the ideal of perfect obedience and pursue holiness with all our might. Our prayer must be, 'Search me, O God, and know my heart: try me, and know my thoughts: and see if there be any wicked way in me, and lead me in the way everlasting' (Ps. 139:23-24).

The Holiness and Higher Life Movements

In the mid-nineteenth century, the Wesleyan doctrine of Christian perfection was adopted and adapted by Methodist authors such as Phoebe Palmer (1807–1874), and in theologians outside of Methodism such as the Oberlin professors Charles Finney (1792–1875) and Asa Mahan (1800–1889) in what came to be known as the Holiness Movement. These teachers linked the doctrine of perfection with a crisis experience of second blessing which they called the baptism of the Holy Spirit for victorious power in sanctification and ministry.[26] This doctrine gained an even wider following through the ministries of Adoniram J. Gordon (1836–1895), Dwight L. Moody (1839–1899), A. B. Simpson (1843–1919), and R. A. Torrey (1856–1928).[27] Finney wrote in 1839 that believers must yield themselves to the Holy Spirit and thus receive Him by faith after their conversion.[28] The promise of God writing His law upon the heart (Jer. 31:33) is nothing less than a promise of entire sanctification in this life.[29] Finney said, 'I shall use the terms entire sanctification to designate a state of confirmed and entire consecration of body, soul and spirit or of the whole being to God ... not in the sense that a soul entirely sanctified cannot sin, but that as a matter of fact, he does not and will not sin.'[30] A key proof text of the Holiness Movement was Paul's prayer that God would 'sanctify you wholly' (1 Thess. 5:23).[31]

---

25. Millard J. Erickson, *Christian Theology*, 3rd ed. (Grand Rapids: Baker Academic, 2013), pp. 901-2.

26. Richard Gilbertson, *The Baptism of the Holy Spirit: The Views of A. B. Simpson and His Contemporaries* (Camp Hill, Pa.: Christian Publications, 1993), pp. 146-57.

27. Gilbertson, *The Baptism of the Holy Spirit*, pp. 55, 62, 157-59, 167-76.

28. Charles G. Finney, 'Lecture XIV: The Holy Spirit of Promise,' *The Oberlin Evangelist* 1, no. 18 (August 14, 1839): p. 138.

29. Charles G. Finney, *Lectures on Systematic Theology, Embracing Ability ... Perseverance* (Oberlin: James M. Fitch, 1847), p. 216

30. Finney, *Lectures on Systematic Theology, Embracing Ability*, p. 201.

31. Phoebe Palmer, *The Way of Holiness* (New York: Piercy and Reed, 1843), pp. 40, 47; Finney, *Lectures on Systematic Theology, Embracing Ability*, pp. 219-20.

Another form of the Holiness Movement, known as the Higher Life Movement, arose from the teachings of W. E. Boardman (1810–1886), Hannah Whitall Smith (1832–1911), and her husband Robert Pearsall Smith (1827–1898). Boardman taught 'a second experience,' 'a second conversion,' and 'a deeper work of grace' than one's initial regeneration.[32] Just as we receive Christ for justification, so justified believers must also receive Christ for sanctification.[33] Boardman said that 'there are Christians of two classes in the world,' some truly converted but not delivered from the bondage of sin described in Romans 7, and others who have found the freedom of Romans 8 by receiving the Spirit of adoption.[34] Hannah Smith said that 'man's part' is nothing but 'surrender and trust, because this is positively all the man can do,' for all the fruit and activity that proceeds from faith is 'not by us, but by Him …. We do not do anything, but He does it.'[35] Sadly, both Robert and Hannah Smith fell away from the faith.[36]

The Early Keswick Movement and Classic Dispensationalism

Despite the tragic collapse of the Smiths, the Higher Life Movement found a rallying point for sympathizers from many Christian denominations at the Keswick (pronounced Keh-zick) Convention in England, which the Smiths had helped to start in 1875. Many prominent evangelicals were closely connected with the Keswick Convention, such as H. C. G. Moule (1841–1920), F. B. Meyer (1847–1929), Andrew Murray (1828–1917), James Hudson Taylor (1832–1905), Frances Ridley Havergal (1836–1879), and Amy Carmichael (1867–1951).[37] Charles Trumbull said, 'What are the conditions of this Victorious Life? Only two, and they are very simple. Surrender and faith. "Let go, and let God."'[38] A number of speakers at the Keswick Convention from the 1920s onward, and especially from the 1960s onward, have presented a more biblical and Reformed view of sanctification.[39]

A view similar to that of the Higher Life-Keswick doctrine was propagated by dispensational teacher Lewis Sperry Chafer (1871–1952). Chafer taught that mankind consists of three groups: natural men, carnal Christians, and spiritual

---

32. W. E. Boardman, *The Higher Christian Life* (Boston: Henry Hoyt, 1858), pp. 47-48.

33. Boardman, *The Higher Christian Life*, pp. 51-52.

34. Boardman, *The Higher Christian Life*, pp. 265-68.

35. Hannah Whitall Smith, *The Christian's Secret to a Happy Life*, rev. ed. (Chicago: F. H. Revell, 1883), pp. 25-26.

36. Andrew David Naselli, *Let Go and Let God? A Survey and Analysis of Keswick Theology* (Bellingham, Wa.: Lexham Press, 2010), pp. 111-15.

37. Andrew David Naselli, 'Keswick Theology: A Survey and Analysis of the Doctrine of Sanctification in the Early Keswick Movement,' *Detroit Baptist Seminary Journal* 13 (2008): pp. 24-25.

38. Cited in Naselli, 'Keswick Theology,' p. 32.

39. See Steven Barabas, *So Great Salvation: The History and Message of the Keswick Conference* (Chicago: Fleming H. Revell, 1952); John C. Pollock and Ian Randall, *The Keswick Story: The Authorized Version of the Keswick Convention*, new ed. (Fort Washington, Pa.: CLC Publications, 2006).

Christians (citing 1 Cor. 2:14-3:1).[40] The carnal Christian, Chafer said, lives 'on the same plane' as the unsaved, though he is born again by the Holy Spirit.[41] In order to become filled with the Spirit and remain so, Chafer taught that the Christian must confess all known sins for cleansing by the blood of Christ, yield his will and dedicate his entire life to God, and rely upon the power of the Holy Spirit.[42] Holiness is not obtained by 'human resolution or struggle'; the only fight in which the believer must engage is the fight to 'maintain an attitude of dependence on Him to do what He alone can do.'[43] In fact, even the love of Christians is really not their own human activity created by grace, but instead God's love 'passing through the heart of the believer out from the indwelling Spirit,' as Christians were passive conduits instead of persons changed by God, so that by His grace they truly loved others.[44] The spiritual life is repeatedly called 'superhuman' instead of recognizing that restoration of the image of God in Christ is a return to true humanity.[45]

Chafer's formulation has been widely influential in American Dispensational evangelicalism through theologians like Charles Ryrie. Its popular appeal is illustrated in a booklet distributed by the thousands that depicts the carnal Christian with self on the throne and 'Christ dethroned and not allowed to direct the life,' until the Christian desires the Spirit's help, confesses his sins, presents his whole life to God, and claims the filling of the Spirit by faith.[46]

Exegetical Response to the Carnal Christian Doctrine

At this point, we need to address the two major texts presented as arguments for so-called carnal Christians. The first is Romans 7:14-25, which begins, 'For we know that the law is spiritual: but I am carnal, sold under sin. For that which I do I allow not: for what I would, that do I not; but what I hate, that do I.'

Some interpreters view Romans 7:14-25 as a continuation of the Paul's description of an unbeliever under the law which he began in verse 7. To be 'sold under sin' is the language of slavery (1 Kings 21:20, 25) or being given to the power of one's enemy (Deut. 32:30; Judg. 2:14). However, it is best to view Paul as now describing a believer because he describes his present experience, using the Greek present tense, as a man who trusts in 'Jesus Christ our Lord' and finds deliverance in Him from the power of sin though still conflicted in himself by the presence of sin (Rom. 7:25). To be 'carnal' or fleshly in some respects (v. 14) is not the same

---

40. Lewis Sperry Chafer, *He That Is Spiritual*, rev. ed. (Philadelphia: Sunday School Times Co., 1919), pp. 3-14.

41. Chafer, *He That Is Spiritual*, pp. 12-13.

42. Chafer, *He That Is Spiritual*, pp. 82-85, 105-108, 119.

43. Chafer, *He That Is Spiritual*, p. 121.

44. Chafer, *He That Is Spiritual*, pp. 50-51.

45. Chafer, *He That Is Spiritual*, pp. 65, 74, 125.

46. Bill Bright, *Have You Made the Wonderful Discovery of the Spirit-Filled Life?* (Peachtree City, Ga.: New Life Resources, 2008), pp. 2-3, 10-11, available at http://crustore.org/downloads/SFL.pdf.

as being 'in the flesh,' and thus lacking the Spirit (Rom. 8:9; cf. 1 Cor. 3:1, 3-4).[47] Peter wrote of believers suffering the inner attacks of 'fleshly' or 'carnal' desires (1 Pet. 2:11). As to being 'sold under sin' (Rom. 7:14), it does not refer in this context to willingly giving oneself to sin (cf. 1 Kings 21:20, 25), but to a man who 'is subjected to a power that is alien to his own will,' as John Murray commented.[48] This man loves God's law and serves it willingly (vv. 16, 19, 22, 25). This accords with the doctrine that the converted person in union with Christ is now a servant of righteousness (Rom. 6:17-18). Paul distinguishes between himself and the 'sin that dwelleth in me' (v. 17), the latter of which wages war against his 'inward man' or 'mind,' which loves God's law (vv. 22-23). James Fraser (1700–1769) of Alness observed, 'The prevailing habitual inclination and determination of his will was towards good.'[49] In sharp contrast, the mindset of the flesh in the person who lacks God's Spirit is 'enmity against God' – he rebels against God's law and cannot do any other (Rom. 8:7-9).[50]

Inward conflict of holy desires and sinful desires is the characteristic of a true Christian (Gal. 5:17). The same condition described in the latter half of Romans 7 continues in Romans 8. In the former, Paul spoke of his condition as living in 'the body of this death' (Rom. 7:24). In the latter, Paul said, 'And if Christ be in you, *the body is dead* because of sin; but the Spirit is life because of righteousness' (8:10). Those under the ruling influence of the Holy Spirit still live in the body of death and must face the reality of indwelling sin, but they are finding progressive, experiential victory by the Spirit who is applying to them the finished work of Christ. Therefore, we conclude that Romans 7:14-25 describes the painful reality of indwelling sin in the believer in spiritual union with Christ.

However, it is at this point that the advocate of the 'carnal Christian' doctrine notes that Paul says as a believer, 'I am carnal, sold under sin. For that which I do I allow not: for what I would, that do I not; but what I hate, that do I' (Rom. 7:14-15). Does Paul here describe a carnal Christian who lives in a state of defeat and subjection to the power of sin until he appropriates the work of the Spirit by faith? We argue that this text does not describe a distinct spiritual state from that found in Romans 8.

1. These two chapters evidence *no transition from defeat to victory*. Such a crisis cannot be read into Paul's exclamation in Romans 7:25, 'I thank God through Jesus Christ our Lord,' because he does not follow it with a description of newly found victory, but with a restatement of the same condition of inward conflict: 'So

---

47. James Fraser, *A Treatise on Sanctification: An Explication of Romans Chapters 6, 7, and 8:1–4*, rev. ed. (1897; Audubon, N.J.: Old Paths, 1992), pp. 270-71.

48. John Murray, *The Epistle to the Romans*, The New International Commentary on the New Testament, 2 vols. (Grand Rapids: Eerdmans, 1968), 1:261.

49. Fraser, *Treatise on Sanctification*, p. 277.

50. William Hendriksen, *Exposition of Paul's Epistle to the Romans, Volume 1, Chapters 1–8*, New Testament Commentary (Grand Rapids: Baker, 1980), 1:226; Murray, *The Epistle to the Romans*, 1:258.

then with the mind I myself serve the law of God; but with the flesh the law of sin.' The Christian overcomes sin by faith in Christ while remaining in that state of inward conflict and frustration. As we noted earlier, 'the body of this death' (v. 24) corresponds to 'the body is dead because of sin' (8:10; cf. 6:12). The Spirit already leads us forward to conquer indwelling sin, not by translating us into a new spiritual state of ease, but by leading us in a battle to the death against 'the deeds of the body' (Rom. 8:13).

2. Paul's frustration reflects *holy ambition for perfect love, not total failure*. Though he wrote, 'For the good that I would I do not: but the evil which I would not, that I do' (Rom. 7:19), this cannot be understood as believers with a complete lack of doing good or a total abandonment to commit sin. Those who live in unrepentant sin are on the pathway to wrath and eternal death, not to life (Rom. 2:5; 6:21-23; 8:13). Rather, 'the good that I would' is entire and perfect obedience to the law (7:22, 25), which he cannot yet render to God. This is not a condition of immaturity, but the tension found in the highest level of godliness. Murray wrote, 'The more sanctified he becomes the more painful to him must be the presence in himself of that which contradicts the perfect standard of holiness.'[51]

As to Paul's statement 'the evil which I would not, that I do' (v. 19), he did not imply that he continually engaged in sinful behaviors. He spoke of the law here not in terms external behavior, but as 'spiritual' (v. 14), that is, from the Holy Spirit and addressing matters of the human spirit.[52] In the larger context, the law which Paul mentioned pertained to inward desires: 'Thou shalt not covet,' and the results were 'concupiscence,' or evil desire (vv. 7-8). The soul of the law was the inner quality of love (Rom. 13:10). Therefore, he described his frustrated desire to live in perfect love and cast out all sinful lust. Fraser said, 'He willed that the love of God should fill his heart, and prevail in it to the most intense degree; that his heart should be wholly spiritual and heavenly, in all its thoughts and affections; ... that vain thoughts, sin and sinful imperfections should never hold him short of such perfect attainment in his duty.'[53]

3. The contrast between Roman 7:14-25 and Romans 8 is between *the weakness of the law and the power of the Spirit, not two states* (carnal and spiritual). Even for the regenerate believer, the law does not supply the power needed to conquer sin but only directs the believer to what is good, holy, and righteous. Christians put sin to death and obey God's law only by the empowerment of the Holy Spirit obtained by Jesus Christ. However, Paul does not know of a category of God's children who are not empowered by the Spirit: 'For as many as are led by the Spirit of God, they are the sons of God' (Rom. 8:14). The only two states that he mentions are those who walk after the flesh and those who belong to Christ and have the Holy Spirit

---

51. John Murray, *The Epistle to the Romans*, 1:258.

52. See Romans 1:11; 15:27; 1 Corinthians 2:13, 15; 9:11; cf. John 4:24.

53. James Fraser, *Treatise on Sanctification*, p. 278.

(vv. 4-9). Only those who walk in the pathway of suffering obedience and self-denial will enter into the eternal glory and life of Christ (vv. 13, 17).

4. When Paul called himself 'carnal' (Rom. 7:14), he expressed *frustration, not an absolute characterization of a spiritual state*. Paul referred to the Corinthians as 'carnal' in order to humble them for their immature and worldly conduct (1 Cor. 3:1-3). It is somewhat akin to telling a fifteen-year-old son that he is acting like a two-year-old, not because he is no longer potty-trained or thinks and acts in every respect like a toddler, but because some of his attitudes and actions are immature and inconsistent with who he is. In the same way, Paul rebuked the Corinthians for their immature attitudes and actions that were inconsistent with their spiritual state in Christ. Paul may have written this epistle three or four years after evangelizing in Corinth and organizing the church there, and therefore many of the believers there may have been only a few years past their conversion from gross paganism.

Therefore, we conclude that there is no special category of believers united to Christ who remain in a state of powerlessness, defeat, and enslavement to sin. Christians who feel discouraged or defeated do not need to be translated into a new state but do need to renew their faith in the finished work of Christ, repent of their sins, and press on in the battle.

Before we proceed to the next point, we must pause to warn of the great danger of considering yourself a Christian if you are not walking in obedience to God. John said, 'Hereby we do know that we know him, if we keep his commandments. He that saith, I know him, and keepeth not his commandments, is a liar, and the truth is not in him' (1 John 2:3-4). John Owen (1616–1683) wrote, 'He will lead none to heaven but whom he sanctifies on the earth. The holy God will not receive unholy persons; this living head will not admit of dead members, nor bring men into the possession of a glory which they neither love nor like.'[54]

You will not go to heaven if you do not seek God's kingdom and His righteousness. Revelation 21:27 says of the city of God, 'And there shall in no wise enter into it any thing that defileth, neither whatsoever worketh abomination, or maketh a lie: but they which are written in the Lamb's book of life.' Therefore, we must 'pursue ... sanctification without which no one will see the Lord' (Heb. 12:14).

Theological Response to Two-Level Christianity

To summarize, Holiness, Higher Life, early Keswick, and some Dispensational writers generally affirm the following principles of sanctification:

(1) Regeneration is insufficient to initiate a significant process of sanctification.

(2) Sanctification is separable from justification and often begins later.

(3) Large numbers of regenerate and justified believers live under the power of sin.

---

54. John Owen, *An Exposition of the Epistle to the Hebrews*, 7 vols. (repr., Edinburgh: Banner of Truth, 1991), 3:417.

(4) Victory is found in a second blessing.

(5) Holiness is not by effort but surrender and faith: 'let go and let God.'

(6) The higher life is superhuman in its divine quality.

In reply, we argue from the Holy Scriptures that:

1. The new birth produces a new life.

One of the concerns driving many advocates of these views is the dismal conduct of many professing Christians. With this concern we greatly sympathize. Their solution, however, is unbiblical, for it denies that the new birth truly produces righteous conduct, turning from sin, Christ-like love, and victory over the world (1 John 2:29; 3:9; 4:7; 5:4). The new birth is a supernatural, miraculous act of God like raising the dead to life. People deny the biblical doctrine of regeneration and dishonor its divine Author when they say that it fails to produce fruit.[55] We must never say that saving grace permits sin so that a person may be saved without Christ seated, so to speak, on the throne of his life. William Hendriksen (1900–1982) said, 'Grace dethrones sin. It destroys sin's lordship.'[56]

2. All in Christ are justified and sanctified.

Sanctification is distinct from justification, but it is never separated from justification, for the justified person is united to Christ by a Spirit-worked faith. If we break this connection, we open ourselves to the charge that justification by faith alone promotes sin. On the contrary, no one may rightly say that we can sin all the more so that justifying grace may abound, for believers are united with Christ in His death and resurrection (Rom. 6:1-14; Gal. 2:16-20).

3. No one in Christ is a slave of sin.

While it may be true that some *professing* believers live under the power of sin, there is no biblical basis to say that true believers, those who are regenerate and justified, live under the power of sin. Paul's words in Romans 6 do not address an elite group in the church, but all those effectually called to belong to Jesus Christ as His holy people (Rom. 1:6-7). Paul did not command them to die to sin by appropriating Christ's death, but to count themselves as already dead to sin because of the crucifixion of Christ (6:2, 6, 11).[57] He did not call them to come out of the dominion of sin, but said that sin will not reign over them (v. 14), for they are no longer slaves of sin, but of righteousness (vv. 17-18). As Paul said in Galatians 5:24, those who belong to Christ have crucified the flesh with its evil desires. Those ruled by sin do not belong to Christ. Those whose lives are characterized

---

55. On the effective power of the new birth, see chapter 12 regarding effectual calling and regeneration.

56. William Hendriksen, *Exposition of Paul's Epistle to the Romans*, p. 203.

57. John Murray, *The Epistle to the Romans*, 1:225-26.

by unrepentant sin are not on the road to heaven, and the only alternative is the wrath of God (1 Cor. 6:9-10; Gal. 5:19-21; Eph. 5:5-6). John Murray commented on Romans 6:1-2, 'This is the identity of the believer – he died to sin ... a definitive act in the past .... A believer cannot therefore live in sin; if a man lives in sin he is not a believer.'[58]

4. Christians do not need a second work of grace.

The Holy Scriptures do not teach the necessity of a second blessing distinct from conversion, either the baptism or filling of the Spirit. Instead, they teach the necessity of a steady walk with God with new blessings of grace each day. What about Paul's prayer for the entire sanctification of the Thessalonian saints? He wrote, 'The very God of peace sanctify you wholly; and I pray God your whole spirit and soul and body be preserved blameless unto the coming of our Lord Jesus Christ. Faithful is he that calleth you, who also will do it' (1 Thess. 5:23-24). Certainly, Paul prayed for God to work holiness through every part of their lives, inward and outward (cf. 2 Cor. 7:1). Paul's prayers for them sought great growth in their love, growth he hoped to see in this life (1 Thess. 3:11-12). We should likewise pray for our sanctification. However, Paul looked for the ultimate answer to these prayers at Christ's 'coming' in glory (1 Thess. 3:13; 5:23). That is our entire sanctification and Christian perfection: when we see Him as He is (1 John 3:2).

5. Sanctification comes by our faith and work.

While it is certainly true that we are sanctified by faith in Jesus Christ, the idea of 'letting go and letting God' unwisely pits faith against effort and works in sanctification. When Paul described the duties of the Christian life, he did not simply tell the readers of his epistles to 'let go and let God' so that the Spirit would carry them along in holiness, but gave them many practical commands to obey while continually pointing them to the sufficiency of Christ. In this regard, sanctification is different from justification, which is by faith alone apart from works of the law (Rom. 3:28). Paul never said, 'Work out your justification,' but with regard to our obedience he did say, 'Work out your salvation with fear and trembling' (Phil. 2:12). Owen wrote that the Holy Spirit 'works in us and with us, not against us or without us; so that his assistance is an encouragement as to the facilitating of the work, and no occasion of neglect as to the work itself.'[59]

Paul's solution for the carnal Corinthians was not to receive holiness by faith without any effort, but for them to become watchful warriors who fight like men to stand in the faith and to labor in love (1 Cor. 16:13-14). He compared the Christian life to an athletic competition where we must run, strive, fight, and discipline

---

58. John Murray, *The Epistle to the Romans*, 1:213.

59. John Owen, *Of the Mortification of Sin in Believers*, in *The Works of John Owen*, ed. William H. Goold (1850–1853; repr., Edinburgh: Banner of Truth, 1965), 6:20.

ourselves in order to win the prize (9:24-27; cf. Heb. 12:1). The pursuit of holiness is warfare against spiritual powers, not a cruise on a luxury ship. To be sure, it can only be won by the strength we find in Christ, but we must still 'wrestle' and 'stand' against the forces pressing upon us if we would win (Eph. 6:10-14).

The second half of 'let go and let God' also demeans the sovereignty of God, as if He cannot work unless we give Him permission. Instead of teaching that God works only if we will, the Bible says that God works our willing (Phil. 2:13). Reversing this order too easily becomes the occasion of spiritual pride. Kenneth Prior warns, 'There is a subtle danger of speaking of sanctification as essentially coming from our own effort or initiative. We can unconsciously do this even while acknowledging our need for the power of the Holy Spirit, by making the operation of that power dependent upon our surrender and consecration.'[60]

6. The life of sanctification is not superhuman but very human in Jesus Christ.

We are not becoming gods but the 'new man' who bears the image of God in the human righteousness and godliness that grace produces (Eph. 4:24). This new humanity was forged for us in the fires of suffering by the human body and soul of Jesus Christ. God's Spirit comes to us as 'the Spirit of life in Christ Jesus' and 'the Spirit of Christ,' that is, of Christ crucified for our sins (Rom. 8:2-3, 9). God's Spirit does not lift us up into a heavenly realm of divine omnipotence but brings divine omnipotence down into our weakness and death, first in Christ, and through Christ in us.

Jesus obeyed God in a manner that involved profound struggle, suffering, tears, and cries to God – and Jesus was without sin (Heb. 2:18; 4:15; 5:7-8). How much more then, is our pathway to holiness full of difficulty and tribulation, and yet also hope through the Holy Spirit (Rom. 5:3-5). Sanctification does not replace our human minds and wills with divine energy but conforms us to the image of God's incarnate and crucified Son (Rom. 8:17, 29). There is no resurrection without the cross, neither for Christ nor for us in union with Christ (Phil. 3:10-11). Martin Luther (1483–1546) said that the Christian is 'tempted to flee when fear overcomes him, or to yield to sinful desire when it entices him … but in the end, he does not surrender, even though it costs him utmost exertion and pain just barely to resist and to come out on top.'[61]

A superhuman view of sanctification may arise from a confused eschatology, as if we had already arrived in glory. Hendriksen said, 'The Christian is living in an era in which two ages, the old and the new, overlap.'[62] We no longer belong to this

---

60. Kenneth Prior, *The Way of Holiness: A Study in Christian Growth* (Downers Grove, Ill.: InterVarsity, 1982), p. 42.

61. Martin Luther, *Lectures on Romans*, ed. and trans. Wilhelm Pauck (Louisville: Westminster John Knox, 1961), p. 189 (on Rom. 6:14).

62. William Hendriksen, *Exposition of Paul's Epistle to the Romans*, 1:232.

world, but we are still in it, and to some extent it is still in us. God's grace teaches that 'denying ungodliness and worldly lusts, we should live soberly, righteously, and godly, in this present world; looking for that blessed hope, and the glorious appearing of the great God and our Savior Jesus Christ' (Titus 2:12-13).

Practical Conclusion

Over the history of the Christian church, some persons with defective views of sanctification have risen to high levels of holiness and performed notable works of service in the mission of the church. We would not in the least deny this, nor fail to thank God for what Christ has done through them. However, doctrine makes a difference in how we live. False doctrines of sanctification can produce a great deal of confusion, sin, and sorrow in the lives of those who embrace them. We have seen in this chapter that both in Roman Catholicism and Evangelicalism there has been a tendency to define Christianity unbiblically on two levels.

One of the great problems with two-level Christianity in any form is that it tends to excuse hypocrites from a life of holiness while thinking they are in Christ, and to confuse believers into thinking they have arrived at a high level of holiness when they in fact are just beginning. These teachings replace the continual duty of spiritual work with a crisis, whether it is a vow of celibacy and poverty, an act of self-dedication, or an emotional experience. The believer is then told that he has arrived at a high spiritual plane and his focus must be on maintaining it, often through a simplistic formula. Since such a doctrine often appeals to God's grace, the believer is made to feel that any questioning of this doctrine is doubting the sufficiency of Christ. People are then launched into Christian service and missions who are poorly equipped to face the reality of their remaining sin with the faith of a persevering spiritual warrior.

The beauty of the Reformed view is that it grounds holiness in grace but calls believers to obedient action on the basis of God's grace. Wilhelmus à Brakel (1635–1711) said:

> There is a union between you and Christ indeed, and you are indeed one Spirit with Him (1 Cor. 6:17). You are indeed grafted into Him as into an olive tree and thus have become a partaker of His life and nature (Rom. 11:17). Should not then the same life of Jesus become manifest in us, and should we not then walk as He has walked? You are indeed the bride of the Lord Jesus .... Would a bride not adorn herself to make herself pleasant and charming to her bridegroom?[63]

Let us, therefore, cast off our sins and run the race that is set before us with our eyes fixed upon Jesus. Let us press on in the upward call of Christ. Let us pursue holiness, without which no one will see the Lord.

---

63. Wilhelmus à Brakel, *The Christian's Reasonable Service*, trans. Bartel Elshout, ed. Joel R. Beeke (Grand Rapids: Reformation Heritage Books, 1992–1995), 3:25.

HOLINESS CONSUMMATED

CHAPTER 27

PERSEVERING IN CHRIST TO THE END[1]

(HEBREWS 12:1-3)

'NEVER, never, never give up!' That was the essence of one of Winston Churchill's commencement addresses. The message was: 'Keep on keeping on.' Never giving up is a tough assignment when it comes to walking as Jesus walked in areas such as cross-bearing, office-bearing, and weeping. How do we persevere in such ways?

It is one thing to begin the Christian life and quite another to persevere in it to the end. It is one thing to repent and believe the gospel and quite another to go on repenting and believing. The miracle of Pentecost in Acts 2:4 is remarkable, but in some ways Acts 2:42 is even more remarkable: 'And they continued steadfastly in the apostles' doctrine and fellowship and in breaking of bread, and in prayers.' Have you, too, discovered that it can be harder to go on believing as a Christian than to become one in the first place? Do you find that enduring can be an enormous challenge?

Perhaps even now you are fearful, telling yourself, 'I love being energized by sermons on perseverance and renewed calls to gospel work, pursuit of holiness, and building up the church. But I know myself all too well. Within a week or two, I am afraid I will fall back into my old routine of living as a mediocre Christian, lacking zeal to walk as Christ walked. I am afraid I will fall back into defeat and say, "I can never measure up to walking as Jesus walked, so what's the use of trying? The poverty of my ongoing faith and sanctification is terribly discouraging. How can I persevere in believing in the absence of anything tangible to confirm my faith? How can I go on believing that God is light in the darkest night? How can I persevere in paying the high cost of faithfulness, enduring persecution, affliction, and loss for the gospel's sake?"'

So how do we endure in the Christian race when the motivation to press on fades and our life of holiness weakens, when we are in danger of giving up the fight against our besetting sin, and when it seems that God is not answering our prayers?

---

1. Revised from Joel R. Beeke, 'Endurance to the End,' in *Walking as He Walked* (Bridgend, Wales: Bryntirion, and Grand Rapids: Reformation Heritage Books, 2007), pp. 87-117.

397

The answer is profound yet simple: We endure as Christ endured when He was tempted to surrender in the battle of spiritual warfare. We walk as He walked, by His grace and His strength.

Hebrews 12 teaches us how Christ endured. Let us focus on verses 1-3: 'Wherefore seeing we also are compassed about with so great a cloud of witnesses, let us lay aside every weight, and the sin which doth so easily beset us, and let us run with patience the race that is set before us, looking unto Jesus the author and finisher of our faith; who for the joy that was set before him endured the cross, despising the shame, and is set down at the right hand of the throne of God. For consider him that endured such contradiction of sinners against himself, lest ye be wearied and faint in your minds.'

Let us explore the subject of persevering in Christ to the end from three aspects: (1) its mission, (2) its manner, and (3) its motives.

THE MISSION

The author of Hebrews ministered to the Jewish Christians around A.D. 68, shortly before the Romans destroyed Jerusalem and its temple. The book was written like a sermon to encourage discouraged Jewish converts who were paying too much attention to Jews who were rejecting Christ. These unbelieving Jews were challenging the spiritual worship that the Jewish Christians enjoyed in Jesus Christ. Many were saying, 'Where is your temple, where are your high priests?' Some were persecuting Jewish believers by marginalizing them socially. Others were persecuting believers more openly, withholding jobs and other benefits from them. As a result, many Jewish Christians suffered 'reproaches and afflictions' (Heb. 10:32-34), and were discouraged and tempted to abandon the faith.

The author of Hebrews encourages these Christian Jews by explaining how all the Old Testament rituals and ceremonial laws have been fulfilled in the Lord Jesus Christ. In the first nine chapters, the writer points believers to Christ, the greatest High Priest who brought a perfect sacrifice and who makes perfect intercession. Chapters 10–13 then focus on how we are to live out of Christ's saving work, freely approaching God's throne of grace. These chapters answer poignant questions: What's the use of going on? Why should we endure in the Christian faith? What consequences does Christ's work have for the lives of believers?

Our world today is surprisingly like that of the Christian Hebrews. Many leaders in the religious world look down on conservative evangelicals and regard us as a kind of modern day 'Puritan killjoy.' Like the Christian Hebrews, we often feel rejected, marginalized, even ostracized and persecuted.

The Christian Hebrews' need for endurance is evident not only from our text, but also from several other chapters in Hebrews. Actually, there are ninety-six verses in Hebrews that encourage Christians to endure in faith. For example, Hebrews 10:23 says, 'Let us hold fast the profession of our faith without wavering.' And 10:36 says, 'For ye have need of patience, that after ye have done the will of

God, ye might receive the promise.' Chapter 11 offers powerful examples of Old Testament stalwarts who endured spiritually 'by faith.' These heroes show us the virtue and power of faith.

Chapter 12 goes on to say: 'Wherefore seeing we also are compassed about with so great a cloud of witnesses, let us lay aside every weight, and the sin which doth so easily beset us, and let us run with patience the race that is set before us.' The Greek word here translated as *patience* is identical with the word used in verses 2 and 3, translated as *endurance*. So each of the first three verses in Hebrews 12 uses the word *endurance*. Verse 1 teaches us, 'We need to run the race with endurance'; verse 2 informs us that Jesus 'endured the cross'; and verse 3 claims that Jesus 'endured contradiction.' *Endurance* is the best translation in this context, since the author obviously wants to emphasize that this patience is an active Christian grace; it doesn't just sit and wait. Endurance involves hard labor and implies faithfully carrying a burden. The emphasis in verse 1 is on the last part of the verse: 'Let us run with patience [or with endurance] the race that is set before us.'

Thus our mission of endurance is to *run our Christian race to its end 'with patience.'* Using the metaphor of a race, the writer has in mind the endurance-testing relay races that took place in great colosseums. Those races didn't focus on who were the fastest sprinters, but on which runners would reach the finish line. Relay races were distance events. The contestants in the Christian race include the author of Hebrews, the Hebrew Christians to whom he writes, and, by mutual faith, *us*. Ultimately, every Christian is in the race. The Christian life is a test in endurance, a long relay in which runners assist each other rather than compete against each other. It's a serious race, a race that involves the testing and taxing of our faith, strength, and character. Life and death are set before us; hence, we must persevere. We must keep on keeping on. We cannot just step out of this race when we tire; we have to run all the way to the finish line.

This race of endurance is to be run 'with patience,' we are told. The Christian race has to be run steadily, deliberately, and actively every day, making use of the means of grace – reading and searching the Scriptures, personal and intercessory prayer, reading sound literature, fellowship among the saints, and Sabbath-keeping. The Christian life is not passive; we must work out our own salvation with fear and trembling, knowing that it is God who works in us both to will and to do of His good pleasure (Phil. 2:12-13).

Because of God's central role in perseverance, some theologians want to speak of the *preservation* of the saints, rather than *perseverance*. These two notions are closely related, but not the same. The preserving activity of God is the foundation or root of the saints' perseverance. God preserves his saints. He keeps them in the faith, preserves them from straying from the faith, and ultimately perfects them (1 Pet. 1:5; Jude 24). We may be confident that God will finish the saving work of grace which He has begun in us (Ps. 138:8; Phil. 1:6); Christ is 'the author and finisher of our faith' (Heb. 12:2); God preserves us through the intercession of the

Lord Jesus (Luke 22:32; John 17:5) and the abiding ministry of the Holy Spirit (John 14:16; 1 John 2:27).

Perseverance itself, however, is the saints' life-long activity, confessing Christ as Savior (Rom. 10:9), bringing forth the fruits of God's grace (John 15:16), enduring to the end (Matt. 10:22; Heb. 10:28, 29). True believers persevere in the 'things that accompany salvation' (Heb. 6:9). They keep themselves from sin (1 John 5:18). They keep themselves in the love of God (Jude 21). They run with patience the race that is set before them (Heb. 12:1).

Without preservation, there can be no perseverance. Thus, perseverance includes and yet extends beyond preservation, underscoring the believer's activity and responsibility.

We believe in both the preservation of the saints *by* God and the perseverance of the saints *before* God. True, our perseverance is a fruit of God's preservation, but that perseverance is still ours. It doesn't happen objectively outside of us; it happens subjectively, by grace, within and through us.

So we cannot remain on the sidelines; we are no mere spectators. We must persevere and continue the race patiently, steadfastly, believing in the Lord – not only in times of prosperity, but also in times of adversity (cf. Phil. 3:13-14). Regardless of circumstance, we must put our trust in the Lord every day. Our challenge is to stay focused on the Lord while we live in the midst of trials (cf. Psalm 46). The word translated as *endured* means to *stay* or to *press on*, even when the burden becomes too heavy. When we carry a burden that becomes too heavy, we want to rest for a while. But the apostle says that we need to 'press on' by faith. That is what endurance is all about – to keep hoping and trusting in the Lord, even when everything seems to go against us. It means to say with Job, 'Though he slay me, yet will I trust in him' (Job 13:15) – that is, to trust in God as my greatest Friend when He seems to be acting as if He were my greatest Enemy. It is easy to trust in the Lord when everything is going well, but how hard it becomes when much in our lives seems to testify against us! How easily our faith weakens and our diligent use of the means of grace is thwarted in times of difficulty!

Those who shall one day enter into glory must face numerous trials here on earth. Revelation 7:14 says that those who enter into heaven come 'out of great tribulation.' The believer has some foretaste of heavenly glory on earth, but this earth is not heaven for him. Here on earth, we do not yet enjoy the full salvation promised to believers. We have not yet received the full measure of God's grace. Here on earth our mission is to endure, to be patient runners in the Christian race. But how do we do that?

THE MANNER

We are to run the Christian race, says our text, with both a negative and a positive perspective. You might notice both positive and negative aspects of perseverance in John Flavel's explanation of perseverance: 'What is perseverance unto the end? It is a steady and constant continuance of Christians in the ways of duty and obedience, amidst all temptations and discouragements to the contrary.'[2]

A Negative Perspective on the Race

Negatively, we must rid ourselves of sin and hindrances. 'Let us lay aside every weight [that is, every hindrance], and the sin which doth so easily beset us [that is, not just our besetting or 'favorite' sin, but all sin], and [so] let us run with patience the race that is set before us' (Heb. 12:1).

The apostle is speaking particularly here to Christians. To run the race and reach the finish line, he tells them, they must not be hindered by anything; they must 'lay aside every weight.' How foolish a runner would be to wear heavy clothing and carry all kinds of paraphernalia while running a race! Like Greek athletes who trained naked or with a minimal amount of clothing, a runner who wants to reach the finish line needs to get rid of everything that hinders him.

And so it is with believers. The race we run is difficult and the battle severe. We need much endurance because there is much that hinders us and stands in our way. Unbelief, fear, worry, love of things, cares of this life, and even legitimate things such as relationships, professional duties, and recreational pursuits, when given an undue proportion of our time and heart, can hinder us in our Christian race.

So it is critical to discard anything that hinders us in this race. As a young man, I had to give up playing basketball for my high school team because of the time it consumed and the pride it engendered. Stuart Olyott says, 'For some of you this will mean canceling your subscription to the Internet, getting rid of your TV or stopping reading certain sorts of books or magazines. For others it will mean giving up football or a favorite sport, or even ending unhelpful friendships. We are all vulnerable, but we are not all vulnerable in the same areas.'[3]

Sin is our great enemy in the Christian race. The words, 'the sin which doth so easily beset us,' can be translated as the sin that *entangles* us, that trips us up. Sin encompasses us and clings to us. It comes out onto the racetrack, hangs onto our neck, and clings to us like clothing. 'Sin,' as John Owen put it, 'is always at our elbow.'

Sin takes our eyes off of our Savior; it interrupts our relationship with God. Sin is anti-God. It makes us worldly, selfish, proud, and unbelieving. Sin is spiritual insanity. Is that how you regard sin?

There is a difference, of course, in how unbelievers and believers regard sin: unbelievers cling to sin, but sin clings to believers. That is to say, unbelievers reach out for sin. They delight in it, look for it, and embrace it. But believers despise and

---

2. John Flavel, *An Exposition of the Assembly's Shorter Catechism*, in *The Works of John Flavel* (Edinburgh: Banner of Truth, 1968), 6:206.

3. Stuart Olyott, *This Way to Godliness: the Message of Romans 6, 7, 8* (Bridgend: Bryntirion Press, 2006), p. 28.

hate sin. They try to stay free from sin and break loose from it, but discover to their dismay that sin clings to them.

To put off sin and all other hindrances is not easy. We can't just put them off as we would take off a coat. And yet, we must do it. We must deny whatever hinders us in the Christian race and use all the means of grace to help us in our race. That is what runners do today. They deny themselves anything that would hinder them. They eat the right foods and get the right exercise. They do anything that will help them run and avoid anything that will distract their minds. If athletes are that serious about running an earthly race, how serious should we be about running the heavenly race?

Perhaps you find this extremely difficult to do. It is, but God never said that the Christian race would be easy. We must realize that we are accountable for what we do and don't do in our race. We must understand that we are not victims of sin; hindrances do not just overcome us. The imperative to lay aside every weight implies that we are responsible for those weights and the sin that still besets us so easily. We must put off the conversation and activities of our old nature and put on the righteousness and holiness of the new man (Eph. 4:22-24). There is simply no other way to run this race.

To run the Christian race with endurance means doing continual battle against every weight and every sin. We must become increasingly conscious of them; every day, we must decide against them, say no to them, and put them to death. We cannot trivialize sin, dumb it down, desensitize our consciences, or let down our guard. We cannot just let sin happen; we cannot let it penetrate our souls and our lives.

As the Puritans would say, we must not let sin into the gates of our soul through our senses; we must guard eye-gate and ear-gate. And when we do open the gates too wide to sin and stumble, we must confess and forsake our sin, immediately. We must put a sword through sin; we must push it back out the gates of our soul and close the gates. We must fear and hate sin. We must realize that it entangles us and hinders our walk with the Lord.

Sometimes we may be tempted to give up this battle against sin. 'What's the use?' we ask. We have fought sin again and again, yet we keep stumbling and falling into it. We fear that we have become nothing but sin, and there is no point in staying in the race. But that reasoning is unbiblical, false, and satanic, dear believer. Thanks be to God that sin can be laid aside! Sin does not belong to you as a believer; it does not belong to your new nature. It clings to you, but it is not you. In Romans 6:11, Paul tells us to 'reckon yourselves to be dead indeed unto sin, but alive unto God through Jesus Christ our Lord.' Sin is not your life – *Christ* is! Sin is a thievish, foreign intruder; you must not let it rest in the home of your new heart. You must not accept it as part of you. An old, now-deceased elder in my congregation used to say, 'My father always told us: as a Christian, you have no business sinning.'

How do you view sin and other hindrances? Do you welcome and tolerate sin, or do you fight it and flee from it? Do you fatalistically resign yourself to other, seemingly lawful hindrances, or do you conscientiously lay them aside?

John Bunyan once said that if sin knocks on your door and you open the door, you have not sinned as long as you shut the door as soon as you recognize sin for what it is. We fall into sin when we welcome sin into the home of our minds and dwell upon it.

A Positive Perspective on the Race

Perhaps you respond, 'I see my need for endurance in the Christian race, and I understand that endurance means laying aside sin and various hindrances, but how do I do that?'

You do that by adopting a positive perspective: by looking to Jesus, by confessing Him, depending upon His grace, and by appropriating forgiveness and learning to live by faith as a forgiven sinner throughout the Christian race. After all, Christ has already obtained for us all we need for perseverance. He has promised by the Spirit to uphold His people, He has won the gift of the Holy Spirit for His people on the basis of His righteousness and blood, not because of our works or merit, and He rules us by the gracious Spirit, supplying all that we need to persevere. Therefore, we have solid grounds to believe the promises of God's Word, such as:

- 'And I will give them one heart, and one way, that they may fear me for ever .... I will put my fear in their hearts, that they shall not depart from me' (Jer. 32:39-40).

- 'I will put my [S]pirit within you, and cause you to walk in my statutes, and ye shall keep my judgments, and do them' (Ezek. 36:27).

- 'Then shall they know that I am the LORD their God .... Neither will I hide my face any more from them: for I have poured out my [S]pirit upon the house of Israel, saith the Lord GOD' (Ezek. 39:28-29).

- 'As for me, this is my covenant with them, saith the LORD; My [S]pirit that is upon thee, and my words which I have put in thy mouth, shall not depart out of thy mouth ... from henceforth and for ever' (Isa. 59:21).

You who belong to Jesus Christ are commanded by Scripture to 'work out your own salvation with fear and trembling. For it is God which worketh in you both to will and to do of his good pleasure' (Phil. 2:11-12). Stand in awe at the wonder of sovereign grace, and stand firm in the fight of faith. Take hold of Christ and His glory, just as He has taken hold of you and will never let you go. Be strong and of good courage to obey God's laws, turning neither to the right nor to the left, that you may prosper in all that you do. Be strong, knowing that the Lord says to you, 'I will be with thee: I will not fail thee, nor forsake thee' (Josh. 1:5; cf. Heb. 13:5).

As Hebrews 12:2 says, 'Let us run with patience the race that is set before us, looking unto Jesus the author and finisher of our faith.' To persevere in the Christian race, we need to look beyond the weights of sin that surround us. We need to look to Jesus who ran before us, endured perfectly, and who by the Spirit communicates to us sustaining grace.

In John Bunyan's tale of *Pilgrim's Progress*, Christian comes to the house of Interpreter, where he sees a fire burning by a wall. Someone stands by the fire, continually pouring water on it to quench the flames, but the fire only burns hotter. Christian asks, 'What means this?' Interpreter explains that the fire is the work of God's grace in the heart, and the devil is constantly seeking to put it out.

Christian and Interpreter then walk around the wall and see a man who is secretly pouring oil on the fire so that it will not go out. Interpreter explains, 'This is Christ, who continually, with the oil of his grace, maintains the work already begun in the heart: by the means of which, notwithstanding what the devil can do, the souls of his people prove gracious still.' The man stands behind the wall to show that it is hard for Christians who are being tempted to see that Christ, by the oil of His Spirit, is sustaining them.[4]

As Christian continues his pilgrimage, he must climb the hill of Difficulty, resist many temptations, fight against Apollyon, endure persecution in Vanity Fair, escape from the Castle of Despair, and press on until he reaches the Celestial City. Meantime, Christ is in the background, ever pouring forth the oil of the Spirit so that His servant will overcome. That is a beautiful picture of the perseverance of the saints.

The context of Hebrews 12 makes plain that to run the Christian race, we need to focus by *faith* on Jesus, in whom we find strength, and who is both our model runner, our coach, and by the Spirit our very source of strength. Just as the Old Testament saints lived by faith in the promises of God (Hebrews 11), so we, surrounded by them as a cloud of witnesses, must focus by faith on Jesus alone, in whom all the promises of God 'are yea and amen.' Enduring is a matter of faith, and this faith depends on Jesus Christ.

The apostle reminds us in verses 2 and 3 that Jesus' endurance and ours are intimately connected. Jesus is called here 'the author and finisher of our faith.' How can we be sure that our faith is not in vain – that we will actually complete this race by faith? We can be sure because of Jesus, our uniquely qualified supplier and sustainer of faith, who evokes and stimulates our faith. Jesus is the pioneer and perfecter of our salvation (Heb. 2:10; 4:14-16). He will not allow a single one

---

4. John Bunyan, *The Pilgrim's Progress*, in *The Works of John Bunyan*, ed. George Offor (1854; repr., Edinburgh: Banner of Truth, 1991), 3:100. For more on Bunyan's view of perseverance, see Joel R. Beeke, 'Bunyan's Perseverance,' in *The Pure Flame of Devotion: The History of Christian Spirituality*, ed. G. Stephen Weaver, Jr., and Ian Hugh Clary (Kitchener, Can.: Joshua Press, 2013), p. 323-40. For a treatment of the Puritan teaching on perseverance, see Joel R. Beeke and Tim Worrell, 'The Puritans on Perseverance of the Saints' in Joel R. Beeke and Mark Jones, *A Puritan Theology: Doctrine for Life* (Grand Rapids: Reformation Heritage Books, 2012), pp. 601-17.

of His children to fall to the side of the road because He is the finisher of the faith of His runners. Because faith is the gift and work of Jesus Christ from its origin to its completion, our faith will never be in vain and we will never appeal to Christ in vain. Therefore, our faith must be directed to and concentrated on Christ, the only Mediator. He is the supreme exponent of faith.

THE MOTIVES

Speaking on behalf of Christ, the author of our text in Hebrews acts like a coach giving a motivational talk to his runners before a big race. We need such talks! There are three parts to his talk: the first and primary motivation for running the race of life is *the example of Christ*. We need to look to Him, 'who for the joy that was set before him endured the cross, despising the shame and is set down at the right hand of the throne of God' (v. 2). Our Savior motivates us to run this race in three important ways.

The Example of Christ

First, we are motivated by *what He endured*. Jesus Christ, the holy Lamb of God, Creator of this world, 'endured the cross'! The cross comprehends the worst punishment Jesus could receive in this world. He suffered throughout all of His earthly life, but the cross was the ultimate suffering. Jesus was nailed to it as the chief of sinners; He bore the punishment of His Father for the sins of His elect; He endured being forsaken by His Father, whom He loved from all eternity.

Jesus Christ hung in the naked flame of His Father's wrath for six long hours on the cross. No eye of mercy was cast toward Him, implying, 'We understand.' Seemingly rejected by heaven, earth, and hell, He endured the cross until its bitter end. No words can begin to capture the extremity of His sufferings, when He cried out, 'My God, my God, why hast thou forsaken me?' (Matt. 27:46). At the cross, He descended into the essence of what hell is; it was the most climactic moment of suffering ever endured, an hour so compacted—so infinite—so horrendous—as to be seemingly unsustainable.

Though we cannot grasp the depth of what this forsakenness was for Jesus, we know that it was far more awful that we can imagine. This forsakenness appears to have included some temporary loss of the sense of His sonship, some loss of filial consciousness. In Gethsemane, and in the first and last words of the cross, Jesus was able to call on God as His Father. But at the height of His dereliction on the cross, His cry was 'Eloi, eloi.' He was aware of the goodness of God, the otherness of God, the power and holiness of God, and even that God was His God, but He lost in some degree His sense of sonship in that dread moment. He knew more of sinnership than sonship at that solemn moment. He felt your sin and my sin, dear believer. In His self-image, He was not the Beloved in whom God was well-pleased, but the cursed one; vile, foul, repulsive – an object of dread. This is the essence of the dereliction. This is what God thinks of sin; the price of what Christ, the God-man, had to pay for sin.

Jesus endured the cross even when He was abandoned by God. As the Eternal Word, Jesus had always been with God; as the incarnate Son, He had always been with the Father. Father and Son had gone up from Bethlehem to Calvary together, like Abraham and Isaac going up the mount in Genesis 22. But now, in the hour of Christ's greatest need, God seemed not to be there. When the Son most needed encouragement, no voice cried from heaven, 'This is my beloved Son.' When He most needed reassurance, no one said, 'I am well pleased.' No grace was felt by Him, no favor shown, no comfort administered, no part of the cup removed. God was present only as one displeased, as one bearing down upon Christ with profound wrath. Every detail declares the irrationality, the heinousness, the dread character of sin. And yet, Christ endured the cross!

Jesus endured the cross, our text says, 'for the joy that was set before him.' This word *for* can also mean *instead of.* From that perspective, the Lord Jesus did not endure the cross to gain joy for Himself. With His Father and the Spirit, He already possessed that joy from all eternity. Certainly He was motivated by love to impart eternal joy for sinners, but our text emphasizes that Jesus endured the cross while He was already partaker of the heavenly joy with His Father and the Holy Spirit.

So the cross was not only a way *to* glory; it was also a way *from* glory. The Lord Jesus Christ was willing to leave the joy that He already enjoyed to travel the Via Dolorosa. The Lamb of God suffered for thirty-three years on this earth, culminating in His suffering on the cross. Four short words – 'Jesus endured the cross' – summarize all of Christ's love and willingness to suffer for sinners. He deserved a crown, but He willingly endured a cross. He did not deserve to dirty His feet with this world's dust, yet He was willing to have them nailed to Calvary's cross. Actively and consciously, He remained faithful to the work the Father laid upon His shoulders. He did not waver; He did not hesitate; He endured.

At one point, Jesus stumbled under the weight of the cross, and Simon had to carry it for Him. But help along the way didn't mean that the cross was less of a punishment for Christ. It only meant that He was meant to die on the cross rather than on the roadside. Our dear Lord Jesus Christ endured every hour, every minute, and every second on the cross. We know that when we have much pain, time seems to slow down. Hours creep by. So it was for Jesus. In all His agony and pain, He accepted every second of suffering. His every breath embraced the cross.

We too must endure in our race, but we do not have to endure the cross like Jesus Christ had to do. His huge crosses make all our crosses small! He endured things more fearful and overwhelming than we will ever have to face. He endured the cross to merit our salvation; we endure our crosses out of gratitude for the gift of His salvation. Nevertheless, Jesus' attitude of being willing to forego joy for the sake of submissive cross-bearing is an attitude that we must cultivate. Daily, we must pray for willingness to bear every cross He deems fit to place upon us. We must endure because He endured, to persevere because He persevered. We are called to endure right now, in the midst of our personal struggles. We are called to pause, to stand in awe, and to watch the Lord Jesus Christ. We are called to look to Jesus and consider how He suffered and died. We can become so accustomed to failure in our battles with sin and so busy attempting to sanctify ourselves in our own strength that we fail to meditate on the suffering of the Lord Jesus Christ. If we fail to focus on Christ, we will lack the mercy and grace we need to run the race.

Second, we are motivated by *what He rejoiced in*. The phrase *for the joy* refers to Jesus' exalted state of glory, where He 'is set down at the right hand of the throne of God.' The cross was not Jesus' end point. He rejoiced under the cross, knowing that He would be the victor in the battle with the powers of evil, and that He would soon be resurrected by His Father and taken home to glory to receive His promised reward. The joy that was set before Him was the joy of His own homecoming, the joy of reunion with His Father, the joy of being crowned with honor and glory and having all things put under His feet (Heb. 2:6-8). It was the joy of bringing many sons to glory (2:10). Jesus rejoiced, knowing that He would gain more than He lost.

Dear believer, as Christ lived out this joy with certitude, so we are to joyously await the eternal weight of glory, knowing that our future home with Christ in heaven is secure. We rejoice by faith (Heb. 11:1), knowing that our eyes have not seen, nor have our ears heard, nor has it entered into our hearts, what God has prepared for those who love Him (1 Cor. 2:9). Our future is to be married to Christ forever! That sure hope of glory and gracious reward in Christ ought to motivate us to run the Christian race.

Third, we are motivated by *what He despised*. Many of us have perhaps thought, 'What a shame! Jesus, the Son of God, on the cross!' And yet the Son of God thought little of the shame the cross brought upon Him. When our first parents, Adam and Eve, fell in Paradise, they felt shame because of their sin. This shame Jesus now bore on the cross, where He was made shameful sin. That shame was more intense than His pain. But He despised that shame and willingly endured the cross. He did not grumble or protest. He did not ask for a retrial because of the punishment and sentence of the cross. He endured the cross, 'despising the shame.'

Dear friends, when others mock us for running the Christian race, despise the shame. Be like Christian in *Pilgrim's Progress*, who began the race by shouting, 'Life, life, eternal life,' even as his family and friends called to him to come back. Let Christ be your mentor. Live by the fear of God, not the fear of man, 'esteeming the smiles and frowns of God to be of greater weight and value than the smiles and frowns of men,' as John Brown put it. Despise the world's shame. Count it all joy when you suffer for Christ's sake. Let Christ's willingness to endure shame motivate you to endure.

The Witness of the Saints

A second important motive that encourages us to endure in the Christian race is *the witness of the saints*. Even as we are surrounded with sin and various impediments while we run the Christian race, we are also surrounded with people in the stands who encourage us to endure. Verse 1 says, 'Wherefore seeing we also are compassed about with so great a cloud of witnesses.' These Old Testament heroes of faith encourage us in three ways. First, they encourage us because they were faithful spiritual athletes in the past. Every one of them was a gold medal winner in the race of life. Their example of running bears witness to enduring faith, so that, like Abel, they 'being dead, yet speak' to us (Heb. 11:4), encouraging us to run.

Second, because they reached the finish line by the endurance of faith, they cheer us on to persevere by putting our faith in God and the Messiah, just as they have done. These witnesses declare to us from the Old Testament pages that the Lord is faithful and willing through His Son to help us, too, despite all our stumblings, to endure to the end of the race.

How great a motivation these Old Testament witnesses are! What motivation Enoch provided in that 'he pleased God' (Heb. 11:5-6)! What motivation Abraham offered by obeying God in following His will to an unknown place, living 'in the land of promise, as in a strange country' (vv. 8-9)! What motivation Joseph provided when he gave 'commandment concerning his bones' (v. 22)! What motivation Moses presented when he chose rather 'to suffer affliction with the people of God, than to enjoy the pleasures of sin for a season, esteeming the reproach of Christ greater riches than the treasures in Egypt' (vv. 25-26). Those Old Testament saints who lived by faith surround us, Hebrews 11 and 12 say, like a crowd of spectators, watching us endure, nodding in encouragement, and saying, 'If I, by grace, endured to the end, so can you.'

As we read the Old Testament, we surround ourselves with saints who have lived by faith. They show us that the Lord is faithful to His own, even in the midst of trials that far supersede our own. Hebrews 11:37 says, 'They were stoned, they were sawn asunder, were tempted, were slain with the sword: they wandered about in sheepskins and goatskins; being destitute, afflicted, tormented.' And yet they endured by faith, clinging to God and His promises (v. 39). The Lord surrounds us with these kinds of people. Now, if they have run the difficult race set before them with patience and with endurance, how much more should we? If they did not give up in the face of insurmountable odds, why should we? If the Lord graciously brought these saints to the finish line, why couldn't He also bring us there – we who have so few discouragements and crosses to bear compared to them?

This cloud of witnesses increases in number throughout the New Testament and church history, with people such as Paul and John, as well as Athanasius, Augustine, Luther, Calvin, Whitefield, Spurgeon, Lloyd-Jones – who pressed forward through life by faith despite formidable obstacles and opposition. What encouragement these Bible saints and great divines throughout the ages are for us today!

Luther was so encouraged by the Psalms when he was going through his own trials that he felt a person could scarcely be a Christian without David being one of his best friends. Moreover, as he read the divines of past generations, Luther felt that some of his best friends were those on his bookshelves. Can you not say the same thing? What encouragement is found in David, Isaiah, Paul, John, Calvin, William Perkins, Wilhelmus à Brakel, Thomas Goodwin, John Owen, Anthony Burgess, John Bunyan, Samuel Rutherford, Mary Winslow, Ruth Bryan, and J. C. Ryle! Praise be to God for this cloud of witnesses who have encouraged us by their lives and writings to endure by gracious faith. Sometimes they have so moved me by the love of Christ or so challenged me by their godliness or so instructed me by their spiritual insights that I scarcely know where I would be without this cloud of God's witnesses.

This cloud of witnesses encourages us to think realistically about the communion of saints (*communio sanctorum*). Could it be that the saints in glory are more deeply interested in how we run the Christian race than we realize and are closer to us than we may think? Certainly, we err in taking little interest in those who have gone before us, for we have much to learn from them about running this great race. They are teammates who have reached the goal, but they will not be crowned until we join their ranks and share in their victory. They are eagerly waiting for that day, and urge us onward and forward by their own examples of endurance. We need to endure because of the cloud of witnesses that surrounds us

Third, living witnesses still surround us today. There are live people in the stands watching us and encouraging us to run the race. My witnesses include my God-fearing wife, my God-fearing friends in my church, and dear children of God around the world. One of the great benefits of the communion of saints and maintaining fellowship among believers is being immersed in a community of living witnesses. God's people were never meant to be lone rangers; we need fellowship with each other. The beginners in faith need the mature in faith for guidance; the mature need the beginners for renewed enthusiasm. We need to speak with each other about the faithfulness of our Savior and the ways of God so that we can encourage each other to be faithful in running the race.

Perhaps you are a widow or widower. It has been years since your spouse passed away. You have church friends, but those long evenings are hard to endure. You feel so alone at times. Take heart; the verse here says that you are surrounded by a great cloud of spectators watching you to encourage you in this struggle. Will you remain faithful? Be encouraged, you are not alone; you belong to a large family.

Recently, a young woman came up to me in tears after I spoke at a conference, saying, 'I am an orphan and an only child. I have only one uncle, who lives on the other side of the world. Lately, I have been weeping myself to sleep because of loneliness. But today, you helped me see that I am part of a big family. God is my Father, Jesus is my older Brother, all the believers in this church are my brothers and sisters. Now I have a new take on life and have courage to go on!'

Some people in this cloud of witnesses encourage us in special ways. They may not be famous and important in the eyes of others, but they are very important to us. For me, Samuel Rutherford is a great witness. His *Letters,* which lie on the nightstand beside my bed, have encouraged me countless times when I felt weighed down by affliction. If Rutherford can see afflictions as signs of Jesus coming, why shouldn't I?

I think also of my father, who often said to me before he died, 'Preach Christ in the simplicity of the gospel. You can never preach Him too much!' Or my dear wife, who notices even on the way to church when I feel harassed by Satan and fear I can't preach. 'You have it again, don't you?' she asks. 'It will be alright; your Savior won't desert you; He'll help you once more.' Oh, how such witnesses encourage me to endure, to strive more diligently, to be more godly! Persevere, dear friends, on account of the cloud of witnesses that compass you about.

Strength and Peace of Mind

Finally, be motivated to endure like Christ for your *own strength and peace of mind*. Hebrews 12:3 says, 'For consider him that endured such contradiction of sinners against himself, lest ye be wearied and faint in your minds.' This refers back to verse 2, telling us how Jesus endured the cross. It says that Jesus endured 'such contradiction,' that is, all the hatred, opposition, gainsaying, and contempt of sinners against Himself. The word *contradiction* here is the same word used in the Septuagint, the Greek translation of the Old Testament, when the rebellious Israelites argued with Moses. In the midst of such rebels—priests, scribes, and soldiers who spoke out against Him—Jesus had to suffer.

Jesus endured such contradiction of sinners because of His great love for them. We are moved when someone surrenders his life for a friend, but Jesus gave His life for enemies (Rom. 5:10) such as you and me, who are prone to talk back to God and to argue about His ways. By nature, we do not surrender and receive what He has done, but rebel against it; but when God penetrates our hearts with His saving grace, we are made willing to receive His gospel grace. We, too, will have to suffer contradiction and hostility from those around us, for all who are in Christ Jesus will suffer persecution. We will never endure the magnitude of Christ's contradiction of sinners, but if we walk as He walked, we will certainly encounter the contradiction of sinners against us. But all of this has a purpose.

Our text concludes: 'lest ye be wearied and faint in your minds.' So many times we faint and grow weary. We don't seem to have the energy to keep going. We are too tired to read, pray, and meditate upon the Word of God. Instead of running, we walk, or crawl, or worse yet, stop moving toward God altogether.

Do you feel weary and fainthearted now? Remember, God knows your every circumstance. He knows all about your weariness and weakness from the contradiction of sinners against you. He will not condemn you, but neither does He want you to remain in that condition. He says, '*Consider him* that endured such contradiction of sinners against himself, lest ye be wearied and faint in your minds' (v. 3). '*Consider Him!*' – that's what you are called to do. If you would endure in the race, consider Jesus' endurance in the race. Jesus is the best antidote for weariness and fainting while you are running the Christian race.

When you are afflicted, look to Jesus. Study the prophecies about Him, but especially the gospels and the epistles that most fully reveal His example and teaching. Consider how He endured affliction, and you will learn from Him how to endure as well.

Are you contemplating Christ as you seek to endure in the Christian race? If not, you will faint and will be overtaken by sin. You will fall and repeatedly backslide so long as you do not consider Him. Pray for grace to look to Christ on a daily basis in every area of your life as you battle against hindrances and sin and strive for righteousness.

Dear young people, it can be so tempting to give up your fight against sin. 'I'll just give in once,' you say, 'because all my friends are committing this sin, and I don't want to be different. I don't want to come across as too holy.' In the end, you lose the energy to say no to sin one more time, to stand up one more time for what is right and good. But dear friends, consider Christ; He did not give in even once. He walked the road to Golgotha without hesitancy. Look to Him, so that you might walk as He walked.

Saints may stumble and fall as they struggle against fierce temptations and doubts, they may even backslide and fall away for a time, but they will come to repentance and persevere in faith to the end. Thomas Watson said, 'Grace may be shaken with fears and doubts, but it cannot be plucked up by the roots.'[5]

And when you do fall, as fall you shall, time and time again, fly to Christ. Fly to Him a thousand times. Do not try to hide from God. When my son was once a small boy, I was going to punish him severely for a serious moral infraction. But before I could do that, he ran to me as soon as he saw me, hugged me, and with tears dripping down my neck, pleaded for my forgiveness. That is how we should run to God.

As parents, office-bearers, or employees, we often feel like we are going to faint. We are weary and preoccupied with obligations in every sphere of life. We don't seem to have time or take time to be holy. Our prayers and Bible readings are pitifully short and shallow. *'Consider Him'* – the great office-bearer who endured the cross. Let your energy and endurance derive from Him.

Do not put your heart in this world. This world will soon end. As Spurgeon said, 'If you had got all the world you would have got nothing after your coffin lid was shut but grave dust in your mouth.'[6]

Dear friends, look to Jesus now; look to Him to persevere in seeking Him. If you say, 'Lord, I have prayed so long and been to church so many times, and I am still not saved, so I will stop using the means of grace' – you will go from bad to worse. Stop trying to persevere in your own strength. Look to Jesus for perseverance and endurance. Remember, He endured the cross to save sinners such as you and me.

---

5. Thomas Watson, *A Body of Divinity* (Edinburgh: Banner of Truth, 1965), p. 285.

6. C. H. Spurgeon, 'The Spiritual Resurrection,' *The Metropolitan Tabernacle Pulpit*, vol. 44, #2554 (Pasadena, Tex.: Pilgrim Publications, 1976), p. 56.

He now invites you to come to Him just as you are. If you do not come to Him, you are despising His endurance and His shame – and would you dare to do *that?* Keep pleading the Word of God; Jesus is faithful and will fulfill His own Word.

We are called to look every day to Jesus, the author and finisher of faith. So consider Him, refocus on Him, and cling to Him. Meditate upon His suffering and upon His victory as the Son of God at the Father's right hand. Let His grace strengthen you from day to day. Inspired by the example of Christ and encouraged by the accomplishment of the saints, your weariness will be banished, and your faintness of mind will be dispelled. In their place, your faith, courage, and strength will be renewed, and by grace, you will walk as He walked.

Oh, to be able to say with Paul as the time of our departure draws near: 'I have fought a good fight, I have finished my course, I have kept the faith; henceforth there is laid up for me a crown of righteousness, which the Lord, the righteous judge, shall give me at that day: and not to me only, but unto all them also that love his appearing' (2 Tim. 4:7-8). Then, on the last day, you will meet Him as He is, and He will say, 'Well done, thou good and faithful servant ... enter thou into the joy of thy lord' (Matt. 25:21). You've endured the race, looking to Jesus.

Jesus will then be all in all in the sin-free land of Beulah. There will be no more sin, no more temptation, no more tears or pain or cross-bearing, but only glory in Emmanuel's land. You will forever walk as the Lord Jesus walks, enjoying Him, basking in His smile, bathing in His love, feasting in His presence. Your soul and body will be absolutely perfect. Jesus Christ will delight in you as His perfect bride, and you will be able to say to Him, 'Finally Lord, I am what I always wanted to be from the moment I was born again, for now I can serve Thee with a perfect eye, a perfect body, and a perfect soul.'

When former President Gerald Ford was buried in his hometown of Grand Rapids in 2007, the newspapers were filled with pictures of some of the tens of thousands of people that lined the streets and paid their last respects. The most common sign they displayed said simply, 'Welcome home!' That, dear believer, is what your Savior will one day say to you. 'Welcome home. Welcome to the eternal joy set before you – the joy of walking perfectly as Jesus walked, eternity without end.'

PRAYING FOR PERSEVERANCE

Having seen that our work of perseverance depends upon God's work of preservation, it is fitting to end this chapter—and to fill our lives—with prayer. The doctrine of perseverance obliges us to pray regularly and fervently for God to grant us more of the Spirit's work in us and in other believers. Our Lord encouraged us to do this in Luke 11:13, 'If ye then, being evil, know how to give good gifts unto your children: how much more shall your heavenly Father give the Holy Spirit to them that ask him?' Believers in Christ, pray to your Father to feed you daily with the food of the Spirit. He is your strength. Ask for the Spirit of wisdom to increase your knowledge of God and your future hope. Pray for the

Father to strengthen you with the power of His Spirit so that Christ may make His presence known in your heart and you may be filled with the fullness of God. Go to God and say, 'O God, Thou art my God. Early I will seek Thee. My soul thirsts for Thee. I long to see Thy power and Thy glory.'

I conclude this chapter with a prayer of John Calvin:

> Grant, almighty God, that as Thou art graciously pleased daily to set before us Thy certain and sure will, we may open our eyes and ears and raise all our thoughts to that which not only reveals to us what is right, but also confirms us in a sound mind, so that we may go on in the race of true religion and never turn aside whatever Satan and his demons may devise against us; but that we may stand firm and persevere, until, having finished our warfare, we shall at length come unto that blessed rest which has been prepared for us in heaven by Jesus Christ our Lord. Amen.[7]

---

7. Dustin W. Benge, ed., *Lifting Up Our Hearts: 150 Selected Prayers from John Calvin* (Grand Rapids: Reformation Heritage Books, 2012), p. 247.

CHAPTER 28

THE UTOPIAN MARRIAGE OF CHRIST AND HIS CHURCH

(REVELATION 19:7-9)

MEDITATION on holiness is not complete without meditation on heaven. Scripture always links our pursuit of holiness to our hope of heaven. Consider how Peter, after saying 'hope to the end for the grace that is to be brought unto you at the revelation of Jesus Christ,' places the command to hope next to a call for holiness: 'But as he which hath called you is holy, so be ye holy in all manner of conversation' (1 Pet. 1:13, 15). Our heavenly hope is grace-saturating fuel for our pursuit of holiness.

Have you ever noticed that the Bible does not speak about dying and going to heaven? It speaks about dying and going to be with Christ. Christ is the sum and substance of heaven's glory. Samuel Rutherford said, 'Suppose that our Lord would manifest His art, and make ten thousand heavens of good and glorious things, and of new joys, devised out of the deep of infinite wisdom, He could not make the like of Christ.'[1]

There are several reasons why heaven is so focused on our glorious Savior. One reason is that no one can get there without Christ's saving work. Anyone who enters heaven must confess with Anne Cousin:

> *I stand upon His merit;*
> *I know no other stand,*
> *Not e'en where glory dwelleth*
> *in Immanuel's land.*[2]

Christ is the centerpiece of heaven because in heaven, faith in Christ will become sight of Christ. Peter describes our present situation: We love a Christ whom we

---

1. *Letters of Samuel Rutherford*, ed. Andrew Bonar (1891; repr., Edinburgh: Banner of Truth, 1984), p. 413.

2. One of the nineteen original stanzas of 'Immanuel's Land,' Anne Cousin's hymn, first published in 1857, and composed of lines gathered from the *Letters and Dying Sayings* of Samuel Rutherford (d. 1661), published in 1664.

have not seen, 'in whom, though now ye see him not, yet believing, ye rejoice with joy unspeakable and full of glory' (1 Pet. 1:8). Faith in the unseen Christ will be rewarded by the joy of looking upon Him, and seeing Him as He is, forever. 'Thine eyes shall see the king in his beauty' (Isa. 33:17).

Heaven is Christ-centered because in heaven every believer will be fully conformed to the image of Christ. We who believe 'shall be like him' (1 John 3:2), and He shall be 'the firstborn among many brethren' (Rom. 8:29). What bliss it will be to be without sin, and to reflect Christ so completely that it will be impossible to be un-Christlike!

Heaven is focused on Christ because His glory will always shine there, and His praises will never grow old. 'And the city had no need of the sun, neither of the moon, to shine in it: for the glory of God did lighten it, and the Lamb is the light thereof' (Rev. 21:23).

But another, all-too-often-forgotten reason that heaven focuses on Christ is that in heaven the living church will be married to Christ and will express the love of a bride toward her husband. Dear believer, your engagement to Jesus Christ in this life will be turned into perfect marital union with Him in heaven. This theme often surfaces in Bible passages.[3] But nowhere is the theme of our utopian marriage to Christ so beautifully unfolded as in Scripture's last chapters.

Revelation 19:7-9 says, 'Let us be glad and rejoice, and give honour to him: for the marriage of the Lamb is come, and his wife hath made herself ready. And to her was granted that she should be arrayed in fine linen, clean and white: for the fine linen is the righteousness of saints. And he saith unto me, Write, Blessed are they which are called unto the marriage supper of the Lamb.'

As *The Reformation Heritage KJV Study Bible* says, 'Redemption is a love story (Isa. 54:4-8; Hosea 3:1-5), the covenant is a vow of betrothal (Hosea 2:19-20), salvation is a wedding dress (Isa. 61:10), and the kingdom is a wedding feast (Matt. 22:1-14).'[4] Let us consider what Scripture says about the wedding, the Bridegroom, the bride, and the guests.

THE WEDDING

Presently, the church is betrothed and waiting for her wedding day. There is a great difference between what we mean by engagement and what the Bible means by betrothal. From the day they were betrothed to each other, the couple would be regarded as husband and wife, but they would not live together. For example, Mary and Joseph were only 'espoused' or betrothed, and he was shocked to discover that she was pregnant, but the angel called her his 'wife' (Matt. 1:18, 20).[5] With the

---

3. Psalm 45:10-15; Isaiah 54:5; 62:4-5; Matthew 9:15; 25:1-13; John 3:28, 29; 2 Corinthians 11:2; Ephesians 5:22-33.

4. *The Reformation Heritage KJV Study Bible* (Grand Rapids: Reformation Heritage Books, 2014), p. 1892.

5. See also Deuteronomy 20:7; 22:23-24; 28:30.

betrothal, the bridegroom would pay the bride's father a dowry, or 'bride-price.'[6] According to Jewish tradition, 'the marriage agreement, drawn up at betrothal, was committed into the hands of the best man.'[7] Then, when the wedding day came, both bride and groom would dress in fine clothing (Isa. 61:10). He would come to her home to get her and her friends, and take them to her new home, where they would all feast and celebrate for as long as a week (Judg. 14:12; Matt. 25:1-13).[8]

All Christians are betrothed to Christ. Paul is thus jealously protective of believers who are being troubled by false apostles who preach another gospel. He said in 2 Corinthians 11:2-4:

> 'I am jealous over you with godly jealousy: for I have espoused you to one husband, that I may present you as a chaste virgin to Christ. But I fear, lest by any means, as the serpent beguiled Eve through his subtlety, so your minds should be corrupted from the simplicity that is in Christ. For if he that cometh preacheth another Jesus, whom we have not preached, or if ye receive another spirit, which ye have not received, or another gospel, which ye have not accepted, ye might well bear with him.'

Paul casts himself in the role of the marriage broker or matchmaker. In his love for Christ, he desires to present Him with a chaste virgin bride; in his concern for the Corinthians, he resents anyone who wants to lead them astray into spiritual adultery.

Paul is not just preaching a set of abstract truths. He is not just presenting people with some philosophy. He is proclaiming the person of Christ, and through his preaching he is presenting that person to the congregation. 'I have betrothed you to Christ,' he says. 'You are engaged to be His.' Samuel J. Stone says so beautifully about the church:

> *From heaven He came and sought her*
> *To be His holy bride;*
> *With His own blood He bought her,*
> *And for her life He died.*

Christ has paid the bride-price for all believers. Therefore, we are legally and inalienably His. He is coming again for His bride, the church, to lead us home to His Father's house where He will present us spotless before His Father in heaven.

---

6. On the dowry or bride-price (KJV 'dowry'), see Genesis 34:12; Exodus 22:16-17; 1 Samuel 18:25; cf. Deuteronomy 22:28-29.

7. D. J. William, 'Bride, Bridegroom,' in *Dictionary of Jesus and the Gospels*, ed. Joel B. Green, Scot McKnight, I. Howard Marshall (Downers Grove, Ill.: InterVarsity, 1992), 86. As a source he cites the Midrash, Rabbah Exodus 46.1.

8. 'It reflects the Jewish custom in which the formal wedding is preceded by a legally binding betrothal. During this period, which normally lasts no longer than a year, the pair were called husband and wife. To dissolve the betrothal required a formal divorce, which Joseph briefly considered doing with Mary (Matt. 1:18-20). As part of the betrothal, gifts were exchanged between the families. The bridegroom paid a bride-price to the family of the bride (Exod. 22:16-17), while the bride's father presented a dowry to his daughter (Judg. 1:14-15). When the wedding day arrived, the bride prepared herself by dressing in finery, such as an embroidered garment (Ps. 45:13-14), jewels (Isa. 61:10), ornaments (Jer. 2:32), and a veil (Gen. 24:65)' (Mark Wilson, 'Revelation,' in *Zondervan Illustrated Bible Backgrounds Commentary*, ed. Clinton E. Arnold [Grand Rapids: Zondervan, 2002], 4:354).

There will be a wedding procession and festivities that will last not for a week or two, but for all eternity. We will be with Christ and behold His glory. The story of salvation is a love story. The covenant of grace is a marriage contract. Before the worlds were made, God the Father chose a bride for His Son and drew up a marriage contract between them. This wedding involves choice, not mutual attraction. God chose us in eternity and gave us to Christ, who bought us at Calvary and took us as His own through the preaching of the gospel; and now He will come back for us. When He comes back to claim us, we will enjoy intimacy and fellowship with Him forever.

The whole Trinity is involved in this marriage. The Father gives us His Son as our Bridegroom and gives us as a bride to the Son. As Ephesians 5:25 says, Christ purchased His bride with His blood and death. Ephesians 1:14 says the Holy Spirit is given to us as an *earnest* or guarantee. That guarantee, in ancient times, was shown by a down-payment. Today, this is commonly symbolized by an engagement ring. When Christ betroths us to Himself, He gives us the Spirit as a kind of engagement ring that guarantees that we shall all arrive at the last day for the actual wedding.

James Hamilton puts it so well when he writes, 'We can scarcely imagine the glory of that wedding day,' noting that:

- Never has there been a more worthy bridegroom.

- Never has a man gone to greater lengths, humbled himself more, endured more, or accomplished more in the great task of winning his bride.

- Never has a more wealthy Father planned a bigger feast.

- Never has a more powerful pledge been given than the pledge of the Holy Spirit given to this bride.

- Never has a more glorious residence been prepared as a dwelling place once the bridegroom finally takes his bride.

- Great will be the rejoicing. Great will be the exultation. There will be no limit to the glory given to the Father through the Son on that great day.[9]

The invitation to this wedding feast is presented in Revelation 19:6-7: 'Alleluia: for the Lord God omnipotent reigneth. Let us be glad and rejoice, and give honour to him: for the marriage of the Lamb is come.'

THE BRIDEGROOM

The term *marriage of the Lamb* is strange because lambs don't get married. But Jesus Christ is presented here in His capacity as Savior. The Lamb of this marriage shows us His love by living for us and dying for us. He first appears as the Lamb in Revelation 5, where we read, 'Thou art worthy to take the book, and to open the

---

9. James M. Hamilton, Jr., *Revelation: The Spirit Speaks to the Churches*, Preaching the Word, ed. R. Kent Hughes (Wheaton, Ill.: Crossway, 2012), p. 351. Select statements from his paragraphs were put in bullet point form.

seals thereof: for thou wast slain, and hast redeemed us to God by thy blood out of every kindred, and tongue, and people, and nation' (vv. 6, 9). This love is a very one-sided affair, at least to begin with. 'We love him,' said John, 'because he first loved us' (1 John 4:19).

When we think of the ideal marriage, we think of two lovers gazing into each other's eyes, starry-eyed with love. That is a Western view of marriage. It is different in many other parts of the world, where the parents of a bride often decide when she is to marry. In some cultures, she may have no say in the matter. She may not even know who her husband will be. She does not meet him until the day they are married. She learns to love him as her husband, and he learns to love her as his wife. We see this pattern, for example, in the marriage of Isaac and Rebekah (Gen. 24).

In some ways, that is the kind of marriage we have with Christ. We love Christ. But we only love Him because He loved us first. He loved us while we were yet sinners and were utterly unattractive and undeserving. He loved us while our carnal minds were still at enmity with Him. Our hearts were against Him, yet He loved us.

The prophet Hosea provides us with a powerful example of this love. God said to Hosea, 'Go, take unto thee a wife of whoredoms and children of whoredoms: for the land hath committed great whoredom, departing from the LORD' (Hosea 1:2). That is what happened. As an adulteress, Gomer had a succession of affairs; and when her youth and attractiveness were spent, she ended up in the slave market. But Hosea found Gomer in the slave market and bought her back – not to exact revenge on her for the rest of her life, but out of sheer love (Hosea 3:2). He was a faithful husband to her despite her unfaithfulness to him.

That is how God loves you, dear believer, in Jesus Christ! When we were still sinners—unclean, unfaithful, adulterous, and promiscuous—He loved us. The apostle John said, 'Having loved his own which were in the world, he loved them unto the end' (John 13:1). He loved them to the farthest limits of love.

We can't measure the length, breadth, height, and depth of the love of God; it surpasses knowledge. Jesus Christ loves us beyond our wildest imagination. He loved us all the way to the cross of Calvary. And there on that cross He paid the dowry to free us from the penalty of sin.

Sometimes when two people marry, one has a substantial bank account, and the other is in debt. But when they marry, they merge their accounts, for 'one flesh' means one bank account. That is precisely what Christ has done for us. When we were up to our necks in debt to a holy God because we had broken His law thousands of times, Christ took our liabilities and our debts and paid the price of all our sins. He was made sin for us. Christ became one flesh with His church. Her sins became His sins, and His perfect righteousness becomes hers through faith.

In his book, *The Best Match*, Edward Pearse seeks to woo sinners to come to Christ as their spiritual Husband. Like a good matchmaker, Pearse extols the virtues of this Bridegroom who calls us to become His, and His alone. Do you want a match who has honor and greatness? He is God and man, the brightness of

His Father's glory, the King of kings and Lord of lords. Do you want riches and treasures? Christ's riches are the best, for they last forever, are infinitely great, and will satisfy all your desires. Are you looking for a generous heart in a spouse? Jesus Christ is willing to lay out His riches for His spouse so that her joy may be full. Do you want wisdom and knowledge? The infinite wisdom of God shines in Him; He is Wisdom itself, and knows perfectly how to glorify Himself and do good to those who love Him. Are you looking for beauty? He is altogether lovely, more than all the beauty of human beings and angels combined. Are you seeking someone who will truly love you? Christ is love itself, love that is higher than the heavens and deeper than the seas. Do you want a husband who is honored and esteemed? This Husband is adored by the saints and angels. Everyone whose opinion really matters treasures Him, and God the Father delights in Him. Do you seek a match who will never die and leave you a widow? Christ is the King immortal and eternal; He is the resurrection and the life.[10]

Behold the Lamb of God! Do you know Christ as the Lamb? Have you received Him as your heavenly Husband? Have you come to Him, repenting of your sin and throwing yourself on His mercy? Will you have Jesus Christ, the Son of God, to be your Savior, to love, honor, and obey, from this day forth and forever more? Will you have the Lamb of God to be your Husband – the Sin-bearer to be your Bridegroom? If you will have Him as your Bridegroom, you are invited to the marriage supper of the Lamb, but if you won't, you will not have Him at all.

THE BRIDE

Revelation 19:7 records these words of the church triumphant: 'Let us be glad and rejoice, and give honour to him: for the marriage of the Lamb is come, and his wife hath made herself ready. And to her was granted that she should be arrayed in fine linen, clean and white: for the fine linen is the righteousness of saints.' The bride asks, 'What shall I wear? What kind of raiment is fitting for someone who is to be married to such a Bridegroom?' So she begins in earnest to seek those things that will honor and please Him. She seeks to be holy as He is holy, by His own sanctifying grace. She can't wait for the wedding. As the days go by, she checks off the days, counting how many are left before the big day. This is the picture you have here of the bride of Christ. She has made herself ready for the Bridegroom long before the wedding.

Paul speaks of this anticipation in 2 Timothy 4:6-8. He says: 'For I am now ready to be offered, and the time of my departure is at hand. I have fought a good fight, I have finished my course, I have kept the faith: henceforth there is laid up for me a crown of righteousness, which the Lord, the righteous judge, shall give me at that day: and not to me only'—and then he widens it out to encompass the

---

10. Edward Pearse, *The Best Match: The Soul's Espousal to Christ*, ed. Don Kistler (Grand Rapids: Soli Deo Gloria, 1994), pp. 56-70.

whole church, every believer—'but unto all them also that love his appearing.' True Christians love Christ's coming, looking forward to that day with joyful anticipation and great longing.

Spurgeon said: 'It ought to be a daily disappointment when our Lord does not come; instead of being, as I fear it is, a kind of foregone conclusion that he will not come just yet.'[11] So are you longing for Christ's return? Here, through the preaching of the gospel, partaking of the Lord's Supper, and in prayer meetings, we see Christ, but through a glass darkly. We prize the means of grace, but how much more we will prize the day when we shall see Christ face to face!

What is most amazing is that Christ loves us and desires to be with us. As a pastor, I counsel young couples who can hardly wait to be married. One young man wondered aloud why he and his fiancée had set their wedding date so far in the future. Likewise, the Lord Jesus Christ yearns for His eternal marriage with His beloved bride. Psalm 45:11 says: 'So shall the king greatly desire thy beauty.' Dear believer, in His great love, Jesus Christ will beautify you now with His own image and holiness because He is looking forward to embracing you one day as His bride.

He is the King of heaven, and the King greatly desires you, for you will be lovely in His sight. The King of kings will make us His queen. He who rules over the whole universe will make us queen of heaven. The angels will be our servants. The King will take us by the hand and lead us to Paradise, His own personal garden, where we will live with Him forever!

Various stories tell about a great prince who marries a lowly maiden. But that is nothing compared to what we will one day experience when—wonder of wonders—the greatest Prince of all, the King of kings, takes the hand of us lowly creatures. That wonder immensely adds to the love and beauty and splendor of this astonishing heavenly marriage. It is truly the story that ends, 'And they lived happily ever after.'

We know both from the Bible and experience that marriage is the closest human relationship. The intimacy between a loving husband and a loving wife is beyond words, for the two indeed become one flesh (Eph. 5:31). But Paul speaks of an even greater mystery 'concerning Christ and his church' (v. 32). In glory, dear believer, our closeness to Christ will far surpass even the intimacy between a husband and wife.

Due to being saved by grace alone from the enormity of our sin, our intimacy with the Lord Jesus Christ will be greater than what He experiences with the holy angels who have been with Him in perfect holiness for thousands of years. We will have a direct, personal, intimate, mystical union with the Lord Jesus Christ, which will allow no distance between us.

When I in righteousness at last
Thy glorious face shall see,
When all the weary night is past,

---

11. C. H. Spurgeon, 'Between the Two Appearings,' Sermon of March 15, 1891, on Hebrews 9:26-28, in *The Metropolitan Tabernacle Pulpit* (1892; repr., London: Banner of Truth, 1970), 37:155.

And I awake with Thee
To view the glories that abide,
Then, then I shall be satisfied.[12]

Ephesians 5:25 says that Christ purchased His bride with His death. The bride will also be beautifully adorned for her Husband (Rev. 21:2). In most weddings a bride wears a special gown, which she has chosen and paid for. But in heaven we do not have to purchase a wedding dress, for that dress is the gift of God's grace. Isaiah 61:10 says, 'I will greatly rejoice in the LORD, my soul shall be joyful in my God; for he hath clothed me with the garments of salvation, he hath covered me with the robe of righteousness, as a bridegroom decketh himself with ornaments, and as a bride adorneth herself with her jewels.'

The robe of righteousness that we wear on our glorious wedding day is the realization of our imputed blamelessness and holiness through Christ (Eph. 5:27), for He has redeemed us from sin's guilt and purifies us to be zealous for Him (Titus 2:14). So, this gown is the robe of Christ's perfect righteousness imputed to us in justification (2 Cor. 5:21). Christ takes off the filthy garments of our guilt and clothes us with the clean and beautiful clothing of His merit (Zech. 3:1-5). His obedience is credited to us. We read in Revelation 7:14 of countless people from every nation who 'have washed their robes, and made them white in the blood of the Lamb.' How did they wash their robes and make them white? By trusting in Christ alone for justification from the guilt of all sin. You can receive this cleansing only through faith – the self-abandonment of trusting Christ alone to make you acceptable to God.

Next, Christ continues to cleanse us from impurity in our sanctification. One day that sanctification process will be perfected, and perfect holiness will be the gown that is given to us. Revelation 19:8 says, 'And to her was granted that she should be arrayed in fine linen, clean and white: for the fine linen is the righteousness of saints.' Literally, the Greek text says 'the righteous deeds [δικαιώματά] of the saints.' Thus getting ready for the day that Christ comes for you does involve effort on your part. We are told in verse 7 that 'his wife has made *herself* ready.' The man who says he belongs to Christ and yet never lifts a finger to purify himself is deceived. The Christian life means getting ready. It means putting off the old way of living and putting on the new.

As Paul says in Colossians 3:8-9, 'But now ye also put off all these; anger, wrath, malice, blasphemy, filthy communication out of your mouth. Lie not one to another, seeing that ye have put off the old man with his deeds.' Then verse 12 says, 'Put on therefore, as the elect of God, holy and beloved, bowels of mercies, kindness, humbleness of mind, meekness, longsuffering.' It is serious business to make ourselves ready for the return of Christ. There are no shortcuts, no secrets, and no easy escape routes. We have to *make ourselves ready*!

---

12. *The Psalter, With Doctrinal Standards, Liturgy, Church Order, and Added Chorale Section* (Grand Rapids: Reformation Heritage Books, 1999), no. 31, verse 7 [Ps. 17:15].

At the same time, this preparation is entirely a matter of grace. Notice here that 'fine linen, clean and white ... the righteousness of saints' (v. 8) is *given* to the bride to wear. You and I ought to be totally involved in the business of sanctification; yet, at the same time, sanctification is entirely a matter of grace. In short, the Lord reigns over His prepared bride, making her willing by His power! Revelation 19:6 puts it this way, 'Alleluia: for the Lord God omnipotent reigneth.'

Christ reigns over every part of our salvation – even our sanctification. As Paul says in Ephesians 5:25-27: 'Christ also loved the church, and gave himself for it; that he might sanctify and cleanse it with the washing of water by the word, that he might present it to himself a glorious church, not having spot, or wrinkle, or any such thing; but that it should be holy and without blemish.'

A wrinkle or spot is a sign of age or disease. People spend a fortune to get rid of spots and wrinkles. We are told here that Christ is going to present His church without a single spot or wrinkle to His Father in heaven. He will come with all His holy angels and will take the church by the hand. He will lead her before God and the assembled hosts of the universe. In eternity He chose us. We do not know why. There is nothing in us to merit His choice. What is more, He bought us with His own blood at Calvary. And now He is beautifying us by the gospel and by His Holy Spirit. We remember that Christ Jesus accomplished complete salvation for us when we partake of the Lord's Supper.

As all the hosts of heaven look at the bride on her wedding day, they will give God all the glory. Revelation 19:6-7 tell us: 'And I heard as it were the voice of a great multitude, and as the voice of many waters, and as the voice of mighty thunderings, saying, Alleluia: for the Lord God omnipotent reigneth. Let us be glad and rejoice, and give honour to him: for the marriage of the Lamb is come, and his wife hath made herself ready.'

THE GUESTS INVITED TO THE SUPPER

If the church is the bride, then who are the guests? Some interpreters give the impression that some will be married to the Lamb, while others will just be onlookers or guests at the wedding. We need to remember that the language of Revelation is symbolic. This is the marriage of the Lamb, but of course lambs don't get married. When Jesus says in John 10, 'I am the good shepherd,' and then He says, 'I am the door,' you wonder how He can be both. But He is really more than that and all the other descriptions and designations in Scripture put together. In the same way, the church is the bride of Christ as well as the company of guests at the wedding.

Heaven is a place of festivity. The Lord's Supper is only a foretaste of heaven's eternal supper (Luke 22:18). You will be thoroughly and profoundly happy in heaven, for it is a place of everlasting happiness, celebration, and festivity. In heaven we will feast both with Christ and upon Christ.

In biblical times, sharing supper with someone was a sign of fellowship and closeness (Rev. 3:20). That's why the Pharisees were so upset with Jesus for eating with publicans and sinners (Luke 15:2). But what Jesus did makes the gospel accessible to us all. 'Hallelujah – this Man receives sinners!' we cry out.

When Jesus invites needy sinners to the marriage supper, He offers us an experience of fellowship that is beyond words. The Bible says that when a couple gets married they are to leave their parents to enter into a new relationship. While they were children, the closest relationship the bride and groom had was with their parents. But now the closest relationship they have is with each other as husband and wife. That is the best metaphor to describe the relationship between Christ and His church. As we feast with Christ in heaven, we will have an intimacy that can only be compared to that between a husband and wife – yet it far surpasses even that.

Unlike human marriage, there will be no sexual relations in heaven (Matt. 22:30). We will not have physical relations, but we will have an intimacy that is even deeper. We will have an eternal, perfectly pure relationship with the Lord Jesus Christ, far beyond anything here on earth. We will enjoy His embraces of love and express our love for Him. There will be heavenly ecstasy without any sin or hindrance. It will be the purest, deepest emotion of love possible between the perfect Husband and the purified, perfected wife. When we are married to Jesus Christ, we will find our greatest delight in Him, and He will be delighted with us. Peter leaves us to ponder on what this will be like, if as he notes, we already have such joy in Him: 'Whom having not seen, ye love; in whom, though now ye see him not, yet believing, ye rejoice with joy unspeakable and full of glory' (1 Pet. 1:8).

In his book, *Heaven Help Us,* Steve Lawson tells about a young aristocrat, William Monteague Dyke, who was stricken with blindness at the age of ten. The boy was very intelligent and went to university. While he was in graduate school, he met the beautiful daughter of a British admiral. The courtship soon flamed into romance. Though he had never seen this woman, William fell in love with the beauty of her soul. The two became engaged.

Shortly before the wedding, at the insistence of the bride's father, William agreed to have eye surgery that had a slight chance of restoring his sight. The doctors operated on William and bandaged his eyes. He was then confined to bed with his eyes covered with bandages until the wedding.

William requested that the bandages be removed from his eyes during the ceremony, just when the bride made her way down the center aisle. As the organ signaled for the bride to come down the aisle, every heart waited to see what would happen. As the bride came down the center aisle, William's father began to unwrap the gauze over his son's eyes. When the last bandage was removed, light flooded into William's eyes. Slowly, William focused on the radiant face of his precious bride. Overcome with emotion, William whispered, 'You are more beautiful than I ever imagined.'[13]

---

13. Steven J. Lawson, *Heaven Help Us!: Truths about Eternity That Will Help You Live Today* (Colorado Springs: NavPress, 1995), pp. 168-69.

Something like that will happen to us when the bandages are taken away from our eyes, and we see Jesus. We will attain to what medieval theologians called the beatific vision, the very thing Christ prayed for when He said, 'Father, I will that they also, whom thou hast given me, be with me where I am; that they may behold my glory' (John 17:24). Then we will worship our heavenly Husband forever. He will gaze upon us as His bride and see only beauty – His own work in us. He will see no sin. We shall be like Him and see Him as He is. We will be as perfect in soul and in body as He is. As 1 Corinthians 2:9 says, 'Eye hath not seen, nor ear heard, neither have entered into the heart of man, the things which God hath prepared for them that love him.' Hallelujah!

COME TO THE WEDDING FEAST

The Lord Jesus offers His hand in marriage to you. Will you receive it by faith and repentance? There is a sense in which everyone is called to this wedding. The gospel is to be preached to all creatures. God freely and lovingly invites *all* to this wedding. The invitations are out. All are welcome to come to Christ.

But to come to this wedding, you must be born again. You must know something of the marks of the Spirit's saving grace in your soul. You must know what it means to respond to God's overtures of salvation with true repentance and saving faith. You must learn of your need of the Bridegroom as your only hope of salvation. You must know something of your own depravity and something of Christ's marvelous deliverance from it. And you must want to live for Him in gratitude if you are going to sit at His table wearing His wedding garment. You must be prepared for this table by being stripped of your righteousness. You must long for the day of your eternal marriage with Christ.

You can get to heaven without money, without education, without beauty, or without friends. But you cannot get there without Christ. Only those now engaged to Christ will be married to Him in heaven one day.

I can't tell you how this world is going to end. But I can tell you that there will be a wedding, the wedding of all time, and you're invited! And the gospel demands a response from you – your RSVP. As Paul says in Ephesians 5: 'For this cause shall a man leave his father and mother, and shall be joined unto his wife, and they two shall be one flesh. This is a great mystery: but I speak concerning Christ and the church' (vv. 31-32). The gospel demands that you repent of your sin and cleave to this only Savior by true saving faith.

Those who do repent and trust in Christ can sincerely confess that their greatest hope is the hope of being with Christ and beholding His glory. David sings of this hope in Psalms 16:11 and 17:15: 'Thou wilt shew me the path of life: in thy presence is fullness of joy; at thy right hand are pleasures for evermore …. As for me, I will behold thy face in righteousness: I shall be satisfied, when I awake with thy likeness.' All who share this faith and cherish this hope can sing:

The King there in His beauty,
Without a veil is seen:
It were a well-spent journey,
Though seven deaths lay between:
The Lamb with His fair army,
Doth on Mount Zion stand,
And glory, glory dwelleth
In Emmanuel's land.

O Christ, He is the fountain,
The deep, sweet well of love!
The streams on earth I've tasted
More deep I'll drink above:
There to an ocean fullness
His mercy doth expand,
And glory, glory dwelleth
In Emmanuel's land.

Let me conclude with three practical lessons we can apply from this truth of Christ, the centerpiece of heaven, to whom we may one day be married in the greatest wedding of all time.

1. Since Christ is the jewel in heaven's crown—for He is what makes heaven, heaven—strive to make Him the center of your life here on earth. You can get to heaven without money, education, beauty, or friends. But you cannot get there without Christ. Only those who are now engaged to Christ will one day be married to Him in heaven. So put all your energy into focusing on Christ in His person, names, natures, states, offices, and benefits.

2. As a bride prepares herself for her wedding, we must do likewise. The more we yearn for our marriage with Christ, the more we shall seek for that holiness without which no man shall see the Lord. But the less we think of it, the less we will follow the Lord Jesus in this life. During an engagement, those who are betrothed to each other are not allowed to court other people. We must not flirt with sin but push it far from us and say, 'I will keep myself pure for the Lord Jesus Christ.' Our heavenly hope energizes and enlivens our pursuit of holiness.

3. Remember that death will soon usher you into glory to be forever with your heavenly Husband. In John 14:2-3 Jesus says, 'In my Father's house are many mansions: if it were not so, I would have told you. I go to prepare a place for you. And if I go and prepare a place for you, I will come again, and receive you unto myself; that where I am, there ye may be also.' Death for believers is our gateway into His throne room, to see the beautiful face of our Lord and Savior and Bridegroom, Jesus Christ. Thus through all our lives and on our deathbeds we can sing:

Whom have I, Lord, in heaven but Thee,
To Whom my thoughts aspire?
And, having Thee, on earth is nought
That I can yet desire.

Though flesh and heart should faint and fail,
The Lord will ever be
The strength and portion of my heart,
My God eternally!

May this meditation on our heavenly marriage to Christ fuel a lifelong, ardent pursuit of holiness.

CHAPTER 29

THE LOVE OF GOD IN HEAVEN

HEAVEN is as popular today as it is misunderstood. TV programs and books that deal with heaven, angels, or nearly any other aspect of the life to come are immensely popular. Even non-evangelical authors are writing on utopian, heavenly themes. But if you evaluate this interest of our culture, it is at best superficial. People long for a better world, so they assume that they will find it. But they have no factual evidence to back up their hopes, nor does their belief in heaven impact the way they live today. Also, most treatments of heaven are pathetically man-centered. In a wonderful book, *Biblical Teaching on the Doctrines of Heaven and Hell*,[1] Edward Donnelly writes of hearing a talk show host interview a panel of celebrities. All of them assumed they were going to heaven. But not one of them even bothered to mention God. You cannot have heaven without God.

Even in the church there is a surprising silence about heaven. If you turn to the standard Reformed systematic theology works, heaven does not receive much discussion either. John Calvin's 1200-page *Institutes* has only two pages on heaven; Berkhof's 800-page *Systematic Theology* devotes only one page to heaven. Few great classics have been written on heaven. Richard Baxter's 600-page *The Saint's Everlasting Rest* is a welcome exception. But until recently, there have been few major Christian works about heaven.

Why this surprising silence in the church? Why are we more silent than the Bible on this subject? Professor Donnelly provides several reasons why we don't focus sufficiently on heaven. For one thing, we are too much in love with and thus too preoccupied with the present world. We are so caught up with temporal things and the pressures of a hectic schedule, that thinking about the world to come can easily sink low on your list of priorities. How can this be? How can something so small and short as this temporary life block out something so large and eternal as heaven? Imagine a boy holding a coin. What is larger, the coin or the sun? The answer is obvious. But if you put the coin in front of your eye, it can block out the sun. Is this not what you and I are doing far too often? This is sinful foolishness.

---

1. Edward Donnelly, *Biblical Teaching on the Doctrines of Heaven and Hell* (Edinburgh: Banner of Truth, 2001).

Another reason is that we are too comfortable. Life is luxurious. We have so many comforts we want to enjoy that we hardly give a thought to the unspeakable love, the solid joys, and the lasting pleasures of heaven. In our instant-gratification society, we have become drugged with our own pleasure-seeking. Other generations spoke of being pilgrims on the earth, but we have put down roots and are too comfortable to spend much time hoping for a better world, or in reaching others with the gospel that is the only way for them to reach heaven.

Finally, and perhaps most of all, the love of heaven is too intimate a theme for us to handle. We have become far too accustomed in every area of life to operate at the level of mediocrity. We are mediocre husbands and wives, who seldom commune together in deep, profound ways. We are mediocre parents who seldom have real talks with our children. We are mediocre in prayer and worship, seldom truly praying in our prayers and truly worshiping in our worship. The love of heaven just seems too intimate; it makes us too vulnerable to feel comfortable; it is too awesome for our minds to grasp, too high for our emotions to sustain. It's too rich, too great, too much for us to seriously contemplate.

And yet, how valuable such contemplation can be. Jonathan Edwards pointed out that if the greatest thing in this life is love, as Paul points out in 1 Corinthians 13, certainly love will characterize heaven. Everyone and everything in heaven will be filled with love – love of a far greater height, and depth, and breadth than we have ever known on earth. Here we taste something of God's love, but Heaven will be a place of perfect love, complete and flawless, and direct. The perfect will come, the imperfect will be done away with. When we meditate upon the love of God in heaven, the smallest foretastes of that heavenly glory can cause us to 'rejoice with joy unspeakable and full of glory' here on earth (1 Pet. 1:8).

THE LOVE OF GOD TO HIMSELF IN HEAVEN

One reason why heaven is a perfect state is because heaven is God's home. Heaven is where God most clearly reveals Himself, His glory, and His love. Heaven is where He shows the fullness of His being, where His attributes shine the brightest. Heaven is God's arena of glory and love. Romans 5:2 calls it 'the glory of God.'

Heaven opens to us God's world of love within His own Trinitarian Being. One of the greatest ways God shows His love in heaven is by letting the focus of heaven be on Himself and His glory. For God to let the light of heaven shine upon Himself is not selfishness, but is the communication of love. God Himself is 'the cause and fountain of love in heaven,' Edwards says, and then goes on to say:

> God is the fountain of love, as the sun is the fountain of light .... There, even in heaven, dwells the God from whom every stream of holy love, yea, every drop that is, or ever was, proceeds. There dwells God the Father, God the Son, and God the Spirit, united as one, in infinitely dear, and incomprehensible, and mutual, and eternal love. There dwells God the Father, who is the father of mercies, and so the father of love, who so loved the world as to give his only-begotten Son to die for it. There dwells Christ, the

Lamb of God, the prince of peace and of love, who so loved the world that he shed his blood, and poured out his soul unto death for men. There dwells the great Mediator, through whom all the divine love is expressed toward men, and by whom the fruits of that love have been purchased, and through whom they are communicated, and through whom love is imparted to the hearts of all God's people. There dwells Christ in both his natures, the human and the divine, sitting on the same throne with the Father. And there dwells the Holy Spirit – the Spirit of divine love, in whom the very essence of God, as it were, flows out, and is breathed forth in love, and by whose immediate influence all holy love is shed abroad in the hearts of all the saints on earth and in heaven. There, in heaven … this glorious God is manifested, and shines forth, in full glory, in beams of love. And there this glorious fountain forever flows forth in streams, yea, in rivers of love and delight, and these rivers swell, as it were, to an ocean of love, in which the souls of the ransomed may bathe with the sweetest enjoyment, and their hearts, as it were, be deluged with love![2]

THE LOVE OF GOD TO HIS PEOPLE IN HEAVEN

In Heaven's Christ-centeredness

Not only is God's love and glory fully displayed there, free from all the stains of sin, but the love of Christ is richly displayed to believers there as well. Heaven is a Christ-centered place. Revelation 21:23 describes heaven like this: the Lamb is the light thereof. If you compare the other chapters in Revelation, you will notice that one of the chief activities of those in heaven is saying 'worthy is the Lamb that was slain to receive glory and wisdom and blessing.' The same theme is found in the entire New Testament. Have you ever noticed that the Bible never speaks about dying and going to heaven? It speaks about dying and going to be with Christ, or of falling asleep in Jesus.

Why does the Bible focus on the centrality of the Lord Jesus Christ in heaven? First, no one can get to heaven without Christ's work. For scripture says that nothing defiled or impure can enter there. This is important, because almost everyone you meet on the street thinks that they deserve heaven, or can earn heaven. They are shocked and offended if you suggest that they can't. However, one glimpse of heaven in all its purity would convince you that you cannot enter as you are. Everyone who reaches heaven, will readily admit, 'I only entered here because of the sovereign, gracious love of God in Jesus Christ. His cross paid for my sins. His Spirit made me holy. His hand held my hand all through life, even when I tried to pull my hand out of His hand. In this way I safely reached glory.' This realization will never get old in heaven. Grace will never stop being amazing there. How a child of God needs this encouragement; at times the gospel hardly seems to make an impact in our hearts. But thanks be to God, in heaven this dullness of heart will never afflict us again.

There is a second reason why Christ is central in heaven. Scripture says that in heaven, faith will turn into sight. Isaiah 33:17 puts it like this: 'Thine eyes shall

---

2. Jonathan Edwards, *Heaven: A World of Love* (Amityville, N.Y.: Calvary Press, 1992), pp. 11-12.

see the king in his beauty.' Now we see in a glass, dimly, the apostle says, but then face to face (1 Cor. 13:12). We will see Him as He is (1 John 3:2). John Bunyan in *Pilgrim's Progress* describes this beautifully when he writes about a certain Mr. Standfast. When this man joins the pilgrims on their way to the celestial city, he bares his heart with these words: 'The thought of what I am going to lies like a glowing coal in my heart.' Later when he is called to cross the Jordan River into the celestial city, he has these parting words for his friends: 'I am going now to see that head that was crowned with thorns and that face that was spat upon for me. I have formerly lived by hearsay and faith, but now I go where I shall live by sight and shall be with him in whose company I delight myself.'

The one who has described this the most beautifully is the Puritan Samuel Rutherford, in words that have been turned into a poem called 'The Sands of Time are Sinking.'[3]

> *The bride eyes not her garment,*
> *But her dear Bridegroom's face;*
> *I will not gaze at glory*
> *But on my King of grace.*
> *Not at the crown He giveth,*
> *But on His pierced hand;*
> *The Lamb is all the glory*
> *Of Emmanuel's land.*

Does your heart thrill at the thought of gazing on your King of Grace? Every true child of God can identify with this. If you can't, then you are still unconverted, and dead to God and grace. And you will not enter heaven, unless God's Spirit teaches you this love for Christ, and this longing for Christ.

Far too little is made of the great scriptural theme that believers will be married to Christ in heaven (see chapter 28). This theme surfaces in so many places in Scripture – Psalm 45; Isaiah 54 and 62; Matthew 9 and 25; John 3; 2 Corinthians 11; Ephesians 5; and then most beautifully in Revelation.

Revelation 19:7-9 says, 'Let us be glad and rejoice, and give honour to him: for the marriage of the Lamb is come, and his wife hath made herself ready. And to her was granted that she should be arrayed in fine linen, clean and white: for the fine linen is the righteousness of saints. And he saith unto me, Write, Blessed are they which are called unto the marriage supper of the Lamb. And he saith unto me, These are the true sayings of God.' In chapter 21, after depicting the second coming, the judgment day has happened, the millennium is over, John now tells us about the beginning of eternity, the new heaven and new earth: 'And I John saw the holy city, new Jerusalem, coming down from God out of heaven, prepared as a bride adorned for her husband' (v. 2). Lastly, verse 9 says, 'And there came unto

---

3. Anne Ross Cousin, *Immanuel's Land and Other Pieces* (1857).

me one of the seven angels which had the seven vials full of the seven last plagues, and talked with me, saying, Come hither, I will show thee the bride, the Lamb's wife.' These are just a number of the verses that tell us that it is the great privilege of believers together and individually to become the bride of Christ.

A third reason why Christ is central in heaven is that Christ will continue to be the one who reveals God to us. Listen to how the Lord Jesus Christ describes heaven in the words of His high priestly prayer in John 17. 'Father, I will that they also whom thou hast given me, be with me where I am; that they may behold my glory, which thou hast given me.' He says earlier in this prayer that this glory is the same glory that He enjoyed with God before the creation of the world. Heaven in the Lord Jesus' own words is sharing in His glory as He makes God's glory known to His people.

Do you remember the beautiful passage in Luke 24 where the men on the road to Emmaus listen to Christ's exposition of the Scriptures? They say later on, 'Did not our hearts burn within us while he talked with us by the way?' This is what heaven is like: Jesus Christ opens the mind of God from Scripture, giving a better understanding of the Bible than we ever had here. Eternity means learning from Christ, with a burning heart. Now sometimes after a church service in which God has revealed His presence, the people of God say to each other, 'I wish we could stay and enjoy the blessings God has given in the opening of His Word.' In heaven that joy will never cease. O that this day would come quickly! How long, O Lord?

There is still a fourth reason why the focus in heaven is on Christ. Those who are in heaven will be fully conformed to the image of Christ (Rom. 8:29; 1 John 3:2). What bliss this will be! No more sin. No more selfishness that taints everything that you do. But in body and soul like the Lord Jesus Christ, made perfect, made glorious. Like Him, those in heaven will say, 'It is my food and drink to do the will of my Father.' Like He did already while He was on earth, those in heaven will grow in wisdom and stature, and in favor with God and man. We will be raised in the likeness of His resurrection, so that our bodies are made like unto His glorious body. Then whatever you do in word, thought, or deed, will be to God's glory. What bliss this will be – to be so conformed to the image of Christ, that it will be impossible to be un-Christlike!

This is part of the blissful love of God in heaven – to interact with the people of God and see Christ always reflected in them. Everyone you meet will remind you of Christ and teach you more about Christ. This is why the language of the Song of Solomon is beautiful. Have you ever read the words of the bridegroom to the bride, and wondered, how can Christ think of His people with such love? Listen to a sample of them: 'Thou art all fair my love, there is no spot in thee.' Or 'as the lily among the thorns, so is my love among the daughters' (Song 4:7; 2:2). It is so hard to imagine as a sinner that Christ can speak this way of us. You wonder, is this not exaggeration? But when Christ sees His perfection mirrored in His bride in heaven, it will be the day of the rejoicing of His heart. His heart will be ravished by His bride, and she will be able to look Him in the eye without shame, and rejoice in His loving glance, and say, 'My beloved is mine and I am his' (Song 2:16).

This is so very hard for a believer to grasp and to hang onto. We may think, 'Can I really be made sinless, never to fall again?' The glory of Jesus Christ can never be dimmed or put out; therefore the glory of the individual believer cannot be dimmed (Rev. 22:5). A new fall into sin will therefore be impossible because of Christ!

'Yes but,' someone will say, 'What about now? What about the times I still sin?' Stop. Don't start there. Start with these words from Scripture, spoken to the Colossians: 'Christ in you, the hope of glory' (Col. 1:27). The converted are joined to Christ. Not just outwardly, but inwardly. His glory already shines in your soul. That is why you love Him. Think of a beautiful tulip bulb. It does not look like much to the naked eye, but inside there is a beautiful tulip on the way. God's grace in the heart now is glory begun below.

The fifth reason why heaven is focused on Christ is connected to the previous reason. Because His glory will always shine undimmed, His praises will never grow old. Through an endless eternity, the people of God will never run out of reasons to sing his praises. The assembly will cry out, 'Thou art worthy, O Lord, to receive glory and honor!' Isaiah 26 says that the saints in heaven sing, 'thou hast wrought all our works in us!' (v. 12). Not unto us, O Lord of heaven, but unto Thee be glory given! Does this focus not make you want to do good works in order that you might bring praise to Christ one day by being able to cast them at His feet?

In Our Perfection

Scripture, in speaking about heaven, does not just speak of God and of Christ. It also speaks about us as believers – about our stupendous perfection. God, in His superlative love, will grant us what we have always longed for from the moment of regeneration: perfect souls and perfect bodies to praise and glorify Him sinlessly.

Consider first that *our souls will be made perfect in holiness*. Describing heaven as that sphere into which we enter when we engage in worship, Hebrews 12:23 tells us that we have come 'to God the Judge of all and to the spirits of just men made perfect.'

So here is basic and immensely encouraging Scripture teaching that all who die in Christ are completely purified in their souls at the moment of death from every trace of sin. This is an amazing act of God's love. No more sin! If we had only one wish surely it would be this. John Owen says, 'He is no true believer unto whom sin is not the greatest burden, sorrow, and trouble.'[4] I trust we know the sense of the horrible corruption inside of us. How we hate ourselves and abhor ourselves and are ashamed of ourselves because of sin!

How our self-centeredness, dishonesty, and impurity fuel thoughts of lust or evil that we would be desperately ashamed for any other human being to know

---

4. John Owen, *The Grace and Duty of Being Spiritually Minded*, in *The Works of John Owen*, ed. William H. Goold (London and Edinburgh: Johnstone and Hunter, 1852), 7:333.

about! Our lack of self-control; the way we snap at our children; the way we fume and fret and get irritated so easily; our obstinacy; our refusal to say that little word, 'sorry'; our cruelty even to those we know and love best; our resentment and our unforgiving spirit – the list is endless. My friend, are you aware of your indwelling sin and your weakness and your corruption?

What about the sins regarding holy things – our hardness of heart; reading the Bible but remaining unmoved; failing to pray for the lost only because it is a duty; letting our thoughts wander while listening to the preaching of the gospel. There is in us a network and complex of sin.

We have to say with Paul, 'Evil is present with me' – until heaven, where I will never sin again, or grieve the Spirit again, or break a single one of God's commandments again. I will never hurt anyone again, or fail my Savior again, or have to ask for forgiveness again. I will never have to weep over myself again, or abhor myself again, or despise myself again. Sinless perfection is a thrilling reality. God has predestined us, in His stupendous love, to be conformed to the image of His Son, and we will be. We pray, 'Deliver us from evil,' and He will deliver us from all evil – the evil inside of us included.

My friends, how much closer to God we will be than we have ever been on this earth. He will look at us with all the love of His Triune Being in heaven and He will delight in us. Our souls will be in a new intimate, joyful communion with God, closer than ever before. No barriers, nothing between us, no sins, no shadow of grief on our souls. We will see our Father's face without a cloud between us.

Then we will say with M'Cheyne,

> *When I see thee as thou art,*
> *love thee with unsinning heart,*
> *then, Lord, shall I fully know.*

Yes, in heaven we will love God with an unsinning heart. No more sin.

My dear friends, does that not encourage you in your struggle against sin? Some of us are very weary of our sins. There is some besetting sin and you have struggled with and wrestled with and it has thrown you down again and again. And you have been tempted to despise yourself and to look upon yourself as a useless, worthless, hopeless thing. Perhaps you have even doubted your salvation. God's Word says to you, child of God: 'Take heart – those sins are doomed, their death sentence has been pronounced.' Look at those sins with the eyes of faith from the perspective of heaven. The moment your soul enters heaven your sins are finished. And when they are remembered in heaven, they will be a cause of joy and worship and love and gratitude for the grace of Christ which forgave them, cancelled them, blotted them out, and threw them into the depths of the sea.

Secondly, not only will our souls be made perfect in holiness, but *we shall be like Christ in that our bodies will be raised in glory*. This, too, is part of God's love to us in glory. The Greek philosopher Plato was surely wrong when he taught that human beings are immortal souls imprisoned in worthless bodies of flesh. We humans are physical-spiritual unities. In Adam, God created both our soul and body as good. We fell in Adam with both our soul and body. When God sent His Son to die for us, it was for our souls *and* our bodies. By regeneration our bodies become temples of the Holy Ghost (1 Cor. 6:19). Our loving Father grants that our bodies will be resurrected in perfect condition immediately to be reunited in sinless perfection with our souls (1 Cor. 15:51-52). Our bodies will be the same and yet different. In 1 Corinthians 15 Paul tells us, first, that our body '*is sown in corruption; and raised in incorruption*' (v. 42b). In the hour of resurrection our bodies shall live forever, never to decay again, never to ache again, and never to feel pain again.

Thirdly, Paul says in verse 43, '*It is sown in dishonour; it is raised in glory.*' It is part of my calling as a pastor to see the bodies of dead people. What does the casket contain? It contains a poor, weak, wasted body of an old person, the body of someone ravaged by disease – empty clay; evidence of the wages of sin. And it is going to be put into the ground, it is going to rot. It is sown in dishonor. There is nothing there of power or of life or of beauty. But says Paul, 'It is raised in glory.' In heaven our bodies will be awesome, radiant, beautiful, young, and marvelous. Jesus said, 'The righteous will shine forth as the sun in the kingdom of heaven' (Matt. 13:43). We will be forever young in the beauty of our strength, our manliness, our womanliness. There will be a glory about us, a magnificence, a beauty. C. S. Lewis says, 'If we could see now fellow believers as we will see them in heaven we would be tempted to fall down and worship them.'[5] The body is raised in glory.

Fourthly, Paul says, '*It is sown in weakness; it is raised in power.*' How weak we are in our lack of strength and energy. But God says that our bodies will pulsate with energy and dynamism and power. We will not know what weariness is. We will be able to carry out all the impulses of our holy wills and our desires in continuous blessed activity forever and ever!

Lastly, '*It is sown a natural body; it is raised a spiritual body*' (v. 44). This verse is widely misunderstood. The word *natural* here means subject to the limitations of this age, weakened, damaged by sin. The word *spiritual* does not mean non-material or non-physical. That is where people go wrong. What Paul means is that we will have physical, material bodies of flesh and blood which are totally dominated by the Holy Spirit, possessed by the Spirit, and energized and ruled by the Spirit. Just for a moment try to imagine the sheer physical well-being of heaven.

And then, best of all, Jesus, in His perfect love, shall gaze upon us in our perfect souls and perfect bodies, and 'He shall see of the travail of his soul, and shall be satisfied' (Isa. 53:11). He will not be disappointed. *God's work in you will be brought to such a pitch of glorious perfection that the Lord will fall in love with you, His church, His bride, with no spot, no wrinkle, no blemish, or any such thing.* It is very, very easy for us to believe that we love the Savior, but sometimes we find it very hard to believe

---

5. C. S. Lewis, *The Weight of Glory* (New York: HarperOne, 2001), p. 45.

that the Savior will love us in heaven. But we will be changed, conformed to His image, swept clean, made perfect and glorious and wonderful, all by God's grace. *It is Himself He sees in us. It is Himself He loves in us. It is His own grace and His own perfections and His own beauty that He admires in us.* He loves Himself in us, and that is why we are told that we shall be like Him.

Friends, it will be heaven indeed to look into the face of Christ, and say, 'Jesus loves me, this I know.' That will be heaven. We shall be like Him and see Him as He is.

In the Societies of Heaven

Our most vital relationship, of course, is with the Triune God, but the Bible also directs us to the saints, to the elect of God, as those with whom we will interact – the great multitude whom no one could number of all nations, tribes, peoples, and languages, whose names are written in the Lamb's book of life.

Now of course, there will be many humans with whom we will not have any relationship in heaven. And those will be the unconverted in hell. Jonathan Edwards says, 'Heaven will have no pity for hell, not because the saints are unloving but because they are perfectly loving. They now love as God loves and whom God loves, being now in perfect conformity with His love.'[6] The saints in heaven will not miss the unconverted or be grieved over them. How urgent therefore is the work of evangelism! In that great multitude in heaven, think of the variety, the saints of all the ages, of all the nations, of all the cultures, all the personalities, all the experiences, and all the stories to tell! Think of the millions upon millions of believers who will be your friends, your brothers and sisters. Think of the unity that will prevail there. There will be no disagreements, no divisions, no denominations, no Presbyterians, or Methodists, or Baptists. There will be no theological arguments or controversies.

There are Christians here on earth whom we try to love but we find it very difficult to like, but everyone in heaven will be admirable and lovable and attractive, appealing, glorious, clothed with the beauty of Christ. We will have the privilege of being friends, fellow members with such glorious beings, practicing forever and ever the grace of love which we were taught to practice on this earth. We will love one another.

How the love of God in heaven in granting us this perfect love of the communion of saints ought to remind us of the importance of loving our fellow Christians on earth. Away with those cursed quarrels, horrible divisions, misunderstandings and criticisms among each other. Remember, we are going to love these people forever, we are going to love them to all eternity. It is our shame that we don't love them now. Can we not try to see fellow believers now the way they are going to be? Can we not try to live with them with the eyes of faith to when all the nonsense

---

6. Edwards, *Heaven: A World of Love*, p. 35.

and shortcomings are swept away, and the image of Christ will be perfect? How confusing it is for the unbeliever to see Christians quarreling with each other, and yet claiming they are going to be together forever, loving each other perfectly in heaven. Let us love our fellow Christians, let us love all our brothers and sisters in Christ, let us forgive them, and ask them to forgive us. Let us strive to live now as we will live then.

In the Beauty of Heaven

When Christ returns, He will bring heaven with Him. He will destroy all the effects of sin, and remake this world on which we now live into a paradise. He will create new heavens, and a new earth. This means that heaven is not an endless worship service where disembodied ghosts float around on clouds. Revelation tells us that the heavenly Jerusalem will descend onto the new earth (Rev. 21:2). The apostle Peter writes in his second epistle that the heavens shall pass away with a great noise, and the elements shall melt with fervent heat, so that the earth and all the works that are therein shall be burned up (2 Pet. 3:10). But he also adds, 'according to his promise, we look for new heavens and a new earth, wherein dwells righteousness' (2 Pet. 3:13). Heaven will be on the new earth.

Here is where Isaiah 11 can help us. Look at how Isaiah describes heaven: the wolf will lie down next to the lamb, the leopard with the goats, and the lions with calves, and a little child shall lead them; 'they shall not hurt nor destroy in all my holy mountain.' Notice why not: 'for the earth shall be full of the knowledge of the LORD, as the waters cover the sea' (Isa. 11:6-9). When you see creation now at its finest, you are catching just a glimpse of what heaven will be like on the new earth, surpassing the glory of this world so much that you might say to yourself, 'Never have I seen real flowers till now. Never have I felt a glorious spring morning like this.' The best moments on this earth are simply a faint picture of what will come.

In the Occupations and Activity of Heaven

Eternity, through all its endless years, will be one long act of worship. Don't think of this too narrowly though. There will be work to do. In the broad sense, however, all that takes place will be an act of worship. Listen to how Revelation 22:3 describes this: 'the throne of God and of the Lamb shall be in it, and his servants shall serve him.' Other texts speak of reigning with Christ (2 Tim. 2:12; Rev. 20:6). There will be work to do. The saints will have dominion over the new earth, as God's stewards. Only work will no longer take place in the sweat of your face, among the thorns. You will not be exhausted by your labors, but energized by them, and rejoice in how they bring glory to God. You will not labor in vain, only to see what you have done crumble to dust. But all that you make and do will be perfect, lovable and pleasing in God's sight.

There will be feasting in heaven, starting with the marriage celebration between Christ and His church. There will be eating and drinking – such that no one will ever go hungry again. There will be joy, untainted by sin. There will be singing. The Psalms describe it like this: 'thou wilt show me the path of life; in thy presence is fullness of joy; at thy right hand are pleasures forevermore' (16:11).

I hope in the life to come should offer such rich comfort. Some of us are sitting here with battle fatigue: the constant fight against temptation, the world, the malice of Satan, and the frailties of our bodies. Let the hope of the new creation cheer and energize the people of God even now.

THE GLORY OF GOD'S LOVE IN HEAVEN

Infinite Love

First, remember that God's love in heaven is infinite love. Edwards said that God's love in heaven is like an ocean without a floor and without a shore. All the love we will enjoy in heaven are but drops from the infinite ocean of divine love. Spurgeon said, 'A fish can more easily drink the oceans dry than we can ever exhaust the love of God in heaven.'[7] Eternally, God will say to us of His love, 'Eat, O friends; drink, yea, drink abundantly, O beloved' (Song 5:1).

Friends, God's love is infinite, but we are finite. We are incapable of receiving something that is infinite in amount, so He will display it for an infinite length of time – all eternity. It will take all eternity to show believers the love of God.

Everlasting Love

God's love is eternal. Paul wonderfully picks up on this theme: 'But God, who is rich in mercy, for his great love wherewith he loved us, Even when we were dead in sins, hath quickened us together with Christ, (by grace ye are saved;) And hath raised us up together, and made us sit together in heavenly places in Christ Jesus' (Eph. 2:4-6). He saved us, Paul says, but for what purpose? 'That in the ages to come he might show the exceeding riches of his grace in his kindness toward us through Christ Jesus' (Eph. 2:7).

Do you see what Paul is saying? God determined to love us from eternity past so that when we get to heaven He will show the exceeding riches of His grace, love, mercy, and kindness to us forever and ever. God's love in heaven is permanent; it is everlasting.

The story has been told of a boy in Sunday School, who, when asked to recite John 3:16, got mixed up in the end, and said, 'Whosoever believeth on him should not perish but have everlasting love.' There you have it – everlasting life is everlasting love.

Progressive Love

God's love is progressive. In heaven there will be an increasing amount of love because the infinity of God's love has to increase so that we receive more of it, increasing our enjoyment of it. And so it will continue more and more. We will

---

7. *Spurgeon's Sermons* (London, 1874), 20:223.

grow in heaven in our capacity to absorb God's love. Just as our minds grow as we learn more, our hearts will grow to receive more of the love of God throughout all eternity. God enlarges our hearts for all eternity.

Responsive Love

God's love in heaven will work a responding love in our minds and hearts in at least two ways.

Loving God

As we are overwhelmed with the love of God in heaven, we will respond in kind. There is a principle in physics that says for every action there is an equal opposite reaction. If you bounce a ball it comes back up. In heaven, when God shows us His love, we will respond with love. In heaven, as God shows us His love, we will reply by obeying His greatest commandment: 'Thou shalt love the Lord thy God with all thy heart, soul, mind and strength; this is the first and great commandment' (Matt. 22:37-38). Being saturated with the love of God, we will love Him in response—naturally and easily and spontaneously—with all that is within us. We won't have to work at it; or battle sin to do it. Here, there are holy moments when we love God fervently, but then ten minutes later our love wanes. We don't always love God, and yet we want to. But in heaven that will all change. We will love God perfectly and unselfishly – not just for what He has done for us, as wonderful as that is, but for who He is in Himself. We will love God for His own sake.

First John 4 says, 'We love him because he first loved us.' That's it; He causes the reaction. Look at the tenses; He loved us before we did, but then causes us to love Him. In eternity He will continue to love us; He will continue to cause us to love Him in reply. God will continue to love us, and we will continue to love Him.

Loving our Neighbor

Secondly, not only will we obey the first commandment to love God in heaven, we will also keep the second, Love your neighbor as yourself. In heaven we will reply by loving all others in heaven perfectly, purely, and unselfishly for all eternity. We will naturally love others in heaven and they will love us. Heaven is not only a world of God's love for us and our love for Him, but our love for each other becomes mutual; the second love commandment is carried out perfectly for all eternity.

Heaven is a universe of God's love. Hell is not. Everybody in hell hates one another. People joke about hell and talk about how they will have a good time with their friends, but they will certainly not! There are no friends in hell! Everybody is everyone's enemy in hell. Love is a good thing, but there is nothing good in hell. No one in hell is capable of love. They would kill each other if they could. But more than that – sinners in hell will experience hatred for one another, and not even the slightest drop of love; they will also experience the greatest hatred of all that the Bible calls 'the holy wrath of God.' And so God will hate them with a holy hatred because of their sins and people will respond in kind by hating God and one another, thereby adding to their own punishment.

HEAVEN ON EARTH: LIVING IN LIGHT OF GOD'S HEAVENLY LOVE

There are several ways in which the love of God in heaven impacts our lives on earth now.

1. Let the love of God move you to cultivate love even now on earth. If we are going to spend eternity loving other Christians in heaven, why should we not start right now by loving them? It is not easy. Maybe you know the old poem that says:

> *To live above with saints we love,*
> *Oh, that will be the glory;*
> *But to live below with saints we know,*
> *Ah, that's another story.*

It is not easy to love them because they are sinners, and it is not easy for them to love us because we are sinners. But God has given us His love whereby we are able to love now above the sins that are in other people, and makes it possible for them to love us in return. So let's cultivate this love, even here on earth.

2. Let the love of God fill you so much that you have no reason to despair the death of another Christian. Some of us have lost very close loved ones who were Christians. You cried, and your tears were an evidence of the depth of your love. There is nothing wrong with that. But we must not despair. Rather than despair we should envy them with a holy envy. They have gone on to heaven!

3. Let the love of God in heaven give you new strength on earth. Think of a traveler stranded on a stormy, rainy night who has to walk the last ten miles to get to where he is going. As he plods along with gusts of wind ripping at him, he thinks of sitting down and giving up. But then he sees ahead the lights of home twinkling through the trees. And with renewed energy he keeps on going. As we meditate on God's love in heaven, God allows the lights of home to twinkle through the darkness of this world: 'Now is our salvation nearer than when we first believed' (Rom. 13:11). Only a little while longer, and the weary night will be past. And you will awake with God, where streams of pleasures ever flow, where boundless joys abide. Keep on!

Caught up in the things of this life, we are so busy with houses and land, with buying and selling, with cooking and cleaning, that we hardly ever think about heaven. Do you know how God prepared the apostle Paul for his labors as missionary? Why did Paul always seem to be ready for one more challenge, sermon, or rebuke? Because God had given him a vision of heaven. Thoughts of heaven are one of the best preparations for usefulness on earth. The more you meditate on heaven, the more heavenly foretastes will be given to you by the Spirit of God, and thus the more fit you will be for the Master's use.

4. Let the love of God encourage you to face your own death with courage. God will give you dying grace when the dying hour comes. He will give you a foretaste of His love, not only in salvation and justification, but He will give you that one last installment that will carry you over to the next life.

5. Let the love of God and the foretastes you have of heaven here make you long more for your eternal home and eternal crowning. In one of his sermons Spurgeon says, 'If we do not get to heaven before we die we shall never get there afterwards.' Have you ever had a foretaste of heaven? Spurgeon gives an illustration of a young prince who one morning was found trying on his father's gold crown before his father got up. His father the king was quite annoyed with him. But Spurgeon says to his readers and listeners, 'Try on your crown. Your Father won't mind. Try it on as often as you can. We must be more in heaven.'[8]

Perhaps you remember what Isaac Walton wrote of the great Puritan writer, Richard Sibbes: 'Of that blessed man let this just praise be given, that heaven was in him before he was in heaven.'[9] Oh, that that could also be said of all of us!

6. Finally, let the love of God, if you are as yet an unbeliever, move you to fly to God today for mercy and forgiveness. You might have always claimed that you are a child of God, but the Word of God has exposed you as a counterfeit Christian. Wake up before it is too late. Wake up before you wake up in hell. Just like there is endless unimaginable happiness in heaven, there is endless unimaginable misery in hell. Don't put off repentance and faith any longer.

Fly to Christ now. Hide from God by hiding in God. Christ died to save sinners like you.

> *Dark, dark had been the midnight*
> *But dayspring is at hand,*
> *And glory, glory dwelleth*
> *In Emmanuel's land.*[10]

---

8. C. H. Spurgeon, *Metropolitan Tabernacle Pulpit* (Pasadena, Tex.: Pilgrim, 1977), 9 (1863), p. 142.

9. Cited in C. H. Spurgeon quoting Isaac Walton, *The Salt-Cellars* (Pasadena, Tex.: Pilgrim, 1975), p. 249.

10. Anne Ross Cousin, 'The Sands of Time are Sinking,' *Immanuel's Land and Other Pieces* (1857).

SCRIPTURE INDEX

SUBJECT INDEX

Also available from Christian Focus Publications...

KNOWING
and GROWING
in
ASSURANCE
of FAITH

Joel R. Beeke

Knowing and Growing in the Assurance of Faith

Joel R. Beeke

In his 100th work, Joel Beeke writes on the power and beauty of true, secure assurance of faith: the heartfelt conviction that one belongs to Christ through faith and will enjoy everlasting salvation. This title opens up Dr. Beeke's expertise and learning for anyone 'trapped in a background of easy believism or trapped in the opposite fear of assurance being the certain mark of being presumptuous and so crushing the young shoots of hope and assurance as they appear.'

Here in this book, with perspicuity and simplicity, and informed by a lifetime of reflection and study of this subject, Dr Beeke lays out the New Testament witness that so thrilled the hearts of the Reformers and our Evangelical forebears. I highly recommend it.

Michael A. G. Haykin
Professor of Church History and Biblical Spirituality,
The Southern Baptist Theological Seminary, Louisville, Kentucky

Here is a book that every person should read, whether they are a believer or an unbeliever. Joel Beeke has once again done a masterful job of presenting a thorough biblical case on this important subject.

Steven J. Lawson
President, OnePassion Ministries and Professor of Preaching,
The Master's Seminary, Sun Valley, California

I'm delighted to see this book make Dr. Beeke's expertise more widely accessible, and hope that many more will now benefit from it as I did. To be fruitful, healthy and happy in Christ, Christians need to know the truths laid out for us here.

Michael Reeves
President and Professor of Theology, Union School of Theology, Oxford, England

ISBN 978-1-7819-1300-0

THE
ADORABLE
TRINITY

Standing for Orthodoxy in
Nineteenth-Century America

MANTLE NANCE

The Adorable Trinity
Standing for Orthodoxy in Nineteenth–Century America
Mantle Nance

The Adorable Trinity investigates the little-known yet fascinating conflict between Trinitarianism and Unitarianism in the nineteenth-century American South. It explores the lives, ministries, and theological contributions of three Southern Presbyterian pastor-scholars associated with Columbia Theological Seminary – James Henley Thornwell, Thomas Smyth, and Benjamin Morgan Palmer – and their winsome, fruitful stands for the Trinitarian faith in response to a burgeoning Southern Unitarian movement. In a readable and engaging way, the author provides readers with intriguing history that illumines the mind and warm theology that moves the heart to adore and serve the Triune God of love.

Mantle Nance's study of the controversy in the Old South between Trinitarians and Unitarians is historically and theologically marked by careful scholarship and, although committed to the supernaturalism of Trinitarian belief, seeks to be fair and judicious throughout. Far from being a good, but dusty, relic of past concerns, it touches on many of the most crucial issues facing human thought and destiny today (or at any time). It is very much alive; a penetrating word for our times...

Douglas F. Kelly

Professor of Theology Emeritus, Reformed Theological Seminary,
Charlotte, North Carolina

This book is a fascinating look at a neglected chapter in the history of the old South. The author offers an inspiring account of southern theologians' convincing arguments that the Trinity is foundational to every aspect of Christian faith and practice. The book will be a delight to anyone interested in this era of America history.

S. Donald Fortson

Professor of Church History and Pastoral Theology, Reformed Theological
Seminary, Charlotte, North Carolina

ISBN 978-1-5271-0518-8

R.E.D.S.
REFORMED,
EXEGETICAL
AND
DOCTRINAL
STUDIES

DEATH IN ADAM, LIFE IN CHRIST

THE DOCTRINE OF IMPUTATION

J.V. FESKO

SERIES EDITORS J.V. FESKO & MATTHEW BARRETT